PAIGE BALTZAN

Daniels College of Business
University of Denver

CAMERON WELSH

Haskayne School of Business
University of Calgary

BUSINESS DRIVEN INFORMATION SYSTEMS

FOURTH CANADIAN EDITION

McGraw-Hill
Ryerson

Business Driven Information Systems
Fourth Canadian Edition

ISBN-13: 978-1-25-903081-9
ISBN-10: 1-25-903081-4

3 4 5 6 7 WEB 20 19 18 17

Printed and bound in Canada.

Care has been taken to trace ownership of copyright material contained in this text; however, the publisher will welcome any information that enables them to rectify any reference or credit for subsequent editions.

Director of Product Management: Rhondda McNabb
Senior Product Manager: James Booty
Marketing Manager: Cathie Lefebvre
Product Developer: Sarah Fulton
Senior Product Team Associate: Stephanie Giles
Supervising Editor: Jessica Barnoski
Photo/Permissions Editor: Robyn Craig Research
Copy Editor: Rodney Rawlings
Plant Production Coordinator: Michelle Saddler
Manufacturing Production Coordinator: Lena Keating
Cover Design: Dianne Reynolds
Cover Image: Rafe Swan/Getty Images
Interior Design: Laserwords Private Limited
Page Layout: Laserwords Private Limited
Printer: Webcom

ABOUT THE AUTHORS

PAIGE BALTZAN

Paige Baltzan teaches in the Department of Business Information and Analytics at the Daniels College of Business at the University of Denver. She holds a B.S.B.A. specializing in Accounting/MIS from Bowling Green State University, and an M.B.A. specializing in MIS from the University of Denver. She is a co-author of several books, including *Business Driven Technology*, *Essentials of Business Driven Information Systems*, *I-Series*, and a contributor to *Management Information Systems for the Information Age*. Before joining the Daniels College faculty in 1999, Paige spent several years working for a large telecommunications company and an international consulting firm, where she participated in client engagements in the United States as well as South America and Europe. Paige lives in Lakewood, Colorado, with her husband, Tony, and daughters, Hannah and Sophie.

CAMERON WELSH

Cameron Welsh is an instructor and Haskayne Teaching Fellow at the Haskayne School of Business at the University of Calgary. In his years at the Haskayne School of Business, Cameron has been a member of the school's MIS area. During those years he has taught introductory business analytics to incoming first-year students, the introductory information systems course, and senior elective MIS courses that include everything from management issues to the school's MIS field projects course. Cameron's industry experience includes a number of years in the retail industry and the founding of a family business. His research and consulting interests are in the development of performance metrics, governance, and blended and e-learning. Cameron is also involved as a management and technical advisor to a number of not-for-profit organizations.

BRIEF CONTENTS

CONTENTS

PREFACE

Business initiatives must be fully considered prior to—and must drive—discussions of how information systems and technology support successful business decisions. This premise that business initiatives should direct information systems choices is ingrained in *Business Driven Information Systems*, Fourth Canadian Edition. By addressing business needs first, and then addressing the information systems that support those needs, this text provides the foundation that will enable students to achieve excellence in business. Whether they major in operations management, manufacturing, sales, marketing, finance, human resources, accounting, or virtually any other business discipline, *Business Driven Information Systems* is designed to give students the ability to understand how information systems can be a source of strength for an organization.

Common business goals associated with information systems projects include reducing costs, improving productivity, improving customer satisfaction and loyalty, creating competitive advantages, streamlining supply chains, global expansion, and so on. Achieving these results is not easy. Implementing a new accounting system or marketing plan is not likely to generate long-term growth or reduce costs across an entire organization. Businesses must undertake enterprise-wide initiatives to achieve broad general business goals such as reducing costs. Information systems play a critical role in deploying such initiatives by facilitating communication and increasing business intelligence. Any individual anticipating a successful career in business, whether it is in accounting, finance, human resources, or operations management, must understand the basics of information systems that can be found in this text.

We have found tremendous success teaching MIS courses by demonstrating the correlation between business and IS. Students who understand the tight correlation between business and IS understand the power of this course. Such understanding informs even non-traditional business as is seen in a few of the new cases in the text including "Moneyball: About More Than Just the Players," the opening case in Chapter 3, and "ERP and Analytics Brings Germany World Cup Success," the first closing case in Chapter 7. These cases outline the way in which information systems and analytics are being used to not only manage customers and ticket sales at the front end of the business but also to manage the on-field talent. Scouting and player development is now more than just observing a player perform; it is a process that involves analyzing the numbers that the player produces during that performance and comparing those numbers to benchmarks. Practices now include the capture of information from sensors on the player's body or even attached to the ball. This data is then analyzed to help not only the player, but also the team as a whole, perform better. Engaging examples like these help students to see that IS can be leveraged to improve businesses in every field.

Students learn 10 percent of what they read, 80 percent of what they personally experience, and 90 percent of what they teach others. The business-driven approach takes the difficult and often intangible MIS concepts, brings them to the student's level, and applies them using a hands-on approach to reinforce the concepts. Teaching MIS with a business-driven focus helps:

- Add credibility to IS
- Open students' eyes to IS opportunities
- Attract majors
- Engage students

As instructors we have reached out to friends in industry to help us understand the skills and knowledge they require in the people they are hiring into their organizations. We have asked, "What are the skills of the ideal business and MIS graduate?" Out of the responses to this question, we have generated a list. These prized skills include those of:

- Critical thinking
- An understanding of business basics

- A process-oriented approach to business
- The comprehension of a number of key MIS skills

This feedback, along with the insights of reviewers, has helped to guide us in the revision of this fourth edition

FORMAT, FEATURES, AND HIGHLIGHTS

Business Driven Information Systems is state-of-the-art in its discussions, presents concepts in an easy-to-understand format, and allows students to be active participants in their learning. The dynamic nature of information systems requires all students, more specifically business students, to be aware of both current and emerging technologies. Students are facing complex subjects and need a clear, concise explanation to be able to understand and use the concepts throughout their careers. By engaging students with numerous case studies, exercises, projects, and questions that enforce concepts, *Business Driven Information Systems* creates a unique learning experience for both faculty and students.

- **Audience.** *Business Driven Information Systems* is designed for use in undergraduate or introductory MBA courses in Management Information Systems, which are required in many Business Administration and Management programs as part of the common body of knowledge for all business majors.

- **Logical Layout.** Students and faculty will find the text well organized with the topics flowing logically from one chapter to the next. The definition of each term is provided before it is covered in the chapter and is supported by an audio file that students click to review the term and its definition. Each chapter offers a comprehensive opening case study, introduction, learning outcomes, closing case studies, key terms, and *Making Business Decisions* questions. The Plug-Ins include the same pedagogical elements, with the exception of opening case and closing case studies.

- **Thorough Explanations.** Complete coverage is provided for each topic that is introduced. Explanations are written so that students can understand the ideas presented and relate them to other concepts.

- **Solid Theoretical Base.** The text relies on current theory and practice of information systems as they relate to the business environment. Current academic and professional journals cited throughout the text are found in the Endnotes section at the end of each chapter—a roadmap for additional pertinent readings that can be the basis for learning beyond the scope of the chapters or Plug-Ins.

- **Material to Encourage Discussion.** All chapters contain a diverse selection of case studies and individual and group problem-solving activities as they relate to the use of information systems in business. Three comprehensive cases at the end of each chapter reinforce content. These cases encourage students to consider the concepts presented and then apply those concepts to a situation they might find in an organizational setting. Different people in an organization often view the same facts from different points of view, and the cases will encourage students to consider some of those various views. The fourth Canadian edition includes 11 new and 3 revised opening and closing cases.

- **Integrative Themes.** Several recurring themes add integration to the material. Among these are value-added techniques and methodologies, ethics and social responsibility, globalization, and gaining a competitive advantage. Such topics are essential to gaining a full understanding of the strategies that a business must recognize, formulate, and in turn implement. In addition to addressing these in the chapter material, many illustrations are provided for their relevance to business practice.

CHANGES TO THE FOURTH CANADIAN EDITION

The fourth Canadian edition makes every effort to support student learning. Key changes made in the fourth edition are as follows.

The fourth edition sees a significant reorganization of the content to better reflect how the material is related. The text is now organized into five modules consisting of one to three chapters each. Starting with an introductory module, the text then moves to a module focused on data and information. This module first deals with such topics as decision making, business processes, knowledge management, and business analytics and then follows with the technologies that support these issues. The next module looks at e-business, the World Wide Web, and the mobile technologies that make these concepts strong enablers of business today. This is followed by a module that looks at enterprise solutions including ERP, SCM, and CRM. The last module follows up with some of the issues around information and technology, and how businesses plan for and implement technology into their organizations.

Chapter 1:

- Updated Opening Case: *Information Technology Helps LCBO Transform Itself*
- Updated figures for currency and to make them more student-friendly
- New Figures 1.4 and 1.10
- New Closing Case One: *Say "Charge It" with your Mobile Device*
- New Closing Case Three: *Apple: Merging Technology, Business, and Entertainment*

Chapter 2:

- Reorganized the material for better flow and to place more-used topics in the first part of the chapter
- New Figures 2.1, 2.3, 2.4, 2.6, 2.11, and 2.17
- New Closing Case Three: *Actionly: Online Brand Management*

Chapter 3:

- New Opening Case: *Moneyball: About More Than Just the Players*
- A revised section on knowledge, business intelligence, and big data
- Second section of chapter refocused on collaboration and the tools used to make this happen
- New Figures 3.6, 3.7, 3.10, 3.16, 3.17, and 3.18

Chapter 4:

- Refocused chapter on databases, data warehouses, and data mining
- New Figures 4.13 and 4.14

Chapter 5:

- New Opening Case: *Pinterest: Billboards for the Internet*
- Reorganized chapter to focus on the business-driven issues that surround how business uses the Internet based on suggestions of reviewers
- Moved ISP and other technology-based content to Chapter 6
- New Figures 5.3, 5.4, 5.11, and 5.18
- Updated Closing Case One: *The Rise and Fall of Canadian Tire's Website Ordering*

Chapter 6:

- New Canadian examples, such as OptikTV and Fibe TV
- Updates on changes in mobile and other technologies like GIS

- New Figures 6.13 and 6.21
- New Closing Case One: *Wireless Bikes*
- New Closing Case Two: *Geoblogging for Chimpanzees and More*
- New Closing Case Three: *Crash Pads*

Chapter 7:

- Added content on ERP failures
- New Figures 7.2 and 7.5
- New Closing Case One: *ERP and Analytics Brings Germany World Cup Success*
- Revised Closing Case Two: *Campus ERP*

Chapter 8:

- Minor updates to SCM-related technologies and examples of how businesses use SCM throughout the chapter
- Updated stats for CareNET Closing Case

Chapter 9:

- New Opening Case: *Twitter: A Social CRM Tool*
- New content on Social CRM (tied to new Opening Case)
- New content on RFID
- New Figure 9.13
- New Closing Case One: *Target: CRM and Big Data*

Chapter 10:

- New Opening Case: *The Privacy Commissioner of Canada's Work*
- New content on backup and recovery material (moved from previous Chapter 11)
- Added content on Chinese hacking, Heartbleed, and Blackshades
- New Figures 10.4, 10.7, 10.8, 10.9, and 10.12
- New Closing Case Two: *Information Ethics and Privacy Issues with Facebook Make Headlines*

Chapter 11:

- New Figures 11.2, 11.8, 11.10, 11.12, 11.13, 11.17, and 11.19
- New Closing Case Two: *Disaster at Denver International Airport*

Chapter 12:

- New Opening Case: *Cloud Computing in Canada*
- Updated content on cloud computing
- New Figures 12.3, 12.10, 12.11, 12.12, 12.13, 12.14, and 12.15
- New Closing Case Two: *Pandora's Music Box*

FEATURES OF THE eBOOK

Content embedded in the eBook includes:

- **Videos.** Twenty videos embedded within the text cover topics from entrepreneurship to disaster recovery. Videos are embedded near related chapter content. Video IMs are available to instructors to help turn the videos into engaging classroom activities.

- **Technology Plug-Ins and Associated Files.** The Technology Plug-Ins offer integration with core chapters and provide critical knowledge using essential business applications such as Microsoft Excel, Microsoft Access, and Microsoft Project. Each Plug-In includes associated data files and an accompanying PowerPoint presentation to aid student learning.

- **Opening Case Scenarios.** Each chapter includes a link to a new Opening Case scenario, putting the student in the role of a business person assigned a task related to the case. Intended to prepare students for increasingly common scenario-based job interview questions, these scenarios help students to connect chapter content to real-world business decisions.

- **Audio Glossary.**

- **Apply Your Knowledge Projects and Associated Files.** Embedded at appropriate places within the text. Apply Your Knowledge Projects challenge students to bring the skills they have learned from the chapter to real business problems. These projects help to develop the application and problem-solving skills of students through challenging and creative business-driven scenarios.

- **Apply Your Knowledge Tools Projects.** These 34 projects focus on student application of core concepts and tools. All tools projects come with a Captivate solution file that walks students step by step through the solution, saving instructors valuable time.

- **Links to the Cohesion Case.** The Broadway Café is a running case instructors can use to reinforce core material such as customer relationship management, supply chain management, business intelligence, and decision making. The case has 15 sections that challenge students to develop and expand their grandfather's coffee shop. Links to relevant sections are embedded at appropriate places in the eBook chapters.

- **Links to the Database Systems Cohesion Case.** This cohesion case mimics the one above with a focus on databases.

- **Live Weblinks.**

- **Additional Appendices.** Three additional appendices, "Designing Databases," "The Systems Development Life Cycle Basics," and "Hardware and Software Basics," are available in PDF format.

ACKNOWLEDGMENTS

I would like to acknowledge the hard work of my co-author and previous authors who gave me an excellent base upon which to build this edition. I would like to extend special thanks to Irene Herremans from the University of Calgary, Graham McFarlane and other members of the Haskayne School of Business MIS Industry Advisory Council, and my mentor Ron Murch, who helped contribute valuable advice and ideas used in some of the case material for this fourth Canadian edition. I would also like to thank the reviewers who in a number of cases made some well-thought-out and very specific suggestions for improvement. I am also grateful to the team at McGraw-Hill Ryerson, particularly Sarah Fulton, James Booty, and Jessica Barnoski, as well as my copy editor, Rodney Rawlings. I would also like to thank Laura McJannet for introducing me to James and the *Business Driven Information Systems* project.

Cameron

Reviewers for the Fourth Canadian Edition

Jennifer Percival, University of Ontario Institute of Technology

Anteneh Ayanso, Brock University

Norman Shaw, Ryerson University

Sheri Adekola, Sheridan Institute of Technology

Bernie Warren, Thompson Rivers University

Gokul Bhandari, University of Windsor

Barbara Eddy, Sheridan Institute of Technology

WALKTHROUGH

Why Do I Need to Know This? and Learning Outcomes

Why Do I Need to Know This? Located on the first page of each chapter, this section clearly outlines for students how the material to be covered in the chapter is relevant to them as business students.

WHY DO I NEED TO KNOW THIS ?

This chapter sets the stage for the textbook. It starts from ground zero by providing a clear description of what information systems are and how they fit into business practice and organizational activities. The chapter then provides an overview of how organizations operate in competitive environments and how firms need to constantly define and redefine their business strategies to create a competitive advantage. Doing so allows organizations to survive and thrive. It is important to note that an

Learning Outcomes. These outcomes focus on what students should learn and be able to communicate upon completion of the chapter.

LEARNING OUTCOMES

LO 1.1 Explain the role information systems have in business.

LO 1.2 Explain information systems basics, and the responsibilities of senior IS personnel.

LO 1.3 Describe the job market in Canada over the next several years for MIS and ICT professionals, and identify the

Chapter Opening Case and Opening Case Study Questions

Chapter Opening Case. To enhance student interest, each chapter begins with an opening case study that highlights an organization or concept that has been time-tested and value-proven in the business world. This feature serves to fortify concepts with relevant examples of outstanding companies. Discussion of the case is threaded throughout the chapters.

opening case study

Moneyball: About More Than Just the Players

Billy Beane was the general manager of the Oakland Athletics in the 2002 and 2003 seasons when the A's went to the playoffs with one-third of the payroll of the New York Yankees. How did he accomplish this? Beane selected what he believed were undervalued players to play on his team. Beane looked for players with high

Opening Case Study Questions. Located at the end of each section, thought-provoking questions connect the Chapter Opening Case Study with important chapter concepts.

> **OPENING CASE QUESTIONS**
>
> **Information Technology Helps LCBO Transform Itself**
>
> 1. What might have happened to the LCBO if its top executives had not supported the investment needed in IT?
> 2. Evaluate the effects on the LCBO if its inventory control and warehouse management systems fail.
> 3. Is it unethical for the LCBO to share its customer information from Vintages.com with other government agencies or departments? Explain your answer.
> 4. Is Mr. Kelly fulfilling his role as senior vice-president of information (CIO) correctly?

Projects and Case Studies

Case Studies. The text is packed with 48 case studies illustrating how a variety of prominent organizations and businesses have successfully implemented many of this text's concepts. All cases are timely and promote critical thinking. Company profiles are especially appealing and relevant to your students, helping to stir classroom discussion and interest.

Making Business Decisions. These small scenario-driven projects help students focus on decision making as it relates to the topical elements in the chapters.

> **MAKING BUSINESS DECISIONS**
>
> **1. Competitive Analysis**
>
> Cheryl O'Connell is the owner of a small, high-end retailer of women's clothing called Excelus. Excelus's business has been successful for many years, largely because of Cheryl's ability to anticipate the needs and wants of her loyal customer base and provide them with personalized service. Cheryl does not see any value in IS and does not want to invest any capital in something that will not directly affect her bottom line. Develop a proposal describing the potential IS-enabled competitive opportunities or threats Cheryl might be missing by not embracing IS. Be sure to include a Porter's Five Forces analysis and discuss which one of the

End-of-Chapter Elements

Each chapter contains complete pedagogical support in the form of:

Summary of Key Themes. These brief bulleted sections offer a tidy recap of the chapter's most important ideas, and their relevance to business.

> **SUMMARY OF KEY THEMES**
>
> The purpose of this chapter was twofold:
>
> 1. To provide you with an introduction to information systems in business.
>   a. Information systems basics were explained.
>   b. Roles and responsibilities in information systems were described.

Key Terms. Key terms are displayed at the end of each chapter.

> **KEY TERMS**
>
> Business-driven information systems
> Business intelligence (BI)
> Business process
> Business-to-business (B2B) marketplace
>
> Buyer power
> Chief information officer (CIO)
> Chief knowledge officer (CKO)
> Chief privacy officer (CPO)

Three Closing Case Studies. These case studies reinforce important concepts with prominent examples from businesses and organizations. Discussion questions follow each case study.

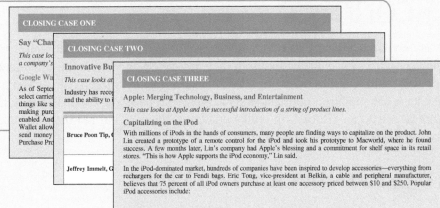

About the Plug-Ins

Located on Connect, the overall goal of the Plug-Ins is to provide an alternative for faculty who find themselves having to purchase an extra book to support Microsoft Office instruction. The Plug-Ins offer integration with the core chapters and provide critical knowledge using essential business applications, such as Microsoft Excel, Access, and Project. Each Plug-In uses hands-on tutorials for comprehension and mastery.

End-of-Chapter Elements

Each Plug-In chapter contains complete pedagogical support in the form of:

Plug-In Summary. Revisits the plug-in highlights in summary format.

Making Business Decisions. Small scenario-driven projects that help students focus individually on decision making as they relate to the topical elements in the chapters.

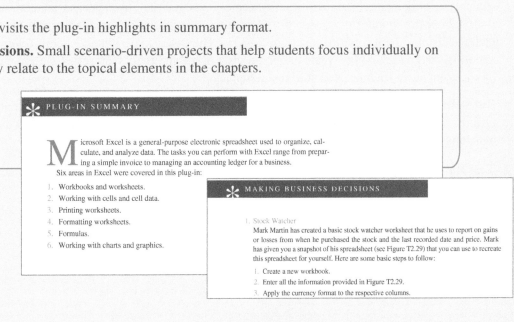

connect

McGraw-Hill Connect™ is a Web-based assignment and assessment platform that gives students the means to better connect with their coursework, with their instructors, and with the important concepts that they will need to know for success now and in the future. With Connect, instructors can deliver assignments, quizzes, and tests easily online. Students can practise important skills at their own pace and on their own schedule. With Connect, students also get 24/7 access to an eBook—an online edition of the text—to aid them in successfully completing their work, wherever and whenever they choose.

LEARNSMART

No two students are alike. Why should their learning paths be? LearnSmart uses revolutionary adaptive technology to build a learning experience unique to each student's individual needs. It starts by identifying the topics a student knows and does not know. As the student progresses, LearnSmart adapts and adjusts the content based on his or her individual strengths, weaknesses, and confidence, ensuring that every minute spent studying with LearnSmart is the most efficient and productive study time possible.

SMARTBOOK

As the first and only adaptive reading experience, SmartBook is changing the way students read and learn. SmartBook creates a personalized reading experience by highlighting the most important concepts a student needs to learn at that moment in time. As a student engages with SmartBook, the reading experience continuously adapts by highlighting content based on what each student knows and doesn't know. This ensures that he or she is focused on the content needed to close specific knowledge gaps, while it simultaneously promotes long-term learning.

Instructor and student resources available within Connect include the following:

Instructor Supplements

- **Treadsoftly Adventures Running Excel Cases:** New to the fourth edition, this series of 8 case assignments gets students to work through "real-life" business problems in Excel. In each case, students are introduced to a business issue facing the founder of Treadsoftly Adventures. With the information provided, they resolve the issue and make decisions about future business operations. The cases begin with decisions relating to the company startup, and run through the first few years of operations. Each assignment features a case and backgrounder video narrated by the company's founder, and an Excel template.

- **Video Exercises:** Each of the videos that accompanies the text is supported by detailed teaching notes on how to turn the videos into classroom exercises in which your students can apply the knowledge they are learning after watching the videos.

- **Test Bank:** This computerized package allows instructors to custom-design, save, and generate tests. The testing program permits instructors to edit, add, and delete questions from the test banks, analyze test results, and organize a database of tests and student results.

- **Instructor's Manual (IM):** The IM includes suggestions for designing the course and presenting the material. Each chapter is supported by answers to end-of-chapter questions and problems, and suggestions concerning the discussion topics and cases.

- **Microsoft® PowerPoint® Presentations:** A set of PowerPoint slides accompanies each chapter and features a lecture outline, key figures and tables from the text, and detailed teaching notes.

- **Technology Plug-Ins and Associated Files.** The Technology Plug-Ins offer integration with core chapters and provide critical knowledge using essential business applications such as Microsoft Excel, Access, and Project. Each Plug-In includes associated data files and an accompanying PowerPoint presentation to aid student learning.

- **Opening Case Scenarios.** For each chapter there is an Opening Case scenario, putting the student in the role of a business person assigned a task related to the case. Intended to prepare students for increasingly common scenario-based job interview questions, these scenarios help students to connect chapter content to real-world business decisions.

- **Audio Glossary.**

- **Apply Your Knowledge Projects and Associated Files.** Apply Your Knowledge Projects challenge students to bring the skills they have learned from the chapter to real business problems. These projects help to develop the application and problem-solving skills of students through challenging and creative business-driven scenarios.

- **Apply Your Knowledge Tools Projects.** These 34 projects focus on student application of core concepts and tools. All tools projects come with a Captivate solution file that walks students step by step through the solution, saving instructors valuable time.

- **Image Library:** Text figures and tables, as permission allows, are provided in a format by which they can be imported into PowerPoint for class lectures.

- **Project Files:** The authors have provided files for all projects that need further support, such as data files.

- **Cohesion Case:** The Broadway Café is a running case instructors can use to reinforce core material such as customer relationship management, supply chain management, business intelligence, and decision making. The case has 15 sections that challenge students to develop and expand their grandfather's coffee shop. Students receive hands-on experience in business and learn technology's true value of enabling business. The case can be found at **www.cohesioncase.com**.

- **Database Cohesion Case:** This case mimics the Broadway Café cohesion case with a focus on databases. The database cohesion case can be found at **www.cohesioncase.com/database**.

- **Video Content:** Twenty videos accompany this text and cover topics from entrepreneurship to disaster recovery. Video IMs are also available so you can turn the videos into engaging classroom activities.

SUPERIOR LEARNING SOLUTIONS AND SUPPORT

The McGraw-Hill Ryerson team is ready to help you assess and integrate any of our products, technology, and services into your course for optimal teaching and learning performance. Whether it's helping your students improve their grades, or putting your entire course online, the McGraw-Hill Ryerson team is here to help you do it. Contact your Learning Solutions Consultant today to learn how to maximize all of McGraw-Hill Ryerson's resources!

For more information on the latest technology and Learning Solutions offered by McGraw-Hill Ryerson and its partners, please visit us online: **www.mheducation.ca/he/solutions**.

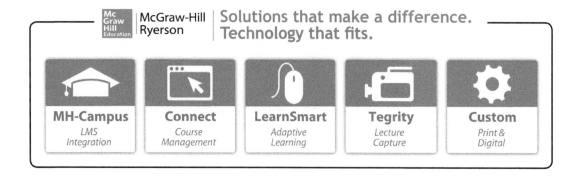

Business-Driven Information Systems

Module 1 introduces us to the use of management information systems (MIS), which most companies rely heavily on to run various aspects of their businesses. Whether they need to order and ship goods, interact with customers, or conduct other business functions, companies often use management information systems as the underlying infrastructure for the activities. MIS allow companies to remain competitive in today's fast-paced world, and especially when conducting business on the Internet. Every organization must adapt to technological advances and innovations to keep pace with today's rapidly changing environment. If it doesn't, its competitors certainly will!

No matter how exciting technology may be, successful companies do not use it simply for its own sake. They should have a solid business reason. The purpose of Module 1 is to raise your awareness of the vast opportunities made possible by the tight correlation between business and technology. Business strategies and processes should always drive technology choices. Although awareness of an emerging technology can sometimes lead us in new strategic directions, the role of information systems, for the most part, is to support existing business strategies and processes.

CHAPTER 1

Information Systems and Business Strategy

LO 1.1 Explain the role information systems have in business.

LO 1.2 Explain information systems basics, and the responsibilities of senior IS personnel.

LO 1.3 Describe the job market in Canada over the next several years for MIS and ICT professionals, and identify the opportunities.

LO 1.4 Describe how business-driven information systems can increase a company's competitive business strategy.

LO 1.5 Explain the various ways organizations can assess their competitive advantage (e.g., the Five Forces Model, three generic strategies, and value chain analysis).

This chapter sets the stage for the textbook. It starts from ground zero by providing a clear description of what information systems are and how they fit into business practice and organizational activities. The chapter then provides an overview of how organizations operate in competitive environments and how firms need to constantly define and redefine their business strategies to create a competitive advantage. Doing so allows organizations to survive and thrive. It is important to note that an information system is shown as a key enabler to help organizations operate successfully in such competitive environments.

As a business student, you should be aware of the tight correlation between business and information systems. First you must understand an information system's role in daily business life, and then realize how information systems can support and implement enterprise-wide initiatives and global business strategies. After reading this chapter, you will acquire a solid understanding of business-driven information systems, information systems fundamentals, and business strategy.

Information Technology Helps LCBO Transform Itself

Liquor Control Board of Ontario

The Liquor Control Board of Ontario (LCBO) transformed itself from a boring, not-so-tech-savvy government-run agency into a pretty sophisticated Canadian retailer, according to its senior vice-president of IT, Hugh Kelly, when ComputerWorld Canada spoke to him back in 2009. Information technology and systems have become an integral part of the business with such things as **LCBO.com** and **Vintages.com**, a warehouse management system, forecast and replenishment systems, and an intranet. This has led to record sales in both 2011–12 and 2012–13. A key aspect of the record dividends are the operational efficiencies that the LCBO is finding. "Net sales growth resulted from consumers trading up to premium products, incremental sales from new stores, an appealing product mix and effective marketing," said LCBO President and CEO Bob Peter. In 2011–12, "[g]ood expense control and inventory management also allowed us to capitalize on increased dollar sales and exceed last year's dividend in a challenging economy." In 2012–13, "[d]espite a challenging retail economy, LCBO was able to deliver these results by managing expense, careful product and inventory control and executing store network improvements." said LCBO President and CEO Bob Peter.[1]

The LCBO also completed its 13th annual social responsibility campaign in 2011–12 with the "Home Bartending Challenge" at **DeflateTheElephant.com**, which resulted in the continued growth of the LCBO's Deflate the Elephant social responsibility campaign. The campaign encouraged hosts to help prevent guests from drinking and driving through a Facebook Pledge photo contest and TV commercials during the summer and holiday seasons.

Vintages

Vintages, along with Vintages.com, is a premium wine and spirits bilingual retailer that has introduced 5,000 new and unique products to the buying public in Ontario. Using the 600-plus LCBO store network and its website, Vintages introduces 125 new products on a biweekly basis to customers while maintaining a stock of its customers' favourites in its Essentials Collection.

Those purchasing online have their orders delivered to their local LCBO store so that the LCBO can maintain its role in ensuring social responsibility and not shipping to minors. To make this happen the LCBO contracted with Robocom Systems International to maintain a real-time inventory of products that directly interfaces with the company's warehouse management system. "So," according to Kelly, "if the system tells you there are ten bottles available, as soon as you order two bottles, it indicates that only eight bottles are left for the next customer." Also needed is a credit card payment system that complies with Payment Card Industry Data Security Standards (PCI DSS) and a process that ensures that once an order is made it is picked from the warehouse and shipped to the customer's nearest store, an automated email is sent to customer, and the credit card is charged for the purpose.

LCBO.com

LCBO.com was revamped to better engage and target its customers. The idea was to have the LCBO become involved in social media, and tailor the site to its individual customers' needs. He also planned to bring this involvement to the customer in the stores with interactive flat-screen kiosks designed to better inform customers about their purchases and to get instant feedback. Today the customer is able to perform a customized search for specific products and determine which stores have those products. The site acts as a hub for LCBO special promotions and contains podcasts such as "Decoding Wine Labels" in its "LCBO Wine 101: Video Podcast Series." It also gives the customer cocktail recipes, food and drink, and entertainment tips, and suggestions for thank-you or corporate gifts, and maintains the LCBO's commitment to social responsibility with a dedicated section of the site.

Supply Chain

Customers see Vintages and LCBO.com first-hand; they do not see behind the scenes where technology also plays a key role in the new LCBO. Systems such as the warehouse management system allow them to distribute products in less than a full case, know when a bottle in a case has been broken, and accurately reflect the inventory levels so that when a customer orders a bottle of wine they can ensure timely delivery. Other systems allow the LCBO to forecast and replenish stock in a timely manner based on over-the-counter sales information that is fed back to head office.

LCBO 2.0

Internally, the company manages its communications with an extensive intranet that reduces the financial and environmental burdens of paper-based memos and forms. It is used to send internal bulletins, memos, and expense reports, or to lessen the burden on employees when distributing LCBO media reports. It is the primary communication vehicle for the company.

Apps

The LCBO introduced the app "LCBO on the Go" for BlackBerry and iPhone users that allows them to search the LCBO inventory, find the closest store, and browse for products from their smartphone. They have Deflate the Elephant's "SpeakUp" iPhone app that helps hosts send friendly reminders about drinking and driving and contains recipes for mocktails. They also lend support for Natalie MacLean's new mobile wine app, which allows users to search 150,000 wines available across the country and get inventory levels in nearby stores.[2]

1.1 INFORMATION SYSTEMS IN BUSINESS

LO1 INFORMATION SYSTEMS' ROLE IN BUSINESS

Did you know that

- The movie *Avatar* took more than four years to create and cost $450 million?
- Lady Gaga's real name is Stefani Joanne Angelina Germanotta?
- Customers pay $2.6 million for a 30-second advertising time slot during the Super Bowl?

A *fact* is the confirmation or validation of an event or object. In the past, people primarily learned facts from books. Today, by simply pushing a button people can find out anything, from anywhere, at any time. We live in the *information age*, when infinite quantities of facts are widely available to anyone who can use a computer. The impact of information technology on the global business environment is equivalent to the printing press's impact on publishing and electricity's impact on productivity. College student startups were mostly unheard of before the information age. Now, it's not at all unusual to read about a business student starting a multimillion-dollar company from his or her dorm room. Think of Mark Zuckerberg, who started Facebook from his dorm, or Michael Dell (Dell Computers) and Bill Gates (Microsoft), who both founded their legendary companies as college students.

You may think only students well versed in advanced technology can compete in the information age. This is simply not true. Many business leaders have created exceptional opportunities by coupling the power of the information age with traditional business methods. Here are just a few examples:

- Amazon is not a technology company; its original business focus was to sell books, and it now sells nearly everything (see Figure 1.1).
- Netflix is not a technology company; its primary business focus is to rent videos.
- Zappos is not a technology company; its primary business focus is to sell shoes, bags, clothing, and accessories.

FIGURE 1.1

Amazon.com

Amazon's founder, Jeff Bezos, at first saw an opportunity to change the way people purchase books. Using the power of the information age to tailor offerings to each customer and speed the payment process, he in effect opened millions of tiny virtual bookstores, each with a vastly larger selection and far cheaper product than traditional bookstores. The success of his original business model led him to expand Amazon to carry many other types of products. The founders of Netflix and Zappos have done the same thing for videos and shoes. All these entrepreneurs were business professionals, not technology experts. However, they understood enough about the information age to apply it to a particular business, creating innovative companies that now lead entire industries.

Students who understand business along with the power associated with the information age will create their own opportunities and perhaps even new industries, as co-founders Jack Dorsey, Evan Williams, Biz Stone, and Noah Glass did with Twitter and Mark Zuckerberg with Facebook. Our primary goal in this book is to arm you with the knowledge you need to compete in the information age.

Information Systems' Impact on Business Operations

Achieving the results such as reducing costs, improving productivity, and generating growth is not easy. Implementing a new accounting system or marketing plan is not likely to generate long-term growth or reduce costs across an entire organization. Businesses undertake enterprise-wide initiatives to achieve broad general business goals such as reducing costs. Information technology plays a critical role in deploying such initiatives by facilitating communication with technologies like WiMax and increasing business analytics through tools like SAS Enterprise Miner.

Understanding information systems begins with an understanding of how businesses function and of information systems' role in creating efficiencies and effectiveness across the organization. Typical businesses operate by functional areas or *silos*. Each silo undertakes a specific core business function (see Figure 1.2).

Functional areas are anything but independent in a business. In fact, functional areas are *interdependent* (see Figure 1.3). Sales must rely on information from operations to understand inventory, place orders, calculate transportation costs, and gain insight into product availability based on production schedules. For an organization to succeed, every department or functional area must work together to share common information and not be a silo. Information systems can enable departments to more efficiently and effectively perform their business operations.

COMMON DEPARTMENTS IN AN ORGANIZATION

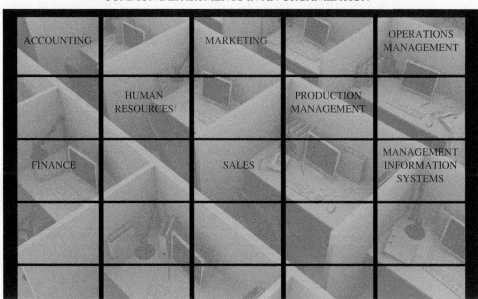

FIGURE 1.2

Departmental Structure of a Typical Organization

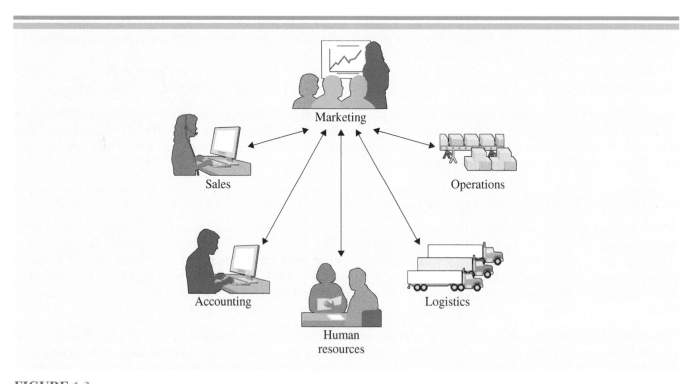

FIGURE 1.3

Marketing Working with Other Organizational Departments

Individuals anticipating a successful business career, whether in accounting, finance, human resources, or operations management, must understand information systems basics and how information systems impact businesses.

LO2 | INFORMATION SYSTEMS BASICS

Information systems (IS) are computer-based tools that people use to work with information and that support the information and information processing needs of an organization. An information system can be an important enabler of business success and innovation. This is not to say that IS *equals* business success and innovation or that IS *represents* business success and innovation. Information systems are most useful when they leverage the talents of people. Information systems in and of themselves are not useful unless the right people know how to use and manage them effectively.

Information technology (IT), on the other hand, is the acquisition, processing, storage, and dissemination of vocal, pictorial, textual, and numerical information by a microelectronics-based combination of computing and telecommunications.[3]

Management information systems is a business function just like marketing, finance, operations, and human resources management. Formally defined, *management information systems (MIS)* is the function that plans for, develops, implements, and maintains IT hardware, software, and applications that people use to support the goals of an organization. To perform the MIS function effectively, almost all organizations today, particularly large and medium-sized ones, have an internal IS department, often called Information Technology (IT), Information Systems (IS), or Management Information Systems (MIS).

Data, Information, Business Intelligence, and Knowledge

The core drivers of the information age are:

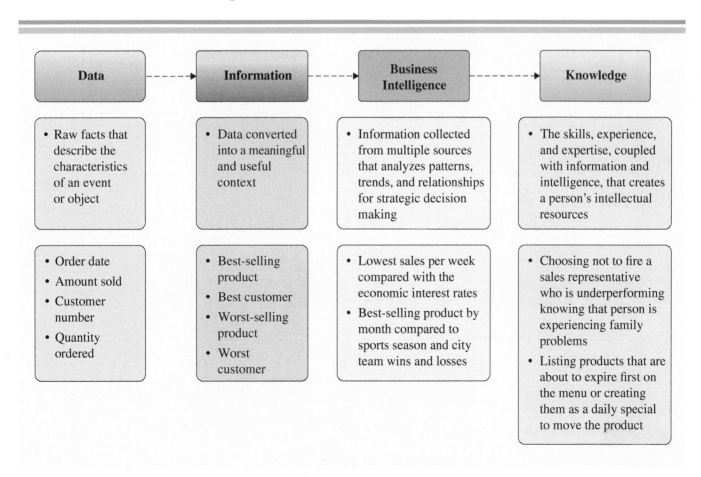

FIGURE 1.4

Data, Information, Business Intelligence, and Knowledge

- Data
- Information
- Business intelligence
- Knowledge (see Figure 1.4)

It is important to distinguish between data, information, and knowledge. **Data** are raw facts that describe the characteristics of an object or event. Characteristics for a sales event could include the date, item number, item description, quantity ordered, customer name, and shipping details. **Information** is data converted into a meaningful and useful context. Information from sales events could include best-selling item, worst-selling item, best customer, and worst customer. **Business intelligence (BI)** is information collected from multiple sources such as suppliers, customers, competitors, partners, and industries that analyzes patterns, trends, and relationships for strategic decision making. BI manipulates multiple variables and in some cases even hundreds of variables including such items as interest rates, weather conditions, and even gas prices. **Knowledge** is information that is acted upon. In this sense, *knowledge* is "actionable information" (see Chapter 3). Information systems applications, such as Microsoft Excel, help display and manage data (see Figure 1.5), turn data into information (see Figure 1.6), and generate knowledge for decision-making purposes (i.e., present information that can be acted upon) (see Figure 1.7).

Order Date	Product Name	Quantity	Unit Price	Total Sales	Unit Cost	Total Cost	Profit	Customer	Sales Rep
04-Jan-10	Mozzarella cheese	41	24	984	18	738	246	The Station	Debbie Fernand
04-Jan-10	Romaine lettuce	90	15	1,350	14	1,260	90	The Station	Roberta Cross
05-Jan-10	Red onions	27	12	324	8	216	108	Bert's Bistro	Loraine Schultz
06-Jan-10	Romaine lettuce	67	15	1,005	14	938	67	Smoke House	Roberta Cross
07-Jan-10	Black olives	79	12	948	6	474	474	Flagstaff House	Loraine Schultz
07-Jan-10	Romaine lettuce	46	15	690	14	644	46	Two Bitts	Loraine Schultz
07-Jan-10	Romaine lettuce	52	15	780	14	728	52	Pierce Arrow	Roberta Cross
08-Jan-10	Red onions	39	12	468	8	312	156	Mamm'a Pasta Palace	Loraine Schultz
09-Jan-10	Romaine lettuce	66	15	990	14	924	66	The Dandelion	Loraine Schultz
10-Jan-10	Romaine lettuce	58	15	870	14	812	58	Carmens	Loraine Schultz
10-Jan-10	Pineapple	40	33	1,320	28	1,120	200	The Station	Loraine Schultz

Rows of data

FIGURE 1.5

Data

Order Date	Product Name	Quantity	Unit Price	Total Sales	Unit Cost	Total Cost	Profit	Customer	Sales Rep
15-Feb-10	Chicken	41	36	1,476	25	1,025	451	Smoke House	Roberta Cross
19-Feb-10	Chicken	50	36	1,800	25	1,250	550	Smoke House	Roberta Cross
03-Mar-10	Chicken	64	36	2,304	25	1,600	704	Pierce Arrow	Roberta Cross
12-Apr-10	Chicken	2	36	72	25	50	22	Laudisio	Roberta Cross
08-Jul-10	Chicken	94	36	3,384	25	2,350	1,034	Pierce Arrow	Roberta Cross
20-Nov-10	Chicken	15	36	540	25	375	165	Two Bitts	Roberta Cross
28-Nov-10	Chicken	6	36	216	25	150	66	Laudisio	Roberta Cross
30-Nov-10	Chicken	51	36	1,836	25	1,275	561	Pierce Arrow	Roberta Cross

This view shows all of Roberta Cross's chicken sales information.

FIGURE 1.6

Information

Distribution Analysis		
Question	Name	Total
Who is Bob's best customer by total sales?	Pierce Arrow	$ 56,789
Who is Bob's worst customer by total sales	Smoke House	$ 3,456
Who is Bob's best customer by profit?	Laudisio	$ 45,777
Who is Bob's worst customer by profit?	Carmens	$ 4,555
What is Bob's best-selling product by total sales?	Chicken	$ 34,234
What is Bob's worst-selling product by total sales?	Black olives	$ 567
What is Bob's best-selling product by profit?	Peppers	$ 22,444
What is Bob's worst-selling product by profit?	Red onions	$ 2,443
Who is Bob's best sales representative by profit?	Loraine Schultz	$ 98,989
Who is Bob's worst sales representative by profit?	Roberta Cross	$ 4,567
What is the best sales representative's best-selling product (by total profit)?	Red onions	$ 24,343
Who is the best sales representative's best customer (by total profit)?	Flagstaff House	$ 1,234
What is the best sales representative's worst-selling product (by total profit)?	Romaine lettuce	$ 45,678
Who is the best sales representative's worst customer (by total profit)?	Bert's Bistro	$ 5,678

Advanced analytical tools uncover business intelligence in the data
that can be acted upon.

FIGURE 1.7

Knowledge

Information Resources and Cultures

The plans and goals of the MIS department must align with the plans and goals of the organization. Information systems can enable an organization to increase efficiency in manufacturing, retain key customers, seek out new sources of supply, and introduce effective financial management.

It is not always easy for managers to make the right choices when using IS to support (and often drive) business initiatives. Most managers understand their business initiatives well, but are often at a loss when it comes to knowing how to use and manage IS effectively in support of those initiatives. Managers who understand what information systems are, and what they can and cannot do, are in the best position for success. In essence:

■ *People* use

■ *processes* to work with

■ *information* systems

■ to produce *information* (see Figure 1.8)

These key resources—people, processes, and information systems (in that order of priority)—are inextricably linked and essential for the creation of information. If one of these fails, they all fail. Most important, if one fails, chances are the business will fail.

An organization's culture also plays a large role in determining how successfully it will share information. Culture influences the way people use information (their information behaviour) and reflects the importance that company leaders attribute to using information in achieving success or avoiding failure. Four common information-sharing cultures exist in organizations today: information-functional, information-sharing, information-inquiring, and information-discovery (see Figure 1.9).[4]

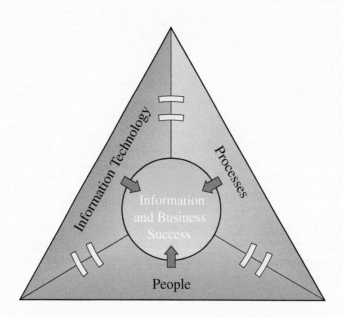

FIGURE 1.8

The Relationships Among People, Processes, Information Technology, and Information

INFORMATION-FUNCTIONAL CULTURE

Employees use information as a means of exercising influence or power over others. For example, a sales manager refuses to share information with marketing. This causes marketing to need whenever the sales manager's input a new sales strategy is developed.

INFORMATION-INQUIRING CULTURE

Employees across departments search for information to better understand the future and align themselves with current trends and new directions.

INFORMATION-SHARING CULTURE

Employees across departments trust each other to use information (especially about problems and failures) to improve performance.

INFORMATION-DISCOVERY CULTURE

Employees across departments are open to new insights about crises and radical changes and seek ways to create competitive advantages.

FIGURE 1.9

Different Information Cultures Found in Organizations

An organization's information culture can directly affect its ability to compete in the global market. If an organization operates with an information-functional culture, it will have a great degree of difficulty operating. Getting products to market quickly and creating a view of its end-to-end (or entire) business from sales to billing is a challenge. If an organization operates with an information-discovery culture it can get products to market quickly and easily see a 360-degree view of its entire organization. Employees can use this view to better understand the market and create new products that offer a competitive advantage.

LO3 | ROLES AND RESPONSIBILITIES IN INFORMATION SYSTEMS

Employees across the organization must work closely together to develop strategic initiatives that create competitive advantages. Understanding the basic structure of a typical IS department—including titles, roles, and responsibilities—helps an organization build a cohesive enterprise-wide team. MIS is a relatively new functional area, having been around formally in most organizations only for about 40 years. Job titles, roles, and responsibilities often differ from organization to organization. Nonetheless, clear trends are developing toward elevating some MIS positions within an organization to the strategic level.

The *chief information officer (CIO)* is an executive-level position that involves high-level strategic planning and management of information systems pertaining to the creation, storage, and use of information by a business. The CIO is responsible for overseeing all uses of information systems, and ensuring the strategic alignment of IS with business goals and objectives. As a result, the CIO must have a deep understanding of both information systems and business; the need for in-depth IS knowledge enables him or her to understand how systems can help business. This requires a solid understanding of every aspect of an organization coupled with tremendous insight into the capability of IS. It is also important for a CIO to be able to communicate to others in the organization how information systems can be used for the benefit of the enterprise—for example, how IS can enable the development of new products and services and yield greater returns on investment for the company. Further, the CIO must be able to successfully implement and make use of information systems to reach such goals.

Due to the strategic importance of this role, more and more CIOs play a key role in the executive suite. The broad roles of a CIO include:

- *Manager.* Ensure the delivery of all IS projects, on time and within budget.
- *Leader.* Ensure the strategic vision of IS is in line with the strategic vision of the organization.
- *Communicator.* Advocate and communicate the IS strategy by building and maintaining strong executive relationships.

Though all CIO positions contain aspects of these three broad roles, it is interesting to note that the CIO role can differ in terms of how CIOs manage their time and the hurdles CIOs face, and the impact CIOs have on their organizations. For example, both Canadian and American CIOs indicate that the bulk of their time is spent meeting with company executives and working with IS vendors and non-IS business partners. However, when polled, American CIOs also state that a large chunk of their time is concentrated on planning strategy. CIOs from both Canada and the United States identify alignment between corporate strategy and IS as a key management priority. Canadians, however, appear to be further ahead in getting business counterparts to share accountability for IS investments, which should have a direct positive effect on alignment. American CIOs rate unrealistic or unknown expectations from business and inadequate budgets as top hurdles to CIO effectiveness.

Although the CIO is considered a position within IS, CIOs must be concerned with more than just IS. In annual industry surveys by industry associations and firms such as CIO Magazine, Gartner, and Forrester, CIOs have consistently ranked attracting and retaining customers and reducing enterprise costs high in their top yearly priorities. Figure 1.10 shows the top three activities for CIOs from CIO Magazine's survey for 2014.[5]

Game-Changing Activities	Service/Cost Centre Activities
Driving business innovation	Improving IT operations
Cultivating IT-business relationship	Developing new systems
Developing business strategy	Controlling IT costs

FIGURE 1.10

Results of CIO Magazine's Top Three Activities of CIOs[6]

The *chief technology officer (CTO)* is responsible for ensuring the throughput, speed, accuracy, availability, and reliability of an organization's information technology. CTOs have direct responsibility for ensuring the efficiency of IT resources used in information systems throughout the organization. Most CTOs possess a well-rounded knowledge of all aspects of IT, including hardware, software, and telecommunications. CTOs typically report to the chief information officer (CIO). The role of CTO is similar to that of CIO, except that CIOs must take on the additional responsibility of ensuring that the technology aligns with the organization's strategic initiatives.

The *chief security officer (CSO)* is responsible for ensuring the security of information systems, and developing strategies and technical safeguards against attacks from hackers and viruses. The role of a CSO has been elevated in recent years because of the number of such attacks. Most CSOs possess detailed knowledge of networks and telecommunications because hackers and viruses usually find their way into information systems through networked computers.

The *chief privacy officer (CPO)* is responsible for ensuring the ethical and legal use of information within an organization. CPOs are the newest senior executive position in IS. Recently, 150 of the Fortune 500 companies added the CPO position to their list of senior executives. Many CPOs are lawyers by training, enabling them to understand the often complex legal issues surrounding the use of information and information technology.

The *chief knowledge officer (CKO)* is responsible for collecting, maintaining, and distributing an organization's knowledge. The CKO designs processes and information systems that make it easy for people to reuse knowledge. These systems create repositories of organizational documents, methodologies, tools, and practices, and they establish methods for filtering information. The CKO must continuously encourage employee contributions to keep the information systems up to date. The CKO can contribute directly to the organization's bottom line by reducing the learning curve for new employees or employees taking on new roles.

Studies conducted at the Institute for Intellectual Capital Research in Hamilton, Ontario, indicate that the CKO position will become commonplace. The Institute surveyed 53 executive search firms in Canada and the United States about their perceptions regarding CKO placements. Almost three-quarters of survey respondents expected that searches for CKO placements will increase significantly.[7]

All of the above IS positions and responsibilities are critical to an organization's success. While many organizations may not have a different individual for each of these positions, they must have leaders taking responsibility for all these areas of concern. The individuals responsible for enterprise-wide IS and IS-related issues must provide guidance and support to the organization's employees.

The Skills Gap in Canada

Beyond the senior roles in MIS, opportunities will exist in MIS or ICT (information, communications, and technology) within Canada over the next number of years, especially for those with a combination of business skills and technical skills.

According to the Information and Communications Technology Council, there will be a need to hire 106,000 ICT workers from 2011 to 2016 in Canada, and because of the unique mix of business skills and technical skills required this will be a serious and pervasive problem in all regions of Canada. The greatest shortages will be for computer and information systems managers, telecommunications carrier managers, and information systems analysts and consultants. According to the report, "the severity of these shortages will increase when employers are looking for individuals with leading edge skills or with particular combinations of domain experience and ICT expertise." Even with the shortages there will be a few areas where supply will exceed demand, such as computer programmers and interactive media designers, computer network technicians, and user support technicians. In these areas programmers that work with Java, .Net, or ERP applications like SAP and Oracle will still be in high demand.

The council also notes that graduates who have experience through a co-op program or internship will have a distinct advantage over graduates from traditional programs without a practicum component in finding employment in the ICT field. The mix of technical skills with a knowledge of business is essential, as the report points out:

> At the heart of the skills shortage challenge is a pervasive mismatch between the capabilities that employers require and the skills and experience (or lack thereof) of many job-seekers. Over the course of the past decade, employers became increasingly dissatisfied with ICT professionals who had suitable technical skills,

but who lacked soft skills or relevant business experience. As a result, a new capabilities profile emerged. This capabilities profile included technical skills, soft skills (team working ability, communications skills, etc.) and context skills, i.e., an understanding of the business needs and business processes to which ICT is applied. By the end of the last decade (if not earlier), this broader capabilities profile had become the new norm for employers seeking to fill ICT jobs.

The report also suggests that the types of skills sets employers are looking for fall into two fairly specific categories:

Two types of skill profiles are in demand. The first combines ICT skills with an understanding of business processes including an understanding of the specific context in which a business or organization operates. The second combines ICT skills with the technical skills that are important to another field, for example, a particular industry or sector.

One of the greatest challenges today is effective communication between business personnel and IT personnel. Figure 1.11 demonstrates the importance of communication for IS executives. Business personnel possess expertise in functional areas such as marketing, accounting, sales, and so forth. IS personnel have the technological expertise. Unfortunately, a communications gap often exists between the two. Business personnel have their own vocabularies based on their experience and expertise, whereas IS personnel's vocabularies consist of acronyms and technical terms. Effective communication between business and IS personnel should be a two-way street, with each side making the effort to understand each other (including written and oral communication).

Skill	What It Means
Communications	The ability to communicate and influence at all levels
Business knowledge	A need to understand and focus on how they can help their businesses grow and not just look at cutting costs and being more efficient
Innovation/creativity	The vision that differentiates a CIO from a more traditional IT director—innovation, creativity, flair, and an entrepreneurial spirit
Leadership	Good leaders who inspire and motivate their teams and drive them to achieve remarkable things
Domain knowledge	A practical understanding of technology fundamentals in order to make the right strategic calls about the deployment and exploitation of IT

FIGURE 1.11

Skills Required by IT Executives and What They Really Mean[8]

At the same time, organizations must develop strategies for integrating IS personnel into the various business functions. Too often, IS personnel are left out of strategy meetings because of the belief they do not understand the business so they will not add any value. That is a dangerous position to take. IS personnel must understand the business if the organization is going to determine which technologies can benefit (or hurt) the business. With a little effort to communicate, IS personnel might provide information on the functionality available in an information system, which could add tremendous value to a meeting about how to improve customer service. Working together, business and IS personnel have the potential to create competitive advantages, reduce costs, and streamline business processes.

It is the CIO's responsibility to ensure effective communications between business and IS personnel. While the CIO assumes the responsibility on an enterprise-wide level, it is each employee's responsibility to communicate effectively on a personal level.

Figure 1.12 lists the median salaries and median salaries with bonuses for information systems careers in Calgary, Alberta, in February 2014. It also lists the number of typical years of experience for someone entering into each of the positions, as reported by corporate HR departments.

Position	Median Salary	Median Salary with Bonuses	Years of Experience
Business Systems Analyst I	$63,303	$67,500	0–2
Business Systems Analyst II	$76,621	$80,785	2–4
Business Systems Analyst III	$88,835	$94,128	4–6
IS Auditor II	$94,261	$101,299	2–4
Web Designer	$81,369	$83,661	2–4
IT Manager	$113,247	$123,566	5
Help Desk Manager	$97,748	$105,171	7
Business Process Consultant	$115,571	$128,554	7
Project Coordinator	$85,593	$89,490	5
IT Director	$163,057	$192,440	8
CIO/CTO	$217,356	$277,637	10–12

FIGURE 1.12

Median Salaries of Selected ICT Positions (2014)[9]

Source: Used with permission of Salary.com, an IBM company.

OPENING CASE QUESTIONS

Information Technology Helps LCBO Transform Itself

1. What might have happened to the LCBO if its top executives had not supported the investment needed in IT?

2. Evaluate the effects on the LCBO if its inventory control and warehouse management systems fail.

3. Is it unethical for the LCBO to share its customer information from Vintages.com with other government agencies or departments? Explain your answer.

4. Is Mr. Kelly fulfilling his role as senior vice-president of information (CIO) correctly?

1.2   BUSINESS STRATEGY

LO4] IDENTIFYING COMPETITIVE ADVANTAGES

To survive and thrive, an organization must create a competitive advantage. A *competitive advantage* is a product or service that an organization's customers put a greater value on than similar offerings from a competitor. Unfortunately, competitive advantages are typically temporary because competitors often seek ways to duplicate the competitive advantage. In turn, organizations must develop a strategy based on a new competitive advantage.

When an organization is the first to market with a competitive advantage, it gains a first-mover advantage. The *first-mover advantage* occurs when an organization can significantly impact its market share by being first to market with a competitive advantage. FedEx created a first-mover advantage by creating its customer self-service software, which allows people and organizations to request parcel pickups, print mailing slips, and track parcels online. Other parcel delivery companies quickly began creating their own online services. Today, customer self-service on the Internet is a standard for doing business in the parcel delivery business.

As organizations develop their competitive advantages, they must pay close attention to their competition through environmental scanning. *Environmental scanning* is the acquisition and analysis of events and trends in the environment external to an organization. Information technology has the opportunity to play an important role in environmental scanning.

Frito-Lay, a premier provider of snack foods such as Cracker Jacks and Cheetos, does not just send its representatives into grocery stores to stock shelves; they carry handheld computers and record the product offerings, inventory, and even the product locations of their competitors. Frito-Lay uses this information to gain business intelligence on everything from how well competing products are selling to the strategic placement of its own products.

Organizations use three common tools to analyze and develop competitive advantages: (1) Five Forces Model, (2) three generic strategies, and (3) value chain analysis.

LO5 | THE FIVE FORCES MODEL: EVALUATING BUSINESS SEGMENTS

Michael Porter's Five Forces Model is a useful tool to aid organizations facing the challenging decision of entering a new industry or industry segment. The *Five Forces Model* helps determine the relative attractiveness of an industry and includes:

- Buyer power
- Supplier power
- Threat of substitute products or services
- Threat of new entrants
- Rivalry among existing competitors (see Figure 1.13)

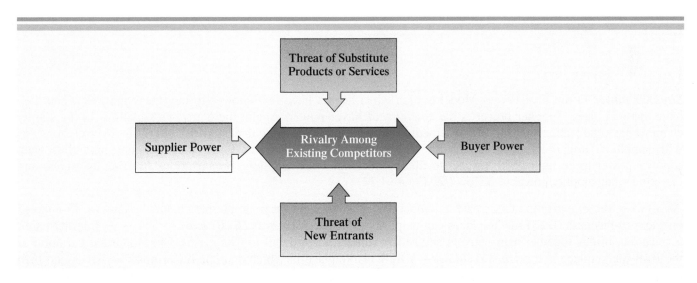

FIGURE 1.13

Porter's Five Forces Model

Buyer Power

Buyer power in the Five Forces Model is high when buyers have many choices of whom to buy from and low when their choices are few. There are two situations in the supply chain where organizations need to be concerned about buyer power: (1) in their relationships with customers; and (2) in their relationships with suppliers (see Figure 1.14). Regarding the relationships with customers, organizations function as suppliers and thus prefer to reduce the buyer power of customers (and create a competitive advantage). In this situation an organization must make it more attractive for customers to buy from it instead of its competition. One of the best IS-based examples of this is **loyalty programs**, which reward customers on the basis of the amount of business they do with a particular organization. The travel industry, for example, has its familiar frequent-flyer programs for airlines and frequent-guest programs for hotels. Keeping track of the activities and accounts of many thousands or millions of customers covered by loyalty programs is not practical without large-scale IS systems. Loyalty programs are a good example of using IS to reduce buyer power; because of the rewards travellers receive (e.g., free airline tickets, upgrades, or hotel stays), customers are more likely to be loyal to or give most of their business to a single organization. With respect to the relationship with suppliers, organizations function as buyers and thus prefer to increase their own buyer power with suppliers (and create competitive advantage). In this situation, organizations want to work with a large pool of suppliers to potentially supply the desired good or service.

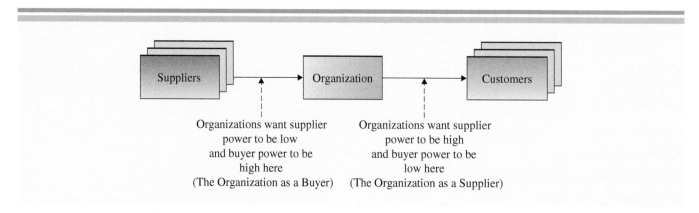

FIGURE 1.14

An Organization Within the Supply Chain

Supplier Power

Supplier power in the Five Forces Model is high when buyers have few choices to buy from and low when they have many choices. Supplier power is the converse of buyer power. Again, there are two situations in the supply chain where organizations need to be concerned: (1) in their relationships with customers; and (2) in their relationships with suppliers. Regarding the relationships with customers, organizations function as suppliers and thus want supplier power to be high. With respect to the relationships with suppliers, organizations function as buyers and therefore want supplier power to be low (see Figure 1.14).

As a buyer, the organization can create a competitive advantage by locating alternative supply sources. IS-enabled business-to-business (B2B) marketplaces can help. A **business-to-business (B2B) marketplace** is an Internet-based service that brings together many buyers and sellers (discussed in detail in Chapter 5). One important variation of the B2B marketplace is a **private exchange**—a B2B marketplace in which a single buyer posts its needs and then opens the bidding to any supplier who cares to bid. Bidding is typically carried out through a **reverse auction**, a format in which increasingly lower bids are solicited from organizations willing to supply the desired product or service at an increasingly lower price. As the bids get lower, more suppliers drop out; ultimately, the organization with the lowest bid wins. Internet-based reverse auctions are an excellent example of how information systems can reduce supplier power for an organization and create a competitive advantage.

Threat of Substitute Products or Services

The *threat of substitute products or services* in the Five Forces Model is high when there are many alternatives to a product or service and low when there are few alternatives from which to choose. Ideally, an organization prefers to be in a market in which there are few substitutes for the products or services it offers. Of course, that is seldom possible today, but an organization can still create a competitive advantage by using switching costs.

Switching costs are costs that can make customers reluctant to switch to another product or service. A switching cost need not have an associated *monetary* cost. **Amazon.ca** offers an example. As customers purchase products over time, Amazon, using IS, develops a profile of their shopping and purchasing habits, enabling it to offer products tailored to a particular customer. If the customer decides to shop elsewhere, there is an associated switching cost because the new site will not have the profile of the customer's past purchases. In this way, Amazon has reduced the threat of substitute products or services by creating a "cost" to the consumer to switch to another online retailer.

The cellphone industry offers another good example of switching costs. Cellphone providers want to keep their customers as long as possible. Many offer their customers free phones or specially priced packages with unlimited minutes, text, and data if they sign a longer-term contract. This creates a cost for the customers if they decide to switch, because they will be required to pay a penalty for breaking their contract. In the past, another switching cost for the customer was losing the actual cellphone number; however, this cost has been removed with the implementation of *local number portability (LNP)* or the ability to "port" numbers to new providers. Within the context of the Five Forces Model, eliminating this switching cost creates a greater threat of substitute products or services for the supplier. That is, cellphone customers can now expect to see more new providers cropping up over the next several years. They will compete on price, quality, and services with the big-name providers such as Rogers, TELUS, and Bell Mobility because cellphone numbers can be moved from one provider to another. When businesses reduce or eliminate switching costs, the consumer gains more power.

Threat of New Entrants

The *threat of new entrants* in the Five Forces Model is high when it is easy for new competitors to enter a market and low when there are significant entry barriers to entering a market. An entry barrier is a product or service feature that customers have come to expect from organizations in a particular industry and must be offered by an entering organization to compete and survive. For example, a new bank must offer its customers an array of IS-enabled services, including ATM use, online bill paying, and account monitoring. These are significant barriers to entering the banking market. At one time, the first bank to offer such services gained a valuable first-mover advantage, but only temporarily, as other banking competitors developed their own IS systems.

Rivalry Among Existing Competitors

Rivalry among existing competitors in the Five Forces Model is high when competition is fierce in a market and low when competition is more complacent. Although competition is always more intense in some industries than in others, the overall trend is toward increased competition in almost every industry.

The retail grocery industry is intensively competitive. While Loblaws, Sobeys, and Metro compete in many different ways, essentially they try to beat or match the competition on price. Most of them have loyalty programs that give shoppers special discounts. Customers get lower prices while the store collects valuable information on buying habits to develop more effective product placement and pricing strategies. In the future, expect to see grocery stores using wireless technology systems to track customer movement throughout the store and match it to products purchased to determine product placement and pricing strategies. Such a system will be a huge competitive advantage to the first store to implement it.

Since margins are low in the retail grocery market, grocers build efficiencies into their supply chains, connecting with their suppliers in IS-enabled information partnerships such as the one between Walmart and its suppliers. Communicating with suppliers over telecommunications networks rather than using paper-based systems makes the procurement process faster, cheaper, and more accurate. That equates to lower prices for customers and increased rivalry among existing competitors.

THE THREE GENERIC STRATEGIES: CREATING A BUSINESS FOCUS

Once the relative attractiveness of an industry is determined and an organization decides to enter that market, it must formulate a strategy for entering the new market. An organization can follow Porter's three generic strategies when entering a new market: (1) broad cost leadership; (2) broad differentiation; or (3) focused strategy. Broad strategies reach a large market segment, while focused strategies target a niche market. A focused strategy concentrates on either cost leadership or differentiation. Trying to be all things to all people, however, is a recipe for disaster, since it is difficult to project a consistent image to the entire marketplace. Porter suggests that an organization is wise to adopt only one of the three generic strategies illustrated in Figure 1.15.

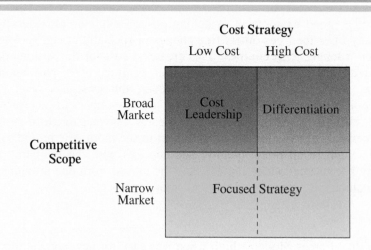

FIGURE 1.15

Porter's Three Generic Strategies

To illustrate the use of the three generic strategies, consider Figure 1.16. The matrix shown demonstrates the relationships among strategies (cost leadership versus differentiation) and market segmentation (broad versus focused).

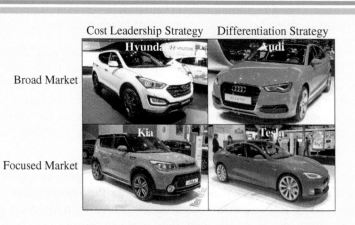

FIGURE 1.16

Porter's Three Generic Strategies in the Auto Industry

- *Hyundai* is following a broad cost leadership strategy. Hyundai offers lower-cost vehicles, in each particular model stratification, that appeal to a large audience.

- *Audi* is pursuing a broad differentiation strategy, with its A-series available at several price points. Audi's differentiation is safety, and it prices its various Quattro models (higher than Hyundai) to reach a large, stratified audience.

- *Kia* has a more focused cost leadership strategy. Kia mainly offers low-cost vehicles in the lower levels of model stratification.

- *Tesla* offers the most focused differentiation strategy of any in the industry.

VALUE CHAIN ANALYSIS: TARGETING BUSINESS PROCESSES

Once an organization enters a new market using one of Porter's three generic strategies, it must understand, accept, and successfully execute its business strategy. Every aspect of the organization contributes to the success (or failure) of the chosen strategy. The business processes of the organization and the value chain they create play an integral role in strategy execution. Figure 1.17 combines Porter's Five Forces and his three generic strategies creating business strategies for each segment.[10]

Industry Force	Generic Strategies		
	Cost Leadership	Differentiation	Focused
Entry Barriers	Ability to cut price in retaliation deters potential entrants.	Customer loyalty can discourage potential entrants.	Focusing develops core competencies that can act as an entry barrier.
Buyer Power	Ability to offer lower price to powerful buyers.	Large buyers have less power to negotiate because of few close alternatives.	Large buyers have less power negotiate because of few alternatives.
Supplier Power	Better insulated from powerful suppliers.	Better able to pass on supplier price increases to customers.	Suppliers have power because of low volumes, but a differentiation-focused firm is better able to pass on supplier price increases.
Threat of Substitutes	Can use low price to defend against substitutes.	Customers become attached to differentiating attributes, reducing threat of substitutes.	Specialized products and core competency protect against substitutes.
Rivalry	Better able to compete on price.	Brand loyalty to keep customers from rivals.	Rivals cannot meet differentiation-focused customer needs.

FIGURE 1.17

Generic Strategies and Industry Forces

Value Creation

A *business process* is a standardized set of activities that accomplish a specific task, such as processing a customer's order. To evaluate the effectiveness of its business processes, an organization can use Michael Porter's value chain approach. An organization creates value by performing a series of activities that Porter identified as the value chain. The *value chain* approach views an organization as a series of processes, each of which adds value to the product or service for each customer. To create a competitive advantage, the value chain must enable the organization to provide unique value to its customers. In addition to the firm's own value-creating activities, the firm operates in a value system of vertical activities, including those of upstream suppliers and downstream channel members. To achieve a competitive advantage, the firm must perform one or more value-creating activities in a way that creates more overall value than its competitors. Added value is created through lower costs or superior benefits to the consumer (differentiation).

Organizations can add value by offering lower prices or by competing in a distinctive way. Examining the organization as a value chain (actually numerous distinct but inseparable value chains) leads to identifying the important activities that add value for customers and then finding IS systems that support those activities. Figure 1.18 depicts a value chain. Primary value activities, shown at the bottom of the graph, acquire raw materials and manufacture, deliver, market, sell, and provide after-sales services. Support value activities, along the top of the graph, such as firm infrastructure, human resources management, technology development, and procurement, support the primary value activities.

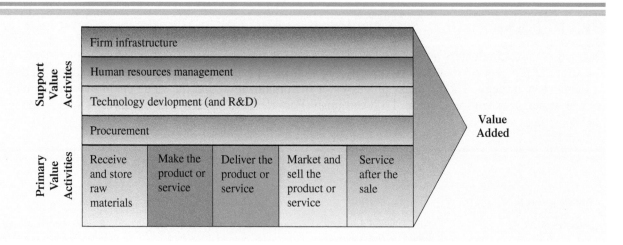

FIGURE 1.18

The Value Chain

Source: Reprinted with the permission of Free Press, a Division of Simon & Schuster, Inc., from Competitive Advantage: Creating and Sustaining Superior Performance by Michael E. Porter. Copyright © 1985, 1998 by Michael E. Porter. All rights reserved.

Organizations should attempt to use information systems to add value to both primary and support value activities. One example of a primary value activity facilitated by IS is the development of a marketing campaign management system that collects data allowing for more effective targeting of marketing campaigns and thereby reducing marketing costs. The system would also help the organization better pinpoint target market needs and potentially increasing sales. One example of a support value activity facilitated by IS is the development of a human resources system that more efficiently rewards employees based on performance. The system could also identify employees who are at risk of leaving their jobs, allowing the organization to find additional challenges or opportunities that would help retain these employees and thus reduce turnover costs.

Value chain analysis is a highly useful tool in that it provides hard-and-fast numbers for evaluating the activities that add value to products and services. An organization can find additional value by analyzing and constructing its value chain in terms of Porter's Five Forces (see Figure 1.19). For example, if an organization wants to decrease its customers' buyer power, it can construct its value chain activity of "service after the sale" by offering high levels of quality customer service. This will increase the switching costs for its customers, thereby decreasing their buyer power. Analyzing and constructing its support value activities can help an organization decrease the threat of new entrants. Analyzing and constructing its primary value activities can help an organization decrease the threat of substitute products or services.

A company can implement its selected strategy by means of programs, budgets, and procedures. Implementation involves organization of the firm's resources and motivation of the employees to achieve objectives. How the company implements its chosen strategy can have a significant impact on its success. In a large company, the personnel implementing the strategy are usually different from those formulating the strategy. For this reason, proper communication of the strategy is critical. Failure can result if the strategy is misunderstood or if lower-level managers resist its implementation because they do not understand the process for selecting the particular strategy.

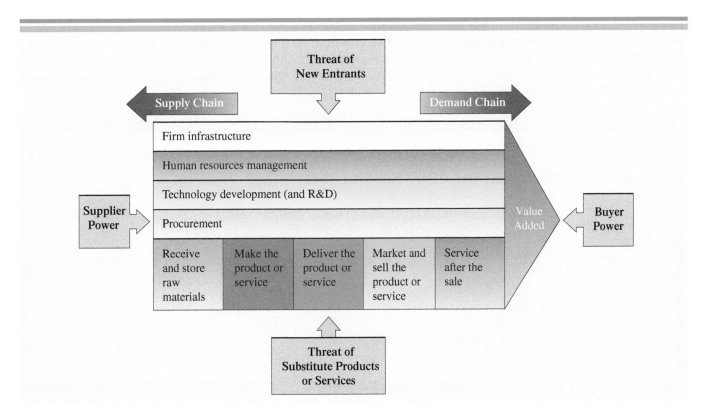

FIGURE 1.19

The Value Chain and Porter's Five Forces

Source: Reprinted with the permission of Free Press, a Division of Simon & Schuster, Inc., from Competitive Advantage: Creating and Sustaining Superior Performance by Michael E. Porter. Copyright © 1985, 1998 by Michael E. Porter. All rights reserved.

An organization must continually adapt to its competitive environment, which can cause its business strategy to change. To remain successful, an organization should use Porter's Five Forces, the three generic strategies, and value chain analysis to adopt new business strategies.

BUSINESS-DRIVEN INFORMATION SYSTEMS AND BUSINESS STRATEGY

The Five Forces Model, the three generic strategies, and value chain analysis are all methods by which organizations can assess their competitive advantage. The Five Forces Model is a framework that helps companies evaluate the relative attractiveness of entering or operating within an industry. It is a framework that can be used to assess the attractiveness of the industry in which a firm competes. The three generic strategies are broad competitive approaches that organizations fall under. Knowing which broad competitive approach an organization is following can help that organization make informed decisions about how the company should compete with other firms. Value chain analysis is a systematic approach organizations can use to assess and improve the value of their business activities. Knowing what value each business activity offers a company can help an organization decide how to change or improve those activities to help it become more competitive.

These three methods, in their own unique ways, give organizations insight into how they can behave more competitively. Armed with this knowledge, organizations can then think about how information systems can be used to facilitate and support this behaviour. For example, an information system can be designed to increase a company's supplier power with its customers, reduce the threat of substitute products or services, or decrease the threat of new entrants to the marketspace. Likewise, an information system can be implemented to help a company function more effectively and efficiently within a certain generic strategy. Similarly, information systems can be developed to enhance poor-performing value activities or strengthen important value chains.

This is what is meant by the term *business-driven information systems*. Information systems are implemented to support a company's competitive business strategy. Organizations do not use information systems for the sake of the systems themselves—they must have a solid business reason for implementing an information system so it improves an organization's competitive position. In other words, it is the business strategies concerning a company's competitive advantage that should drive information systems choices.

OPENING CASE QUESTIONS

Information Technology Helps LCBO Transform Itself

5. Which of Porter's Five Forces is the LCBO trying to use to establish and maintain its competitive advantage?

6. What does the LCBO's primary value chain look like, using specific examples of its value chain to describe it?

7. Which of the three generic strategies is the LCBO using?

8. How does the fact that the LCBO is a monopoly affect its use of Porter's Five Forces? Its use of the Three Generic Strategies?

SUMMARY OF KEY THEMES

The purpose of this chapter was twofold:

1. To provide you with an introduction to information systems in business.

   a. Information systems basics were explained.

   b. Roles and responsibilities in information systems were described.

   c. Ways in which information systems may affect your career were discussed, along with the potential in the ICT field in Canada.

2. To raise awareness of the ability of information systems to enable companies to sustain competitive advantage.

   a. Businesses must be aware of the various forces that determine whether organizations should enter a new industry or segment and how information systems can be used to reduce or enhance the strength of those forces.

   b. Firms need to set strategies and recognize how information systems can be used to add value to those activities that help organizations reach their strategic goals.

KEY TERMS

Business-driven information systems	**Buyer power**
Business intelligence (BI)	**Chief information officer (CIO)**
Business process	**Chief knowledge officer (CKO)**
Business-to-business (B2B) marketplace	**Chief privacy officer (CPO)**

Chief security officer (CSO)

Chief technology officer (CTO)

Competitive advantage

Data

Environmental scanning

Fact

First-mover advantage

Five Forces Model

Information

Information age

Information systems (IS)

Information technology (IT)

Knowledge

Loyalty programs

Management information systems (MIS)

Private exchange

Reverse auction

Rivalry among existing competitors

Supplier power

Switching costs

Threat of new entrants

Threat of substitute products or services

Value chain

CLOSING CASE ONE

Say "Charge It" with Your Mobile Device

This case looks at the competitive advantage of using a specific information technology (mobile devices) to improve a company's business strategy.

Google Wallet

As of September 19, 2011, Google Wallet with the Tap and Pay feature became available on select devices on select carrier networks in the United States. With Google Wallet the user stores all their credit and debit cards, and things like savings offers and gift cards, in their Wallet and then accesses them right from their smartphone when making purchases by simply tapping the phone on a specially enabled checkout terminal. It requires an NFC-enabled Android device with a secure element chip running the most recent Android operating system. Google Wallet allows the user to buy online, buy in stores through either Tap and Pay or with a Google Wallet Card, and send money to friends and family. It offers 24/7 fraud monitoring and instant transaction notification, and the Purchase Protection plan covers 100 percent of eligible unauthorized transactions.

CIBC Mobile App with Rogers, suretap™ SIM card

In Canada we have seen the first venture into mobile app payment with a partnership between CIBC, Rogers Communication, and TELUS in the form of the CIBC Mobile Payment App for credit card purchases on eligible smartphones for purchases up to $50. This payment option, which links the user's phone to his or her credit card, is available at thousands of locations across the country including gas stations and grocery stores.

To use the new CIBC Mobile Payment App, you must have:

- An eligible CIBC credit card.
- A Rogers or TELUS Samsung Galaxy Note II™, HTC One™, Samsung Galaxy S4™, Samsung Galaxy S III™ with Near Field Communication (NFC); it is also available with Rogers BlackBerry® Q10, BlackBerry® Z10, BlackBerry® Bold™ 9900 with Near Field Communication (NFC), and TELUS BlackBerrty devices will also be eligible in the near future.
- A data plan and an activated suretap™ SIM card from Rogers Communications or TELUS.

The CIBC Mobile Payment App has multiple layers of security protection, making it just as secure as using a CIBC credit card. The security features include:

- Ability to lock the CIBC Mobile Payment App with an optional passcode.

- Cardholder protection for unauthorized transactions.

- Trusted encryption technology to store your credit card information on the chip of the smartphone.[11]

Questions

1. Using Porter's Five Forces, describe the barriers to entry and switching costs for this new technology.

2. Which of Porter's three generic strategies is this new technology following?

3. Describe the value chain of using cellphones as a payment method.

4. What types of regulatory issues might occur due to this type of technology?

CLOSING CASE TWO

Innovative Business Managers

This case looks at various examples of successful business strategies led by innovative managers.

Industry has recognized several innovative managers in Canada and abroad who have demonstrated talent, vision, and the ability to identify excellent opportunities (see Figure 1.20).

Bruce Poon Tip, G Adventures	▪ Recognized a market segment (adventure seekers) with needs underserved by the travel industry. ▪ Took advantage of Web information technologies to market the business and conduct business transactions.
Jeffrey Immelt, General Electric (GE)	▪ Repositioned GE's portfolio with major acquisitions in health care, entertainment, and commercial finance. ▪ Created a more diverse, global, and customer-driven culture.
Steve Reinemund, PepsiCo	▪ Developed strong and diverse leadership that helped PepsiCo tap new markets. ▪ Attained consist ent double-digit growth through productive innovation and smart marketing.
Philip Knight, Nike	▪ Transformed a volatile, fad-driven marketing and design icon into a more shareholder-friendly company.

FIGURE 1.20
Innovative Business Managers

Bruce Poon Tip, G Adventures

Back in 1990, Bruce Poon Tip launched G Adventures (**www.gadventures.com**) in the belief that other travellers would share his desire to experience authentic adventures in the real world. G Adventures is a tour operator in more than 100 countries and specializes in small-group adventures. It boasts revenues of $100 million a year. The business started out of Poon Tip's Toronto apartment and has since grown from a one-man show to a company of over 300, and from a handful of trips in Latin America to hundreds of adventures on all seven continents. Poon Tip's commitment to in-house information technology, bold acquisitions like the purchase of an Antarctica expedition ship, strong industry partnerships, and innovative marketing strategies has led him to carve out a unique market niche. G Adventures takes advantage of serving the needs of an untapped market through Web technologies that allow clients to customize their trips via a personalized trip planner and to browse trip opportunities through an innovative search tool that classifies trips by destination, activity (e.g., culture, biking, kayaking, hiking, rafting), trip style (e.g., active, comfort, exploratory, family, gourmet), duration, and dates.[12]

Jeffrey Immelt, General Electric (GE)

In May 2013, Jeff Immelt was on stage to explain why software innovation is so crucial to the GE's future. He is predicting that the "consumer Internet" is giving way to the "industrial Internet." According to Immelt we are about to see a decade that will see foundational changes to how we do things. "There is a massive business opportunity in using software to anticipate industrial equipment maintenance needs," Immelt said. "Take the jet engine. It has about 20 sensors that capture real-time continuous data—temperature, engine performance, etc. If I can take that data and use it to model a consumer outcome—say, more time on the wing or less fuel burn—that's worth an awful lot of money to my customers. A 1 percent change in fuel burn for an airline is worth hundreds of millions of dollars."

The industrial Internet is using big data analytics to track changes and provide "guaranteed outcomes," as Immelt puts it—that is, things like less unplanned downtime and better fuel performance. It is improved productivity, smarter machines, and more lucrative services, which according to Immelt are big business for GE. "[T]ell an oil guy you can use software to save him one percent on something, and that guy will be your friend for life."

Immelt has made a massive financial commitment, and with the money GE has been pushing hundreds of millions of dollars into this effort and hiring all manner of mathematicians and data scientists to drive big data analytics.

"People have told companies like GE for years that they can't be in the software business," Immelt said. "We're too slow. We're big and dopey. But, you know what? We are extremely dedicated to winning in the markets we're in. And this is a to-the-death fight to remain relevant to our customers." In other words, to Immelt, the industrial Internet is the future engine of GE's services business.[13]

Steven Reinemund, PepsiCo

Steven Reinemund has turned PepsiCo into a $27 billion food and beverage giant. "To be a leader in consumer products, it's critical to have leaders who represent the population we serve," said Reinemund, who created a diverse leadership group that defines the strategic vision for the company. Reinemund also takes a major role in mentoring and teaching his employees and demands that all senior executives do the same. The payoff: consistent double-digit earnings and solid sales at a time when many of the company's staple products—potato chips and soft drinks—are under attack for fears about childhood obesity and health concerns.[14]

Philip Knight, Nike

Philip Knight, who got his start by selling Japanese sneakers from the trunk of his car, built the $14 billion sports behemoth Nike. Knight and his team transformed high-performance sports equipment into high-fashion gear and forever changed the rules of sports marketing with huge endorsement contracts and in-your-face advertising. Then, just as suddenly, Nike lost focus. In early 2000, kids stopped craving the latest sneaker, the company's image took a huge hit from its labour practices, sales slumped, and costs soared.

Thus began Knight's second act. He revamped management and brought in key outsiders to oversee finances and apparel lines. Knight devoted more energy to developing new information systems. Today, Nike's earnings are less volatile and less fad-driven. In 2004, Nike's earnings increased by $1.2 billion.[15]

Questions

1. Choose one of the companies listed above and explain how it could use a chief information officer (CIO), chief technology officer (CTO), and chief privacy officer (CPO) to improve business.

2. Why is it important for all of G Adventures's functional business areas to work together? Provide an example of what might happen if the G Adventures's marketing department failed to work with its sales department.

3. Why are information systems important to an organization like G Adventures?

4. Which of Porter's Five Forces is most important to Nike's business?

5. Which of the three generic strategies is PepsiCo following?

6. Explain the value chain and how a company like GE can use it to improve operations.

Apple: Merging Technology, Business, and Entertainment

This case looks at Apple and the successful introduction of a string of product lines.

Capitalizing on the iPod

With millions of iPods in the hands of consumers, many people are finding ways to capitalize on the product. John Lin created a prototype of a remote control for the iPod and took his prototype to Macworld, where he found success. A few months later, Lin's company had Apple's blessing and a commitment for shelf space in its retail stores. "This is how Apple supports the iPod economy," Lin said.

In the iPod-dominated market, hundreds of companies have been inspired to develop accessories—everything from rechargers for the car to Fendi bags. Eric Tong, vice-president at Belkin, a cable and peripheral manufacturer, believes that 75 percent of all iPod owners purchase at least one accessory priced between $10 and $250. Popular iPod accessories include:

- Speakers and recharger docks
- High-end earphones
- FM transmitters
- iPod holders
- Digital camera connectors

Capitalizing on the iPhone

Looking at someone using an iPhone is an interesting experience, because there is a good chance they are not making a phone call. They might be doing any of number of things, from playing a game to trading stocks, watching a TV show, or even conducting business with a mobile version of **Salesforce.com**'s customer-management software. In a brilliant strategic move, Apple let outsiders offer software for the iPhone, and in less than six months from its introduction more than 10,000 applications had been created.

Early on, developers like Jeff Holden of Pelago Inc., a social networking company, fully intended to follow the conventional wisdom for how to build a sizable, fast-growing software company: get your programs on as many platforms and devices as possible. But when he crunched the numbers he came to an interesting business conclusion: the 13 million iPhone owners had already downloaded more applications than the 1.1 billion other cellphone owners! To entrepreneurs, developing a program for the iPhone automatically provided a significantly larger market. "Why would I ever build for anything but the iPhone" Holden asked. One might ask if this is still a wise strategy today.

Capitalizing on the iPad

The iPad is a lightweight, portable tablet computer, similar to the iPhone, that allows customers to download applications, check email, and play music—all at the touch of a button. Both the iPhone and the iPad can multitask, allowing customers to read a Web page while downloading email in the background over wireless networks. The arrival of the iPad brought a simultaneous expansion of the network of accessories. Because the iPad was designed with an exposed screen, and without a separate keyboard, memory card slots, or expansion ports, one might say it was specifically built for accessories. Many owners will modify it in some way, whether for mere decoration or hardcore protection. A few of the accessories are:

- Clear Armor screen protector
- Antique book case cover
- Wireless keyboard
- Joule luxury stand

Apple has consistently outperformed its key MP3 player rivals with the iPod, and continues to make its products attractive to the consumer, while providing complementary features such as games and applications. For the iPhone, Apple developed a unique application called Siri, a voice-activation system capable of recognizing voice commands. Siri can perform all kinds of functions from dialling a contact and creating an email to location services such as "Find my Phone," ensuring lost phones are found quickly.

Apple also offers a service called the iCloud. The iCloud has the ability to collect all of the content, including videos, photos, songs, books, etc., from customer devices such as iPods, iPads, and iPhones in one secure location in "the cloud." Apple customers no longer have to worry about backing up their applications or data because everything is automatically uploaded and stored in the iCloud when using an Apple device. In a fast-paced, technology-driven sector, with competitors quickly following suit, Apple is constantly pressured to develop new products and product extensions. Apple tries to maintain its competitive advantage by focusing on the following key areas:

- *Customer focus.* Apple is driven by customer satisfaction and ensures customers are deeply involved in product development and application development.
- *Resources and capabilities.* Apple continues to invest heavily in research and development to take advantage of new technologies, improved facilities, and cloud infrastructures.
- *Strategic vision.* Apple has a clear alignment of its vision, mission, and business leadership and goals.
- *Branding.* Apple is the leader in brand loyalty as it has achieved cult status with its authentic product image.
- *Quality focus.* Apple has an outstanding commitment to quality.[16]

Questions

1. Do you agree or disagree that Apple's iTunes, iPhone apps, and iPad apps give the company a competitive advantage? Be sure to justify your answer.

2. Why are data, information, business intelligence, and knowledge important to Apple? Give an example of each type in relation to the iPad.

3. Analyze Apple using Porter's Five Forces Model.

4. Which of the three generic strategies is Apple following?

5. Which of Porter's five forces did Apple address through its introduction of the iPhone?

MAKING BUSINESS DECISIONS

1. Competitive Analysis

Cheryl O'Connell is the owner of a small, high-end retailer of women's clothing called Excelus. Excelus's business has been successful for many years, largely because of Cheryl's ability to anticipate the needs and wants of her loyal customer base and provide them with personalized service. Cheryl does not see any value in IS and does not want to invest any capital in something that will not directly affect her bottom line. Develop a proposal describing the potential IS-enabled competitive opportunities or threats Cheryl might be missing by not embracing IS. Be sure to include a Porter's Five Forces analysis and discuss which one of the three generic strategies Cheryl should pursue.

2. Applying the Three Generic Strategies

This chapter discussed several examples of companies that pursue differentiated strategies so that they are not forced into positions where they must compete based solely on price. In a team, choose an industry and find and compare two companies, one that is competing on price and another pursuing a differentiated strategy enabled by the creative use of IS. Some industries you may want to consider are clothing retailers, grocery stores, airlines, and personal computers. Prepare a presentation for the class on the ways that the company is using IS to help it differentiate and compete against the low-cost provider. Before you begin, spend some class time to make sure each team selects a different industry.

3. Using Information and Knowledge

You are the CEO of a 500-bed acute care general hospital. Your internal IS department is responsible for running applications that support both administrative functions (e.g., patient accounting) and medical applications (e.g., medical records). You need assurance that your IS department is a high-quality operation in comparison to similar hospitals. What information should you ask your CIO to provide to give the assurance you seek? Provide the reasoning behind the suggested information. Also, determine how the interrelationship between information and knowledge can drive your business's success.

4. Building Business Relationships

Synergistics Inc. is a startup company that specializes in helping businesses build successful internal relationships. You have recently been promoted to senior manager of the Business and IS Relationship area. Sales for your new department have dwindled over the last ten years for a variety of reasons, including the burst of the technological stock bubble, recent economic conditions, and a poorly communicated business strategy. Your first task on the job is to prepare a report detailing the following:

- Fundamental reasons for the gap between IS and the business.
- Strategies you can adopt to convince the business that this is an area critical to success.
- Strategies the business can follow to ensure synergies exist between the two sides.

5. Determining MIS Organizational Structures

You are the chief executive officer for a startup telecommunications company. The company currently has 50 employees and plans to ramp up to 3,000 by the end of the year. Your first task is to determine how you are going to model your organization. You decide to address the MIS department's organizational structure first. You need to consider if you want to have a CIO, CPO, CSO, CTO, and CKO, and if so, what the reporting structure will look like and why. You also need to determine the responsibilities for each executive position. Once you have compiled this information, put together a presentation describing your MIS department's organizational structure.

6. The Five Forces Model

Your team is working for a small investment company that specializes in information systems investments. A new company, Geyser, has just released an operating system that plans to compete with Microsoft's operating systems. Your company has a significant amount of capital invested in Microsoft. Your boss, Jan Savage, has asked you to compile a Porter's Five Forces analysis for Microsoft to ensure that your company's Microsoft investment is not at risk.

connect LEARNSMART SMARTBOOK

For more information on the resources available from McGraw-Hill Ryerson, go to www.mheducation.ca/he/solutions.

ENDNOTES

1. "LCBO Sales Top $4.7 Billion in 2011–12," May 16, 2012, http://lcbo.com/lcbo-ear/media_releases/content?content_id=1481, accessed July 9, 2013; "LCBO Transfers All-Time High $1.7 Billion Dividend," June 17, 2013, http://lcbo.com/lcbo-ear/media_releases/content?content_id=2421, accessed February 4, 2014.

2. Rafeael Ruffolo, "Vintage Technology: Inside the LCBO: How IT Powers the Liquor Control Board of Ontario," *ComputerWorld Canada*, May 14, 2009; "About Vintages," www.vintages.com/about_vintages.shtml, accessed July 20, 2011; "New Technology Allows You to Scan 150,000 Wines at LCBO," www.ourhometown.ca/lifestyle/LF0026.php, May 15, 2011, accessed July 20, 2011.

3. Dennis Longley and Michael Shain, *Dictionary of Information Technology*, 2nd ed. (Macmillan Press, 1985), p. 164.

4. Charles W. L. Hill and Gareth R. Jones, *Strategic Management: An Integrated Approach*, 8th ed. (Boston: Houghton Mifflin, 2008).

5. Kim Nash, "State of the CIO 2014: The Great Schism," http://www.cio.com/article/744601/State_of_the_CIO_2014_ The_Great_Schism, January 1, 2014, accessed February 6, 2014.

6. Ibid.

7. Nick Bontis, "The Rising Star of the Chief Knowledge Officer," *Ivey Business Journal,* Volume 66, Issue 4, March/April 2002, p. 20.

8. Andy McCue, "Five Skills You Need to Be CIO: The Skills That Pay the Bills …," www.silicon.com/management/cio-insights/2007/08/06/five-skills-you-need-to-be-cio-39167994, August 6, 2011, accessed July 20, 2011.

9. "Canada Salary Calculator," www.canadavisa.com/canada-salary-wizard.html, accessed February 14, 2014.

10. Michael E. Porter, *Competitive Strategy: Techniques for Analyzing Industries and Competitors* (New York: The Free Press, 1980).

11. CIBC Mobile Payment™ App, https://www.cibc.com/ca/features/mobile-payment.html, accessed March 23, 2014; "Making Our Money Mobile," February 26, 2012, http://www.cbc.ca/spark/2012/02/repeat-of-spark-151-february-16-29-2012, accessed February 5, 2014; Google Wallet, http://www.google.com/wallet/index.html, accessed February 5, 2014.

12. Andrew Wahl, "The Next Best Managers," *Canadian Business*, Volume 79, Issue 20, October 9–October 22, 2006, p. 66; Libby Znaimer, "Adventures Come with the Territory," *Financial Post: Weekend, National Post*, November 18, 2006, p. FW8.

13. John Paczkowski, "GE CEO Jeff Immelt's Big Data Bet," May 29, 2013, http://allthingsd.com/20130529/ge-ceo-jeff-immelts-big-data-bet, accessed February 6, 2014.

14. "The Best Managers," *BusinessWeek*, January 10, 2005, Issue 3915.

15. "Innovative Managers," *BusinessWeek*, April 24, 2005.

16. "Apple Profit Surges 95 Percent on iPod Sales," Yahoo! News, http://news.yahoo.com/s/afp/20060118/bs_afp/uscompanyearningsit _060118225009, accessed January 18, 2005; "Apple's IPod Success Isn't Sweet Music for Record Company Sales," Bloomberg.com, http://quote.bloomberg.com/apps/news?pid5nifea&&sid5aHP5Ko1pozM0, accessed November 2, 2005; www.apple.com/iphone, accessed June 7, 2007; news.com/NikeiPod1raises1RFID1privacy1concerns/2100-1029 _3-6143606.html, accessed June 7, 2007.

Decisions, Data, Information, and Business Intelligence

Module 2 concentrates on the data and information components of information systems. Most people view IS strictly from a technological paradigm, but in fact, IS's power and influence is not so much a result of its technical nature, but rather on what that technical infrastructure carries, houses, and supports: information.

The purpose of this module is to highlight this point and to raise awareness about the importance of information to organizational success. Understanding the significance of information is a fundamental lesson of this module. Companies that properly manage information as a key organizational resource have a definite advantage over competitors that don't. Treating information as a corporate asset can yield success in the market place. In short, this module deals with the concept of information and underscores the point that information does matter to organizational success.

The module first focuses on the types of decisions that business make and how information systems can support an organization in making and measuring the success of those decisions. Included in this part to the module are the different types of artificial intelligence that can either support decision making or make the decisions on their own. Next, the chapter discusses the importance of business processes and how companies can go about designing good business process that help support the decision-making process.

Next is a discussion of how organizations go about sharing and using information. In doing this how organizations can ensure that employees have access to the business intelligence they need, share that information with others, and best use that information by turning information into knowledge is described. When employees are armed with knowledge, they become empowered to deliver innovations, forge best practices, and develop new products and services for the company.

Finally, how organizations must properly manage transactional data stored in relational databases and how that data can be transformed into analytical information by implementing enterprise-wide data warehouses is illustrated. Doing so allows companies to data mine this information and uncover business intelligence that was discussed in the previous chapter.

Decisions and Processes: Value-Driven Business

LO 2.1 Explain how organizations use transaction processing systems (TPS), decision support systems (DSS), and executive information systems (EIS) to make decisions and how each can be used to help make unstructured, semi-structured, and structured decisions.

LO 2.2 Explain the difference between transactional data and analytical information, and between online transaction processing (OLTP) and online analytical processing (OLAP).

LO 2.3 Describe what artificial intelligence (AI) is and the five types of artificial intelligence systems used by organizations today.

LO 2.4 Describe how the five types of AI systems differ from TPS, DSS, and EIS.

LO 2.5 Describe the importance of business process improvement, business process re-engineering, business process modelling, and business process management to an organization and how information systems can help in these areas.

This chapter describes various types of business information systems found across the enterprise used to run basic business processes and used to facilitate sound and proper decision making. Using information systems to improve decision making and re-engineer business processes can significantly help organizations become more efficient and effective.

As a business student, you can gain valuable insight into an organization by understanding the types of information systems that exist in and across enterprises. When you understand how to use these systems to improve business processes and decision making, you can vastly improve organizational performance. After reading this chapter, you should have gained an appreciation of the various kinds of information systems employed by organizations and how you can use them to help make informed decisions and improve business processes.

opening case study

Information Systems Improve Business Processes at Grocery Gateway

Grocery Gateway is Canada's leader in the online retailing of home and office delivered groceries. Founded by a group of entrepreneurs with the idea that people had better things to do in life than grocery shop, Grocery Gateway started out with only a handful of employees and a couple of rental trucks. In 2004, Grocery Gateway was acquired by Longo Brothers Fruit Market Inc., a family-owned independent grocery business that has operated physical grocery stores since 1956.[1] Today, Grocery Gateway continues to serve customers throughout the Greater Toronto Area. Quite a bit of growth for a startup company founded only in 1996 by a bunch of classmates and rugby mates in a basement of a house.[2]

Like other online grocers, Grocery Gateway's strategy is all about the last mile of service. Online grocers sell groceries over the Internet and deliver them directly to your door. In this sense, groceries are used to initiate the customer relationship and create a pipeline to the home. The online grocer then leverages this pipeline to introduce complimentary products to the consumer.[3]

What is attractive to consumers is that the online grocery store is open 24 hours, 7 days a week, and that there is greater simplicity in clicking a mouse to get the food you want than trekking down to a physical store and pushing a grocery cart. Though prices are competitive with those of supermarkets, price is not the value proposition for the consumer. Rather, shopping online for groceries is a timesaver. Consumers—generally busy people without time on their hands—are looking to find easier and quicker ways to do chores. Also, people who find it physically challenging to do grocery shopping (such as the elderly and the disabled), and those who choose not to own a car, find the service that Grocery Gateway provides to be quite beneficial.

Information Systems Are at the Heart of the Company's Business Processes

Grocery Gateway realizes the critical role that information systems play in the health and viability of their electronic business and the running of their business processes. Technology is used for Grocery Gateway's business processes such as supporting online merchandising, single-item picking, home delivery operations, and customer service. For example, Grocery Gateway has built several key features into its website to attract and retain its customers, such as an online shopping demo, a getting-started tutorial, and email customer support. Moreover, the site offers a suite of electronic commerce functionality that allows consumers to browse or find grocery items, see pictures and descriptions (including prices), and select items in a shopping basket and check out those items for delivery.[4] To work effectively, the various functions, such as item searching, grocery ordering, customer profiling, electronic payments, and delivery scheduling, must be tightly integrated and coordinated for the website to function as a cohesive whole.

Additionally, one electronic commerce research study suggests that online grocery retailers should be looking to improve ordering processes and delivery mechanisms as a means of securing a solid and repeating customer base.[5]

Using Information Systems to Manage Logistics Business Processes

In addition, Grocery Gateway is well aware that what will make or break it is the logistics of quick delivery. Thus, the company has turned to the Descartes Systems Group, an on-demand logistics management solutions provider, to optimize its selection of delivery routes. The goal is to maximize efficiency in route selection by considering historical delivery data and real-time information. Real-time data are obtained through a combination of sophisticated routing, tracking, planning, and dispatching functionality. The technology allows Grocery Gateway to guarantee its customers a specific 90-minute window of delivery to their doors, much narrower than what is offered by other retail delivery operations.

Imagine the complexity of coordinating the delivery of groceries. With thousands of active customers, Grocery Gateway delivery trucks make roughly 500 stops to customer homes and offices per day. Descartes's On-Demand Fleet Management Solution software ensures that these orders are delivered within the 90-minute window. To do so, the software needs to take into account not only unpredictable delays such as traffic jams and road accidents but also last-minute customer requests or cancellations. GPS-enabled mobile phones allow the logistics software to know the exact position and location of drivers to make the best decisions on routes.

Using Descartes's software has improved the bottom line. Since deploying the On-Demand Fleet Management Solution, Grocery Gateway has improved its on-time delivery performance by 14 percent and is exceeding its yearly stops per paid hour by 12.4 percent. Routes are continually optimized for maximum efficiency. Access to historical data ensures that business processes are optimized and customer service needs are responded to more proactively.[6]

2.1 DECISION MAKING AND INFORMATION SYSTEMS

MAKING BUSINESS DECISIONS

Business is accelerating at a breakneck pace. However, the more information a business acquires, the more difficult it becomes to make decisions, and the amount of information people must understand to make good decisions is growing exponentially. In the past, people could rely on manual processes to make decisions because they had limited amounts of information to process.

Today, with massive volumes of available information, it is almost impossible for people to make decisions without the aid of information systems. Highly complex decisions—involving far more information than the human brain can comprehend—must be made in increasingly shorter time frames. Figure 2.1 highlights the primary challenges associated with depending on information systems to make decisions. The challenges are growing and will continue to grow.

What is the value of information? The answer to this important question varies, but Karsten Solheim would say the value of information is its ability to lower a company's handicap. Solheim, an avid golfer, invented a putter with a "ping," which led to a successful golf equipment company and the PING golf clubs. PING Inc., a privately held corporation, was the first to offer customizable golf clubs. The company prides itself on being a just-in-time manufacturer that depends on flexible information systems to make informed production decisions. PING's production systems scan large amounts of information and pull orders that meet certain criteria such as order date (this week), order priority (high), and customer type (Gold). PING then manufactures the appropriate products, allowing it to carry less than 5 percent of inventory in its warehouse. PING depends on its flexible information systems for production decision support and thanks information systems for the growth of its business.[7]

LO1 | Decision-Making Essentials

A few key concepts about organizational structure will help our discussion of MIS decision-making tools. The structure of a typical organization is similar to a pyramid, and the different levels require different types of information to assist in decision making, problem solving, and opportunity capturing (see Figure 2.2).

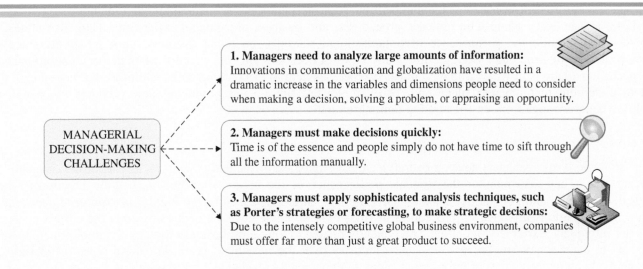

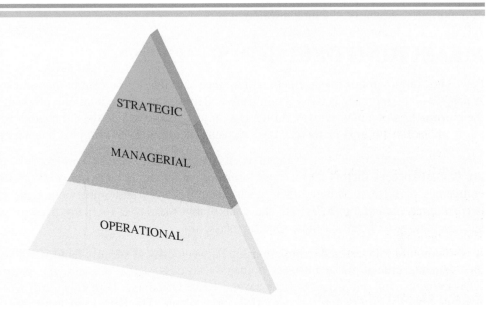

FIGURE 2.1

Managerial Decision Making Challenges

FIGURE 2.2

Common Company Structure

Operational

At the operational level, employees develop, control, and maintain core business activities required to run day-to-day operations. Operational decisions are considered *structured decisions*, which arise in situations where established processes offer potential solutions. Structured decisions are made frequently, are almost repetitive in nature, and they affect short-term business strategies. Reordering and creating employee staffing and weekly production schedules are examples of routine structured decisions.

Managerial

At the managerial level, employees are continuously evaluating company operations to hone the firm's ability to identify, adapt to, and leverage change. A company that has a competitive advantage needs to constantly adjust and revise its strategy to remain ahead of the competition. Managerial decisions cover short- and medium-range plans, schedules, and budgets, along with policies, procedures, and business objectives for the firm. They also allocate resources and monitor the performance of organizational subunits, including business units, divisions, process teams, project teams, and other work groups. These types of decisions are considered *semi-structured decisions* and they occur in situations in which a few established processes help to evaluate potential solutions, but not enough to lead to a definite recommended decision. For example, decisions about producing new products or changing employee benefits range from unstructured to semi-structured.

Strategic

At the strategic level, managers develop overall business strategies, goals, and objectives, as part of the company's strategic plan. They also monitor the strategic performance of the organization and its overall direction in the political, economic, and competitive business environment. Strategic decisions are highly *unstructured decisions*, occurring in situations in which no procedures or rules exist to guide decision makers towards the correct choice. They are infrequent, extremely important, and typically related to long-term business strategy. Examples include the decisions to enter a new market or even a new industry over the next three years. For these types of decisions, managers rely on many sources of information, along with personal knowledge, to find solutions.

Decision making and problem solving in today's electronic world encompass large-scale, opportunity-oriented, strategically focused solutions. The traditional "cookbook" approach to decision making will simply not work. This is also reflected when one surveys highly regarded executive education programs in Canada where decision making and problem solving consistently appear as important aspects of each program and, in turn, as skills that are regarded as important to executives' career development.[8]

MEASURING DECISION SUCCESS

Peter Drucker, a famous management writer, once said that if you cannot measure something, you cannot manage it. A *project* is a temporary activity a company undertakes to create a unique product, service, or result. For example, the construction of a new subway station is a project, as is a movie theatre chain's adoption of a software program to allow online ticketing. How do managers measure the progress of complex business project like these?

Metrics are measurements that evaluate results to determine whether a project is meeting its goals. Two core metrics are critical success factors and key performance indicators. *Critical success factors (CSFs)* are the crucial steps companies perform to achieve their goals and objectives and implement their strategies (see Figure 2.3). *Key performance indicators (KPIs)* are the quantifiable metrics a company uses to evaluate progress toward critical success factors. KPIs are far more specific than CSFs.

It is important to understand the relationship between critical success factors and key performance indicators. CSFs are elements crucial for a business strategy's success. KPIs measure the progress of CSFs with quantifiable measurements, and one CSF can have several KPIs. Of course, both categories will vary by company and industry. Imagine *improve graduation rates* as a CSF for a college. The KPIs to measure this CSF can include:

■ Average grades by course and gender

■ Student dropout rates by gender and major

■ Average graduation rate by gender and major

■ Time spent in tutoring by gender and major

KPIs can focus on external and internal measurements. A common external KPI is *market share*, or the proportion of the market that a firm captures. We calculate it by dividing the firm's sales by the total market sales for the entire industry. Market share measures a firm's external performance relative to that of its competitors. For example, if a firm's total sales (revenues) are $2 million and sales for the entire industry are $10 million, the firm has captured 20 percent of the total market or a 20 percent market share.

A common internal KPI is *return on investment (ROI)*, which indicates the earning power of a project. We measure it by dividing the profitability of a project by the costs. This sounds easy, and for many departments where the projects are tangible and self-contained it is; however, for projects that are intangible and cross departmental lines (such as MIS projects), ROI is challenging to measure. Imagine attempting to calculate the ROI of a fire extinguisher. If the fire extinguisher is never used, its ROI is low. If the fire extinguisher puts out a fire that could have destroyed the entire building, its ROI is astronomically high.

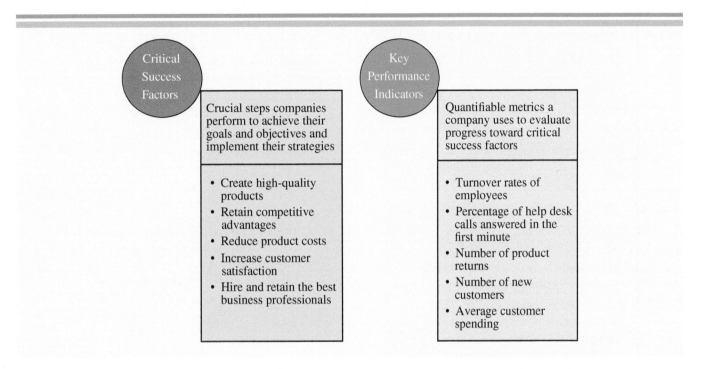

FIGURE 2.3

CSF and KPI Metrics

Creating KPIs to measure the success of an MIS project offers similar challenges. Think about a firm's email system. How could managers track departmental costs and profits associated with company email? Measuring by volume does not account for profitability, because one sales email might land a million-dollar deal while 300 others might not generate any revenue. Non-revenue-generating departments such as human resources and legal require email but will not be using it to generate profits. For this reason, many managers turn to higher-level metrics, such as efficiency and effectiveness, to measure MIS projects. *Best practices* are the most successful solutions or problem -solving methods that have been developed by a specific organization or industry. Measuring MIS projects helps determine the best practices for an industry.

Efficiency and Effectiveness Metrics

Efficiency IS metrics measure the performance of MIS itself, such as throughput, transaction speed, and system availability. **Effectiveness IS metrics** measure the impact MIS has on business processes and activities, including customer satisfaction and customer conversion rates. Efficiency focuses on the extent to which a firm is using its resources in an optimal way, while effectiveness focuses on how well a firm is achieving its goals and objectives. Peter Drucker offers a helpful distinction between efficiency and effectiveness: Doing things right addresses efficiency—getting the most from each resource. Doing the right things addresses effectiveness—setting the right goals and objectives and ensuring they are accomplished. Figure 2.4 describes a few of the common types of efficiency and effectiveness MIS metrics. KPIs that measure MIS projects include both efficiency and effectiveness metrics. Of course, these metrics are not as concrete as market share or ROI, but they do offer valuable insight into project performance.[9]

Large increases in productivity typically result from increases in effectiveness, which focus on CSFs. Efficiency MIS metrics are far easier to measure, however, so most managers tend to focus on them, often incorrectly, to measure the success of MIS projects. Consider measuring the success of automated teller machines (ATMs). Thinking in terms of MIS efficiency metrics, a manager would measure the number of daily transactions, the

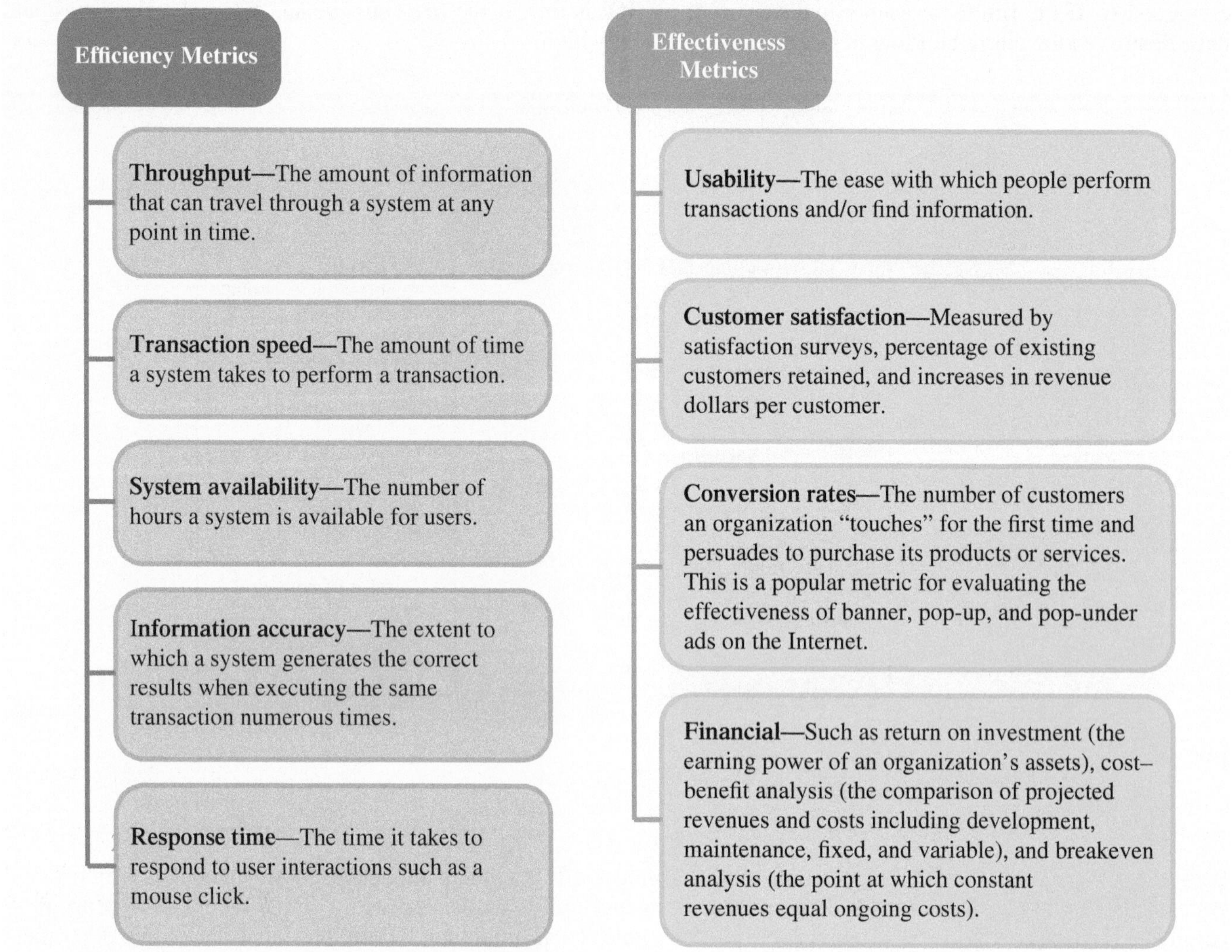

Efficiency Metrics

Throughput—The amount of information that can travel through a system at any point in time.

Transaction speed—The amount of time a system takes to perform a transaction.

System availability—The number of hours a system is available for users.

Information accuracy—The extent to which a system generates the correct results when executing the same transaction numerous times.

Response time—The time it takes to respond to user interactions such as a mouse click.

Effectiveness Metrics

Usability—The ease with which people perform transactions and/or find information.

Customer satisfaction—Measured by satisfaction surveys, percentage of existing customers retained, and increases in revenue dollars per customer.

Conversion rates—The number of customers an organization "touches" for the first time and persuades to purchase its products or services. This is a popular metric for evaluating the effectiveness of banner, pop-up, and pop-under ads on the Internet.

Financial—Such as return on investment (the earning power of an organization's assets), cost–benefit analysis (the comparison of projected revenues and costs including development, maintenance, fixed, and variable), and breakeven analysis (the point at which constant revenues equal ongoing costs).

FIGURE 2.4
Common Types of Efficiency and Effectiveness Metrics

average amount per transaction, and the average speed per transaction to determine the success of the ATM. Although these offer solid metrics on how well the system is performing, they miss many of the intangible or value-added benefits associated with ATM effectiveness. Effectiveness MIS metrics might measure how many new customers joined the bank due to its ATM locations or the ATMs' ease of use. They can also measure increases in customer satisfaction due to reduced ATM fees or additional ATM services such as the sale of stamps and movie tickets, significant time savers and value-added features for customers. Being a great manager means taking the added viewpoint offered by effectiveness MIS metrics to analyze all benefits associated with an MIS project.

Interrelationship Between Efficiency and Effectiveness MIS Metrics

Efficiency and effectiveness are definitely related. However, success in one area does not necessarily imply success in the other. Efficiency MIS metrics focus on the technology itself. While these efficiency MIS metrics are important to monitor, they do not always guarantee effectiveness. Effectiveness MIS metrics are determined according to an organization's goals, strategies, and objectives. Here, it becomes important to consider a company's CSFs, such as a broad cost leadership strategy (Walmart, for example), as well as KPIs such as increasing new customers by 10 percent or reducing new-product development cycle times to six months. In the private sector, Canadian Tire continuously benchmarks its MIS projects for efficiency and effectiveness. Maintaining constant website availability and optimal throughput performance are CSFs for Canadian Tire.

Figure 2.5 depicts the interrelationships between efficiency and effectiveness. Ideally, a firm wants to operate in the upper right-hand corner of the graph, realizing both significant increases in efficiency and effectiveness. However, operating in the upper left-hand corner (minimal effectiveness with increased efficiency) or the lower right-hand corner (significant effectiveness with minimal efficiency) may be in line with an organization's particular strategies. In general, operating in the lower left-hand corner (minimal efficiency and minimal effectiveness) is not ideal for the operation of any organization.

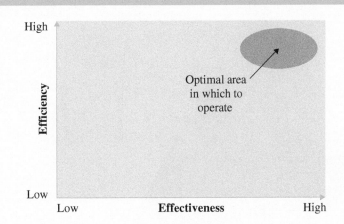

FIGURE 2.5

The Interrelationships Between Efficiency and Effectiveness

Benchmarks regardless of what process is measured, how it is measured, and whether it is performed for the sake of efficiency or effectiveness, managers must set **benchmarks**, or baseline values the system seeks to attain. **Benchmarking** is a process of continuously measuring system results, comparing those results to optimal system performance (benchmark values), and identifying steps and procedures to improve system performance. Benchmarks help assess how an MIS project performs over time. For instance, if a system held a benchmark for response time of 15 seconds, the manager would want to ensure response time continued to decrease until it reached that point. If response time suddenly increased to 1 minute, the manager would know the system was not functioning correctly and could start looking into potential problems. Continuously measuring MIS projects against benchmarks provides feedback so managers can control the system.

LO2 | TYPES OF INFORMATION

Besides understanding the types of decisions organizations make and how to measure the success of the decisions there is also a need to better understand how organizations use data and information to make decisions. It is important to understand the difference between transactional data and analytical information (see Figure 2.6). **Transactional data** encompass all the raw facts contained within a single business process or unit of work, and their primary purpose is to support performing daily operational tasks. Examples of events where transactional data are captured include purchasing stocks, making an airline reservation, or withdrawing cash from an ATM. Examples of transactional data for these events include a stock purchase price, an airline reservation number, and a bank account balance. Organizations use transactional data when performing operational tasks and routine decisions, such as analyzing daily sales reports to determine how much inventory to carry.

Analytical information encompasses all summarized or aggregated transactional data, and its primary purpose is to support performing analysis tasks. Analytical information also includes external information such as that obtained from outside market and industry sources. Examples of analytical information include trends, aggregated sales amounts by region, product statistics, and future growth projections. Examples of analytical information include the largest-growing basket of stocks over the last quarter on the TSX (e.g., energy stocks, technology stocks), the most popular destination of travel for British Columbia residents, and projections of cash withdrawals made from ATMs for the upcoming holiday weekend. Organizations use analytical information when making important ad hoc decisions such as whether the organization should build a new manufacturing plant or hire additional sales personnel.

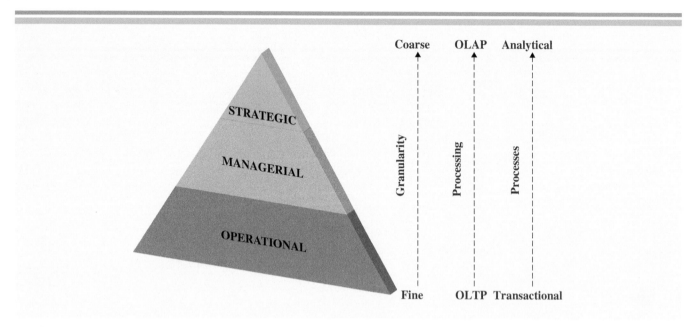

FIGURE 2.6

Information Levels Throughout an Organization

Two different types of processing occur in an organization with respect to transactional data and analytical information: online transaction processing and online analytical processing.

Revisiting Figures 2.2 and 2.6 we find that at the operational level, people perform online transaction processing. *Online transaction processing (OLTP)* is the capturing of transaction and event data using information systems to (1) process the data according to defined business rules, (2) store the data, and (3) update existing data to reflect the new data entered. During OLTP, the organization must capture every detail of transactions and events.

At the managerial and strategic level, people conduct online analytical processing that deals less with raw transactional details and more with meaningful aggregations of data. This summarization or aggregation of raw data from transactional processing systems is when data is given a context, becomes meaningful, and is turned into information. Working with less "fine" (detailed) and more "coarse" (summarized) information allows employees to make broader decisions for the organization. Whether information is fine or coarse refers to the granularity of that information. Those higher up the organizational pyramid tend to work with information that has coarser granularity. *Online analytical processing (OLAP)* is the analysis of summarized or aggregated information sourced from transaction processing systems data, and sometimes external information from outside industry sources, to create business intelligence in support of analytical and strategic (non-operational) decision making. *Business intelligence* is a broad, general term describing information that people use to support their analytical and strategic decision-making efforts. Further discussion of business intelligence is seen in Chapter 3.

A few of the capabilities associated with OLAP are consolidation, drill-down, and slice-and-dice.

■ *Consolidation* involves the aggregation of information and features simple rollups to complex groupings of interrelated information. Many organizations track financial information at a regional level and then consolidate the information at a single global level.

- *Drill-down* enables users to view details, and details of details, of information. Viewing monthly, weekly, daily, or even hourly information represents drill-down capability.

- *Slice-and-dice* is the ability to look at information from different perspectives. One slice of information could display all product sales during a given promotion. Another slice could display a single product's sales for all promotions.

Walmart consolidates point-of-sale details from its thousands of stores and uses OLAP to transform this information into business intelligence. Data mining systems (covered in detail in Chapter 4) sift instantly through summarized data (information) to uncover patterns and relationships that would elude an army of human researchers. The results enable Walmart to predict sales of every product at each store with uncanny accuracy, translating into huge savings in inventories and maximum payoff from promotional spending. Data mining tools apply algorithms to information sets to uncover inherent trends and patterns in data and information. Business analysts use data mining to develop new business strategies to build models that, when exposed to new information sets, perform a variety of data analysis functions. The analysts provide business solutions by combining the analytical techniques and the business problem at hand, which often reveals important new correlations, patterns, and trends in information. A few of the more common forms of data mining analysis capabilities include cluster analysis, association detection, and statistical analysis.

ENHANCING DECISION MAKING WITH MIS

Where does the information to make decisions and measure performance come from? Traditionally, it is from three major classes of information systems that are found in organizations: transaction processing systems (TPS), decision support systems (DSS), and executive information systems (EIS).

A *transaction processing system (TPS)* is the basic business system that serves the operational level (clerks and analysts) in an organization. A TPS performs OLTP and handles transactional data. The most common example of a TPS is an operational accounting system such as a payroll system or an order-entry system. In terms of decision making, a TPS supports operational types of decisions such as: How much did a specific customer order on July 1? What unit price was paid? To what address was the product delivered?

A *decision support system (DSS)*, on the other hand, models data and information to support managers, analysts, and other business professionals during the decision-making process for more analytical purposes. A DSS can be used on transactional data or analytical information, depending on the level and depth of analysis desired. A more robust DSS performs OLAP and works with analytical information. For example, at the limousine and transportation company Boston Coach, managers must dispatch fleets of hundreds of vehicles as efficiently as possible. Boston Coach requires a real-time dispatching system that considers inventory, customer needs, and soft dimensions such as weather and traffic. Researchers at IBM built Boston Coach a mathematical algorithm for a custom dispatch DSS that combines information about weather, traffic conditions, driver locations, and customer pickup requests and determines which cars to assign to which customers. The system is so efficient that, after launching it, Boston Coach experienced a 20 percent increase in revenues.[10]

Three quantitative models often used by DSS include:

1. *Sensitivity analysis*—the study of the impact that changes in one (or more) part(s) of the model have on other parts of the model. Users change the value of one variable repeatedly and observe the resulting changes in other variables.

2. *What-if analysis*—checking the impact of a change in an assumption on the proposed solution. For example, "What will happen to the supply chain if a blizzard in Alberta reduces holding inventory from 30 percent to 10 percent?" Users repeat this analysis until they understand all the effects of various situations. Figure 2.7 displays an example of what-if analysis using Microsoft Excel. The tool calculates the net effect of a predefined set of input variables or scenarios (e.g., best, most likely, worst) such as tax rate, interest rate, and sales growth on a company's bottom line.

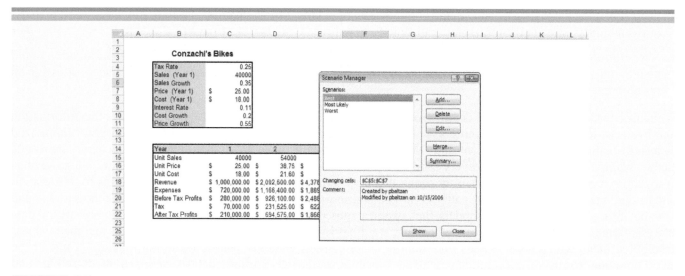

FIGURE 2.7

Example of What-If Analysis in Microsoft Excel

3. *Goal-seeking analysis*—finding the inputs necessary to achieve a goal such as a desired level of output. Instead of observing how changes in a variable affect other variables, as in a what-if analysis, goal-seeking analysis sets a target value (a goal) for a variable and then repeatedly changes other variables until the target value is achieved. For example, "How many customers are required to purchase a new product to increase gross profits to $5 million?" Figure 2.8 displays a goal-seeking scenario using Microsoft Excel. The model determines how many bikes Hauger will need to sell to break even, or have a profit of zero. Hauger needs to sell 46 bikes at $3,500 each to break even.

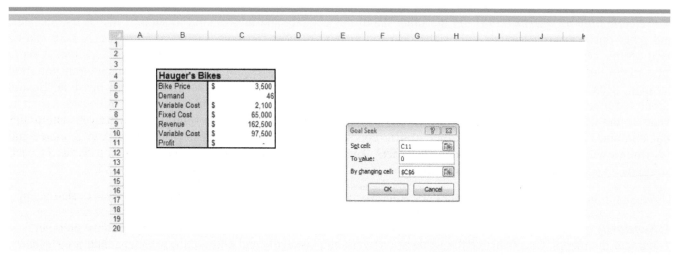

FIGURE 2.8

Example of Goal-Seeking Analysis in Microsoft Excel

One national insurance company uses a DSS to analyze the amount of risk the company is undertaking when it insures drivers who have a history of driving under the influence of alcohol. The DSS discovered that only 3 percent of married male homeowners in their forties received more than one Driving Under the Influence (DUI) offence. The company decided to lower rates for customers falling into this category, which increased its revenue while mitigating its risk.[11]

Figure 2.9 displays how a TPS is used in conjunction with a DSS. Each TPS in the figure supplies transaction-based data to the DSS. The DSS summarizes and aggregates the data sourced from many different TPS systems into information, which assists managers and analysts in making informed decisions. Canadian Pacific Railway uses a DSS to analyze the movement of all its railcars and to track shipments against delivery commitments. Without this tool, the job of integrating and analyzing transaction-based data would be difficult.[12]

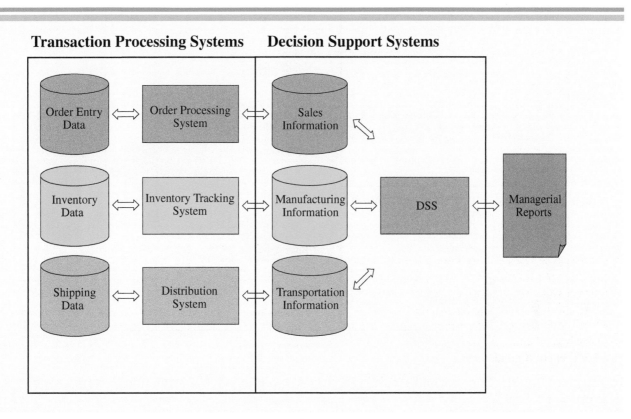

FIGURE 2.9

Interaction Between Transaction Processing Systems and Decision Support Systems

An *executive information system (EIS)* is a specialized DSS that supports senior-level executives within the organization. An EIS differs from a DSS because an EIS typically contains information from external sources as well as information from internal data sources, supports executive end-users exclusively, contains primarily very coarse (highly summarized) information, and is used more often for strategic purposes (see Figure 2.10).

Today many of these systems use *visualization* to produce graphical displays of patterns and complex relationships in large amounts of data. Executive information systems use visualization to deliver specific key information to top managers at a glance, with little or no interaction with the system. A common tool that supports visualization is a *digital dashboard*, which tracks KPIs and CSFs by compiling information from multiple sources and tailoring it to meet user needs. Following is a list of features included in a dashboard designed for a senior executive of an oil refinery:

■ A hot list of KPIs, refreshed every 15 minutes

■ A running line graph of planned versus actual production for the past 24 hours

■ A list of outstanding customer complaints and their resolution status

■ A chart of West Texas Intermediate Crude prices

■ Scrolling news headlines from Bloomberg News, a financial news service

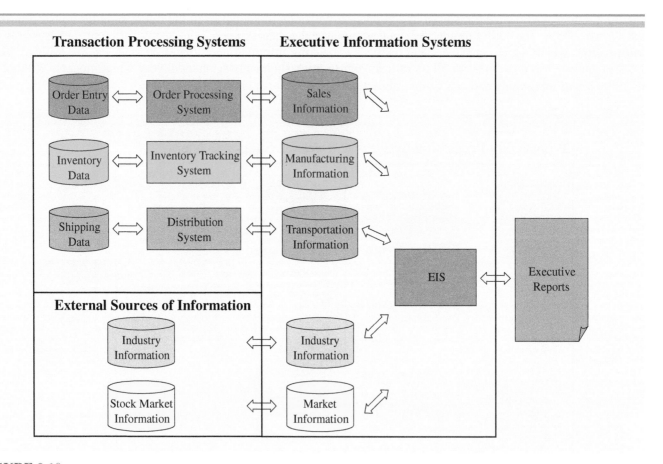

FIGURE 2.10

Interaction Between Transaction Processing Systems and Executive Information Systems

Digital dashboards, whether basic or comprehensive, deliver results quickly. As digital dashboards become easier to use, more executives can perform their own analysis without inundating IS personnel with questions and requests for reports. According to an independent study by Nucleus Research, there is a direct correlation between the use of digital dashboards and companies' return on investment (ROI). Figures 2.11 and 2.12 display two different digital dashboards.

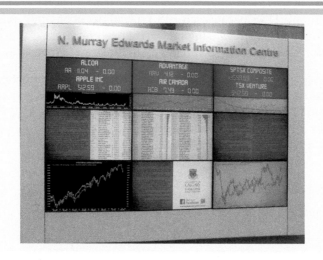

FIGURE 2.11

Stock Market Dashboard

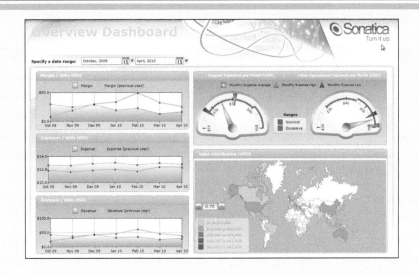

FIGURE 2.12

Sales Executive Dashboard

Source: Dundas Data Visualization, Inc., www.dundas.com.

EIS systems, such as digital dashboards, allow executives to move beyond reporting to using information to directly impact business performance. Digital dashboards help executives react to information as it becomes available and make decisions, solve problems, and change strategies daily instead of monthly.

At Verizon Communications, CIO Shaygan Kheradpir tracks 100-plus major information systems on a single screen called "The Wall of Shaygan." Using real-time processing, a new set of charts communicating Verizon's performance is produced every 15 seconds, flashing onto a giant LCD screen in Kheradpir's office. The 44 screenshots cycle continuously, all day long, every day. The dashboard includes more than 300 measures of business performance that fall into one of three categories:

1. *Market pulse.* Examples include daily sales numbers, market share, and subscriber turnover.

2. *Customer service.* Examples include problems resolved on the first call, call centre wait times, and on-time repair calls.

3. *Cost drivers.* Examples include number of repair trucks in the field, repair jobs completed per day, and call centre productivity.

Kheradpir has memorized the screens and can tell at a glance when the lines on the charts are not trending as expected. The system informs him of events such as the percentage of customer calls resolved by voice systems, number of repair trucks in the field, and amount of time to resolve an information system issue. The dashboard works the same way for 400 managers at every level of Verizon.[13] Executives must be mindful of their dashboards as not all dashboards process data in real time; they may process data in a batched manner on a nightly, weekly, or even monthly basis.

Note that the classification of information systems as TPS, DSS, or EIS is just one classification of information systems found in organizations. Later on in the textbook, different classifications of information systems used in organizations will be introduced (e.g., Section 2.2 classifies various types of enterprise information systems according to their business functionality, such as customer relationship management, supply chain management, and enterprise resource planning). However, the classification of systems as TPS, DSS, or EIS is useful in demonstrating which class of systems work with transactional data and which with analytical information. This classification is also useful in identifying who the typical users of these systems are and what decision-making purposes they are typically used for (see Figure 2.13).

	Transaction Processing System (TPS)	Decision Support System (DSS)	Executive Information System (EIS)
Type of data or information typically found in the system	Transactional data	Transactional data or analytical information	Analytical information
Who typically makes the decision using the system?	Clerk or analyst	Analyst or manager	Executive
Type of decision typically handled	Operational	Analytical or managerial	Strategic

FIGURE 2.13

TPS, DSS, and EIS Differences

Figure 2.13 showcases how decision making occurs at all levels of an organization and how various types of information systems can facilitate different types of decision making. For instance, a TPS is useful for decisions at the operational level, while the other types are more appropriate for decisions at the managerial and strategic levels.

Though each system supports different types of decisions and different types of users, it is important to understand that these various systems need to be tightly integrated and that the underlying data found in a TPS must be accurate and reliable for higher-level decision-making systems to be effective. The reason for this is that data stored in a TPS are often used to source the data and information contained in decision support and executive information systems. Thus, it is imperative that transactional data found in TPS be accurate and reliable, and that the data in these systems be consistent across the enterprise. Otherwise, data used to source any DSS or EIS might lead to misguided decisions by management and analysts. This might hamper the organization in its pursuit of strategic goals and objectives—not a position any firm wants to be in.

LO3 | ARTIFICIAL INTELLIGENCE

Today, companies are taking advantage of artificial intelligence to help employees make better operational, managerial, and strategic decisions. **RivalWatch.com** offers a strategic business information service using artificial intelligence that enables organizations to track the product offerings, pricing policies, and promotions of online competitors. Clients can determine the competitors they want to watch and the specific information they wish to gather, ranging from products added, removed, or out of stock, to price changes, coupons offered, and special shipping terms. Clients can check each competitor, category, and product either daily, weekly, monthly, or quarterly.

"Competing in the Internet arena is a whole different ballgame than doing business in the traditional brick-and-mortar world because you're competing with the whole world rather than the store down the block or a few miles away," said Phil Lumish, vice-president of sales and marketing at RivalWatch. "With new products and campaigns being introduced at a breakneck pace, e-businesses need new tools to monitor the competitive environment, and our service is designed specifically to meet that need."[14]

Executive information systems are starting to take advantage of artificial intelligence to facilitate unstructured strategic decision making. *Artificial intelligence (AI)* simulates human thinking and behaviour, such as the ability to reason and learn. Its ultimate goal is to build a system that can mimic human intelligence.

Intelligent systems are various commercial applications of artificial intelligence. They include sensors, software, and devices that emulate and enhance human capabilities, learn or understand from experience, make sense of ambiguous or contradictory information, and even use reasoning to solve problems and make decisions effectively. Intelligent systems perform such tasks as boosting productivity in factories by monitoring equipment and signalling when preventive maintenance is required. They are beginning to show up everywhere:

- At Manchester Airport in England, the Hefner AI Robot Cleaner alerts passengers to security and no-smoking rules while it scrubs up to 6,094 square metres of floor per day. Laser scanners and ultrasonic detectors keep it from colliding with passengers.

- Shell Oil's Smart Pump keeps drivers in their cars on cold, wet winter days. It can service any automobile built after 1987 that has been fitted with a special gas cap and a windshield-mounted transponder that tells the robot where to insert the pump.

- Companies such Walgreens, Amazon, The Gap, and Staples use Kwa Robots to fulfill orders in their distribution centres.

- The FireFighter AI Robot can extinguish flames at chemical plants and nuclear reactors with water, foam, powder, or inert gas. The robot puts distance between the human operator and the fire.[15]

AI systems dramatically increase the speed and consistency of decision making, solve problems with incomplete information, and resolve complicated issues that cannot be solved by conventional computing. There are many categories of AI systems; five of the most familiar are (1) expert systems, (2) neural networks, (3) genetic algorithms, (4) intelligent agents, and (5) virtual reality. Figure 2.14 gives examples of each type.

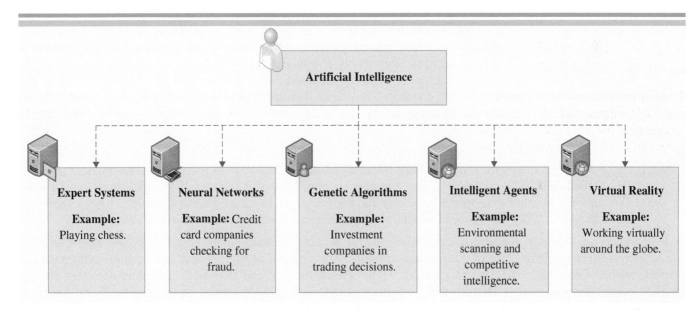

FIGURE 2.14

Examples of Artificial Intelligence

LO4 | Expert Systems

Expert systems are computerized advisory programs that imitate the reasoning processes of experts in solving difficult problems. Human expertise is transferred to the expert system, and users can access the expert system for specific advice or answers. Most expert systems reflect expertise from many humans and can therefore perform better analysis than any single expert. Typically, the system includes a knowledge base containing various accumulated experience and a set of rules for applying the knowledge base to each particular situation. The best-known expert systems play chess and assist in medical diagnosis. Expert systems are the most commonly used form of AI in the business arena because they fill the gap when human experts are difficult to find or retain, or are too expensive.

Neural Networks

A *neural network*, also called an *artificial neural network*, is a category of AI that attempts to emulate the way the human brain works. The types of decisions for which neural networks are most useful are those that involve pattern or image recognition, because a neural network can learn from the information it processes. Neural networks analyze large quantities of information to establish patterns and characteristics in situations where the logic or rules are unknown. Neural network features include:

■ Learning and adjusting to new circumstances on their own

■ Lending themselves to massive parallel processing

■ Functioning without complete or well-structured information

■ Coping with huge volumes of information with many dependent variables

■ Analyzing nonlinear relationships (they have been called fancy regression analysis systems)

The biggest problem with neural networks to date has been that the hidden layers are hidden; it is difficult to see how the neural network is learning and how the neurons are interacting. Newer neural networks no longer hide the middle layers. With these systems, users can manually adjust the weights or connections, giving them more flexibility and control.

The finance industry is a veteran in neural network technology and has been relying on various forms of it for over two decades. The industry uses neural networks to review loan applications and create patterns or profiles of applications, which fall into two categories: approved or denied. Other industries are following suit:

■ Physicians at the Children's Hospital of Eastern Ontario use a neural network to help keep watch over newborns' progress. The hospital, in collaboration with Carleton University, has spent more than a decade developing a machine-intelligence system that can scour through reams of data looking for patterns. In this instance, vital signs and other medical information from babies are digitally recorded every few seconds and housed in one of the most complex medical databases in the country. Vital-signs data from newborns with particular heart defects, body weights, and blood-pressures are analyzed by the neutral network to help reliably predict valid patient outcomes.[16]

■ Banks use neural networks to find opportunities in financial markets. By carefully examining historical stock market data with neural network software, bank financial managers can learn of interesting coincidences or small anomalies (called *market inefficiencies*). For example, it may be that whenever IBM stock goes up, so does Unisys stock. Or a treasury note might be selling for one cent less in Japan than in Canada. These snippets of information can make a big difference to a bank's bottom line in a competitive financial market.

■ Researchers are actively engaged in developing neural network systems for business purposes. One Canadian research team at the University of Alberta has developed an artificial neural network information system, called the Canadian Construction Claim Tracker (CCCT), to collect, classify, and analyze Canadian construction claims. The research team extracted 567 detailed Canadian construction claim contracts from Provincial and Supreme Courts of Canada records, and using CCCT were able to predict the outcome of a contract dispute with 65 percent accuracy. As researchers become better at designing neural network algorithms, this is expected to improve, although such systems can never be expected to attain 100 percent accuracy. For example, the prediction of court decisions will always be influenced by social, political, cultural, psychological, and environmental factors that neural networks may have difficulty assessing.[17]

■ Mail-order companies use neural networks to determine which customers are likely, or not likely, to order from their catalogues. Companies find that fine-tuning their mailing lists in this manner is effective, and expect to generate millions of dollars.

■ Fraud detection widely uses neural networks. Visa, MasterCard, and insurance companies are able to spot suspicious activity in individual accounts by their use. MasterCard, for example, estimates neural networks save the company $50 million annually.

Neural networks are often combined with "fuzzy logic" to express complicated and subjective concepts in a form that makes it possible to simplify the problem and apply rules that are executed with a level of certainty.[18] *Fuzzy logic* is a mathematical method of handling imprecise or subjective information. The basic approach is to assign values between zero and one to vague or ambiguous information. The higher the value, the closer it is to one. The value zero represents non-membership, and the value one represents membership, in the group the data represents. For example, fuzzy logic is used in washing machines, which determine by themselves how much water to use or how long to wash (they continue washing until the water is clean). In accounting and finance, fuzzy logic allows people to analyze information with subjective financial values (e.g., intangibles such as goodwill) that are important considerations in economic analysis.

Genetic Algorithms

A *genetic algorithm* is an artificial intelligence system that mimics the evolutionary, survival-of-the-fittest process to generate increasingly better solutions to a problem. A genetic algorithm is essentially an optimizing system: it finds the combination of inputs that gives the best outputs.

Genetic algorithms are best suited to decision-making environments in which thousands, or perhaps millions, of solutions are possible. Genetic algorithms can find and evaluate solutions with many more possibilities, faster and more thoroughly than a human. Organizations face decision-making environments for all types of problems that require optimization techniques, such as the following:

- Business executives use genetic algorithms to help them decide which combination of projects a firm should invest in, taking complicated tax considerations into account.
- Investment companies use genetic algorithms to help in trading decisions.
- Telecommunication companies use genetic algorithms to determine the optimal configuration of fibre-optic cable in a network that may include as many as 100,000 connection points. The genetic algorithm evaluates millions of cable configurations and selects the one that uses the least amount of cable.[19]

Intelligent Agents

An *intelligent agent* is a special-purpose knowledge-based information system that accomplishes specific tasks on behalf of its users. Intelligent agents use the knowledge base to make decisions and accomplish tasks in a way that fulfills the intentions of a user. Intelligent agents are usually symbolized by a suitable graphic such as a likeness of Sherlock Holmes.

One of the simplest examples of an intelligent agent is a *shopping bot*—software that searches several retailer websites and provide a comparison of each retailer's offerings, including price and availability. Increasingly, intelligent agents handle the majority of a company's Internet buying and selling and handle such processes as finding products, bargaining over prices, and executing transactions. Intelligent agents also have the capability of handling all supply chain buying and selling.

Another application of intelligent agents is in environmental scanning and competitive intelligence. For instance, an intelligent agent can learn the types of competitor information users want to track, continuously scan the Web for it, and alert users when a significant event occurs.

What do cargo transport systems, book distribution centres, the video game market, a flu epidemic, and an ant colony have in common? They are all complex adaptive systems that share some characteristics and use multi-agent systems and agent-based modelling to solve problems. By observing parts of the ecosystem, such as ant or bee colonies, AI scientists can use hardware and software models that incorporate insect characteristics and behaviour to (1) learn how people-based systems behave, (2) predict how they will behave under a given set of circumstances, and (3) improve human systems to make them more efficient and effective. This concept of learning from ecosystems and adapting their characteristics to human and organizational situations is called *biomimicry*.

In the last few years, AI research has made much progress in modelling complex organizations as a whole with the help of *multi-agent systems*, in which groups of intelligent agents have the ability to work independently and interact. The simulation of a human organization using a multi-agent system is called *agent-based modelling*. In agent-based modelling, each of the intelligent agents follows a set of simple rules and can adapt to changing conditions.

Agent-based modelling systems are used to model stock market fluctuations, predict the escape routes that people seek in a burning building, estimate the effects of interest rates on consumers with different types of debt, and anticipate how changes in conditions will affect the supply chain, to name just a few. Examples of companies that have used agent-based modelling to their advantage are:

- Southwest Airlines—to optimize cargo routing
- Procter & Gamble—to overhaul its handling of what the company calls its "supply network" of five billion consumers in 140 countries
- Air Liquide America—to reduce production and distribution costs of liquefied industrial gases
- Merck & Co.—to find more efficient ways of distributing anti-AIDS drugs in Africa
- Ford Motor Co.—to build a model of consumer preferences and find the best balance between production costs and customer demands

Virtual Reality

Virtual reality is a computer-simulated environment that can be a simulation of the real world or an imaginary world. This fast-growing area of artificial intelligence originated in efforts to build more natural, realistic, multisensory human–computer interfaces. Virtual reality enables telepresence, whereby users can be anywhere in the world and work alone or together at a remote site. Typically, this involves using the system to enhance the sight and touch of a human who is remotely manipulating equipment to accomplish a task. Examples range from virtual surgery, wherein surgeon and patient may be on opposite sides of the globe, to the remote use of equipment in hazardous environments such as chemical plants and nuclear reactors.

Augmented reality is the viewing of the physical world with computer-generated layers of information added to it.

Examples of a *virtual workforce* include Microsoft's headquarters in Redmond, Washington, where traffic congestion occurs daily for the 35,000 commuters. To alleviate the problem Microsoft is offering its employees the ability to work virtually from home. Over 42 percent of IBM's 330,000 employees work virtually, saving over $100 million per year in real-estate-related expenses. The idea offers several advantages: fewer cars on the road, increases in productivity, and decreased real estate expenses. Drawbacks include the fear among workers that they will jeopardize their careers by working from home, and the fact that some workers need a busy environment to stay productive. Virtual workers also tend to feel alone, secluded, and deprived of vital training and mentoring.

OPENING CASE QUESTIONS

Information Systems Improve Business Processes at Grocery Gateway

1. What information systems are used at Grocery Gateway to help staff make decisions? Would you classify these systems as TPS, DSS, or EIS?

2. How do these systems support operational-, managerial-, or strategic-level decisions?

3. What steps could the company take to leverage the transactional data collected by the information systems outlined in the case to help make managerial and strategic decisions for the company?

4. Identify a few key metrics a Grocery Gateway executive might want to monitor on a digital dashboard. How can these metrics be used to improve organizational decision making?

2.2 BUSINESS PROCESSES

LO5) EVALUATING BUSINESS PROCESSES

Businesses gain a competitive edge when they minimize costs and streamline their business processes. Columbia Sportswear Company is a global leader in the design, production, marketing, and distribution of outdoor apparel and footwear. The company is always looking to make the members of its highly mobile workforce more responsive and efficient while also helping them enjoy better work–life balance. Columbia Sportswear wanted new ways to streamline its operations to get up-to-the-minute information to employees working across multiple time zones. The company deployed innovative Microsoft messaging software to give its workers flexible, safeguarded access to messages from anywhere in the world. This helps the company speed every aspect of its business, and gives employees more freedom to enjoy an active lifestyle.[20]

Most organizations pride themselves on providing breakthrough products and services for customers. Unfortunately, if customers do not receive what they want quickly, accurately, and hassle-free, even fantastic offerings will not save an organization from annoying its customers and ultimately eroding the firm's financial performance.

The best way for an organization to satisfy customers and spur profits is by completely understanding all of its business processes. A *business process* is a standardized set of activities that accomplish a specific task, such as processing a customer's order.[21] Business processes transform a set of inputs into a set of outputs (goods or services) for another person or process by using people and tools. Waiting in line at a grocery store is a great example. The purpose of the *checkout* process is to pay for and bag groceries; it begins when a customer steps into line and ends when he or she gets the receipt and leaves. The *steps* of the process are the activities the customer and store personnel do to complete the transaction.

Automatic checkout systems at grocery stores are an excellent example of business process improvement. Imagine other, more complex business processes—developing new products, building a new home, ordering clothes from mail-order companies, requesting new telephone service from a telephone company, and administering CPP payments.

Examining business processes helps an organization determine bottlenecks, eliminate duplicate activities, combine related activities, and identify smooth-running processes. Organizations are only as effective as their business processes, and to stay competitive they must optimize and automate. Developing logical business processes can help an organization achieve its goals. For example, an automobile manufacturer might have the goal of reducing the time it takes to deliver a car to a customer. It cannot hope to meet this goal with an inefficient ordering process or a convoluted distribution process. Sales representatives might be making mistakes when completing order forms, data entry clerks might not accurately code order data, and dock crews might be inefficiently loading cars onto trucks. All of these errors increase the time it will take to get the car to the customer. Improving any one of these processes can have a significant effect on the total distribution process, made up of the order entry, production scheduling, and transportation processes. Figure 2.15 displays several sample business processes, and Figure 2.16 shows the entire customer order process across business units.[22]

Some processes (such as a programming process) may be wholly contained within a single department. However, most (such as ordering a product) are cross-departmental, spanning the organization. Figure 2.17 displays the different categories of cross-departmental business processes. *Customer-facing processes* result in a product or service that is received by an organization's external customer and can be specific to an industry. *Business-facing processes* are invisible to the external customer but essential to the effective management of the business and include goal setting, day-to-day planning, performance feedback, rewards, and resource allocation.[23]

A company's strategic vision should provide guidance on which business processes are core, that is, which are directly linked to the firm's critical success factors. Mapping these core business processes to the value chain reveals where the processes touch the customers and affect their perceptions of value. This type of map conceptualizes the business as a value delivery system, allowing managers to ensure all core business processes are operating as efficiently and effectively as possible.

ACCOUNTING and FINANCE

Paying accounts payable
Collecting accounts receivable
Creating financial statements

ENVIRONMENTAL MANAGEMENT

Environmental protection
Hazardous waste disposal
Air/water/soil resource management

HUMAN RESOURCES

Hiring employees
Enrolling employees in health benefits
Tracking vacation and sick leave

MANAGEMENT INFORMATION SYSTEMS

Making backups
Managing service agreements
Enforcing Internet use policy

FIGURE 2.15

Sample Business Processes

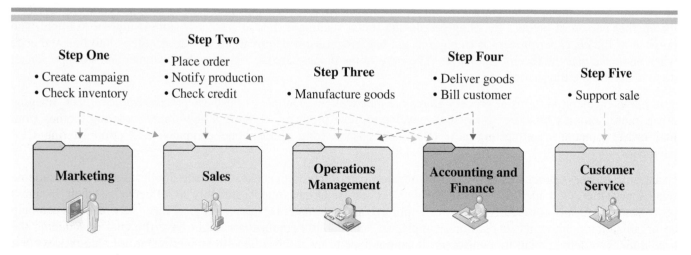

Step One
• Create campaign
• Check inventory

Step Two
• Place order
• Notify production
• Check credit

Step Three
• Manufacture goods

Step Four
• Deliver goods
• Bill customer

Step Five
• Support sale

Marketing | Sales | Operations Management | Accounting and Finance | Customer Service

FIGURE 2.16

Five Steps in the Order-to-Delivery Business Process

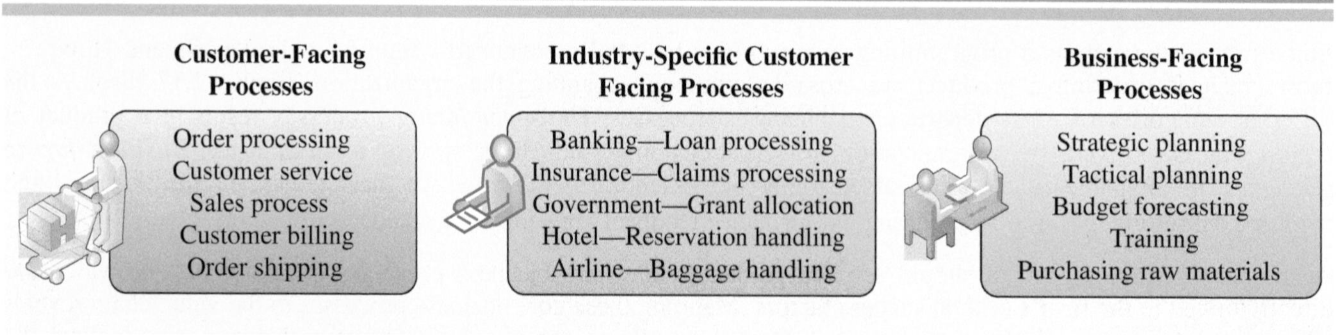

Customer-Facing Processes

Order processing
Customer service
Sales process
Customer billing
Order shipping

Industry-Specific Customer Facing Processes

Banking—Loan processing
Insurance—Claims processing
Government—Grant allocation
Hotel—Reservation handling
Airline—Baggage handling

Business-Facing Processes

Strategic planning
Tactical planning
Budget forecasting
Training
Purchasing raw materials

FIGURE 2.17

Examples of Customer-Facing, Industry-Specific, and Business-Facing Processes

A *business process patent* is a patent that protects a specific set of procedures for conducting a particular business activity. A firm can create a value chain map of the entire industry to extend critical success factors and business process views beyond its boundaries. *Core processes* are business processes, such as manufacturing goods, selling products, and providing service, that make up the primary activities in a value chain. Evaluating core processes allowed National Semiconductor to identify the core business processes required to move assembly plants to Southeast Asia. The map identified logistics and distribution as critical to the success of the move. Thus, to ensure reliable delivery of its products, the company contracted with Federal Express, combining its outstanding manufacturing process and Federal Express's exceptional distribution processes. The move allowed National Semiconductor to save money by closing nine warehouses while maintaining excellence in logistics and distribution. As this example demonstrates, changing business processes can generate significant competitive advantages across the value chain.[24]

BUSINESS PROCESS MODELLING

To determine whether a process is appropriately structured, organizations should create a cross-functional team to build process models that display input–output relationships among process-dependent operations and departments. They should create business process models documenting a step-by-step process sequence for the activities required to convert inputs to outputs for the specific process.

Business process modelling (or *mapping*) is the activity of creating a detailed flowchart, workflow diagram, use case diagram, or process map showing process inputs, tasks, and activities, in a structured sequence. A *business process model* is a graphic description of a process, showing the sequence of tasks that complete the process from a selected viewpoint. A set of one or more process models details the many functions of a system or subject area with graphics and text, and its purpose is to:

■ Expose process detail gradually and in a controlled manner

■ Encourage conciseness and accuracy in describing the process model

■ Focus attention on the process model interfaces

■ Provide a powerful process analysis and consistent design vocabulary[25]

Business process modelling usually begins with a functional process representation of *what* the process problem is, or an As-Is process model. *As-Is process models* represent the current state of the operation that has been mapped, without any specific improvements or changes to existing processes. The next step is to build a To-Be process model that displays *how* the process problem will be solved or implemented. *To-Be process models* show the results of applying change improvement opportunities to the current (As-Is) process model. This approach ensures that the process is fully and clearly understood before the details of a process solution are decided. The To-Be process model shows *how* the *what* is to be realized. Figure 2.18 displays the As-Is and To-Be process models for ordering a hamburger.[26]

Analyzing As-Is business process models leads to success in business process re-engineering since these diagrams are powerful for visualizing the activities, processes, and data flow of an organization. As-Is and To-Be process models are integral in process re-engineering projects. Figure 2.19 illustrates an As-Is process model of an order-fulfillment process developed by a process modelling team representing all departments that contribute to the process. The process modelling team traces the process of converting the input (orders) through all the intervening steps until the final required output (payment) is produced. The map displays the cross-functional departments involved in a typical order-fulfillment process.[27]

It is easy to get bogged down in excessive detail when creating an As-Is process model. The objective is to aggressively eliminate, simplify, or improve the To-Be processes. Successful process improvement efforts result in positive answers to the key process design or improvement question: Is this the most efficient and effective process for accomplishing the process goals? This process modelling structure allows the team to identify all the critical interfaces, overlay the time to complete various processes, start to define the opportunities for process simulation, and identify disconnects (illogical, missing, or extraneous steps) in the processes. Figures 2.20 and 2.21 illustrates a model for improving the business process.

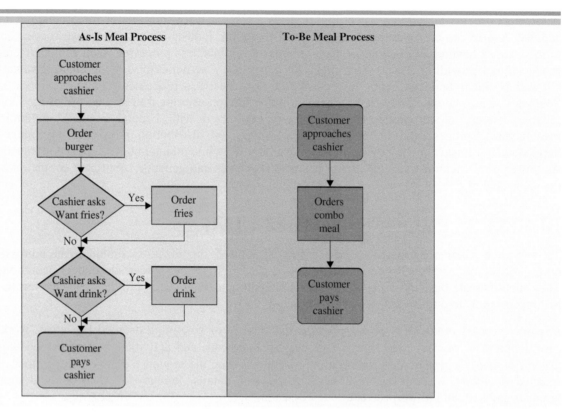

FIGURE 2.18

As-Is and To-Be Process Model for Ordering a Meal at a Burger Restaurant

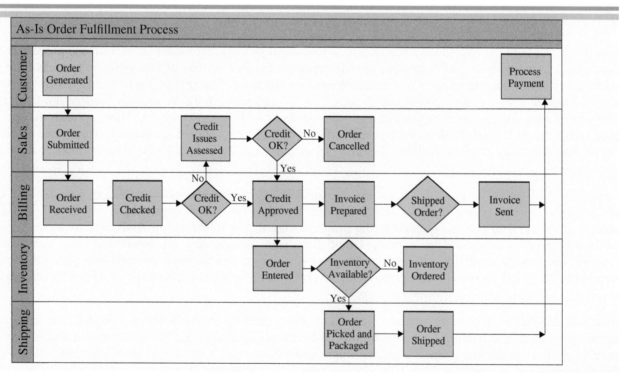

FIGURE 2.19

As-Is Process Model for Order Fulfillment

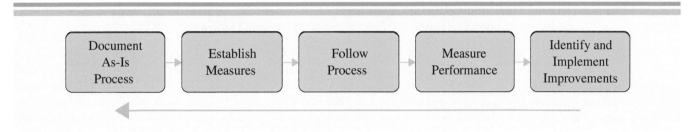

FIGURE 2.20

Steps in Business Process Improvement

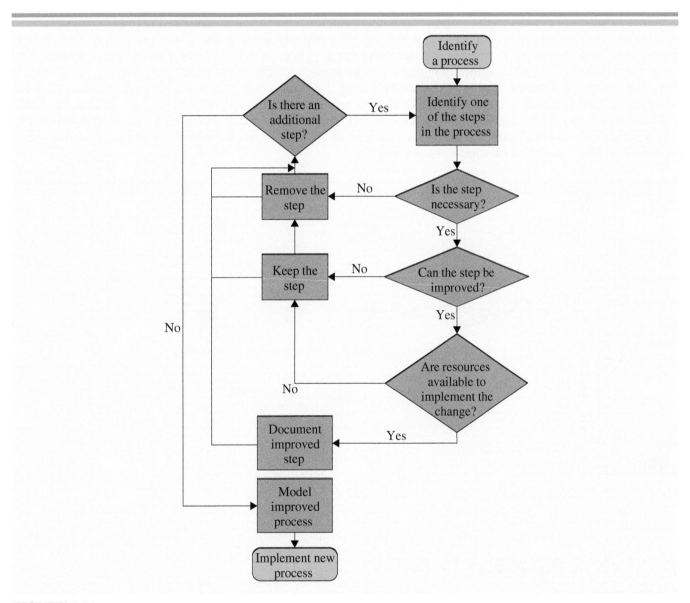

FIGURE 2.21

Business Process Improvement Model

The consulting firm KPMG uses process modelling as part of its business re-engineering practice. They used process modelling to help a large financial services company slash costs and improve productivity in its Manufactured

Housing Finance Division. Turnaround time for loan approval was reduced by half, using 40 percent fewer staff members.

Modelling helped the team analyze the complex aspects of the project. "In parts of the loan origination process, a lot of things happen in a short period of time," according to team leader Bob Karrick of KPMG. "During data capture, information is pulled from a number of different sources, and the person doing the risk assessment has to make judgment calls at different points throughout the process. There is often a need to stop, raise questions, make follow-up calls, and so on and then continue with the process modelling effort. Modelling allows us to do a thorough analysis that takes into account all these decision points and variables."[28]

BUSINESS PROCESS MODELLING EXAMPLES

A picture is worth a thousand words. Just ask Wayne Kendrick, a systems analyst for Mobil Oil Corporation. Kendrick, whose work involves planning and designing complex processes, was scheduled to make a presentation to familiarize top management with a number of projects his group was working on. "I was given 10 minutes for my presentation, and I had 20 to 30 pages of detailed documentation to present. Obviously, I could not get through it all in the time allocated." Kendrick turned to business process models to help communicate his projects. "I think people can relate to pictures better than words," Kendrick said. He applied his thinking to his presentation by using Microsoft's Visio to create business process models and graphs to represent the original 30 pages of text. "It was an effective way to get people interested in my projects and to quickly see the importance of each project," he stated. The process models worked and Kendrick received immediate approval to proceed with all of his projects. Figures 2.22 through 2.26 offer examples of business process models.

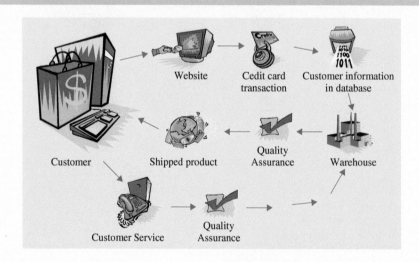

FIGURE 2.22

Online Sales Process Model

BUSINESS PROCESS IMPROVEMENT

Workflow includes the tasks, activities, and responsibilities required to execute each step in a business process. Understanding workflow, customers' expectations, and the competitive environment provides managers with the necessary ingredients to design and evaluate alternative business processes in order to maintain competitive advantages when internal or external circumstances change.

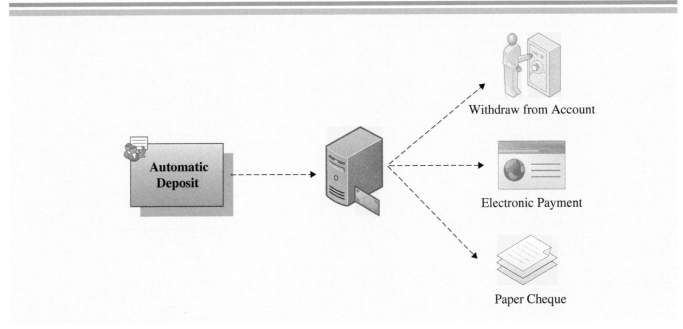

FIGURE 2.23

Online Banking Process Model

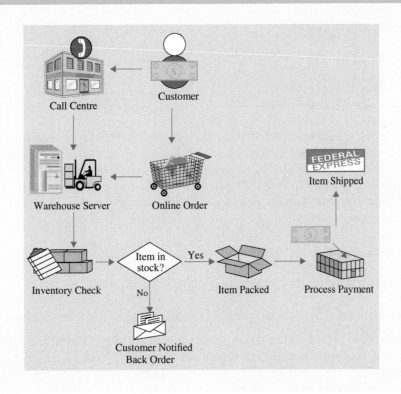

FIGURE 2.24

Order Fulfillment Process Model

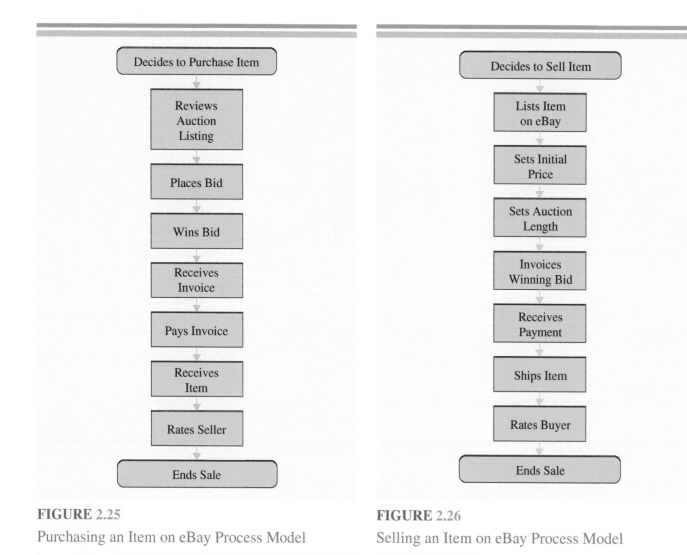

FIGURE 2.25

Purchasing an Item on eBay Process Model

FIGURE 2.26

Selling an Item on eBay Process Model

Alternative business processes should be effective (they deliver the intended results) and efficient (they consume the least amount of resources for the intended value). They should also be adaptable or flexible and support change as customers, market forces, and technology shift. Changes in business processes need to consider the change available to the firm and the business areas in which the change will be most often effective. How does a company know whether it needs to undertake the giant step of changing core business processes? Three conditions indicate the time is right to initiate a business process change:

1. There has been a pronounced shift in the market the process was designed to serve.

2. The company is markedly below industry benchmarks on its core processes.

3. To regain competitive advantage, the company must leapfrog competition on key dimensions.[29]

Improving business processes is paramount to staying competitive in today's electronic marketplace. Organizations must improve their business processes because customers are demanding better products and services. If customers do not receive what they want from one supplier, they can simply mouse-click and have many other choices. ***Business process improvement*** attempts to understand and measure the current process and make performance improvements accordingly.

Business processes should drive information systems choices, not the other way around. Businesses that choose information systems and then attempt to implement business processes based on the information systems typically fail. All business processes should be based on business strategies and goals. After determining the most efficient and effective business process, an organization can find the information system to use to support the business process. Of course, this does not always happen and often individuals find themselves in the difficult position of changing a business process because the information system cannot support the ideal solution.

This method for improving business processes is effective for obtaining gradual, incremental improvement. However, several factors have accelerated the need to radically improve business processes. The most obvious is information technology. New information technologies (like the Internet and wireless) yield new capabilities and improved functionalities in information systems. These, in turn, rapidly bring new capabilities to businesses, raising the competitive bar and the need to improve business processes dramatically. For example, **Amazon.com** reinvented the supply chain of selling books by using information systems that took advantage of the Internet. Amazon is a book-selling business, yet information systems that took advantage of Internet technology fundamentally changed the way customers purchase books.

Another apparent trend is the flattening of the global world through technology, bringing more companies and more customers into the marketplace and greatly increasing competition. A customer today can just as easily order a bottle of wine from a winery in France as from a wholesaler in the United States. In today's marketplace, major technological and business changes are required just to stay in the game. As a result, companies have requested methods for faster business process improvement. Also, companies want breakthrough performance changes, not just incremental changes, and they want it now. Because the rate of change has increased for everyone, few businesses can afford a slow change process. One approach for rapid change and dramatic improvement is business process re-engineering.

BUSINESS PROCESS RE-ENGINEERING

Business process re-engineering (BPR) is the analysis and redesign of workflow within and between enterprises. BPR relies on a different school of thought than business process improvement. In the extreme, BPR assumes the current process is irrelevant, does not work, or is broken and must be overhauled from scratch. Such a clean slate enables business process designers to dissociate themselves from today's process and focus on a new process. It is like the designers projecting themselves into the future and asking: What should the process look like? What do customers want it to look like? What do other employees want it to look like? How do best-in-class companies do it? How can a new information system facilitate the process?[30]

Figure 2.27 displays the basic steps in a business process re-engineering effort. It begins with defining the scope and objectives of the project, and then goes through a learning process (with customers, employees, competitors, non-competitors, and new information systems). Given this knowledge base, the designers can create a vision for the future and design new business processes by creating a plan of action based on the gap between current processes, information systems, structures, and process vision. It is then a matter of implementing the chosen solution.[31]

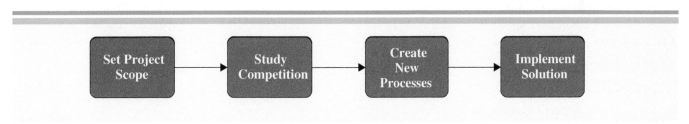

FIGURE 2.27
Business Process Re-engineering Model

Opportunities for Using BPR

Companies frequently strive to improve their business processes by performing tasks faster, cheaper, and better. Figure 2.28 displays different ways to travel the same road. A company can improve the way that it travels the road by moving from foot to horse and then from horse to car. However, true BPR looks at taking a different path. That same company could forget about travelling on the same old road and use an airplane to get to its final destination. Companies often follow the same indirect path for doing business, not realizing there might be a different, faster, and more direct way of doing business.[32]

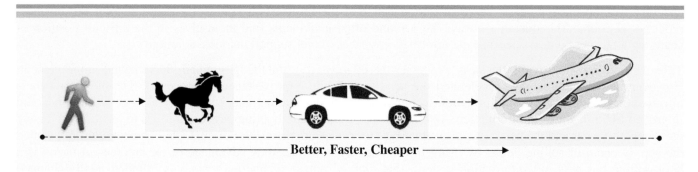

FIGURE 2.28

Different Ways to Travel the Same Route

Creating value for the customer is the leading factor for instituting BPR, and information systems often play important enabling roles. Radical and fundamentally new business processes enabled Progressive Insurance to slash claim settlement time from 31 days to four hours. Typically, car insurance companies follow this standard claims resolution process: The customer gets into an accident, has the car towed, and finds a ride home. He or she then calls the insurance company to begin the process, which usually takes over a month (see Figure 2.29).

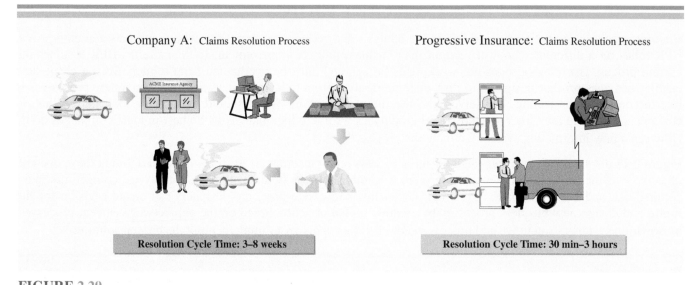

FIGURE 2.29

Auto Insurance Claims Processes

Progressive Insurance improved service to its customers by offering a mobile claims process. When a customer has a car accident, he or she calls in the claim on the spot. The Progressive claims adjuster goes to the accident location and performs a mobile claims process, surveying the scene and taking digital photographs. The adjuster then offers the customer on-site payment, towing services, and a ride home (see Figure 2.29).[33]

A true BPR effort does more for a company than simply improve it by performing a process better, faster, and cheaper. Progressive Insurance's BPR effort redefined best practices for its entire industry by changing the way that information systems support the claims process. Figure 2.30 displays the different types of change an organization can achieve, along with the magnitude of change and the potential business benefit.[34]

An organization can re-engineer its cross-departmental business processes or an individual department's business processes according to its needs. When selecting a business process to re-engineer, wise organizations focus on those core processes that are critical to their performance and potential add to the organizations competitive

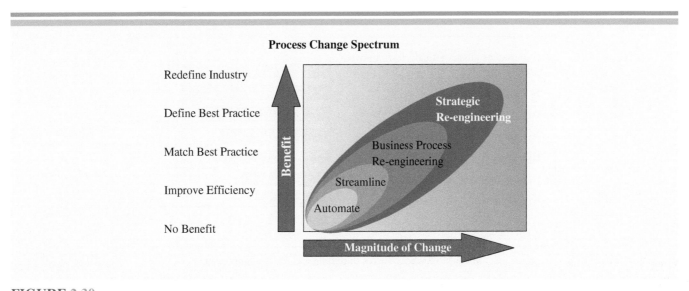

FIGURE 2.30

Process Change Spectrum

advantage, rather than marginal processes that have little impact. Re-engineering practitioners use several criteria to determine the importance of a process:

■ Is the process broken?

■ Is it feasible that re-engineering this process will succeed?

■ Does it have a high impact on the agency's strategic direction?

■ Does it significantly impact customer satisfaction?

■ Is it antiquated?

■ Does it fall far below best-in-class?

■ Is it crucial for productivity improvement?

■ Is the return on investment high and quickly obtained?

THE FUTURE: BUSINESS PROCESS MANAGEMENT

A key advantage of information systems is their ability to improve business processes. Working faster and smarter has become a necessity for companies. Initial emphasis was given to areas such as production, accounting, procurement, and logistics. The next big areas to discover information systems' value in business processes were sales and marketing automation, customer relationship management, and supplier relationship management. Some of these processes involve several departments of the company and some are the result of real-time interaction of the company with its suppliers, customers, and other business partners. The latest area to discover the power of information systems in automating and re-engineering business processes is business process management. ***Business process management (BPM)*** integrates all of an organization's business processes to make individual processes more efficient. BPM can be used to solve a single glitch or to create one unifying system to consolidate a myriad of processes.

Many organizations are unhappy with their current mix of software applications and dealing with business processes that are subject to constant change. These organizations are turning to BPM systems that can flexibly automate their processes and glue their enterprise applications together. Figure 2.31 outlines a few key reasons organizations are embracing BPM systems.

BPM systems effectively track and orchestrate the business process. BPM can automate tasks involving information from multiple systems, with rules to define the sequence in which the tasks are performed as well as responsibilities, conditions, and other aspects of the process. BPM can benefit an organization by updating processes in real time,

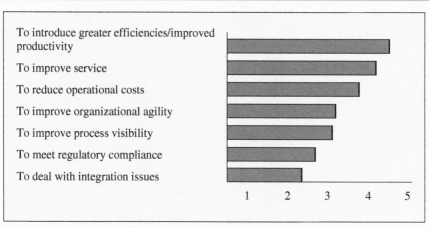

Scale 1 to 5 where 1 = not important and 5 = very important

FIGURE 2.31
Key Reasons for BPM

reducing expenses, automating key decisions, and improving productivity. BPM not only allows a business process to be executed more efficiently, but it also provides the tools to measure performance and identify opportunities for improvement—as well as to easily make changes in processes to act upon those opportunities, such as:

- Bringing processes, people, and information together.

- Breaking down the barriers between business areas and finding owners for the processes.

- Managing business processes within the enterprise and outside the enterprise with suppliers, business partners, and customers.

- Looking at systems horizontally instead of vertically.[35]

BPM: A Collaborative Process

A good BPM solution requires two great parts to work together as one. Since BPM solutions cross application and system boundaries, they often need to be sanctioned and implemented by the IS organization, while at the same time BPM products are business tools that business managers need to own. Therefore, confusion often arises as to whether business or IS managers should be responsible for driving the selection of a new BPM solution.

The key requirement for BPM's success in an organization is understanding that it is a collaboration of business and IS, and thus both parties need to be involved in evaluating, selecting, and implementing a BPM solution. IS managers need to understand the business drivers behind the processes, and business managers need to understand the impact the BPM solution may have on the infrastructure. Generally, companies that have successfully deployed BPM solutions are those whose business and IS groups have worked together as a cohesive team.

All companies can benefit from a better understanding of their key business processes, analyzing them for areas of improvement and implementing improvements. BPM applications have been successfully developed to improve complex business issues of some medium- to large-sized companies. Like many large-scale implementation projects, BPM solutions are most successful in companies with a good understanding of their information systems landscape, and management willing to approach business in a new way. BPM solutions are truly driven by the business process and the company's owners.[36]

Effective BPM solutions allow business owners to manage many aspects of the information system through business rules they develop and maintain. Companies that cannot support or manage cultural and organizational changes may lack positive BPM results.

BPM Risks and Rewards

If an organization is considering BPM, it must be aware of the risks involved in implementing these systems. One factor that commonly derails a BPM project has nothing to do with information systems and everything to do with people. BPM projects involve cultural and organizational changes that companies must make to support the new management approach required for success. Where ten area leaders once controlled ten pieces of an end-to-end process, now a new group is involved in implementing a BPM solution across all these areas. Suddenly the span of control is consolidated and all are accountable to the whole process, not just one piece of the puzzle.

The added benefit of BPM is not only an information systems solution, but also a business solution. BPM is a new business architecture and approach to managing the process and enabling proactive, continuous improvement. The new organizational structure and roles created to support BPM help maximize the continuous benefits to ensure success.

An MIS director from a large financial services company gave this feedback when asked about his experience in using a BPM solution to improve the company's application help desk process. "Before BPM, the company's application help desk was a manual process, filled with inefficiencies, human error, and no personal accountability. In addition, the old process provided no visibility into the process. There was absolutely no way to track requests, since it was all manual. Business user satisfaction with the process was extremely low. A BPM solution provided a way for the company to automate, execute, manage, and monitor the process in real time. The biggest technical challenge in implementation was ensuring that the user group was self-sufficient. While the company recognized that the IS organization is needed, it wanted to be able to maintain and implement any necessary process changes with little reliance on IS. It views process management as empowering the business users to maintain, control, and monitor the process. BPM goes a long way to enable this process."[37]

OPENING CASE QUESTIONS

Information Systems Improve Business Processes at Grocery Gateway

5. What does Grocery Gateway's customer order process look like?

6. Describe how Grocery Gateway's customer website supports Grocery Gateway's business processes.

7. Describe how Descartes's fleet management software improved Grocery Gateway's logistics business processes.

8. How does the business process affect the customer experience? The company's bottom line?

9. What other kinds of information systems could be used by Grocery Gateway to improve its business processes?

10. Comment on the need for integration between the various types of information systems at Grocery Gateway. What benefits from integration do you see for the company's various business processes? What challenges do you think will exist in facilitating such integration?

SUMMARY OF KEY THEMES

The purpose of this chapter was to explain the concepts of decision making and business processes. Information systems were showcased in terms of their ability to support organizational decision making at all levels in the company and for all types of decisions. The differences between decision types and transactional data, analytical information, TPS, DSS, EIS, and AI were explained. Information systems were also shown to be excellent vehicles by which to assess business processes and implement improved business processes. Business process re-engineering was introduced and how it can yield positive results on an organization's operations was discussed.

After reading this chapter, you, the business student, should have detailed knowledge of the types of decision-making information systems that exist in an organization. You should have a better understanding of how information systems and business processes can improve decision making that affects organizational performance. You should have a good grasp of how business processes integrate the various information systems together and improve organizational efficiency and effectiveness.

You should understand that investment in business process improvement, business process re-engineering, or business process management is the same as any other information systems-related investment. Planning the project properly, setting clear goals, educating those people who have to change their mindset once the system is implemented, and retaining strong management support will help with a successful implementation generating a solid return on investment. You should know that organizations must go beyond the basics when implementing business process improvement and realize that it is not a one-time project. Managing and improving end-to-end business processes is difficult and requires more than a simple, one-time effort. Continuously monitoring and improving core business processes will guarantee performance improvements across an organization.

KEY TERMS

Analytical information

Artificial intelligence (AI)

As-Is process models

Augmented reality

Benchmarking

Benchmarks

Business-facing processes

Business intelligence

Business process

Business process improvement

Business process management (BPM)

Business process model

Business process modelling (mapping)

Business process patent

Business process re-engineering (BPR)

Core processes

Consolidation

Critical success factors (CSF)

Customer-facing processes

Decision support system (DSS)

Digital dashboard

Drill-down

Effectiveness IS metrics

Efficiency IS metrics

Executive information system (EIS)

Expert systems

Fuzzy logic

Genetic algorithm

Goal-seeking analysis

Intelligent agent

Intelligent systems

Key performance indicators (KPIs)

Market share

Neural network (artificial neural network)

Online analytical processing (OLAP)

Online transaction processing (OLTP)

Project

Return on investment (ROI)

Semi-structured decisions

Sensitivity analysis

Shopping bot

Slice-and-dice

Structured decisions

To-Be process models

Transaction processing system (TPS)

Transactional data

Unstructured decisions

Visualization

Virtual reality

Virtual workforce

What-if analysis

Workflow

CLOSING CASE ONE

Information Systems Are Critical for Takeoff in Canada's Airline Industry

This case highlights the critical role revenue management information systems play in running the enterprise and their use for decision support.

When asked about the Canadian airline industry's reliance on information systems, Stephen Smith sits up straight. As a seasoned airline executive with over 25 years of experience working for such airlines as Air Canada, Zip Air, WestJet, Air Ontario, and Air Toronto, Smith knows that the airline industry has long been an intensive user of information systems—a direct result of airlines like Air Canada that carry over 20 million passengers every year, on 200,000 flights. "In the old days, the inventory system to maintain passenger records and numbers booked on a flight were done on paper and hung on nails. While this system worked, it certainly wouldn't work in a day and age like today. Computerized information systems are essential."

Think about it. From a process perspective, each flight must be allocated an aircraft, with x economy seats and y executive class seats. Then, against that inventory, names, record locators, and payment information must be matched to generate a ticket. That ticket must be then turned over to a gate agent, who then forwards it to the revenue accounting office, who then takes the money into revenue, because at this point the revenue is earned.

When questioned about how airlines go about maximizing the revenue generated on every flight, Smith explains how airlines rely heavily on using revenue management information systems. "Airlines, including Air Canada, invest heavily in revenue management systems. These systems forecast the demand for a flight at various fare levels based on historical demand. Without computers, this task would be next to impossible."

The reason for this is simply the proliferation of data involved. For a large airline carrier having hundreds of routes and multiple fare classes, the mathematical modelling required is beyond that of a human being. As a result, airlines invest millions of dollars into building and maintaining their revenue management systems in order to handle the vast amounts of data that must be processed. With hundreds or thousands of departures per day, the need for quick and accurate revenue management systems is critical for airlines in terms of helping them figure out what inventory to sell given the demand for flights and forecasts.

In fact, the need to manage revenue has become critical ever since deregulation of the airline industry in Canada occurred. Since deregulation, carriers have been free to set their own airfares, and rather than trying to fill planes, airlines now try to maximize their revenue. Thus, the emphasis for airlines these days is to fill planes with enough high-paying customers to cover costs and make a profit, as opposed to ensuring that all flights are simply full.[38]

What are revenue management systems? These are information systems used by airlines to calculate how many seats in each fare class are offered on particular legs of a flight at a given time, taking into account current demand, historical data, and special one-time events that influence demands for travel. According to Smith, "the process of revenue management is a very, very sophisticated form of revenue control, which, based on historical booking trends, attempts to forecast the passenger demand for a flight, and what they might be willing to pay. The ideal scenario is that a passenger shows up at the last minute, there is one open seat on the flight, and they are willing to pay the amount the airline is asking for that last seat."

With the advent of the Web, airlines are well aware that customers are increasingly able to compare fares from all competitors with a few mouse clicks. An airline's fares have become almost totally visible and thus airlines are forced to implement competitive fares in their revenue management systems. If a fare is too high, a potential customer will buy from the competition; if a fare is too low, the airline loses out on potential revenue earned.[39]

These revenue management systems also need to set overbooking levels. Stephen Smith explains, "some people simply do not show up for their designated flights. Approximately 10 percent of passengers do not show up. These no-shows force airlines to overbook their flights, otherwise, 10% of an airline's revenue would not be realized—which means that for most airlines, they would become very unprofitable, very quickly."

Further, when taking into account cancelled flights, people changing bookings, delays, and rebookings, the logic built into revenue management systems becomes very complicated, very fast. This complexity is exacerbated when one considers the fact that revenue systems must also deal with different fare structures for different types of passengers. In general, there are two types of passengers: those who must fly on that flight, on that day; and those who are willing to move flights, days, and even destinations. An example of the former are business travellers or those with medical appointments. An example of the latter are those on vacation, or going to meet friends and relatives. Obviously, those in the first group are far more willing to pay more for their flight, as the convenience of a flight on that day to their destination at that time is far more important than the cost of the flight. The second group is far more likely to gravitate to the cheapest flight, regardless of when it leaves (within reason) either by day or time; in fact, vacation travellers will even change countries based upon which flight is the cheapest. In addition, the first group normally books flights closer to flight time, as planning travel a month ahead for most businesses is not normal; this group rarely stays over weekends and wants to be able to change flights if plans change (which they frequently do). The second group is completely different, planning much further ahead, staying over weekends, and rarely changing plans.

As a result, airlines came up with various fare levels, and various requirements to obtain those fares. Revenue management must handle these requirements. The first fare was the "full fare economy fare," which was the most one could pay for an economy seat, but could be bought up to the last minute, and allowed the traveller to change flights without a penalty. Then there were 3-day advance fares, 7-day advance fares, and 14-day advance fares, each with a number of fares in the category, allowing the traveller to change/not change/pay for a change as well as the requirement to stay over a Saturday night, or not. You can imagine that doing this inventory for each flight, for 660 flights per day, for 365 days (most airlines only keep inventory of flights up to one year in advance) would be impossible without the help of computerized information systems.

To handle these different fare scenarios, the airlines set up fare "buckets" and "nest" them within broad groups, so that they allowed, for instance, a 3-day fare (normally more than a 7-day fare) to outsell its bucket, if there were 7-day fares still remaining. Once a flight booking goes above the expected higher booking rate, the lower fare inventory is shut down, as the flight is booking up faster than expected. Conversely, if the booking levels go below an expected lower booking rate, then the lower fares are opened up, as the flight is booking slower than expected. This analysis is done on every flight for every day for the entire year, every hour, otherwise airlines could be caught flatfooted and oversell, or undersell, a large number of flights for the entire year.

This sophistication has been taken to the next level. The airlines' most loyal passengers (e.g., Air Canada Elite or Super Elite passengers) can now book a flight even if it has been overbooked or a certain fare group is sold out. This allows the airline to repay its most loyal customers with something not available to all customers.

In the future, airlines hope to be able to set up a fare schedule for each customer, depending on buying habits and loyalty to the airline. This is just another attempt, in a fixed-cost industry, to buy loyalty, as almost every dollar of revenue drops to the bottom line of the airline, and the more a customer flies with the airline, the more revenue is generated. A case in point is Air Canada's decision to implement a data warehouse to enhance its yield marketing intelligence and provide the company with a scalable platform that facilitates future growth in CRM and finance analytics applications.[40]

In addition to revenue management, revenue accounting for an airline is critical, as revenue cannot be taken into account until the customer has flown. This is another area where, since the demise of paper tickets (most travel is now ticketless), computer systems must be able to match the customer with the fare that has been paid, to ensure he or she has followed the appropriate rules, and to take that fare into revenue.

Stephen Smith relaxes in his chair and summarizes his thoughts on the airline industry's reliance on information systems: "As you can imagine, the ability to forecast passenger demand for a flight, at all different fare levels, is a very sophisticated process which was never considered back in the days that people counted tags for their flight inventory. For this reason, I can [assure] you that information systems have become fundamentally critical to the daily operations of an airline. There's no turning back to paper now."

Questions

1. What advantages are there for an airline to use a revenue management system?

2. Are revenue management systems a competitive advantage or simply a new necessity for doing business in the airline industry today?

3. What type of decisions could be made with the help of a revenue management system?

4. Is a revenue management system a TPS, DSS, or an EIS?

5. Would the revenue management system described in the case contain transactional data or analytical information?

6. What types of metrics would an airline executive want to see in a digital dashboard displaying revenue information?

7. How could AI enhance the use of an airline's revenue management system for decision support?

CLOSING CASE TWO

Leveraging the Power and Avoiding the Pitfalls of BPM

This case illustrates the potential and hazards associated with BPM initiatives.

John, the CEO of a large Canadian distribution firm with worldwide distribution of oil and gas drilling equipment, has recently been searching the Web for examples of places where BPM is being used. The other day he approached his CIO, Sheila, with a number of examples where it has been used successfully.

After a few conversations and some additional research, they developed a list of a few areas in their firm where they think using BPM could help. They assigned a small project team to investigate these areas further and asked them if implementing BPM into the company could improve its business processes and whether it could be successfully implemented. They also added a list of a few precautions against actions that seem to result in project failure.

Global Outsourcing

Organizations, in hopes of reducing costs of skilled labour and getting work done more quickly by having tasks executed on a 24/7 basis, are redistributing work processes over a global workforce. The tricky part for companies to figure out is deciding which tasks to redistribute globally and which tasks should remain local. This being so, many organizations are turning to BPM to help them figure things out. A recent industry report predicts a dramatic resurgence in interest in business process management will happen as companies turn to BPM to figure out which jobs in a company can remain local and which can be outsourced across the globe.[41]

Records Management

Many organizations have formal records management programs in place to manage and deal with a company's vast amount of paper documents. Historically, this function was primarily concerned with the long-term storage of contracts, invoices, and purchase agreements. However, today, greater emphasis is being put on a more holistic view of the records management function, one that involves managing company records across the information life cycle from creation, use, and storage to final disposition. A recent industry report indicates that BPM may offer great improvements for managing a company's records if records were associated with each stage of a business process. So, rather than worrying about storing a contract after it is signed, sealed, and delivered by all parties, a better approach is to create a contract document at the beginning of contract negotiations and maintain it throughout each stage of the contract life cycle. The report encourages companies to develop records management programs that are tightly coupled with underlying business processes and views BPM as the right tool to get the job done.[42]

Supply Chain Management

Market trends indicate that supply chains that link multiple suppliers of goods and services together to create, distribute, and sell finished products need tighter process integration to be successful. According to industry insiders, tighter process integration in supply chain processes is becoming increasingly important in order to meet rising market demand, and warrants the need for information systems applications to automatically connect to other applications, whether these applications exist inside or outside the enterprise, and to execute the functions necessary to complete a specific business process.[43]

Potential Problems

Despite the potential benefits that BPM can provide, some industry experts caution haste and point to five pitfalls that lessen the likelihood of BPM project success:[44]

1. *Failure to properly estimate the scope of the project.* This is typically done either by overestimating expectations of business process improvement and failing to achieve them, or underestimating the complexity, time, and costs involved in changing existing business processes. Is the company ready to change? Does the company have the requisite resources required to implement the change? How long will it take to implement the change? It is these types of questions that underlie the reasons why a business process re-engineering project succeeds or fails.

2. *Failure to develop and obtain sign-off on a sound business case for the project.* Without proper analysis and buy-in from all key stakeholders involved in a business process re-engineering initiative, the project is more likely to fail. Due diligence and buy-in result in a more successful implementation of the business process redesign project. A sound business case will also serve as a guide during project implementation and a measuring stick by which to assess whether or not the project is on track.

3. *Failure to identify and engage a strong sponsor for the project.* Upper management support or buy-in from a powerful project sponsor is vital in ensuring that naysayers of a business process improvement project are kept at bay.

4. *Failure to identify and properly manage project stakeholders.* Stakeholder buy-in and engagement are critical, along with rallying support from others in the organization to start the project and keep the project afloat and alive during turbulent times.

5. *Shortchanging, or entirely skipping, the all-important task of documenting and analyzing the "As-Is" process before designing the "To-Be" process.* Not fully understanding the reasons why certain things are done in an existing business process can lead to serious design flaws or missing functionality in a newly developed business process.

Questions

1. How can BPM help improve global outsourcing? Records management? Supply chain management?

2. What other business activities are excellent candidates for BPM?

3. Which of the five pitfalls do you think is the most important? Why?

4. Which of the five pitfalls do you think is the most common pitfall that organizations face when undergoing BPM? Why?

5. What is the advantage of treating BPM as a project, as opposed to some other type of business activity?

CLOSING CASE THREE

Actionly: Online Brand Management

This case illustrates the use of online brand management.

Data are all over the Internet! Tons and tons and tons of data! For example, over 152 million blogs are created each year, along with 100 million Twitter accounts resulting in 25 billion tweets, 107 trillion emails are sent, and 730 billion hours of YouTube videos are watched. This arena, known as the social media sector, is by far one of the fastest-growing and most influential sectors in business. Companies are struggling to understand how the social media sector impacts it both financially and strategically.

Data are valuable to any company, and the data on the Internet are unique because the information comes directly from customers, suppliers, competitors, and even employees. As the social media sector takes off, companies are finding themselves at a disadvantage when attempting to keep up with all of the "online chatter" about their goods and services on the many different social media websites, including Facebook, Twitter, Flickr, LinkedIn, Yelp, Google, blogs, etc.

Any time there is a problem there is a potential business solution, and **Actionly.com** chooses to capitalize on the data glut problem. Actionly monitors multiple social media channels through one tracking service looking for specific keywords for industries, brands, companies, and trends. Actionly customers choose a keyword to monitor—such as a brand, product names, industry terms, or competitors—and then Actionly constantly collects the data from these social channels and pulls that data into a cohesive digital dashboard. The digital dashboard tracks the desired information, such as marketplace trends, specific companies, competitive brands, entire industries (e.g., clean technology), by simultaneously searching Twitter, Facebook, Google, YouTube, Flickr, and blogs. After completing a search, Actionly uses Google Analytics to create graphs and charts indicating how frequently each keyword was found throughout the various channels. Additionally, it links each respective channel to the dashboard and filters them with "positive" and "negative" connections, allowing users to respond to any comments.

Actionly's business model sets it up for success in this emerging industry. Actionly has a first-mover advantage, because it was the first online brand management company offering this service to customers. And the company benefits by using its own services to ensure its brand stays number one on all social media websites. Actionly uses Google Analytics to help transform the data it collects from the various social media websites into valuable business intelligence. Its digital dashboard monitors several key metrics, including:

- *Reputation management.* Actionly's easy to use digital dashboard allows customers to observe and analyze trends and track mentions about brands based on historical data as well as continuously updated data. For example, a customer can view graphs that highlight key trends across 30 days for specific brands, products, or companies.

- *Social ROI.* By connecting to Google Analytics from Actionly, a customer can analyze its campaign performance for individual tweets or Facebook posts to determine which are successful and which are failing. Actionly analyzes every post and click to track page views, visitor information, goal completions, and so on, through its digital dashboard, allowing users to customize reports tracking the performance of daily posts.

- *Twitter analytics.* After adding Twitter accounts to the dashboard, a user can drill down into the data to view graphs of followers, mentions, and retweets. This eliminates the need to manually track a number of Twitter accounts, and a user can view the data in graphs or export the data in Excel for further analysis.

- *Marketing campaign tracking.* If a company is launching a big promotion or contest, it can post messages across multiple Facebook or Twitter accounts; all the user has to do is select which Twitter or Facebook accounts it wants to use and when. Actionly's Campaign Tracking helps a user view which posts are resonating well with customers and measure metrics such as page views, signups, conversions, and revenue by post. Actionly even segments the data by post, account, campaign, or channel, allowing users to measure performance over time.

- *Click performance.* Actionly tracks performance by hour and day of week, allowing customers to view which clicks are getting the most attention. Its algorithm automatically assigns a sentiment to tweets, allowing the customer to immediately filter positive or negative or neutral posts to react to information quickly.

- *Sentiment analysis.* Reviewing positive and negative feedback helps gauge how a brand is doing over time, allowing the client to try to increase the positive sentiment. However, no sentiment scoring is 100 percent accurate due to the complexities of interpretation, culture, sarcasm, and other language nuances. For example, if Actionly is incorrectly tracking a metric, it can change it, allowing users to assign their unique sentiments directly to their tweets. A user can also select to have positive or negative alerts for keywords emailed as soon as the keyword is posted to help manage online brand and company reputations.

- *Competitive analysis.* Actionly tracks competitor intelligence by watching new-product releases, acquisitions, or customer feedback, allowing a company to stay on top of market entrants, market-related blogs, news, or industry-related seminars/webinars.

■ *Find influencers.* Actionly's digital dashboard allows a user to engage directly with key influencers or people who are driving the online chatter about goods and services. Actionly identifies influencers and determines their relevance to the company, brand, or product. It then compiles a list of influencers based on users with the most followers and who have been most active for the specific searches in the past 30 days.[45]

Questions

1. Define the three primary types of decision-making systems, and explain how a customer of Actionly might use them to find business intelligence.

2. Describe the difference between transactional and analytical information, and determine which types Actionly uses to create a customer's digital dashboard.

3. Illustrate the business process model used by a customer of Actionly following Twitter tweets.

4. Explain business process re-engineering and how Actionly used it to create its unique business model.

5. Formulate different metrics Actionly uses to measure the success of a customer's marketing campaign.

MAKING BUSINESS DECISIONS

1. Making Decisions

You are the vice-president of human resources for a large consulting company. You are compiling a list of questions that you want each interviewee to answer. The first question on your list is "How can information systems enhance your ability to make decisions at our organization?" Prepare a one-page report to answer this difficult question.

2. DSS and EIS

Dr. Rosen runs a large dental conglomerate—Teeth Doctors—that staffs more than 700 dentists in four provinces. Dr. Rosen is interested in purchasing a competitor called Dentix that has 150 dentists in three additional provinces. Before deciding whether to make the purchase, Dr. Rosen must consider several issues:

■ The cost of purchasing Dentix

■ The location of the Dentix offices

■ The current number of customers per dentist, per office, and per province

■ The merger between the two companies

■ The professional reputation of Dentix

■ Other competitors

Explain how Dr. Rosen and Teeth Doctors can benefit from using information systems to make an accurate business decision regarding the potential purchase of Dentix.

3. Finding Information on Decision Support Systems

You are working on the sales team for a small catering company that maintains 75 employees and generates $1 million in revenues per year. The owner, Pam Hetz, wants to understand how she can use decision support systems (DSS) to help grow her business. Pam has an initial understanding of DSS and is interested in learning more about what types are available, how they can be used in a small business, and the cost associated with different systems. In a group, research the website **www.dssresources.com** and compile a presentation that discusses systems in detail. Be sure to answer all Pam's questions on DSS in the presentation.

4. Artificial Intelligence Versus TPS, DSS, and EIS

In your new job as a business analyst, you have been asked by your boss, Amanda Krokosky-Gentry, to make a presentation to the MIS executive team about the difference between artificial intelligence and TPS, DSS, and EIS systems. In particular she is interested in how the systems help users make decisions and which systems lead to better decision making. Compile a presentation examining these topics.

connect **LEARNSMART** **SMARTBOOK**

For more information on the resources available from McGraw-Hill Ryerson, go to www.mheducation.ca/he/solutions.

ENDNOTES

1. www.grocerygateway.com/common/about.aspx, accessed July 3, 2011.

2. http://investing.businessweek.com/research/stocks/private/snapshot.asp?privcapId=2917, accessed June 27, 2011.

3. "The Challenges Confronting a Successful e-Business Start-Up: The Grocery Gateway Story," presentation given by Scott Bryan, Executive Vice-President, Grocery Gateway on September. 22, 2003, at the DeGroote School of Business, McMaster University.

4. www.grocerygateway.com/common/about.aspx, July 3, 2011.

5. www.descartes.com/cases/cs_grocery_gateway.html, accessed July 3, 2011.

6. Nathalie Kilby and Tim Maton, "Grocers Fail to Deliver Online," *Marketing Week*, Volume 29, Issue 19, 2006, pp. 38–39; http://executive.mcgill.ca/seminars/essential-management-skills, accessed June 27, 2011; "Ivey Executive Development Decision Making Skills," www.youtube.com/watch?v=utqa-FPIYfI, accessed June 27, 2011; Henry L. Kutarna, "The Leadership Skill Set," www.banffcentre.ca/departments/leadership/library/pdf/skill_set_6-7.pdf, accessed June 27, 2011.

7. "The Visionary Elite," *Business 2.0*, December 2003, pp. S1–S5.

8. http://executive.mcgill.ca/seminars/essential-management-skills, accessed June 27, 2011; "Ivey Executive Development Decision Making Skills," www.youtube.com/watch?v=utqa-FPIYfI, accessed June 27, 2011; Henry L. Kutarna, "The Leadership Skill Set," www.banffcentre.ca/departments/leadership/library/pdf/skill_set_6-7.pdf, accessed June 27, 2011.

9. Ken Blanchard, "Effectiveness vs. Efficiency," Wachovia Small Business, www.wachovia.com, accessed July 9, 2010

10. "Boston Coach Aligns Service with Customer Demand in Real Time," www-935.ibm.com/services/au/index.wss/casestudy/igs/a1006084?cntxt=a1005848, accessed November 4, 2003.

11. "Industry Facts and Statistics," Insurance Information Institute, www.iii.org, accessed December 2005.

12. "Canadian Pacific Railway Uses Business Objects to Improve Asset Utilization," *Reuters Significant Developments*, January 10, 2001.

13. Christopher Koch, "How Verizon Flies by Wire," *CIO Magazine*, November 1, 2004.

14. http://rivalwatch.com/solutions/index.php, accessed July 3, 2011.

15. Neil McManus, "Robots at Your Service," *Wired*, January 2003, p. 59.

16. Marlene Orton, "Health-Care Getting Wired," *The Ottawa Citizen*, October 19, 2005, p. F2.

17. Amir Camille Chehayeb and Mohamed Al-Hussein, "Using Artificial Neural Networks for Predicting the Outcome of Canadian Construction Litigated Claimes," *AACE International Transactions*, 2006, pp. 18.1–18.6.

18. S. Begley, "Software au Natural," *Newsweek*, May 8, 2005.

19. Beth Bacheldor, "Steady Supply," *InformationWeek*, November 3, 2003, www.informationweek.com, accessed June 27, 2011.

20. www.columbia.com, accessed July 3, 2011.

21. "What Is BPR?," http://searchcio.techtarget.com/definitions/business-process-reengineering, accessed July 4, 2011; BPR Online, www.prosci.com/mod1.html, accessed July 4, 2011; Business Process Reengineering Six Sigma, www.isixsigma.com, accessed July 9, 2010; SmartDraw.com, www.smartdraw.com, accessed July 9, 2010.

22. Ibid.

23. Ibid.

24. Michael Hammer, *Beyond Reengineering: How the Process-Centered Organization Is Changing Our Work and Our Lives* (New York: HarperCollins Publishers, 1996); Richard Chang, *Process Reengineering in Action: A Practical Guide to Achieving Breakthrough Results*, Quality Improvement Series (San Francisco: Pfeiffer, 1996).

25. Ibid.

26. Ibid.

27. H. James Harrington, *Business Process Improvement Workbook: Documentation, Analysis, Design and Management of Business Process Improvement* (New York: McGraw-Hill, 1997); Michael Hammer, *Beyond Reengineering: How the Process-Centered Organization Is Changing Our Work and Our Lives* (New York: HarperCollins Publishers, 1996).

28. Ibid.

29. Michael Hammer, *Beyond Reengineering: How the Process-Centered Organization Is Changing Our Work and Our Lives* (New York: HarperCollins Publishers, 1996); Richard Chang, *Process Reengineering in Action: A Practical Guide to Achieving Breakthrough Results*, Quality Improvement Series (San Francisco: Pfeiffer, 1996).

30. Michael Hammer, *Beyond Reengineering: How the Process-Centered Organization Is Changing Our Work and Our Lives* (New York: HarperCollins Publishers, 1996).

31. Richard Chang, *Process Reengineering in Action: A Practical Guide to Achieving Breakthrough Results*, Quality Improvement Series (San Francisco: Pfeiffer, 1996); H. James Harrington, *Business Process Improvement Workbook: Documentation, Analysis, Design and Management of Business Process Improvement* (New York: McGraw-Hill, 1997); Michael Hammer, *Beyond Reengineering: How the Process-Centered Organization Is Changing Our Work and Our Lives* (New York: HarperCollins Publishers, 1996); Michael Hammer and James Champy, *Reengineering the Corporation: A Manifesto for Business Revolution* (New York: HarperBusiness Essentials, 1993); *Government Business Process Reengineering (BPR) Readiness Assessment* (Washington, DC: General Services Administration, 1996); "Real World Process with Hammer and Company," www.hammerandco.com/HammerAndCompany.aspx?id=19, accessed July 4, 2011.

32. Ibid.

33. Ibid.

34. Ibid.

35. Ibid.

36. Bjorn Andersen, *Business Quality Improvement Toolbox* (Milwaukee, WI: ASO Quality Press, 1999).

37. "What Is BPR?," http://searchcio.techtarget.com/definition/business-process-reengineering, accessed July 4, 2011; BPR Online, www.prosci.com/mod1.html, accessed July 4, 2011; Business Process Reengineering Six Sigma, www.isixsigma.com, accessed July 9, 2010; SmartDraw.com, www.smartdraw.com, accessed July 9, 2010.

38. Mark Fray, "Seat Science," *Business Travel World*, February 2004, pp. 26–27.

39. Losef Loew, "Draining the Fare Swamp," *Journal of Revenue and Pricing Management*, 2004, Volume 3, Number 1, pp. 18–25.

40. "Air Canada Selects Teradata Warehouse for Revenue Management Analytics Applications," *Reuters Significant Developments*, September 28, 2006.

41. James Watson, Jeetu Patel, and Bill Chamber, "Enterprise Content Management Forecast 2009: Compliance and Ediscovery, Advanced Search, Sharepoint, and Business Process Management Dominate Christmas Wish Lists," *Infonomics*, Volume 22, Issue 6, November/December 2008, pp. 44–49.

42. Nishan Desilva and Ganesh Vednere, "Benefits and Implementation of Business-Process-Driven Records Management," *Infonomics*, Volume 22, Issue 6, November/December 2008, pp. 52–55.

43. Geoff Keston, "Supply Chain Management Market Trends," *Market* (Faulkner Information Services), October 2008.

44. Bill Brasington, "Implementing Business Process Management: Five Not-So-Easy Pieces," *Infonomics*, Volume 22, Issue 6, November/December 2008, pp. 20–22.

45. www.actionly.com, accessed March 16, 2014; www.socialmedia.biz/2011/01/12/top-20-social-media-monitoring-vendors-for-business, accessed March 16, 2014; http://www.salesforcemarketingcloud.com/products/social-media-listening, accessed March 16, 2014; http://www.oracle.com/us/solutions/social/overview/index.html, accessed March 16, 2014.

3

CHAPTER

Data, Information, and Knowledge

LO 3.1 Explain the defining value characteristics of both transactional data and analytical information, and the need for organizations to have data and information that are timely and of high quality.

LO 3.2 Describe the difference between knowledge management and knowledge management systems.

LO 3.3 Explain what business intelligence is and how it is impacting the way organizations are making decisions in today's business environment.

LO 3.4 Describe what is meant by a collaboration system, and how such systems can support both structured and unstructured collaboration.

LO 3.5 Explain the differences between, and business advantages of, various types of collaboration systems, such as groupware, content management systems, and workflow management systems.

This chapter discusses the concepts of data and information and their relative importance to organizations. It distinguishes between data, information and knowledge and the use of data and information in producing business intelligence. It also looks at how many organizations strive to find ways to help employees, customers, and business partners access the information they need, share this information with others, and use and incorporate it in their daily work. Doing so allows companies to not only get work done, but also encourages sharing and generating new ideas that lead to the development of innovations, improved work habits, and best practices.

Information systems are pivotal in making all this happen. They can improve the access and flow of information in a company, thus helping to facilitate business processes and growth.

This is the focus of this chapter—to showcase how information systems can help organizations capitalize on the power of information by providing mechanisms for improved accessing, sharing, and understanding of the information and data collected. This includes accessing and using structured and unstructured information.

As a business student, you need to be aware of how information systems, especially knowledge management systems, can help a company's bottom line by leveraging the power of information. By being conscious of the usefulness of information access and sharing tools, you will appreciate the opportunities for success they afford and will see the need to champion their use in companies to help organizations better succeed in the marketplace.

opening case study

Moneyball: About More Than Just the Players

Billy Beane was the general manager of the Oakland Athletics in the 2002 and 2003 seasons when the A's went to the playoffs with one-third of the payroll of the New York Yankees. How did he accomplish this? Beane selected what he believed were undervalued players to play on his team. Beane looked for players with high slugging percentages and on-base percentages—which had been statistically demonstrated as good predictors of offensive success—and low salary expectations to field his playoff-bound teams and thus brought business analytics and "sabermetric" analysis to baseball. Was Beane more successful than other general managers or did he revolutionize baseball or sport? Let's take a look.[1]

Getting Fans to the Games: The NHL

Every summer when the National Hockey League releases its schedule for the upcoming season, Carolina Hurricane's director of ticketing operations, Bill Nowicki, can immediately tell which games are going to be difficult to market to fans. The reasons vary: there may be game conflicts with a Carolina Panthers of the NFL home game, or the game may be against an opponent with low drawing power in the Raleigh, North Carolina, area. Some games are just a tougher sell. Given that the Hurricanes lack the lucrative fan base of teams like the Toronto Maple Leafs or the Vancouver Canucks, they need help to fill the seats. To this end, the Hurricanes, like other pro sports teams across North America, are implementing many of the same software and data analytics technologies currently used by insurance companies to nab fraudsters or by large corporations to identify new business trends.

In the past the process of selling tickets to those outside of the Hurricanes' core fan base wasn't scientific. Decisions about when to hold a promotion or offer a new ticket package were based on instinct, and those instincts were often based on trends the team's management felt they could identify from the success or failure of past practices. In 2005, the Hurricanes implemented a new ticketing technology that enabled the team to track all the purchases made by an individual fan. It was not until the team started to apply various software algorithms and analytics technologies to the data that Mr. Nowicki and his team were able to use it to develop new insights about fan behaviours. Nowicki noted that "we had years and years of data that we had uploaded into that system but we hadn't really mined any of it to really look at our customers. So what we've done now is we've begun to create a profile of our ticket plan holders using demographic criteria that is available to us and really create a picture about what our plan holders look like." Today the Hurricanes can look at individual fans and determine certain elements of their demographics. For example, if a particular fan lives within 50 kilometres of the PNC arena, has a certain level of discretionary income, and attends five games per season, the team can tailor its offerings to that individual. According to Nowicki, "we can put you up against that profile and see where your best fit would be and it allows our sales guys to sell more efficiently and score those leads so that we're not spinning our wheels and cold calling. We're really going after certain people for certain products."[2]

Getting Fans to the Game: The NBA

The Orlando Magic is among the top revenue earners in the NBA, despite being in the 20th-largest market. The Magic accomplishes this feat by studying the resale ticket market to price tickets better, to predict season ticket holders at risk of defection (and lure them back), and to analyze concession and product merchandise sales to make sure the organization has what the fans want every time they enter the arena. The club has even used analytics to help coaches put together the best line up. "Our biggest challenge is to customize the fan experience, and analytics helps us manage all that in a very robust way. The Magic uses analytics to help manage the basketball team by analyzing the efficiency of certain lineups. The 'Moneyball' approach, if you will," says CEO Alex Martins.[3]

Getting the Right Players on the Field

Pro teams aren't just using these software tools to figure out what to charge for a lower bowl seat or when to offer a special promotion; indeed, teams are following Beane and turning to analytics to help scout potential draftees, figure out what to pay for a potential free agent, and predict how a given player might perform in specific situations.

Analytics is coming to the NFL. In 2013, the NFL's Buffalo Bills announced the team would be creating an analytics department following earlier moves by the Baltimore Ravens and Jacksonville Jaguars to do the same. In 2012, the San Francisco 49ers utilized an application developed by SAP to help their college scouts prepare for the annual entry draft.

According to Rishi Diwan, vice-president and head of product management for sports at SAP, the technology developed for the NFL and the 49ers allows college scouts to input information on a potential draftee while the scout is watching a game or practice. This information then becomes instantly available to the team's front office. The application takes certain measurable data points collected about each player. Data points include things such as their 40-yard dash time, their stats from the previous season, or the size of their hands. The system then compares those metrics with starters currently playing in the NFL. According to Diwan "each position has certain metrics that you're looking at. Today, if you did a search, you'd get a list of players and a table of numbers, and [teams] have to process all these numbers, retain them in their head and remember how this stacks up to other players. There was no easy way to compare that." Diwan believes the next step will be to create algorithms that will determine whether a player's score on a particular metric or scores on a combination of metrics, such as running 4.28 in the 40-yard dash, is predictive of pro football success.[4]

New Challenges

Still, there are challenges to the adoption of this kind of new technology inside organizations. According to Diwan, "when you're looking at technology and its application in sports, you're talking about a cultural shift more than the ability to process that much data. You can create all kinds of analytics, but if people don't understand them, they'll never use them. In sports, you're dealing with a lot of intuition and a lot of experiences, so there's many things you have to think about to get the technology accepted."

This is part of the reason for events like the MIT Sports Analytics Conference. Sports analytics have primarily been focused on players and determining factors such as which ones to seek in the draft, or put in the game, or which ones might be overpaid. Most statistics measure individual player performance but ultimately it's all about how the team performs, not the individuals on the team. It is hoped by getting together at conferences like the one at MIT, progress will be made toward identifying and refining the next steps of applying these measures to team performance given particular lineups.

Despite the success of Billy Beane's Oakland A's acceptance among coaches, managers, and team owners to make player decisions based on data and analysis is progressing much more slowly than the technology. Most teams are not taking full advantage of the data they have, and the fact that contact between the analysts working on team and player performance and those working on business analytics is not nurtured limits the results that teams see. It might be better to combine these groups of analysts and prioritize the problems they work on. This may also lead to improvements in the critical area of communications. Coaches and general managers say that analytics are useless in sports unless the analysts are good at explaining their analyses and results in clear, sports-related terms. At conferences like the MIT Sloan Sports Analytics Conference coaches and general managers often argue that if you don't know baseball [or basketball or football or soccer] you're not going to be able to relate your analytics to those who make decisions.[5]

3.1 DATA, INFORMATION, KNOWLEDGE, AND INTELLIGENCE

INTRODUCTION

Data and information are powerful. They are useful in telling an organization how its current operations are performing, as well as estimating and strategizing how future operations might perform. New perspectives open up when people have the right data and information on hand and know how to use them. The ability to understand, digest, analyze, and filter data and information is key to success for any professional in any industry.

However, it is important to distinguish between data and information. **Data** are raw facts that describe the characteristics of an event. Characteristics for a sales event can include a date, item number, item description, quantity ordered, customer name, or shipping details. **Information** is data converted into a meaningful and useful context. Information from sales events could include the best-selling item, the worst-selling item, the best customer, or the worst customer.

LO1 ORGANIZATIONAL DATA AND INFORMATION

Ford's European plant manufactures more than 5,000 vehicles a day and sells them in over 100 countries worldwide. Every component of every model must conform to complex European standards, including passenger safety standards and pedestrian and environmental protection standards. These standards govern each stage of Ford's manufacturing process from design to final production. The company needs to obtain many thousands of different approvals each year to comply with the standards. Overlooking just one means the company cannot sell the finished vehicle, which brings the production line to a standstill and could potentially cost Ford up to one million euros per day. Ford built the Homologation Timing System (HTS), based on a relational database, to help it track and analyze these standards. The reliability and high performance of the HTS have helped Ford substantially reduce its compliance risk.[6]

Data and information are everywhere in an organization. When addressing a significant business issue, employees must be able to obtain and analyze all the relevant data and information available, so they can make the best decisions possible. Organizational data and information come at different levels, formats, and "granularities." **Granularity** refers to the extent of detail within the data and information (fine and detailed versus coarse and abstract). On one end of the spectrum is coarse granularity, or highly summarized data or information. At the other end is fine granularity, or data or information that contains a great amount of detail. If employees are using a supply chain management system to make decisions, they might find that their suppliers are sending data and information in different formats and granularities, and at different levels. One supplier might send detailed data in a spreadsheet, another supplier might send summary information in a Word document, and yet another might send aggregate information from data stored in a database. Employees must be able to correlate the different levels, formats, and granularities of data and information when making decisions.

Successfully collecting, compiling, sorting, and finally analyzing data and information from multiple levels, in varied formats, exhibiting different granularities can provide tremendous insight into how an organization is performing. Taking a hard look at organizational data and information can yield exciting and unexpected results such as potential new markets, new ways of reaching customers, and even new ways of doing business. Figure 3.1 displays the different types of data and information found in organizations.

Samsung Electronics took a detailed look at over 10,000 reports from its resellers to identify "lost deals," or orders lost to competitors. The analysis yielded the enlightening result that 80 percent of lost sales occurred in a single business unit, the health care industry. Furthermore, Samsung was able to identify that 40 percent of its lost sales in that industry were going to a certain competitor. Before performing the analysis, Samsung was heading into its market blind. Armed with new information, Samsung changed its selling strategy in the health care industry by implementing a strategy to work more closely with hardware vendors to win back lost sales.[7]

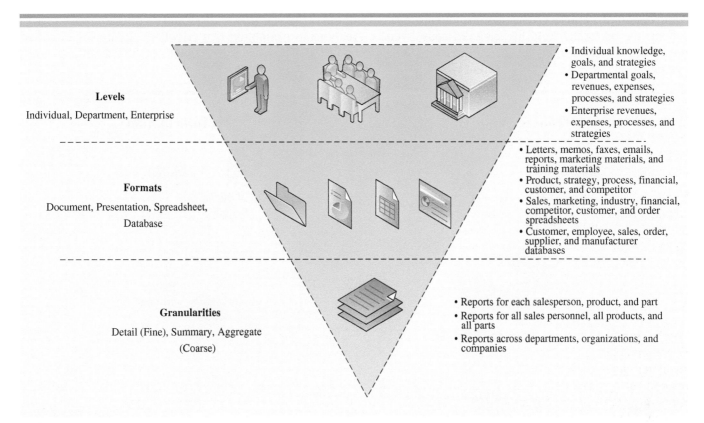

Levels

Individual, Department, Enterprise

Formats

Document, Presentation, Spreadsheet,
Database

Granularities

Detail (Fine), Summary, Aggregate
(Coarse)

- Individual knowledge, goals, and strategies
- Departmental goals, revenues, expenses, processes, and strategies
- Enterprise revenues, expenses, processes, and strategies
- Letters, memos, faxes, emails, reports, marketing materials, and training materials
- Product, strategy, process, financial, customer, and competitor
- Sales, marketing, industry, financial, competitor, customer, and order spreadsheets
- Customer, employee, sales, order, supplier, and manufacturer databases
- Reports for each salesperson, product, and part
- Reports for all sales personnel, all products, and all parts
- Reports across departments, organizations, and companies

FIGURE 3.1

Levels, Formats, and Granularities of Organizational Data and Information

Not all companies are successful at managing data and information, but they can be. For example, outfitting customers since 1856, Orvis is the oldest American mail-order company. The company was experiencing issues with understanding their customers due to natural growth in both marketing channels and product lines. Orvis features an extensive lineup of products, from the traditional fishing gear they are known for to home furnishings, dog products, and adventure travel packages. Their channels had expanded, with millions of customers receiving their catalogues every year, the addition of customers purchasing products on the Web, and others who shop in Orvis's 93 retail and outlet stores in the United States and United Kingdom. With their multi-channel approach to sales, Orvis needed to get an overview of their customers.

The problem, however, was that Orvis was relying on a complex web of tools that few in the organization understood. They needed to replace a series of fragmented legacy systems with something that extended across all their channels. The change involved first building new marketing databases that mapped the available data so that new analytic tools could be used to support the evolved Orvis' customer base.[8]

In addition to understanding how data and information can differ in level, format, and granularity, it is important to understand three additional characteristics that help determine the value of data and information: type (transactional and analytical), timeliness, and quality.

The Value of Transactional Data and Analytical Information

As discussed previously, there is a difference between transactional data and analytical information. *Transactional data* encompasses all of the data contained within a single business process or unit of work, and its primary purpose is to support performing daily operational tasks. Organizations capture and store transactional data in databases, and they use it when performing operational tasks and repetitive decisions, such as analyzing daily sales figures and production schedules to determine how much inventory to carry.

Analytical information, on the other hand, encompasses all organizational information, and its primary purpose is to support the performance of higher-level analysis tasks. Analytical information is used when making important ad hoc decisions such as whether the organization should build a new manufacturing plant or hire additional sales personnel. Figure 3.2 displays different types of transactional and analytical information.

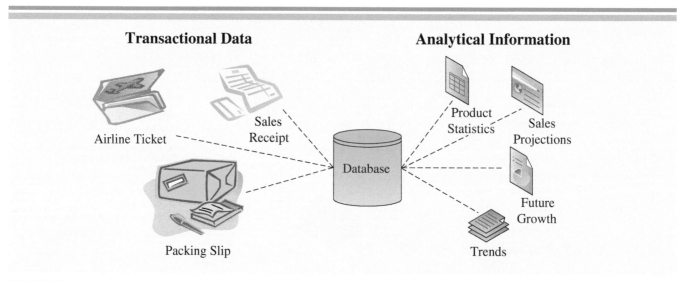

FIGURE 3.2

Transactional Data Versus Analytical Information

The Value of Timely Data and Information

The need for timely data and information can change for each business decision. Some decisions require weekly or monthly data and information, while others require daily data or information. Timeliness is an aspect of data and information that depends on the situation. In some industries, data or information that is a few days or weeks old can be relevant, while in other industries data or information that is a few minutes old can be almost worthless. Some organizations, such as 911 centres, stock traders, and banks, require consolidated, up-to-the-second data and information, 24 hours a day, seven days a week. Other organizations, such as insurance and construction companies, require only daily or even weekly data and information.

Real-time data are immediate, up-to-date data. *Real-time information* is immediate, up-to-date information. A *real-time system* provides real-time transactional data and/or real-time analytical information in response to query requests. Many organizations use real-time systems to exploit key corporate transactional data. For example, a survey of 1,500 chief information officers led by Gartner Group found that systems that mine, benchmark, and measure real-time performance data continue to be among the top spending priorities for these CIOs.[9]

The growing demand for real-time data and information stems from organizations' need to make faster and more effective decisions, keep smaller inventories, operate more efficiently, and track performance more carefully. But timeliness is relative. Organizations need fresh, timely data and information to make good decisions. Data and information also need to be timely so that they meet employees' needs—but no more. If employees can absorb data or information only on an hourly or daily basis, there is no need to gather real-time data or information in smaller increments. The payments industry is experiencing a change in business needs in terms of real-time payment processing. Traditionally, banks collect payments from customers and then process the payments using batch processing. The new realities of the global economy raised concerns around improving the risk management of payments, especially where liquidity, fraud, and money laundering are concerned. As a result, central banks like the Bank of Australia are changing regulations, requiring banks to adapt to real-time payment processing so that banks are aware of what is happening in their payment divisions in real time, not 24 hours later. This has also been aided by the pressure from new forms of competition in the payment industry and the demands from bank shareholders to reduce costs. The high cost of maintaining outdated mainframes that perform the batch processing is one area that has been targeted for cost reductions.[10]

Most people request real-time data and information without understanding one of the biggest pitfalls associated with real-time data and information—continual change. Imagine the following scenario. Three managers meet at the end of the day to discuss a business problem. Each manager has gathered data and information at different times during the day to create a picture of the situation. Each manager's picture may be different because of this time discrepancy. Their views on the business problem may not match since the data and information they are basing their analysis on are continually changing. This approach may not speed up decision making, and may actually slow it down.

The timeliness of the data and information required must be evaluated for each business decision. Organizations do not want to find themselves using real-time data and information to make a bad decision faster.

The Value of Quality Data and Information

When we think of the value of quality data and information, we often think of how we collect data and information that is of high quality; and that is discussed later on in this section. We must also consider how we deliver this data so that its value can be realized. Take Swisscom Event Solution, a provider of temporary integrated communication networks at meetings, conventions, and special events. The event teams at Swisscom have to set up complex networks in short periods of time. Their project managers were seeing many information-based challenges in the process that resulted in team members not being able to get to the quality data and information in their systems. These challenges included:

■ Tasks and timelines were difficult to track.

■ Looking for information was time-consuming.

■ Reporting of SOX data visibility in the data was taking too long.

■ Sharing information was challenging, especially with non-employees.

The challenge was not only to identify and collect the high-quality data required, but to get that data to the right person at the right time, so that Swisscom could benefit from the value of the information.[11]

Business decisions are only as good as the quality of the data and information used to make the decisions. Figure 3.3 reviews five characteristics common to high-quality data and information: accuracy, completeness, consistency, uniqueness, and timeliness. Figure 3.4 displays these issues in a sample data set.

Accuracy	Are all the values correct? For example, is the name spelled correctly? Is the dollar amount recorded properly?
Completeness	Are any of the values missing? For example, is the address complete including street, city, province, and postal code?
Consistency	Does aggregate or summary information agree with detailed information? For example, do all total fields equal the true total of the individual fields?
Uniqueness	Is each transaction, entity, and event represented only once in the information? For example, are there any duplicate customers?
Timeliness	Is the information current with respect to the business requirements? For example, is information updated weekly, daily, or hourly?

FIGURE 3.3

Characteristics of High-Quality Data and Information

Figure 3.4 highlights several issues with low-quality data that might occur in a particular example, including:

1. The first issue is *missing* data; the customer's first name is missing. (See item 1 in Figure 3.4.)

2. The second issue is *incomplete* data; the street address contains only a number and not a street name.

3. The third issue is definitely an example of *inaccurate* data; a phone number is located in the email address field.

4. The fourth issue is probably *duplicate* data; the only slight difference between the two customers is the spelling of the last name. Similar street addresses and phone numbers make this likely.

5. The fifth issue is potentially *wrong* data; the customer's phone and fax numbers are the same. Some customers might have the same number for phone and fax line, but the fact that the customer also has this number in the email address field is suspicious.

6. The sixth issue is, again, *incomplete* data; there is not a valid area code for the phone and fax numbers.

1. *Missing* data (no first name)   2. *Incomplete* data (no street)   3. *Inaccurate* data (invalid email)

ID	Last Name	First Name	Street	City	Province	Postal Code	Phone	Fax	Email
113	Smith		116 Lakewood Pl SE	Calgary	AB	T2J 4T7	(403) 777-1258	(403) 777-5544	ssmith@yahoo.ca
114	Jones	Jeff	ZZA	Calgary	AB	T2M 3X5	(403) 666-6868	(403) 666-6868	(403) 666-6868
115	Roberts	Jenny	507 Cantrell Dr SW	Calgary	AB	T2W 2K9	527-1122	759-5654	jr@msn.ca
116	Robert	Jenny	507 Cantrell Dr SW	Calgary	AB	T2W 2K9	527-1122	759-5654	jr@msn.ca

4. Probable *duplicate* data (similar names, same address, phone number)   5. Potential *wrong* data (are the phone and fax numbers the same or is this an error?)   6. *Incomplete* data (missing area codes)

FIGURE 3.4

Examples of Low-Quality Data

Recognizing how quality issues occur allows organizations to begin to correct them. Some of the sources of low-quality data and information, or dirty data, are:

1. Customers, especially when online, intentionally entering inaccurate data or information to protect their privacy

2. Data or information from different systems having different data or information entry standards and formats

3. Employees entering abbreviated or erroneous data or information by accident or to save time

4. Third-party and external data or information that contains inconsistencies, inaccuracies, and errors

Addressing the sources of data and information inaccuracies will significantly improve the quality of organizational data and information and the value extracted from the data and information.

Understanding the Costs of Poor Data and Information   Using the wrong data or information can lead to making the wrong decision. Making the wrong decision can cost time, money, and even reputations. Every business decision is only as good as the data or information used to make the decision. Bad data or information can cause serious business ramifications such as:

- Inability to accurately track customers, which directly affects strategic initiatives such as customer relationship management (CRM) and supply chain management (SCM)
- Difficulty identifying the organization's most valuable customers
- Inability to identify selling opportunities and wasted revenue from marketing to non-existent customers and non-deliverable mail
- Difficulty tracking revenue because of inaccurate invoices
- Inability to build strong relationships with customers, which increases their buyer power

Understanding the Benefits of Good Data and Information   Lillian Vernon is a leading catalogue and online retailer that sells gifts, household goods, children's goods, and fashion accessory items. It has been doing so for over 50 years and its success has been due to customer care and the goal of creating the best customer interaction possible. The problem was that customer interaction was suffering from their customer care agents' lack of access to good data. This in turn led to inefficient interaction, which meant long wait times for customers and overall poor customer service, along with dissatisfied customer care agents and a high agent turnover rate. The solution was to put a complete view of the customer at agents' fingertips so they could more efficiently help customers with their orders. The result was a minimum 17 percent reduction in average customer handling times, a 50 percent reduction in customer agent training times, and a reduction in customer agent turnover.[12]

EMCO Corporation—founded in London, Ontario in 1906 as the Empire Brass Manufacturing Company Limited—is one of Canada's largest integrated distributors of products for the construction industry. The company uses visualization software developed by Vancouver-based Antarctica Systems to display all the company's data at a glance. The software allows top management to view company-critical data, such as inventory levels and profit margins, on an interactive map instead of a spreadsheet. Further, once a trouble spot is identified, management can click and zoom to drill down to lower-level data to investigate and understand the underlying data better. Such software tools allow companies like EMCO to quickly make sense of the transactional data they collect, identify problem areas, and make better-informed decisions about how to address trouble spots.[13]

There are numerous examples of companies that use their high-quality data and information to make solid strategic business decisions. Quality data and information do not automatically guarantee that every decision made is going to be a good one, since it is people who ultimately make the decisions. But high-quality data and information ensure that the basis of the decisions is accurate. The success of the organization depends on appreciating and leveraging the true value of timely and quality data and information.

Data Governance

Data is a vital resource and users need to be educated on what they can and cannot do with it. To ensure a firm manages its information correctly, it will need special policies and procedures establishing rules on how the data is organized, updated, maintained, and accessed. Every firm, large and small, should create an information policy concerning data governance. *Data governance* refers to the overall management of the availability, usability, integrity, and security of company data. A company that supports a data governance program has a defined a policy that specifies who is accountable for various portions or aspects of the data, including its accuracy, accessibility, consistency, timeliness, and completeness. The policy should clearly define the processes concerning how to store, archive, back up, and secure the data. In addition, the company should create a set of procedures identifying accessibility levels for employees. Then, the firm should deploy controls and procedures that enforce government regulations and compliance with mandates such as *Sarbanes-Oxley.*

LO2 ⌐ KNOWLEDGE

In the previous section the difference between data and information was described. Data were described as "raw facts" that portray the characteristics of an event, such as a date, item number, or quantity ordered. Information was described as data converted into a meaningful and useful context. In this sense, information can be thought of as "meaningful data," such as the identification of the best-selling item or worst-selling item from sales data collected by a company. ***Knowledge*** on the other hand is described as "actionable information." Simply put, information becomes knowledge when it can be acted upon.

Consider carpenters. They are knowledgeable individuals who know a lot about woodworking—they can pull together all the information they have gathered over the years about woodworking and put that information into action by actually knowing how to build something. However, if we wrote down all the information about woodworking in a book and gave it to a non–woodworking expert, that person would not necessarily be any more knowledgeable about woodworking and able to build something. He or she would definitely be more informed, but would not be considered knowledgeable unless he or she was able to understand the information in the book and put that information into action.

The point of this example is to showcase that having information about a topic does not make a person knowledgeable. Rather, to be considered knowledgeable, a person needs to understand that information, be able to make inferences between various tidbits of information presented and, most important, be able to apply that information into action.

In this light, information can be viewed as the building block or stimulus for knowledge. Knowledge is created when information is understood, when disparate facts are connected, and when insights are gleaned. Information is truly the foundation for generating new knowledge.

It is important to understand the distinction between information and knowledge because it raises important questions for organizations as they try to capitalize on the information they collect. For example, where does knowledge reside? Is it stored in databases and data warehouses? Inside textual documents, reports, and email messages? Or is it stored in the heads of organization's workers?

There are two trains of thought about the answer. A computer scientist would argue that knowledge is contained within formalized data structures, and that technologies exist today, such as artificial intelligence and intelligent agents, that are capable of understanding the meaning of the information stored in those formalized data structures and taking actions based on this understanding. A humanist or information scholar would argue the opposite, saying that knowledge resides in human beings and that, though information systems can store and process data and information quite well, it is up to users to interpret and make sense of the information these systems provide.

Both viewpoints are valid, and it will be interesting to see how this plays out as more advances in computing are made over the decades. However, information systems today are limited in their capacity to turn information into knowledge, and most organizations realize this. In response, organizations grapple with ways to extract information out of their massive data and information repositories, document collections, customer communications, and consultant reports and turn that information into knowledge.

What most organizations have found is that helping employees access, share, and use information is perhaps the best way to convert information into knowledge. Organizations are realizing that having information sit in a database, document, or email archive does little for knowledge creation. They are beginning to understand that to be knowledgeable and act knowingly they must find ways to help their employees get at information as quickly and efficiently as possible, easily share that information with others, and use that information in their work.

Types of Knowledge

Not all information is valuable. Individual companies must determine what information qualifies as intellectual and knowledge-based assets. In general, intellectual and knowledge-based assets fall into one of two categories: explicit or tacit. As a rule, *explicit knowledge* consists of anything that can be documented, archived, and codified, often with the help of information systems. Examples of explicit knowledge are assets such as patents, trademarks, business plans, marketing research, and customer lists.

Tacit knowledge is the knowledge contained in people's heads. The challenge inherent in tacit knowledge is figuring out how to recognize, generate, share, and manage knowledge that resides in people's heads. While information technology in the form of email, instant messaging, and related technologies can facilitate disseminating tacit knowledge, identifying it in the first place can be a major obstacle.

Knowledge Management

Knowledge management (KM) involves capturing, classifying, evaluating, retrieving, and sharing information assets in a way that provides context for effective decisions and actions. KM is the systematic, effective management and use of an organization's information resources that contain or embody knowledge. These sources include people (human experts), paper documents, electronic documents, presentations, and spreadsheets, and data warehouse solutions.

It is best to think of KM in the broadest context. KM is the process through which organizations generate value from their intellectual and knowledge-based assets. Most often, generating value from such assets involves codifying what employees, partners, and customers know, and sharing that know-how among employees, departments, and even with other companies to devise best practices. However, codification is not always the goal of KM—often organizational knowledge resides within human experts and it is best to cultivate and use that expertise in that form rather than trying to explicitly document or codify that know-how in some formal manner.

It is important to note that the above description of KM is not all about information systems. While KM is often facilitated by IS, information systems by themselves are not KM. Knowledge management is about how companies cultivate and promote practices (behaviours), and use information systems that help capture, store, organize, and make the best use of information within and across the enterprise to increase and leverage organizational knowledge and know-how.

Think of a golf caddie as a simplified example of a knowledge worker. Good caddies do more than carry clubs and track down wayward balls. When asked, a good caddie will give advice to golfers, such as, "The wind makes the ninth hole play 15 yards longer." Accurate advice may lead to a bigger tip at the end of the day. The golfer, having derived a benefit from the caddie's advice, may be more likely to play that course again. If a good caddie is willing to share what he knows with other caddies, then they all may eventually earn bigger tips. How would KM work to make this happen? The caddie master may decide to reward caddies for sharing their knowledge by offering them credits for pro-shop merchandise. Once the best advice is collected, the course manager would publish the information in notebooks (or make it available on mobile devices, like a Blackberry via an app) and distribute them to all the caddies. The result of a well-designed KM program is that everyone wins. In this case, caddies get bigger tips and deals on merchandise, golfers play better because they benefit from the collective experience of caddies, and the course owners win because better scores lead to repeat business.

Knowledge Management in Business

KM has assumed greater urgency in Canadian business over the past few years as millions of baby boomers prepare to retire. When they punch out for the last time, the knowledge they gleaned about their jobs, companies, and industries during their long careers will walk out with them—unless companies take measures to retain their insights. In addition, CIOs who have entered into outsourcing agreements must address the thorny issue of transferring the knowledge of their full-time staff members, who are losing their jobs because of an outsourcing deal, to the outsourcer's employees.

Knowledge can be a competitive advantage for an organization. Information technology can distribute an organization's knowledge base by connecting people and digitally gathering their expertise. The primary objective of KM is to be sure that a company's knowledge of facts, sources of information, and solutions are readily available to all employees whenever it is needed.

Such KM requires that organizations go well beyond providing information contained in spreadsheets, databases, and documents. It must include expert information that typically resides in people's heads. A *knowledge management system (KMS)* supports capturing, organizing, and disseminating knowledge (i.e., know-how) throughout an organization. It is up to the organization to determine what information qualifies as knowledge.

Shadowing and joint problem solving are two best practices for transferring or recreating tacit knowledge inside an organization. In many companies, KM is performed through *mentoring*. Shadowing and joint problem solving also allow companies to enact mentoring within their organizations.

Shadowing   With *shadowing*, less experienced staff observe more experienced staff to learn how their more experienced counterparts approach their work. Dorothy Leonard and Walter Swap, two KM experts, stress the importance of having the protégé discuss his or her observations with the expert to deepen the dialogue and crystallize the knowledge transfer.

Joint Problem Solving   Another sound approach is *joint problem solving* by expert and novice. Because people are often unaware of how they approach problems or do their work and therefore cannot automatically generate step-by-step instructions for doing whatever they do, having a novice and expert work together on a project will bring the expert's approach to light. The difference between shadowing and joint problem solving is that shadowing is more passive. With joint problem solving, the expert and the novice work hand in hand on a task.

Information is of little use unless it is analyzed and made available to the right people, at the right place, and at the right time. To get the most value from intellectual assets, knowledge must be shared. An effective KMS system should help do one or more of the following:

■ Foster innovation by encouraging the free flow of ideas

■ Improve customer service by streamlining response time

■ Boost revenues by getting products and services to market faster

■ Enhance employee retention rates by recognizing the value of employees' knowledge

■ Streamline operations and reduce costs by eliminating redundant or unnecessary processes

A creative approach to KM can result in improved efficiency, higher productivity, and increased revenues in practically any business function.

Software is helping ChevronTexaco improve how it manages the assets in oil fields by enabling employees in multiple disciplines to easily access and share the information they need to make decisions. ChevronTexaco teams of 10 to 30 people are responsible for managing the assets, such as the drilling equipment, pipelines, and facilities, for a particular oil field. Within each team, earth scientists and various engineers with expertise in production, reservoir, and facilities work together to keep the oil field up and running. Each member of the asset team needs to communicate with other members to make decisions based on the collection and analysis of huge amounts of information from various departments. Individual team members can look at information from the perspective of their own department.

This has helped ChevronTexaco achieve a 30 percent productivity gain, a 50 percent improvement in safety performance, and more than $2.0 billion in operating cost reductions. Through KMSs, ChevronTexaco has restructured its gasoline retailing business and now drills oil and gas wells faster and cheaper.[14]

Not every organization matches ChevronTexaco's success with KM. Numerous KM projects have failed, generating an unwillingness to undertake—or even address—KM issues among many organizations. However, KM is an effective tool if it is tied directly to discrete business needs and opportunities. Beginning with targeted projects that deliver value quickly, companies can achieve the success that has proved elusive with many big-bang approaches. Successful KM projects typically focus on creating value in a specific process area, or even just for a certain type of transaction. Companies should start with one job at a time—preferably the most knowledge-oriented one—and build KM into a job function in a way that actually helps employees do their work better and faster, then expand to the next most knowledge-intensive job, and so on. Celebrating even small success with KM will help build a base of credibility and support for future KM projects.

KM Technologies

KM is not a purely technology-based concept. Organizations that implement a centralized database system, electronic message board, Web portal, or any other collaborative tool in the hope that they have established a KMS are wasting both time and money.

Although tools don't make a KMS, such a system does need tools, from standard, off-the-shelf email packages to sophisticated collaboration tools designed specifically to support community building and identity. Generally, KMS tools fall into one or more of the following categories:

■ Knowledge repositories (databases)

■ Expertise tools often involving some form of artificial intelligence

■ E-learning applications

■ Discussion and chat technologies

■ Search and data mining tools

In some instances new tools are being developed and implemented that blur the boundaries between the categories, such as Open Text Connectivity. Companies such as Fairchild Semiconductor have benefited from this system, which allows its engineers to control their circuit integration simulations. They can stop the simulation at any time, make corrections, and restart the simulation instead of waiting for a simulation to finish (which might take days) before they can make corrections. It also allows Fairchild to operate remote design centres.[15]

Knowledge Management Outside the Organization

Companies also look to collect knowledge from outside the organization. The most common form of collective intelligence found outside the organization is **crowdsourcing**, which refers to the wisdom of the crowd. The idea that collective intelligence is greater than the sum of its individual parts has been around for a long time (see Figure 3.5). With Web 2.0 tools, the ability to efficiently tap into its power is emerging. For many years organizations believed that good ideas came from the top. CEOs collaborated only with heads of sales and marketing, the quality assurance expert, or the road warrior salesperson. The organization chart governed who should work with whom and how far up the chain of command a suggestion or idea would travel. Today this belief is being challenged, as firms capitalize on crowdsourcing by opening up a task or problem to a wider group to find better or cheaper results from outside the box.

FIGURE 3.5

Crowdsourcing: The Crowd Is Smarter Than the Individual

Today, people can be continuously connected, a driving force behind collaboration. Traditional business communications were limited to face-to-face conversations and one-way technologies that used **asynchronous communications**, or communications that occur at different times, such as discussion boards. Ask a group of postsecondary students when they last spoke to their parents. For many the answer is less than an hour ago, as opposed to the traditional response of a few days ago. In business, too, continuous connections are now expected in today's collaborative world.

KM and Social Networking   Companies that have been frustrated by traditional KM efforts are increasingly looking for ways to find out how knowledge flows through their organization, and social networking analysis can show them just that. **Social networking analysis (SNA)** is a process of mapping a group's contacts (whether personal or professional) to identify who knows whom and who works with whom. In enterprises, it provides a clear picture of how far-flung employees and divisions work together and can help identify key experts in the organization who possess the knowledge needed to, say, solve a complicated programming problem or launch a new product.

Mars, manufacturer of M&Ms, used SNA to identify how knowledge flows through its organizations, who holds influence, who gives the best advice, and how employees share information. The Canadian government's central IT unit used SNA to establish which skills it needed to retain and develop, and to determine who, among the 40 percent of the workforce that was due to retire within five years, had the most important knowledge and experience to begin transferring to others.[16]

SNA is not a replacement for traditional KM tools such as knowledge databases or portals, but it can provide companies with a starting point for how best to proceed with KM initiatives. As a component to a larger KM strategy, SNA can help companies identify key leaders and then set up a mechanism, such as communities of practice, so that those leaders can pass on their knowledge to colleagues. To identify experts in their organizations, companies can use software programs that track email and other kinds of electronic communication.[17]

LO3) BUSINESS INTELLIGENCE AND BIG DATA

Business intelligence refers to applications, techniques, and technologies that are used to gather, provide access to, and analyze information to support people's decision-making efforts. For example, in Chapter 7, business intelligence was described as an extended component of ERP systems where transactional data are collected, organized, and summarized into analytical information, and where analytical tools are used to mine and understand this information to assist managers and analysts in their decision-making efforts. An early reference to business intelligence occurs in Sun Tzu's book titled *The Art of War*. Sun Tzu claims that to succeed in war, one should have full knowledge of one's own strengths and weaknesses and full knowledge of the enemy's strengths and weaknesses. Lack of either one might result in defeat. A certain school of thought draws parallels between the challenges in business and those of war, specifically:

- Collecting information
- Discerning patterns and meaning in the information
- Responding to the resultant information[18]

Many organizations today find it next to impossible to understand their own strengths and weaknesses—let alone their enemies'—because of the enormous volume of organizational data and information that is still inaccessible to all but the IS department. For example, organizational data and information include far more than simple fields in a database; they also include voice mail, customer phone calls, text messages, and video clips, along with numerous other new forms of data and information.

Business intelligence (BI) or ***big data*** is information collected from multiple sources such as suppliers, customers, competitors, partners, and industries that analyzes patterns, trends, and relationships for strategic decision making. ***Business analytics (BA)***, on the other hand, is the practice of using iterative, methodical techniques to explore an organization's data, with emphasis on predictive, applied, and statistical analysis. Big data, business intelligence, and business analytics are becoming big business in Canada. Some believe that in the next five years there will be a significant number of new Data Analytic positions created annually in Canada. The term "big data," which has become very popular in the past year or so, encompasses a number of other areas such as data warehousing, business analytics, business intelligence, and decision making. Figure 3.6 represents the combined thoughts of some big data providers in Calgary, Alberta, such as IBM and Quattro Integration Group (purchased by Deloitte in 2013), on what "big data" looks like in practice today and where a number of the terms that are batted around fit into the big picture.[19]

Business intelligence tools allow for data to be changed into information and knowledge through the use of data mining techniques and advancements in algorithms. Companies such as SAP, Microsoft, and Oracle continue to add analytics to their ERP systems to compete with companies like SAS and take more complete advantage of the data collected in their ERP systems.

The Importance of Decision-Making Speed and Big Data

The trend toward speed in decision making is not going away. In August 2013, Cisco announced 4,000 job cuts in middle management, decreasing the size of its teams, it said, in order to speed up decision making and execution. Earlier, Cisco had announced the formation of "councils" to oversee parts of the company's business, but this decision had been reversed because it negatively impacted the speed of decision making.[20]

Target has been analyzing its data for many years in an attempt to capture more customers. In recent years the company has been using its data to target women in their second trimester of pregnancy so that it can acquire them and their families as regular customers after the birth. It sends expectant mothers special pregnancy-related ads early to get them into the stores. Then, when the child arrives and the mothers' regular buying habits are in flux due to their exhausted and overwhelmed state, Target takes advantage of the opportunity to get them to start buying things other than the targeted specials; they are already in the store and the goods are convenient.[21]

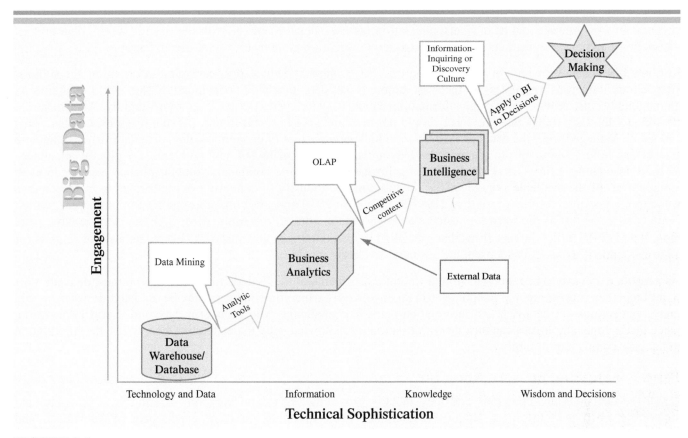

FIGURE 3.6

Big Data: A Visual Description

SUPPORTING DECISIONS WITH BUSINESS INTELLIGENCE

Many organizations today find it next to impossible to understand their own strengths and weaknesses, let alone their biggest competitors, because the enormous volume of organizational data is inaccessible to all but the MIS department. Organization data include far more than simple structured data elements in a database; they also include unstructured data such as voice mail, customer phone calls, text messages, video clips, and numerous new forms such as tweets from Twitter.

The Problem: Data-Rich, Information-Poor

An ideal business scenario would be as follows. A business manager, on his way to meet with a client, reviews historical customer data and realizes that the client's ordering volume has substantially decreased. Drilling down into the data, he notices the client has had a support issue with a particular product. He quickly calls the support team and learns that a replacement for the defective part can be shipped in 24 hours, and that the client has visited the website and requested information on a new product line. Armed with all this information, the business manager is now prepared for a productive meeting. He understands the client's needs and issues, and can address new sales opportunities with confidence.

For many companies the above example is simply a pipe dream. All of that client information would actually take hours or even days to compile. With so much data available, it is surprisingly hard for managers to get information such as inventory levels, order history, or shipping details. Managers send their information requests to the MIS department where a dedicated person puts together the various reports. In some situations, responses can take days, by which time the information may be outdated and opportunities lost. Many organizations find themselves in the position of being data-rich and information-poor. Even in today's electronic world, managers struggle with the challenge of turning their business data into business intelligence.

As businesses increase their reliance on enterprise systems such as CRM and ERP, they are rapidly accumulating vast amounts of transactional data. Every interaction between departments or with the outside world, data on past transactions, and external market data are entered into information systems for future use and access.

Just how fast is data growing? In a special report in *The Economist* dedicated to managing information, the authors, after citing numerous examples of the vast amounts of data available, concluded: "The world contains an unimaginably vast amount of digital information which is getting ever vaster ever more rapidly. This makes it possible to do many things that previously could not be done: spot business trends, prevent diseases, combat crime and so on. Managed well, the data can be used to unlock new sources of economic value, provide fresh insights into science and hold governments to account. But they are also creating a host of new problems. Despite the abundance of tools to capture, process and share all this information—sensors, computers, mobile phones and the like—it already exceeds the available storage space." In addition, the industry of delivering rich information from rich data was already estimated to be more than US$100 billion in 2010 and growing at about 10 percent a year, which is about twice as fast as the software business as a whole. No wonder Microsoft, IBM, SAP, and Oracle have spent more than US$15 billion buying firms that specialize in managing data and analytics.[22] Data are a strategic asset for a business, and if the asset is not used, the business is wasting resources.

As a result, data have to be requested from different departments or the IS department itself, who must dedicate staff to pull together various reports. Responses can take weeks, by which time the data may be outdated. It has been said that organizations are data-rich and information-poor. The challenge is to transform data into useful information. Once that's done, employees can turn that information into knowledge by understanding how to use the information to increase company profitability.

Business Intelligence as a Solution

Employee decisions are numerous and they include providing service information, offering new products, and supporting frustrated customers. Employees can base their decisions on data, experience, or knowledge and preferably a combination of all three. Business intelligence can provide managers with the ability to make better decisions. A few examples of how different industries use business intelligence are:

- *Airlines.* Analyze popular vacation locations with current flight listings
- *Banking.* Understand customer credit card usage and non payment rates
- *Health care.* Compare the demographics of patients with critical illnesses
- *Insurance.* Predict claim amounts and medical coverage costs
- *Law enforcement.* Track crime patterns, locations, and criminal behaviour
- *Marketing.* Analyze customer demographics
- *Retail.* Predict sales, inventory levels, and distribution
- *Technology.* Predict hardware failures

Figure 3.7 displays how organizations using BI can find the cause too many issues and problems simply by asking "Why?" The process starts by analyzing a report such as sales amounts by quarter. Managers will drill down into the report looking for why sales are up or why sales are down. Once they understand why a certain location or product is experiencing an increase in sales, they can share the information in an effort to raise enterprise-wide sales. Once they understand the cause for a decrease in sales, they can take effective action to resolve the issue. Here are a few examples of how managers can use BI to answer tough business questions:

- *Where has the business been?* Historical perspective offers important variables for determining trends and patterns.
- *Where is the business now?* Looking at the current business situation allows managers to take effective action to solve issues before they grow out of control.
- *Where is the business going?* Setting strategic direction is critical for planning and creating solid business strategies.

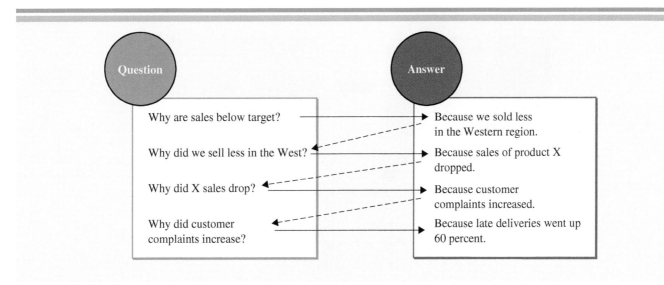

FIGURE 3.7

How BI Can Answer Tough Customer Questions

Ask a simple question—such as who is my best customer or what is my worst-selling product—and you might get as many answers as you have employees. Databases, data warehouses, and data marts can provide a single source of "trusted" data that can answer questions about customers, products, suppliers, production, finances, fraud, and even employees. They can also alert managers to inconsistencies or help determine the cause and effects of enterprise-wide business decisions. All business aspects can benefit from the added insights provided by business intelligence, and you, as a business student, will benefit from understanding how MIS can help you make intelligent decisions.

Operational, Tactical, and Strategic BI

Claudia Imhoff, president of Intelligent Solutions, Inc., believes it is useful to divide the spectrum of data mining analysis and BI into three categories: operational, tactical, and strategic. Two trends are displayed when viewing the spectrum from operational through tactical to strategic. First, the analysis becomes increasingly complex and ad hoc—that is, less repetitive, less predictable, and requiring varying amounts and types of information. Second, both the risks and the rewards of the analysis increase. That is, the often time-consuming, more strategic queries produce value less frequently but when they do the value can be extraordinary. Figure 3.8 illustrates the differences between operational, tactical, and strategic BI.[23]

None of these forms are performed in isolation; they must work with each other, feeding results from strategic to tactical to promote better operational decision making. For example, strategic BI may be used in the planning stages of a marketing campaign. The results of these analytics form the basis for the beginnings of a new campaign, targeting specific customers or demographics for example. The daily analyses of the campaign are used by the more tactical form of BI to change the course of the campaign if its results are not tracking where expected. Perhaps a different marketing message is needed, or the inventory levels are not sufficient to maintain the current sales pace, so the scope of marketing might be changed. These results are then fed into the operational BI for immediate actions—offering a different product, optimizing the sale price of the product, or changing the daily message sent to selected customer segments.

For this synergy to work, the three forms of BI must be tightly integrated. Minimal time should be lost transporting the results from one technological environment to another. Seamlessness of information and process flow is a must. TruServ, the parent company of True Value Hardware, has used BI software to improve efficiency of its distribution operations and reap a US$50 million reduction in inventory costs. The marketing department uses BI to track sales promotion results such as which promotions were most popular by store or by region. Now that TruServ is building promotion histories in its data warehouses, it can ensure that all stores are fully stocked with adequate inventory. TruServ was able to achieve a positive return on investment in about five to six months.[24]

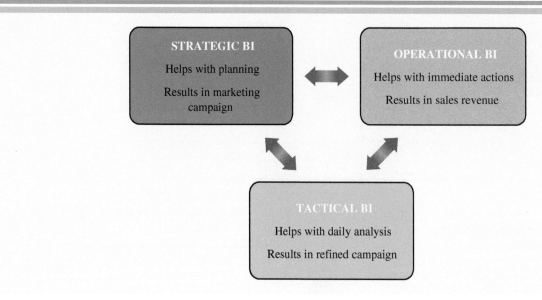

FIGURE 3.8

The Three Forms of BI Must Work Toward a Common Goal

BI's Operational Value

A leading risk insurance company allows customers to access account information over the Internet. Previously, the company sent paper reports and diskettes to all of its customers. Any errors in the reports would take one to two months to correct because customers would first have to receive the report, catch the mistake, and then notify the company of the error. Now customers spot the errors in real time and notify the insurance company directly through the extranet, usually within a couple of days.[25]

Richard Hackathorn, of Bolder Technologies, developed an interesting graph to demonstrate the value of operational BI. Figure 3.9 shows the three latencies that affect the speed of decision making: data, analysis, and decision latencies.

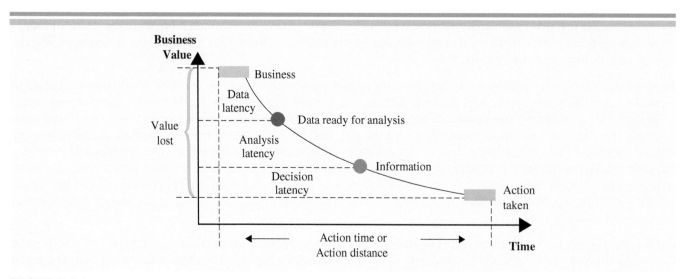

FIGURE 3.9

The Latency Between a Business Event and an Action Taken

- *Data latency* is the time needed to make transactional data ready for analysis (i.e., the time for extracting, transforming, and cleansing the data) and for loading the summarized, aggregated, cleansed data (analytical information) into a data warehouse. The time is takes depends on the state of the transactional data to begin with.

- *Analysis latency* is the length of time from when the analytical information is made available to when analysis is complete. This depends on the time it takes a business to do analysis. Usually, we think of this as the time it takes a human to do it, but this can be decreased by using automated analytics that have thresholds. When the thresholds are exceeded, alerts or alarms are issued to appropriate personnel, or they cause exception processes to be initiated without any need for human intervention.

- *Decision latency* is the time it takes a human to comprehend the analytic result and determine an appropriate action. This form of latency is difficult to reduce. The ability to remove the decision-making process from the human and automate it greatly reduces the overall decision latency. Many forward-thinking companies are doing just that. For example, rather than send a high-value customer a letter about a bounced cheque (which takes days to get to the customer), an automated system can simply send an immediate email or voice message informing the customer of the problem.

The key is to shorten these latencies so that the time frame for opportunistic influences on customers, suppliers, and others is faster, more interactive, and better positioned. As mentioned above, the best time to influence customers is not after they have left the store or the website; it is while they are still in the store or navigating the site.

For example, a customer searching a website for travel deals is far more likely to be influenced by appropriate messaging actions then and there. Actions taken immediately, while customers are still in the site, might include:

- Offering customers an appropriate coupon for the trip they showed interest in while searching for cheap airfares
- Giving customers information about their current purchase such as the suggestion that visas are needed
- Congratulating customers on reaching a certain frequent-buyer level and giving them 10 percent off an item

A website represents another great opportunity to influence a customer, if the interactions are appropriate and timely. For example:

- A banner announcing the next-best product on offer right after the customer puts an item in her basket
- The customer receiving an offer for a product he has just removed from the basket
- Displaying on-screen appropriate instructions for using a product; perhaps warning a parent that it should not be used by children under age 3[26]

Rapid innovations in systems and data mining tools are putting operational, tactical, and strategic BI at the fingertips of employees across the enterprise. With the successful implementation of BI systems, an organization can expect to benefit from the following:

- **Single Point of Access to Information for All Users** With a BI solution, organizations can unlock information held within their transactional databases by giving authorized users a single point of access to analytical information stored in a data warehouse. Whether this information resides in a data warehouse or data mart, users can prepare reports and drill deep down into the information to understand what drives their business, without technical knowledge of the underlying data structures. The most successful BI applications allow users to do this with an easy-to-understand, non-technical, graphical user interface.

- **BI Across Organizational Departments** There are many different uses for BI and one of its greatest benefits is that it can be used at every step in the value chain. All departments across an organization from sales to operations to customer service can benefit from the value of BI.

  Volkswagen AG uses BI to track, understand, and manage information in every department—from finance, production, and development, to research, sales and marketing, and purchasing. Users at all levels of the organization access supplier and customer reports relating to online requests and negotiations, vehicle launches, and vehicle capacity management and tracking.[27]

- **Up-to-the-Minute Information for Everyone** The key to unlocking information is to give users the tools to quickly and easily find immediate answers to their questions. Some users will be satisfied with standard reports that are updated on a regular basis, such as current inventory reports, sales per channel, or customer status reports. However, the answers these reports yield can lead to new questions. Some users will want dynamic access to information. The information that a user finds in a report will trigger more questions, and these questions will not be answered in a pre-packaged report.

While users may spend 80 percent of their time accessing standard or personalized reports, for 20 percent of their tasks they need to obtain additional information not available in the original report. To address this need and to avoid frustration (and related report backlog for the MIS department), a BI system should let users autonomously make ad hoc requests for information from an enterprise data warehouse or departmental data mart.

For merchants of MasterCard Worldwide, access to BI offers the opportunity to monitor their businesses more closely on a day-to-day basis. Advertising agencies can use information from the extranet when developing campaigns for merchants. On the authorization side, a call centre can pull up cardholder authorization transactions from a data warehouse to cut down on fraud. MasterCard expects that in the long term, and as business partners increasingly demand access to system data, the system will support more than 20,000 external users.[28]

Categories of BI Benefits

Management is no longer prepared to sink large sums of money into building BI systems without proof that these systems will yield significant contributions to the bottom line. When looking at how BI affects the bottom line, an organization should analyze not only the organization-wide business benefits, but also the various benefits it can expect to receive from BI deployment. A practical way of breaking down these numerous benefits is to separate them into direct, indirect, unpredictable, and intangible benefits.

Direct Quantifiable Benefits   Direct quantifiable benefits include working time saved in producing reports, selling information to suppliers, and so on. A few examples are:

- Moët et Chandon, the famous champagne producer, reduced its IS costs from approximately 30 cents to 15 cents per bottle.

- A leading risk insurance company provides customers with self-service access to their information in the insurance company's database and no longer sends paper reports. This one benefit alone saves the organization $400,000 a year in printing and shipping costs. The total three-year ROI for this BI deployment was 249 percent.[29]

Indirect Quantifiable Benefits   Indirect quantifiable benefits can be evaluated through indirect evidence—improved customer service means new business from the same customer, and differentiated service brings new customers. A few examples are:

- A customer of Owens & Minor cited extranet access to the data warehouse as the primary reason for giving the medical supplies distributor an additional $44 million in business.

- "When salespeople went out to visit TaylorMade's customers at golf pro shops and sporting goods retail chains, they didn't have up-to-date inventory reports. The sales reps would take orders for clubs, accessories, and clothing without confidence that the goods were available for delivery as promised," said Tom Collard, information systems director with TaylorMade. "The technology has helped TaylorMade not only reduce costs by eliminating the reporting backlog … it has eliminated a lot of wasted effort that resulted from booking orders that it couldn't fill."[30]

Unpredictable Benefits   Unpredictable benefits are the result of discoveries made by creative users. A few examples are:

- Volkswagen's finance BI system allowed an interesting discovery to take place that later resulted in significant new revenue. The customers of a particular model of the Audi product line had completely different behaviours than customers of other cars. Based on their socioeconomic profiles, they were thought to want long lease terms and fairly large upfront payments. Instead, the information revealed that Audi customers actually wanted shorter leases and to finance a large part of the purchase through the lease. Consequently, the company immediately introduced a new program combining a shorter lease, larger upfront payments, and aggressive leasing rates, especially for that car model. The interest in the new program was immediate, resulting in over $2 million in new revenue.

- Peter Blundell, former knowledge strategy manager for British Airways, and various company executives had a suspicion that the carrier was suffering from a high degree of ticket fraud. To address this problem, Blundell and his team rolled out BI. "Once we analyzed the information, we found that ticket fraud was not an issue at all. What we had supposed was fraud was in fact either information quality issues or process problems," Blundell said. "What it did was give us so many unexpected opportunities in terms of understanding our business." Blundell estimated that the BI deployment has resulted in around $100 million in cost savings and new revenues for the airline.[31]

Intangible Benefits   Intangible benefits include improved communication throughout the enterprise, improved job satisfaction of empowered users, and improved knowledge sharing. A few examples are:

- The corporate human resources department at ABN AMRO Bank uses BI to gain insight into its workforce by analyzing information on such items as gender, age, tenure, and compensation. Thanks to this sharing of intellectual capital, the HR department is in a better position to demonstrate its performance and contribution to the business successes of the corporation as a whole.

- Ben & Jerry's uses BI to track, understand, and manage information on the thousands of consumer responses it receives on its products and promotional activities. Through daily customer feedback analysis, Ben & Jerry's is able to identify trends and modify its marketing campaigns and its products to suit consumer demand.

Visual Business Intelligence

Informing is accessing large amounts of data from different management information systems. **Infographics (information graphics)** displays information graphically so it can be easily understood. Infographics can present the results of large data analysis looking for patterns and relationships that monitor changes in variables over time. **Data visualization** describes technologies that allow users to "see" or visualize data to transform information into a business perspective. **Data visualization tools** (see Figure 3.10) move beyond Excel graphs and charts into sophisticated analysis techniques such as pie charts, controls, instruments, maps, time series graphs, and more. Data visualization tools can help uncover correlations and trends in data that would otherwise go unrecognized. **Business intelligence dashboards** track corporate metrics such as critical success factors and key performance indicators and include advanced capabilities such as interactive controls allowing users to manipulate data for analysis. The majority of business intelligence software vendors offer a number of different data visualization tools and business intelligence dashboards.

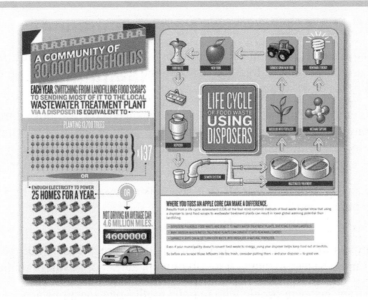

FIGURE 3.10
Emerson's Food Waste Infographic

Source: 2012 InSinkErator is a division of Emerson Electroc Co. All rights reserved.

Trends in Decision-Making Tools

The world's leading business analytics firm is still SAS. Tools like SAS Enterprise Miner are being used for many business analytics tasks by companies in many industries and even in the not-for-profit sector. In recent years other software giants, such as Microsoft with MS Share Point and their Microsoft Dynamic software and SAP with HANA, are making huge inroads in the business analytics and decision-making software world. Microsoft has purchased former leaders in this segment, such as Great Plains and FRx Software, to expand their customer base. At SAP about 35 percent of their sales are now in business analytics and it likely will see this segment of its business grow to at least 50 percent in the next few years. There have also been developments like Deloitte purchasing niche consulting companies, for example Quattro Integration Group, one of the leading SAP implementation firms in western Canada, with a focus on big data, especially in the oil and gas sector.[32]

OPENING CASE QUESTIONS

Moneyball: About More Than Just the Players

1. What data do you think would be important to a business manager of a team in your favourite professional sport?

2. How would your answer to the first question differ for the general manger of the same team?

3. What types of data do think would be good metrics for prospective player identification in your favourite professional sports league?

4. What do you see as the primary role of business intelligence in your favourite professional sports league in the next few years?

3.2 DELIVERING INFORMATION, KNOWLEDGE, AND INTELLIGENCE ACROSS THE ORGANIZATION

LO4) COLLABORATION SYSTEMS

Heineken has shortened its inventory cycle time for beer production and distribution from three months to four weeks. By using its collaborative system to forecast demand and expedite shipping, the company has dramatically cut inventory levels and shipping costs while increasing sales.

Over the past few years most business processes have changed on various dimensions (e.g., flexibility, interconnectivity, coordination style, autonomy) because of market conditions and organizational models. Frequently, information is located within physically separated systems as more and more organizations spread their reach globally. This creates a need for a software infrastructure that enables collaboration systems.

A *collaboration system* is an IT-based set of tools that supports the work of teams by facilitating the sharing and flow of information. Collaboration solves specific business tasks such as telecommuting, online meetings, deploying applications, and remote project and sales management (see Figure 3.11).

Collaboration systems allow people, teams, and organizations to leverage and build upon the ideas and talents of staff, suppliers, customers, and business partners. It involves a unique set of business challenges that:

- Include complex interactions between people who may be in different locations and want to work across function and discipline areas

- Require flexibility in work process and the ability to involve others quickly and easily

- Call for creating and sharing information rapidly and effortlessly within a team

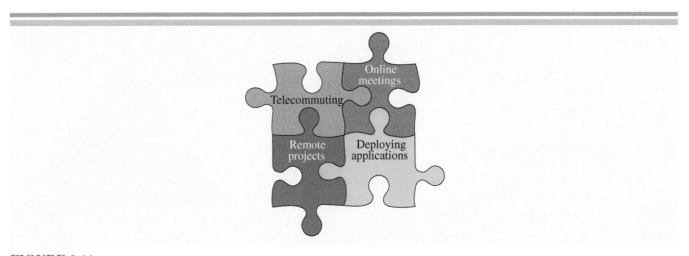

FIGURE 3.11

Ways Business Is Using Collaboration

Most organizations collaborate with other companies in some capacity. Consider the supplier–customer relationship, which can be thought of as a continuous life cycle of engagement, transaction, fulfillment, and service activities. Rarely do companies excel in all four life cycle areas, either from a business-process or technology-enabled aspect. Successful organizations identify and invest in their core competencies, and outsource or collaborate for those competencies that are not core to them. Collaboration systems fall into one of two categories:

1. *Unstructured collaboration* (sometimes referred to as *information collaboration*) includes document exchange, shared whiteboards, discussion forums, and email. These functions can improve personal productivity, reducing the time spent searching for information or chasing answers.

2. *Structured collaboration* (or *process collaboration*) involves shared participation in business processes, such as workflow, in which knowledge is hard-coded as rules. This helps improve automation and the routing of information.

Regardless of location or format—be it unstructured or structured—relevant accurate information must be readily and consistently available to those who need it anytime, anywhere, and on any device. Integrating information systems enables an organization to provide employees, partners, customers, and suppliers with the ability to access, find, analyze, manage, and collaborate on content. The collaboration can be done across a wide variety of formats, languages, and platforms. Lockheed Martin Corporation's ability to share complex project information across an extended supply chain in real time was key in its successful bid of a $19 billion contract with the U.S. Department of Defense (DoD) to build 21 supersonic stealth fighters. American government procurement rules require defence contractors to communicate effectively to ensure that deadlines are met, costs are controlled, and projects are managed throughout the life cycle of the contract.[33]

In anticipation of the contract, the Fort Worth, Texas, unit of Lockheed developed a real-time collaboration system that can tie together its partners, suppliers, and DoD customers via the Internet. The platform lets participants work together on product design and engineering tasks as well as supply chain and life cycle management issues. Lockheed will host all transactions and own the project information. The platform will let DoD and Lockheed project managers track the daily progress of the project in real time. This is the first major DoD project with such a requirement. The contract, awarded to the Lockheed unit and partners Northrop Grumman Corp. and BAE Systems, is the first installment in what could amount to a $200 billion program for 3,000 jet fighters over 40 years.

To be successful—and avoid being eliminated by the competition—an organization must undertake new initiatives, address both minor and major problems, and capitalize on significant opportunities. To support these activities, an organization will often create and use teams, partnerships, and alliances, because the expertise needed is beyond the scope of a single individual or organization. These groups can be formed internally among a company's employees or externally with other organizations (see Figure 3.12).

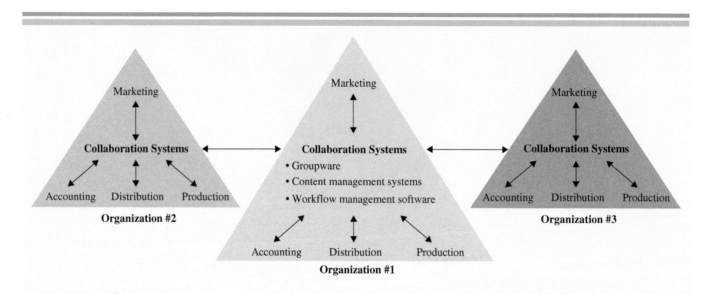

FIGURE 3.12

Collaboration Within and External to an Organization

Businesses of all sizes and in all markets have witnessed the benefits of leveraging their IS assets to create competitive advantage. Whereas information systems efforts in the past were aimed at increasing operational efficiency, the advent and proliferation of network-based computing (the Internet being the most visible but not the only example) has enabled organizations to build systems with which all sorts of communities can interact. The ultimate result will allow organizations to do business with customers, business partners, suppliers, governments and regulatory agencies, and any other community relevant to their particular operation or activity.

Just as organizations use internal teams, so they are increasingly forming alliances and partnerships with other organizations. The ***core competency*** of an organization is its key strength, a business function that it does better than any of its competitors. Research in Motion is highly regarded for its research and development and innovation, while Bombardier Aerospace's core competencies lie in product design and manufacturing. A ***core competency strategy*** is one in which an organization chooses to focus specifically on what it does best (its core competency) and forms partnerships and alliances with other specialist organizations to handle non-strategic business processes. Strategic alliances enable businesses to gain competitive advantages through access to a partner's resources, including markets, technologies, and people. Teaming up with another business adds complementary resources and capabilities, enabling participants to grow and expand more quickly and efficiently, especially fast-growing companies that rely heavily on outsourcing many areas of their business to extend their technical and operational resources. In the outsourcing process, they save time and boost productivity by not having to develop their own systems from scratch. They are then free to concentrate on innovation and their core business.

Information systems make such business partnerships and alliances easier to establish and manage. An ***information partnership*** occurs when two or more organizations cooperate by integrating their information systems, thereby providing customers with the best of what each can offer. The advent of the Internet has greatly increased the opportunity for IS-enabled business partnerships and alliances.

For example, an information partnership between the federal government (Industry Canada), provinces and territories (Ontario, British Columbia, and Yukon), and local governments (City of Kamloops, Regional Municipality of Halton and its two municipalities Milton and Halton Hills, and City of Whitehorse) has simplified the task of obtaining permits for large and small Canadian enterprises. These partners worked together to develop the BizPal (Business Permits and Licences) solution to provide a single point for businesses to obtain the necessary information when applying for permits and licences across all levels of government. Before this one-stop shopping solution, businesses were forced to enter the same information several times and make multiple payments. By collaborating and allowing information to be shared, these government partners have successfully deployed an integrated information systems solution that benefits Canadian companies wishing to start up a business.[34] The strengths of the collaboration process lie with the integration of many systems, namely:

- Content management systems
- Workflow management systems
- Groupware systems

Social Business, Collaboration, and Knowledge Management

IBM defines *social business* as business that puts people and the value of human connections front and centre. A social business is one that operates for the benefit of addressing social needs and enables society to function more effectively.

On IBM's Social Business Web page you see the following statement about the benefits of social business and why companies should adopt it: "When you inspire your workforce to innovate and collaborate more productively, you create tangible business value. When you anticipate needs and deliver exceptional experiences, you delight your customers and create advocates. When you integrate your business processes with the right social tools, you secure a competitive advantage and pioneer new ways of doing business." In other discussions authors tell us that knowledge management and collaboration drive the same benefits that IBM has posted on their page.

Knowledge management and collaboration involve mostly people and technology. Increasingly there is the application of artificial intelligence being applied to the knowledge management side of the equation. Another trend is the use of social business apps to help business and the people involved in the businesses collaborate and share knowledge more easily. Large consulting firms like Accenture have identified a number of tools that will help business progress in this area over the near future:

1. Wikis to enhance topic-centric knowledge management and collaborative content creation

2. Social tools that include rich user profiles, discussion forums, personal spaces, activity feeds, and status updates

3. Semantic resources that include faceted search tools, visual navigation, temporal analysis, and rules-based inference engines

4. Text mining tools that include document ingestion, automatic link identification, and automatic page categorization, all crowdsourced for maintenance efficiency and improved accuracy[35]

LO5   Content Management Systems

A ***content management system*** provides tools to manage creating, storing, editing, searching, and publishing information in a collaborative environment. As a website grows in size and complexity, the business must establish procedures to ensure that things run smoothly. At a certain point, it makes sense to automate this process and use a content management system to manage this effectively. The content management system marketplace is complex, incorporating document management, digital asset management, and Web content management. Figure 3.13 highlights the three primary types of content management systems. Major content management system vendors include EM Corporation, Autonomy Interwoven, Percussion, Open Text, and Oracle.

With two hospitals, numerous physicians' offices, and a variety of health centres and treatment program locations, Summit Health, the largest health care provider in Franklin County, Pennsylvania, looked to provide its customers with a personalized Web experience. Summit Health also looked for a way that internal staff could easily update the website without needing any IT resources. The solution that Summit Health developed started with a content management system, which not only allowed Summit Health to launch a new site but also included a number of added benefits for both its customers and its internal staff. The benefits Summit Health realized were:

- Internal users having the power to author website content

- An enhanced technical infrastructure that supported new features and, most importantly, made the site easier for customers to use

- Completely updated content using tools such as an enhanced provider directory

- The primary goal of increased engagement with visitors through interactive tools such as physician finders, online class schedules, the ability to send e-cards to patients, online ordering of gift shop items for patients, and a health information library

Document management system (DMS)	A *document management system (DMS)* supports the electronic capturing, storage, distribution, archiving, and accessing of documents. It optimizes the use of documents within an organization independently of any publishing medium (e.g., the Web). A DMS provides a document repository with information about other information. The system tracks the editorial history of each document and its relationships with other documents. A variety of search and navigation methods are available to make document retrieval easy. A DMS manages highly structured and regulated content, such as pharmaceutical documentation.
Digital asset management system (DAM)	Though similar to document management, a *digital asset management system (DAM)* generally works with binary rather than text files, such as multimedia file types. DAMs emphasize allowing file manipulation and conversion—for example, converting GIF files to JPEG.
Web content management system (WCM)	A *Web content management system (WCM)* adds a layer to document and digital asset management that enables publishing content both to intranets and to public websites. In addition to maintaining the content itself, WCMs often integrate content with online processes such as e-business systems.

FIGURE 3.13

Common Types of Content Management Systems

According to Michele Zeigler, Summit Heath's vice-president of Information Services and CIO, "as we establish more content ownership throughout the Summit organization, our site becomes more and more timely, accurate, and dynamic."[36]

Workflow Management Systems

A *workflow* defines all the steps or business rules, from beginning to end, required for a business process; *workflow management systems* facilitate the automation and management of business processes and control the movement of work through the business process. Work activities can be performed in series (consecutively in sequence) or in parallel (at the same time) and can involve both people and automated computer systems. In addition, many workflow management systems allow the opportunity to measure and analyze the execution of the process because the systems allow the flow of work to be defined and tracked. Workflow software helps automate a range of business tasks and electronically route the right information to the right people at the right time. Users are notified of pending work, and managers can observe status and route approvals through the system quickly.

There are two primary types of workflow systems: messaging-based and database-based. *Messaging-based workflow systems* send work assignments through an email system. The workflow system automatically tracks the order for the work to be assigned and each time a step is completed, the system automatically sends the work to the next individual in line. For example, every time a team member completes a piece of the project, the system automatically sends the document to the next team member.

Database-based workflow systems store documents in a central location and automatically ask the team members to access the document when it is their turn to edit the document. Project documentation is stored in a central location and team members are notified by the system when it is their turn to log in and work on their portion of the project.

Either type of workflow system helps present information in a unified format, improves teamwork by providing automated process support, and allows team members to communicate and collaborate within a unified environment.

Prior to its restructuring, Fraser Papers (now Twin Rivers Paper Company) was a Canadian forestry giant with operations across Canada and the United States. As one of the largest producers of printing and publishing paper products at the time, it had facilities in Connecticut, Maine, Ohio, Wisconsin, Quebec, and New Brunswick. The company managed more than 81,000 hectares of forest and operated a nursery, numerous sawmills, and multiple pulping facilities. Fraser's involvement in manufacturing, forest management, and pulping resulted in a demanding IT environment where streamlining workflow was a top priority.

One example of the need to streamline workflow was at Fraser Papers's main facility in Maine. This facility included 400 users and produced thousands of mission-critical documents including cheques, purchase orders, invoices, accounts payable (A/P) documentation, and inventory control documentation. When the company looked more closely at just part of this workflow—writing and printing cheques—Fraser Papers discovered it had special needs. When producing cheques for A/P there was a need to work in multiple currencies; A/P worked mostly with Canadian and American vendors but also with global suppliers and two banks, one in Canada and one in the United States. Another workflow feature was the need to manage cheques centrally and keep cheque printing secure while still allowing users to do their jobs and create A/P cheques, paycheques, and direct deposit receipts without extra work. Also due to nature of the Fraser Papers's business was the need to allow for the secure printing of paycheques to remote locations, eliminating delays in getting paycheques to employees and reducing mailing costs.[37]

Groupware

Groupware is software that supports team interaction and dynamics including calendaring, scheduling, and videoconferencing. Organizations can use this technology to communicate, cooperate, coordinate, solve problems, compete, or negotiate. While traditional technologies like the telephone qualify as groupware, the term refers to a specific class of technologies relying on modern computer networks, such as email, newsgroups, videophones, and chat rooms.

Groupware users can work together at the same time (synchronous groupware) or different times (asynchronous groupware), and work together in the same place (co-located) or in different places (distance).

Figure 3.14 shows the types of technologies that can be used in the different quadrants of collaborative communication.

	Same time "Synchronous"	Different time "Asynchronous"
Same place "Co-located"	Presentation support	Shared computers
Different place "Distance"	Videophones, Chat	Email, Workflow

FIGURE 3.14

Supporting Technologies for the Different Quadrants of Collaborative Communication

The groupware concept integrates various systems and functionalities into a common set of services or a single (client) application. In addition, groupware can represent a wide range of systems and methods of integration. Figure 3.15 displays the advantages groupware systems offer an organization over single-user systems.

Facilitating communication (faster, easier, clearer, more persuasive)
Enabling telecommuting
Reducing travel costs
Sharing expertise
Forming groups with common interests where it would not be possible to gather a sufficient number of people face to face
Saving time and cost in coordinating group work
Facilitating group problem solving

FIGURE 3.15

Advantages of Groupware Systems

In today's business environment there is numerous software available to help companies with their collaborative efforts. The leading vendors of these types of software are Microsoft, IBM, and Oracle.

Allianz Suisse is one of Switzerland's largest insurance companies with about 1,100 independent sales agents in 70 different locations across Switzerland. The company markets, sells, and services its insurance products using a dedicated insurance application running on local notebook PCs. Data on those PCs are synchronized with servers at its Zurich headquarters. As the agents sell insurance, the required forms are completed, submitted, and processed using this application. Of course, agents spend most of their time on the road, visiting with prospects and customers. In order to maximize their efficiency and effectiveness, they require access to customer information and appointment schedules, which are maintained on the company's server. They also require the ability to schedule new meetings from the road and synchronize this new information with the information already on the server. Finally, they need remote access to their email. As they call on customers and prospects, the agents prefer not to lug their laptop computers along with them. Instead, most have purchased their own smart phones or tablets, and rely on Allianz Suisse to provide the ability to download contact, scheduling, and email information to those devices. According to Robert Spaltenstein, head of groupware at Allianz Suisse, "to help streamline the way they work and provide them with access to their Lotus Domino email and PIM, we needed a reliable and secure solution that would provide anywhere, anytime wired or wireless synchronization between their devices and our Lotus Domino system."[38]

Videoconferencing and Web Conferencing

Videoconferencing, also called *telepresence*, uses telecommunications to bring people at different sites together for a meeting. It uses a type of groupware, a set of interactive telecommunication technologies that allow persons at two or more locations to interact via two-way video and audio transmissions simultaneously. The interaction can be as simple as a conversation in private offices (*point-to-point*), or it might involve several sites (*multi-point*) with more than one person in large rooms at the different sites. Besides the audio and visual transmission of conversations, videoconferencing can be used to share documents, computer-displayed information, and whiteboards.[39]

Simple analog videoconferences were being established as early as the invention of television. These systems consisted of two closed-circuit television systems connected via cable. During the first manned space flights, NASA used two radio-frequency (UHF or VHF) links, one in each direction; TV channels routinely use this kind of technology when reporting from distant locations, for instance. Then mobile links to satellites using special trucks became common (see Figure 3.16 for an example of videoconferencing).

Videoconferencing is part of online networking websites to help businesses form profitable relationships quickly and efficiently without involving travel. Several factors support business use of videoconferencing, including:[40]

■ Over 60 percent of face-to-face communication is nonverbal. Therefore, an enriched communications tool such as videoconferencing can promote an individual's or a team's identity, context, and emotional situation.

■ It is estimated that the average worker loses 2.1 hours a day to interruptions and inefficient communications.

■ The latest technology available lends itself to reliable and easy-to-use conferencing, fostering collaboration at meetings.

■ Enterprises that fail to use modern communications technologies run the risk of falling behind their competition.[41]

Web conferencing blends audio, video, and document-sharing technologies to create virtual meeting rooms. There, people can chat in video conference calls or use real-time text messages. They can mark up a shared document as if using a whiteboard, and even watch live software demos or video clips.

Perhaps the biggest surprise about Web conferencing is its simplicity. Users need only set up an account and download a few small software files. The best part about a Web conference is that attendees do not have to have the same hardware or software. Every participant can see what is on anyone else's screen, regardless of the application being used (see Figure 3.17 for an example of Web conferencing).[42]

FIGURE 3.16
Videoconferencing

FIGURE 3.17
Web Conferencing

Even with its video features, Web conferencing is not quite like being there, nor is it like being in a sophisticated (and pricey) videoconferencing facility; but it does offer the benefit of mobility. You do not have to be sitting in a conference facility to participate.

A growing number of companies are offering Web conferencing. Leaders in this industry include WebEx, Same Time, Skype, and Elluminate Live. Additionally, offerings like Goggle Hangouts and Apple's Face time have expanded the ability to hold a Web conference anywhere, as this software is included on your Android or iOS device when you purchase it.

Enterprise Portals

As a means of improving information sharing, and use, many organizations have implemented *enterprise portals*, quite often as a feature of the organization's ERP system. These are single-point Web browser interfaces used within an organization to promote gathering, sharing, and disseminating information throughout an enterprise.[43] Gartner describes enterprise portals as Web software that provides access to, and interaction with, relevant information resources (such as documents, reports, data warehouses, and employees), by selected target audiences within and across the extended enterprise, delivered in a highly personalized manner.[44]

These information systems provide employees with a path to all-encompassing content, services, and applications through one access point. Unlike department-based Web sites hosted on a company's intranet or internal Web-based network, an enterprise portal's primary purpose is to provide a transparent directory of information located throughout an organization, not act as a separate source of information itself. In this sense, the primary purpose of an enterprise portal is to function as an information gateway or launch pad for employees to various sorts of information. In recent years, such gateways have become organizational necessities due to the proliferation of department-based Web sites throughout the firm and the desire to provide employees with both internal and external company-related information. Figure 3.18 shows an example of an enterprise portal.

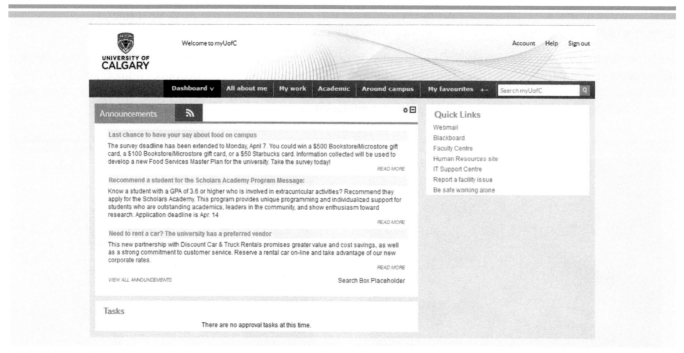

FIGURE 3.18

A Typical Enterprise Portal for a University

Source: University of Calgary 2014, www.ucalgary.ca.

Enterprise portals are described as applications that enable companies to unlock internally and externally stored information, and provide users a single gateway to personalized information needed to make informed business decisions."[45] The primary purpose of a portal is to help people navigate organizational information; its secondary purpose is to provide unique content. This is in contrast to other types of Internet sites, such as external or departmental websites, where the primary purpose is to disseminate information and keep people at that specific site.

More advanced portal features include access to workgroup productivity tools such as email, calendars, workflow and project management software, expense reporting and travel reservation applications, and more specialized functions for transaction-based information processing in which users can read, write, and update corporate data directly through the portal interface.

In addition to the above, enterprise portals can possess a variety of other features that help support information and knowledge, sharing, and use (see Figure 3.19), including:

1. A *publishing facility* that enables users to post and index information directly into the portal themselves

2. An *automatic indexing facility* that classifies information items posted on the portal using an algorithm

3. A *subscription facility* that notifies and distributes relevant information on a regular basis to a specific user or a group of users

4. *Intelligent agents* that understand a user's preferences and roles, help him or her to find relevant information, and tailor the presentation of information on the interface in the most helpful way.

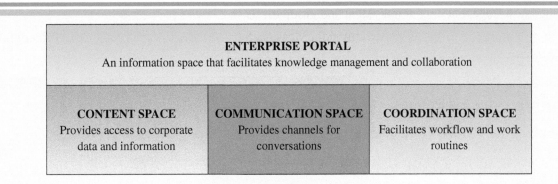

FIGURE 3.19

An Enterprise Portal as an Information Space for Knowledge Management and Collaboration

Instant Messaging

Email is by far the dominant collaboration application, but real-time collaboration tools like instant messaging are creating a new communication dynamic within organizations. ***Instant messaging*** (also ***IM*** or ***IMing***) is a type of communications service that enables someone to create a kind of private chat room with another individual in order to communicate in real time over the Internet. Most of the popular instant messaging programs provide a variety of features, such as:

■ *Web links.* Share links to favourite websites

■ *Images.* Look at an image stored on someone else's computer

■ *Sounds.* Play sounds

■ *Files.* Share files by sending them directly to another IM user

■ *Talk.* Use the Internet instead of a phone to talk

■ *Streaming content.* Receive real-time or near-real-time stock quotes and news

■ *Instant messages.* Receive immediate text messages

Software tools like IBM's Same time are now unifying business communication with their real-time platform and inclusion of IM, Web conferencing, and mobile collaboration tools. These built-for-business products let an organization offer presence awareness, secure instant messaging, and Web conferencing. These products give employees instant access to colleagues and company information regardless of time, place, or device.

The bigger issue in collaboration for organizations is cultural. Collaboration unites teams from different regions, departments, and even companies—people who bring different skills, perceptions, and capabilities. A formal collaboration strategy helps create the right environment and the right systems for team members.

The Role of Mobile Devices

M-learning uses portable computing devices with wireless capability to enable mobility and mobile learning. This allows teaching and learning to extend beyond the traditional classroom. The academic world is looking at the role of mobile devices like smart phones and tablets in knowledge management. In more traditional areas like m-commerce and m-government, mobile phones are not used for knowledge management but rather only for information management through activities such as information dissemination, storage, and, retrieval. According to case study and literature search research by Mzwandile Shongwe focused on using mobile phones for knowledge management and m-learning, some of the trends we are seeing are:

■ The use of SMS (Short Message Service) mostly for information dissemination and retrieval, and the inbox for information storage

■ The use, in m-learning, of mobile phones for information and knowledge management, such as creating and transferring knowledge, but only at individual and group levels

■ The use in m-learning of SMS, MMS (Multimedia Message Service), camera, video, email, Web conferencing, and chat services[46]

OPENING CASE QUESTIONS

Moneyball: About More Than Just the Players

5. How could a team incorporate social media collaboration in its player scouting?

6. What technologies mentioned could scouts use to better collaborate with each other while preparing for a player draft?

7. If you were in Billy Beane's position today, how do you think you might convince your team's upper management that sport analytics will assist your team in both marketing the team and fielding a better team?

SUMMARY OF KEY THEMES

This chapter discussed various ways that information systems can help organizations access, share, and use information. Specifically, this chapter described:

■ *How information systems can help companies turn information into knowledge, and build partnerships, teams, and alliances.* Information comes in many different shapes and sizes. It can be structured data found in transactional databases; unstructured information found in documents and memos (in paper or electronic form); or thoughts and ideas that employees possess. Information systems offer organizations a means to manage and leverage this wide range of complex information. Though this can be a challenging and difficult pursuit, there is a real payoff for organizations that do. When employees are armed with the right information at the right time, they become empowered to turn that information into "action" by delivering innovations, forging best practices, and developing new products and services, not only for the company but for its partnerships, teams, and alliances as well.

■ *The difference between knowledge management and knowledge management systems.* Knowledge management is the management of the processes through which organizations generate value from what their employees know, and from what information is collected and stored within the organization. This can be accomplished through IT and non-IT ways. Information technology is an enabler of knowledge management. Recognizing that knowledge resides in individuals, rather than in information systems and databases themselves, knowledge management systems are information systems that help humans understand the information collected and stored in databases across the enterprise, and that connect them with human experts who can provide interpretations and insight.

■ *Business intelligence, data mining, data visualization, and the relationship between business intelligence and the enterprise data repository.* Business intelligence leverages the information stored in data warehouses and data marts for strategic advantage and more effective business practice. The goal of BI is to provide the enterprise with tools to explore and mine the repository of trusted information found in data repositories— information that can be used in a multitude of applications to answer questions about customers, products, supply and demand chains, production inefficiencies, financial trends, fraud, and even employees. BI can be used to flag anomalies via alerts, provide visualization and statistical models, and understand the cause and effects of decisions upon the enterprise.

■ *What is meant by a collaboration system, and how such systems can support both structured and unstructured collaboration.* A collaboration system is an information system that supports the work of teams by facilitating the sharing and flow of information. This collaboration can be structured, as in the coordination of workflow, or unstructured, as in the exchange of information on an ad hoc basis through document exchange, discussion forums, and email.

■ *The differences between, and business advantages of, various types of collaboration systems, such as groupware, content management systems, and workflow management systems.* Groupware is software that supports team interaction and dynamics, including calendaring, scheduling, and videoconferencing. Content management systems provide tools to manage the creation, storage, editing, and publication of information in a collaborative environment. Workflow management systems facilitate automating and managing business processes, as well as moving work through the business process. Together these systems offer efficiency and effectiveness gains in how work and coordinated activities get done in organizations.

As a business student, you need to know all this, since you will soon be working in organizations yourself. If you recognize the importance of facilitating information access, promoting information sharing, and encouraging information use in a company (especially with the help of information systems), you will be better prepared to help your organization work collaboratively and promote knowledge generation, sharing, and use across the enterprise.

KEY TERMS

Analysis latency	Data latency
Analytical information	Decision latency
Asynchronous communications	Digital asset management system (DAM)
Big data	Document management system (DMS)
Business analytics (BA)	Enterprise portals
Business intelligence (BI)	Explicit knowledge
Collaboration system	Granularity
Content management system	Groupware
Core competency	Information
Core competency strategy	Information collaboration
Crowdsourcing	Information partnership
Data	Instant messaging (IM, IMing)
Database-based workflow systems	Joint problem solving
Data governance	Knowledge

Knowledge management (KM)	**Structured collaboration (process collaboration)**
Knowledge management system (KMS)	**Tacit knowledge**
M-learning	**Transactional data**
Messaging-based workflow systems	**Unstructured collaboration (information collaboration)**
Process collaboration	**Videoconferencing**
Real-time data	**Web conferencing**
Real-time information	**Web content management system (WCM)**
Real-time system	**Wikis**
Shadowing	**Workflow**
Social networking analysis (SNA)	**Workflow management systems**

CLOSING CASE ONE

DreamWorks's Animation Collaboration

This case showcases the use of collaboration software in an organization.

Hewlett-Packard (HP) and DreamWorks Animation SKG (DreamWorks) were the first to introduce a collaboration studio for simulating face-to-face business meetings across long distances. Vyomesh Joshi, executive vice-president at HP, and Jeffrey Katzenberg, CEO of DreamWorks, officially unveiled the HP Halo Collaboration Studio in New York City in 2005. Halo enables people in different locations to communicate in a vivid, face-to-face environment in real time. Whether across a country or across the ocean, users can see and hear one another's physical and emotional reactions to conversation and information.

By giving participants the remarkable sense that they are in the same room, the Halo Collaboration Studio transformed the way businesses such as PepsiCo, Advanced Micro Devices, and DreamWorks communicate across the globe. Halo significantly increases team effectiveness, provides faster decision-making capabilities, and decreases the need for travel.

"The HP Halo Collaboration Studio enables remote teams to work together in a setting so lifelike that participants feel as though they are in the same room," Joshi said. "To create this experience, HP is harnessing its expertise in colour science, imaging, and networking in this new category of innovation. It is something we believe will not only disrupt the traditional videoconferencing market, but will also change the way people work in a global market."

Early in the production of the animated film *Shrek 2*, DreamWorks realized a significant return on investment using the Halo technology. By connecting its California teams in Glendale and Redwood City, DreamWorks was able to speed up many aspects of the production.

"In 2002, while we were producing *Shrek 2*, we realized that DreamWorks needed face-to-face collaboration between key creative talent in different locations," Katzenberg said. "We weren't satisfied with the available videoconferencing systems, so we designed a collaboration solution that would fulfill our needs. HP took the system and turned it into Halo, a solution that allowed for very effective communication." The Halo system become HP's telepresence and videoconferencing solution for its customers through 2011 when they sold it to Polycom, one of the leaders in telepresence and videoconferencing.

Halo Connection

To connect via Halo, organizations purchase at least two Halo rooms set up for six people each. Three plasma displays in each room enable participants to see those they are collaborating with in life-size images. The rooms come equipped with studio-quality audio and lighting, and participants use a simple onscreen user interface to collaborate, with just a few mouse clicks.

An intricate software control system ensures Halo rooms work easily and seamlessly together. The control system also provides precise image and colour calibration, so participants see each other as they appear in real life. A dedicated HP Halo Video Exchange Network provides a high-bandwidth experience with imperceptible delays between Halo studios worldwide.

To ensure a 24/7 connection and eliminate the need for enterprises to manage operating and maintaining a Halo room, services offered include network operations and management, remote diagnostics and calibration, concierge, equipment warranty, and ongoing service and repair.

Participants can easily share documents and data directly from their notebook PCs with individuals in other rooms, using a collaboration screen mounted above the plasma displays. The rooms also contain a high-magnification camera, which enables individuals to zoom in on objects on a table revealing the finest of details and colour shading, and a phone that opens a conference call line to those not in one of the Halo rooms.

"We believe there is a personal connection that comes with Halo that just clearly doesn't come from any other kind of technology we've used in the past," said Steve Reinemund, CEO of PepsiCo. "Halo is one of the best investments we've made to improve the effectiveness of our business and work/life balance for our people."[47]

Questions

1. How can companies use Halo to increase their business efficiency?

2. Explain how a company like PepsiCo can use Halo to gain a competitive advantage in its industry.

3. How can knowledge management be increased by using a product such as Halo?

4. Why would a company like DreamWorks, which is not IT-focused, be interested in collaboration systems?

5. What are a few of the security issues surrounding this type of information system?

CLOSING CASE TWO

Enterprise Content Management at Statoil

This case illustrates the use and benefits of using a content management system in an organization.

Statoil is one of the world's largest exporters of crude oil and the second-largest supplier of natural gas to the European market. The company has approximately 30,000 employees in locations scattered over 40 countries. Based in Norway, Statoil is the leading operator on the Norwegian continental shelf and experiencing strong growth in international production.[48]

Since 2002, the company has adopted an e-collaboration strategy. The goal of the strategy is to create a corporate "knowledge reservoir" that provides global access to a common pool of digital assets and is used to support work processes and share information between Statoil and its customers, employees, and business partners.

Access to this knowledge reservoir is provided through an information portal and controlled through the assignment of end-user roles. For instance, a customer would have much more limited access to information housed in the knowledge reservoir than a Statoil employee would.

The need for this strategy arose from the information overload that burdened the company. As is typical for many decentralized organizations, Statoil's information was scattered across a number of different storage media and applications. The total number of databases exceeded 5,500.

The core foundation of the knowledge reservoir is content management. This involves the ability to support a content life cycle in the company that effectively deals with the capture, transformation, storage, security, distribution, retrieval, and eventual destruction of documents. Though Statoil made great gains in facilitating such content management practices, it also faced challenges getting there.

The largest problem was how content was maintained throughout the company. There were literally thousands of heterogeneous content databases involving stand-alone intranet and extranet applications and over 800 databases containing archived documents. Though technically these were all accessible across the enterprise, logically people were unaware that these documents were available. Hence, much of the material was never loaded into a centralized, shared-content management system. Having so much content reside outside a shared, centralized content management system has negative implications for archiving, version management, publication, and workflow.

Another difficulty was that people tended to use personal email folders to manage document attachments, rather than posting documents once in a central location for others to use. Emailing attachments caused network congestion and chewed up precious file storage space. If stored centrally, a document is stored just once and people can reference the document there if needed.

Another challenge was that storing files in their original production format made retrieving these items difficult after a few years. This is because content management system technologies change and the format of these production files do not. On the flipside, updating the format to be compatible with content management system technologies may make these files unusable for retrieval by the original application that produced them. The best solution would be to store content in application-independent formats.

Difficulties also stemmed from the lack of embedded routines that could potentially delete unwanted information stored across production or archiving systems. This results in the redundant storage of information and the over-accumulation of content. To clean up content, Statoil had to issue "campaigns" to encourage employees to delete unnecessary information.

Another challenge pertained to searches. There was no single, integrated search facility that could retrieve documents across the thousands of other heterogeneous content-based systems. This was largely a result of different business units using different taxonomies to classify their content and storing their content in different physical structures. Hence, information retrieval across business units was problematic, despite the best intentions of the company.

Though these challenges were obstacles to effectively managing corporate content, Statoil made great strides in overcoming them. To date, the e-collaboration strategy yielded several successes for the company, including:

- A basic content management solution
- Automatic archiving
- Long-term storage of content with separate data indices
- Automatic security levels of information based on metadata
- Integration of existing standard office tools
- A corporate yellow pages
- One common portal framework
- Training services for the content management solution
- Implementation of content management guidelines for use by third-party solution providers (i.e., for working on projects with partners)
- The establishment of required e-learning modules for employees

In this sense, Statoil did well in creating and managing information content, regardless of whether it is sourced internally within the organization or externally from information suppliers; and in automating the content life cycle, from creation to archive, with information delivered to the recipient independent of time, place, or media.[49]

Questions

1. Why do you think content management is such a critical part of Statoil's strategy?

2. Comment on the utility and importance of Statoil's use of an information portal to promote enterprise-wide content management.

3. To what extent do you think Statoil's predicament of information overload is typical for organizations in Canada?

4. What lessons learned and insights from the chapter's discussion on the factors affecting the adoption and use of enterprise portal could help promote Statoil's adoption and use of its content management initiative?

CLOSING CASE THREE

Leveraging Knowledge at Bell Canada

This case showcases how a company can use a knowledge management system to enable its employees to be more knowledgeable in performing their jobs.

Bell Canada is Canada's largest telephone and telecommunications company. Servicing both consumer and business customer markets, the company provides broadcast and cable television, local telephone, long distance, wireless communications, Internet access, and satellite television. The telecommunications giant operates in a fast-paced and highly competitive environment. New competitors and innovative technologies constantly threaten to capture Bell's stronghold on the Canadian marketplace. To stay ahead of the pack, Bell recognizes the importance of providing its employees with easy access to the most current information.

In response, Bell has built the Market Knowledge Centre (MKC)—a one-stop, self-directed learning tool—to help employees attain high levels of competency and enable knowledge sharing at Bell. The MKC provides employees with easy access to high-quality, relevant information in a forum where this information can be personalized, pushed, pulled, shared, discussed, summarized, and integrated with other pieces of information. Bell believes that such a tool increases the chance of employees making new discoveries, learning new insights, and strengthening their know-how. In this way, Bell envisions the portal as a tool that helps employees turn information into knowledge.

The objectives of the MKC are to:

- Enable Bell to meet competitive challenges in the marketplace
- Enrich the company's hiring and training programs
- Increase technological literacy among employees
- Provide resources to employees that can help them develop their knowledge and competencies[50]

In short, the MKC is an electronic library on Bell's intranet that gives employees access to authoritative and recent information on topics pertaining to their interests and work-related tasks. Employees visit to read the latest publications from in-house experts and outside consultants. The documentation available varies widely, covering telecommunications, technologies, business, marketing, and management. Information is not limited just to text-based documents; other forms include audio conferences and invitations to live briefings or seminars. The beauty of this tool is that it provides information access from each employee's desktop. Employees are not constrained by physical geography, unavailable copies, or hours of operation—typical problems voiced in the past by employees trying to access paper-based collections housed in traditional corporate libraries.

Further, employees can, by creating personal folders, customize the MKC to have access to the subjects of interest to them. When users find documents of interest, they can tag or bookmark them, save them in their folders, and create annotations or comments to organize their reading choices. The MKC also facilitates search and browse functions. Employees can locate documents of interest through a keyword search. End-users can browse the library collection by broad subject category, author, and date; such a facility helps employees get an overview of what is contained in the collection—kind of like what happens when someone strolls through the stacks of a traditional library getting a sense of things and randomly finding material of interest.

Through these features, the MKC helps employees do their jobs better. The MKC provides key strategic and tactical information needed by employees to support their projects. A large chunk of this information is research-related. Given the fast-changing environment, Bell recognizes the need to provide current research results to employees, so the portal's content is updated daily. Employees can sign up for weekly email alerts to keep them informed about the latest additions to the library. In fact, this form of "push" technology—where the MKC informs end-users about new material rather than the end-users having to "pull" the information out themselves by constantly checking—can be targeted so that only new material matching a user's profile of interest is reported.

There are savings for the company with the MKC. It eliminates duplicate spending on consultant reports, trade magazines, and industry documents across the enterprise by centralizing subscriptions to online databases and electronic journals and negotiating corporate-wide distribution licences with suppliers. The portal has also done away with the need to maintain and staff physical library locations within Bell at its Montreal, Toronto, and Ottawa locations.

A dedicated staff of trained information specialists maintains the MKC to keep it fresh, current, and robust. This entails major updates of the portal in the release of new versions (about once every three years) and smaller updates that offer incremental enhancements to the portal interface and its collections. The current version engages users by giving them the ability to comment on reports they receive from the site and to discuss the findings contained in these reports. The new version will also provide a usage count for each report so that users can filter their search for information by accessing the most viewed reports. Features that have been added to the MKC include:

1. Incorporating Google's Mini Search Appliance, which has proved more accurate than the search tool formerly used

2. Integrating news feeds, which allows users to subscribe to a number of news sources and a daily email news digest

3. Creating subject pages that are a compilation of important pieces of information the MKC has on any specific subject (usually a hot issue)

To ensure the MKC is responsive to company needs, performance measures of client satisfaction are conducted regularly. Employee feedback is critical for evaluating the utility of this tool and figuring out what enhancements are needed. This can be done by polling end-users through client surveys and interviews and/or analyzing portal server logs to understand employee usage behaviour with various portal functions and visits to portal pages. Both information support staff and the portal tool itself need to be measured.

Overall, the MKC portal offers many benefits to Bell. The tool ensures more informed decision making, increased distribution of research and corporate materials, higher employee satisfaction through the provision of continual online learning, savings in duplicate spending on publication dissemination and maintaining multiple physical library locations, and improved collaboration between departments and work teams. Moreover, this tool helps employees turn information into knowledge by giving workers easy access to high-quality and relevant information, and the ability to work with, share, and discuss this information with others, leading to gains in understanding and the ability to put this understanding into action.[51]

Questions

1. Do you think employing social networking software will be commonplace in corporate environments in the future? What are the drivers of the use of such software? What are the inhibitors of its use?

2. Why is email not conducive to collaborative work? How are Web 2.0 technologies better suited to support collaborative work?

3. What is the advantage of having Web 2.0 software functionality built upon a strong underlying ECM platform?

4. What factors contribute to the current low levels of adoption of enterprise content management software by corporations?

MAKING BUSINESS DECISIONS

1. Collaboration on Intranets

MyIntranet.net is a worldwide leader providing online intranet solutions. The MyIntranet online collaboration tool is a solution for small businesses and groups inside larger organizations that need to organize information, share files and documents, coordinate calendars, and enable efficient collaboration, all in a secure, browser-based environment. MyIntraneth as just added conferencing and group scheduling features to its suite of hosted collaboration software. Explain why infrastructure integration is critical to the suite of applications to function within this environment.

2. Gaining Efficiency with Collaboration

During the past year, you have been working for a manufacturing firm to help improve its supply chain management by implementing enterprise resource planning and supply chain management systems. For efficiency gains, you are recommending that the manufacturing firm should be turning toward collaborative systems. The firm needs to share intelligent plans and forecasts with supply chain partners, reduce inventory levels, improve working capital, and reduce manufacturing changeovers. Given the collaboration systems presented to you in this unit, what type of system(s) would you recommend to facilitate your firm's future needs?

3. Working with the Flow

Calgary Stampede organizers must plan every year to host a 10-day, world-renowned event involving rodeo competitions, a midway, stage shows, concerts, chuckwagon races, agricultural competitions, First Nations exhibitions, and pancake breakfasts. The Stampede involves myriad tasks such as advertising, creating a program schedule, and working with hundreds of volunteers to pull off "The Greatest Outdoor Show on Earth" every July. The event attracts more than 1.2 million visitors each year. As the event grows in magnitude and complexity, Calgary Stampede organizers are turning to the use of a workflow management system to help plan and carry out this event. Given the work that needs to be done, what types of features would the workflow management system need to provide, and what types of tasks would the workflow management system need to handle to help organizers effectively manage the Calgary Stampede?

4. Managing Manuscripts

A prestigious international academic information systems journal, *IS Quarterly Canada*, receives hundreds of manuscripts every year from authors around the globe wishing to publish their research findings. You have been hired by the editor-in-chief to design a content management system to organize and keep track of the manuscript submission and review process. Every manuscript is first screened by an editor to see if it is worthy of review. If so, two to three reviewers are sent a copy for feedback. Once their comments are received, the editor makes a decision to reject the manuscript, request revisions, or accept the manuscript for publication. Revised manuscripts might either undergo further rounds of review or be accepted by the editor for publication as is. What features and functions would you include in such a system? Justify the selection of your choices.

5. Knowledge Audit

A leading management IT consulting firm, Know IT, headquartered in Montreal, Quebec, provides its clients with solutions to a host of business information systems problems and issues. The firm maintains a shared document repository, accessible only to internal workers and consultants, of past solutions to problems, common workarounds, and links to useful Web resources. The firm also maintains an experts' database that profiles each employee in the firm and identifies each person's skills and areas of expertise. You have been hired by Know IT to conduct a knowledge audit. This involves identifying both tacit and explicit knowledge sources within the firm, as well as the processes and procedures in place that facilitate the collection, retention, and retrieval of knowledge across the enterprise. What kinds of things would you be looking for in your assessment? What barriers can you think of that might deter workers from contributing or sharing their knowledge with others? Would these barriers be more predominant in a consulting firm, less predominant, or the same as in other types of companies? What incentives or changes could you put in place to increase knowledge collection, retention, sharing, and use within the firm?

connect **LEARNSMART** **SMARTBOOK**

For more information on the resources available from McGraw-Hill Ryerson, go to www.mheducation.ca/he/solutions.

ENDNOTES

1. Richard Van Zandt," Billy Beane's Perfect Draft," April 13, 2006, http://baseballevolution.com/guest/richard/rvzbeane1.html, accessed April 7, 2014; http://en.wikipedia.org/wiki/Moneyball, accessed April 7, 2014.

2. Matt Hartley, "How Pro Sports Teams Are Using Data Analytics to Draft Better Players," *Financial Post*, September 3, 2013, http://business.financialpost.com/2013/09/03/pro-sports-teams-turning-to-data-anlaytics-to-fill-seats/?__lsa=3f15-bfa8, accessed April 7, 2014.

3. www.sas.com/en_us/customers/orlando-magic.html, accessed April 7, 2014.

4. Ibid.; www.sas.com/en_us/industry/sports.html, accessed April 7, 2014.

5. Thomas Davenport, "Learning from Analytics in Sports in CIO Journal of *The Wall Street Journal*," March 5, 2014, http://blogs.wsj.com/cio/2014/03/05/learning-from-analytics-in-sports, accessed April 7, 2014; Susan Slusser, "Michael Lewis on A's 'Moneyball' Legacy," September 17, 2011, www.sfgate.com/athletics/article/Michael-Lewis-on-A-s-Moneyball-legacy-2309126.php, accessed April 7, 2014.

6. "Ford's Vision," http://donate.pewclimate.org/docUploads/Ford.pdf, accessed June 18, 2003.

7. Mitch Betts, "Unexpected Insights,"*Computerworld*, April 14, 2003, www.computerworld.com, accessed September 4, 2003.

8. "Orvis Uses Unica Campaign, eMessage, and NetInsight to Achieve Greater Customer Intimacy—and Record Profits," 2010, http://ibm.com, accessed August 15, 2011.

9. "Data Mining: What General Managers Need to Know," *Harvard Management Update*, October 1999.

10. "Real Time Payments Processing: Reshaping the Payments Industry Landscape," www.distra.com, accessed August 15, 2011.

11. Meridith Levinson, "Harrah's Knows What You Did Last Night," *Darwin Magazine*, May 2001; "Harrah's Entertainment Wins TDWI's 2000 DW Award," www.hpcwire.com, accessed October 10, 2003; Gary Loveman, "Diamonds in the Data Mine," *Harvard Business Review*, May 2003, p. 109; "NCR—Harrah's

Entertainment, Inc.," www.ncr.com, accessed October 12, 2003; "Cognos and Harrah's Entertainment Win Prestigous Data Warehousing Award," 2002 news release, www.cognos.com, accessed October 14, 2003; Kim Nash, "Casinos Hit Jackpot with Customer Data," www.cnn.com, accessed October 14, 2003; Michael S. Malone, "IPO Fever," *Wired*, March 2004.

12. "An Exceptional Customer Experience Each and Every Time," 2009, www.jacada.com/customers/case-study_lillian-vernon.htm?AspxAutoDetectCookieSupport=1, accessed August 16, 2011.

13. "More Insight, Better Decisions," *KMWorld*, April 2004, Volume 13, Issue 4, p. 6.

14. "Knowledge Management Research Center," *CIO Magazine*, www.cio.com/research/knowledge, accessed December 2005.

15. http://connectivity.opentext.com, accessed September 6, 2011; "Open Text Exceed on Demand Empowers Fairchild Semiconductor," 2011, http://connectivity.opentext.com/resource-centre/success-stories/Success_Story_ Empowers_Fairchild_Semiconductor_to_Work_Faster_and_Smarter.pdf, accessed September 6, 2011.

16. Megan Santosus, "In the Know," *CIO Magazine*, January 2006.

17. Ibid.

18. "The Critical Shift to Flexible Business Intelligence," used with permission; Claudia Imhoff, Intelligent Solutions, Inc., "What Every Marketer Wants—and Needs—from Technology," used with permission; Claudia Imhoff, Intelligent Solutions, Inc., "Enterprise Business Intelligence," May 2006, used with permission; Jill Dyche, Baseline Consulting Group, "The Business Case for Data Warehousing," 2005, used with permission.

19. Alvin Szott, Business Executive, IBM, personal communication, May 2013; Guillermo Salazar, Managing Director, Quattro Integration Group (Now Director, Deloitte Canada), personal communication, May 2013; Bill Laycock, Director Database Marketing, ATB Financial Services, personal communication, April2013; Virginia Galt, "The Fastest-Growing Job Market You've Never Heard Of," July 4, 2013, www.theglobeandmail.com/report-on-business/careers/career-advice/the-fastest-growing-job-market-youve-never-heard-of/article10505923, accessed July 12, 2013.

20. Stephan Lawson, "Cisco to Slash 4,000 Jobs in Bid to Move Faster," August 14, 2013, www.itworld.com/it-management/369162/cisco-slash-4000-jobs-bid-move-faster?source=ITWNLE_nlt_today_2013-08-15, accessed August 15, 2013.

21. Charles Duhigg, "How Companies Learn Your Secrets," February 16, 2012, www.nytimes.com/2012/02/19/magazine/shopping-habits.html?pagewanted=all, accessed July 12, 2013.

22. "Data, Data Everywhere," special report, *The Economist*, February 25, 2010, www.economist.com/node/15557443, accessed August 24, 2011.

23. Ibid.

24. Ibid.

25. Ibid.

26. Ibid.

27. Ibid.

28. Ibid.

29. Ibid.

30. Ibid.

31. Ibid.

32. "SAS Software by Industry," www.sas.com/industry, accessed July 15, 2013; Kelly McDonald, Manager Consulting—Technology Strategy & Architecture, Deloitte, personal communication, March, 2013; Sean Hennesey, Managing Director, Quattro Integration (Now Director, Deloitte), personal communication, November, 2012; "Deloitte Acquiring Quattro Integration: Strengthens Energy, Resource Capability," *Edmonton Journal*, July 8, 2013, www.edmontonjournal.com/business/Deloitte+acquiring+Quattro +Integration+strengthens+energy/8629210/story.html accessed August 19, 2013.

33. "D-FW Defense Contractors Show Mixed Fortunes since September 11," 2002, www.bizjournals.com/dallas/ stories/2002/09/09/focus2.htm, accessed June 8, 2004; Steve Konicki, "Collaboration Is Cornerstone of $19B Defense Contract," 2000, www.business2.com/content/magazine/indepth/2000/07/11/17966, accessed June 8, 2004.

34. Andrea Di Malo, "Joining Up Government Across Tiers: Canada's BizPal," *Gartner Industry Research*, February 2006.

35. www.ibm.com/social-business/us/en, accessed August 15, 2013; Lisa Quast, "Why Knowledge Management Is Important to the Success of Your Company," August 20, 2012, www.forbes.com/sites/lisaquast/2012/08/20/ why-knowledge-management-is-important-to-the-success-of-your-company, accessed August 15, 2013; "Transforming Knowledge Management and Collaboration in the Intelligence Community," 2012, www.accenture.com/SiteCollectionDocuments/PDF/Accenture-Semantic-Wiki-PoV.pdf, accessed August 15, 2013.

36. "FatWire Content Server Helps Summit Health Offer a Personalized Web Experience to Their Customers," www.fatwire.com/customers/industries/healthcare# tab2, accessed August 26, 2011.

37. "Formtastic: Paper Company Cuts Own Paper Consumption," www.quadrantsoftware.com/resources/success-stories/fraser-paper-success, accessed August 26, 2011; "Fraser Papers Seeks Bankruptcy Protection," June 18, 2009, www.cbc.ca/news/business/story/2009/06/18/fraser-bankruptcy-protection.html, accessed August 28, 2011; Scott Vallely, "Fraser Paper to Emerge with New Name," March 9, 2010, http://psvallely. blogspot.com/2010/03/fraser-paper-to-emerge-with-new-name.htm, accessed August 28, 2011.

38. "Customer Success Stories: Allianz Suisse," 2008, http://m.sybase.com/files/Success_Stories/Sybase_ Allianz_SS_022108.pdf, accessed August 26, 2011.

39. www.allconferenceservices.com/business-video-conferencing.html, accessed June 23, 2010.

40. Ibid.

41. Ibid.

42. Ibid.

43. Brian Detlor, *Towards Knowledge Portals: From Human Issues to Intelligent Agents* (Dordrecht, The Netherlands: Kluwer Academic Publishers, 2004).

44. David Gootzit, "Key Issues for Enterprise Portals, 2008,"*Gartner Research*, ID Number G00154863.

45. C. C. Shilakes and J. Tylman, *Enterprise Information Portals*, white paper (New York: Merrill Lynch, 1998).

46. Mzwandile Shongwe, "Can Mobile Phones Be Used for Knowledge Management?," 2010, presentation at the Moi University Conference 2010, www.mu.ac.ke/academic/schools/is/muconference2010/mzwandile.pdf, accessed August 29, 2011; "M-Learning and Mobility," www.educause.edu/ELI/ LearningTechnlologies/ MLearningandMobility/12397, accessed August 29, 2011.

47. "HP Unveils Halo Collaboration Studio," December 12, 2005, www.hp.com; "HP Halo Telepresence and Video Conferencing Solutions," http://h71028.www7.hp.com/enterprise/cache/570006-0-0-31-338.html, accessed May 11, 2014; Robert Mullins, "Polycom Buys HP's Halo Videoconferencing Unit," June 1, 2011, www.networkcomputing.com/unified-communications/polycom-buys-hps-halo-videoconferencing-unit/d/d-id/1098065, accessed May 11, 2014.

48. www.statoil.com, accessed November 17, 2009.

49. Bjorn Erik Munkvold, Tero Paivarinta, Anne Kristine Hodne, and Elin Stangeland, "Contemporary Issues of Enterprise Content Management: The Case of Statoil," *Scandinavian Journal of Information Systems*, Volume 18, Issue 2 (2006), pp. 69–100, www.cs.aau.dk/SJIS/journal/volumes/volume18/no2/munkvoldetal-18-2.pdf; Kristian Korsvik, "Enterprise Content Management in Practice: A Case Study in Statoil Oil Trading and Supply" (Kristiansand, Norway: University of Agder, 2010).

50. www.conferenceboard.ca/education/best-practices/pdf/BellCanada.pdf, accessed November 1, 2009.

51. www.conferenceboard.ca/education/best-practices/pdf/BellCanada.pdf, accessed November 1, 2009; Jouamaa Khalid, Associate Director, Market Knowledge Centre, Bell Canada, personal email communication, October 28, 2009.

Databases, Data Warehouses, and Data Mining

LO 4.1 | Describe the structure of a relational database.

LO 4.2 | Describe the advantages to storing data in a relational database.

LO 4.3 | Explain how users interact with a database management system, the advantage of data-driven websites, and the primary methods of integrating data and information across multiple databases in organizations.

LO 4.4 | Describe data warehouse fundamentals and advantages.

LO 4.5 | Describe data mining, and explain the relationship between data mining and data warehousing.

Information is a powerful asset, a key organizational resource that enables companies to carry out business initiatives and plans. Companies that are able to manage this key resource well are primed for competitive advantage and success. This chapter provides an overview of database fundamentals and the steps required to integrate various bits of data stored across multiple, operational data stores into a comprehensive and centralized repository of summarized information.

As a business student, you must understand the tools that help manage information and the different types of questions you would use a transactional database or enterprise data warehouse to answer. You need to be aware of the complexity of storing transactional data in relational databases and the level of effort required to transform operational data into meaningful, summarized analytical information. You need to realize the power of data and information and the competitive advantage a data warehouse brings to an organization in terms of facilitating business intelligence. Understanding this power will help you compete better in a global marketplace, and will help you make smarter, more informed, data- and information-supported managerial decisions.

The Case for Business Intelligence at Netflix

As a consumer you see analytics or business intelligence at work on a regular basis. Examples are everywhere, such as when you go to the Web and sign in at sites such as **Amazon.ca** or **Netflix.com**, and get a personalized Web page of items that you might be interested in purchasing. If you are a regular visitor and Total Rewards member at one of the casinos owned by Caesars Entertainment, you might notice that when you sit down at a slot machine and insert your Total Rewards card the attendant arrives shortly with your favourite drink. Other examples are customer segmentation strategies used at Best Buy, or the strategies used at RBC Financial to identify the most profitable customers and ways to turn less profitable customers into more profitable ones. All of these companies and many more use databases or data warehouses to collect your search data, purchase data, or track your activities (like the drinks you order while gambling in the casino), and then by using data mining tools and business intelligence they turn this data into information that can boost their bottom lines.

Reed Hastings and a $40 Late Fee

So let's go back to a time before Netflix. Reed Hastings, co-founder and CEO of Netflix and a former math teacher, was hit with a $40 late fee for *Apollo 13* at Blockbuster Video, which got him thinking about the video rental business model. Why did video stores not work like health clubs where you could use the service as much or as little as you wanted for a flat monthly fee? So, armed with US$750 million from the sale of a former venture, Hastings co-founded Netflix in 1997. As of early 2014, Netflix had more than 40 million subscribers with over 33million members in the United States and over 1 million in Canada, and was the world's leading Internet subscription service for watching movies and TV shows. It expanded to service Latin America—the Caribbean, Mexico, and Central and South America in September 2011. In January 2012 it launched streaming-only services in the United Kingdom and Ireland, and reached the million-subscriber mark eight months later. In October 2012 it expanded into Norway, Denmark, Sweden, and Finland, and has since expanded services to the Netherlands with plans for Germany and France. In 2013, Netflix also became a "streaming TV network service" in the United States.[1]

The Science and the Art of Netflix

There is more than just art to the personalized page that appears when you sign in to Netflix. Like a number of other companies using analytics these days—Amazon, Caesars Entertainment, Capital One, and the New England Patriots—Netflix is led by a CEO with a background in math or analytics. Due to this leadership, Netflix is a company with a strong scientific culture, and when it comes to choosing which movies to distribute, analytics plays a large role. That said, there is also an art to picking movies, according to Tom Sarandos, Netflix's chief content officer. Sarandos says choosing which movies to distribute is 70 percent science and 30 percent art.

The question then becomes: How does the movie selection process work? Before we start, one must understand that the box office success of a movie is only a proxy for awareness of a movie's existence; it does not necessarily translate into demand for the movie in the rental market, and box office success or failure does not mean success or failure of the movie in the rental market. Because of these two facts, distribution managers use their experience to formulate a hypothesis of a movie's possible success in the rental market. They then follow this up with the science of analytics to help them make the final decision as to what movies to distribute.

The Analytics

Where do the analytics come from? First, all of the Netflix customers' searching behaviours, movie rankings, and click behaviours are recorded in Netflix's NoSQL database. Then, using tools such as Cinematch, Netflix's algorithm, the data collected are analyzed and used to help match customers to movie recommendations. In fact, at one point Netflix offered a million-dollar prize to anyone that could improve Cinematch's accuracy by 10 percent.

So what does Cinematch do? It defines clusters of movies, connects customer movie rankings to the clusters, and then uses this connection to recommend movies to a particular customer. It does all of this in the blink of an eye, because it can evaluate thousands of ratings per second. The result is a personalized Web page with movie rankings for each customer that visits the Netflix-website.

In addition, Cinematch also considers Netflix's inventory condition in its recommendations. Netflix will often recommend movies that fit the customer's profile but that are not in high demand, in order to take advantage of "the long tail." In addition to the movie clusters, rankings, and inventory condition, Netflix uses a somewhat controversial practice called "throttling" in its analysis. In throttling, infrequent customers are given priority over frequent customers for DVD rentals. This might seem strange, but since shipping is free to customers and the monthly charge is fixed, infrequent customers are Netflix's most profitable customers, and as in any business it's best to keep your most profitable customers satisfied.

What Does This Mean?

Business intelligence is important to Netflix, as it is part of its secret of success. According to Hastings, "if the Starbucks secret is a smile when you get your latte, ours is the Web site adapts to the individual's taste." By collecting customer data in their database and then analyzing the data, Netflix is able to have its website adapt to the personal tastes of each of its over 40 million.[2]

4.1 DATABASES

LO1 STORING TRANSACTIONAL DATA

Transactional data are stored in a database. Operational-based information systems, such as SCM and CRM systems, access and maintain these data. Records retrieved from the databases can be used to provide answers to questions and help make decisions. The computer program used to manage and query a database is known as a *database management system (DBMS)*. The properties and design of DBMSs are included in the studies of information science, information systems, and computer science.

The central concept of a database is that of a collection of records. Typically, a given database has a structural description of the type of raw facts it holds, known as a *schema*. The schema describes the objects represented and the relationships among them. There are a number of different ways of organizing a schema, that is, of modelling the database structure. These are known as *database models* (or *data models*). The most commonly used model today is the relational model, which represents all data in the form of multiple related tables each consisting of rows and columns. This model represents relationships by using values common to more than one table. Other models, such as the hierarchical model and the network model, use a more explicit representation of relationships.

Many professionals consider a collection of data to constitute a database only if it has certain properties; for example, if the data are managed to ensure integrity and quality, if there is shared access by a community of users, if the collection has a schema, or if it supports a query language. However, there is no universally agreed upon definition of these properties.[3]

RELATIONAL DATABASE FUNDAMENTALS

There are many different models for organizing data in a database, including the hierarchical database, the network database, and the most prevalent, the relational database model. Broadly defined, a ***database*** maintains data about various types of objects (e.g., inventory), events (e.g., transactions), people (e.g., employees), and places (e.g., warehouses). In a ***hierarchical database model***, data are organized into a treelike structure that allows repeating data using parent–child relationships, in such a way that it cannot have too many relationships. Hierarchical structures were widely used in the first mainframe database management systems. However, owing to their restrictions, hierarchical structures often cannot be used to relate to structures that exist in the real world. The ***network database model*** is a flexible way of representing objects and their relationships. Where the hierarchical model structures data as a tree of records, each record having one parent record and many children, the network model allows each record to have multiple parent and child records, forming a lattice structure. The ***relational database model*** is a type of database that stores data in the form of logically related two-dimensional tables. This text focuses on the relational database model, because that is the most prevalent form used in business.

Consider how a bottling company might implement an inventory-tracking database to improve order accuracy, decrease order response time, and potentially increase sales.

Traditionally, the company sent distribution trucks to each customer's premises to take orders and deliver stock. Many problems were associated with this process, including numerous data entry errors, which caused filling orders to take longer than expected. To remedy the situation, the bottling company created pre-sales teams equipped with handheld devices to visit customers and take orders electronically. On returning to the office, the teams synchronized orders with the company's inventory tracking database to ensure automated processing and rapid dispatch of accurate orders to customers.

Entities, Tables, Fields, and Records

Figure 4.1 illustrates the primary concepts of the relational database model based on the terminology used in Microsoft Access—entities, tables, fields, records, keys, and relationships. An ***entity*** is a person, place, thing, transaction, or event about which data are stored. A ***table*** (also known as an ***entity class*** or file) is a collection of similar entities. The tables of interest in Figure 4.1 are CUSTOMER, ORDER, ORDER LINE, PRODUCT, and DISTRIBUTOR. Notice that in each table the collection of similar entities is stored in a different two-dimensional structure. ***Fields***, also called ***attributes*** or columns, are characteristics or properties of a table. In Figure 4.1, the fields for CUSTOMER include *Customer ID*, *Customer Name*, *Contact Name*, and *Phone*. Fields for PRODUCT include *Product ID*, *Product Description*, and *Price*. The columns in the table contain the fields. ***Records***, also called ***instances***, is the data about each entity in a table like Dave's Sub Shop in the CUSTOMER table and occupies one row in its respective table. Each row contains a record.

Keys and Relationships

To manage and organize various tables within the relational database model, developers must identify primary keys and foreign keys and use them to create logical relationships. A ***primary key*** is a field (or group of fields) that uniquely identifies a given entity in a table. In CUSTOMER, the *Customer ID* uniquely identifies each record (customer) in the table and is the primary key. Primary keys are important because they provide a way of distinguishing each record in a table by making each record unique.

A ***foreign key*** in the relational database model is a primary key of one table that appears as a field in another table and acts to provide a logical relationship between the two tables. Consider Manitoba Shipping, one of the distributors listed in the DISTRIBUTOR table. Its primary key, *Distributor ID*, is MB8001. Notice that *Distributor ID* also appears as an attribute in the ORDER table. This establishes the fact that Manitoba Shipping (*Distributor ID* MB8001) was responsible for delivering orders 34561 and 34562 to the appropriate customer(s). Therefore, *Distributor ID* in the ORDER table creates a logical relationship (who shipped what order) between ORDER and DISTRIBUTOR.

Using the database structure in Figure 4.1 the bottling company is able to collect the right data together to create an individual invoice for each of its clients, such as Dave's Sub Shop.

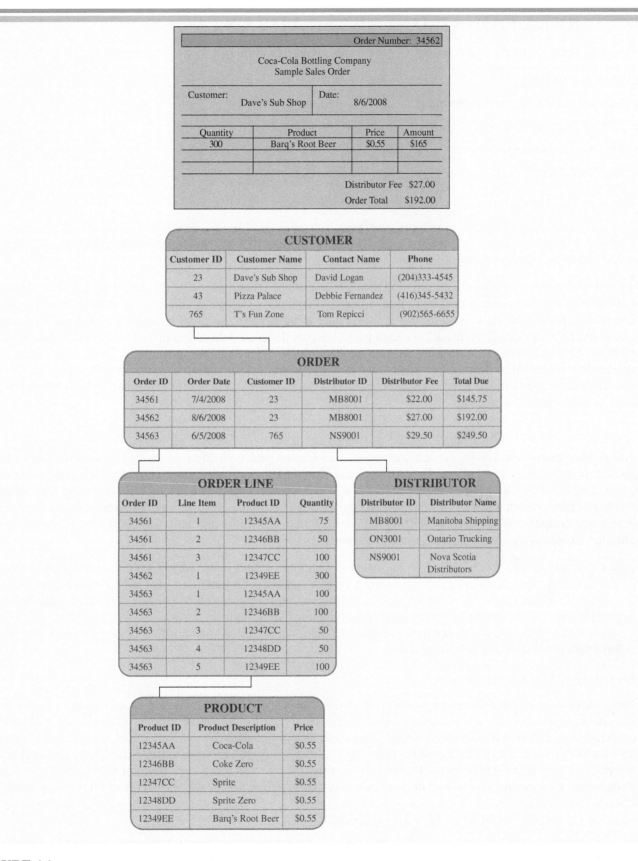

FIGURE 4.1

Potential Relational Database for the Coca-Cola Bottling Company

LO2 | RELATIONAL DATABASE ADVANTAGES

From a business perspective, databases offer many advantages, including:

- Increased flexibility
- Increased scalability and performance
- Reduced data redundancy
- Increased data integrity (quality)
- Increased data security

Increased Flexibility

Good databases mirror business structures, and handle changes quickly and easily, just as any good business needs to be able to handle changes quickly and easily. Equally importantly, databases provide flexibility in allowing each user to access the data in whatever way best suits his or her needs.

The distinction between logical and physical views is important in understanding flexible database user views. The *physical view* of data deals with the physical storage of data on a storage device such as a hard disk. The *logical view* of data focuses on how users logically access data to meet their particular business needs. This separation of logical and physical views is what allows each user to access database data differently. That is, while a database has only one physical view, it can easily support multiple logical views. One user might want a customer report presented in alphabetical format, in which case last name appears before first name. Another user might want customer names appearing as first name and then last name. Both are easily achievable, but they are different logical views of the same physical data.

Increased Scalability and Performance

Unlike other provinces that piggyback income tax calculation and collection on federal government tax returns, Quebec directly levies and collects its own personal income tax. This autonomy gives Quebec greater leeway in applying taxation as a tool of public policy, but it also burdens the province with the task of storing and protecting swelling, terabyte-sized amounts of taxpayer data managed in separate databases and deployed across a multitude of servers and desktops. When Quebec's Revenue Ministry recognized this problem it implemented a single, scalable solution that would satisfy the province's database needs.[4]

Only a database could "scale" to handle the massive volumes of data involved in Quebec's collection of personal income tax data. *Scalability* refers to how well a system can adapt to increased demands. *Performance* measures how quickly a system performs a certain process or transaction. Some organizations, such as eBay, must be able to support hundreds or thousands of online users including employees, partners, customers, and suppliers, who all want to access and share data. Databases today scale to exceptional levels, allowing all types of users and programs to perform data processing and searching tasks.

Reduced Data Redundancy

Data redundancy is the duplication of data, or storing the same data in multiple places. Redundant data occurs because organizations frequently capture and store the same data in multiple locations. The primary problem with redundant data is that it is often inconsistent, making it difficult to determine which values are the most current or most accurate. Not having correct data is confusing and frustrating for employees and disruptive to an organization. One primary goal of a database is to eliminate data redundancy by recording each piece of data in only one place in the database. Eliminating data redundancy saves space, makes performing updates easier, and improves quality.

Increased Data Integrity (Quality)

Data integrity is a measure of the quality of data. Within a database environment, *integrity constraints* are rules that help ensure the quality of data. Integrity constraints are defined and built into the database. The database (more appropriately, the DBMS) ensures that users can never violate these constraints. There are two types of integrity constraints: (1) relational integrity constraints, and (2) business-critical integrity constraints.

Relational integrity constraints are rules that enforce basic and fundamental data constraints. For example, a referential integrity constraint would not allow someone to create an order for a non-existent customer, provide a mark up percentage that was negative, or order zero pounds of raw materials from a supplier.

Business-critical integrity constraints enforce business rules vital to an organization's success and often require more insight and knowledge than relational integrity constraints. Consider a supplier of fresh produce to large grocery chains such as Safeway. The supplier might implement a business-critical integrity constraint stating that no produce returns are accepted after 15 days past delivery. That would make sense because of the chance of spoilage of the produce. These types of integrity constraints tend to mirror the very rules by which an organization achieves success.

Specifying and enforcing integrity constraints produces higher-quality data that provide better support for business decisions. Organizations that establish specific procedures for developing integrity constraints typically see a decline in data error rates and an increase in the use of organizational data.

Increased Data Security

Data are organizational assets. Like any asset, an organization must protect its data from unauthorized users or misuse. As systems become increasingly complex and more available over the Internet, security becomes a bigger issue. Databases offer many security features, including passwords, access levels, and access controls.

Passwords provide authentication of the user who is gaining access to the system. Access levels determine who has access to the different types of data, and access controls determine what type of data access they have. Customer service representatives might need read-only access to customer order data so they can answer customer order inquiries; they might not have or need the authority to change or delete order data. Managers might require access to employee files, but they should have access only to their own employees' files, not the employee files for the entire company. Various database security features ensure that individuals have only certain types of access to certain types of data.

As well as data security, databases can impact personal security. For example, the National Integrated Interagency Information (N-III) system allows police and law enforcement agencies from coast to coast to produce consolidated database search results across multiple police databases from a single seamless query. In this way, N-III helps ensure Canadian homes and communities remain safe by delivering complete and accurate data to Canadian law enforcement agencies.[5]

LO3 | DATABASE MANAGEMENT SYSTEMS

The Beer Store is the primary distribution and sales channel for beer in Ontario. It operates 447 stores and serves around 17,000 licensed customers, 638 Liquor Control Board of Ontario stores and 142 retail partners, 76 northern agents, and 8 distribution centres. The Beer Store offers over 477 beer brands from 104 brewers around the world. Using a number of applications on top of a database management system, the Beer Store modernized its operations with a new point of sale system. The new system not only restored employee confidence but is able to communicate with each of the 447 stores on a per-transaction basis. This has allowed the Beer Store to achieve accurate and timely inventory reporting, and build routine opening and closing procedures at each location. It has also made it possible to better manage inventories and reduce wage costs in each of its retail locations.[6]

A database management system accesses data from a database. A *database management system (DBMS)* is software through which users and application programs interact with a database. The user sends requests to the DBMS and the DBMS performs the actual manipulation of the data in the database. There are two primary ways users can interact with a DBMS, (1) directly and (2) indirectly, as displayed in Figure 4.2. In either case, users access the DBMS and the DBMS accesses the database.

DATA-DRIVEN WEBSITES

For websites with continually changing information—press releases, new product information, updated pricing, etc.—it is best to build a data-driven website. The pages on such a site must change according to what a visitor is interested in browsing. Consider a company selling sports cars. A database is created with data on each of the currently available cars (e.g., make, model, engine details, photograph, etc.). A visitor to the site selects Porsche, enters the price range he or she is interested in, and clicks "Go." He or she is presented with information on available cars within the price range and an invitation to purchase or request more information from the company. Via a secure administration area on the site, the company has the ability to modify, add cars to, or remove cars from the database. Examples of data-driven websites are Environment Canada's Weather Office (**www.weatheroffice.ec.gc.ca/canada_e.html**) and Statistics Canada (**www.statcan.gc.ca**).[7]

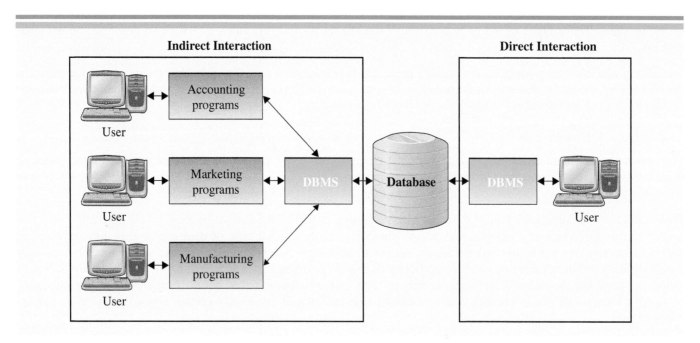

FIGURE 4.2

Interacting Directly and Indirectly with a Database Through a DBMS

A *data-driven website* is an interactive website kept constantly updated and relevant to customer needs by use of a database. Such sites are especially useful when they offer a great deal of information, products, or services. Visitors are frequently angered if they are buried under an avalanche of information when searching a site. A data-driven website invites visitors to select and view what they are interested in by means of a query. The site analyzes the query and then builds a customized Web page in real time that satisfies it. In this sense, data-driven websites are *dynamic* in nature.

Figure 4.3 displays a Google user querying the term "business intelligence" and the database sending back the appropriate Web page.[8] There are many advantages associated with data-driven websites or pages beyond the abilities to collect and query data (see Figure 4.4).[9]

Integrating Data Among Multiple Databases

At one time, every department in the U.K.'s Ministry of Defence (MOD) and army headquarters had its own systems, each system had its own database, and sharing data among the departments was difficult. Manually inputting the same data multiple times into the different systems was time-consuming and inefficient. In many cases, management could not even compile the data it required to answer questions and make decisions.

The army solved the problem by integrating its systems, building connections between its many databases. These integrations allow the army's multiple systems to automatically communicate by passing data between the databases, eliminating the need for manual data entry into multiple systems, because after entering the data once the integrations send the data immediately to all other databases. The integrations have not only enabled the different departments to share data, but also dramatically increased the quality of the data. The army can now generate reports detailing its state of readiness and other vital issues, nearly impossible tasks before building the integrations.[10]

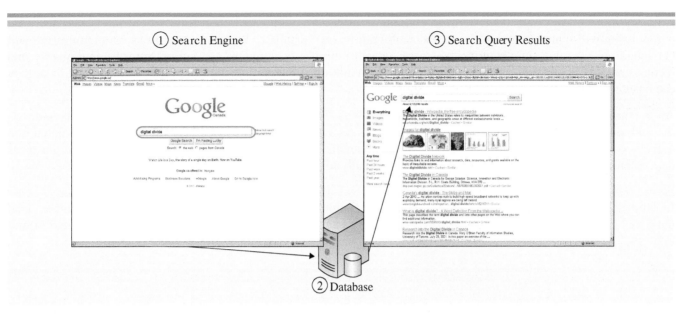

FIGURE 4.3

Google: A Data-Driven Website

- *Development capability.* Allows the website owner to make changes anytime—all without having to rely on a developer or knowing HTML programming. A well-structured data-driven website enables updating with little or no training.

- *Content management capability.* A static website requires a programmer to make updates. This adds an unnecessary layer between the business and its Web content, which can lead to misunderstandings and slow turnaround for desired changes.

- *Future expandability.* A data-driven website can grow faster than would be possible with a static site. Changing the layout, displays, and functionality of the site (adding more features and sections) is easier.

- *Minimization of human error.* Even the most competent programmer, given the task of maintaining many pages, will overlook things and make mistakes. This leads to bugs and inconsistencies that can be time-consuming and expensive to track down and fix. Unfortunately, users who come across these bugs will likely get irritated and leave the site. A well-designed data-driven website has "error trapping" mechanisms to ensure that required information is filled out correctly and that content is entered and displayed in its correct format.

- *Less production and update costs.* A data-driven website can be updated and "published" by any competent data entry or administrative person. In addition to being convenient and more affordable, changes and updates will take a fraction of the time that they would with a static site. While training a competent programmer can take months or even years, a data entry person can be trained in 30 to 60 minutes.

- *More efficiency.* By their very nature, computers are excellent at keeping volumes of information intact. With a data-driven solution, the system keeps track of the templates, so users do not have to. Global changes to layout, navigation, or site structure need to be programmed only once, in one place, and the site itself will take care of propagating those changes to the appropriate pages and areas. A data-driven infrastructure improves the reliability and stability of a website, while greatly reducing the chance of "breaking" some part of the site when adding new areas.

- *Better stability.* Any programmer who has to update a website from static templates must be organized to keep track of all the source files. If a programmer departs unexpectedly, it might involve re-creating existing work if those source files cannot be found. Also, if there have been any changes to the templates, the new programmer must be careful to use only the latest version. With a data-driven website, there is peace of mind. Content is never lost—even if your programmer is.

FIGURE 4.4

Data-Driven Website Advantages

An *integration* allows separate systems to communicate directly with each other. Similarly to the U.K.'s army, an organization will maintain multiple systems, each with its own database. Without integrations, an organization will (1) spend considerable time entering the same data in multiple systems and (2) suffer from the low quality and inconsistency typically embedded in redundant data. While most integrations do not eliminate redundant data, they can ensure its consistency across multiple systems.

An organization can choose from two integration methods. The first is to create forward and backward integrations that link processes (and their underlying databases) in the value chain. A *forward integration* takes data entered into a given system and sends it automatically to all downstream systems and processes. A *backward integration* takes data entered into a given system and sends it automatically to all upstream systems and processes.

Figure 4.5 demonstrates how this method works across the systems or processes of sales, order entry, order fulfillment, and billing. In the order entry system, for example, an employee updates the data for a customer. That data, via the integrations, is sent upstream to the sales system and downstream to the order fulfillment and billing systems.

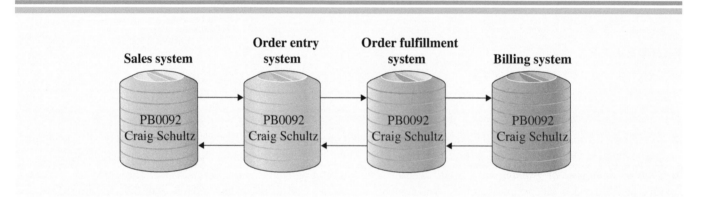

FIGURE 4.5

Forward and Backward Customer Data Integration

Ideally, an organization wants to build both forward and backward integrations, which provide the flexibility to create, update, and delete data in any of the systems. However, integrations are expensive and difficult to build and maintain, and most organizations build only forward integrations (sales through billing in Figure 4.5). Building only forward integrations implies that a change in the initial system (sales) results in changes in all the other systems. Integration of data is not possible for any changes occurring outside the initial system, which again can result in inconsistent organizational data. To address this issue, organizations can enforce business rules that all systems, other than the initial system, have read-only access to the integrated data. This requires users to change data in the initial system only, which always triggers the integration and ensures that organizational data does not get out of sync.

The second integration method builds a central data repository. Figure 4.6 provides an example of customer data integrated using this method across four different systems in an organization. Users can create, update, and delete customer information only in the central customer database. As users perform these tasks on the central customer database, integrations automatically send the new and/or updated customer data to the other systems. The other systems limit users to read-only access of the customer data stored in them. Again, this method does not eliminate redundancy, but it does ensure consistency of the same data among multiple systems.

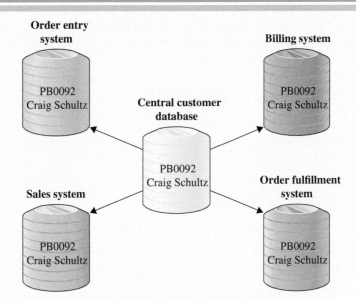

FIGURE 4.6
Integrated Customer Data

OPENING CASE QUESTIONS

The Case for Business Intelligence at Netflix

1. What is the impact to Netflix if the information contained in its database is of low quality?

2. Review the five common characteristics of high-quality information and rank them in order of importance to Netflix.

3. How might Netflix resolve issues of poor information in their customer movie reviews?

4. Identify the different types of entities that might be stored in Netflix's database.

5. Why is database technology so important to Netflix and its business model?

4.2 DATA WAREHOUSING

LO4 ACCESSING ORGANIZATIONAL INFORMATION

When Hardee's introduced the Monster Thick burger across the United States, the burger contained 1,420 calories in its two third-pound Angus beef patties, three slices of processed cheese, and four slices of bacon topped with a dollop of mayonnaise on a sesame seed bun. Why does a national restaurant chain introduce such an artery-clogging item in a nation with a growing epidemic of obesity and do it with the confidence that they have a winning product?

The quick answer is that CKE Restaurants, the parent company of Hardee's, used its organizational data to help it make the decision—through the use of its business intelligence systems, ironically called CPR (CKE Performance Reporting). CKE was also able to determine with CPR whether the burger would be cannibalizing the sales of other burgers and whether it was worth the cost of production. In test markets, the burger exceeded expectations, which led to the decision for a nationwide launch supported by a US$7 million advertising campaign. Sales at Hardee's restaurants went up an average 5.8 percent year over year, the Monster Thick burger being responsible for most of the increase.[11]

HISTORY OF DATA WAREHOUSING

In the 1990s, as organizations began to need more timely information about their business, they found that traditional operational information systems were too cumbersome to provide relevant information efficiently and quickly. Operational systems typically include detailed accounting, order entry, customer service, and sales data, and are not appropriate for business analysis for the following reasons:

- Data from other operational applications are not included.
- Operational systems are not integrated, or not available in one place.
- Operational data are mainly current—do not include the history that is required to make good decisions.
- Operational data frequently have quality issues (errors)—the data need to be cleansed.
- Without data history, it is difficult to tell how and why things change over time.
- Operational systems are designed to handle transaction processing, not analysis and decision support.

During the latter half of the 20th century and even through the first decade of the 21st century, the numbers and types of databases increased. Many large businesses found themselves with data scattered across multiple platforms and variations of technology, making it almost impossible for any one individual to use data from multiple sources. Completing reporting requests across operational systems could take days or weeks using antiquated reporting tools that were designed, more or less, to execute the business rather than run the business. From this idea, the data warehouse was born as a place where relevant summarized and aggregated data (information) could be held for completing strategic reports for management. The key here is the word *strategic*, because most executives were less concerned with the day-to-day operations than they were with a more overall look at the model and business functions.

A key idea within data warehousing is to take data from multiple platforms/technologies (as varied as spreadsheets, databases, and Word files) and put them in a common location that uses a common querying tool. In this way, operational databases could be held on whatever system was most efficient for the operational business, while the reporting/strategic information could be held in a common location using a common language. Data warehouses take this a step further, giving the information stored in the data warehouse commonality by defining what each term means and keeping it standard. An example of this is gender: it can be referred to in many ways (Male, Female, M/F, 1/0), but should be standardized in a data warehouse with one common way of referring to each sex (M/F).

This design makes decision support more readily available without affecting day-to-day operations. One aspect of a data warehouse that should be stressed is that it is *not* a location for *all* of a business's information, but rather a location for information that is interesting, or that will assist in making strategic decisions relative to the organization's overall mission.

Data warehousing is about extending the transformation of transactional data into analytical information. Data warehouses offer strategic level, external, integrated, and historical information so businesses can make projections, identify trends, and decide key business issues. The data warehouse collects and stores integrated sets of historical data from multiple operational systems and feeds them to one or more data marts. It may also provide end-user access to support enterprise-wide views of information.

DATA WAREHOUSE FUNDAMENTALS

A *data warehouse* is a logical collection of analytical information—gathered from many different operational databases—that supports business analysis activities and decision-making tasks. The term *data warehouse* was coined in 1990 by Bill Inmon, known as the "Father of Data Warehousing." He describes a data warehouse as a subject-oriented, integrated, time-variant, and non-volatile collection of information used to support organizational decision making, where:

- *Subject-oriented* means that information is organized around major subject areas of the company (e.g., customer, vendor, product) instead of around a company's ongoing business operations or business applications found in transactional processing systems.

- *Integrated* means that information is gathered into a data warehouse from a variety of operational data sources and merged into a coherent and consistent whole.

- *Time-variant* means that all information in a data warehouse is time-stamped with a particular time period, such as weekly, monthly, quarterly, or yearly.

- *Non-volatile* means that information in a data warehouse is stable and, once loaded, never changes, so as new information is added, old information is never removed or modified.[12]

The primary purpose of a data warehouse is to aggregate transactional data into analytical information throughout an organization into a single repository in such a way that employees can make decisions and undertake business analysis activities. Therefore, while operational databases store the details of all transactions (e.g., the sale of a product) and events (e.g., hiring a new employee), data warehouses store that same data but in an aggregated form better suited to supporting decision-making tasks. Aggregation, in this instance, can include totals, counts, averages, and the like.

The data warehouse modelled in Figure 4.7 compiles data from internal databases or transactional/operational databases and external databases through *extraction, transformation, and loading (ETL)*, which is a process that extracts data from internal and external databases, transforms that data into information using a common set of enterprise definitions, and loads the information into a data warehouse. The data warehouse then sends subsets of the information to data marts. A *data mart* contains a subset of data warehouse information. To distinguish between data warehouses and data marts, think of data warehouses as having a more organizational focus and data marts as having focused information subsets particular to the needs of a given business unit, such as finance, or production and operations.

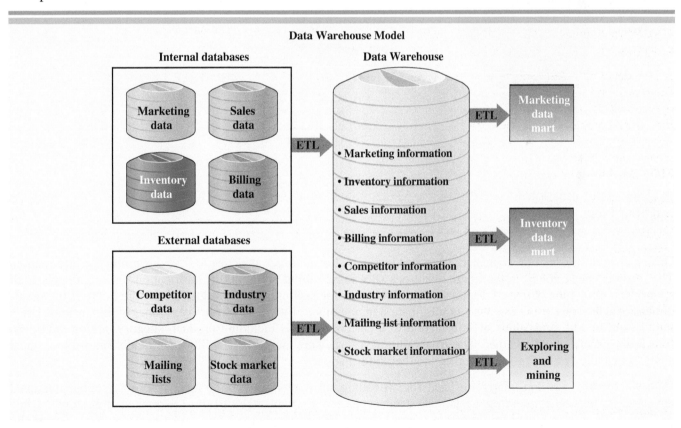

FIGURE 4.7
Model of a Typical Data Warehouse

Lands' End was experiencing issues with its customer data. The data were spread across a number of systems and as the business grew over the years, new business rules were added, which led to rule conflicts in their legacy systems. Lands' End was looking for a solution that would lead to cost efficiencies by automating tasks, but it also wanted to give the marketing staff the power to manage operational aspects of the marketing campaigns and free up resources to focus on strategic marketing. In addition, the company was looking to reduce customer acquisition costs and grow the average revenue per transaction and customer. The solution was to move the customer data for all Lands' End sources into a customer data mart so that their staff could actually work with the data to make better decisions. The results included, among other things, a marketing staff that was empowered to carry out marketing campaigns.[13]

Multi-dimensional Analysis

A relational database contains data in a series of two-dimensional tables. In a data warehouse and data mart, information is multi-dimensional, meaning it contains layers of columns and rows. For this reason, most data warehouses and data marts are **multi-dimensional databases**. A **dimension** is a particular attribute of information. Each layer in a data warehouse or data mart represents information according to an additional dimension. A **cube** is the common term for the representation of multi-dimensional information. Figure 4.8 displays a cube (*Cube a*) that represents store information (the layers), product information (the rows), and promotion information (the columns).

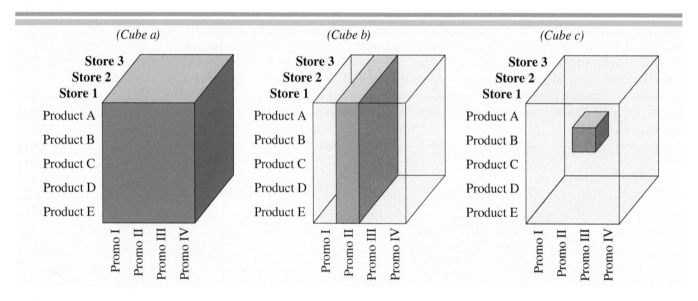

FIGURE 4.8

A Cube of Information for Performing a Multi-dimensional Analysis on Three Stores for Five Products and Four Promotions

Once a cube of information is created, users can begin to slice-and-dice the cube to drill down into the information. The second cube (*Cube b*) in the figure displays a slice representing promotion II information for all products at all stores. The third cube (*Cube c*) displays only information for promotion III, product B, at store 2. By using multi-dimensional analysis, users can analyze information in a number of ways and with any number of dimensions. Users might want to add dimensions of information to a current analysis including product category, region, and even forecasted versus actual weather. The true value of a data warehouse is its ability to provide multi-dimensional analysis that allows users to gain insights into their information.

Data warehouses and data marts are ideal for offloading some of the querying against a transactional relational database. For example, querying a relational database to obtain an average of sales for product B at store 2 while promotion III is under way might create a considerable processing burden for a relational database, essentially slowing down the time it takes another person to enter a new sale into the same relational database. If an organization performs numerous queries against a relational database (or multiple relational databases), aggregating that transactional data into analytical information that can be stored in a data warehouse is beneficial.

Information Cleansing or Scrubbing

Maintaining quality information in a data warehouse or data mart is extremely important. A survey in 2009 by The Data Warehouse Institute (TDWI) showed that most organizations are overly optimistic about the quality of their data, and that there was a lack of support from senior management to correct the problem of bad data quality. According to the survey, "the top problems related to data quality included a lack of clear ownership and responsibility for data, duplicate data, and data in silos throughout the organizations. Participants also listed as critical concerns the absence of a data governance policy, and a lack of understanding of what data was accessible and how to access it." The survey indicated that few companies have an idea of how much bad data quality costs them. The results of a classic survey by the TDWI estimated that poor data quality cost American businesses US$611 billion a year. Ina more recent survey, the participants "indicated that poor data quality negatively affects productivity as well as the ability to manage assets and inventory, and results in incorrect billing for products and services. It also raises possible regulatory issues."[14]

To increase the quality of organizational information and thus the effectiveness of decision making, businesses must formulate a strategy to keep information clean. This is the concept of *information cleansing (scrubbing)*, a process that weeds out and fixes or discards inconsistent, incorrect, or incomplete information.

Specialized software tools exist that use sophisticated algorithms to parse, standardize, correct, match, and consolidate data warehouse information. This is vitally important because data warehouses often contain information from several different databases, some of which can be external to the organization. In a data warehouse, information cleansing occurs first during the ETL process and second on the information once it is in the data warehouse. Companies can choose information cleansing software from several different vendors, including Oracle, SAS, IBM, and Pitney Bowes Business Insight. Ideally, scrubbed information is error-free and consistent.

Dr Pepper Snapple Group manufactures, markets, and distributes more than 50 brands of soft drinks across Canada, the United States, Mexico, and the Caribbean, with approximately US$6 billion in annual revenues. With 20,000 employees, 24 manufacturing facilities, and 200 distribution centres across North America, they needed better visibility of their manufacturing process so they could identify bottlenecks, resolve operational issues, and optimize their business performance. The challenge was not only to collect production line data but also be able to analyze and report on that data so they could keep production lines running efficiently 24 hours a day. The solution included a data mart (cube) and metadata to support the reports and dashboard that plant managers used to gain the visibility they need into their production lines.[15]

Looking at customer data stored in multiple transactional database systems highlights why information cleansing is necessary. Customer data exist in several operational systems. In each system, all details of this customer data could change from the customer ID to contact details (see Figure 4.9). Determining which customer data are accurate and correct for a customer depends on the business process that is being executed.

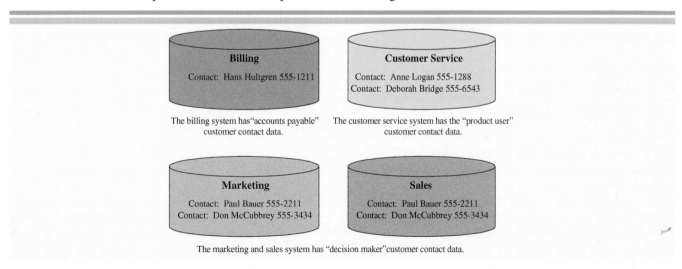

FIGURE 4.9
Customer Contact Data in Operational Systems

Figure 4.10 displays a customer name entered differently in multiple operational systems. Information cleansing allows an organization to fix these types of inconsistencies and cleans the information in the data warehouse. Figure 4.11 displays the typical events that occur during information cleansing.

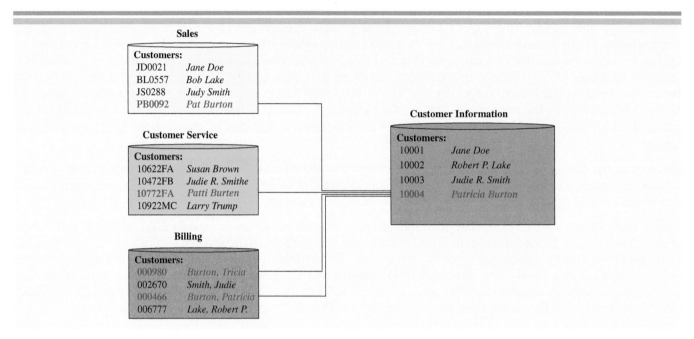

FIGURE 4.10

Standardizing Customer Name from Operational Systems

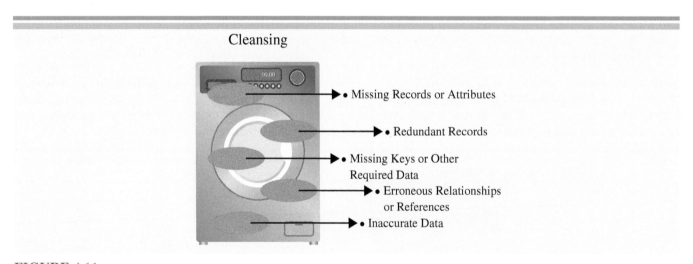

FIGURE 4.11

Information Cleansing Activities

Achieving perfect information is almost impossible. The more complete and accurate an organization wants its information to be, the more it costs (see Figure 4.12). The trade-off for perfect information lies in accuracy versus completeness. Accurate information means it is correct, while complete information means there are no blanks. A birth date of 31/02/1991 is an example of complete but inaccurate information (February 31 does not exist). An address containing Charlottetown, P.E.I., without a postal code is an example of incomplete information that is accurate. For their information, most organizations determine a percentage high enough to make good decisions at a reasonable cost, such as 85 percent accurate and 65 percent complete.

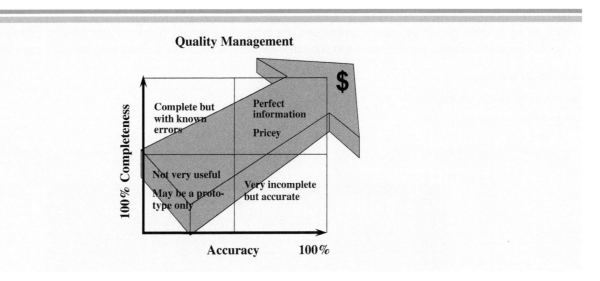

FIGURE 4.12

Accurate and Complete Information

LO5 DATA MINING

At the centre of any operational, tactical, or strategic BI effort is data mining. Scotiabank is working with SAS to mine its customer's data and as a result it has increased its incremental accounts by 80,000 to 100,000 accounts a year. The data mining allows them to put together 30 to 60 campaigns a year versus the 5 or 6 it was doing before and generate half a million leads a month. Ruf Strategic Solutions a provider of data mining marketing intelligence that helps organizations employ statistical approaches to large data warehouses to identify customer segments that display common traits. Marketers can then target these segments with specially designed products and promotions. *Data mining* is the process of analyzing information to extract insights not necessarily evident from the information alone. Data mining can also begin at a summary information level (coarse granularity) and progress through increasing levels of detail (drilling down), or the reverse (drilling up). Data mining is the primary tool used to uncover BI in vast amounts of analytical information stored in data warehouses.[16]

To perform data mining, users need a variety of techniques, called *data mining tools*, to find patterns and relationships in large volumes of information and infer rules from them that predict future behaviour and guide decision making. These specialized technologies and functionalities include query tools, reporting tools, multi-dimensional analysis tools, statistical tools, and intelligent agents. Data mining approaches decision making with a few different activities in mind, including:

■ *Classification*—assigns records to one of a predefined set of classes.

■ *Estimation*—determines values for an unknown continuous variable behaviour or estimated future value.

■ *Affinity grouping*—determines which things go together.

■ *Clustering*—segments a heterogeneous population of records into a number of more homogeneous subgroups.[17]

Sega of America, one of the largest publishers of video games, uses data mining and statistical tools to distribute its advertising budget. Using its data warehouse, product line specialists and marketing strategists drill into trends of each retail store chain. Their goal is to find buying trends that help them determine which advertising strategies are working best and how to reallocate advertising resources by media, territory, and time.[18]

Data mining tools apply algorithms to information sets to uncover inherent trends and patterns in the information, which analysts use to develop new business strategies. Analysts use the output from data mining tools to build models that, when exposed to new information sets, perform a variety of information analysis functions. The analysts provide business solutions by putting together the analytical techniques and the business problem at hand, which often reveals important new correlations, patterns, and trends (such as the pattern of shifts in consumer environmental behaviours; see Figure 4.13). The more common forms of data mining analysis capabilities include:

- Cluster analysis
- Association detection
- Statistical analysis

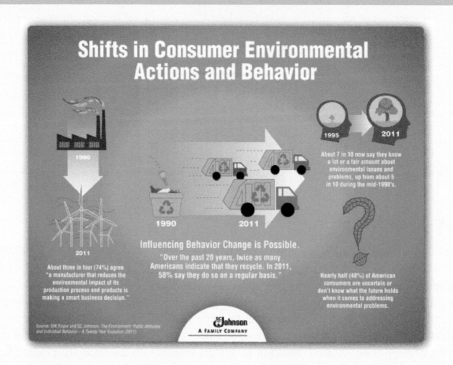

FIGURE 4.13

SC Johnson: Changes in Consumer Environmental Behaviours

Cluster Analysis   *Cluster analysis* is a technique used to divide an information set into mutually exclusive groups so that the members of each group are as close together as possible to one another, and the different groups are as far apart as possible. Cluster analysis is frequently used to segment customer information for CRM systems to help organizations identify customers with similar behavioural traits, such as clusters of best customers or one-time customers. Cluster analysis also has the ability to uncover naturally occurring patterns in information.

Data mining tools that "understand" human language are finding unexpected applications in medicine. IBM and the Mayo Clinic unearthed hidden patterns in medical records, discovering that infant leukemia has three distinct clusters, each of which probably benefits from tailored treatments. Caroline A. Kovac, general manager of IBM Life Sciences, expects that mining the records of cancer patients for clustering patterns will turn up clues pointing the way to "tremendous strides in curing cancer."[19]

A great example of cluster analysis occurs when attempting to segment customers on the basis of postal codes. Understanding the demographics, lifestyle behaviours, and buying patterns of the most profitable segments of the population at the postal code level is key to a successful target marketing strategy. Targeting only those who have a high propensity to purchase products and services will help a high-end business cut its sales and marketing costs tremendously. Understanding each customer segment by postal code allows a business to determine the importance of each segment.[20]

Association Detection   Whirlpool Corporation a US$19 billion home and commercial appliance manufacturer, employs hundreds of R&D engineers, data analysts, quality assurance specialists, and customer service personnel who all work together to ensure that each generation of appliances is better than the previous generation. Whirlpool is an example of an organization that is gaining BI with association detection data mining tools.[21]

Association detection reveals the degree to which variables are related and the nature and frequency of these relationships in the information. Whirlpool's warranty analysis tool uses statistical analysis to automatically detect potential issues, provide quick and easy access to reports, and perform multi-dimensional analysis on all warranty information. This tool enables managers to take proactive measures to control product defects before most customers are aware of the defect. It also allows personnel to devote more time to value-added tasks such as ensuring high quality on all products rather than waiting for or manually analyzing monthly reports.[22]

Many people refer to association detection algorithms as *association rule generators*, because they create rules to determine the likelihood of events occurring together at a particular time or following each other in a logical progression. Percentages usually reflect the patterns of these events, for example, "55 percent of the time, events A and B occurred together," or "80 percent of the time that items A and B occurred together, they were followed by item C within three days."

One of the most common forms of association detection analysis is **market basket analysis**, which analyzes such items as websites and checkout scanner information to detect customers' buying behaviour and predict future behaviour by identifying affinities among customers' choices of products and services (see Figure 4.14). Market basket analysis is frequently used to develop marketing campaigns for cross-selling products and services (especially in banking, insurance, and finance) and for inventory control, shelf product placement, and other retail and marketing applications.

FIGURE 4.14

Data Collection for Market Basket Analysis

Statistical Analysis   *Statistical Analysis* performs such functions as information correlations, distributions, calculations, and variance analysis, to name just a few. Data mining tools offer knowledge workers a wide range of powerful statistical capabilities so they can quickly build a variety of statistical models, examine the models' assumptions and validity, and compare and contrast the various models to determine the best one for a particular business issue.

Kraft is the producer of instantly recognizable food brands such as Oreo, Ritz, Delissio, and Kool-Aid. The company implemented two data mining applications to assure consistent flavour, colour, aroma, texture, and appearance for all of its food lines. One application analyzed product consistency and the other analyzed process variation reduction (PVR).

The product consistency tool called Sensory and Experimental Collection Application (SENECA) gathers and analyzes information by assigning precise definitions and numerical scales to such qualities as chewy, sweet, crunchy, and creamy. SENECA then builds models, histories, forecasts, and trends based on consumer testing, and evaluates potential product improvements and changes.

The PVR tool ensures consistent flavour, colour, aroma, texture, and appearance for every Kraft product, since even small changes in the baking process can result in huge disparities in taste. Evaluating every manufacturing procedure, from recipe instructions to cookie-dough shapes and sizes, the PVR tool has the potential to generate significant cost savings for each product. Using these types of data mining techniques for quality control and cluster analysis makes sure that the billions of Kraft products that reach consumers annually will continue to taste the same.[23]

Forecasting is a common form of statistical analysis. Formally defined, *forecasts* are predictions made on the basis of time series information. *Time series information* is time-stamped information collected at a particular frequency. Examples of time series information include Web visits per hour, sales per month, and calls per day. Forecasting data mining tools allow users to manipulate the time series for forecasting activities.

When discovering trends and seasonal variations in transactional information, companies use a time series forecast to change the transactional information by units of time, such as transforming weekly information into monthly or seasonal information or hourly information into daily information. They base production, investment, and staffing decisions on a host of economic and market indicators in this manner. Forecasting models allow organizations to take into account all sorts of variables when making decisions.

Nestlé Italiana is part of the multinational giant Nestlé S.A. and currently dominates Italy's food industry. The company improved sales forecasting by 25 percent with its data mining forecasting solution, which enables the company's managers to make objective decisions based on facts instead of subjective decisions based on intuition. Determining sales forecasts for seasonal confectionery products is a crucial and challenging task. During Easter, Nestlé Italiana has only four weeks to market, deliver, and sell its seasonal products. The Christmas time frame is a little longer, lasting from six to eight weeks, while other holidays such as Valentine's Day and Mother's Day have shorter time frames of about one week.

The company's data mining solution gathers, organizes, and analyzes massive volumes of information to produce powerful models that identify trends and predict confectionery sales. The BI created is based on five years of historical information and identifies what is important and what is not important. Nestlé Italiana's sophisticated data mining tool predicted Mother's Day sales forecasts that were 90 percent accurate. The company has benefited from a 40 percent reduction in inventory and a 50 percent reduction in order changes, all due to its forecasting tool. Determining sales forecasts for seasonal confectionery products is now an area in which Nestlé Italiana excels.[24]

Today, vendors such as Business Objects, Cognos, SAP, Microsoft, and SAS offer complete data mining decision-making solutions. Moving forward, these companies plan to add more predictive analytical capabilities to their products. Their goal is to give companies more what-if scenario capabilities based on internal and external information.

OPENING CASE QUESTIONS

The Case for Business Intelligence at Netflix

6. Why must Netflix cleanse or scrub the information in its database?

7. Choose one of the three common forms of data mining analysis and explain how Netflix is using it to gain BI.

8. How might Netflix be using tactical, operational, and strategic BI?

SUMMARY OF KEY THEMES

The purpose of this chapter was to provide you, the business student, with a detailed discussion about databases, data warehouses, and data mining, specifically:

- *The defining value characteristics of both transactional data and analytical information, and the need for organizations to have data and information that are timely and of high quality.* Transactional data are the raw facts contained within business operational processes. Analytical information is meaningful data that support non-operational business tasks. Organizations should strive for data and information that are accurate, complete, consistent, unique (non-duplicated), and timely to facilitate operational efficiency and effectiveness. Further, ensuring data and information are timely and of high quality gives companies the ability to make sound decisions based on accurate and reliable information, and ultimately helps uncover business intelligence.

- *Relational database fundamentals and advantages.* Relational databases store data in logically related two-dimensional tables made up of columns and rows. Tables represent business entities. Columns represent attributes or characteristics of those entities. Rows are instantiations of actual business entities (e.g., a specific order, a specific customer). Primary keys (one or more columns in a table) define a unique instantiation (row) within a table. Foreign keys are columns in tables that are primary keys in other tables; foreign keys are the mechanisms through which relationships between tables are defined. The advantage of relational databases is that they facilitate business transaction processing and the ad hoc reporting of data.

- *How users interact with a database management system, the advantage of data-driven websites, and the primary methods of integrating data and information across multiple databases in organizations.* A DBMS is software through which users and application programs access data and information stored in a database. Users access a DBMS either directly or indirectly. One way users interact with a DBMS is through a data-driven website. Data-driven websites source the content displayed on these sites from data and information stored in databases. Typically, the display of data and information is customized to reflect user interactions (e.g., queries). In this way, the rendering of content on these sites is up to date, dynamic (non-static), and relevant to users' information needs. In many organizations, databases were built independently and thus there is a need to integrate the data and information stored across these disparate databases to ensure the data and information between them is consistent. This facilitates consistent reporting and use of that data and information (such as in the case of a data-driven website). The two primary methods of integration are forward and backward integration, where data in a given information system is sent downstream or upstream.

- *Data warehouse fundamentals and advantages.* Data warehouses (and data marts) contain summarized, analytical information sourced from transactional relational databases. That is, raw transactional data from different operational relational databases are extracted, transformed, and loaded into data warehouses so that the information stored in a data warehouse can be easily queried and reported on. The primary reason organizations are building data warehouses and data marts is that most corporations today are inundated with data—from their own internal operational systems, their vendors, suppliers, and customers, and from other external sources such as credit bureaus or industry sales data.

- *Data mining fundamentals and advantages.* Data mining allows organizations to deal with the vast amounts of data they collect so that it can easily be digested or comprehended. Today it is easy to answer and ask questions like "Who are the best customers?" or "What are the most profitable products?" Data mining allows organizations to take data that has been organized in its database or data warehouse and apply various statistical techniques to answer questions like those.

KEY TERMS

Affinity grouping	**Business-critical integrity constraints**
Association detection	**Classification**
Attributes	**Cluster analysis**
Backward integration	**Clustering**

Cube

Database

Database management system (DBMS)

Data-driven website

Data integrity

Data mart

Data mining

Data mining tools

Data redundancy

Data warehouse

Dimension

Entity

Entity class

Estimation

Extraction, transformation, and loading (ETL)

Field

Forecasts

Foreign key

Forward integration

Hierarchical database model

Information cleansing (scrubbing)

Instances

Integration

Integrity constraints

Logical view

Market basket analysis

Multi-dimensional databases

Network database model

Performance

Physical view

Primary key

Records

Relational database model

Relational integrity constraints

Scalability

Statistical analysis

Table

Time series information

CLOSING CASE ONE

Scouting for Quality

This case illustrates how one organization improved data and information quality through centralization and standardization of its databases.

Scouts Canada, the country's leading organization for youth aged 5 to 26, has been part of the national landscape for over 100 years. There are approximately 3,600 boy scout groups scattered across most cities and towns in Canada. Over 69,000 young people enjoy Scouts Canada's programs today.[25]

A scout's motto is to "be prepared" and Scouts Canada's national office located in Ottawa did just that in their endeavour to integrate Scouts Canada's fragmented membership systems.

This project produced a single, integrated membership system for the whole country. Before that, each of Scouts Canada's 27 separate councils had its own membership systems that fed information to national headquarters. This data feed was not automatic. Rather, information was sent to the national office by fax. Not only did the national office receive an overwhelming amount of paper, staff were also burdened with the task of manually re-entering this data into their own database system. This consumed a great amount of labour and time. According to Tom Obright, Director of Information Management for Scouts Canada, "it was one full week [spent] grabbing all these sheets and throwing them together into some kind of presentable format."

The problem was exacerbated when Scouts Canada decided to reduce staff. As a result, a pilot membership management system was developed and tested with four participating councils. After that, the other 23 councils started using the new membership management system. By doing so, Scouts Canada had standardized its registration for new members across all 27 councils.

Before this, each of the 27 councils had subtly different formats. One problem was the way each council went about entering insurance coverage information for new members. As a result, when there were 27 different membership systems, it took as much as six months to straighten out the data. Until then, it was dangerously open to interpretation when a new registrant was actually covered by insurance.

The new centralized system improved things dramatically. Duplicated data entry efforts were eliminated. The registration process is much quicker. And the new system resolved the insurance coverage issue by properly coding when insurance coverage becomes effective for each new member.

The 27 separate councils like the system very much. It has empowered them to do more with the data they collect. With the new centralized membership management system, each council can extract and download a copy of the system's baseline data and use that data on their own computers to generate whatever reports they wish.

By conducting this integration project, Scouts Canada successfully turned 27 separate databases into one quality unifying database that improved business performance and reporting. Having access to information that is accurate, current, and standardized across all areas of the company allows Scouts Canada to make better informed decisions.[26]

Questions

1. Explain the importance of high-quality data and information for Scouts Canada.

2. Review the five common characteristics of quality data and information and rank them in order of importance for Scouts Canada.

3. How could data warehouses and data marts be used to help Scouts Canada improve the efficiency and effectiveness of its operations? Its decision making?

4. What kind of data marts might Scouts Canada want to build to help the association analyze its operational performance?

5. Do the managers at Scouts Canada actually have all the information they require to make an accurate decision? Explain the statement "it is never possible to have all of the information required to make the best decision possible."

CLOSING CASE TWO

Searching for Revenue: Google

This case illustrates how database technology underlies Google's business strategy and operations.

Google was founded by Sergey Brin and Larry Page back in 1996 when both were Ph.D. students at Stanford University. Today, Google has put both these founders on *Forbes* magazine's list of world billionaires. Google, famous for its highly successful search engine, strives to organize the world's information and make this information universally accessible and useful for everyone.

How Google Works

Google's Web server sends the query to Google's index servers. The content inside the index server is similar to the index at the back of a book; it tells which pages contain the words that match any particular query term. The query then travels to the document servers where the documents physically reside (these could be anywhere in the world on any server—not just Google's), retrieves snippets of information from the stored documents there (such as name of the page/document, the first few sentences on the page/document) that are useful to describe each search result. Finally, the search engine returns the results (hits) to the user. The user then decides on and selects the individual hits to explore and visits these documents directly from the various document servers themselves. The generation of a returned hit list only takes a fraction of a second because Google has previously created its index information. Without doing this indexing ahead of time, Google could not generate a returned hit list of relevant documents for a query in such a short time.

Google consists of three distinct parts:

1. The Web crawler, known as Googlebot, finds and retrieves Web pages (documents) and passes them to the Google indexer for indexing. Googlebot functions much like a Web browser. It sends a request for a Web page to a Web server, downloads the entire page, and then hands it off to Google's indexer. Googlebot can request thousands of different Web pages simultaneously.

2. The indexer indexes every word on each page and stores the resulting index of words in a huge database. This index is sorted alphabetically by search term, with each index entry storing a list of documents in which the term appears and the location within the text where it occurs. Indexing the full text of Web pages allows Google to go beyond simply matching single search terms. Google gives more priority to pages that have search terms near each other and in the same order as the query. Google can also match multi-word phrases and sentences.

3. The query processor compares the search query to the index and recommends the documents that it considers most relevant. Google considers more than a hundred factors in determining which documents are most relevant to a query, including the popularity of the page, the position and size of the search terms within the page, and the proximity of the search terms to one another. The query processor has several parts, including the user interface (search box), the "engine" that evaluates queries and matches them to relevant documents, and the results formatter.

Selling Words

Google's primary line of business is its search engine; however, the company does not generate revenue from people using its site to search the Internet. It generates revenue from the marketers and advertisers that are paying to place their ads on the site.

It is estimated that there are three billion searches on Google every day performed by people all over the world. AdWords, a part of the Google site, allows advertisers to bid on common search terms. The advertisers simply enter in the keywords they want to bid on and the maximum amounts they want to pay per click, per day. Google then determines a price and a search ranking for those keywords based on how much other advertisers are willing to pay for the same terms. Pricing for keywords ranges from a few cents to an unlimited ceiling per click. A general search term like *tropical vacation* costs less than a more specific term like *Hawaiian vacation*. Whoever bids the most for a term appears in a sponsored advertisement link either at the top or along the side of the search results page.

Paid search is the ultimate in targeted advertising, because consumers type in exactly what they want. One of the primary advantages of paid-search Web programs such as AdWords is that customers do not find it annoying, as is the problem with some forms of Web advertising, such as banner ads and pop-up ads. According to the Interactive Advertising Bureau, overall industry revenues from paid search surpassed banner ads in the third quarter of 2003.

It is Salar Kamangar, Google's director of product management, who came up with the AdWords concept and who oversees that part of the business. "A big percentage of queries we get are commercial in nature," said Kamangar. "It is a marketplace where the advertisers tell us about themselves by telling us how much each lead is worth. They have an incentive to bid how much they really want to pay, because if they underbid, their competitors will get more traffic." AdWords accounts for the majority of Google's annual revenue, up from zero in 2002.

Expanding Google

Google has a secret weapon working for its research and development department—hackers. Hackers actually develop many of the new and unique ways to expand Google. The company elicits hacker ideas through its application program interface (API), a large piece of the Google code. The API enables developers to build applications around the Google search engine. By making the API freely available, Google has inspired a community of programmers that are extending Google's capabilities. "It's working," said Nelson Minar, who runs the API effort. "We get clever hacks, educational uses, and wacky stuff. We love to see people do creative things with our product."

In addition to these projects are Google Maps, Google Earth, and Google Street View. These freely available data-driven websites (applications) allow users to query and interact with fairly up-to-date map information stored in Google's databases. Google Maps is Google's Web mapping service application that powers many map-based services; the application offers street maps, and a route planner for travelling by foot, car, or public transit. Google

Earth is a virtual globe, map, and geographic information program that superimposes satellite and aerial photographic images of the Earth. Google Street View is a technology featured in both Google Maps and Google Earth. This feature provides panoramic photographs of locations taken at street level from a fleet of specially adapted cars (and sometimes tricycles and snowmobiles for those hard-to-reach places). These vehicles are installed with multiple directional cameras to facilitate the rendering of 360-degree views of the location being shot, and several GPS units to determine location positioning on a map.

Stopping Google

As part of its Google Print Library Project, the company is working to scan all or parts of the book collections of the University of Michigan, Harvard University, Stanford University, the New York Public Library, and Oxford University. It intends to make those texts searchable on Google and to sell advertisements on the Web pages.

The Authors Guild has filed a lawsuit against Google, alleging that its scanning and digitizing of library books constitutes a massive copyright infringement. "This is a plain and brazen violation of copyright law," Nick Taylor, president of the New York–based Authors Guild, said in a statement about the lawsuit, which is seeking class action status. "It's not up to Google or anyone other than the authors, the rightful owners of these copyrights, to decide whether and how their works will be copied."

In response, Google defended the program in a company blog posting. "We regret that this group chose to sue us over a program that will make millions of books more discoverable to the world—especially since any copyright holder can exclude their books from the program," wrote Susan Wojcicki, vice-president of product management. "Google respects copyright. The use we make of all the books we scan through the Library Project is fully consistent with both the fair use doctrine under U.S. copyright law and the principles underlying copyright law itself, which allow everything from parodies to excerpts in book reviews and was ruled as such in 2013."[27]

Questions

1. Review the five common characteristics of high-quality information and rank them in order of importance to Google's business.

2. What would be the ramifications of Google's business if the search information it presented to its customers was of low quality?

3. Describe the different types of databases. Why should Google use a relational database?

4. Identify the different types of entities, entity classes, attributes, keys, and relationships that might be stored in Google's AdWords relational database.

5. How might Google use a data warehouse to improve its business operations?

6. Why would Google need to scrub and cleanse the information in its data warehouse?

7. Identify a data mart that Google's marketing and sales department might use to track and analyze its AdWords revenue.

CLOSING CASE THREE

Caesars: Gambling Big on Technology

This case illustrates how database technologies can support an organization's business strategy.

The large investment made by Caesars Entertainment Corporation, formerly Harrah's (which changed its name in 2010 when it went public) in its information technology strategy has been tremendously successful. The results of Caesars's investment at the time included:

■ 10 percent annual increase in customer visits

- 33 percent increase in gross market revenue

- Yearly profits of over US$208 million

- Highest three-year ROI in the industry

- A network that links over 42,000 gaming machines in 26 casinos across 12 states in the United States

- Recipient of a Leadership in Data Warehousing Award from The Data Warehousing Institute (TDWI), the premier association for data warehousing

The casino industry is highly competitive—rivalry among existing competitors is fierce. Bill Harrah was a man ahead of his time when he opened his first bingo parlour in 1937 with the commitment of getting to know each one of his customers. In 1984, Phil Satre, president and CEO of Harrah's, continued that. In search of its competitive advantage, Harrah's invested in an enterprise-wide technology infrastructure to maintain Bill Harrah's original conviction: "Serve your customers well and they will be loyal."

Caesars's Commitment to Customers

Caesars's patented Total Rewards™ program was designed to help build strong relationships with its customers. It rewarded customers for their loyalty by tracking their gaming habits across the company's then 26 properties and currently maintains information on over 19 million customers, information the company uses to analyze, predict, and maximize each customer's value.

At Caesars the program continues to be a success because of its implementation of a service-oriented strategy. Total Rewards allows Caesars to give every customer the appropriate amount of personal attention, whether it's leaving sweets in the hotel room or offering free meals. It works by providing each customer with an account and a corresponding card to swipe each time he or she plays a casino game. The program collects information on the amount of time the customers gamble, their total winnings and losses, and their betting strategies. Customers earn points based on the amount of time they spend gambling, which they can then exchange for complimentary items such as dinners, hotel rooms, tickets to shows, and even cash.

Total Rewards helps employees determine which level of service to provide each customer. When a customer makes a reservation at any of Caesars's brands, the service representative taking the call can view the customer's detailed information, including loyalty level, games typically played, past winnings and losses, and potential net worth. If the service representative notices that the customer has a Diamond loyalty level, he or she knows that the customer should never have to wait in line and should always get free upgrades to the most expensive rooms.

"Almost everything we do in marketing and decision making is influenced by technology," says Gary Love man, Caesars's chairman and CEO. "The prevailing wisdom in this business is that the attractiveness of property drives customers. Our approach is different. We stimulate demand by knowing our customers. For example, if one of our customers always vacations at Harrah's in April, they will receive a promotion in February redeemable for a free weekend in April."

Gaining Business Intelligence with a Data Warehouse

Millions of customers visit Caesars resorts each year, and tracking a customer base larger than the population of Germany is a challenge. To tackle this challenge, Caesars began developing a system called WINet (Winner's Data Network), which links all Caesars properties, allowing the company to collect and share customer information on an enterprise-wide basis. WINet collects customer data from all the company transactions, game machines, and hotel management and reservations systems, transforms and cleanses it, and then puts the results in a central data warehouse. Information there includes both customer and gaming information recorded in hourly increments. The marketing department uses the data warehouse to analyze customer information for patterns and insights, which allows it to create individualized marketing programs based on spending habits. Most importantly, the data warehouse allows the company to make business decisions based on information, not intuition.

Casinos traditionally treat customers as though they belong to a single property, typically the place the customer most frequently visits. Harrah's was the first casino to realize the potential of rewarding customers for visiting more than one property. Today, Caesars has found that customers who visit more than one of its properties represent the fastest-growing revenue segment. In the first two years of the Total Rewards program, the company received a $100 million increase in revenue from customers who gambled at more than one casino.

Caesars also uses BI to determine gaming machine performance. Using the data warehouse, Caesars examines the performance and cost structure of each individual gaming machine. The company can quickly identify games that do not deliver optimal operational performance and can make a decision to move or replace the games. The capability to assess the performance of each individual slot machine has provided Caesars with savings in the tens of millions of dollars. Former CIO Tim Stanley has stated, "As we leverage more information from our data warehouse and increase the use and sophistication of our decision science analytical tools, we expect to have many new ways to improve customer loyalty and satisfaction, drive greater revenues, and decrease our costs as part of our ongoing focus on achieving sustainable profitability and success."

Security and Privacy

Some customers have concerns about Caesars's data and information collection strategy since they want to keep their gambling information private. The good news for these customers is that casinos are actually required to be more mindful of privacy concerns than most companies. For example, casinos cannot send marketing material to any underage persons. To adhere to strict government regulations, casinos must ensure that the correct information security and restrictions are in place. Many other companies actually make a great deal of money by selling customer information. Caesars has not joined this trend, since its customer data and information are part of the company's competitive advantage.

The Future of Caesars

In the future, Caesars hopes to become device-independent by allowing employees to access the company's data warehouse via mobile devices. "Managing relationships with customers is incredibly important to the health of our business," Stanley says. "We will apply whatever technology we can to do that."

For example, Caesars has been undergoing efforts to develop systems described as "patron-based technology" that foster communication with customers through slot machines. Ultimately, such data collected through slot machines can be stored in a data warehouse and later analyzed to gain further insight into customers and their needs.[28]

Questions

1. Identify the effects poor information might have on Caesars's service-oriented business strategy.

2. How does Caesars use database technologies to implement its service-oriented strategy?

3. Caesars was one of the first casino companies to find value in offering rewards to customers who visit multiple locations. Describe the effects on the company if it had not built any integrations among the databases located at each of its casinos. How might Caesars use distributed databases or a data warehouse to synchronize customer information?

4. Estimate the potential impact to Caesars's business if there is a security breach in its customer information.

5. Identify three different types of data marts Caesars might want to build to help it analyze its operational performance.

6. What might occur if Caesars fails to clean or scrub its information before loading it into its data warehouse?

7. Describe cluster analysis, association detection, and statistical analysis, and explain how Caesars could use each one to gain insights into its business.

MAKING BUSINESS DECISIONS

1. Explaining Relational Databases

You have been hired by Vision, a startup recreational equipment company in British Columbia. Your manager, Holly Henningson, is unfamiliar with databases and their associated business value. Holly has asked you to create a report detailing the basics of databases. Holly would also like you to provide a detailed explanation of relational databases along with their associated business advantages.

2. Entities and Attributes

Martex Inc. is a Canadian manufacturer of athletic equipment, and its primary lines of business include running, tennis, golf, swimming, basketball, and aerobics equipment. Martex currently supplies four primary vendors including Sam's Sports, Total Effort, The Underline, and Maximum Workout. Martex wants to build a database to help it organize its products. In a group, identify the different types of entities, entity classes, attributes, keys and relationships Martex will want to consider when designing its database.

3. Integrating Information

You are currently working for the Public Transportation Department of Winnipeg. The department controls all forms of public transportation including buses, subways, and trains. Each department has about 300 employees and maintains its own accounting, inventory, purchasing, and human resources systems. Generating reports across departments is a difficult task and usually involves gathering and correlating the information from the many different systems. It typically takes about two weeks to generate the quarterly balance sheets and profit and loss statements. Your team has been asked to compile a report recommending what the Public Transportation Department of Winnipeg can do to alleviate its information and system issues. Be sure that your report addresses the various reasons departmental reports are presently difficult to obtain as well as how you plan to solve this problem.

4. Data and Information Timeliness

Data and information timeliness is a major consideration for all organizations. Organizations need to decide the frequency of backups and the frequency of updates to a data warehouse. In a team, describe the timeliness requirements for backups and updates to a data warehouse for each of the following:

- Weather tracking systems
- Car dealership inventories
- Vehicle tire sales forecasts
- Interest rates
- Restaurant inventories
- Grocery store inventories

5. Improving Data and Information Quality

HangUps Corporation designs and distributes closet organization structures. The company operates five systems—order entry, sales, inventory management, shipping, and billing. The company has severe data and information quality issues including missing, inaccurate, redundant, and incomplete data and information. The company wants to implement a data warehouse containing information from the five different transactional systems to help maintain a single customer view, drive business decisions, and perform multi-dimensional analysis. Identify how the organization can improve its data and information quality when it begins designing and building its data warehouse.

connect **LEARNSMART** **SMARTBOOK**

For more information on the resources available from McGraw-Hill Ryerson, go to www.mheducation.ca/he/solutions.

ENDNOTES

1. Lilly Vitorovich, "Netflix Reaches 1 Million Membership Milestone in UK, Ireland," *The Wall Street Journal*, August 20, 2012; "Netflix Watch Instantly Streaming Coming to Norway, Denmark, Sweden and Finland This Year," www.engadget.com/2012/08/15/netflix-watch-instantly-streaming-scandinavia, accessed July 15, 2013; "Bloomberg: Netflix Launches in Sweden, Denmark, Norway and Finland," www.bloomberg.com/article/2012-10-18/aqIpfZEcO.os.html, accessed July 15, 2013; "Netflix Streaming Heads to the Netherlands in Late 2013," http://news.cnet.com/8301-1023_3-57590000-93/netflix-streaming-heads-to-the-netherlands-in-late-2013, accessed July 15, 2013; Mathilde Hamel, "Netflix Bets on International Expansion to Keep Growing," March 13, 2014, www.cnbc.com/id/101487231, accessed April 18, 2014.

2. Thomas Davenport and Jeanne Harris, *Competing on Analytics: The New Science of Winning* (Boston: Harvard Business Publishing Corporation, 2007); Thomas Davenport, Jeanne Harris, and Robert Morrison, *Analytics at Work: Smarter Decisions Better Results* (Boston: Harvard Business Publishing Corporation, 2010); "Media Center," https://signup.netflix.com/MediaCenter, accessed August 10, 2011; Jennifer Saba, "Netflix Inc Is Expanding Its Online Video Service to 43 Countries in Latin America and the Caribbean, Sending Its Shares to an All-Time High," *Reuters US Edition*, July 5, 2011, www.reuters.com/article/2011/07/05/us-netflix-idUSTRE7642VV20110705, accessed August 15, 2011.

3. http://searchsqlserver.techtarget.com/definition/database, accessed August 15, 2011; www.webopedia.com/TERM/D/database.html, accessed August 15, 2011.

4. "Success Stories in Government Using VERITAS Software," 2001, http://sysdoc.doors.ch/VERITAS/quebec.pdf, accessed August 15, 2011.

5. "Preliminary Privacy Impact Assessment National Integrated Interagency Information System (N-III—Integrated Query Tool [IQT])," April 11, 2011, www.cbsa-asfc.gc.ca/agency-agence/reports-rapports/pia-efvp/atip-aiprp/niii-eng.html, accessed August 15, 2011.

6. "The Beer Store Achieves High-Performance Processing Targets to Handle Increased Data Volume from 440 Stores," March 2010, www.oracle.com/us/corporate/customers/customersearch/index.html?xCountry=Canada, accessed August 24, 2011; www.thebeerstore.ca/about-us/did-you-know, accessed May 10, 2014.

7. http://searchsqlserver.techtarget.com/definition/database, accessed August 15, 2011; www.webopedia.com/TERM/D/database.html, accessed August 15, 2011.

8. Lance Loveday and Sandra Niehaus, *Web Design for ROI: Turning Browsers into Buyers and Prospects into Leads* (Berkeley, CA: New Riders, 2008).

9. Ibid.

10. "Oracle Success Stories," www.oracle.com/successstories/army, accessed May 15, 2003.

11. Meridith Levinson, "The Brain Behind Big Bad Burger and Other Tales of Business Intelligence," May 15, 2007, www.cio.com/article/109454/TheBrain&_;Behind_the_Big_Bad_Burger_and_Other_Tales_of_Business_Intelligence, accessed August 16, 2011.

12. W. H. Inmon and Richard D. Hackathorn, *Using the Data Warehouse* (Mississauga, ON: John Wiley & Sons Canada, 1994).

13. "Lands' End Uses Unica Campaign to Implement Customer-Centric Strategies," 2003–2009, www.unica.com, accessed August 16, 2011.

14. The Data Warehouse Institute (Renton, WA), http://tdwi.org/articles/2009/11/10/qa-survey-shows-organizations-overly-optimistic-about-data-quality.aspx?sc_lang=en, accessed May 10, 2014.

15. "Information to Reporting to Smarter Operations: Performance Management at Dr Pepper Snapple Group," 2009, www.ibm.com, accessed August 16, 2011.

16. "Scotiabank Mines Data to Generate Leads," www.sas.com/en_us/customers/scotiabank.html, accessed May 10, 2014; http://bi.ruf.com, accessed May 10, 2014.

17. The Data Warehouse Institute (Renton, WA), "Question and Answer: Survey Shows Organizations Overly Optimistic About Data Quality," November 10, 2009; http://tdwi.org/articles/2009/11/10/qa-survey-shows-organizations-overly-optimistic-about-data-quality.aspx?sc_lang=en, accessed August 24, 2011; Graham Rhind, "Poor Quality Data: The Pandemic Problem That Needs Addressing" (Worcester, UK: Postcode Anywhere, 2007), www.grcdi.nl/PCAwhitepaper.pdf, accessed August 24, 2011.

18. Ibid.

19. Ibid.

20. Ibid.

21. Ibid.; "Whirlpool Corp (WHR: New York)," http://investing.businessweek.com/research/stocks/earnings/earnings.asp?ticker=WHR:US, accessed August 24, 2011.

22. Claudia Imhoff and Ray Pettit, Intelligent Solutions, Inc., "The Critical Shift to Flexible Business Intelligence," 2004, used with permission; Claudia Imhoff and Ray Pettit, Intelligent Solutions, Inc., "What Every Marketer Wants—and Needs—from Technology," used with permission; Claudia Imhoff, Intelligent Solutions, Inc., "Enterprise Business Intelligence," May 2006, used with permission; Jill Dyche, Baseline Consulting Group, "The Business Case for Data Warehousing," 2005, used with permission.

23. Ibid.

24. Ibid.

25. www.scouts.ca, accessed May 10, 2014; Scouts Canada Annual Report, 2012–13, www.scouts.ca/sites/default/files/AR2012-13-Web-en.pdf, accessed May 10, 2014.

26. Joshua Weinberger, *Customer Relationship Management*, Volume 9, Issue 1 (January 2005), pp. 45–46.

27. "Google Knows Where You Are," *BusinessWeek*, February 2, 2004, www.google.com, accessed October 28, 2009; Cade Metz, "8 Years Later, Google's Book Scanning Crusade Ruled 'Fair Use,'" November 14, 2013, www.wired.com/2013/11/google-2, accessed May 10, 2014.

28. Meridith Levinson, "Harrah's Knows What You Did Last Night," *Darwin Magazine*, May 2001; "Harrah's Entertainment Wins TDWI's 2000 DW Award," www.hpcwire.com, accessed October 10, 2003; Gary Loveman, "Diamonds in the Data Mine," *Harvard Business Review*, May 2003, p. 109; "NCR—Harrah's Entertainment, Inc.," www.ncr.com, accessed October 12, 2003; "Cognos and Harrah's Entertainment Win Prestigious Data Warehousing Award," 2002 news release, www.cognos.com, accessed October 14, 2003; Kim Nash, "Casinos Hit Jackpot with Customer Data," www.cnn.com, accessed October 14, 2003; Michael S. Malone, "IPO Fever," *Wired*, March 2004.

E-Business, Networks, and Mobile Business

M odule 3 explores how businesses in today's environment use the Internet and other networks to take advantage of e-business and mobilize business processes. The impact of e-business can range from transforming industries to adding efficiency and effectiveness to business processes. In the media we often hear about how companies like Google, Amazon, and Facebook have transformed industries or created new industries, but with most businesses, e-business allows them to improve and reduce the cost of day-to-day activities like reaching out to and interacting with their customers and business partners. In many instances companies are taking advantages of technologies like cellular phones, GIS, and RFID to further the impacts of the Internet on their organizations. Today these technologies are allowing companies and their employees to become more mobile, track goods remotely and, in the case of transportation companies, plan the most effective and efficient routes.

This module first looks at the impact of the Internet on business through the advent of e-business. How has e-business impacted businesses not only in terms of reaching their customers also in the way companies operate in their day-to-day activities? This part of the module should also encourage the reader to think about how organizations can take advantage of the various e-business models and the features of e-business that are discussed.

Once the Internet and e-business are described, the module provides an overview of networks, telecommunications, and mobile technology basics—aspects that make up an organization's underlying communications infrastructure and that must be understood and managed correctly to develop and maintain useful and usable information systems. This part of the module also shows how these technologies can be used to support businesses as they become more mobile.

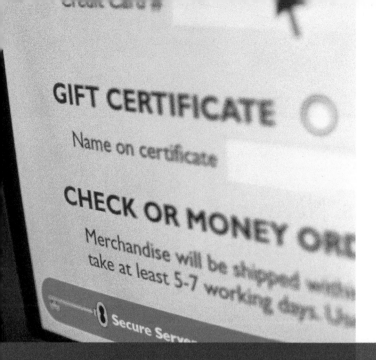

The Internet and E-Business

LO 5.1 Explain the differences between disruptive and sustaining technologies.

LO 5.2 Explain how the Internet and the World Wide Web have evolved over the years and disrupted traditional ways of doing business.

LO 5.3 Describe how an organization's various departments can use e-business to increase revenues or reduce costs, and how organizations can measure e-business success.

LO 5.4 Compare the four types of e-business models.

LO 5.5 Describe the benefits and challenges of Web 2.0, and the new trends happening in e-business today.

Managers must understand the importance of doing business on the Internet and how it has revolutionized the way business is performed. E-business offers new opportunities for growth and new ways of performing business activities that were simply not possible before the Internet. More than just giving organizations a means of conducting transactions over the Web, electronic business provides companies with the ability to develop and maintain relationships with customers, supply partners, and even employees, between and within enterprises.

As a business student, you should understand the fundamental impact of the Internet on business. As a future manager and organizational knowledge worker, you need to understand what benefits electronic business can offer an organization and your career. In addition, you need to understand the challenges that come along with adopting Web technologies and how Web 2.0 is affecting communication. You need to be aware of the various strategies organizations can use to deploy electronic business, as well as recent trends and methods of measuring e-business performance. This chapter will give you this knowledge and help prepare you for success in today's electronic global marketplace.

Pinterest: Billboards for the Internet

Pinterest has been called the latest addiction for millions of people around the world. Pinterest, a visual social media network, allows users to create "interest boards" where they "pin" items of interest found on the Web. Terms you need to understand to use Pinterest include:

- *Pin.* A link to an image from a computer or a website. Pins can include captions for other users. Users upload, or "pin," photos or videos to boards.
- *Board.* Pins live on boards and users can maintain separate boards, which can be categorized by activity or interests, such as cooking, do-it-yourself activities, fitness, music, movies, etc.
- *Repin.* After pinning an item, it can be repinned by other Pinterest users, spreading the content virally. Repinning allows users to share items they like with friends and family.

Pinning is simply done by clicking on a photo or video that captures the attention of a user, whether it be by uploading personal photos or repinning a photo or video from a fellow user. Started in 2010, Pinterest has already attracted over 10 million users with the majority being women between the ages of 25 and 54. Millions of people visit the website each day to find what new items will spark their interest as there are always more and more things to see.

Pinterest is considered a social network, but unlike other social networks, such as Twitter and Facebook, Pinterest is open to invited users only; meaning it is an invitation-only website and users must "ask" for an invitation before gaining access. Upon accepting the invitation, users can gain access to the website and begin inviting their own "friends" with whom they have connections on Facebook or Twitter. Pinterest's primary mission is to:

> connect everyone in the world through the "things" they find interesting. We think that a favourite book, toy, or recipe can reveal a common link between two people. With millions of new pins added every week, Pinterest is connecting people all over the world based on shared tastes and interests.

Just like on other social networks, Pinterest users can compile a list of people they want to follow. A user can link a Pinterest board to a Facebook account, allowing instant access to quickly see which of his or her Facebook friends are on the social network. Adding bookmarks allows the user to pin images to other websites such as a book at Barnes & Noble or a set of mugs at Pier 1 Imports. The image is automatically linked to the retailer's website, and if another users clicks on the image, that user receives additional information on the product or service. If users pin a specific image of a plate or sweater, they can add the item's price in the description, which will automatically place a banner ad on the image and show the listed price. If users are unsure of what they are looking for, they can search for a specific event or theme such as "21st birthday party" for a whole array of ideas.

Essentially, Pinterest allows users to paint a visual picture. Just imagine a wedding planner talking to a bride about her upcoming event, and the bride mentions she would like a "classic modernism" wedding. If the wedding planner was confused on what exactly the bride meant by classic modernism, she could quickly visit Pinterest to find an entire suite of photos and videos to spark ideas of how to coordinate the event.

The Business Value of Pinterest

Visual Communication

Pinterest is by far one of the hottest social media spaces available today. Offering all kinds of valuable information from useful cleaning tips to fantastic recipes to beautiful photos and videos, the website is extremely valuable for sharing anything visual. Pinterest is in no way simply a passing fad as companies begin to use the website for social marketing.

One of the best business uses of Pinterest is allowing employees to visually communicate and brainstorm. Visual communication is a new experience for many employees, and the phrase "A picture is worth a thousand words" can help a company perform many tasks from generating new products to transforming business processes. In fact, many companies are using Pinterest to solicit feedback directly from employees, customers, and suppliers to ensure the company is operating efficiently and effectively. Soliciting feedback directly from customers allows companies to have a customer service support team handle problems before they become mainstream issues. Giving customers a new channel to post their thoughts and concerns about products or services can provide valuable feedback for any company. Companies typically state that they may not respond to every question or comment, but that they take each and every concern into account, demonstrating that they are devoted to creating a bond between themselves and their customers.

Driving Traffic

Pinterest drives traffic—it is that simple! Even though the website operates under an invitation-only model, it has attracted more than 10 million users in less than two years. That number might seem small compared to powerhouses such as Facebook, Twitter, or Google, but it demonstrates there is enough of an audience to send a decent amount of traffic to any business. The images a business pins up should be linked to the relevant page of its website. If users are attracted by it, they may click on it to find out more.

Pinterest also drives traffic by providing higher rankings on search engine optimization as companies appear higher and higher on search lists the more users are pinning to their boards. Linking is one of the key factors search engines consider, and with Pinterest gaining in popularity, it is also growing as a trustworthy domain. The number of Pinterest users combined with its ability to increase search rankings will play an important role when a company is looking to increase visibility and drive traffic to its website. Data from Shareaholic found that Pinterest sent more referral traffic to bloggers than Google, YouTube, and LinkedIn combined, falling just behind Twitter.

Product Branding

Pinterest is an extraordinary branding tool, offering a place where companies can create a presence and community around a product, idea, event, or company. Just like other social networking websites, Pinterest allows a company to reach out and engage its customers, vendors, suppliers, and even employees to communicate about its products and services. Recently the National Football League's Minnesota Vikings began using Pinterest to create a following of favourite photos, statistics, and even game-day recipes!

Pinterest recently deployed an iPhone application that allows users to pin photos and video from their cameras instantly on their boards. Pinterest's unique competitive advantage is its ability to host billions of images and redirect users to the appropriate sources in a user-friendly interface.

Pinterest's Dilemma

Since its inception, Pinterest has been under fire from sites such as Flikr, Photobucket, and Instagram over attributing credit to those who own the images that are pinned. Many users are concerned that they may one day be sued for the improper use of an image they pinned.

The Pinterest Terms of Use state, "If you are a copyright owner, or are authorized to act on behalf of one, or authorized to act under any exclusive right under copyright, please report alleged copyright infringements taking place on or through the Site by completing the following DMCA Notice of Alleged Infringement and delivering it to Pinterest's Designated Copyright Agent."

To Protect Pinterest from third-party litigation claims (such as those from authors claiming copyright infringement), Pinterest has incorporated the following statement into its indemnity clause: "You agree to indemnify and hold harmless Pinterest and its officers, directors, employees and agents, from and against any claims, suits, proceedings, disputes, demands, liabilities, damages, losses, costs and expenses, including, without limitation, reasonable legal and accounting fees (including costs of defence of claims, suits or proceedings brought by third parties), arising out of or in any way related to (i) your access to or use of the Services or Pinterest Content, (ii) your User Content, or (iii) your breach of any of these Terms."

Pinterest is well aware of the probability that many of the pinned images might be violating copyright infringement and is attempting to protect itself against any litigation claims resulting from users intentionally or unintentionally breaking the law through its site.[1]

5.1 BUSINESS AND THE INTERNET

INTRODUCTION

In the past, such pop stars as Usher, Britney Spears, and Justin Timberlake used TV programs (e.g., *Star Search*, *Mickey Mouse Club*) to launch themselves from obscurity to stardom. In this era of the Internet, the entertainment business has also been affected and how new talents are discovered has changed.

At age 12, Justin Bieber started posting homemade music videos to You Tube, and when the number of views went from hundreds to thousands to tens of thousands, industry insiders such as Usher and Timberlake started to notice. Eventually he was signed with Usher's Island Deft Jam Recordings. His first two albums *My World* and *My World 2.0* debuted at number six and number one respectively on the Billboard 200 Album Chart, making Bieber the youngest solo male act to reach number one there since Stevie Wonder did it in 1963.[2]

LO1 | WEB 1.0: DISRUPTIVE TECHNOLOGY

Polaroid, founded in 1937, produced the first instant camera in the late 1940s. The camera was one of the most exciting technological advances the photography industry had ever seen. With it, customers no longer had to depend on others to develop their pictures. The company eventually went public, becoming one of Wall Street's most prominent enterprises, with its stock trading above $70 in 1997. However, in 2002 the stock was down to 8 cents and the company declared bankruptcy.[3]

How could a company like Polaroid, which had innovative technology and a captive customer base, go bankrupt? Perhaps its executives had failed to use Porter's Five Forces to analyze the threat of substitute products or services. If they had, would they have noticed the two threats—one-hour film processing and digital cameras—that eventually stole Polaroid's market share? Would they have understood that their customers—people who want instant access to their pictures without having a third party involved—would be the first to use one-hour film processing and the first to purchase digital cameras? Could the company have found a way to compete with one-hour film processing and the digital camera?

Most organizations face the same dilemma: the criteria an organization uses to make business decisions for its present business could possibly create issues for its future business—what is best for the current business might ruin it in the long term. Some observers of our business environment have an ominous vision of the future—digital Darwinism. *Digital Darwinism* implies that organizations that cannot adapt to the new demands put on them for surviving in the information age are doomed to extinction.[4]

Disruptive Versus Sustaining Technology

A *disruptive technology* is a new way of doing things that initially does not meet the needs of existing customers. Disruptive technologies tend to open new markets and destroy old ones. A *sustaining technology*, on the other hand, produces an improved product that customers are eager to buy, such as a faster car or larger hard drive. Sustaining technologies tend to provide us with better, faster, and cheaper products in established markets. Incumbent companies most often lead sustaining technology to market, but virtually never lead in markets opened by disruptive technologies. Figure 5.1 displays companies that are expecting future growth to occur from new investments (disruptive technology) and companies that are expecting future growth to occur from existing investments (sustaining technology).

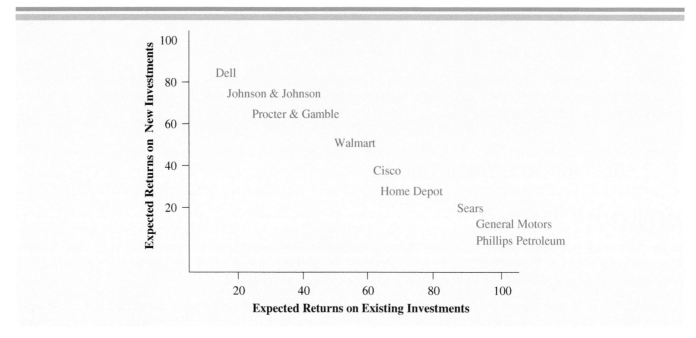

FIGURE 5.1

Expected Returns on Disruptive and Sustaining Technologies

Source: Reprinted by permission of Harvard Business School Press. From *The Innovator's Dilemma*, by Clayton Christensen. Boston, MA. © 1997 by the Harvard Business School Publishing Corporation. All rights reserved.

Disruptive technologies typically cut into the low end of the marketplace and eventually evolve to displace high-end competitors and their reigning technologies. Sony is a perfect example of a company that entered the low end of the marketplace and eventually evolved to displace its high-end competitors. Sony started as a tiny company that built portable, battery-powered transistor radios people could carry around with them. The sound quality of Sony's transistor radios was poor because the transistor amplifiers were of lower quality than traditional vacuum tubes, which produce a better sound; but customers were willing to overlook sound quality for the convenience of portability. With the experience and revenue stream from the portables, Sony improved its technology to produce cheap, low-end transistor amplifiers that were suitable for home use and invested those revenues to improve the technology further, which produced better radios.[5]

The Innovator's Solution by Clayton M. Christensen discusses how established companies can take advantage of disruptive technologies without hindering existing relationships with customers, partners, and stakeholders. Xerox, IBM, Sears, and Kodak all listened to existing customers, invested aggressively in technology, had their competitive antennae up, and still lost their market-dominant positions. Christensen states that these companies may have put too much emphasis on satisfying customers' current needs, while neglecting to adopt new disruptive technology that would meet customers' future needs, causing the companies to eventually lose market share. Figure 5.2 highlights several companies that launched new businesses by capitalizing on disruptive technologies.[6]

THE INTERNET AND WORLD WIDE WEB: BUSINESS DISRUPTORS
LO2

When the Internet was in its early days, no one had any idea how massive it would become. Computer companies did not think it would be a big deal; neither did the phone or cable companies. Difficult to access and operate, it seemed likely to remain an arcane tool of the U.S. Department of Defense and academia. However, the Internet grew, and grew, and grew. It began with a handful of users in the mid-1960s and by the end of 2013 had reached an estimated 2.7 billion users and an estimated 2.1 billion mobile broadband subscriptions (see Figure 5.3 and Figure 5.4).

Company	Disruptive Technology
Apple	iPod, iPhone, iPad
Charles Schwab	Online brokerage
Hewlett-Packard	Microprocessor-based computers, inkjet printers
IBM	Minicomputers and personal computers
Intel	Low-end microprocessors
Intuit	QuickBooks software; TurboTax software; Quicken software
Microsoft	Operating system software
Oracle	Database software
Sony	Transistor-based consumer electronics

FIGURE 5.2

Companies That Capitalized on Disruptive Technologies[7]

Source: Reprinted by permission of Harvard Business School Press. From *The Innovator's Dilemma,* by Clayton Christensen. Boston, MA. Copyright © by the Harvard Business School Publishing Corporation; all rights reserved.

Much of the future growth in users is going to come from developing nations and trends like villages in Indonesia and India having Internet access before they have electricity will likely continue.[8] Figure 5.5 displays several ways the Internet is changing business.

Evolution of the Internet and World Wide Web

During the Cold War, in the mid-1960s, the American military decided it needed a bomb-proof communications system, and the concept for the Internet was born. The system would link computers throughout the country, allowing messages to get through even if a large section of the country was destroyed. In the early days, the only

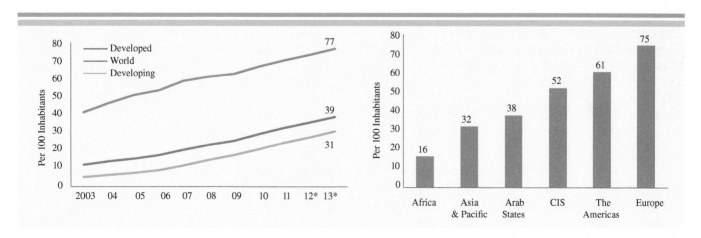

FIGURE 5.3

World Internet Growth and Penetration[9]

Source: ITU World Telecommunication/ICT Indicators database.

linked computers were at government think tanks and a few universities. The Internet was essentially an emergency military communications system operated by the U.S. Department of Defense's Advanced Research Project Agency (ARPA) and was called ARPANET.

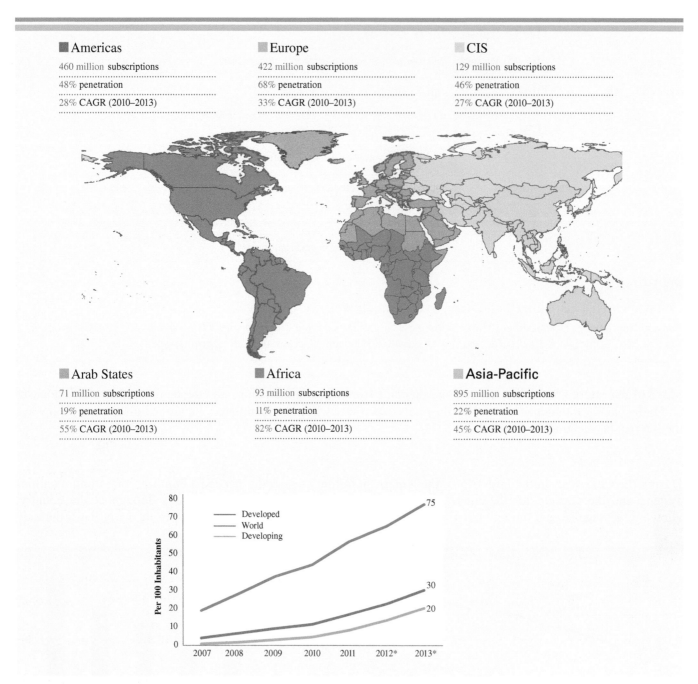

FIGURE 5.4

World Mobile Broadband Subscriptions Penetration and Growth[10]

Source: ITU World Telecommunication/ICT Indicators database.

Formally defined, the **Internet** is a global public network of computer networks that pass information from one to another using common computer **protocols**—which are standards that specify the format of data as well as the rules to be followed during transmission.

Industry	Business Changes Due to Technology
Auto	**AutoTrader.ca** is Canada's used-car marketplace, listing millions of cars from both private owners and dealers. It actually helps to increase used-car dealer's business, as it drives millions of qualified leads (potential used-car buyers) to participating automotive dealers and private sellers.
Publishing	With the Internet, anyone can publish online content. Traditionally, publishers screened many authors and manuscripts and selected those that had the best chances of succeeding. **Lulu.com** turned this model around by providing self-publishing along with print-on-demand capabilities.
Education and training	Continuing medical education is costly, and just keeping up-to-date with advances often requires taking training courses and travelling to conferences. Now continuing education in many fields is moving online, and by 2016 over 50 percent of doctors will be building their skills through online learning. Companies such as Cisco save millions by moving training to the Internet.
Entertainment	The music industry was hit hard by e-business, and online music traders such as iTunes average billions of annual downloads. Unable to compete with online music, the majority of record stores closed. The next big entertainment industry to feel the effects of e-business will be the multibillion-dollar movie business. Video rental stores are closing their doors as they fail to compete with online streaming and home rental delivery companies such as Netflix.
Retail	Forrester Research predicts e-business retail sales will grow at a 10 percent annual growth rate through 2014. Online retail sales in Canada were $18.9 billion in 2012.[11]
Travel	Travel site **Expedia.ca** is one of Canada's biggest leisure-travel agencies. The majority of Canadians use online travel sites to plan vacations and Expedia.ca leads the way with almost 15 percent of this traffic, more than its leading three competitors combined. By mid-2013, 57 percent of travel sales was done online.[12]

FIGURE 5.5

E-Business Disruption of Traditional Industries[13]

In time, every university in the United States that had defence-related funding installed ARPANET computers. Gradually, the Internet moved from a military pipeline to a communication tool for scientists. As more scholars came online, system administration transferred from ARPA to the National Science Foundation. Years later, businesses began using the Internet, and the administrative responsibilities were once again transferred.

Today, no one party operates the Internet; however, several entities oversee it and set standards, including:

- *Internet Engineering Task Force (IETF)*—the protocol engineering and development arm of the Internet

- *Internet Architecture Board (IAB)*—responsible for defining the overall architecture of the Internet, providing guidance and broad direction to the IETF

- *Internet Engineering Steering Group (IESG)*—responsible for technical management of IETF activities and the Internet standards process

People often use the terms *Internet* and *World Wide Web* interchangeably, but they are not synonymous. Throughout the 1960s, 1970s, and 1980s, the Internet was primarily used by the U.S. Department of Defense to support activities such as email and transferring files. It was restricted to non-commercial activities, and its users included government employees, researchers, university professors, and students.

The **World Wide Web (WWW)**, a global system that uses the Internet as its transport mechanism, changed the purpose and use of the Internet. Exchange of information on the WWW, also known as the *Web*, takes place through a standard known as the **hypertext transfer protocol (HTTP)**, which enables authors to embed hyperlinks in Web documents by defining *uniform resource locators (URLs)* and how they can be used to retrieve resources anywhere on the Internet. HTTP defines the process by which a Web client, called a *browser*, originates a request for information and sends it to a Web server, a program designed to respond to HTTP requests and provide the desired information. In a hypertext system, users navigate by clicking a hyperlink embedded in the current document. The action displays a second document in the same or a separate browser window.

The Web has quickly become the ideal medium for publishing information on the Internet, and it serves as the platform for the electronic economy. Figure 5.6 displays the reasons for the popularity and growth in the WWW.

- The microcomputer revolution have made it possible for an average person to own a computer.
- Advances in networking hardware, software, and media have made it possible for business PCs to be inexpensively connected to larger networks.
- Browser software such as Microsoft's Internet Explorer and Netscape Navigator have given computer users an easy-to-use graphical interface to find, download, and display Web pages.
- The speed, convenience, and low cost of email have made it an incredibly popular tool for business and personal communications.
- Basic Web pages are easy to create and are extremely flexible.
- Smart phones and other mobile devices create easy, anywhere access.

FIGURE 5.6

Reasons for World Wide Web Growth

The WWW remained primarily text-based until 1991, when two events occurred that would forever change the Web and the amount and quality of information available (see Figure 5.7). First, on August 6, 1991, Tim Berners-Lee built the first website (**http://info.cern.ch**—the site has been archived). The site provided details about the WWW, including how to build a browser and set up a Web server. It also housed the world's first Web directory, since Berners-Lee later maintained a list of other sites apart from his own.[14]

Easy to compile	Searching for information on products, prices, customers, suppliers, and partners is faster and easier when using the Internet.
Increased richness	*Information richness* refers to the depth and breadth of information transferred between customers and businesses. Businesses and customers can collect and track more detailed information when using the Internet.
Increased reach	*Information reach* refers to the number of people a business can communicate with, on a global basis. Businesses can share information with numerous customers all over the world.
Improved content	A key element of the Internet is its ability to provide dynamic, relevant content. Buyers need good content descriptions to make informed purchases, and sellers use content to properly market and differentiate themselves from the competition. Content and product description establish the common understanding between both parties to the transaction. As a result, the reach and richness of that content directly affects the transaction.

FIGURE 5.7

The Internet's Impact on Information

Second, Marc Andreesen developed a new computer program called the NCSA Mosaic (National Center for Supercomputing Applications at the University of Illinois) and gave it away! The browser made it easier to access the websites that had started to appear. Soon, sites contained more than just text; they also had sound and video files. These pages, written in the *hypertext mark-up language (HTML)*, had links that allowed the user to quickly move from one document to another, even when the documents were stored on different computers. Web browsers read the HTML text and converted it into a Web page.[15]

By eliminating time and distance, the Internet makes it possible to perform business in ways not previously imaginable. The ***digital divide*** occurs when those with access to technology have great advantages over those without access to technology. People living in the village of Siroha, India, must cycle 8 kilometres to find a telephone. For over 700 million rural people living in India, the digital divide was a way of life, until recently. Media Lab Asia sells telephony and email services via a mobile Internet kiosk mounted on a bicycle, which is known as an "infothelas." The kiosk has an onboard computer equipped with an antenna for Internet service and a specially designed all-day battery. Over 2,000 villages purchased the kiosk for $1,200, and another 600,000 villages were interested.

Bear in mind that even when access to technology is made available, cultural and language differences may serve as barriers to bridging the digital divide. In response, computer interfaces are being developed that do not require the ability to read text. Such interfaces instead rely on videos and animated cartoons that speak in local languages as a way to encourage first-time, non-literate computer and mobile phone users to adopt these technologies.[16]

LO3 | E-BUSINESS BASICS

In 1994, Jeff Bezos started to change the business of book retailing with the introduction of **Amazon.com**. In 2001, Apple released its first version of iTunes, and in 2003, Tom Anderson and Chris DeWolf started MySpace (now Myspace), both of which greatly impacted the music business model that had been around for decades. iTunes introduced a new way of distributing and purchasing music while MySpace introduced social networking to its members' information about the independent music scene around the United States. In 2004, Facebook was developed for college and university students to share photos in a "social network." Today, Facebook has over 1.23 billion registered users worldwide and has impacted how people interact and communicate with each other, as can be seen in some of Facebook's user statistics. About 50 percent of Facebook's active users log on on any given day and each user has on average 130 friends. Altogether, people spend over 700 billion minutes per month on Facebook.[17]

For businesses, the biggest benefit of the Internet is its ability to allow organizations to perform business with anyone, anywhere, anytime. *E-commerce* is the buying and selling of goods and services over the Internet; it refers only to online transactions. *E-business*, a term derived from *e-commerce*, is the conduct of business on the Internet, not only buying and selling, but also serving customers and collaborating with business partners. That is, the primary difference between e-commerce and e-business is that e-business also refers to online exchanges of information—for example, a manufacturer allowing its suppliers to monitor production schedules or a financial institution allowing its customers to review their banking, credit card, and mortgage accounts.

E-business has permeated every aspect of daily life. Both individuals and organizations have embraced Internet technologies to enhance productivity, maximize convenience, and improve communications globally. From banking to shopping to entertainment, the Internet has become integral to daily life. Figure 5.8 provides examples of a few of the industries using e-business.

ADVANTAGES OF E-BUSINESS

Expanding Reach

Easy access to real-time information is a primary benefit of e-business. Businesses use the Web to expand their *information reach*, the measure of the number of people a firm can communicate with all over the world. With today's technology, companies can also increase the *information richness*—the depth and breadth of details contained in a piece of textual, graphic, audio, or video information. Buyers use information *richness* to make informed purchases, and sellers need information *reach* to properly market and differentiate themselves from the competition.

E-businesses operate 24/7. This availability directly reduces transaction costs, since consumers no longer have to spend a lot of time researching purchases or travelling great distances to make them. The faster delivery cycle for online sales helps strengthen customer relationships, improving customer satisfaction and ultimately sales.

A firm's website can be the focal point of a cost-effective communications and marketing strategy. Online promotion allows a company to precisely target its customers whether they are local or around the globe. A physical location is restricted by size and limited to those customers who can get there, while an online store has a global marketplace with customers and information seekers already waiting in line.

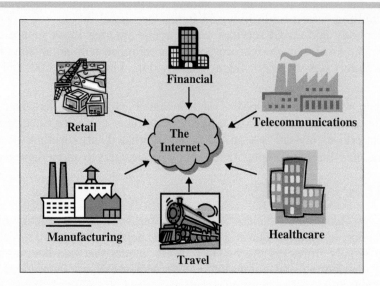

FIGURE 5.8

Overview of Industries Using E-Business

Opening New Markets

E-business is perfect for increasing niche-product sales. ***Mass customization*** is the ability of an organization to tailor its products or services to the customers' specifications. For example, customers can order M&Ms in special colours or with customized sayings such as "Marry Me." ***Personalization*** occurs when a company knows enough about a customer's likes and dislikes that it can fashion offers more likely to appeal to that person, say by tailoring its website to individuals or groups on the basis of profile information, demographics, or prior transactions. Amazon uses personalization to create a unique portal for each of its customers.

Chris Anderson, editor-in-chief of *Wired* magazine, describes niche-market e-business strategies as capturing the ***long tail***, referring to the tail of a typical sales curve. This strategy demonstrates how niche products can have viable and profitable business models when selling via e-business. In traditional sales models, a store is limited by shelf space when selecting products to sell. For this reason, store owners typically purchase products that will be wanted or needed by the masses, and the store is stocked with broad products because there is no room on the shelf for products that only a few customers might purchase. E-businesses such as Amazon and eBay have eliminated the shelf-space dilemma and are able to offer an infinite number of products.

Netflix offers an excellent example of the long tail. Let's assume that an average mom-and-pop video store maintains 3,000 movies in its inventory, whereas Netflix, without physical shelf limitations, can maintain 100,000 movies in its inventory. Looking at sales data, the majority of video store revenue comes from new releases that are rented daily, whereas older selections are rented only a few times a month and don't repay the cost of keeping them in stock. Thus Rogers Plus's sales tail ends at title 3,000 (see Figure 5.9). However, Netflix, with no physical limitations, can extend its tail beyond 100,000 (and with streaming video, perhaps 200,000 or more). In this way, Netflix increases sales, even if a title is rented only a few times.[18]

Intermediaries are agents, software, or businesses that provide a trading infrastructure to bring buyers and sellers together. The introduction of e-business brought about ***disintermediation***, which occurs when a business sells directly to the customer online and cuts out the intermediary (see Figure 5.10). This business strategy lets the company shorten the order process and add value with reduced costs or a more responsive and efficient service. The disintermediation of the travel agent occurred as people began to book their own vacations online, often at a cheaper rate. At Lulu.com anyone can publish and sell print-on-demand books, online music, and custom calendars, making the publisher obsolete.[19]

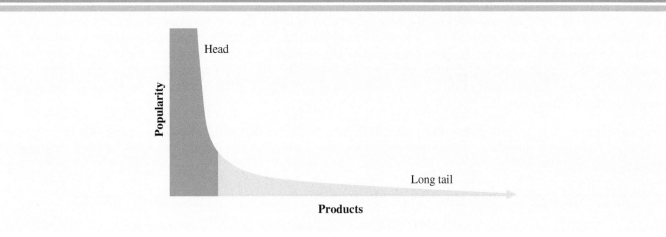

FIGURE 5.9

The Long Tail

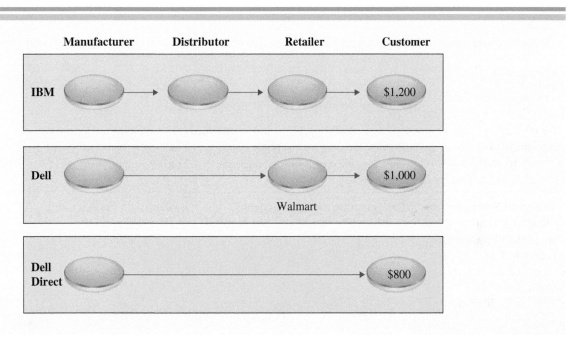

FIGURE 5.10

Business Value of Disintermediation

In *reintermediation*, steps are *added* to the value chain as new players find ways to add value to the business process. Levi Strauss originally thought it was a good business strategy to limit all online sales to its own website. A few years later, the company realized it could gain a far larger market share by allowing all retailers to sell its products directly to customers. As e-business matures it has become evident that to serve certain markets in volume, some reintermediation may be desirable. One example is **Biddingo.com**, a Canadian online marketplace that enables suppliers providing various goods and services to locate bid opportunities from various Canadian government agencies. Government agencies in Canada spend over $100 billion annually on various products and services and post over 1,000 of these opportunities on Biddingo at any given time. The marketplace notifies registered suppliers in Biddingo about new bids through daily alerts. The system not only helps government agencies find the most competitive bids from suppliers who have registered as pre-qualified vendors with them; it also allows suppliers to know about bid opportunities they may miss out on otherwise. This is important because governmental bid opportunities are typically open only for two to three weeks.[20] Figure 5.11 lists some intermediary forms of e-business and their functions.

Cybermediation refers to the creation of new kinds of intermediaries that simply could not have existed before the advent of e-business, including comparison-shopping sites such as **Kelkoo.com** and bank account aggregation services such as Citibank.[21]

Form	Description	Examples
Content providers	Generate revenues by providing digital content such as news, music, photos, or videos.	Netflix.com, iTunes.com, CNN.com
Infomediaries	Provide specialized information on behalf of producers of goods and services and their potential customers.	Edmunds.com, BizRate.com, Bloomberg.com, Zillow.com
Online marketplaces	Bring together buyers and sellers of products and services.	Amazon.com, eBay.com, Priceline.com
Portals	Operate central website for users to access specialized content and other services.	Google.com, Yahoo.com, MSN.com
Service providers	Provide services such as photo sharing, video sharing, online backup, and storage.	Flickr.com, Mapquest.com, YouTube.com
Transaction brokers	Process online sales transactions.	Etrade.com, Charlesschwab, Fidelity.com

FIGURE 5.11

E-Business Forms

Reducing Costs

Operational benefits of e-business include business processes that require less time and human effort or can be eliminated. Compare the cost of sending out 100 direct mailings (paper, postage, labour) to the cost of a bulk email campaign. Think about the cost of renting a physical location and operating phone lines versus the cost of maintaining an online site. Switching to an e-business model can eliminate many traditional costs associated with communicating by substituting systems, such as Live Help, that let customers chat live with support or sales staff.

Online air travel reservations cost less than those booked over the telephone. Online ordering also offers the possibility of merging a sales order system with order fulfillment and delivery so customers can check the progress of their orders at all times. E-businesses can also inexpensively attract new customers with innovative marketing and retain present customers with improved service and support.[22]

One of the most exciting benefits of e-business is its low startup costs. Today, anyone can start an e-business with just a website and a great product or service. Even a dog-walking operation can benefit from being an e-business.

Improving Operations

E-business has had some of its biggest impacts on customer service. Communication is often faster, more available, and more effective, encouraging customers to learn more about the product. Customers can often help themselves, using the content richness only a website can provide, and they can both shop and pay online without having to leave the house. Companies can also use email, special messages, and private password access to special areas for top customers.

Improving Effectiveness

Just putting up a simple website does not create an e-business. E-business sites must create buzz, be innovative, add value, and provide useful information. In short, they must build a sense of community and collaboration.

IT measures of efficiency, such as the amount of traffic on a site, don't tell the whole story. For example, they do not necessarily indicate large sales volumes. Many sites with lots of traffic have minimal sales. The best way to measure e-business success is to use *effectiveness* IT metrics, such as the revenue generated by Web traffic, the number of new customers acquired by Web traffic, and reductions in customer service calls resulting from Web traffic.

Interactivity measures advertising effectiveness by counting visitor interactions with the target ad, including time spent viewing the ad, number of pages viewed, and number of repeat visits to the advertisement. Interactivity measures are a giant step forward for advertisers, since traditional advertising methods—newspapers, magazines, radio, and television—provide few ways to track effectiveness. Figure 5.12 displays the e-business marketing initiatives that allow companies to expand their reach while measuring effectiveness.[23]

Marketing via E-Business
An *associate (affiliate) program* allows a business to generate commissions or referral fees when a customer visiting its website clicks on a link to another merchant's site. For example, if a customer on company A's site clicks on a banner ad to another vendor's site, company A will receive a referral fee or commission when the customer performs the desired action, typically making a purchase or completing a form.
A *banner ad* is a box running across a website that advertises the products and services of another business, usually another e-business. The banner generally contains a link to the advertiser's site. Advertisers can track how often customers click on a banner ad resulting in a click-through to their site. Often the cost of the banner ad depends on the number of customers who click on the ad. Web-based advertising services can track the number of times users click the ad, generating statistics that enable advertisers to judge whether the advertising fees are worth paying. Banner ads are like live classifieds. Tracking the number of clicks is an excellent way to understand the effectiveness of the ad.
A *click-through* is a count of the number of people who visit one site and click on an advertisement that takes them tadvertiser. Tracking effectiveness based on click-throughs guarantees exposure to target ads; however, it does not guarantee that the visitor liked the ad, spent any substantial time viewing the ad, or was satisfied with the information contained in the ad.
A *cookie* is a small file deposited on a hard drive by a website containing information about customers and their browsing activities. Cookies allow sites to record the comings and goings of customers, usually without their knowledge or consent.
A *pop-up ad* is a small Web page containing an advertisement that appears outside of the current site loaded in the browser. A *pop-under ad* is a form of a pop-up ad that users do not see until they close the current browser screen.
Viral marketing is a technique that induces websites or users to pass on a marketing message to other sites or users, creating exponential growth in the message's visibility and effect. One example of successful viral marketing is Hotmail, which promotes its service and its own advertisers' messages in every user's email notes. Viral marketing encourages users of a product or service supplied by an e-business to encourage friends to join. Viral marketing is a word-of-mouth type of advertising program.

FIGURE 5.12

Types of E-Business Marketing Initiatives

The ultimate outcome of any advertisement is a purchase. Organizations use metrics to tie revenue amounts and the number of new customers created directly back to the websites or banner ads. Through **clickstream data** they can observe the exact pattern of a consumer's navigation through a site. Figure 5.13 displays different types of clickstream metrics, and Figure 5.14 provides definitions of common metrics based on clickstream data. To interpret such data properly, managers try to benchmark against other companies. For instance, consumers seem to visit their preferred sites regularly, even checking back multiple times during a given session.[24]

Number of page views (i.e., the number of times a particular page has been presented to a visitor)
Pattern of websites visited, including most frequent exit page and most frequent prior website
Length of stay on the website
Dates and times of visits
Number of registrations filled out per 100 visitors
Number of abandoned registrations
Demographics of registered visitors
Number of customers with shopping carts
Number of abandoned shopping carts

FIGURE 5.13

Clickstream Data Metrics

Website Visit Metrics	
Stickiness (visit duration time)	Length of time a visitor spends on a website
Raw visit depth (total Web pages exposure per session)	Total number of pages a visitor is exposed to during a single visit to a website
Visit depth (total unique Web pages exposure per session)	Total number of unique pages a visitor is exposed to during a single visit to a website
Website Visitor Metrics	
Unidentified visitor	A visitor is an individual who visits a website. "Unidentified visitor" means that no information about that visitor is available.
Unique visitor	A unique visitor is one who can be recognized and counted only once within a given period of time.
Identified visitor	An ID is available that allows a user to be tracked across multiple visits to a website.

FIGURE 5.14

Metrics Measuring Website Success

LO4 ⎤ E-BUSINESS MODELS

An *e-business model* is an approach to conducting electronic business on the Internet. E-business transactions take place between two major entities—businesses and consumers. All e-business activities happen within the framework of two types of business relationships: (1) the exchange of products and services between businesses (business-to-business, or B2B) and (2) the exchange of products and services with consumers (business-to-consumer, or B2C) (see Figure 5.15).

E-Business Term	Definition		Business	Consumer
Business-to-business (B2B)	Applies to businesses buying from and selling to each other over the Internet.	Business	B2B	B2C
Business-to-consumer (B2C)	Applies to any business that sells its products or services to consumers over the Internet.			
Consumer-to-business (C2B)	Applies to any consumer that sells a product or service to a business over the Internet.	Consumer	C2B	C2C
Consumer-to-consumer (C2C)	Applies to sites primarily offering goods and services to assist consumers interacting with each other over the Internet.			

FIGURE 5.15
Basic E-Business Models

The primary difference between B2B and B2C is the nature of the customers; B2B customers are other businesses while B2C markets to consumers. Overall, B2B relations are more complex and have higher security needs; plus B2B is the dominant e-business force, representing 80 percent of all online business.[25] Figure 5.16 illustrates all of the e-business models: business-to-business, business-to-consumer, consumer-to-consumer, and consumer-to-business.

Business-to-Business (B2B)

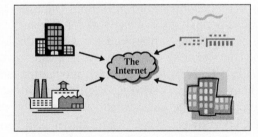

Business-to-Consumer (B2C)

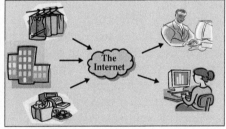

Consumer-to-Business (C2B)

Consumer-to-Consumer (C2C)

FIGURE 5.16
E-Business Models

Business-to-Business (B2B)

Business-to-business (B2B) applies to businesses buying from and selling to each other over the Internet. Online access to data, including expected shipping date, delivery date, and shipping status, provided either by the seller or a third-party provider is widely supported by B2B models. A new wave in B2B models called ***electronic marketplaces*** or ***e-marketplaces*** comprises interactive business communities providing a central market where multiple buyers and sellers can engage in e-business activities (see Figure 5.17). E-marketplaces present structures for conducting commercial exchange, consolidating supply chains, and creating new sales channels. Their primary goal is to increase market efficiency by tightening and automating the relationship between buyers and sellers. Existing e-marketplaces allow access to various mechanisms in which to buy and sell almost anything, from services to direct materials.

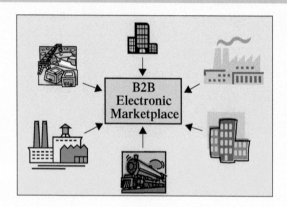

FIGURE 5.17

Business-to-Business E-Marketplace Overview

Business-to-Consumer (B2C)

Business-to-consumer (B2C) applies to any business that sells its products or services to consumers over the Internet. **Cyberflowers.com**, an e-business Canadian success story headquartered in Bolton, Ontario, is an Internet retailer of flowers and speciality gifts selling directly to consumers. It uses a network of florists for same-day delivery anywhere in the United States and Canada and two-business-day turnaround for worldwide delivery. The company's website provides customers with an online floral and specialty gift store. As a means of creating the Web's "most desirable online floral and gift community," the site is primed for easy navigation and provides interesting and targeted content. For example, Cyberflowers helps customers send ideal gifts to important people in their lives by offering a large selection of products, information about the latest trends and concepts, personalized service, and reasonable prices.[26] CellieGonsalves, owner of Cyberflowers, says, "the Internet is full of untapped opportunities for florists ... the medium fits with the flower purchaser's needs." For example, consumers can view flower arrangements on their computer screens to help them decide which one they prefer, these arrangements can be viewed day or night, prices in both American and Canadian currencies can be displayed, and shoppers can sign up for email reminders for upcoming holidays and anniversaries.[27] Common B2C e-business models aree-shops and e-malls (see Figure 5.18).

Consumer-to-Business (C2B)

Consumer-to-business (C2B) applies to any consumer that sells a product or service to a business over the Internet. One example of this model is **Priceline.com**, in which bidders (or customers) name their prices for items such as airline tickets or hotel rooms, and a seller decides whether to supply them. The demand for C2B e-business will increase over the next few years due to customers' desire for greater convenience and lower prices. The C2B business model is a complete reversal of the traditional business model where companies offer goods and services to consumers.

Brick-and-Mortar Business
A business that operates in
a physical store without an
Internet presence.
Example: T. J. Maxx

Click-and-Mortar Business
A business that operates
in a physical store and on
the Internet.
Example: Barnes & Noble

Pure-Play (Virtual) Business
A business that operates on
the Internet only without a
physical store.
Example: Google

FIGURE 5.18

Forms of B2C Operations

Consumer-to-Consumer (C2C)

Consumer-to-consumer (C2C) applies to sites primarily offering goods and services to assist consumers interacting with each other over the Internet. eBay, the Internet's most successful C2C online auction website, links like-minded buyers and sellers for a small commission.

C2C online communities, or virtual communities, interact via email groups, Web-based discussion forums, or chat rooms. C2C business models are consumer-driven and opportunities are available to satisfy most consumers' needs, ranging from finding a mortgage to job hunting. They are global swap shops based on customer-centred communication. C2C communities like **Kickstarter.com** and **Kiva.com** connect those wishing to make microloans or small investments to those in need of them. Figure 5.19 highlights the different types of C2C communities thriving on the Internet.

- *Communities of interest.* People interact with each other on specific topics, such as golfing and stamp collecting.

- *Communities of relations.* People come together to share certain life experiences, such as cancer patients, senior citizens, and car enthusiasts.

- *Communities of fantasy.* People participate in imaginary environments, such as fantasy football teams and playing one-on-one with Michael Jordan.

FIGURE 5.19

Types of C2C Communities

ORGANIZATIONAL STRATEGIES FOR E-BUSINESS

To be successful in e-business, an organization must master the art of electronic relationships. Traditional means of customer acquisition such as advertising, promotions, and public relations are just as important with a website. Primary business areas taking advantage of e-business include:

- Marketing/sales
- Financial services
- Procurement
- Customer service
- Intermediaries

Marketing/Sales

Direct selling was the earliest type of e-business, and it has proven to be a stepping stone to more complex commerce operations. Successes such as eBay, Indigo, Dell Inc., and Travelocity have sparked the growth of this segment, proving customer acceptance of e-business direct selling. Marketing and sales departments are initiating some of the most exciting e-business innovations.

Sears Canada introduced 58-inch Skype-enabled screens into 10 of its "modern store" fashion outlets with another 25 planned that allows their customers to ask their "fashion gurus" what they think when they are not physically present with the shopper. In 2010, Sears Canada found a 32 percent year-over-year growth in sales of brands in store that featured Skype online viewing screens. Sears is looking to expand on the outlets that have the Skype technology.[28]

Financial Services

Financial services websites are enjoying rapid growth, as they help consumers, businesses, and financial institutions distribute information with greater convenience and richness than is available in other channels. Consumers in e-business markets pay for products and services using a credit card or one of the methods outlined in Figure 5.20. Online business payments differ from online consumer payments because businesses tend to make large purchases (from thousands to millions of dollars) and typically do not pay with a credit card. Businesses make online payments using electronic data interchange (EDI) (see Figure 5.21). Transactions between businesses are complex and typically require a level of system integration between the businesses.

Financial cybermediary	A *financial cybermediary* is an Internet-based company that facilitates payments over the Internet. PayPal is the best-known example.
Electronic funds transfer	An *electronic funds transfer* is a mechanism for sending a payment from a chequing or savings account. There are many implementations of it, such as Interac E-Transfers.
Electronic bill presentment and payment (EBPP)	An *electronic bill presentment and payment (EBPP)* is a system that sends bills over the Internet and provides an easy-to-use mechanism (such as clicking on a button) to pay the bill. EBPP systems are available through local banks or online services such as epost and Quicken.
Digital wallet	A *digital wallet* is both software and information—the software provides security for the transaction, and the information includes payment and delivery information (e.g., the credit card number and expiration date) such as with RBC Secure Cloud.

FIGURE 5.20

Types of Online Consumer Payments

Electronic data interchange (EDI) is a standard format for exchanging business data. One way an organization can use EDI is through a *value-added network (VAN)*, which is a private network, provided by a third party, for exchanging information through a high-capacity connection. VANs support electronic catalogues (from which orders are placed), EDI-based transactions (the actual orders), security measures such as encryption, and EDI mailboxes.

Financial EDI (financial electronic data interchange) is a standard electronic process for B2B market purchase payments. National Cash Management Systems is an automated clearinghouse in the United States that supports the reconciliation of the payments.

FIGURE 5.21

Types of Online Business Payment

Many organizations are now turning to providers of electronic trading networks for enhanced Internet-based network and messaging services. Electronic trading networks are service providers that manage network services. They support business-to-business integration information exchanges, improved security, guaranteed service levels, and command centre support (see Figure 5.22). As electronic trading networks expand their reach and the number of Internet businesses continues to grow, so will the need for managed trading services. Using these services allows organizations to reduce time to market and the overall development, deployment, and maintenance costs associated with their integration infrastructures.

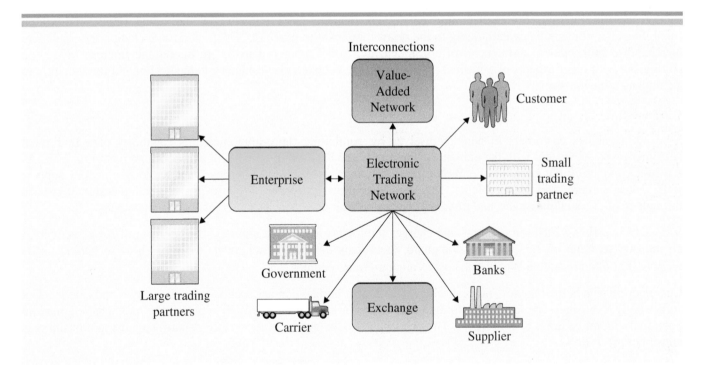

FIGURE 5.22

Diagram of an Electronic Trading Network

Traders at Vanguard Petroleum Corporation [U.S.] used to spend most days on the phone, patrolling the market for pricing and volume information to strike the best possible deal. The process was slow and tied up traders on one negotiation at a time, making it difficult to stay on top of quickly changing prices. One winter, for example, the weather got cold and stayed cold, causing propane prices to increase dramatically. The price was moving so fast that Vanguard was missing opportunities to buy, sell, and execute deals because it was able to complete only one deal at a time.

To bridge these shortcomings and speed the process, Vanguard became one of the first users of Chalkboard, a commodity markets electronic trading network that is now part of ChemConnect, a B2B e-marketplace. Vanguard uses Chalkboard to put bids and offers in front of hundreds of traders and complete various trades at multiple delivery points simultaneously. Vanguard now completes deals in real time and is able to access a broader audience of buyers and sellers.[29]

Procurement

Maintenance, repair, and operations (MRO) materials (also called ***indirect materials***) are materials necessary for running an organization but do not relate to the company's primary business activities. Typical MRO goods are office supplies (such as pens and paper), equipment, furniture, computers, and replacement parts. In the traditional approach to MRO purchasing, a purchasing manager received a paper-based request for materials. The purchasing manager then needed to search a variety of paper catalogues to find the right product at the right price. Not surprisingly, the administrative cost for purchasing indirect supplies often exceeded the unit value of the product itself. According to the Organisation for Economic Co-operation and Development (OECD), companies with more than $500 million in revenue spend an estimated $75 to $150 to process a single purchase order for MRO supplies.[30]

E-procurement is the B2B purchase and sale of supplies and services over the Internet. The goal of many e-procurement applications is to link organizations directly to pre-approved supplier catalogues and to process the entire purchasing transaction online. Linking to electronic catalogues significantly reduces the need to check the timeliness and accuracy of supplier information.

An ***electronic catalogue*** presents customers with information about goods and services offered for sale, bid, or auction on the Internet. Some electronic catalogues manage large numbers of individual items, and search capabilities help buyers navigate quickly to the items they want to purchase. Other electronic catalogues emphasize merchandise presentation and special offers, much as a retail store is laid out to encourage impulse or add-on buying. As with other aspects of e-business, it is important to match electronic catalogue design and functionality to a company's business goals.

Customer Service

E-business enables customers to help themselves by combining the communications capability of a traditional customer response system with the content richness only the Web can provide—all available and operating 24/7. As a result, conducting business via the Web offers customers the convenience they want while freeing key support staff to tackle more complex problems. The Web also allows an organization to provide better customer service through email, special messages, and private password—Web access to special areas for top customers.

Vanguard manages $2 trillion in assets and charges the lowest fees in the industry: 0.19 percent of net assets versus an industry average of 1.51 percent. Vanguard keeps fees down by teaching its investors how to better use its website. For good reason: a Web logon costs Vanguard mere pennies.[31]

Customer service is the business process whereby the most human contact occurs between a buyer and a seller. Not surprisingly, e-business strategists are finding that customer service via the Web is one of the most challenging and potentially lucrative areas of e-business. The primary issue facing customer service departments using e-business is consumer protection.

E-BUSINESS BENEFITS AND CHALLENGES

According to **Internetworldstats.com**, the Internet links over 2.4 billion people worldwide. Experts predict that over the next several years, global Internet use will triple, making e-business a more significant factor in the global economy. As e-business improves, organizations will experience benefits and challenges alike. Figure 5.23 details e-business benefits for an organization.

Highly accessible	Businesses can operate 24 hours a day, 7 days a week, 365 days a year.
Increased customer loyalty	Additional channels to contact, respond to, and access customers contributes to customer loyalty.
Improved information content	In the past, customers had to order catalogues or travel to a physical facility before they could compare price and product attributes. Electronic catalogues and Web pages present customers with updated information in real time about goods, services, and prices.
Increased convenience	E-business automates and improves many of the activities that make up a buying experience.
Increased global reach	Business, both small and large, can reach new markets.
Decreased cost	The cost of conducting business on the Internet is substantially lower than traditional forms of business communication.

FIGURE 5.23

E-Business Benefits

The Internet is forcing organizations to refocus their information systems from the inside out. A growing number of companies are already using the Internet to streamline their business processes, procure materials, sell products, automate customer service, and create new revenue streams. Although the benefits of e-business systems are enticing, developing, deploying, and managing these systems is not always easy. Unfortunately, e-business is not something a business can just go out and buy. Figure 5.24 details the challenges facing e-business.

Protecting consumers	Consumers must be protected against unsolicited goods and communication, illegal or harmful goods, insufficient information about goods or their suppliers, invasion of privacy, and cyberfraud.
Leveraging existing systems	Most companies already use information technology to conduct business in non-Internet environments, such as marketing, order management, billing, inventory, distribution, and customer service. The Internet represents an alternative and complementary way to do business, but it is imperative that e-business systems integrate existing systems in a manner that avoids duplicating functionality and maintains usability, performance, and reliability.
Increasing liability	E-business exposes suppliers to unknown liabilities because Internet commerce law is vaguely defined and differs from country to country. The Internet and its use in e-business have raised many ethical, social, and political issues, such as identity theft and information manipulation.
Providing security	The Internet provides universal access, but companies must protect their assets against accidental or malicious misuse. System security, however, must not create prohibitive complexity or reduce flexibility. Customer information also needs to be protected from internal and external misuse. Privacy systems should safeguard the personal information critical to building sites that satisfy customer and business needs. A serious deficiency arises from using the Internet as a marketing means. Sixty percent of Internet users do not trust the Internet as a payment channel. Making purchases via the Internet is considered unsafe by many. This issue affects both the business and the consumer. However, with encryption and the development of secure websites, security is becoming less of a constraint for e-businesses.
Adhering to taxation rules	The Internet is not yet subject to the same level of taxation as traditional businesses. While taxation should not discourage consumers from using electronic purchasing channels, it should not favour Internet purchases over store purchases either. Instead, a tax policy should provide a level playing field for traditional retail businesses, mail-order companies, and Internet-based merchants. The Internet marketplace is rapidly expanding, yet it remains mostly free from traditional forms of taxation.

FIGURE 5.24

E-Business Challenges

Consumer Protection

An organization that wants to dominate by using superior customer service as a competitive advantage must not only consider how to service its customers, but also how to protect its customers. Organizations must recognize that many consumers are unfamiliar with their digital choices, and some e-businesses are well aware of these vulnerabilities. For example, 17-year-old high school senior Francis Cornworth offered his "Young Man's Virginity" for sale on eBay. The offer attracted a $10 million phony bid. Diana Duyser sold half of a grilled cheese sandwich that resembles the Virgin Mary to the owners of an online casino for US$28,000 on eBay. Figure 5.25 highlights the different protection areas for consumers.[32]

- Unsolicited goods and communication
- Illegal or harmful goods, services, and content
- Insufficient information about goods or their suppliers
- Invasion of privacy
- Cyberfraud

FIGURE 5.25
Consumer Protection Issues

Regardless of whether the customers are other businesses or end consumers, one of their greatest concerns is the security level of their financial transactions. This includes all aspects of electronic information, but focuses mainly on the information associated with payments (e.g., a credit card number) and the payments themselves, that is, the "electronic money." An organization must consider such issues as encryption, secure socket layers (SSL), and secure electronic transactions (SET), as explained in Figure 5.26.

Encryption scrambles information into an alternative form that requires a key or password to enable reading the information. It is achieved by scrambling letters, replacing letters, replacing letters with numbers, and other ways.

A *secure socket layer (SSL)* (1) creates a secure and private connection between a client and server computer, (2) encrypts the information, and (3) sends the information over the Internet. SSL is identified by a website address that includes an "s" at the end—https.

A *secure electronic transaction (SET)* is one using a transmission security method that ensures the transaction is secure and legitimate. Similarly to SSL, SET encrypts information before sending it over the Internet. However, SET also enables customer authentication for credit card transaction. SETs are endorsed by major e-commerce players including MasterCard, Visa, Netscape, and Microsoft.

FIGURE 5.26
E-Business Security Methods

A key element of e-marketplaces is their ability to provide not only transaction capabilities but also dynamic, relevant content to trading partners. The first e-business websites provided shopping cart capabilities built around product catalogues. Now, as a result of the complex e-marketplace that must support existing business processes and systems, content is becoming even more critical for e-marketplaces. Buyers need good content description to make informed purchases, and sellers need content to properly market and differentiate themselves from the competition. Content and product description establish the common understanding between both parties to the transaction. As a result, the accessibility, usability, accuracy, and richness of that content directly affect the transaction. Figure 5.27 displays the different benefits and challenges of various e-marketplace revenue models.

Revenue Model	Benefits	Challenges
Transaction fees	■ Can be directly tied to savings (both process and price savings) ■ Important revenue source when high level of liquidity (transaction volume) is reached	■ If process savings are not completely visible, use of the system is discouraged (incentive to move transactions offline) ■ Transaction fees likely to decrease with time
Licence fees	■ Creates incentives to do many transactions ■ Customization and back-end integration leads to lock-in of participants	■ Upfront fee is a barrier to entry for participants ■ Price differentiation is complicated
Subscription fees	■ Creates incentives to do transactions ■ Price can be differentiated ■ Possibility to build additional revenue from new user groups	■ Fixed fee is a barrier to entry for participants
Fees for value-added services	■ Service offering can be differentiated ■ Price can be differentiated ■ Possibility to build additional revenue from established and new user groups (third parties)	■ Cumbersome process for customers to continually evaluate new services
Advertising fees	■ Well-targeted advertisements can be perceived as value-added content by trading participants ■ Easy to implement	■ Limited revenue potential ■ Overdone or poorly targeted advertisements can be disturbing elements on the website

FIGURE 5.27

The Benefits and Challenges of Various E-Marketplace Revenue Models

---

OPENING CASE QUESTIONS

Pinterest: Billboards for the Internet

1. Do you consider Pinterest a form of disruptive or sustaining technology?

2. Describe the e-business model and revenue model for Pinterest.

3. What is open source software and how might Pinterest take advantage of it?

5.2   WEB 2.0 AND BEYOND

LO5   WEB 2.0

Web 2.0's vast disruptive impact is just beginning. *Web 2.0* is a set of economic, social, and technology trends that collectively form the basis for the next generation of the Internet—a more mature, distinctive medium characterized by user participation, openness, and network effects. Although the term suggests a new version of the WWW, it does not refer to an update to Web technical specifications; instead, it refers to changes in the ways software developers and end users use the Web as a platform. According to Tim O'Reilly, "Web 2.0 is the business revolution in the computer industry caused by the move to the Internet as platform, and an attempt to understand the rules for success on that new platform." Figure 5.28 displays the move from Web 1.0 to Web 2.0.[33]

	Web 1.0		Web 2.0
	Doubleclick	→	Google AdSense
	Ofoto	→	Flickr
	Akamai	→	Bittorrent
	Mp3.com	→	Napster
	Britannica Online	→	Wikipedia
	Personal Websites	→	Blogging
	Evite	→	Upcoming.org and EVDB
	Domain Name Speculation	→	Search Engine Optimization
	Page Views	→	Cost per Click
	Screen Scraping	→	Web Services
	Publishing	→	Participation
	Content Management Systems	→	Wikis
	Directories (Taxonomy)	→	Tagging ("Folksonomy")
	Stickiness	→	Syndication

FIGURE 5.28
The Move from Web 1.0 to Web 2.0

More than just the latest technology buzzword, Web 2.0 is a transformative force that is propelling companies across all industries toward a new way of doing business. Those who act on the Web 2.0 opportunity stand to gain an early-mover advantage in their markets. What is causing this change? Consider the following raw demographic and technological drivers:

■ Billions of people around the globe now have access to the Internet.

■ According to Morgan Stanley, in 2015 the Web will be accessed by mobile devices more than by desktop computer. As of 2013, 17.4 percent of users accessed the Web via mobile phones with those in Asia accessing the Web 26.6 percent via mobile phones.[34]

■ As of the end of 2013, 87.3 million American households had broadband connections.[35]

Combine these drivers with the fundamental laws of social networks and lessons from the Web's first decade, and you get Web 2.0, the next-generation, user-driven, intelligent Web:

■ As of late 2013, **Facebook.com** had 1.19 billion subscribers and was the site most visited by American Web surfers. It surpassed Google with 8.93 percent of all American visits in late 2010 to gain this status.

■ Google+ (**plus.google.com**), introduced in late June 2011 on an invitation-only basis, topped 540 million active users in late 2013.

■ **Twitter.com** on an average day delivers 58 million tweets; on its first day it delivered 224.[36]

Mashups

A **Web mashup** is a website or Web application that uses content from more than one source to create a completely new service. The term is typically used in the context of music; putting Jay-Z lyrics over a Radiohead song makes something old new. The Web version of a mashup allows users to mix map data, photos, video, news feeds, blog entries, and so on. Content used in mashups is typically sourced from an ***application programming interface (API)***, which is a set of routines, protocols, and tools for building software applications. A good API makes it easier to

business." This being so, plans for improvements to the intranet had to be part of a larger communications strategy for the company—one that addressed email communications and people and manager communications as well as the intranet.[41]

Four common tools for accessing Internet information are:

- Intranets
- Extranets
- Portals
- Kiosks

Intranets

An *intranet* is an internalized portion of the Internet, protected from outside access, that allows an organization to provide access to information and application software to only its employees. An intranet is an invaluable tool for presenting organizational information, as it provides a central location where employees can find information. It can host all kinds of company-related information such as benefits, schedules, strategic directions, and employee directories. At many companies, each department has its own Web page on the intranet for departmental information sharing. An intranet is not necessarily open to the external Internet, but it enables organizations to make internal resources available using familiar Internet clients, such as Web browsers, newsreaders, and email.

Intranet publishing is the ultimate in electronic publishing. Companies realize significant returns on investment (ROI) simply by publishing information, such as employee manuals or telephone directories, on intranets rather than printed media.

Canadian telecommunications giant Bell Canada created an intranet for its employees to facilitate information access, creation, sharing, and use across the enterprise. Bell also uses its intranet for a variety of business purposes. For example, customer service representatives use it to retrieve rate plan information, phone specifications, and promotions details, improving the speed and accuracy of the service they provide to customers. To ensure the information shared is accurate and current, approximately 500 Bell Canada employees are able to update the intranet's content. The content management system language translation capabilities allow Bell Canada to offer content in both French and English. Bell Canada's intranet is accessible to customer service representatives across four divisions, improving communication among its users.[42]

Extranets

An *extranet* is an intranet that is available to strategic allies (such as customers, suppliers, and partners). Many companies are building extranets as they begin to realize the benefit of offering individuals outside the organization access to intranet-based information and application software such as order processing. Having a common area where employees, partners, vendors, and customers access information can be a major competitive advantage.

Walmart created an extranet for its suppliers, who can view detailed product information at all Walmart locations. Suppliers log on to the extranet and view metrics on products such as current inventory, orders, forecasts, and marketing campaigns. This helps the company's suppliers maintain their supply chains and ensure Walmart never runs out of products.[43]

Portals

A *portal* is a website that offers a broad array of resources and services, such as email, online discussion groups, search engines, and online shopping malls.

Not so long ago, the only way to get any return on the junk in your garage was to hold a yard sale. eBay changed all that. Now tens of thousands of small and medium-size businesses use eBay as their primary storefront, bringing e-commerce to the people. According to eBay lore, the first item auctioned was a broken laser pointer that sold for $14.83, proving that some one somewhere will buy just about anything. Several billion dollars' worth of transactions later, the proof is on firmer ground than ever.

There are general portals and specialized or niche portals. Leading general portals include **Yahoo.com**, **TheLoop.ca**, and **Canoe.ca**. Examples of niche portals are **Garden.com** (for gardeners), and **Fool.com** (for investors).

Pratt & Whitney, one of the largest aircraft-engine manufacturers in the world, has sales and service field offices geographically scattered around the globe that at one time were connected via expensive dedicated lines. The company saved $2.6 million annually by replacing the dedicated lines with high-speed Internet access to its field service portal. Field staff can find information they need in a fraction of the time it took before. The company estimates this change will save another $8 million per year in "process and opportunity" savings.[44]

Kiosks

A *kiosk* is a publicly accessible computer set up to allow interactive information browsing. In a kiosk, the operating system has been hidden from view, and the program runs in full-screen mode with a few simple tools for navigation.

Indigo Books & Music Inc., Canada's largest books retail chain, offers in-store customers access to Web kiosks as part of its commitment to providing a stress-free, service-driven approach to satisfying book and music lovers. Customers can search and buy books, DVDs, videos, gifts, and music; choose home or store delivery; and find out about upcoming events at stores. The company operates over 600-plus kiosks across Canada in its Indigo and Chapters stores. To improve the customer experience, Indigo is constantly updating the kiosks with new functionality, such as offering more product lines; creating category pages and boutiques; and allowing customers to use discount cards and review and manage their accounts. In addition, the kiosks have resulted in small increases in customer conversion rates and sales.[45]

NEW TRENDS IN E-BUSINESS: E-GOVERNMENT AND M-COMMERCE

Recent business models that have arisen to enable organizations to take advantage of the Internet and create value are within e-government. *E-government* uses strategies and technologies to transform government(s) by improving the delivery of services and enhancing the quality of interaction with the citizen-consumer within all branches of government (see Figure 5.31).

One example of an e-government portal, **www.canada.gc.ca**, the official Canadian gateway to all federal government information, is the catalyst for a growing electronic government. Its powerful search engine and ever-growing collection of topical and customer-focused links connect citizens and businesses, as well as visitors and people immigrating to Canada, to millions of Web pages from the federal government. Figure 5.29 highlights specific e-government models.

M-Commerce

Today, Internet-enabled mobile devices out number PCs. *Mobile commerce*, or *m-commerce*, is the ability to purchase goods and services through a wireless Internet-enabled device. The emerging technology behind m-commerce is a mobile device equipped with a Web-ready micro-browser or smartphone. Using new forms of technology, smartphones offer fax, email, and phone capabilities all in one, paving the way for m-commerce to be accepted by an increasingly mobile workforce. Figure 5.30 gives a visual overview of m-commerce.

Constituent-to-government (C2G)	C2G mainly constitutes the areas where a constituent interacts with the government. It includes community spaces where people themselves can post information and opinions about government and talk to politicians and government decision makers directly.
Government-to-business (G2B)	This model includes all government interaction with business enterprises, whether it be procurement of goods and services from suppliers or information regarding legal and business issues that is transmitted electronically.
Government-to-constituent (G2C)	Governments around the world are now dealing with constituents electronically, providing them with updated information. Governments are also processing applications for visas, renewal of passports and driver's licences, advertising of tender notices, and other services online.
Government-to-government (G2G)	Governments around the world are now dealing with other governments electronically. This e-business model, still at the inception stage, will enhance international trade and information retrieval—for example, on criminal records of new migrants. At the provincial level, information exchange and processing of transactions online will enable enhanced efficiencies.

FIGURE 5.29

E-Government Models

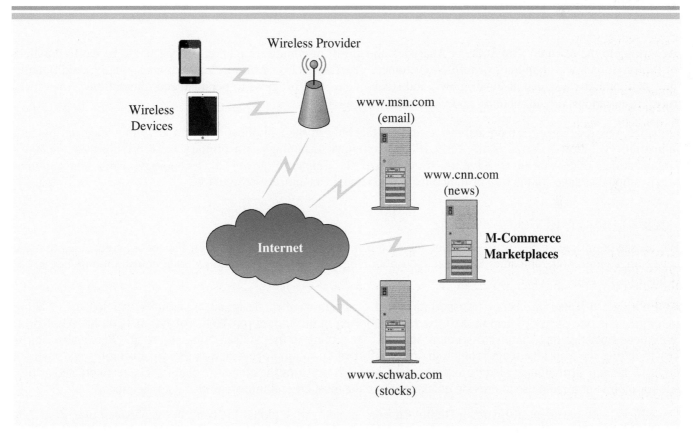

FIGURE 5.30

M-Commerce Technology Overview

	Business	Consumer (constituent)	Government
Business	B2B canbiotech.com	B2C canadiantire.ca	B2G lockheedmartin.com
Consumer (constituent)	C2B priceline.com	C2C ebay.ca	C2G hamiltoncatch.org
Government	G2B canadabusiness.gc.ca	G2C servicecanada.gc.ca	G2G gateway.gov.uk

FIGURE 5.31

Extended E-Business Models

According to the research firm Strategy Analytics, the global m-commerce market is expected to be worth hundreds of billion dollars with hundreds of million customers generating tens of billion transactions annually. Additionally, information activities such as email, news, and stock quotes will progress to personalized transactions, "one-click" travel reservations, online auctions, and video conferencing.[46]

Organizations face changes more extensive and far-reaching in their implications than anything since the modern industrial revolution occurred in the early 1900s. Computer technology is a primary force driving these changes. Organizations that want to survive must recognize the immense power of technology, carry out required organizational changes in the face of it, and learn to operate in an entirely different way.

Social Media and Business

We all see companies advertising on Facebook, companies with their own pages on Facebook, companies that are active on Twitter, and companies that have their own blogs for both internal and external consumption—but where is business in terms of social media?

At Enbridge, a leader in energy transportation and distribution, they designed an intranet that led to its being recognized as one of the 10 best in 2010 by Jakob Nielsen in his annual top 10 list of intranets on his Alert Box. Why does Enbridge have an award-winning intranet? According to the Nielsen Norman group: "Personalization is key to letting the Enbridge team provide the right information to employees across the organization's six business units. Content contributors are led by an Editor-in-Chief, who ensures the content's quality. The team created a 'lite' site for mobile or remote use to provide quick access to the most critical information and applications."

Dave Fleet, vice-president of Edelman Digital Canada, an innovative global PR firm, in his personal blog describes trends to watch for on the social media front with business. In addition to the listing the top trends, he describes the best practices needed to ensure that a company will be able to take advantage of the trends. Some of the more interesting trends are: (1) integrating social media with all other forms of corporate communication and business functions; (2) using social customer support; (3) realizing that its influence is maturing and that it is no longer about reaching out, but about providing thought leadership and expertise, and social media can be the tool to do this; and

(4) realizing that social impacts drive reputation (think of BP and the Gulf of Mexico in 2010 or the Fukushima nuclear disaster in Japan in 2011). For a complete list you can visit Fleet's blog at **DaveFleet.com**.

Edelman Digital conducts a yearly worldwide Trust Barometer survey. In 2011 Edelman found that how people structure trust is changing. It found that people look at factors like transparency, engagement, and profit with a purpose in messages they receive to gauge their trustworthiness.[47] Edelman has also found in recent years that the overall trust levels of Canadians are declining. Companies need to be aware of these changes and how they might impact the use of social media for business purposes.

The Future

Mozilla, the organization that brings us tools such as the Firefox browser and the Thunderbird email client, also collects big data on the use of the Internet. According to Mozilla's figures, in 2012 there were 81 million new websites, 634 million websites in total, and 2.7 billion Internet users worldwide. In addition, there were an estimated 2.1 billion mobile broadband subscriptions by the end of 2013. Just how prevalent are mobile devices? According to the International Communications Union and the United Nations in 2013, of the 7.1 billion people on earth, 6 billion have access to a mobile phone (with a total of 6.8 billion mobile subscriptions worldwide), while only 4.5 billion have access to a toilet.

It took 22 years for the Internet to see its first two billion users, but in the next five years it will have gained another two billion. Of those two billion, 65 percent will be from the developing world and 50 percent will be living below the poverty line. In 2012–13 emerging markets like the Philippines, Indonesia, and India have seen the strongest growth. What will the Internet look like in five years? What will be the predominate languages used? How are the WWW and the Internet going to be used?

An example today of use in the developing world comes from Brazil. In the slums of cities like Rio and Brasilia, one sees houses with satellite dishes on them. These dishes are not for television but for Internet connections. Neighbours pool the money saved by going without one meal a week so that they can share the Internet between a group of five or six households. Why? In one case it is because the homeowner is a bricklayer and with Internet access he can have a business website to attract high-end clients who would not come to his place of business in the slums.

In the developing world the Internet is even allowing everyone to time shift and/or place-shift more and more. In 2013 former Mozilla CEO Gary Kovacs wrote that his family had just cancelled their cable subscription because they can get everything they watch on television from Internet sources, and watch what they want when they want.[48]

OPENING CASE QUESTIONS

Pinterest: Billboards for the Internet

4. Categorize Pinterest as an example of Web 1.0 (e-business) or Web 2.0.

5. Create a plan for how a startup company could take advantage of Web 3.0 and generate the idea for the next great website that would be similar to Pinterest.

6. Evaluate the challenges facing Pinterest and identify ways the company can prepare to face these issues.

7. How have social networking sites used technology to change how people communicate with each other?

SUMMARY OF KEY THEMES

The purpose of this chapter was to provide you with an overview of doing business on the Internet. Understanding how Web-based technologies have revolutionized the way organizations conduct business is key to a successful future in business. Internet technologies have not only improved (and sometimes replaced) traditional ways of doing business, but also introduced new business opportunities and ventures.

From this overview, you should now have a better understanding of the benefits and challenges afforded by the Internet, recent trends that have occurred and are occurring in the market-place, and the various strategies and models that organizations use to deploy electronic business. Armed with this knowledge, you, the business student, should be better prepared to place the material presented in the remainder of this textbook in context of the larger e-business picture—the global marketplace.

KEY TERMS

Application programming interface (API)

Associate (affiliate) program

Banner ad

Business-to-business (B2B)

Business-to-consumer (B2C)

Click-through

Clickstream data

Consumer-to-business (C2B)

Consumer-to-consumer (C2C)

Cookie

Cyber mediation

Digital Darwinism

Digital divide

Digital wallet

Disintermediation

Disruptive technology

E-business

E-business model

E-commerce

E-government

E-procurement

Electronic bill presentment and payment (EBPP)

Electronic catalogue

Electronic data interchange (EDI)

Electronic marketplaces (e-marketplaces)

Encryption

Extranet

Financial cybermediary

Financial EDI (financial electronic data interchange)

Hypertext transfer protocol (HTTP)

Information reach

Information richness

Interactivity

Intermediaries

Internet

Intranet

Kiosk

Long tail

Maintenance, repair, and operations (MRO) materials (indirect materials)

Mashup editors

Mass customization

Mobile commerce (m-commerce)

Personalization

Pop-under ad

Pop-up ad

Portal

Protocols

Reintermediation

Secure electronic transaction (SET)

Secure socket layer (SSL)

Semantic Web

Service-oriented architecture (SOA)

Sustaining technology

Value-added network (VAN)

Viral marketing

Web 2.0

Web 3.0

Web mashup

World Wide Web (WWW)

The Rise and Fall and Rise of Canadian Tire's Website Ordering

This case illustrates how a company can change and reposition its strategic use of its B2C website over time.

The Launch of Shopping on CanadianTire.ca

In November 2000, Canadian Tire was one of the last of Canada's leading retailers to launch its online B2C shopping site, **www.CanadianTire.ca**. The site was promoted as offering great convenience and access to product information and Canadian Tire money rewards. For example, shoppers could go online to browse and purchase thousands of home, automotive, and sports and leisure products. Additionally, there were perks such as being able to have purchases gift-wrapped and delivered to any address in Canada, and searching for products in various ways (e.g., by product or lifestyle category, by price range, and by what's on special). Added-value features included displaying related products on the returned pages of a search query, and providing a comprehensive amount of information on each product viewed. This included colour photographs of products, detailed descriptions of product features, customer reviews, warranty information, and of course, pricing details. Items on sale were highlighted in red. Additionally, the site could be personalized if shoppers registered in the "My Canadian Tire" section of the site. Doing so allowed customers to earn Canadian Tire money rewards on purchases, just as shoppers would if they purchased goods in person at a physical store. Significantly, Canadian Tire allocated a dedicated inventory to fulfill online orders with real-time inventory management that allowed shoppers to track the progress of their orders online from shipment right through to delivery. By providing such a strong and robust website for shoppers, Canadian Tire believed its B2C site offered a competitive and strategic advantage over its competitors, particularly the country's perennial retail giant Walmart Canada, which developed its B2C site to showcase products but did not sell them online at the time.[49]

Changes in the Wind

Fast-forward to 2009 and Canadian Tire's B2C website strategy changed. The company decided to stop selling its merchandise on the Web, and to promote and use its site as strictly a consumer research tool. Canadian Tire's experience found that most customers were just using the site to browse and search for products and compare prices, and then visiting a Canadian Tire store to purchase. This makes sense, considering that Canadian Tire had more than 450 retail stores across the country within a 15-minute drive of 85 percent of the Canadian population at the time. Having such a strong network of stores conveniently located to consumers undermined the need to purchase products over the Web. This was especially true of large purchase items, such as patio furniture sets, which are expensive to ship. Further, the company found that shoppers who lived far away from a physical store were not likely to order products online anyway, since the shipping costs made the purchase price of goods prohibitive. Also, Canadian Tire found that it was spending too much money on third-party help to fulfill Web orders and on dedicated warehouse space allocated strictly to the online business.

The Landscape Changes Again

In late 2011 after Canadian Tire's acquisition of Forzani Group, the acquisition of Zellers by Target, and changes in Canadians' online shopping habits such as ordering tires from U.S. websites and having them shipped to mechanics in Canada for installation, Canadian Tire re-examined its Web strategy.[50] Additionally, Walmart was introducing its new fully functional e-commerce site **Walmart.ca**. Today, Canadian Tire's site offers a pay-and-pickup model for select items in its stores. With this model customers can purchase certain items from the website and get them at their local store when the items are ready for pickup. The items treated this way are ones that Canadian Tire thinks suitable for such handling, and the items must be in stock at the store selected by the customer. Individual stores may ship items to customers depending on that franchisee's policy.

Questions

1. How could Canadian Tire use e-business metrics to monitor its B2C website's performance?

2. What was Canadian Tire's original strategy for its B2C website?

3. Why did this strategy fail?

4. What is Canadian Tire's current strategy? Why is this strategy more conducive to the Canadian marketplace?

5. Explain the e-business benefits and challenges facing Canadian Tire.

CLOSING CASE TWO

Hamilton's GIS-Enhanced Website

This case shows how Web technologies can improve the traditional way of doing business.

The City of Hamilton, Ontario, uses a geographic information system (GIS) in almost every one of its departments for sewer, water, and road projects; urban and regional planning; emergency planning preparedness and dispatch; economic development; taxation; municipal elections; and even tracking of public health risks such as the West Nile Virus. A GIS contains a computer database that stores both digital mapping and descriptive text information about geographic features. Public use of this GIS is through a website, Map.Hamilton (**www.map.hamilton.ca**), that enables people to perform a variety of tasks, such as locate municipal services, verify the location of a particular address, view aerial photos for land use, measure distances and areas, investigate tax and other property information, etc. For example, the site can be used by parents to locate child care centre information within the City of Hamilton (see Figure 5.32). Businesses can use the site to show customers where they are and what other services are nearby. Developers around the world can use the information at Map.Hamilton to help find appropriate development opportunities.[51]

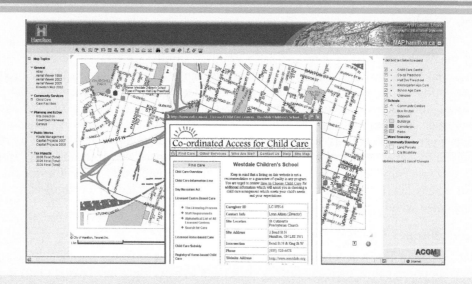

FIGURE 5.32

Finding Child Care Centre Information on Map.Hamilton.ca

The City's GIS-enhanced site renders more than 78,000 maps per month. To accomplish this task without the aid of a website would be a large drain on human resources and time by city staffers. The site thus provides a great cost savings to the city, since thousands of citizens can access the maps they need at their convenience. The strategic goals in providing citizens with these maps and associated services (e.g., giving citizens access to thematic maps of property taxes showing tax impacts and reassessments along with tools for looking up assessment values and taxes payable) are to spend money more wisely and to use technology to improve business processes. The City's GIS solutions are doing just that by improving customer service, aiding economic development, and helping staff members work more efficiently. The maps are a convenient way for staff and constituents to communicate and collaborate on issues—when solving problems over the phone or online, city staffers and citizens can look at the same map or picture on the Web at the same time. Plans for future map-based Web services could include "Where should I invest in Hamilton?" "Where's my snowplow?" and tools for finding a given location such as the closest library, park, or other municipal service.[52] Since newer Web-based mapping technologies, such as those provided by Google Earth, have raised end-user expectations on how online mapping tools should look and function, the City is currently reviewing options for streamlining the use of the site and its workflows. According to James Rickert, Supervisor of Business Applications at the City of Hamilton, "we are trying to address this issue by introducing new technology to help integrate what users are requesting with what information the City can provide."

The use of a GIS-enhanced website is part and parcel of the City's vision to provide Hamiltonians with convenient and reliable access to information and services via Map.Hamilton. The City is currently in the process of establishing a framework for the delivery of citizen services across all channels, including the Web. This framework will provide the guiding principles under which a new Web strategy will be developed, and under which new and improved customer-focused services will be implemented. These portal improvements, as well as the City's plans for future map-based Web services, speak to the constant and never-ending need to keep up with the development of new technologies, address end-user expectations, and deliver information and services in more efficient and effective ways. According to Rickert, these improvements, though required, can take considerable time and energy as the amount of work to implement the changes is "large, complex, and needs to be delivered in a way that does not cause confusion to portal users."[53]

Questions

1. How is technology being used by the City to support its strategic goals and operations?

2. What barriers likely exist in rolling out these technologies and securing their successful use and adoption?

3. How can the City leverage its GIS functionality for m-commerce?

4. What performance metrics should the City collect to assess the viability and robustness of its maps website (**map.hamilton.ca**)? Its City of Hamilton site (**hamilton.ca**)?

5. Why would the City want to develop a Web strategy that adheres to broad citizen services delivery guidelines that deal with non-Web channels?

CLOSING CASE THREE

eBay: The Ultimate E-Business

This case illustrates how eBay has successfully garnered business success with its e-business strategies but needs to be constantly on guard to adapt and respond to an ever-changing marketplace.

Pierre Omidyar was just 28 when he sat down over a long holiday weekend to write the original computer code for what eventually became an Internet super-brand—the auction site eBay. Omidyar viewed auctions as a fair mechanism for Internet commerce where sellers could set their minimum prices, and buyers could then determine an item's market value by bidding up to what they were willing to pay. A novel feedback system could allow buyers and sellers to rate each other, helping minimize fraud by enabling the community to police itself. "I really wanted to give the individual the power to be a producer as well. It was letting the users take responsibility for building the community," Omidyar would later explain.

The site launched on Labour Day, September 4, 1995, under the title of Auction Web, soon to be renamed after the site's domain name—**eBay.com** (a shortening of Echo Bay, Omidyar's consulting firm). The service was free at first, but started charging to cover Internet service provider costs.

A Viable Marketplace

eBay.com took off. It provided something novel that its users craved: an efficient, viable marketplace with a strong community built on fairness and trust. A photography student looking for a used camera could choose from various models across the nation and trust the timely delivery of the product. The owner of a vintage clothing store could sell to collectors living in different time zones. The community would expose a deceptive or fraudulent user and ban them from the marketplace.

Entrepreneurs in record numbers began setting up shop on eBay. For example, according to a survey conducted for eBay by ACNielsen International Research, 75,000 people supported themselves by selling items on eBay in 2002; however, by early 2008, the website boasted hundreds of millions of registered users, over 15,000 employees, and revenues of almost US$7.7 billion.

The stock market value of Omidyar's innovative company grew to US$2 billion in its first three years, and his site's staying power as an economic engine was evident. Jeffrey Skoll, a Stanford MBA, joined the company in 1996 after the site was already profitable. In March 1998, Meg Whitman took over as president and CEO. In September 1998, eBay launched a successful public offering, making both Omidyar and Skoll billionaires—three years after Omidyar created eBay. After nearly 10 years at eBay, Whitman decided to enter politics. On January 23, 2008, the company announced that Whitman would step down on March 31, 2008, and John Donahoe was selected to become president and CEO.

Business Ventures via eBay

This e-business has launched several sub-business ventures that add value for its customers, such as payments and communications. Over the years, eBay has had to create and adapt these businesses in response to changing marketplace conditions.

The Payment Business: PayPal

Founded in 1998, PayPal, a subsidiary eBay company that eBay purchased in 2002 for US$1.5 billion, enables any individual or business with an email address to securely, easily, and quickly send and receive payments online. PayPal's service builds on the existing financial infrastructure of bank accounts and credit cards, and uses the world's most advanced proprietary fraud prevention systems to create a safe, global, real-time payment solution. According to Scott Thompson, PayPal's president, the company's key advantage over rival payment systems is its fraud management capabilities and its global reach.

PayPal.com has quickly become a global leader in online payment solutions with almost 112.3 million active account members worldwide. Buyers and sellers on eBay, online retailers, online businesses, and traditional offline businesses are transacting with PayPal. It is available in 190 markets and operates in 25 currencies worldwide.

To grow this successful subsidiary even further to become one of the top global brands, PayPal plans to incorporate Bill Me Later Inc., which offers its own online payment service. Several merchants support both PayPal and Bill Me Later as separate payment options, and PayPal wants to strategically combine these services into a single option to promote uptake and usage. According to John Donahoe, there are only three global payment networks winners (Visa, American Express, and MasterCard) and he believes the same thing is going to happen in the online payment world—few winners will exist, perhaps only one—and there is a strong desire to take steps now to ensure PayPal is in that winning group. Further, PayPal plans to roll out an open development platform that will let other companies create Web applications that accept PayPal payments. The company believes this will not only let merchants experiment with the ways they will accept and process online payments, but also decrease PayPal's development costs as it enables millions of developers worldwide to build profitable and sustaining businesses with PayPal.

The Communication Business: Skype

Skype, a global Internet communications company, allows people everywhere to make free, unlimited, superior quality voice calls via its innovative peer-to-peer software. Launched in August 2003, today Skype boasts 299 million users.

In September 2005, eBay acquired Skype for approximately US$2.6 billion, anticipating that Skype would streamline and improve communications between buyers and sellers as it is integrated into the eBay marketplace. With Skype, buyers gained an easy way to talk to sellers quickly and get the information they need, and sellers could more easily build relationships. The auction company hoped the acquisition would strengthen its global marketplace and payments platform, while opening several new lines of business and creating significant new opportunities for the company.

In April 2009, eBay announced plans to sell off Skype. The reason for the spin off was a desire for eBay to focus on its core business of e-commerce. According to John Donahoe, Skype was a "great stand-alone business" but had "limited energies" with eBay. By selling Skype, the company was able to hone its efforts on improving its e-commerce site. One area of expansion is international e-commerce. Operations from outside North America account for more than half of eBay's revenue and there is certainly continued growth opportunity in this area, though competition is fast increasing.

Can eBay Retain Its Tech Savvy?

In the early days of the Web, eBay poured most of its resources into building a sophisticated infrastructure and auction system that could sustain large amounts of traffic and transactions. Later, eBay turned its energies toward acquisitions and expansions, such as PayPal and Skype, at the expense of delivering new technological tools and features to the eBay interface. Today, eBay's strategy is to reorient itself to a focus on e-commerce. More services have been developed for PayPal such as the addition of smartphone application and striking partnerships with thousands of Internet shopping sites.

Some industry analysts question whether eBay can revive its technical elegance in time to attract and retain customers toward its online auctions. For example, many customers complain that a search on eBay's site does not yield results that are as relevant as a search on Google, and that the tools available on eBay do not enable people to interact with others as easily as they can on social networking sites such as Facebook. Inside the company, some workers lament the exhaustive vetting process required to test new ideas that stifles and creates barriers to launching innovative technical solutions.

In response, eBay has made changes within the company. It has hired key senior personnel who have first-hand knowledge of how to translate customer requirements into technical solutions and restructured the organizational chart to ensure better cross-pollination of technological know-how and ideas across various business units. Such steps are aimed at promoting an internal culture and environment that is open and receptive to launching new technological innovations. Examples of technical solutions that aim to enhance the customer experience are the delivery of a "daily deal" widget that tips off shoppers to one-day deals on certain products, and an "email-a-friend" button next to each item posted on eBay that provides a simple way for customers to remind themselves and their friends of bargain details.[54]

Questions

1. What is eBay's e-business model and why has it been so successful?

2. How has eBay's strategy changed over the years?

3. eBay has long been an e-marketplace for used goods and collectibles. Today, it is increasingly a place where major businesses come to auction their wares. Why would a brand-name vendor set up shop on eBay?

4. What are the three different types of online auctions and which one is eBay using?

5. What are the different forms of online payment methods for consumers and business? How might eBay's customers benefit from the different payment methods?

6. Which metrics would you use if you were hired to assess the efficiency and effectiveness of eBay's website?

MAKING BUSINESS DECISIONS

1. Leveraging the Competitive Value of the Internet

Physical inventories have always been a major cost component of business. Linking to suppliers in real time dramatically enhances the classic goal of inventory "turn." The Internet provides a multitude of opportunities for radically reducing the costs of designing, manufacturing, and selling goods and services. **E-mango.ca**, a fruit e-marketplace, must take advantage of these opportunities or find itself at a significant competitive disadvantage. Identify the disadvantages that confront E-mango if it does not leverage the competitive value of the Internet.

2. Implementing an E-Business Model

The Genius is a revolutionary mountain bike with full suspension and shock-adjustable forks that is being marketed via the Internet. The Genius needs an e-business solution that will easily enable internal staff to deliver fresh and relevant product information throughout its website. To support its large audience, the company also needs the ability to present information in multiple languages and serve over one million page views per month to visitors in North America and Europe. Explain what e-business model you would use to market The Genius on the Internet.

3. Assessing Internet Capabilities

Sports Rentals is a small, privately owned business that rents sports equipment in Calgary. The company specializes in winter rentals, including ski, snowboarding, and snowmobile equipment. It has been in business for 20 years and, for the first time, it is experiencing a decline in rentals. The company's owner is puzzled by the recent decreases. The snowfall for the last two years has been outstanding, and the ski resorts have opened earlier and closed later than most previous years. Reports say tourism in Alberta is up, and the invention of loyalty programs has significantly increased the number of local skiers. Overall, business should be booming. The only reason for the decrease in sales might be the fact that big retailers such as Walmart and SportChek are now renting winter sports equipment. The company's owner would like your team's help in determining how he can use the Internet to help his company increase sales and decrease costs to compete with these big retailers.

4. Online Auction Sites

You are working for a new Internet startup company, eGoodMarket (**eGoodMarket.ca**), an online marketplace for selling goods and services. The company offers a wide variety of features and services that enable online members to buy and sell their goods and services quickly and conveniently. The company's mission is to provide a global trading platform where anyone can trade practically anything. Suggest some ways that eGoodMarket can extend its market reach beyond that of its competitor, eBay.com.

5. Everybody Needs an Internet Strategy

An Internet strategy addresses the reasons businesses want to "go online." "Going online" because it seems like the right thing to do now or because everyone else is doing it is not a good enough reason. A business must decide how it will best use the Internet for its particular needs. It must plan for where it wants to go and how best the Internet can help shape that vision. Before developing a strategy, a business should spend time on the Internet, see what similar businesses have grown, and what is most feasible, given a particular set of resources. Think of a new online business opportunity and answer the following questions:

1. Why do you want to put your business online?

2. What benefits will going online bring?

3. What effects will being connected to the Internet have on your staff, suppliers, and customers?

6. Searching for Disruption

SchedulesRUs.ca is a large corporation that develops software that automates scheduling and record keeping for medical and dental practices. SchedulesRUs.ca currently holds 48 percent of its market share, has more than 8,700 employees, and operates in six countries.

You are the vice-president of product development at SchedulesRUs.ca. You have just finished reading *The Innovator's Dilemma* by Clayton Christensen and you are interested in determining what types of disruptive technologies you can take advantage of, or should watch out for, in your industry. Use the Internet to develop a presentation highlighting the types of disruptive technologies you have found that have the potential to give the company a competitive advantage or could cause the company to fail.

7. Finding Innovation

Along with disruptive technologies, there are also disruptive strategies. The following are a few examples of companies that use disruptive strategies to gain competitive advantages:

- *Ford.* Henry Ford's Model T was so inexpensive that he enabled a much larger population of people, that historically could not afford cars, to own one.

- *JetBlue.* Whereas Southwest Airlines initially followed a strategy of new-market disruption, JetBlue's approach is low-end disruption. Its long-range viability depends on the major airlines' motivation to run away from the attack, as integrated steel mills and full-service department stores did.

- *McDonald's.* The fast-food industry has been a hybrid disrupter, making it so inexpensive and convenient to eat out that it created a massive wave of growth in the "eating out" industry. McDonald's earliest victims were mom-and-pop diners.

- *Circuit City and Best Buy.* These two companies disrupted the consumer electronics departments of full-service and discount department stores, which has sent them upmarket into higher-margin goods. Circuit City is also an example of what can happen to a company when its disruptive strategy fails to maintain competitive advantage after about 60 years of business.

There are numerous other examples of corporations that have used disruptive strategies to create competitive advantages. In a team, prepare a presentation highlighting three additional companies that used disruptive strategies to gain a competitive advantage.

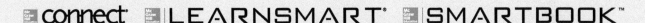

For more information on the resources available from McGraw-Hill Ryerson, go to www.mheducation.ca/he/solutions.

ENDNOTES

1. Ingrid Lunden, "Pinterest Updates Terms of Service as It Preps an API and Private Pinboards: More Copyright Friendly," *Tech Crunch*, April 2012; Chad McCloud, "What Pinterest Teaches Us About Innovation in Business," *Bloomberg Business Week*, May 2012; Courteney Palis, "Pinterest Traffic Growth Soars to New Heights: Experian Report," *The Huffington Post*, April 6, 2012.

2. "Popstar Justin Bieber Is on the Brink of Stardom," http://abcnews.go.com/GMA/Weekend/teen-pop-star-justin-bieber-discovered-youtube/story?id=9068403, accessed July 19, 2011; "Justin Bieber Tops Billboard 200 with 'My World 2.0,'" www.billboard.com/news/justin-bieber-tops-billboard-200-with-my-1004079496.story#/news/justin-bieber-tops-billboard-200-with-my-1004079496.story, accessed July 19, 2011.

3. Adam Lashinsky, "Kodak's Developing Situation," *Fortune*, January 20, 2003, p. 176.

4. www.wired.com, accessed November 15, 2003.

5. Adam Lashinsky, "Kodak's Developing Situation," *Fortune*, January 20, 2003, p. 176.

6. Clayton Christensen, *The Innovator's Solution* (Boston: Harvard Business Review Press, 2003).

7. Ibid.

8. Reprinted by permission of Harvard Business School Press. From *The Innovator's Dilemma*, by Clayton Christensen. Boston, MA. © 1997 by the Harvard Business School Publishing Corporation. All rights reserved.

9. "The World in 2013: ICT Facts and Figures," February 2013, International Telecommunications Union, Geneva, Switzerland.

10. Ibid.

11. "Canadians Spent $18.9B Online in 2012, Stats Can Says," October 28, 2013, http://www.cbc.ca/news/business/canadians-spent-18-9b-online-in-2012-statscan-says-1.2254150, accessed February 8, 2014.

12. "Internet Travel Hotel Booking Statistics," June 16, 2013, http://www.statisticbrain.com/internet-travel-hotel-booking-statistics, accessed March 23, 2014.

13. www.newmediatrendwatch.com/world-overview/91-online-travel-market?start=1, accessed October 2011.

14. http://info.cern.ch, accessed July 19, 2011.

15. "Internet Pioneers," www.ibiblio.org/pioneers/andreesen.html, accessed July 19, 2011.

16. Gunjan Bagla, "Bringing IT to Rural India One Village at a Time," *CIO Magazine*, March 1, 2005; Max Martin, "Text-Free Software to Bridge Digital Divide," http://indiatoday.intoday.in/site/story/Text-free+software+to+bridge+digital+divide/1/88480.html, accessed July 19, 2011.

17. www.facebook.com/press/info.php?statistics, accessed July 19, 2011.

18. Chris Anderson, Editor-in-Chief of *Wired* Magazine, "The Long Tail: Why the Future of Business Is Selling Less of More," www.longtail.com/2006.

19. "Disintermediation," TechTarget, http://whatis.techtarget.com/definition/0,,sid9_gci211962,00.html, accessed April 4, 2010.

20. www.biddingo.com/*.main?toPage=ScMenuWhatIs BnXP.jsp, accessed July 19, 2011.

21. "Reintermediation," *PC Magazine*, www.pcmag.com/encyclopedia_term/0,2542, t=reintermediation&i=50364,00.asp, accessed April 4, 2010.

22. Scott McCartney, "You Paid What for That Flight?," *The Wall Street Journal*, August 26, 2010, http://online.wsj.com/article/ SB10001424052748704540904575451653489562606.html.

23. "The Complete Web 2.0 Dictionary," www.go2web20.net, accessed June 24, 2007; "Web 2.0 for CIOs," www.cio.com/article/16807; www.emarketer.com, accessed January 2006.

24. Ibid.

25. www.emarketer.com, accessed July 2010.

26. www.cyberflowers.com/cyberflowers/about_us.php, accessed July 19, 2011.

27. Rolph Mali, "Florists Bloom Online," *Canadian Florist Magazine*, March 2002, http://florist.hortport.com/Past_Issues.htm?ID=778.

28. "Sears Canada Introduces In-Store Skype," www.powerretail.com.au/multichannel/sears-canada-introduces-in-store-skype, accessed February 9, 2014.

29. Frank Quinn, "The Payoff Potential in Supply Chain Management," www.ascet.com, accessed June 15, 2003.

30. www.oecd.org, accessed June 2005.

31. "At-Cost Investing," https://personal.vanguard.com/us/whatweoffer, accessed July 19, 2011; https://about.vanguard.com/who-we-are/fast-facts, accessed March 26, 2014.

32. "Watch Your Spending," *Business Week*, May 23, 2004.

33. Tim O'Reilly, "What Is Web 2.0: Design Patterns and Business Models for the Next Generation of Software," www.oreillynet.com/pub/a/oreilly/tim/news/2005/09/30/what-is-web-20.html, accessed July 19, 2011; "Web 2.0 for CIOs," *CIO Magazine*, www.cio.com/article/16807, accessed July 19, 2011.

34. JoliOdel, "New Study Shows the Mobile Web Will Rule by 2015," April 13, 2010,http://mashable.com/2010/04/13/mobile-web-stats, accessed March 23, 2014; Zoe Fox, "17.4% of Global Web Traffic Comes Through Mobile," August 23, 2013, http://mashable.com/2013/08/20/mobile-web-traffic, accessed March 23, 2014.

35. Emil Protalinski, "Over 70% of US Households Now Have Broadband Internet Access, with Cable Powering over 50% of the Market," December 9, 2013, http://thenextweb.com/insider/2013/12/09/70-us-households-now-broadband-internet-access-cable-powering-50-market/#!A3fHy, accessed March 23, 2014.

36. "Facebook Passes Google as Most Visited Site of 2010," www.computerworld.com/s/article/9202938/Facebook_passes_Google_as _most_visited_site_of_2010, accessed July 19, 2011; "Google+ Tops 10 Million Users, Confirms CEO Larry Page," www.wired.co.uk/news/archive/2011-07/18/google-plus-ten-million-visitors, accessed July 19, 2011; "Number of Active Users at Facebook over the Years," http://news.yahoo.com/number-active-users-facebook-over-230449748.html, accessed March 23, 2014; http://newsroom.fb.com/Key-Facts, accessed March 23, 2014; Jeff Bulas,"12 Awesome Social Media Facts and Statistics for 2013," September 20, 2013, http://www.jeffbullas.com/2013/09/20/12-awesome-social-media-facts-and-statistics-for-2013, accessed March 23, 2014; "Twitter Statistics," January 1, 2014, www.statisticbrain.com/twitter-statistics, accessed March 23, 2014.

37. "The Complete Web 2.0 Directory," www.go2web20.net, accessed July 19, 2011; "Web 2.0 for CIOs," www.cio.com/article/16807, accessed June 19, 2011.

38. Anne Zelenka, "The Hype Machine, Best Mashup of Mashup Camp 3," www.gigaom.com/2007/01/18/the-hype-machine-best-mashup-of-mashup-camp-3, accessed June 14, 2007; www.webmashup.com, accessed June 14, 2007; www.web3d.org/realtime-3d, accessed July 19, 2011.

39. Anne Zelenka, "The Hype Machine, Best Mashup of Mashup Camp 3," www.gigaom.com/2007/01/18/the-hype-machine-best-mashup-of-mashup-camp-3, accessed June 14, 2007; www.webmashup.com, accessed June 14, 2007.

40. Ibid.

41. André R. Robillard and Toby Ward, "Turning the Dream into Reality: Harnessing People Power to Create a High Productivity Intranet," Information Highways Conference, Toronto, Ontario, March 29, 2006.

42. "Bell Canada Manages Content for Its Call Centre," *Transform Magazine*, www.transformmag.com/techselections/showArticle.jhtml?articleID=16101051, accessed February 26, 2007.

43. Amy Johnson, "A New Supply Chain Forged," *Computerworld*, September 30, 2002.

44. "Pratt & Whitney," *Business Week*, June 2004.

45. "Case Study: Indigo Books & Music Inc.," www.microsoft.com/canada/casestudies/indigo.mspx, accessed February 26, 2007; www.creativeleap.ca/pages/folio/kiosk.html, accessed March 26, 2014.

46. "E-Commerce Taxation," www.icsc.org/srch/government/ECommerceFebruary2003.pdf, accessed July 19, 2011.

47. "2014 Edelman Trust Barometer Findings," http://edelman.ca/2014/01/30/2014-edelman-trust-barometer-canadian-findings, accessed April 3, 2014.

48. "The Socioeconomic Impact of the Mobile Internet," www.youtube.com/watch?v=1lUbyH2AOOg, accessed March 15, 2014; Gary Kovacs, "The Role and Use of Technology in the Delivery of Education," talk at University of Calgary, May 17, 2013; Jim Daly, "The Internet Has More Than 2 Billion Users and It's Just Getting Started," January 2, 2013, www.fedtechmagazine.com/article/2013/01/internet-has-more-2-billion-users-and-its-just-getting-started, accessed March 23, 2014.

49. Jim Fox, "Canadian Tire and Hudson's Bay: Latecomers to e-Commerce Game," *DSN Retailing Today,* December 11, 2000, pp. 10, 22.

50. www.canadiantire.ca/en/instore-pickup.html?adlocation=HP_slmmb2_Affiliate_Product_Ecomm14311_en, accessed March 9, 2014; Chris Sorenson, "Canadian Tire's Baffling Strategy to Sell You Everything," October 11, 2011, www.macleans.ca/economy/business/so-wrong-that-its-right, accessed on March 9, 2014.

51. http://map.hamilton.ca/maphamilton/GISServ/GISServices.aspx, accessed July 19, 2011.

52. A. Little, "Hamilton, Ontario, Canada, Uses a GIS-Enhanced Web Site," *Public Management*, March 2006, pp. 34–35.

53. James Rickert, personal communication, July 13, 2009.

54. Robert Hof, "Pierre M. Omidyar: The Web for the People," *Business Week*, December 6, 2004; Margaret Kane, "eBay Picks Up PayPal for 1.5 Billion," *CNET News*, www.news.com, accessed July 8, 2002; John Blau, "Are eBay and Skype a Good Fit?," *InfoWorld*, www.infoworld.com/t/networking/are-ebay-and-skype-good-fit-073, accessed July 19, 2011; "Better Ask: IRS May Consider eBay Sales as Income," *USA Today*, March 27, 2005; eBay news release, January 23, 2008, http://news.ebay.com/releasedetail.cfm?ReleaseID=289314; CrunchBase, www.crunchbase.com/person/john-donahoe, accessed July 9, 2009; PayPal, "Corporate Fast Facts," www.paypal media.com/documentdisplay.cfm?DocumentID=2260, accessed July 9, 2009; Daniel Wolfe, "eBay Set to Merge PayPal and Bill Me Later Systems," *American Banker*, Volume 174, Issue 49, March 13, 2009, p. 4; Brad Reed, "How the Skype Spinoff Could Change the Market," *Network World*, April 20, 2009, pp. 12, 14; Geoffrey A. Fowler and Evan Ramstad, "eBay Looks Abroad for Growth-Online Auctioneer to Buy Korean Site As It Refocuses on E-Commerce," *The Wall Street Journal*, April 16, 2009, p. B2; Douglas MacMillan, "Can eBay Get Its Tech Savvy Back?," *Business Week*, June 22, 2009, pp. 48–49.

6
CHAPTER

Telecommunications and Mobile Technology

LO 6.1 Explain network basics and how networks enable data sharing to occur.

LO 6.2 Describe the use of networks and telecommunications in business (i.e., VoIP, networking businesses, increasing the speed of business, and the challenges associated with securing business networks).

LO 6.3 Describe the business drivers for using mobile technologies, and the advantages and disadvantages of using cellular technologies in business.

LO 6.4 Describe how satellite technologies are used in business, and how LBS, GPS, and GIS help create business value.

LO 6.5 Explain Wi-Fi, WiMAX, and RFID technologies, their use in business, as well as mobile business trends.

The pace of technological change never ceases to amaze. What only a few years ago would have been considered Star Trek technology is becoming normal. What used to take hours to download over a dial-up modem connection can now transfer in a matter of seconds through an invisible, wireless network connection from a computer thousands of miles away. We are living in an increasingly wireless present and hurtling ever faster toward a wireless future. The tipping point of ubiquitous, wireless, handheld, mobile computing is not far away.

As a business student, you must understand the concepts of network architecture and mobile technology to be able to understand how information technology can be used to support your business decisions. This is a critical skill for business executives, whether you're a novice or a seasoned Fortune 500 employee. By learning about the various concepts discussed in this chapter, you will develop a better understanding of how business can leverage technologies to compete in today's mobile world.

In addition, after reading this chapter, you should have many of the skills needed to become directly involved in analyzing current networking architectures, in recommending needed changes in mobile business processes, and in evaluating alternative networking options.

opening case study

The Ironman

World Triathlon Corporation (WTC), owner of the Ironman Triathlon World Championship, is in the business of fulfilling dreams—the dreams of endurance athletes to complete one of the world's most gruelling events. The most well-known event, the Ironman Triathlon World Championship on Kona, brings more than 1,700 of the world's top endurance athletes to rugged Kailua-Kona, Hawaii, for a world championship race every fall. Athletes attempt to swim 3.86 kilometres, cycle 180.25 kilometres, and run a full 42.20 kilometre marathon— all in a single day. The event features a remote course that threads around the side of an active volcano and offers breathtaking vistas, but also rough terrain, shimmering heat, and shifting trade winds.

For most of its history, it wasn't easy for family and friends to know how their son, sister, friend, or colleague was faring in the contest. Even those who could afford the trip to Hawaii were in the dark about their athletes' progress. "As a spectator, you'd see the start, and then the athletes would disappear, and that was pretty much it until the finish line," recalls Dave Scott, who ran his first triathlon in 1976. The Ironman Triathlon World Championship has changed all that. Using mobile technology, long-range WiMAX networks, Wi-Fi–enabled hotspots, and timing technology, the Ironman is transforming the way audiences and athletes experience the race. By using WiMAX to enable remote cameras at locations along the course, Ironman raised the bar for professional sports broadcasting. It also spotlighted a technology many say will help bring the next billion users into the Internet community.

Now people worldwide can look at any athlete and find out where he or she is on the course and at what speed the athlete is moving at any of WTC's 70.3—"half ironman"—or "full ironman" events. WTC makes this possible by using WiMAX to provide high-speed broadband connections in various locations along the 113 or 226 kilometre courses at all of the WTC's approximately 100 events each year. The company uses radio frequency identification (RFID) to track the athlete's progress and high-bandwidth communications to transmit professional-quality video and other data, and makes the information accessible over the Ironman LIVE (**www.ironman.com/triathlon/coverage/past.aspx#axzz 308lMsmNH**) website.

The First Kona Race Broadcast

Networking the Kona course was a challenge, because of the same factors that make the race challenging for the athletes. "We're on a very rough, rugged course on an island with an active volcano," explains Dan Gerson, Ironman LIVE production manager. "It's hot, it's windy, and there's no infrastructure. If you can deploy WiMAX here, you can probably deploy it pretty much anywhere." Airspan Networks provided the WiMAX infrastructure, using its high-performance base stations and subscriber stations to create a high-throughput network backbone capable of transmitting data rates required for top-quality video. The team set up its base station atop the hotel that served as the event's starting point and finish line, which also happened to be one of the lowest geographical points of the course. The team was operating in a non-line-of-sight environment and highly porous volcanic rock absorbed the wireless signals more than other types of rock would.

Airspan set up relays on the ridge sides of the volcano, the side of the road, the sides of buildings—anywhere to keep the fidelity of the signals. Some cameras were in locations without power, so they used generators. This was a wireless deployment in every sense of the word, and a great demonstration of the viability of WiMAX technology. Athletes were filmed as they passed by the WiMAX-enabled video stations equipped with network video cameras. That footage was incorporated into the live webcast, along with pre-event interviews, commentary, footage shot from cameras on motorcycles and helicopters, and other content produced by the Ironman team. WTC produced the broadcast at the event site in a live production studio that streamed the video data to the global servers that run the Ironman LIVE site.

In addition to these, Ironman used other wireless technologies to bring the athletes and their fans closer. For example, Ironman employed RFID technology, called the My Laps Champion Chip, to track each athlete's progress along the event route and maximize accuracy and safety. Each athlete wore an ankle bracelet with an RFID tag, and as a competitor crossed over one of 12 timing mats spread throughout the course, the RFID tag communicated to a reader that captured the athlete's times, and relayed that data over the wireless network to a database. Seconds later, data on an athlete's progress were available on the Ironman LIVE website, where spectators and viewers at home could see the athlete's pace and timing. Many viewers stayed on the website throughout the event, monitoring their athlete's progress. Today all North American Ironman events continue to use the My Laps technology through a Canadian provider, **SportStats.ca**.

WTC also set up eight wireless hotspots, including five along the event course and at the finish line. An Internet café was stocked with notebook and handheld computers, providing convenient, wireless access to event information and the Ironman LIVE site. Two giant screen displays showed the live program coverage from Ironman LIVE. Staff used additional notebooks and handheld devices to manage the race and access information on each athlete's progress. For example, if athletes needed medical care, the health care team used a RFID scanner to scan their RFID tags and instantly access medical records and local contact information.

Other Advantages

Ironman's transformative use of wireless computing makes business sense. The compelling programming solidifies the respect WTC earns for its sports broadcasting leadership. It also drives larger audiences and higher advertising revenues for WTC and the host broadcasters, which use WTC's Ironman Triathlon programming in its television broadcasts of the events. Larger audiences and better experiences for athletes and their families ultimately lead to greater participation in Ironman and Ironman 70.3 Triathlons and the dozens of qualifying races, and to growing popularity for the sport.[1]

6.1 NETWORKS AND TELECOMMUNICATIONS

INTRODUCTION

Change is everywhere in the information technology domain, but nowhere is change more evident and more dramatic than in the realm of telecommunications and networking. Most information systems today rely on digital networks to communicate information in the form of data, graphics, video, and voice. Companies large and small from all over the world use networked systems and the Internet to locate suppliers and buyers, to negotiate contracts with them, and to provide bigger, better, and faster services than ever before. The continued development of smart-phones and tablets capabilities are one of the factors driving the need for bigger and faster services.

For example, CBC provided its customers with unprecedented access to the Sochi 2014 Olympic and Paralympic Winter Games on both CBC TV, TSN, and Sports Net along with **CBC.ca** and the Sochi app. This was a great value-add to CBC customers, because they were given both live and on-demand access on their television, mobile phones, computers, and tablets from all the competition venues. Much of the non-television coverage was via dedicated feeds that provided unedited, uninterrupted coverage of the competitions, allowing CBC customers to have complete control over their Olympic Games experience and watch what they wanted, when they wanted, and how they wanted. CBC's coverage also expanded on coverage of the 2010 games in Vancouver, where the host broadcaster Bell allowed TV hockey fans to enjoy access to two player-cams that focused on individual players on every men's hockey team, as well as prepackaged hockey-related content; and Bell Mobility featured seven networks so fans could watch the events live on enabled mobile devices through live streams and exclusive Web video content.[2]

Telecommunication systems enable the transmission of data over public or private networks. A *network* is a communications, data exchange, and resource-sharing system created by linking two or more computers and establishing standards, or protocols, so that they can work together. Telecommunication systems and networks are traditionally complicated and historically inefficient. However, businesses can benefit from today's modern network infrastructures, which provide reliable global reach to employees and customers. Businesses around the world are moving to network infrastructure solutions that allow greater choice in how they go to market—solutions with global reach. These alternatives include wireless, Voiceover Internet Protocol (VoIP), and radio-frequency identification (RFID). This chapter takes a detailed look at the key telecommunication, network, and wireless technologies being integrated into businesses around the world.

LO1 ⌉ NETWORK BASICS

Networks range from small two-computer networks to the biggest network of all, the Internet. A network provides two principal benefits: the ability to communicate and the ability to share. Music is the hot product line at coffee retailer Starbucks. In Starbucks stores, customers can shop for music wirelessly through iTunes free, thanks to the company's own increasingly sophisticated in-store network.

Today's corporate digital networks include a combination of local area networks and the Internet. A *local area network (LAN)* is designed to connect a group of computers in close proximity to each other as in an office building, a school, or a home. A LAN is useful for sharing such resources as files, printers, games, or other applications. It often connects to other LANs, and to the Internet or wide area networks. A *wide area network (WAN)* spans a large geographic area, such as a state, province, or country. WANs often connect multiple smaller networks, such as LANs or metropolitan area networks (MANs). A *metropolitan area network (MAN)* is a large computer network usually spanning a city.

Direct data communication links between a company and its suppliers or customers, or both, have been successfully used to give the company a strategic advantage. The Sabre airline reservation system is a classic example of a strategic information system that depends upon communication provided through a network. The Sabre system pioneered technological advances for the industry in such areas as revenue management, pricing, flight scheduling, cargo, flight operations, and crew scheduling. In addition, not only did Sabre help invent e-commerce (now referred to as *e-business*) for the travel industry, but it also holds claim to progressive solutions that defined—and continue to revolutionize—the travel and transportation marketplace, as they have with travel booking through their Travelocity brand.[3]

INTERNET PROVIDERS

An *Internet service provider (ISP)* is a company that provides individuals and other companies access to the Internet along with additional related services, such as website-building. An ISP has the equipment and the telecommunication line access required to have a point of presence on the Internet for different geographic areas. Larger ISPs have their own high-speed leased lines so they are less dependent on telecommunication providers and can deliver better service to their customers. Among the largest national and regional ISPs are Bell Internet, Shaw, TELUS, Rogers, Videotron, and Cogence.

Navigating the different options for an ISP can be daunting and confusing. There are hundreds of ISPs in Canada; some are large with household names, and others are literally one-person operations. Although Internet access is viewed as a commodity service, in reality features and performance can differ tremendously among ISPs. Common ISP features are Web hosting, availability, and support.

Another member of the ISP family is the *wireless Internet service provider (WISP)*, an ISP that allows subscribers to connect to a server at designated hotspots or access points using a wireless connection. This type of ISP offers access to the Internet and the Web from anywhere within the zone of coverage provided by an antenna, usually a radius of about a kilometre. Figure 6.1 displays a brief overview of how this technology works.

One example of a WISP is Shaw that provides access to wireless laptop users in more than 40,000 locations across western Canada. A wireless service called Shaw Go Wi-Fi allows customers to access the Internet and via a wireless network from convenient locations away from their home or office.[4]

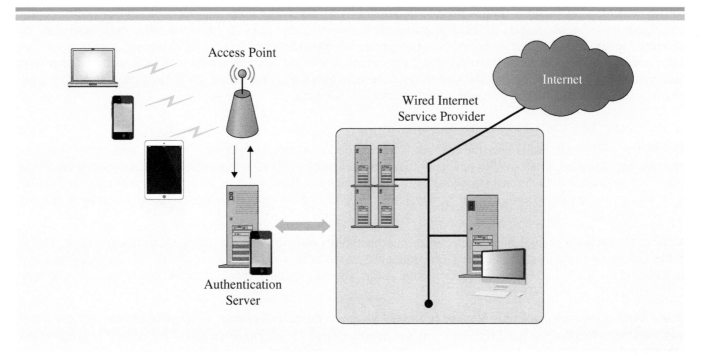

FIGURE 6.1
Wireless Access Diagram

An *online service provider (OSP)* offers an extensive array of unique services such as its own version of a Web browser. The term *online service provider* helps to distinguish ISPs that offer Internet access and their own online content, such as AOL Inc, from ISPs that simply connect users directly with the Internet, such as EarthLink. Connecting to the Internet through an OSP is an alternative to connecting through a national ISP, such as Bell Internet, or a regional or local ISP.

An *application service provider (ASP)* is a company that offers an organization access over the Internet to systems and related services that would otherwise have to be located in personal or organizational computers. Employing the services of an ASP is essentially outsourcing part of a company's business logic. Hiring an ASP to manage a company's software allows the company to hand over the operation, maintenance, and upgrade responsibilities for a system to the ASP.

One of the most important agreements between the customer and the ASP is the service level agreement. *Service level agreements (SLAs)* define the specific responsibilities of the service provider and set the customer expectations. SLAs include such items as availability, accessibility, performance, maintenance, backup/recovery, upgrades, equipment ownership, software ownership, security, and confidentiality. For example, an SLA might state that the ASP must have the software available and accessible from 7 a.m. to 7 p.m. Monday through Friday. It might also state that if the system is down for more than 60 minutes, there will be no charge for that day.

LO2 NETWORKS ENABLE DATA SHARING

The key advantage of providing data communication links between a company and its suppliers or customers is the sharing of data. For example, a LAN or a WAN permits users on the network to get data (if they are authorized to do so) from other points on the network, but it is the sharing of data itself—not the data communication links themselves—that provides the most benefit to the business. In this sense, data communication links (technology) enable data sharing to occur, and it is this data sharing that allows companies to be competitive and successful. For example, it is important for managers to be able to retrieve overall corporate sales forecasts from corporate databases to use in developing spreadsheets (or any other program used for business analysis) to project future activity. To satisfy customers, automobile dealers need to be able to locate particular vehicle models and colours with specific equipment installed. Managers at various points in a supply chain need to have accurate, up-to-date data on inventory levels and locations. Accountants at corporate headquarters need to be able to retrieve summary data on sales and expenses from each of the company's divisions. The chief executive officer (CEO), using an executive information system, needs current data on business trends from the corporate network. Data communication links enable such activities and help companies gain competitive advantage.

Voice over Internet Protocol

Originally, phone calls made over the Internet had a reputation of offering poor call quality, lame user interfaces, and low call-completion rates. With new and improved technology and IT infrastructures, Internet phone calls now offer similar quality to traditional telephone calls. Today, many consumers are making phone calls over the Internet with *Voice over Internet Protocol (VoIP)*, which uses TCP/IP technology to transmit voice calls over long-distance telephone lines.

VoIP's standards allow for easier development, interoperability among systems, and application integration. This is a big change for an industry that relies on proprietary systems to keep customers paying for upgrades and new features. The VoIP and open-standards combination should produce more choices, lower prices, and new applications.

Many VoIP companies, including Vonage (Canada), Skype, and Brama Telecom VoIP, offer calling within Canada and the United States for a fixed fee and a low per-minute charge for international calls.[5] Broadband Internet access (broadband is described in detail later in this chapter) is required, and regular house phones plug into an analog telephone adapter provided by the company or purchased from a third party (such as D-Link or Linksys), as displayed in Figure 6.2. In the case of Skype, calls can be made directly to mobile and landlines from a computer, tablet or smartphone.

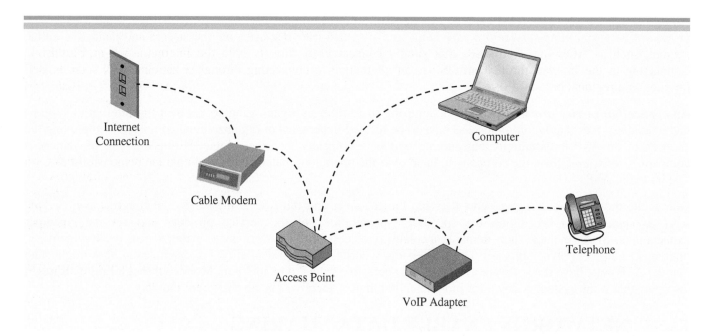

FIGURE 6.2

Diagram of VoIP Connection

Since VoIP uses existing network and Internet infrastructure to route telephone calls more efficiently and inexpensively than traditional telephone service, VoIP offers businesses significant cost savings, productivity gains, and service enhancements.

Unfortunately, VoIP routes calls through the same paths used by network and Internet traffic, and therefore has the same vulnerabilities and is subject to the same Internet threats. Much like data, VoIP traffic can be intercepted, captured, or modified. Any threat that slows or degrades service even slightly disrupts business. As a result, VoIP traffic must be secured.

Skype has long been one of the most popular VoIP options for consumers—largely because of its low cost. Now, it is gaining popularity in the business world as well. Microsoft purchased Skype in late 2011 and has bundled 60 minutes of calls a month to landlines into its Microsoft Office 365 package.

Rip Curl is one of the greatest surf and snow brands in the world. With more than 1,200 staff members and a retail presence in more than 60 countries, the company faces communications challenges in keeping abreast of global industry trends, sharing global marketing plans, coordinating events, and collaborating on design initiatives across many region. Rip Curl's finance and marketing divisions have been using Skype's free instant messaging and video calls for several years now to track communications with international colleagues.[6]

Skype already includes many features that make it attractive to business users, including call forwarding and the ability to filter and block unwanted calls. In addition, Skype's conference calling feature lets users have conversations with multiple people, mixing participants who are using Skype, regular landline phones, and mobile phones.

Skype allows users to do more than just place voice calls. For instance, users with computers equipped with webcams can make video calls to get "face time" with co-workers or clients—without the hassle or expense of travelling. In addition to features built into the Skype software, many useful add-in programs are available to download that add functionality and enhance productivity.[7]

Skype also uses a file transfer feature that makes it easier to collaborate with colleagues over the phone; users can send copies of reports, pictures, or other files they need to share—with no limits on file size. This feature can be disabled if an administrator does not want users to be able to transfer files, due to security or privacy issues.[8]

Networking Businesses

Retailer REI (Recreational Equipment Inc.) reports that one-third of all customers who buy online and pick up at the store make another purchase while in the store. Other online retailers, such as Mountain Equipment Co-op, Future Shop, and Canadian Tire, offer in-store pickup as a result of their inventory integration technologies; Canadian Tire offers in-store pickup only. In-store pickup needs to have some level of inventory integration to work effectively. The integration of data is critical for being able to display to the consumer the availability of products at the closest store.[9]

To set up an e-business a decade ago would have required an individual organization to assume the burden of developing the entire network infrastructure. Today, industry-leading companies have developed Internet-based products and services to handle many aspects of customer and supplier interactions. Customers now expect seamless retailing just as they expect stores that are clean and well stocked. Retailers are integrating their e-business sites with their inventory and point-of-sale (POS) systems so that they can accept in-store returns of merchandise bought online and also allow customers to buy on the Web and pick up in the store.

Many companies, such as Best Buy, The Running Room, and Canadian Tire, have integrated their physical and online stores. These companies have been the fast movers, because they already had an area in their stores for merchandise pickup (usually for big, bulky items like televisions and appliances), and because, long before the Web, they had systems and processes in place that facilitated the transfer of a sale from one store to another. To take on the challenge of e-business integration, an organization needs a secure and reliable IT infrastructure for mission-critical systems (see Figure 6.3).

A *virtual private network (VPN)* is a way to use the public telecommunication infrastructure (e.g., the Internet) to provide secure access to an organization's network (see Figure 6.4). A *value-added network (VAN)* is a private network, provided by a third party, for exchanging information through a high-capacity connection.

Organizations engaging in e-business have relied largely on VPNs, VANs, and other dedicated links handling electronic data interchange transactions. These traditional solutions are still deployed in the market and for many companies will likely hold a strategic role for years to come. However, conventional technologies present significant challenges:

- By handling only limited kinds of business data, they contribute little to a reporting structure intended to provide a comprehensive view of business operations.

- They offer little support for the real-time business process integration that will be essential in the digital marketplace.

- Relatively expensive and complex to implement, conventional technologies make it difficult to expand or change networks in response to market shifts.

- Transparent exchange of data with suppliers, trading partners, and customers

- Reliable and secure exchange information internally and externally via the Internet or other networks

- End-to-end integration and provide message delivery across multiple systems, in particular databases, clients, and servers

- Scalable processing power and networking capacity to meet high demands

- Integrator and transaction framework for both digital businesses and traditional brick-and-mortar businesses that want to leverage the Internet for any type of business

FIGURE 6.3

E-Business Network Characteristics

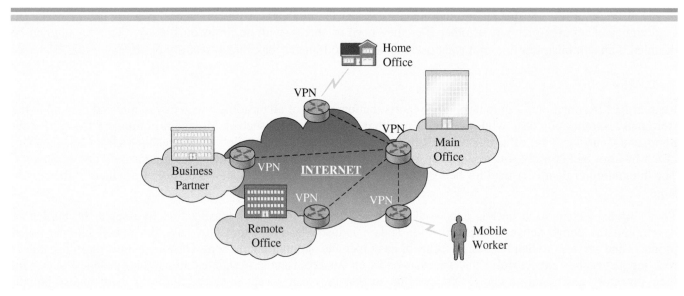

FIGURE 6.4

Virtual Private Network Overview

Increasing the Speed of Business

Transmission can occur at different speeds. By speed we do not mean how fast the signal travels in terms such as kilometres per hour, but rather the volume of data that can be transmitted per unit of time. Various terms are used to describe transmission speed. ***Bandwidth*** is the difference between the highest and the lowest frequencies that can be transmitted on a single medium, and is a measure of the medium's *capacity*; ***hertz*** is cycles per second; and ***bits per second (bps)*** is the number of signals (bits) sent per second. If each cycle sends one signal that transmits exactly one bit of data, which is often the case, then all these terms are identical. For example, 2.36 Hz is the same as 2.3 billion bps.

The notion of bandwidth, or capacity, is important for telecommunications. For example, approximately 50,000 bits (0s and 1s) are required to represent one page of data. Transmitting this page over a 128,000 bps (128 Kbps) digital subscriber line (DSL) would take only four-tenths of a second. Graphics require approximately 1 million bits for one page. This requires about 8 seconds over a 128 Kbps DSL. Full-motion video transmission requires the enormous bandwidth of 12 million bps, thus data compression techniques must be employed to be able to send video over the existing telephone network. The bandwidth determines what types of communication—voice, data, graphics, full-motion video—can reasonably be transmitted over a particular medium.

Figure 6.5 outlines the typical transmission speeds found in business today. Figure 6.6 gives an overview of the average time required to download specific Internet functions.[10]

Transmission Medium	Typical Speeds*
Twisted pair—voice telephone	14.4 Kbps–56 Kbps
Twisted pair—digital telephone	128 Kbps–1.544 Mbps
Twisted pair—LAN	10 Mbps–100 Mbps
Coaxial cable—LAN	10 Mbps–1 Gbps
Wireless—LAN	6 Mbps–54 Mbps
Microwave—WAN	50 Kbps–100 Mbps
Satellite—WAN	50 Kbps–100 Mbps
Fibre-optic cable—WAN	100 Mbps–100 Gbps

*bps = bits per second, Kbps = one thousand bits per second, Mbps = one million bits per second, Gbps = one billion bits per second.

FIGURE 6.5
Telecommunications Transmission Speeds

Internet Function	Dial-up (56K)	Satellite (512K)	DSL (1M)	Cable (5M)	Wireless (5M)
An email	1 sec	< 1 sec			
A basic Web page (25K)	10 sec	< 1 sec			
One five-minute song (5M)	15 min	2 min	1 min	40 sec	
One two-hour movie (500M)	20 h	4 h	2 h	70 min	

FIGURE 6.6
Internet Function Average Download Time

High-speed Internet, once an exotic and expensive service used only by larger companies, is now an inexpensive mainstream offering. The term ***broadband*** generally refers to high-speed Internet connections transmitting data at speeds greater than 200 kilobytes per second (Kbps), compared to the 56 Kbps maximum speed offered by traditional dial-up connections. While traditional dial-up access (using normal voice telephone line technology) is sufficient for some consumers, many need or want the much faster connections that technological advances now allow. The right option for Internet access depends on a company's needs and on which services are available. Figure 6.7 lists some of the advantages and disadvantages of current available conventional broadband technology.[11]

Technology	Typical Download Speed (Mbps)	Typical Upload Speed (Mbps)	Advantages	Disadvantages
Digital subscriber line (DSL)	0.5–3	0.25–1.0	■ Good upload rates ■ Uses existing telephone lines	■ Speeds vary depending on distance from telephone company's central office ■ Slower downloads than less expensive alternatives
Cable	0.5–250	0.5–15	■ Uses existing cable infrastructure ■ Low-cost equipment	■ Shared connections can overload system, slowing upload times
TI/T3 dedicated line	1.5–3	1.5–3	■ Uses existing phone wiring	■ Performance drops significantly with range ■ Susceptible to crosstalk
Fibre-to-the-home	5–300	1–15	■ Fast data speeds ■ Infrastructure has long life expectancy ■ Low maintenance ■ Low power costs	■ Not widely available yet ■ Significant deployment cost (for company)
Fixed wireless	0.5–12	0.5	■ Typically inexpensive to install, no underground digging	■ Weather, topography, buildings, and electronics can cause interference
Satellite	0.5–2	0.05	■ Nearly universal coverage ■ Available in otherwise inaccessible areas	■ Expensive service/ equipment ■ Upload/download delays

FIGURE 6.7

Advantages and Disadvantages of Broadband Technology

The town of Olds, Alberta, has Canada's first Gigabit Internet service. The town has rolled out 1,000 Mbps Internet service to the whole town by the town building its own fibre-optic network and then becoming its own ISP. It is expected that 100 percent of the town's residents and business will have access to the service sometime in 2014. The monthly cost for service will be $57 to $90 depending on if service is bundled with Internet phone and television.[12]

Securing Business Networks

Networks are a tempting target for mischief and fraud. An organization has to be concerned about proper identification of users and authorization of network access, the control of access, and the protection of data integrity. A firm must identify users before they are granted access to a corporate network, and that access should be appropriate for the given user. For example, an organization may allow outside suppliers access to its internal network to learn about production plans, but the firm must prevent them from accessing other data, such as financial records. In addition, the organization should preserve the integrity of its data; users should be allowed to change and update only well-specified data. These problems are exacerbated on the Internet where individuals must be concerned about fraud, invalid purchases, and misappropriation of credit card data.

Providing network security is a difficult challenge. Almost all networks require some kind of logon, including a username and password, but many people are casual with their passwords, making them easy to guess. (A good password has both upper- and lowercase letters and numbers, along with a few punctuation marks [where allowed] for added security.) Most corporate security goes far beyond passwords. One common approach is a firewall, a computer that sits between an internal network and the Internet. The firewall allows access to internal data from specified incoming sites but tries to detect unauthorized access attempts and prevent them from occurring.

For highly secure communications, a sender can *encrypt* data—that is, encode it so that someone without the "key" to decode cannot read the message. There are a number of encryption approaches, and there is controversy over how strong the encryption should be. The most secure approaches use longer keys, making it much more difficult for intruders to compute them. But governments are concerned about terrorists and criminals getting access to strong encryption methods that are beyond the capabilities of law enforcement authorities to decrypt, so there are export restrictions on encryption programs.

For Internet commerce, various schemes have been proposed for sending credit card or other payments over the network securely. Some involve encryption; others use various forms of digital certificates or digital cash. Many firms worry that customers will not want to complete transactions on the Internet because they fear that their credit card numbers might be stolen. However, the law does limit individual liability for misuse of one's credit card to $50.

OPENING CASE QUESTIONS

The Ironman

1. Why is sharing real-time data of an athlete's progress in a race important to the Ironman championship? How does WTC's use of networks and telecommunications promote the sharing of this data?

2. How is WTC using telecommunications and networks to improve its competitive advantage in the professional sports broadcasting industry?

3. How could WTC employ VoIP to enhance the experience of family and friends watching the triathlon?

4. What disadvantages or challenges would WTC likely face implementing broadband technologies?

5. What security issues does WTC likely need to address in its use of network technologies?

6.2 MOBILE TECHNOLOGY

LO3) BUSINESS DRIVERS FOR MOBILE TECHNOLOGIES

Today vending machine operators monitor their vending machines by installing specialized hardware and software along with wireless technology in the machines. The software collects inventory, sales, and " machine health" data at each machine and reports wirelessly to the operators centre. The data are aggregated and stored at a separate facility. With client software installed on their PCs, managers and sales personnel can access the data via a secure website. Management at companies like City Vending Company are excited about the business value of the data being collected, both for daily operations and in the potential for data mining (see Chapter 4). Information like this is helpful when considering new placements of vending machines or locations where multi-vendor machines might be warranted, such as in front of a retail store or high-traffic supermarket. The vendors can also use the data to plan loading of trucks and truck routes.[13]

Rapid and widespread growth of mobile technology in the 21st century has shaped one of the largest technology markets after the PC revolution in the 1980s and 1990s. Untethered connectivity, anytime, anywhere, has fuelled a major market and technology disruption, which has permeated almost every consumer market worldwide. The domino effect of the success of mobile technology has resulted in opportunities for innovation and creativity in technology, marketing, and business strategy.

Companies worldwide are going mobile to increase productivity, speed delivery to market, and reduce operating costs. Retail, distribution, and manufacturing businesses are no exception. Wireless transmissions rely on radio waves (e.g., cellular technology), microwaves, and satellites to send data across high-frequency radio ranges that later connect to wired media.

United Parcel Service (UPS) and FedEx have been using mobile technologies for years, making it possible for data about dispatching and deliveries to travel between couriers and central stations. FedEx's famous tracking system, which can find a package's location from its tracking number, uses a wireless courier-management system.

The terms *mobile* and *wireless* are often used synonymously, but actually denote two different technologies. *Mobile* means the technology can travel with the user, but not necessarily in real time; users can download software, email messages, and Web pages onto their smartphone, laptop, or other mobile device for portable reading or reference. Data collected while on the road can be synchronized with a PC or corporate server.

Wireless, on the other hand, refers to any type of electrical or electronic operation that is accomplished without the use of a "hard-wired" connection. Figure 6.8 displays the factors inspiring the growth of wireless technologies.

Universal access to data and applications	People are mobile and have more access to data than ever before, but they still need to get to the point where they can access all data anytime, anywhere, anyplace.
The automation of business processes	Wireless technologies have the ability to centralize critical data and eliminate redundant processes.
User convenience, timeliness, and ability to conduct business 24/7/365	People delayed in airports no longer have to feel cut off from the world or their office. Through wireless tools and wireless solutions, such as an iPad or Android device, they can access their data anytime, anywhere, anyplace.

FIGURE 6.8

Drivers of Wireless Growth

Provincial government agencies, such as transportation departments, use wireless devices to collect field data, tracking inventory, reporting times, monitoring logistics, and completing forms—all from a mobile environment. The transportation industry is using wireless devices to help determine current locations and alternate driving routes.

Mobile technologies are transforming how we live, work, and play. Handheld devices continue to offer additional functionality, and cellular networks are advancing rapidly in their increased speed and throughput abilities (cellular networks will be described in detail in the next section). These enabling technologies are fuelling the widespread adoption and creation of new and innovative ways to perform business. The big changes that will recreate workplaces, industries, and organizations are coming from mobile and wireless technologies. Figure 6.9 displays a few common examples of wireless technologies that are changing our world.

- *Wireless local area network (wLAN).* Uses radio waves rather than wires to transmit data across a local area network.
- *Smartphones and tablets.* Provide connectivity for portable and mobile applications, both personal and business.
- *Wireless computer peripherals.* Connect wirelessly to a computer, such as a cordless mouse, keyboard, or printer.
- *Satellite television.* Allows viewers in almost any location to select from hundreds of channels.
- *WiMAX wireless broadband.* Enables wireless networks to extend as far as 48 kilometres and transfer information, voice, and video at faster speeds than cable. It is perfect for Internet service providers (ISPs) that want to expand into sparsely populated areas, where the cost of bringing in cable wiring or DSL is too high.
- *Security sensor.* Alerts customers to break-ins and errant pop flies. Its dual sensors record vibration and acoustic disturbances—a shattered window—to help avoid false alarms.

FIGURE 6.9

Mobile Devices Changing Business

The retail industry is fiercely competitive. With the advent of the World Wide Web, non-traditional companies such as **Amazon.com** have emerged and have made brick-and-mortar companies rethink their strategy. Competition is also driving profit margins down. The success of a retailer depends on inventory management, cost control, and proactive customer service. To gain the competitive advantage, more and more retailers are turning to mobile applications to enhance worker productivity, operational efficiencies, and anytime, anywhere customer service. On the sales floor and in the warehouse, mobile solutions can help track materials and shipments from suppliers and distributors to the customers, manage inventory, and support point-of-sales activities. Since vast amounts of data can be collected in an automated fashion, analysis can be done much faster and the results can be used to continuously improve operations and customer service. When companies are looking to develop a mobile strategy there are a number of important questions that need to be answered before proceeding. These questions include:

1. What are the company's objectives?

2. How can mobile initiatives help the company achieve its corporate objectives?

3. Does the company have a mobile strategy? If it does, who owns the mobile strategy? If not, who will own the mobile strategy?

4. What is the company looking to implement for consumers (mobile commerce, mobile interactive marketing) and employees (mobile enterprise applications)?

5. What should the consumer and employee experiences be? Are they different? If so, how and why are they different?

6. What do the company's consumer and employee mobile demographics look like?

Once these questions are answered and the decision is made to go ahead with a mobile strategy, there are a number of important considerations that need to be made in order to formulate an effective mobile strategy. These factors are listed in Figure 6.10.[14]

Step	Description
Defining risks	Before a realistic assessment of any mobile strategy can be put in place, companies must define evaluation criteria. Many companies look at technology and applications in isolation, without defining any potential risks to the organization: risks both if the project is undertaken and if it is not.
Knowing the limits of technology	It is imperative that companies examine the abilities of any technology not only to provide needed functionality but also to explore any limits of the chosen technology. Setting realistic expectations for any mobile technology, both to IT resources deploying the solution and to the ultimate users, is a necessary component of any successful mobile strategy.
Protecting data from loss	Companies must take concrete and immediate steps to assure protection of mobile corporate data assets. Security must be a multi-faceted approach and encompass a variety of techniques covering all areas of exposure.
Compliance in the mobile enterprise	The move to mobility, with far more devices "free to roam wild," will cause a major upsurge in occurrences of data breaches, some of which may not even be discovered, or not discovered for a significant period. Companies must formulate a mobile security strategy before the problem becomes overwhelming.
Staying flexible and embracing change	Companies should not assume that, once created, a mobile strategy is a fixed and/or finished product. With the high rate of change in the marketplace (e.g., devices, connection types, applications), it is incumbent upon the organization to monitor and modify the policy on a regular basis.

FIGURE 6.10

Factors to Consider When Deploying Mobile Strategies

A small number of enterprises have a specific mobile strategy in place. Most struggle with individual mobile projects or try to link mobility to a broader IT strategy. Companies must focus on building a mobile strategy that addresses the peculiarities inherent in mobile computing. The strategy should leverage a number of uses across a variety of lines of businesses within the company to maximize the return on investment (ROI), standardize on architectures and platforms, and provide the most secure infrastructure available to eliminate (as much as possible) extremely costly data loss and security breaches inherent in mobile business. Understanding the different types of mobile technologies available will help executives determine how to best equip their workforce. These mobile technologies are discussed in the remainder of this section and include:

- Using cellular technologies in business
- Using satellite technologies in business
- Using wireless technologies in business
- Mobile business trends

USING CELLULAR TECHNOLOGIES IN BUSINESS

Both Air Canada and West Jet passengers are able to board flights using just a smartphone or other mobile device instead of a regular boarding pass. Instead of a paper pass, Air Canada and West Jet let passengers show a barcode the airline has sent to their mobile device. The two-dimensional code, a jumble of squares and rectangles, stores the passenger's name and flight information. A gate agent confirms the code's authenticity with a handheld scanner, and passengers show photo identification. The electronic boarding pass also works at airport gates. If a passenger's cellphone or mobile device loses power, the passenger can get a paper boarding pass from a kiosk or a customer service agent.[15]

Many small businesses are looking for ways to take mobile payments now have the option of Square, a device that connects to iOS and Android mobile devices and allows the business to accept customer credit card payments in any location in which they have a network connection along with many other features. The Square device is free; the merchant is charged 2.75 percent per transaction for swiped transactions with no other fees, monthly minimums, or service charges.[16]

In less than 20 years, the mobile telephone has gone from being rare, expensive equipment of the business elite to a pervasive, low-cost personal item. Several countries, including those in the United Kingdom, now have more mobile phones than people. There are over 1.2 billion active mobile phone accounts in China. Russia has the highest mobile phone penetration rate in the world at 155.5 percent. The total number of mobile phone subscribers in the world was estimated at 6 billion at the end of 2013, and is expected to reach 7.3 billion in 2014. Sub-Saharan Africa has seen a large growth rate of cellular subscribers due to the availability of prepaid or pay-as-you-go services. With prepaid cellular, the subscribers are not committed to a long-term contract, which has helped fuel the growth in Africa as well as in other continents.[17]

Cellular telephones work by using radio waves to communicate with radio antennas (or towers) placed within adjacent geographic areas called *cells*. A telephone message is transmitted to the local cell by the phone and then is passed antenna to antenna, or cell to cell, until it reaches the cell of its destination, where it is transmitted to the receiving telephone. As a signal travels from one cell into another, a computer that monitors signals from the cells switches the conversation to a radio channel assigned to the next cell.

In a typical digital cellphone system in Canada, the cellphone carrier is granted numerous frequencies to use across the city. The carrier chops up the city into cells, each typically 26 square kilometres in area and normally thought of as a hexagon in a large grid of interlocking hexagons, as illustrated in Figure 6.11. Each cell has a base station that consists of a tower and a small building containing the radio equipment.[18]

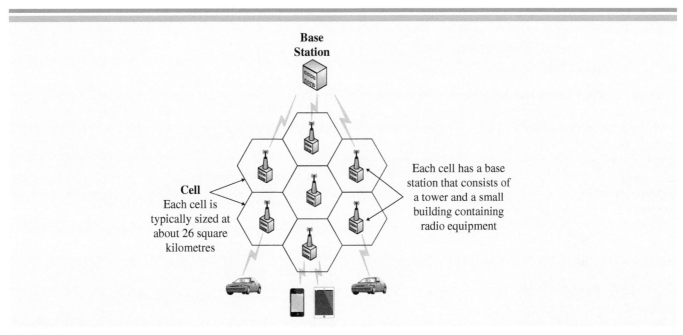

FIGURE 6.11

Cellular Technology Overview

Digital cellular service was introduced by personal communication services (PCS), which were entirely digital phones that could transmit both voice and data, and operate in a higher frequency range (1,900 MHz) than analog cellular telephones. They also introduced short message service (SMS), which is the capability of sending and receiving short text messages. Cellphone providers like digital phones, because they can carry 3–10 times more phone calls on the same systems than they could with analog phones.

PCS was a second-generation (2G) mobile communications technology, and analog cellular systems were first-generation (1G). Second-generation cellular networks are circuit-switched digital networks that can transmit data at about 10 kilobits per second (Kbps), which is extremely slow. Third-generation (3G) networks use a newer packet-switched technology that is much more efficient (and hence faster) than dedicated circuit-switched networks. Third-generation networks have speeds ranging from 120 to 144 Kbps for mobile users in, for example, a car, and up to 2 gigabits per second (Gaps) for stationary users. The next stage was 3G networks designed for high-speed transmission of multimedia data and voice.

Today, companies have fourth-generation (4G) mobile phone systems. 4G technology takes mobile communication another step to integrate radio and television transmissions, and to consolidate the world's phone standards into one high-speed technology. In Canada, companies such as Bell, TELUS, and Rogers have 4G networks with LTE and HSPA+ technologies. 4G LTE cellular service is entrenched in Canada, with estimates that 97 percent of the Canadian population has access to LTE service. Speeds for this service vary, but a provider like Bell says that its network has reached speeds of 75 Mbps in 2012 and that part of its network reached 150 Mbps by the end of 2013.

Most of the LTE service available is in urban areas, but companies like TELUS are planning to roll it out elsewhere in their coverage areas.

Figure 6.12 displays many of the cellular technologies along with their advantages and disadvantages.[19]

Generation	Technology	Advantages and Disadvantages
1G	AMPS (Advanced Mobile Phone Service)	■ Analog voice service only
2G	CDMA (Code Division Multiple Access) TDMA (Time Division Multiple Access) GSM (Global Systems for Mobile Communications PDC (Personal Digital Cellular)	■ Digital voice service ■ 9.6 Kbps to 14.4 Kbps data service ■ Enhanced calling features (such as caller ID) ■ No always-on data connection
3G	W-CDMA (Wideband Code Division Multiple Access)	■ Superior voice quality ■ Always-on data connection up to 7–11 Mbps ■ Broadband data services (such as streaming audio and video)
4G	HSPA+ (Evolved High-Speed Packet Access) WiMAX LTE (Long-Term Evolution)	■ Wi-Fi access networks ■ Always-on data connection 20–300 Mbps ■ Converged data and voice over IP

FIGURE 6.12

Cellular Technology Advantages and Disadvantages

The latest trends in smartphones reflect a convergence of voice, video, and data communications. By blending information with entertainment, smartphones and tablets are centre stage in the evolving trend of mobile infotainment. Android phones and Apple's iPhone are examples of mobile phones that allow users to make calls, surf the Web over a Wi-Fi connection, email a photo, and use touch controls to use various forms of content—including music, audio books, videos, TV shows, and movies.

As the old saying goes, "Timing is everything." Nowhere is that truer than in the real estate business. Real estate agents continue to look for tools that will give them an edge. Real-time access to their area's multiple listing service (MLS) provides one way for some agents to take advantage of timing. MLS offers a database of local properties for sale, with the ability to sort them by a variety of criteria. An agent who accesses a home's listing as soon as it hits the MLS gains a key advantage against the competition, because he or she can immediately request a viewing or, at minimum, simply drive by the location with a client.

Real estate agents are rarely in their offices, so they require technology that not only provides real-time access to their local MLS but also enables them to manage contacts, keep their calendars current, send and receive emails, view documents, calculate basic mortgage numbers, and more. The lighter the solution, the better, so that they can leave the laptop behind when necessary. In addition, if they can combine that with mobile functionality, they need only one device to conduct business.

Many real estate agents are using smartphones as a solution to their needs. Easy to carry and dependable, smartphones give them real-time access to their local MLS, enabling them to learn about properties as soon as they are listed for sale.

Tablets

A *tablet* is a mobile computer larger than a smartphone having an integrated flat touch-screen. It also uses a virtual keyboard, a passive stylus pen, or a digital pen rather than a physical keyboard, and has a Wi-Fi or 4G cellphone connection.

Tablets were actually introduced as early as 1968, but with limited success until Apple came out with the iPad in 2010. Since then, other computer manufacturers have introduced their own tablets.

Business is adopting tablets. By 2017 it is predicted that one in five business devices will be tablets, according to Forrester Research.[20] Adoption of tablets by business has given business more mobility options, especially with the development of apps such as Mobile Office, which is giving workers the same applications they have in the office on their mobile devices.

Bluetooth

Electronic devices can connect to one another in many different ways. The various pieces and parts of computers, entertainment systems, and telephones, make up a community of electronic devices. These devices communicate with each other using a variety of wires, cables, radio signals, and infrared light beams, and an even greater variety of connectors, plugs, and protocols. *Bluetooth* technology eliminates the need for wires that tangle everyday lives. Bluetooth is a telecommunications industry specification that describes how mobile phones, computers, and tablets can be easily interconnected using a short-range wireless connection. Special headsets allow users to cut the cord and make calls even while their cellphones are tucked away in a briefcase. Wireless printing allows users of a Bluetooth-enabled device to connect to a printer via an adapter connected to the printer's communication port.

Since Bluetooth's development in 1994 by the Swedish telecommunications company Ericsson, more than 1,800 companies worldwide have signed on to build products to the wireless specification and promote the new technology in the marketplace. (The engineers dubbed the technology "Bluetooth" to honour Harald Bluetooth, a 10th-century Viking king credited with uniting Denmark and bringing order to the country.)

Bluetooth capability is enabled in a device by means of an embedded chip and supporting software. Although Bluetooth is slower than competing wireless LAN technologies, and its maximum range is 9 metres, limiting it to gadget-to-gadget communication, the chip enables networking to be built into a wide range of devices—even small devices such as cellular phones.

One challenge to wireless devices is their size. Everyone wants their mobile devices to be small, but many also curse the tiny, cryptic keyboards manufacturers squeeze onto smartphones. The laws of physics have proved a significant barrier to solving this problem, but VKB Inc.'s Bluetooth Virtual Keyboard offers a possible solution (see Figure 6.13): it uses a red laser to flash the outline of a keyboard on any surface. Despite its futuristic look, the laser is really just a visual guide to where users put their fingers. A separate illumination and sensor module invisibly tracks when and where each finger touches the surface, translating that into keystrokes and other commands.

FIGURE 6.13

The Bluetooth Virtual Keyboard

LO4 | USING SATELLITE TECHNOLOGIES IN BUSINESS

A special variation of wireless transmission employs satellite communication to relay signals over very long distances. A communications *satellite* is a big microwave repeater in the sky; it contains one or more transponders that listen to a particular portion of the electromagnetic spectrum, amplifying incoming signals, and retransmitting them back to Earth. A *microwave transmitter* uses the atmosphere (or outer space) as the transmission medium to send the signal to a microwave receiver. The microwave receiver then either relays the signal to another microwave transmitter or translates the signal to some other form, such as digital impulses. Microwave signals follow a straight line and do not bend with the curvature of the Earth; therefore, long-distance terrestrial transmission systems require that microwave transmission stations be positioned about 60 kilometres apart, making this form of transmission expensive.

This problem can be solved by bouncing microwave signals off communication satellites, enabling them to serve as relay stations for microwave signals transmitted from terrestrial stations (as illustrated in Figure 6.14). Communication satellites are cost-effective for transmitting large quantities of data over very long distances, and are typically used for communication in large, geographically dispersed organizations that would be difficult to tie together through cabling media or terrestrial microwave. Originally, this microwave technology was used almost exclusively for satellite and long-range communication. However, recent developments in cellular technology now allow complete wireless access to networks, intranets, and the Internet via microwave transmission.

Conventional communication satellites move in stationary orbits approximately 35,000 kilometres above Earth. A newer satellite medium, the low-orbit satellite, travels much closer to Earth and is able to pick up signals from weak transmitters. Low-orbit satellites also consume less power and cost less to launch than conventional satellites. With such wireless networks, businesspeople almost anywhere in the world have access to full communication capabilities, including voice communication via satellite phones, videoconferencing, satellite radio, and multimedia-rich Internet access.

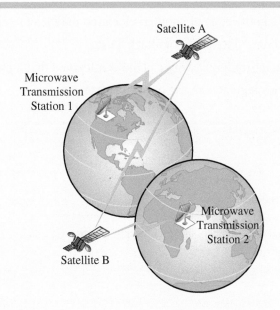

FIGURE 6.14

Satellite Microwave Link

The devices used for satellite communication range from handheld units to mobile base stations to fixed satellite dish receivers. The peak data transmission speeds range from 2.4 Kbps to 2 Mbps, depending on the solution being sought. For the everyday mobile professional, satellite communication does not provide a compelling benefit, but for people requiring voice and data access from remote locations or guaranteed coverage in non-remote locations, satellite technology may be worthwhile. Also, some satellite service providers offer roaming between existing cellular systems and satellite systems.[21]

Satellite-based location will shape the future, creating new applications. Besides emergency call location and navigation in cars and on mobile phones, a range of new services will appear: personal assistance and medical care, localized presence services, finding friends, gaming, localized blogs, and so on. To enable the wide commercial success of each service, several key technological challenges need to be met: accuracy; ubiquity of service, including in dense urban areas and inside buildings; and instantaneous delivery of data.

Location-Based Services

Location-based services (LBS) are wireless mobile content services that provide location-specific data to mobile users moving from location to location. The market for LBS is tremendous, with a variety of available and future services in a number of market segments: mobile telephony, enterprise, vertical markets, and automotive and consumer devices. Figure 6.15 highlights many of the LBS market segments that are currently pushing this technology.

Have you ever needed an ATM and not known where to find one? For tourists and businesspeople travelling far from home, that is an all-too-familiar predicament. Every year, millions of customers contact banks or companies like MasterCard via telephone or its website looking for the location of nearby ATMs; with MasterCard some 70 percent of inquiries are received from international travellers venturing outside their home countries.

Most major banks now provide customers with a mobile, location-based search and directory service, so they can request the location of the nearest ATM or branch. A user that employs location-based services on a regular basis faces a potential privacy problem. Many users consider location data to be highly sensitive and are concerned about a number of privacy issues, including:

- *Target marketing.* Mobile users' locations can be used to classify customers for focused marketing efforts.
- *Embarrassment.* One customer's knowledge of another's location may lead to embarrassing situations.
- *Harassment.* Location data can be used to harass or attack a user.
- *Service denial.* A health insurance firm might deny a claim if it learned that a user visited a high-risk area.
- *Legal restrictions.* Some countries regulate the use of personal data.

Mass Market	
Emergency services	■ Locate emergency call ■ Roadside assistance
Navigation services	■ Navigation to point of interest (directions, maps) ■ E-tourism ■ Avoidance of traffic jams
Tracking services	■ Find-a-friend ■ Tracking of children ■ Tracking of the elderly
Location advertising	■ Located video push
Gaming	■ N-Gage (allows multiple gamers to play against each other over Bluetooth or wireless phone network connections)
Professional Market	
Workforce organization	■ Field force management ■ Optimization of routes ■ Logistics ■ Enterprise resource planning
Security	■ Field tracking ■ Worker protection

FIGURE 6.15

Location-Based Services Market Segments

Unlike other data in cyberspace, location data have the potential to allow others to physically locate a person. Therefore, most wireless subscribers have legitimate concerns about personal safety: What if such data fell into the wrong hands? Laws and rules of varying clarity, offering different degrees of protection, have been enacted in Canada, the United States, the European Union, and Japan.

Global Positioning Systems

The most popular location-based service used today is the ***global positioning system (GPS)***, a constellation of 24 well-spaced satellites that orbit Earth and make it possible for people with ground receivers to pinpoint their geographic location. The location accuracy is anywhere from 10 to 100 metres for most equipment. Accuracy can be pinpointed to within one metre with special military-approved equipment. Figure 6.16 illustrates the GPS architecture.

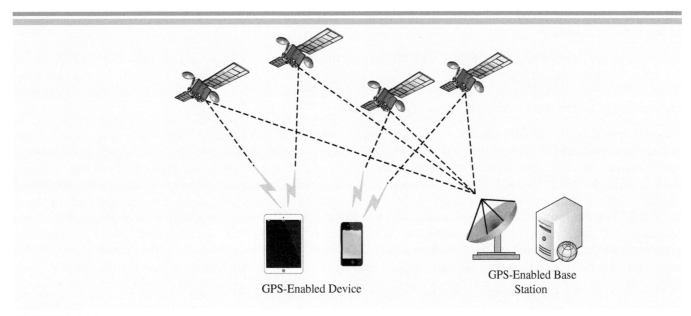

FIGURE 6.16

Global Positioning System Architecture

The GPS is owned and operated by the U.S. Department of Defense (DoD), but it is available for general use around the world. In 1993, the DoD made this technology available for commercial use to anyone with a GPS-enabled device, which has special microprocessors that analyze satellite signals. The current system of GPS satellites is under stress and aging, and there are questions about whether the current service will continue without interruption. According to reports from the Government Accountability Office, the U.S. Air Force has struggled to successfully build new GPS satellites that are part of a $2 billion GPS system modernization program. As of early 2014 the Air Force had begun launching their new satellites.[22]

Applications include a golf GPS that helps golfers calculate the distance from the tee to the pin, or to know exactly where they are in relation to features such as hidden bunkers, water hazards, or greens. The U.S. Golf Association permits distance-measuring devices for use in tournaments at the discretion of the organizers. There are also GPS-enabled watches for runners and cyclists that give their users up-to-the-second measures of distance, speed, and pace.[23]

The market for GPS services will grow to $26.67 billion by the end of 2016. Tracking, navigation, and hardware promise to be multibillion-dollar markets. UPS has outfitted its drivers with GPS-enabled handhelds to help them reach destinations more efficiently. The handhelds will also trigger email alerts if a company vehicle speeds or ventures into unauthorized areas. ZingoTaxi, in the U.K., uses GPS-enabled cars and text messaging to help subscribers hail cabs.

Geographic Information Systems

A *geographic information system (GIS)* is designed to work with data that can be shown on a map. Companies that deal in transportation use GISs combined with database and GPS technology. Airlines and shipping companies can plot routes with up-to-the-second data on the location of all their transport vehicles. Hospitals can keep track of where personnel are by using a GIS and sensors in the ceiling that pick up the transmission of badges worn by hospital staff.

Automobiles have GPSs linked to maps that display driving directions and the exact location of the vehicle in a screen on the dashboard. GM offers the OnStar system, which sends a continuous stream of data to the OnStar centre about the car's exact location. The OnStar Vehicle Diagnostics automatically performs hundreds of diagnostic checks on four key operating systems—the engine/transmission, antilock brakes, airbags, and OnStar systems—in GM vehicles. The vehicle is programmed to send the results via email to the owner each month. The unique email report also provides maintenance reminders based on the current odometer reading, remaining engine oil life, and other relevant ownership data. OnStar now offers secondary-market OnStar systems that can be installed in any make of vehicle.[24]

Smartphone providers equip their phones with GPS chips that enable users to be located to within a geographical location about the size of a tennis court. This allows emergency services such as 911 to find a smartphone user. Marketers are monitoring smartphone GPS development, hoping to be able to call potential customers when they are walking past their store to let them know of a special sale.

Leading-edge farmers use GPS satellite navigation to map and analyze fields, telling them where to apply the proper amounts of seeds, fertilizer, and herbicides. In the past, farmers managed their business on a per-field basis; now they can micro-manage. One farmer found after monitoring the soil that parts of his fields did not need any fertilizer. Less fertilizer lowers costs and reduces pollution from water runoff. One application is to use geographic fixes from the GPS and a computerized counter to record how much grain is being harvested each second from each metre of the field. Then the farmer downloads this data into a personal computer, which produces a contour map that shows variations of, say, more than 60 bushels an acre. Cross-referencing this data to other variables, such as characteristics of the soil, allows the farmer to analyze why some land is less productive. The farmer combines this data with GPS navigational fixes to precisely apply herbicides or fertilizer only where they are really needed.[25]

A GIS is useful for mobile applications, but it offers benefits that go well beyond what is required in a mobile environment. For example, using a GIS, users can decide what data are and are not relevant to them, and formulate their queries based on their personal criteria. Unlike a paper map, a GIS allows for in-depth analysis and problem solving that can make marketing, sales, and planning much more successful. The following are some common GIS uses:

- *Finding what is nearby.* This is the most common use for mobile users. Given a specific location, the GIS finds sources within a defined radius. This may include entertainment venues, medical facilities, restaurants, or gas stations. Users might also use the GIS to locate vendors that sell a specific item they want. This promotes m-commerce by matching buyers with sellers.

- *Routing information.* This is another common use for mobile users. Once users have an idea of where they want to go, a GIS can provide directions on how to get there. Once again, this can be provided graphically using a map or with step-by-step instructions. For mobile applications, it is often helpful to provide routing information in conjunction with search services.

- *Information alerts.* Users may want to be notified when data that are relevant to them become available based on their location. For example, a commuter might want to know if he or she is entering a section of the highway that has traffic congestion, or a shopper might want to be notified if his or her favourite store is having a sale on a certain item.

- *Mapping densities.* For business analysis, knowing population densities can be extremely useful. This allows users to find out where high concentrations of a certain population may be. Densities are typically mapped based on a standard area unit, such as hectares or square miles, making it easy to see distributions. Examples of density mapping may include the location of crime incidents for police to determine where additional patrolling is required, or of customers to help determine ideal field delivery routes.[26]

A GIS can provide data and insight to both mobile users and people at fixed locations, using the location coordinates provided by GPS positioning technologies to give details that are relevant to a specific user at a specific moment. Many of the location-based services discussed earlier in this section would benefit from data and information provided by a GIS.

LO5 USING WIRELESS TECHNOLOGIES IN BUSINESS

Denver International Airport (DIA), like many airports across Canada and the United States, is betting that travellers will like getting something free, and so far it looks like a good bet. DIA. Within a week, and with no public notice of the change, Wi-Fi use grew tenfold. Today DIA offers both free Wi-Fi that is advertising-supported and enhanced Wi-Fi that has a monthly fee.

Wireless Fidelity

Wireless fidelity (Wi-Fi) is a means of linking computers using infrared or radio signals. Wi-Fi, or what is sometimes referred to as *wireless LANs*, represent a rapidly growing proportion of LANs in operation today. Wi-Fi technology has obvious advantages for people on the move who need access to the Internet in airports, restaurants, and hotels. Wi-Fi has also gained acceptance as a home or neighbourhood network, permitting an assortment of laptop and desktop computers, mobile devices, and other Wi-Fi–enabled devices to share a single broadband access point to the Internet. Wireless LANs are also moving into the corporate and commercial world, especially in older buildings and confined spaces where it would be difficult or impossible to establish a wired LAN or where mobility is paramount. Even in newer buildings, wireless LANs are being employed as overlay networks. In such cases, Wi-Fi is installed in addition to wired LANs so that employees can easily move their laptops, tablets, or even smartphones from office to office and can connect to the network in places such as lunchrooms and patios.

After years of discussion and delay, airlines are starting to offer in-flight Internet connections, instant messaging, and wireless email, turning the airplane cabin into a Wi-Fi hotspot. Helping to lead many of the airlines into the new era is Aircell, which in June 2006 won exclusive air-to-ground Wi-Fi rights by plunking down $31.3 million for 3 MHz of terrestrial digital wireless spectrum at a Federal Communications Commission (FCC) auction in the United States. All American airlines that offer Wi-Fi services do so with Aircell's GoGo service, except for Southwest Airlines. Approximately one-third of 2,800 planes in the U.S. are Wi-Fi–equipped. Airlines like Virgin America have their full fleet of aircraft fitted out with Wi-Fi.

Figure 6.17 illustrates how "Wi-Fi in the sky" works. In Canada, Air Canada offers GoGo service on flights from Montreal and Toronto to Los Angeles while over U.S. airspace and as of the time of writing WestJet is launching the service in late 2014.[27]

Another example of how Wi-Fi is changing the competitive landscape is happening in western Canada, where TELUS now offers Optik TV, which is Internet-protocol TV. This allows TELUS to compete with the traditional cable companies like Shaw. In eastern Canada, Bell is offering the same type of service through Fibe TV service.[28]

WiMAX

The main problems with broadband access are that it is expensive and it does not reach all areas. The main problem with Wi-Fi access is that hotspots are small, so coverage is sparse. An evolving technology that can solve all of these problems is called WiMAX. *WiMAX*, or Worldwide Interoperability for Microwave Access, is a telecommunications technology aimed at providing wireless data over long distances in a variety of ways, from point-to-point links to full mobile cellular-type access. WiMAX can cover as much as 4,800 square kilometres depending on the number of users. In Vancouver, for example, many base stations will be required around the city to meet the heavy demand, while a sparsely populated region will need fewer.

A significant application of WiMAX is Internet access in rural areas. One of the first projects in Canada was a trial in the 21,000 square kilometre "Special Areas" in southeastern Albertain 2006. The result was a successful WiMAX implementation with towers being able to transmit signals in the range of 15 to 20 kilometres and customers getting speeds of 1.5 to 3 Mbps. This led to an expansion of WiMAX services in the Special Areas, and in Starland County and the Municipal District of Acadia. Since the trial, the ISP Net ago is offering 5 Mbps and 10 Mbps services. There are now several WiMAX service providers in Canada, including British Columbia, Alberta, Ontario, Quebec, and the Yukon. In fact, a number of activities involved in creating the third and fourth editions of this book were carried out using WiMAX Internet connections![29]

WiMAX offers Web access speeds five times faster than those of typical wireless networks, though they are still slower than wired broadband. Higher-end notebook computers will have WiMAX technology built in, though WiMAX cards that plug into a slot in the computer will also be available. Companies such as Nokia and Samsung Electronics are also making mobile devices and infrastructure with WiMAX technology.

WiMAX may erase the suburban and rural blackout areas that currently have no broadband Internet access because phone and cable companies have not yet run the necessary wires to those remote locations.

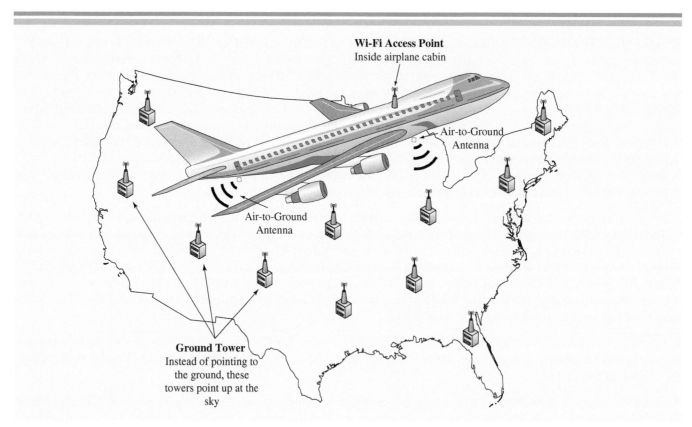

Wi-Fi Access Point
Inside airplane cabin

Air-to-Ground
Antenna

Air-to-Ground
Antenna

Ground Tower
Instead of pointing to
the ground, these
towers point up at the
sky

FIGURE 6.17
Wi-Fi in the Sky

A WiMAX system consists of two parts:

■ *A tower.* A single WiMAX tower can provide coverage to a large area—as big as 4,800 square kilometres.

■ *A receiver.* The receiver and antenna might be built into a laptop the way Wi-Fi access is today.[30]

A WiMAX tower station can link directly to the Internet using a high-bandwidth, wired connection. It can also connect to another WiMAX tower using a line-of-sight microwave link. It is this latter connection (often referred to as a *backhaul*) that allows WiMAX to provide coverage to remote rural areas. Figure 6.18 illustrates WiMAX architecture.

Wi-Fi–style access will be limited to a 6–10 kilometre radius (60 square kilometres of coverage, which is similar in range to a cellphone zone). Through the stronger line-of-sight antennas, the WiMAX transmitting station would send data to WiMAX-enabled computers or routers set up within the transmitter's 48 kilometre radius. This is what allows WiMAX to achieve its maximum range. The benefits of the WiMAX technology include long range up to 48 kilometres, low cost, high wireless bandwidth (up to 70 Mbps), and the fact that it can operate in both line-of-sight and non-line-of-sight environments.[31]

Radio Frequency Identification (RFID)

Radio frequency identification (RFID) technologies use active or passive tags in the form of chips or smart labels that can store unique identifiers and relay this data to electronic readers. ***RFID tags***, often smaller than a grain of sand, combine tiny chips with an antenna. When a tag is placed on an item, it automatically radios its location to RFID readers on store shelves, checkout counters, loading bay doors, and shopping carts. With RFID tags, inventory is taken automatically and continuously. RFID tags can cut costs by requiring fewer workers for scanning items; they can also provide more current and more accurate data to the entire supply chain. On average, Walmart saves $8.4 billion a year by installing RFID in many of its operations. Figure 6.19 illustrates one example of an RFID architecture.

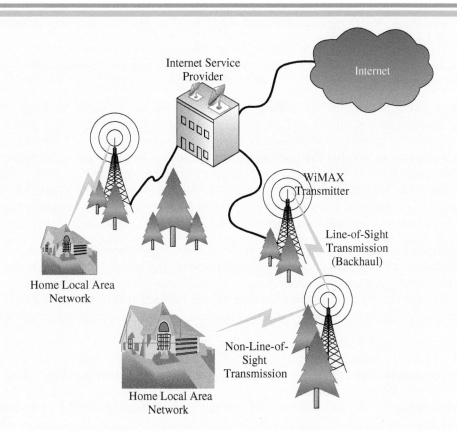

FIGURE 6.18

WiMAX Architecture

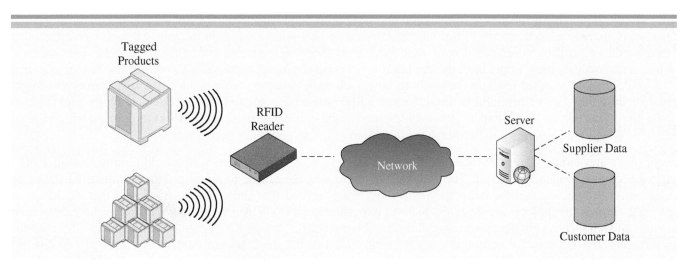

FIGURE 6.19

RFID Architecture

RFID tags represent the next big step forward from bar codes, the ubiquitous stripes on the sides of packages that provide basic product and pricing data. The simplest tags, passive RFID tags, require no internal power supply. Incoming radio frequency signals from RFID readers can transmit a minute electrical current, enough to power the integrated circuit in the tag and transmit a response. The key benefit is that the bar code on a case or pallet no longer needs to be swiped to identify the contents; the tag just needs to come within range of a reader—anywhere from a few metres up to 18. In addition, RFID tags can transmit far more data about a product, including price, serial number, and even when and where it was made.

Much of the recent interest surrounding RFID has arisen from mandates and recommendations by government agencies, and from a few private-sector mega corporations.

RFID technologies offer practical benefits to almost anyone who needs to keep track of physical assets. Manufacturers improve supply chain planning and execution by incorporating RFID technologies. Retailers use RFID to control theft, increase efficiency in their supply chains, and improve demand planning. Pharmaceutical manufacturers use RFID systems to combat the counterfeit drug trade and reduce errors in filling prescriptions. Machine shops track their tools with RFID to avoid misplacing tools and to track which tools touched a piece of work. RFID-enabled smart cards help control perimeter access to buildings. In the last couple of years, owing in large part to Walmart and DoD mandates, many major retail chains and consumer goods manufacturers have begun testing pallet- and case-level merchandise tagging to improve management of shipments to customers.[32]

RFID tags differ from conventional bar code tags in a number of ways, differences that have shown the benefit of adopting the technology but simultaneously also greatest concern over the privacy issues involved. For example, under today's bar code technology, a pack of Wrigley's gum sold in Edmonton has the same bar code as a pack sold in St. John's. With RFID, however, each pack would have a unique ID code that could be tied to the purchaser of that gum when the buyer uses an "item registration system," such as a frequent-shopper card or a credit card.

The purchaser could then be tracked if he or she entered that same store again, or, perhaps more frighteningly, entered any other store with RFID reading capability. Unlike bar codes, RFID tags can be read from much greater distances and the reading of such devices is non-directional. This means that if someone enters a store with a pack of gum in a pocket or purse, the RFID reader can identify that pack of gum, the time and date it was purchased, where it was purchased, and how frequently the consumer comes into the store. If a credit card or a frequent-shopper card was used to purchase the gum, the manufacturer and store could also tie that data to the consumer's name, address, and email, and then direct targeted advertisements by gum companies as the shopper walks down the aisles, or send mailings through email or regular mail about other products.

As the technology behind RFID advances, so does the potential for privacy infringement. RFID already has the capability to determine the distance of a tag from the reader location. With such technology already available, it is not difficult to imagine a situation in which retailers could determine the location of individuals within the store, and thus target specific advertisements to that customer based on past purchases (as in the gum example). In effect, that store would be creating a personal log of past purchases, shopping patterns, and, ultimately, behaviour patterns. While such data gathering would be considered intrusive enough by many consumers' standards, the danger that such data could be sold to other retailers (similarly to how such profiles are currently sold in Internet commerce) might create devastating data vulnerabilities. Though some RFID critics have pointed out that the technology could lead to some sort of corporate "Big Brother," more widespread is the concern that allowing RFID to develop without legal restrictions will eliminate the possibility for consumers to refuse to give such data to retailers.[33]

Some steps are being taken to mitigate these issues. For example, a recent proposal would require that all RFID-tagged products be clearly labelled. This would give consumers the choice to select products without RFID, or, at minimum, to recognize that the items they select are being tracked. For those not satisfied with that disclosure, a growing number of products are designed to limit exposure to RFID-tagged products. With RFID becoming both smarter and smaller, its possible uses are endless (see Figure 6.20). Though RFID poses certain ethical dilemmas for government and commercial operations, it also simplifies life for the common person. As medical benefits are explored further, RFID tags will be used not only for convenience and profit, but also for saving lives.[34]

CHALLENGES OF BUSINESS MOBILITY

The mobile employee has become the norm rather than the exception, driven by lifestyle choices, productivity gains, and technology improvements. Although the advantages of using wireless networks are significant, added challenges exist such as protecting against theft, protecting wireless connections, preventing viruses on mobile devices, and addressing privacy concerns with RFID and LBS (see Figure 6.21).

RFID Use	Description
Preventing toilets from overflowing	You can purchase a "smart" toilet, one that shuts itself off when it is close to overflowing. According to Aqua One, its RFID-enhanced toilets not only are convenient, but also prevent health risks in public facilities such as hospitals and nursing homes.
Identifying human remains	Hurricane Katrina left behind many unclaimed casualties, despite the tireless searches by countless people. Thanks to the Positive ID, RFID tags are now being used to locate bodies in an effort to reunite loved ones. This helps to identify cadavers during transport, and coroners are now able to collect body parts for burial in their rightful places.
Getting into nightclubs	Barcelona's Baja Beach Club is now implanting RFID tags in the arms of patrons who want instant access to the exclusive hangout. The tag also functions as a debit card.
Tracking wheels of cheese	To track cheese through each process and handler until it is sold, RFID tags are being put just under the edges of the wheels. While the idea of black-market cheese may sound ridiculous, consider this—just one wheel of Parmesan can be worth several hundred dollars. The industry is having problems with theft, loss, and even counterfeit cheese.
Issuing passports	Over 100 governments have approved of passports with microchips inside, and the technology is already being used. While government maintains that its purpose is to improve communication between law enforcement agencies, others feel there will be more sinister repercussions. Canada started to issue e-passports in July 2013 but has been issuing e-passports as a trial since 2009 with diplomatic passports.

FIGURE 6.20

Some Unusual Uses of RFID

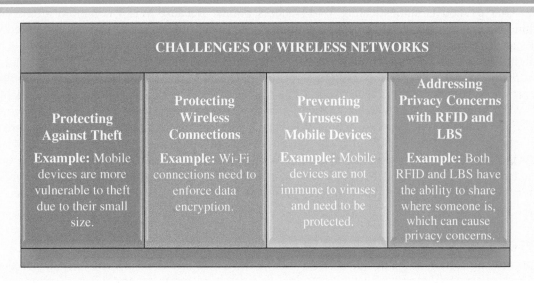

FIGURE 6.21

Challenges of Business Mobility

Protecting Against Theft

Any mobile device is vulnerable to loss no matter how big or small it is. The company may face significant exposure from stolen IDs, passwords, encryption keys, and confidential information if the device falls into the wrong hands, especially if the theft is not discovered or reported immediately and the company does not have time to revoke access.

Power-on passwords—passwords implemented at the hardware level that must be entered before gaining access to the computer—are the first line of defense against unauthorized use. Companies should activate these passwords before giving their workforce the devices. They should also prohibit storing passwords on devices and periodically monitor compliance with the policy. Companies need to consider encrypting and password-protecting data stored on the device, including any flash drives or other mobile storage devices. In addition, some device management tools can send messages to a device to lock it or destroy its contents, which can be an attractive security feature.

Protecting Wireless Connections

Network intrusions can occur if access codes or passwords are stored on a device that is lost or stolen. However, anytime a wireless network connects to a wired one, the wireless network can serve as a conduit for a hacker to gain entry into an otherwise secure wired network. This risk is especially high if the network is not sufficiently secure in its own right.

Before the emergence of the Internet, hackers generally had to be physically present within the corporate complex to gain access to a wired network. The thousands, if not millions, of access points enabled by the Internet now allow hackers to work from a distance. This threat has spawned a variety of different security techniques from firewalls to VPNs to SSL and HTTPS.

War chalking is the practice of tagging pavement with codes displaying where Wi-Fi access is available. The codes for war chalking tell other users the kind of access available, the speed of the network, and if the network is secured. *War driving* is deliberately searching for Wi-Fi signals while driving by in a vehicle. Many individuals who participate in war driving simply map where Wi-Fi networks are available. Other individuals with a more malicious intent use war driving to hack or break into these networks. War driving has been a controversial practice since its inception and has raised the awareness of the importance of wireless network security.

Several techniques can secure wireless networks from unauthorized access whether used separately or in combination. One method is authenticating Wi-Fi access points. Because Wi-Fi communications are broadcast, anyone within listening distance can intercept communications. Every time someone uses an unsecured website via a public Wi-Fi access point, his or her logon name and password are sent over the open airwaves, with a high risk that someone might "eavesdrop" or capture logon names, passwords, credit card numbers, and other vital information. *Wired equivalent privacy (WEP)* is an encryption algorithm designed to protect wireless transmission data. If using a Wi-Fi connection, WEP encrypts the data using a key that converts the data into non-human-readable form. The purpose of WEP was to provide wireless networks with the equivalent level of security as wired networks. Unfortunately, the underlying technology behind WEP has been demonstrated to be relatively insecure compared to newer protocols such as WPA. WLANs that use Wi-Fi have a built-in security mechanism called *Wi-Fi Protected Access (WPA),* a wireless security protocol to protect Wi-Fi networks. It is an improvement on the original Wi-Fi security standard, Wired Equivalent Privacy (WEP), and provides more sophisticated data encryption and user authentication. Anyone who wants to use an access point has to know the WPA encryption key to access the Wi-Fi connection.

Preventing Viruses on a Mobile Device

The need for virus protection at the device level on mobile devices has become critical. Any device that can access the Internet or receive email at risk of catching a virus and passing it on to other devices. Because of the memory limitations of most mobile devices, antivirus software has typically been hosted on a PC or laptop, with the mobile device physically connecting to a PC or laptop to perform a virus scan. The first known mobile phone virus, named Cabir, appeared several years ago and infected only a small number of Bluetooth-enabled phones. It carried out no malicious action; the virus had been created by a group of malware developers to prove it could be done. These developers sent Cabir to antivirus researchers so that they could begin to develop a solution to a problem that promises to get a lot worse. At present, mobile phone viruses do not do much damage, but if protective measures are not taken, they might become as devastating as their computer counterparts.[35]

The best way to protect against mobile phone viruses is the same way users protect themselves from computer viruses—never open anything that seems suspicious. Another method is to turn Bluetooth's "discoverable mode" off by setting it to "Hidden," so that other devices cannot detect it and send it the virus. In addition, one might install some type of security software on the device.

Many of the mobile phone manufacturers, such as Nokia and Samsung, have developed security software for their mobile phones that detects and removes viruses and can protect it from getting certain viruses in the first place.

Addressing Privacy Concerns with RFID and LBS

As technology advances, the potential for privacy infringement does as well. RFID already has the capability to determine the distance of a tag from the reader location. It is not difficult to imagine that retailers could determine the location of individuals within the store and target specific advertisements to them based upon past purchases and shopping and behaviour patterns. Many consumers would consider gathering such information intrusive enough, but the possibility that it could be sold to other retailers might lead consumers to refuse to give retailers any information.

Several steps are being taken to address these privacy concerns. For example, one proposal would require all RFID-tagged products to be clearly labelled. This would act as an alert mechanism to which items are being tracked. Another measure being considered is "Kill Codes," which would turn off all RFID tags when someone comes into contact with them. Another measure is "RSA Blocker Tags," which try to address privacy concerns while maintaining the integrity of the product. Only that store's authorized reader can track items with these tags; customers cannot be tracked outside the store in which they made a purchase.[36]

Location-based services (LBS) can track and monitor objects much like RFID. Tracking vulnerable individuals and company assets is beneficial. But the dark side of LBS risks the invasion of privacy and security caused by indiscreet location tracking. For example, if a company is using LBS to know where each employee is on duty, it must not observe their positions when they are off duty. Advertising at random to users in a specific area may violate privacy if mobile users in the area do not want to receive these advertisements. Criminals might also take advantage of illegal location tracking. And because LBS are based on message exchange in a wireless network, there are always security risks because location information cane stolen, lost, or modified.

Security mechanisms must eliminate or minimize the potential for attacks against LBS entities and reduce exposure of the user's identity and location. One way to solve the problem is to provide strong privacy practices that counterbalance the invisible nature of location collection in the wireless world. LBS policies should specify that:

- Direct marketing purposes are permitted only with the business or service a user has a contract with.
- Electronic messages cannot hide the identity of the sender.
- Solicitation is allowed only if the user has given prior consent.
- The location service must tell the user about the type, duration, and purpose of the data they are collecting.
- The user must be given the opportunity to reject any direct marketing opportunities.[37]

For mobile service providers, an unwelcome push can lead to increased customer care cost. When a user has issues with her PC, she tries to fix it herself. However, when a user's mobile phone is not working, she usually contacts the service provider. As a result, subscribers receiving unsolicited messages through LBS would contact their mobile service providers with complaints.

With the power of a network, business professionals can share data and resources around the globe. With the power of a wireless network, business professionals can take advantage of mobility allowing them to work from anywhere, at any time, using many different devices.

Watching people work in airports, restaurants, stores, trains, planes, and automobiles is common, and soon even remote villages in Africa, South America, and Asia will have access to the Internet along with all the power that comes with wireless networking.

MOBILE BUSINESS TRENDS

Airplane seats. Car dashboards. Digital cameras. Kiosks at shopping malls, school campuses, and hotels. Stadium bleachers. Handheld calculators. Kitchen appliances. Watches. These are just a few of the mobile devices and locations nowadays being set up for wireless. The visionary images of yesterday are giving way to a reality in which connectivity is nearly ubiquitous. Real-time data is now the currency of business and the enabler of groundbreaking changes in education, entertainment, and media, including widespread use of mobile social networks, greater choice in multi-function devices, and more wireless home entertainment options.

- *Social networking gets mobilized.* Mobility is added to existing Internet business models, services, and behaviours, driving traffic for wireless operators. Those in their teens and twenties accustomed to constant connectivity and habit-forming websites, such as Twitter and Facebook, lead a wave of membership in mobile social networks. Social networking location applications, including friend and event finder services, are gaining popularity, even in the professional and over-50 segments. Social networking applications are pre-loaded on many mobile devices sold.

- *Mobile TV.* Cable companies and traditional broadcasters are now competing with the Internet. The newest trend with Broadcaster apps that is developing is the need to subscribe to the app content via your cable or internet provider. Broadcasters are squaring off with content providers over control of the subscriber relationship and user experience.

- *Multi-function devices become cheaper and more versatile.* Intense competition and margin pressure will continue in the handset market, forcing prices of fourth-generation (4G) handsets below $100 and making them affordable for a wide range of users. Seeking to replicate the success of camera phones, device manufacturers will produce more multi-function units with music-playing, location, video, and other capabilities.

- *Location-based services.* GPS is the location technology of choice for the wireless industry. Handset manufacturers will continue to push GPS-enabled handsets as the technology evolves from popular in-car satellite navigation systems like TomTom, to a broadly accepted feature in wireless phones. With bandwidth available to support new multimedia services, location-based service providers are building critical mass. Since there are 10 to 20 times more mobile phones sold than any other consumer electronics device, wireless is a huge driver for GPS adoption.

- *Mobile advertising.* Major brands are shifting from basic SMS marketing to more sophisticated multimedia advertising. RBC Capital Markets expects mobile marketing revenues to balloon. With the technological ability to target and measure the effectiveness of mobile advertising, brands are more strategic in their approach. Rich content, video services, and accuracy advancements in GPS-based location services deliver further value to brands targeting existing and potential customers in innovative ways.

- *Wireless providers move into home entertainment.* Mobile makes headway against fixed broadband operators, which have dominated Internet and cheaper voice service provision in the home. Wi-Fi will remain the primary wireless access technology. The fixed operators may be strengthened by Wi-Fi capabilities in consumer electronics devices (set-top boxes, game consoles, and MP3 players) that enable cost-effective content downloads.

- *Wireless security moves to the forefront.* There is a monumental need to put strong security measures in place. This could be the year that hackers really start paying attention to millions of wireless devices, the growth in mobile data usage, and vulnerable points between mobile and fixed networks. CIOs consistently cite security as their number one concern in extending network access to wireless devices. Attacks, viruses, and data security now exceed device loss or theft as concerns. Services, such as VoIP and mobile payments, provide additional challenges. Vulnerabilities directly affect the bottom line, corporate image, regulatory compliance, and competitive advantage.

- *Enterprise mobility.* Enterprises are taking advantage of the convenient, reliable, attractively priced, bundled mobile solutions entering the market. Corporations are adopting mobile solutions for transactions, data collection, and messaging for a wide variety of employees. Many voice communications processes, such as order placement and delivery notifications, dispatch operations, and remote asset monitoring, continue to shift to wireless data.

OPENING CASE QUESTIONS

The Ironman

6. How is WTC using mobile (cellular) technologies to improve its operations?

7. How is WTC using satellite technologies to improve its operations?

8. Explain how WTC is using WiMAX and RFID wireless technologies in its operations. To what extent do these technologies offer business value?

9. Identify the ethical and security dilemmas that WTC faces in using wireless technologies in its business operations.

SUMMARY OF KEY THEMES

The purpose of this chapter was to provide you, the business student, with a detailed overview of the various telecommunications technologies employed by organizations today. This included discussion on VoIP, business networks, network security, wireless fidelity, and mobile technologies. Organizations are taking advantage of these technologies in the information systems applications they are building. It is important to understand which technologies are available and how businesses can leverage these technologies in their daily and long-term strategic operations.

Specifically, this chapter described:

■ *Network basics and how networks enable data sharing to occur.* Network basics include LANs, WANs, and MANs. Networks offer organizations the ability to share data with customers and suppliers. It is this data sharing, not the network infrastructures themselves, that offer companies the most business benefit. In this sense, networks are an enabler of business success.

■ *The use of networks and telecommunications in business, including Voice over Internet Protocol (VoIP), networking businesses, increasing the speed of business, and the challenges associated with securing business networks.* VoIP facilitates the development and rollout of new business applications at significant cost savings, and provides productivity gains to organizations and service enhancements to customers. Network infrastructures such as VPNs and VANs alleviate the burden of organizations setting up their own entire network infrastructures and help overcome significant challenges in using conventional telecommunication technologies. Organizations need to properly secure their networks because they are tempting targets for mischief and fraud.

■ *Mobile workforce business drivers and the use of cellular technologies in business.* Mobile technologies help organizations increase productivity, speed to market, and reduce operating costs. These technologies create new and innovative ways to perform business. Popular cellular technologies in business include tablets, smartphones, and Bluetooth devices.

■ *The use of satellite technologies in business, and how LBS, GPS, and GIS create business value.* Satellites and microwave transmitters offer businesses a cost-effective way to send and receive large quantities of data over great distances. Location-based services, such as global positioning systems, allow the identification of a person's location to be known so that new business applications, such as geographic information systems, can be offered that depend on knowledge of a person's physical locale.

■ *The use of Wi-Fi, WiMAX, and RFID technologies in business, and other mobile business trends.* New wireless technologies, such as Wi-Fi, WiMAX, and RFID, facilitate the use and development of mobile business applications that offer convenience to customers and operational enhancements to businesses. Mobile business trends, such as mobile social networking, mobile TV, mobile advertising, and the development of cheaper and more versatile mobile devices, have set the stage for increased development and use of mobile applications for business.

KEY TERMS

Application service provider (ASP)	Online service provider (OSP)
Bandwidth	Radio frequency identification (RFID)
Bits per second (bps)	RFID tags
Bluetooth	Satellite
Broadband	Service level agreements (SLAs)
Geographic information system (GIS)	Tablet
Global positioning system (GPS)	Telecommunication systems
Hertz	Value-added network (VAN)
Internet service provider (ISP)	Virtual private network (VPN)
Local area network (LAN)	Voice over Internet Protocol (VoIP)
Location-based services (LBS)	Wide area network (WAN)
Metropolitan area network (MAN)	WiMAX
Microwave transmitter	Wireless fidelity (Wi-Fi)
Network	Wireless Internet service provider (wISP)

CLOSING CASE ONE

Wireless Bikes

This case illustrates an organization's novel use of RFID, GPS, and Wi-Fi technologies.

Bike-sharing programs have been a popular trend in many countries for years but are just beginning to take hold in the United States, driven mainly by the desire to provide zero-emissions transportation for commuters and tourists in urban areas. In Denver, Colorado, Denver B-cycle offers one of the largest bike-sharing programs in the United States. The company has more than 500 bikes, all made by Trek, that are available through more than 50 bike stations, or B-stations as they are called, in the Denver metropolitan area. Each B-station is fully operated through the use of a variety of wireless technologies, such as RFID, GPS, and Wi-Fi, and has a number of locking docks that might hold as few as 5 bikes or as many as 25—the number depending on the amount of use expected.

There are several methods by which a user can access a bike. One is to use the B-station kiosk to unlock a bike with a credit card. This method is preferred for those who seek infrequent usage for short-term rentals. Here, the user receives a pass that is good for a 24-hour rental. Another option is to purchase a 7-day, 30-day, or annual membership online or at the kiosk. This is good for those planning to use bikes on a regular basis. Members receive an RFID-enabled card that allows them to retrieve any of the available bikes from the B-stations located around the city. Members can also download an iPhone app with the added convenience of using the device to unlock and locate bikes.

Once a user selects a bike by using the day pass, RFID-enabled membership card, or iPhone application, the transaction must be validated before the bike is unlocked. This is all done using RFID readers and Wi-Fi–enabled devices that validate the transaction with the company's main database. An RFID reader collects the ID number encoded to a tag attached to the bike. The device then forwards the ID using Wi-Fi to the company's central database, so that the system knows which bike to associate with which user. The user is then alerted with a beep and a green light, indicating the selected bike is unlocked and available for use. When a user wants to return a bicycle, he or she only needs to find an empty dock at any B-station to roll the bike into the locking position. A beep and green light will signal that the bike has been securely locked, and the RFID reader records the tag ID from the bike and sends this information to the company database to complete the transaction.

In addition to having an RFID tag on each bike, embedded GPS units record the routes that a user travels. When a user returns the bike, the GPS information is uploaded to the company database, along with that bike's trek ID number. These data help Denver B-cycle understand the most common routes its users take in addition to allowing the company to collaborate with Denver merchants to target product or service offerings to members, based on their daily routes. For example, a coffee shop might email a coupon to a user who rides by each day. The GPS units also help to protect the company in case a user does not return a bike, or a bike is stolen. Denver B-cycle can use location-based systems to help find the "missing" bike.[38]

Questions

1. What advantages does a wireless network provide Denver B-cycle?

2. What challenges does a wireless network create for Denver B-cycle?

3. What information not described in the case can Denver B-cycle use with RFID and LBS data?

4. How could Denver B-cycle use other wired or wireless network technologies to gain a competitive advantage?

CLOSING CASE TWO

Geoblogging for Chimpanzees and More

This case illustrates the use of location-based data and geodata to change the way people can interact with maps.

Jane Goodall loved Tarzan and Dr. Dolittle when she was a young girl and dreamed of living in Africa among the wild chimpanzees. The Jane Goodall Institute continues her pioneering chimpanzee research that fundamentally changed the way many humans view these wild animals. Using Google Earth, you can now zoom right into the Gombe National Park in Tanzania to watch for yourself the amazing interaction among chimpanzees. Innovative blogs such as Google Earth's geoblog allow users to simply click on an entry, which, in the case of the Institute's blog, causes the globe image to spin toward eastern Africa and then slowly zooms in on the park, allowing users to view satellite images of the animals. The Jane Goodall Institute was the first to create such a Google geoblog.[39] The Institute's blog can be found at **www.janegoodall.org/blogs-publications**.

Google quietly introduced geoblogs back in 2007, and has an official Google "geo" blog at Google LatLong that keeps the world updated on all the new ways that geo data can be used. An April 2014 post on LatLong, for instance, showcases some uses to which the ability to take a look at a location over time can be put. Imagine you are in New York City next to the Freedom Tower and want to see the progress of its construction. You can use your smartphone's GPS to locate your position and then Google Maps Street View images to go back in time and see prior images of the same location. In Gombe National Park, scientists with the Jane Goodall Institute are using Google's Maps Engine and Earth Engine through their smartphones and Android tablets to monitor forest habitat changes that affect chimpanzee populations.[40]

The ability to combine Google Maps with multiple sources of data adds great flexibility to what can be mapped and how those maps can be delivered. Through new interfaces and by making those interfaces available to mobile platforms many new possibilities are added to mapping technologies, from a map on a website to sophisticated heat maps and info graphics. Some examples include simple maps that guide men to the best men's restrooms on Syracuse University campus or an interactive info graphic map of the United States that shows the percentage of the population over 25 that has completed high school.[41]

Questions

1. Imagine what you could do with Google Earth if you added GPS. What other types of research might be accomplished using GPS?

2. How could other nonprofits use geoblogs and GPS to help their cause?

3. How could a business user Google Earth and GPS to create a competitive advantage?

4. Are there any ethical or security concerns with this type of geoblog?

CLOSING CASE THREE

Crash Pads

This case shows use of Wi-Fi technologies to help sports team coaches and officials determine the severity of the contact that players experience during play or practice.

For years now, many National Football League teams have used wireless devices for communicating between players and coaches, and now new devices can be used to assess just how hard players are being hit in the head. In 2010 the Chicago Bears, Dallas Cowboys, and Jacksonville Jaguars tucked Wi-Fi sensors into players' helmets that will send data to the sidelines every time a player is hit or tackled. The sensors have been programmed to detect hard hits, triggering a warning to pull the player for further assessment.

The sensors look like marshmallows stuffed between the helmet's padding and the outside shell. Each sensor can measure the acceleration of a player's head during a hit, and determine the direction, duration, location on the head, magnitude, and time of impact. Once a player's helmet is hit, the sensors immediately transmit the data to staff on the sidelines, who use tablets and smartphones to receive the information. If the data sent determine that the hit exceeds a certain threshold, a mobile device lights up, alerting staff that a player's condition needs to be assessed. The NFL's new injury-related rules state that if a player exhibits any signs of a concussion, he must leave the field for the day.[42]

Such sensors are now appearing on the helmets of college football players and younger players. In Canada, the Western University Mustangs were the first team, professional or amateur, to start using them. Greg Marshall, head coach of the Mustangs, agreed to take part in a research study during the 2013 season in which players' helmets we refitted with a GForce tracker that monitors blows to the head. The Canadian-manufactured tracker used in the study is an unobtrusive device about the size of a domino that is fastened to the inside of the helmet. The study is aimed at gaining clues about helping to reduce the number of concussions.[43]

Today the concern is about becoming reliant on these devices as the be-all and end-all for head injury prevention. "These technologies can be useful if used cautiously, as long as you don't over-interpret what they mean," said Dr. Jeffrey Kutcher, director of the Michigan NeuroSport Program. "It could be really dangerous to rely on this too much." In tests, conditions that should trigger the sensors have sometimes not done so, which could result in undetected concussions in players.[44]

Questions

1. How else can wireless devices be used to prevent injury?

2. Should all football teams, including professional, academic, and recreational, use wireless sensors in helmets? Why or why not?

3. Should other sports such as hockey and cycling start using this technology? Why or why not?

4. How would you suggest that coaches and staff be trained so that they don't become over-reliant on these devices as the primary indicator of a potential head injury?

MAKING BUSINESS DECISIONS

1. Wireless Fitness

Sandifer's Fitness Club is located in beautiful British Columbia. Rosie Sandifer has owned and operated the club for 20 years. The club has three outdoor pools, two indoor pools, ten racquetball courts, ten tennis courts, and an indoor and outdoor track, along with a four-storey exercise equipment and massage therapy building. Rosie has hired you as a summer intern specializing in information technology. The extent of Rosie's current technology includes a few PCs in the accounting department and two PCs with Internet access for the rest of the staff. Your first assignment is to create a report detailing networks and wireless technologies. The report should explain how the club could gain a business advantage by implementing a wireless network. If Rosie likes your report, she will hire you as the full-time employee in charge of information technology. Be sure to include all of the different uses for wireless devices that the club could implement to improve its operations.

2. Secure Access

Organizations that have traditionally maintained private, closed systems have begun to look at the potential of the Internet as a ready-made network resource. The Internet is inexpensive and globally pervasive—every phone jack is a potential connection. However, the Internet lacks security. What obstacles must organizations overcome to allow secure network connections?

3. Integrating Wireless Worlds

Tele-Messaging is a next-generation integrated Internet and wireless messaging service that offers services to ISPs, telecommunications carriers, and portal companies. According to Tele-Messaging's research, the primary reason that 90 percent of the people go online is for email. However, the challenge for Tele-Messaging is how to successfully attract and retain these customers. Customers want more than free calls to sign up and are looking for a host of additional services with whiz-bang technology to give them the information they want, when they want it, anywhere, and in the method most convenient to them. List the infrastructures needed to deliver the technology with the necessary reliability, availability, and scalability demanded by Tele-Messaging's customers.

4. Shipment Routes

Mary Conzachi works in planning for Loadstar, a large trucking company and barge operator in Ontario and Quebec. She has looked into a variety of systems to keep track of the location of trucks and barges so that the company can route shipments better and answer customer inquiries faster. Mary's major concern is with the trucks; the barges have commodities and take weeks to move something. She states that it is much harder to keep up with trucking. Mary has collected information on a variety of products that can help track trucks. For example, the GPS service used for air and marine navigation would allow Loadstar to pinpoint the exact location of a truck. Loadstar would need a system that could identify the truck and send the ID and GPS data to headquarters. Another possibility is to use a cellphone in each truck and have the driver call in at certain hours. Mary said she didn't need to know that a truck is at a certain latitude and longitude. If the driver says he or she is near at certain exit ramp on highway 401, that's good enough. What solution do you recommend? Why?

5. Network Analysis

Global Manufacturing is considering a new technology application. The company wants to process orders in a central location and then assign production to different plants. Each plant will operate its own production scheduling and control system. Data on work in process and completed assemblies will be transmitted back to the central location that processes orders.

At each plant, Global uses PCs that perform routine applications, such as payroll and accounting. The production scheduling and control systems will be a package program running on a new computer dedicated to this application. Global has a high-level systems design for data transmission from the central computer to the plants and for the plant data transmission back to central planning.

The systems staff at Global has retained you as a consultant to help with further analysis. What kind of computer configuration seems most appropriate? What kind of transmission network is needed? What data should be collected? Prepare a plan showing the information Global must develop to establish this telecommunications system. Should Global use a private network or can it accomplish its objectives through the Internet?

connect   LEARNSMART·   SMARTBOOK™

For more information on the resources available from McGraw-Hill Ryerson, go to www.mheducation.ca/he/solutions.

ENDNOTES

1. www.ironman.com, accessed May 7, 2014; http://timepoint.mylaps.com/about.jsf, accessed September 23, 2011; www.mylaps.com/index.php/us_eng/Websites/home, accessed September 23, 2011; www.sportstats.ca/about.xhtml, accessed May 7, 2014.

2. www.news.bce.ca/data/olympicmediakit/pdf/091117_ BellConsortium_Release_EN.pdf, accessed April 8, 2010; "CBC Reveals Sochi Olympics Coverage Plans," October 13, 2013, www.cbc.ca/sports/cbc-reveals-sochi-olympics-coverage-plans-1.2287312, accessed August 22, 2014; "CBC Announces Broadcast Plans for the Sochi 2014 Olympic Winter Games Starting February 6 on CBC," January 9, 2014, www.cbc.ca/mediacentre/cbc-annouces-broadcast-plans-for-the-sochi-2014-olympic-winter-games-starting-february-6-on-cbc.html, accessed August 22, 2014.

3. "Who We Are," www.sabreairlinesolutions.com/about, accessed September 23, 2011; "About Us," www.sabre-holdings.com/aboutUs/index.html, accessed September 23, 2011.

4. www.shaw.ca/wifi, accessed May 6, 2014.

5. www.voipchoices.com/voip-canada.html, accessed April 8, 2010.

6. "Rip Curl Turns to Skype for Global Communications," July 7, 2006, www.voipinbusiness.co.uk/rip_curl_turns_to_skype_for_gl.asp, accessed January 21, 2008; Scott Davison "Case Study—Rip Curl," November 26, 2008, http://blogs.skype.com/business/2008/11/case_study_rip_curl.html, accessed September 23, 2011.

7. "VoIP Business Solutions," www.vocalocity.com, accessed June 28, 2010.

8. https://support.skype.com/en/faq/FA631/can-i-disable-particular-features-of-skype, accessed June 4, 2014.

9. www.rei.com, accessed February 23, 2008.

10. Enrique De Argaez, "What You Should Know About Internet Broadband Access," www.internetworldstats.com/articles/art096.htm, accessed September 23, 2011.

11. "Broadband Technology Overview," June 2005, www.corning.com/docs/opticalfiber/wp6321.pdf, accessed September 23, 2011.

12. www.cbc.ca/news/technology/story/2013/07/17/technology-gigabit-internet-olds.html, accessed August 14, 2013; Darren Barefoot, "Is Canada Missing Out on a Gigabit Internet Future?," *Vancouver Sun*, July 26, 2013, at www.vancouversun.com/technology/Canada+missing+gigabit+Internet+ future/8713981/story.html, accessed August 19, 2013; www.o-net.ca/manage, accessed August 19, 2013; Tamara Gignac, "Superfast Web Service Puts Olds on World Map," *Calgary Herald*, July 24, 2013, at www.calgaryherald.com/news/alberta/Superfast+service+puts+ Olds+world/8703980/story.html, accessed August 19, 2013.

13. "Fresh Snack Facts: Insights into Food and Beverage Vending," April 1, 2011, http://tapmag.com/2011/04/01/fresh-snacks-fast-insights-into-food-and-beverage-vending, accessed September 28, 2011.

14. Scott Cooper, "Navigating the Mobility Wave," October 2006, www.busmanagement.com/article/Navigating-the-mobility-wave, accessed September 23, 2011; Kevin Conway, "What Is Your Company's Mobile Strategy?," May 10, 2011, http://blog.savvis.net/2011/05/what-is-your-companys-mobile-strategy.html, accessed September 28, 2011.

15. "WestJet Announces New Mobile Check-In Option," May 17, 2007, www.flyertalk.com/forum/westjet-frequent-guest/694168-westjet-announces-new-mobile-check-option.html, accessed September 23, 2011; www.aircanada.com/en/travelinfo/traveller/mobile/mci.html, accessed September 23, 2011.

16. https://squareup.com/ca, accessed May 7, 2014.

17. Joshua Pramis, "Number of Mobile Phones to Exceed World Population by 2014," February 28, 2013, www.digitaltrends.com/mobile/mobile-phone-world-population-2014/#!zFyGe, accessed March 2014; Devon Maylie, "Sub-Saharan Africa's Mobile-Phone Growth Faces Challenges," November 11, 2013, http://online.wsj.com/news/articles/SB10001424052702303914304579191500020741652, accessed March 14, 2014.

18. "How Cell Phones Work," www.howstuffworks.com/cell-phone.htm, accessed September 23, 2011.

19. http://network.bell.ca/en, accessed August 14, 2013; https://mobility.telus.com/en/AB/network/index.shtml, accessed August 14, 2013.

20. Liam Tung, "One in Every Five Tablets Will Be an Enterprise Device by 2017," August 6, 2013, www.zdnet.com/one-in-every-five-tablets-will-be-an-enterprise-device-by-2017-7000019038, accessed March 14, 2014; "Enterprise Tablet Adoption Picks Up Steam; Bring Your Own PC Doesn't," March 24, 2011, www.zdnet.com/blog/btl/enterprise-tablet-adoption-picks-up-steam-bring-your-own-pc-doesnt/46481, accessed September 28, 2011.

21. V. Cagri Güngör and Frank C. Lambert, "A Survey on Communication Networks for Electric System Automation," *The International Journal of Computer and Telecommunications Networking*, May 15, 2006, pp. 877–897.

22. United States Government Accountability Office, "Global Positioning System: Significant Challenges in Sustaining and Upgrading Widely Used Capabilities," GAO-09-670T, May 7, 2009; United States Government Accountability Office, "Global Positioning System: Significant Challenges in Sustaining and Upgrading Widely Used Capabilities," GAO-09-325, April 30, 2009; "US Air Force Launches New GPS Satellite," February 21, 2014, www.space.com/24767-gps-satellite-launch-success-delta4-rocket.html, accessed March 14, 2014.

23. "CenterCup Releases PDA Caddy to Leverage Legalized Golf GPS," February 23, 2006, www.golfgearreview.com/article-display/1665.html, accessed September 23, 2011.

24. www.onstar.com, accessed February 10, 2008.

25. Laura McGinnis, "Keeping Weeds in Check with Less Herbicide," August 1, 2006, www.ars.usda.gov/is/AR/archive/aug06/weeds0806.htm, accessed September 23, 2011.

26. www.gis.rgs.org/10.html, accessed February 7, 2008.

27. Bob Tedeschi, "Trying Out Wi-Fi in the Sky," June 22, 2010, http://travel.nytimes.com/2010/06/27/travel/27Prac.html, accessed September 28, 2011; Amanda Stephenson, "WestJet Will Offer In-Flight Wi-Fi in 2014: CEO Saretsky," December 13, 2013, www.calgaryherald.com/business/WestJet+will+offer+flight+2014+Saretsky/9293025/story.html, accessed March 14, 2014.

28. Christine Dobby, "Bell Introduces Wireless IPTV in Bid to Win Subscribers from Competitors," May 27, 2013, http://business.financialpost.com/2013/05/27/bell-introduces-wireless-iptv-in-bid-to-win-subscribers-from-competitors/?__lsa=e724-1981, accessed May 10, 2014; www.telus.com/content/tv/optik/clients, accessed May 10, 2014.

29. Mahdi Smaoui, "Case Study: WiMAX in Rural and Remote Areas: Netago Wireless—Special Areas in Alberta, Canada," ITU-D Q10 2/2, rapporteur's meeting, Geneva, Switzerland, May 7–9, 2007; "Wireless Broadband," www.netago.ca/Wireless_Broadband.aspx, accessed September 30, 2011; "WiMAX Activity in Canada," April 4, 2011, www.crc.gc.ca/en/html/crc/home/info_crc/publications/wimax_2007/ wimax_2007, accessed September 30, 2011.

30. Deepak Pareek, "WiMAX: Taking Wireless to the MAX," *CRC Press*, 2006, pp. 150–51.

31. www.wimax.com, accessed September 28, 2011.

32. Michael Dortch, "Winning RFID Strategies for 2008," *Benchmark Report*, December 31, 2007.

33. Ibid.

34. "RFID Roundup," www.rfidgazette.org, accessed June 28, 2010.

35. RFID Security Alliance, www.rfidsa.com, accessed June 15, 2010; "Mobile Malware Evolution: An Overview, Part 1," September 29, 2006, www.securelist.com/en/analysis/200119916/Mobile_Malware_ Evolution_An_Overview_Part_1, accessed June 4, 2014.

36. "RFID Privacy and You," www.theyaretrackingyou.com/rfid-privacy-and-you.html, accessed June 28, 2010.

37. RFID Security Alliance, www.rfidsa.com, accessed June 15, 2010; "Mobile Malware Evolution: An Overview, Part 1," September 29, 2006, www.securelist.com/en/analysis/200119916/Mobile_Malware_ Evolution_An_Overview_Part_1, accessed June 4, 2014.

38. Alissa Walker, "The Technology Driving Denver's B-cycle Bike Sharing System," *Fast Company*, June 3, 2010, www.fastcompany.com/1656160/the-technology-driving-denvers-new-b-cycle-bike-sharing-system?partner=rss; https://denver.bcycle.com/default.aspx, accessed April 27, 2014; http://denverbikesharing.org/Denver_Bike_Sharing/Denver_Bike_Sharing-_Owner_%26_Operator_of_Denver_B-cycle.html, accessed April 27, 2014.

39. Google Earth, "Jane Goodall Institute–Gombe Chimpanzee Blog," http://earth.google.com/outreach/cs_jgi_blog.html, accessed April 27, 2014.

40. "Go Back in Time with Street View," April 23, 2014, http://google-latlong.blogspot.ca, accessed May 6, 2014; "From Lake Tanganyika to Google Earth: Using Tech to Help Our Communities," April 3, 2014, http://google-latlong.blogspot.ca, accessed May 6, 2014.

41. Geoblog Experiment—Google, https://maps.google.com/maps/ms?ie=UTF8&t=k&oe=UTF8&msa=0&msid=217071296076381043554.0004d8f2c5c9633e41782&dg=feature, accessed May 6, 2014; "Build a Map Infographic with Google Maps & JavaScript," April 9, 2014, http://googlegeodevelopers.blogspot.ca, accessed May 6, 2014.

42. Michael Copeland, "Let the Helmet Make the Call," *Fortune*, February 4, 2010, http://money.cnn.com/galleries/2010/technology/1002/gallery.football_ helmets_sensors.fortune/index.html; www.theshockbox.com, accessed April 27, 2014.

43. Robert MacLeod, "New Football Helmet Sensors Monitor Brain Injuries," November 14, 2013, www.theglobeandmail.com/sports/football/helmet-sensors-monitor-brain-injuries/article15453952, accessed May 7, 2014.

44. Stephanie Smith, "Head Impact Sensors: On-the-Field Placebo or Danger?," November 21, 2013, www.cnn.com/2013/11/15/health/youth-head-sensors, accessed April 27, 2014.

Enterprise MIS Systems

M odule 4 explores how organizations use various types of information systems to help run their daily operations. These are primarily transactional systems that concentrate on the management and flow of low-level data items pertaining to basic business processes such as purchasing and order delivery. The data are often rolled up and summarized into higher-level decision support systems to help firms understand what is happening in their organizations and how best to respond. To achieve seamless handling of the data, organizations must ensure that their enterprise information systems are tightly integrated. Doing so allows organizations to manage and deal with basic business processes as efficiently and effectively as possible and to make better informed decisions.

This module highlights the various types of enterprise information systems found in organizations and the new trends found in enterprise computing today. First, new trends are discussed to showcase how organizations are reacting to and taking advantage of technological changes and challenges. From there, the chapters in this module speak to various types of enterprise information systems and their role in helping firms reach their strategic goals. Though each chapter is devoted to specific types of enterprise systems (e.g., those used for enterprise resource planning, supply chain management, and customer relationship management), these systems must work in tandem with each other, giving enterprise-wide or 360-degree views of the business. Organizations that can process transactional data effectively and summarize this transactional data into enterprise-wide information are better prepared to run efficiently, meet their strategic business goals, and outperform their competitors.

Enterprise Computing Challenges and Enterprise Resource Planning

LEARNING OUTCOMES

LO 7.1 Explain what enterprise computing challenges are happening in organizations today (e.g., innovation, going green, social networks, and virtual worlds).

LO 7.2 Describe enterprise resource planning as a management approach and how information systems can help promote ERP.

LO 7.3 Describe the components of ERP systems and the differences between them.

LO 7.4 Explain the business value of integrating supply chain management, customer relationship management, and enterprise resource planning systems together.

LO 7.5 Explain how an organization can measure ERP success, choose ERP software, and use ERP in SME markets.

WHY DO I NEED TO KNOW THIS ?

This chapter introduces you to trends in enterprise computing and the concept of enterprise resource planning. In terms of trends, it is important for organizations to keep abreast of technological changes and challenges that affect competitor and consumer behaviours, and offer new ways of doing things. This includes continually monitoring and being aware of new innovations in the marketplace.

ERP involves integrating an organization's internal operational processes, such as distribution, accounting, and human resources, into an integrated set of information systems. The ERP concept emerged in response to the massive fortunes, time, and energy spent by organizations trying to support their back-office operations. Prior to this, systems were built in isolation, and organizations struggled to link them because they were often incompatible. They spent hundreds of millions of dollars trying to integrate their internal departmental processes, by building highly customized interfaces between systems and their stand-alone database structures. ERP answered this dilemma by combining the diverse needs of an organization's business units into a single, integrated software program that operated on a single database. Departments could thereby better share data and communicate with one another more easily, resulting in cost savings and competitive advantages.

As a business student, you need to know about trends in enterprise computing and how ERP systems are the backbone of many business operations today. Staying aware of and reacting to technological trends help a firm function competitively and strategically in the marketplace. ERP systems are constantly evolving and it is important that you understand why they exist, what they do, and the real benefits they can offer a company.

Shell Fuels Productivity with ERP

Shell is one of the nation's largest integrated petroleum companies and is a leading manufacturer, distributor, and marketer of refined petroleum products. The company, with its Canadian operations based in Calgary, produces natural gas, natural gas liquids, and bitumen. Shell is also the country's largest producer of sulfur. There is a Canada-wide network of about 1,800 Shell-branded retail gasoline stations and convenience food stores from coast to coast.

Mission-Critical ERP

To run such a complex and vast business operation successfully, the company relies heavily on a mission-critical ERP system. Using such a system is a necessity to help the company integrate and manage its daily operations—operations that span from wells and mines, to processing plants, to oil trucks and gas pumps.

For example, the ERP system has helped the company immensely in reducing and streamlining the highly manual process of third-party contractors submitting repair information and invoices. On average, there are between 2,500 and 4,000 service orders handled by these contractors per month on a nationwide basis.

Life at Shell Before ERP

Prior to implementing the ERP system, contractors had to send Shell monthly summarized invoices that listed maintenance calls the contractors made at various Shell gasoline stations. Each one of these invoices took a contractor between eight and 20 hours to prepare. Collectively, the contractors submitted somewhere between 50 and 100 invoices every month to Shell. This involved each invoice being reviewed by the appropriate territory manager and then forwarded to head office for payment processing. This alone consumed another 16 to 30 hours of labour per month. In Calgary, another 200 hours of work was performed by data entry clerks who had to manually enter batch invoice data into the payment system.

And this was the amount of time needed if things went smoothly! More hours of labour were required to decipher and correct errors if any mistakes were introduced from all the manual invoice generation and data re-entry involved. Often, errors concerning one-line items on an invoice would deter payment of the whole invoice. This irritated the contractors and did not help to foster healthy contractor relationships.

To make matters worse, despite the hours involved and the amount of human data-handling required, detailed information about the service repairs that contractors did was often not entered into the payment system. And if it was entered, the information was not timely—it was often weeks or even months old by the time it made it into the payment processing system. As a result, Shell was not collecting sufficient information about what repairs were being done, what had caused the problem, and how it had been resolved.

ERP Is Solving Issues

Fortunately, ERP solved these inadequacies by providing an integrated Web-based service order, invoice, and payment submission system. With this tool, third-party contractors can enter service orders directly into Shell's ERP system via the Web. When this is done, the contractors can also enter detailed information about the work that was performed—sometimes even attaching photos and drawings to help describe that work. With the ERP system, it takes only a few minutes for a contractor to enter details about a service order. Further, this information can be transmitted through a mobile device to the appropriate Shell manager for immediate approval—shaving off extra time in unnecessary delays.

Another bonus of the ERP system is that the contractors' monthly, summarized invoices can now be generated automatically and fed directly into the ERP system's accounts payable application for processing. No re-keying of data required! Even better, if there is an issue or concern with one invoice item, the other items on the invoice can still be processed for payment.

Shell's ERP system also handles other operational tasks. For example, the system can help speed up maintenance and repair operations at the company's refineries. With the ERP system in place, rather than trying to use a variety of disparate internal systems to access blueprints, schematics, spare parts lists, and other tools and information, workers at the refineries can now use the ERP system to access these things directly from a centralized database.

An added benefit of the ERP system is its ease of use. Past systems refinery workers used were complex and difficult to search for information. The ERP system in place now has a portal-like interface that allows refinery workers to access the functions and information they need to keep operations running. The Web interface allows workers access to this information with one or two clicks of a mouse.

An important part of any successful ERP implementation is training end-users to learn how to use the system and to teach them about the functions and abilities of the ERP system. Recognizing this, Shell offered its personnel both formal and informal ERP training. These proved to be invaluable in teaching end-users the mechanics of the system, raising awareness of the system benefits, and the efficiencies that the ERP system could offer Shell. This not only helped promote end-user acceptance of the ERP system, but also greatly increased employees' intentions to use the system in their daily work.

Shell executives are pleased with the advantages of the ERP system. With the system, employees across the company have gained fast and easy access to the tools and information they need to conduct their daily operations.[1]

7.1 ENTERPRISE COMPUTING CHALLENGES

INTRODUCTION

Many people have no idea how they would get any work done on business trips if they did not have a laptop, tablet, or smartphone; these devices are crucial to their jobs. It is hard to conceive of getting through the day without Google, or text messaging, or using Facebook to stay in touch with an extended network of colleagues. In just a decade or less, information technology has fundamentally changed the way we work.

And in the next decade, the relentless march of computer power and Internet connection speeds will bring more profound changes to work than anything seen so far. Consider just a few of the breakthroughs that technology visionaries think will occur in coming years. Picture your smartphone shrunken to the size of a credit card. Then imagine it can connect not only to contacts on the latest social network, but also to billions of pea-sized wireless sensors attached to buildings, streets, retail products, and clothes—all simultaneously sending data over the Internet. This will allow tracking and managing more than static data; users will be able to track events in the physical world, from production on a factory floor to colleagues' whereabouts, to how customers are using products. All that data will be much easier to view and analyze, using voice or hand and arm gestures to control commands, and viewing results with special glasses that make it seem as if the user is gazing at a life-size screen. Just imagine producing design ideas or actual products via a 3D printer that creates plastic or carbon fibre models from computerized specs as easily as a paper printer spews out reports today.[2]

Organizations are facing technological changes and challenges more extensive and far-reaching in their implications than anything since the modern industrial revolution occurred in the early 1900s. Enterprises that want to survive in the 21st century must recognize these technological changes and challenges, carry out required organizational changes in the face of it, and learn to operate in an entirely different way. Today's organizations focus on defending and safeguarding their existing market positions in addition to targeting new market growth. A few of the changes and challenges organizations are focusing on in the 21st century are:

■ Innovation

■ Social responsibility

■ Social networks

LO1) INNOVATION

In the past, a company was primarily focused on operational excellence. Now innovation drives the wheels of IT. **Innovation** is the introduction of new equipment or methods. The current impetus to innovate comes from the need to cut costs, while still creating a competitive advantage. Fundamental shifts in technology will make it possible for businesses to realize IT's promise of technology-enabled innovation, responsiveness, and speed.

For instance, consider big-wave surfers from around the world who converged on Mavericks at Pillar Point, just a few miles from San Francisco, to challenge each other on the big waves that have made this a legendary surfing destination. The sixth Mavericks Surf Contest had been announced only 48 hours earlier to ensure optimal wave conditions for the contestants. Surfers from as far away as Australia, Brazil, and South Africa scrambled to make their way to this invitation-only competition. It was magical to watch these athletes challenge enormous waves with an ease and grace that made it all seem so natural.

Beneath the surface, however, was a different story, one that contains important lessons for business executives. While all attention was on the athletes riding their surfboards, the technology and techniques used to master big-wave surfing have evolved over decades, driven by dedicated, perhaps even obsessed, groups of athletes and craftsmen. Executives can gain significant insight into the innovation process by looking at this sport and following the six best practices of innovation (see Figure 7.1).[3]

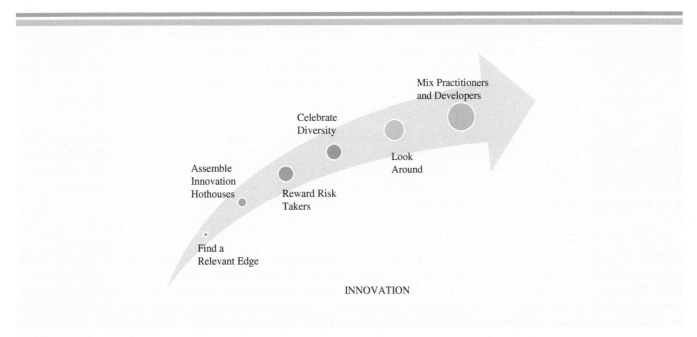

FIGURE 7.1

Six Best Practices of Innovation

Find a Relevant Edge

First, to push performance levels, organizations must find the relevant edge. In the case of big-wave surfers, there has been an ever-expanding search for the breaks that would produce bigger and rougher waves to test new board designs and surfing practices.

Following the lead of surfers, business executives need to find relevant edges that will test and push their current performance. For example, companies making diesel engines and power generators should be actively engaged in finding ways to more effectively serve lower-income customers in remote rural areas of emerging economies. These demanding customers could prompt significant innovation in both product design and distribution processes in an effort to deliver greater value at lower cost. The innovations resulting from these efforts on the edge could lead to significant improvements in product lines.

Assemble Innovation Hothouses

Second, attract motivated groups of people to these edges to work together on challenging performance issues. In the late 1950s, Waimea Bay, on the north shore of Oahu, became the test bed for athletes seeking to push the boundaries of big-wave surfing. In the isolation of the north shore, dedicated surfers spent eight to ten hours each and every day, challenging themselves and each other on the big waves. The real advances in surfing technology and practices occurred at the breaks where surfers gathered and formed deep relationships over extended periods. They learned rapidly from each other and pushed each other to go to the next level.

Large companies have become adept at establishing remote outposts in places like Beijing, Hyderabad, Haifa, and St. Petersburg to attract local talent and push forward challenging research and development projects. Often, though, these outposts either become disconnected from their parent companies or fail to establish deep links with other leading-edge participants in the area. The key challenge is to connect these company-owned facilities more effectively with their local environments as well as with each other through challenging and sustained innovation initiatives that build long-term, trust-based relationships. Performance improvement generally comes first in the form of tacit knowledge that is difficult to express and communicate more broadly. To gain access to this tacit knowledge, people have to be there.

Reward Risk Takers

Third, recognize that the people who are likely to be attracted to the edge are risk takers. This is a key reason the edge becomes such a fertile ground for innovation. It attracts people who are not afraid to take risks and to learn from their experiences. Executives need to be thoughtful about how to attract these people, provide them with environments to support risk taking, and reward them for both successes and failures.

Celebrate Diversity

Fourth, recognize that the edge fosters not just risk taking, but different cultures that are edgy. The advances in big-wave surfing did not come from the casual surfers but from those who developed an entire lifestyle and culture, fostered by intense and even obsessive concentration on pushing the envelope. Executives need to find ways to protect and honour these edgy cultures, whether they are inhabited by Web designers or the next generation of employees who learned how to innovate as members of guilds in World of Warcraft.

Look Around

Fifth, find ways to appropriate insights from adjacent disciplines and even more remote areas of activity. Early advances in surfing technology came from the aerospace industry because some of the employees in this industry were also avid surfers. Some of surfer Laird Hamilton's greatest insights came from his experiences as an expert windsurfer and his colleagues' experiences with snowboarding. By attracting diverse backgrounds and experiences to the edge, executives can foster creative breakthroughs.

Mix Practitioners and Developers

Sixth, bring users and developers of technology together. It is no accident that the most innovative surfers also tended to be expert shapers of surfboards. These folks not only designed surfboards but also shaped the materials into the finished product and then took them out to life-threatening breaks to test and refine them. They were relentless tinkerers, integrating experience, intuition, and craft to come up with creative new boards. Technology and practice are intimately linked—very little performance improvement comes directly out of the technology itself. It is only when seasoned practitioners engage with the technology, especially in close-knit communities, and evolve their practices to use it better, that the real performance breakthroughs occur.

SOCIAL RESPONSIBILITY

Social responsibility implies that an entity, whether it is a government, corporation, not-for-profit organization, or individual, has a responsibility to society. *Corporate policy* is a dimension of social responsibility that refers to the position a firm takes on social and political issues. *Corporate social responsibility* is a dimension of social responsibility that includes everything from hiring minority workers to making safe products. *Sustainable* or *"green" IT* describes the manufacture, management, use, and disposal of information technology in a way that minimizes damage to the environment, which is a critical part of a corporation's responsibility. As a result, the term has many different meanings, depending on whether you are a manufacturer, manager, or user of technology. This portion of the chapter covers energy consumption, recycling IT equipment, and greener IT.

Energy Consumption

Corporate computing's fast-growing power consumption is a threat to operations and the bottom line, and is forcing companies to adopt green energy practices. In 1992 Hewlett-Packard (HP) launched its Design for Environment program with the goals of energy efficiency, materials innovation, and recycling. Through this program HP created a number of products and programs that help consumers save on energy consumption and make recycling old products and consumables easier. Another push of the program, since about 2004, has been aimed at data centres and making them more energy efficient. It is estimated that 65 percent of the energy used in a modern data centre is wasted in idle server time.[4] To combat inefficient energy use, HP has introduced innovations like dynamic smart cooling and Eco POD prefab data centres that can reduce energy consumption by about 50 percent from about 2.0 PUE (power usage effectiveness) to as low as 1.05 PUE.[5] With this thinking, engineers at HP made a startling realization about the servers running the company's computing systems—that surging power consumption, along with rising energy costs, will soon make it more expensive to keep a server going for a year than to acquire one in the first place.[6]

When HP began constructing a 4,645 square metre building in California to house high-powered computers, it sought advice from Pacific Gas & Electric (PG&E). By following the California power company's recommendations, HP saves US$1 million a year in power costs for that data centre alone, PG&E says.

Like HP, companies across the globe are adding equipment to keep up with surging computing needs, and then are forced to make substantial changes to curtail the leap in costs associated with running the big buildings, or data centres, housing all that gear. "Data centres use 50 times the energy per square foot than an office," said Mark Bramfitt, principal program manager at PG&E. Figure 7.2 gives the breakdown of power use in a typical data centre.[7]

The pressure is on for tech companies, utilities, and builders to come up with new ways of cutting energy consumption. The following are some of the ways they are responding.

Sun Microsystems: Throughput Computing   A decade ago, the chip industry had a single focus: making the digital brains of computers process data ever faster. But Sun Microsystems chip architect Marc Tremblay saw a fatal flaw in that strategy. Faster chips would run hotter, and eventually they would burn out. So he designed what's known as a multi-core chip, which has several processors on a single sliver of silicon, each running cooler and sucking less energy but collectively getting more work done.[9] Now, chip manufactures are focused on not only processing power but also the amount of energy their chips are using. Since 2007 companies like Intel and AMD continue to introduce chips that are more power-efficient in each new generation.

Virtualization   It used to be possible to run only one application at a time on a given server. That meant if the application was not needed at any given time, the server was not being used. Analysts estimate only 10 to 20 percent of the typical server's capability is used. *Virtualization* is a framework of dividing the resources of a computer into multiple execution environments. Virtualization software allows IT managers to easily load multiple programs on a single machine and move programs from one computer to another on the fly to make maximum use of a cluster of servers. This significantly reduces energy use, some analysts suggesting up to 80 percent, because fewer servers are needed.[10]

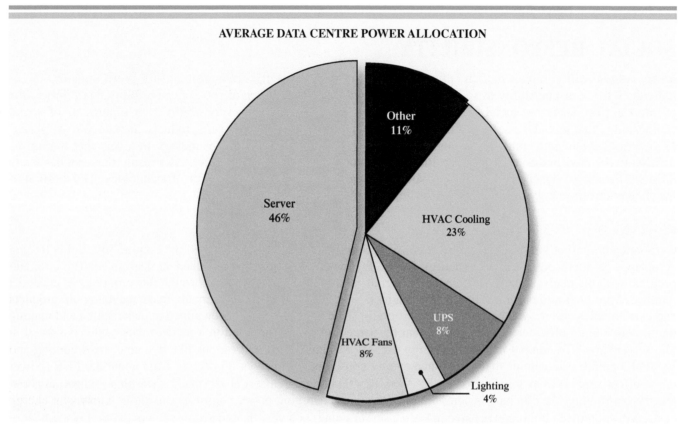

FIGURE 7.2

Breakdown of Power Use in the Typical Data Centre[8]

Source: Roger Allan, "The Greening of Server Farms," *Power Electronics*, September 1, 2009, http://powerelectronics. com/markets/greening-server-farms, accessed May 2014.

Energy Rebate Programs   The province of Ontario offers businesses a number of incentive programs aimed at reducing energy consumption. The programs range from lighting upgrades for small businesses, to incentives for businesses to upgrade systems to hold on to energy savings, and to high performance new construction that exceeds the Ontario building code energy efficiency requirements.[11]

Smart Cooling   HP Research Fellow Chandrakant Patel came up with a new approach to data centre energy use: think of the data centre as one giant machine. Out of that came HP's Dynamic Smart Cooling technology. Thousands of heat sensors monitor temperatures, and software directs the air-conditioning system to put the big chill on the places that need it most. Projected energy savings on cooling costs is 20 to 40 percent.[12]

Alternative Energy Sources   Web-search giant Google, which operates some of the largest data centres in the world, has committed to using cutting-edge technologies to power and cool its data centres, including wind (powers a data centre in the Netherlands) and solar power. Even though Google announced that it was ceasing its efforts to advance alternative energy, it continues its efforts to achieve more efficient energy consumption in its own data centres, using clean energy sources.[13]

Biology Meets Chips   IBM researcher Bruno Michel and his team at the IBM Research-Zurich laboratory are applying biological principles to deal with the heat problem in computing. Just as the human vascular system cools our bodies, Michel is designing devices that cool chips using liquid delivered through capillary-like circulation systems. Typically, the processors in server computers are air-cooled; chilled air is blown over metal caps on top of the chips, where tiny fins dissipate heat. One of Michel's inventions is a metal cap that fits over a processor and sprays jets of water out of 50,000 nozzles into microscopic channels etched in the metal. The channels behave like capillaries, circulating the liquid efficiently and cutting the energy required to pump the water.[14]

Government Involvement   The European Union has imposed limits on carbon emissions. Since 2005, the Emission Trading Scheme has required 12,000 iron, steel, glass, and power plants to buy CO_2 permits, which allows them to emit the gas into the atmosphere. If a company exceeds its limit, it can buy unused permits from other companies that have successfully cut their emissions. If they are unable to buy spare permits, however, they are fined for every excess tonne of CO_2. Because IT contributes to the total carbon emissions in a company, carbon cap-and-trade or tax laws will affect how technology is managed.[15]

Recycle IT Equipment

Sustainable IT disposal refers to the safe disposal of IT assets at the end of their life cycles. It ensures that *e-waste*, or old computer equipment, does not end up in a landfill, where the toxic substances it contains can leach into groundwater, among other problems. Many of the major hardware manufacturers offer take-back programs, so IT departments do not have to take responsibility for disposal. For example, Dell, and Sony will take back any of their products for free and Apple offers gift cards for old equipment that still has monetary value. HP has an extensive recycling program for both consumers and businesses. Printer manufactures like Brother, HP, and Lexmark all have programs for consumers to recycle their printer cartridges.

Furthermore, in Canada, provincial laws require that e-waste be recycled. In response, an industry association called Electronic Product Stewardship Canada (EPSC) was created to promote harmonization among provincial electronic waste regulatory programs and encourage strong environmental standards for the treatment of end-of-life electronics. Many provinces passed legislation requiring recycling surcharges be paid on designated electronic goods shipped or sold into their provinces. Figure 7.3 lists the websites of some of these provincial programs. Current programs have targeted five general categories for end-of-life product recycling: PCs, notebooks, monitors, printers, and televisions, with additional items to be phased in. Although efforts are taken to harmonize e-waste recycling efforts between provinces, the products affected and associated fees vary by province.[16]

Alberta	www.albertarecycling.ca
British Columbia	www.encorp.ca
Nova Scotia	www.acestewardship.ca
Ontario	www.ontarioelectronicstewardship.ca
Saskatchewan	www.sweepit.ca

FIGURE 7.3

Examples of Provincial E-Waste Recycling Programs

Complying with e-waste regulations should become easier for IT managers due to new manufacturing regulations. For example, the EU Directive on the Restriction of the Use of Certain Hazardous Substances in Electrical and Electronic Equipment, which took effect July 1, 2006, restricts the use of six hazardous materials in the manufacture of certain electronics: lead, mercury, cadmium, hexavalent chromium, polybrominated biphenyls, and polybrominated diphenyl ether (the last two materials are flame retardants used in plastics). Such requirements reduce the toxicity of the e-waste produced.[17]

E-waste is expected to continue to grow until 2015, when it is predicted that 73 million tonnes of e-waste will be produced, and in 2016 the world will see the first dip in this growing trend as a number of e-waste initiatives start to take place.[18]

According to National Geographic's *The Green Guide*, 50 to 80 percent of recycled electronics end up in developing nations, where they are disassembled by untrained workers without the proper equipment. This exposes the workers to toxic substances such as mercury, cadmium, and lead. If the equipment is left in landfills, those same toxins end up in water sources.

Green IT

At Sun Microsystems prior to its purchase by Oracle, Openwork, a telecommuting program, provided employees with shared office space, home equipment, and subsidies for Internet connections and electricity. More than 56 percent of Sun's employees used the program. Sun estimated it saved 52,000 tonnes of CO_2 per year due to reduced employee commuting.

Dow Chemical's process control automation system will shut down a plant if it does not comply with air and water emissions requirements. Dow also uses a monitoring system to measure the air and water emissions at its plants and is deploying an environmental reporting system to manage the reporting of this data to authorities, says CIO and Chief Sustainability Officer David Kepler.

IT systems can also help save energy by controlling heat and air-conditioning in office buildings. Wireless sensors and smart dust can be used to measure airflow and room occupancy. If the occupancy sensors (which turn lights on and off when people enter or leave a room) are networked to airflow sensors, the amount of air conditioning used when people are not in a room can be reduced, said David Kepler. "The basic idea is to collect data on how the facility is using energy and use that information to define patterns that can help change what you are doing and reduce operating costs."

To keep up with its explosive growth, Google is building data centres off the beaten path, in places such as Lenoir, North Carolina, Mount Holly, South Carolina, and Council Bluffs, Iowa. For example, its 30-acre facility in The Dalles, Oregon, a town of about 12,000, provided the perfect location, with its hydroelectric dam, affordable land, and a 15-year tax incentive. An industrial-strength power grid connects the dam to Google's complex, where massive cooling systems rise above two data centre buildings.[19] Some of the ways companies save energy in data centres are listed in Figure 7.4.

Use outside air for cooling.

Cool high-density areas.

Use low-power processors.

Incorporate cooling solutions.

Use server power management.

Buy high-efficiency power supplies.

Use virtualization to consolidate servers.

FIGURE 7.4

Ways to Save Energy in a Data Centre

SOCIAL NETWORKS

Encover CEO Chip Overstreet was on the hunt for a new vice-president of sales. He found a promising candidate and dispensed with the glowing but unsurprising remarks from references. Now it was time to dig for any dirt. So he logged on to **LinkedIn.com**, an online business network. "I did 11 back-door checks on this guy and found people he had worked with at five of his last six companies," said Overstreet, whose firm sells and manages service contracts for manufacturers. "It was incredibly powerful."

So powerful, in fact, that many other sites like LinkedIn have cropped up in recent years. They are responding to a growing impulse among Web users to build ties, communities, and networks online, fueling the popularity of sites such as Facebook.

Corporations and smaller businesses have not embraced online business networks with nearly the same abandon as teens and university students who have flocked to social sites. Yet companies are steadily overcoming their reservations and are starting to use these sites and related technologies to craft potentially powerful business tools. Take Twitter, which allows people to exchange short public messages ("tweets") to give others status updates on what's happening in their lives at the moment. Businesses are using this technology to push "real-time" advertising for sales on products that consumers have identified an interest in and that are happening now, or at least for the next few minutes. Many consumers love receiving breaking news on items for sale via tweets they receive, and retailers are reaping the rewards. However, it is still early days. Startups planning to leverage the Twitter phenomenon are still working out their business models. One successful venture is StockTwits, a real-time stock discussion site that allows consumers to search real-time discussions from some of the Web's savviest investors.[20]

Passive Search

Recruiters at Microsoft and Starbucks troll online networks such as LinkedIn for potential job candidates. Goldman Sachs and Deloitte run their own online alumni networks for hiring back former workers and strengthening bonds with alumni-cum–possible clients. Boston Consulting Group and law firm Duane Morris deploy enterprise software that tracks employee communications to uncover useful connections in other companies. And companies such as Intuit have created customer networks to build brand loyalty.

Many companies are leery of online networks. Executives do not have time to field the possible influx of requests from acquaintances on business networks. Employees may be dismayed to learn their workplace uses email monitoring software to help sales associates' target pitches. Companies considering building online communities for advertising, branding, or marketing will need to give up some degree of control over content.

None of those concerns are holding back Carmen Hudson, manager of enterprise staffing at Starbucks, who said she swears by LinkedIn. "It's one of the best things for finding mid-level executives," she said.

The holy grail in recruiting is finding so-called passive candidates, people who are happy and productive working for other companies. LinkedIn is a virtual Rolodex of these types. Hudson says she has hired three or four people this year as a result of connections through LinkedIn. "We've started asking our hiring managers to sign up on LinkedIn and help introduce us to their contacts," she says. "People have concerns about privacy, but once we explain how we use it and how careful we would be with their contacts, they're usually willing to do it."

Boomerangs

Headhunters and human resources departments are taking note. "LinkedIn is a tremendous tool for recruiters," said Bill Vick, the author of *LinkedIn for Recruiting*. So are sites such as **Ryze.com**, **Spoke.com**, and **XING.com**. Many companies are turning to social networks and related technology to stay in touch with former employees. Consulting firm Deloitte strives to maintain ties with ex-workers and has had a formal alumni-relations program for years. It bolsters these efforts with the use of Oracle's Taleo Social Sourcing Cloud Service.

Ex–Deloitte employees can go to the site to browse postings for jobs at a range of companies. They can also peruse open positions at Deloitte. The online network is an extension of an offline program that includes networking receptions and seminars. Deloitte makes no bones about its aim to use the network to lure back some former employees, or *boomerangs*. "Last year, 20 percent of our experienced hires were boomerangs," said Karen Palvisak, a national leader of alumni relations for Deloitte.

Boomerangs cost less to train than new hires and they tend to hit the ground running. As the labour market tightens, alumni become an increasingly attractive source of talent given the following information. According to Accenture 54 percent of companies that have laid off employees are having a hard time finding the skilled workers for new positions and the U.S. department of Labor states that 38 percent of companies are looking to rehire laid-off employees.[21]

Marketing Networks

Business-oriented networks help executives find employees, and they're increasingly useful in other areas, such as sales and marketing. When Campbell Soup Co. asked independent location booker Marilyn Jenett to select a castle in Europe for a promotion, she put a note on Ryze.com, offering a finder's fee to anyone who could suggest the right place.

Jenett got seven responses, including one pointing her to Eastnor Castle. She was so pleased with the location that she booked it again for another event. Jenett said Ryze also helped her develop another small business, a personal mentoring program called Feel Free to Prosper.

Social networks also help forge community with, and among, would-be customers. A group of Mini Cooper owners joined MINI USA for its two-week cross-country car rally. Participants took part in company-sponsored events, such as the official wrap party overlooking the Hudson River and the Manhattan skyline in New Jersey.

But they also planned their own side events along the way with the help of the community forums on the MINI Owner's Lounge site, sponsored by MINI USA. Every month, about 1,500 to 2,000 new owners become active in the community. "Our very best salespeople are Mini owners, and they like to talk about their cars," said Martha Crowley, director of consulting for Beam Interactive, which provides various Internet marketing services for MINI USA.[22]

VIRTUAL WORLDS

Virtuality is the theme of Web 2.0. Two primary types of itmust be considered when looking at the 21st-century world: virtual workforces and virtual worlds (see Figure 7.5).

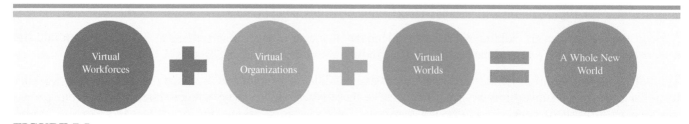

FIGURE 7.5
It's a Whole New World

Virtual Workforce

"Sunday morning and Tuesday afternoon are becoming completely the same," said KLM CIO BoetKreiken. At the same time, employees throughout organizations are becoming much more comfortable with a range of technologies.

In years past, employees might have had only a PC at home. Today they may juggle a network linking several computers, printers, and backup devices including a personal cloud connected to a high-speed Internet connection—in addition to an HD-PVR, several gaming consoles, high-definition TVs, and all manner of other Web-based services such as YouTube and Facebook. The benefits for businesses include lower costs and greater productivity, but figuring out how to communicate with off-site employees is crucial.

Traffic surrounding Microsoft headquarters in Redmond, Washington, has become so congested that State Governor Chris Gregoire nearly missed a 9 a.m. speech at the company's main campus. Roads leading to the software maker were simply not designed to handle the 35,000 commuters who report for work there each day. The gridlock that greeted Gregoire was just the latest reminder that Microsoft needs to tackle its commuter crisis—and quickly.

Microsoft has embarked on a program aimed at getting more employees to work from home and other off-site locales, joining the growing ranks of companies to catch the virtual-workplace wave. According to the telework Research Network, more than 30 million American employees telecommuted at least one day a week, and this number is expected to increase by 63 percent in the next five years.[23]

Letting employees work from outside the office keeps cars off the road, and in addition the practice can foster employee retention, boost worker productivity, and slash real estate costs. At IBM, in 2012 about 24 percent of the company's 430,000 employees used the mobile employees program or work at home program. This resulted in 220 million litres of fuel savings and 45,000 tonnes of CO_2 emissions in the United States alone. VIPdesk, an employer of at-home customer service reps, hangs onto 85 percent of its employees each year, as against the 10 to 20 percent rate for traditional call centres, according to consulting firm IDC. And virtual workers are about 16 percent more productive than office workers, according to Grantham's research.

For all the benefits of freeing workers from the office, drawbacks abound. First, not everyone wants to leave. Some fear they will step off the corporate ladder, while others need a busy environment to stay productive. Some managers are reluctant to scatter direct reports because keeping tabs on a virtual workforce can be harder than managing those close at hand. Some virtual workers can feel lonely, isolated, or deprived of vital training and mentoring. And communication breakdowns can impede innovation, trust, job satisfaction, and performance.

Obstacles like these have prompted IBM and other companies to seek a host of creative solutions to the problems that virtual work presents. Some turn to a combination of mobile devices, email, instant messaging, and collaboration software to help colleagues stay in touch.

Tools for the Virtual Workforce   Mobility and wireless capabilities are the tools of the virtual workforce and include:

- *Mobile commerce (m-commerce)*, the ability to purchase goods and services through a wireless Internet-enabled device.

- *Telematics*, the blending of computers and wireless telecommunications technologies with the goal of efficiently conveying information over vast networks to improve business operations. The most notable example of telematics may be the Internet itself, since it depends on a number of computer networks connected globally through telecommunication devices.

- *Electronic tagging*, a technique for identifying and tracking assets and individuals via technologies such as radio frequency identification (RFID) and smart cards.

Other companies, including Microsoft, WebEx, and Cisco, also specialize in online conferencing and collaboration software that makes it easier for people in different locations to work together and conduct meetings.

For the virtual worker, a laptop, tablet, or smartphone and high-speed Internet access are required. But some companies go the extra mile to outfit virtual employees. IBM provides a universal messaging service that lets executives give a single phone number to clients and colleagues. The service then forwards calls to wherever that executive might be—at home, on a cell phone, or in a so-called e-mobility centre, one of the temporary offices set up by IBM in locations around the world. Patrick Boyle, director of health care and life sciences sales at IBM, spends about half his time travelling, working from taxis, airport lounges, planes, and coffee shops. He is also a frequent user of e-mobility centres and considers headsets an essential tool of the trade.

Virtual Worlds

Virtual worlds are not as sprawling as they were a few years ago. Atits peak of user shipin 2006 to 2008, Second Life attracted a lot of attention from both the media and business; companies such as Wired, Adidas, Dell, and Lego all had digitized islands and buildings in Second Life's virtual world. Today, when you look at Second Life there are spots where you can hold virtual meetings, events, or training sessions. There are also places like the Reality Check Café where one can check out how much physical activity it takes to offset the calories from menu items or visit Stanford's virtual library.

In the first quarter of 2014, Second Life's user base is down to about 1 million visits a month. But it remains one of the most popular virtual worlds, and it is interesting to look back to see how companies used their space in Second Life's virtual world to compete in the global economy:[24]

- *Warner Bros. Records.* Warner Bros. promoted singer Regina Spektor's fourth album, *Begin to Hope*, by building a chic Manhattan loft within Second Life. As Spektor's music played, the loft's lighting and decor changed to roughly illustrate the song lyrics—a new marketing experience that was part video game, part music video.[25]

- *Adidas.* Adidas worked on selling virtual gym shoes in Second Life. The company test-marketed styles before rolling them out in the real world, tracking which colour combinations or designs prove popular among Second Lifers.[26]

- *Toyota.* Toyota's marketing plan for its hip, boxy Scion includes an art gallery in Los Angeles (Scion Space) and sponsored screenings of indie films (the Scion Independent Film Series). The pop-culture-aware car maker is also a presence in Second Life, where it offered a virtual version of the Scion xB.[27]

- *Educational institutions.* Educational institutions such as York University in Toronto, Loyalist College in Belleville, Ontario, and Harvard Law School in Cambridge, Massachusetts, had a presence in the virtual world. York University built a virtual campus in which students couldattend virtual lectures. York professor Ali Asgary created York's site and used it to help teach his course in emergency management. He simulated real-time disasters, like propane explosions or swine-flu epidemics, in Second Life and had his students role-play and problem-solve. The time required to simulate a real-time disaster in Second Life is a fraction what it would take to organize similar simulations in the real world. Instructors at Loyalist College train border agents using a virtual border crossing in Second Life. Harvard Law School held mock trials in a virtual courtroom in Second Life.[28]

OPENING CASE QUESTIONS

Shell Canada Fuels Productivity with ERP

1. How can large organizations like Shell use innovation to fuel productivity?

2. What advantages are there for Shell to recycle its IT equipment? How might recycling IT equipment potentially be threatening to Shell?

3. How could Shell use social networking to boost productivity and increase profits?

4. How might Shell use virtual worlds such as Second Life to make the company more successful? Give specific examples.

7.2 ENTERPRISE RESOURCE PLANNING

LO2 | INTRODUCTION

Enterprise resource planning (ERP) integrates all departments and functions throughout an organization into a single information system (or integrated set of systems) so that employees can make decisions by viewing enterprise-wide data on all business operations. Figure 7.6 highlights a few reasons ERP solutions have proven to be such a powerful force.

ERP is a logical solution to the mess of incompatible applications that had sprung up in most businesses.

ERP addresses the need for global information sharing and reporting.

ERP is used to avoid the pain and expense of fixing legacy systems.

FIGURE 7.6

Reasons ERP Systems Are Powerful Organizational Tools

ERP as a business concept resounds as a powerful internal data management nirvana. Everyone involved in sourcing, producing, and delivering the company's product works with the same data, which eliminates redundancies, reduces wasted time, and removes inconsistencies in the data.

Legacy Systems and ERP

Before we discuss ERP in detail, it is good to understand what ERP systems are replacing—legacy systems. What is a legacy system? An Internet search would retrieve a number of different definitions.

A common definition of a *legacy system* is: older computer technology that remains in use even though there are newer systems available. Legacy systems can be any older technologies that together create an information system. These technologies often remain in place because they still accomplish the job they were designed to do, because they respond adequately to user requests, or because the expense of replacing them is high.

The challenges with legacy systems when a company is moving to an ERP system are twofold. The first is that the important data needing to be converted to the new system is often not compatible as it currently exists. The second is that this data is usually stored in *functional systems*—information systems that serve single business units, such as accounting.[29] This means that the data is not integrated; each business unit has its own set of data, and replication needs to be sorted out. Within the functional systems the same data is also often stored in different formats which compounds this second challenge.

ENTERPRISE RESOURCE PLANNING

Today's business leaders need significant amounts of data to be readily accessible with real-time views into their businesses so that decisions can be made when they need to be, without the added time of tracking data and generating reports.

Many organizations fail to maintain consistency across business operations. If a single department, such as sales, decides to implement a new system without considering the other departments, inconsistencies can occur throughout the company. Not all systems are built to talk to each other and share data, and if sales suddenly implements a new system that marketing and accounting cannot use or is inconsistent in the way it handles data, the company's operations become "siloed." Figure 7.7 displays sample data from a sales database, and Figure 7.8 displays samples from an accounting database. Notice the differences in data formats, numbers, and identifiers. Correlating this data would be difficult, and the inconsistencies would cause numerous reporting errors from an enterprise-wide perspective.

Los Angeles is a city of 3.8 million people, with 30,000 city employees, and a budget of $7 billion. Yet before its ERP implementation each department conducted its own purchasing. That meant that 2,000 people in 600 city buildings and 60 warehouses were ordering material. Some 120,000 purchase orders (POs) and 50,000 cheques per year went to more than 7,000 vendors. Inefficiency was rampant.

"There was a lack of financial responsibility in the old system, and people could run up unauthorized expenditures," said Bob Jensen, the city's ERP project manager. Each department maintained its own inventories on different systems. Expense item mismatches piled up. One department purchased one way, others another. Mainframe-based systems were isolated. The city chose an ERP system as part of a $22 million project to integrate purchasing and financial reporting across the entire city. The project resulted in reducing the cheque processing staff by half, processing POs faster than ever, reducing the number of workers in warehousing by 40 positions, decreasing inventories from $50 million to $15 million, and providing a single point of contact for each vendor. In addition, $5 million a year has been saved in contract consolidation.

Figure 7.9 shows how an ERP system takes data from across the enterprise, consolidates and correlates it, and generates enterprise-wide organizational reports. Original ERP implementations promised to capture all data into one true "enterprise" system, with the ability to touch all the business processes within the organization. Unfortunately, ERP solutions have fallen short of these promises, and typical implementations have penetrated only 15 to 20 percent of the organization. The issue ERP intends to solve is that data within a majority of organizations currently reside in silos that are maintained by a select few, without the ability to be shared across the organization, causing inconsistency across business operations.

	A	B	C	D	E	F	G
1	Order Date	Product Name	Quantity	Unit Price	Unit Cost	Customer ID	Sales Rep ID
2	Monday, January 04, 2010	Mozzarella cheese	41.5	$ 24.15	$ 15.35	AC45	EX-107
3	Monday, January 04, 2010	Romaine lettuce	90.65	$ 15.06	$ 14.04	AC45	EX-109
4	Tuesday, January 05, 2010	Red onions	27.15	$ 12.08	$ 10.32	AC67	EX-104
5	Wednesday, January 06, 2010	Romaine lettuce	67.25	$ 15.16	$ 10.54	AC96	EX-109
6	Thursday, January 07, 2010	Black olives	79.26	$ 12.18	$ 9.56	AC44	EX-104
7	Thursday, January 07, 2010	Romaine lettuce	46.52	$ 15.24	$ 11.54	AC32	EX-104
8	Thursday, January 07, 2010	Romaine lettuce	52.5	$ 15.26	$ 11.12	AC84	EX-109
9	Friday, January 08, 2010	Red onions	39.5	$ 12.55	$ 9.54	AC103	EX-104
10	Saturday, January 09, 2010	Romaine lettuce	66.5	$ 15.98	$ 9.56	AC4	EX-104
11	Sunday, January 10, 2010	Romaine lettuce	58.26	$ 15.87	$ 9.50	AC174	EX-104
12	Sunday, January 10, 2010	Pineapple	40.15	$ 33.54	$ 22.12	AC45	EX-104
13	Monday, January 11, 2010	Pineapple	71.56	$ 33.56	$ 22.05	AC4	EX-104
14	Thursday, January 14, 2010	Romaine lettuce	18.25	$ 15.00	$ 10.25	AC174	EX-104
15	Thursday, January 14, 2010	Romaine lettuce	28.15	$ 15.26	$ 10.54	AC44	EX-107
16	Friday, January 15, 2010	Pepperoni	33.5	$ 15.24	$ 10.25	AC96	EX-109
17	Friday, January 15, 2010	Parmesan cheese	14.26	$ 8.05	$ 4.00	AC96	EX-104
18	Saturday, January 16, 2010	Parmesan cheese	72.15	$ 8.50	$ 4.00	AC103	EX-109
19	Monday, January 18, 2010	Parmesan cheese	41.5	$ 24.15	$ 15.35	AC45	EX-107
20	Monday, January 18, 2010	Romaine lettuce	90.65	$ 15.06	$ 14.04	AC45	EX-109
21	Wednesday, January 20, 2010	Tomatoes	27.15	$ 12.08	$ 10.32	AC67	EX-104
22	Thursday, January 21, 2010	Peppers	67.25	$ 15.16	$ 10.54	AC96	EX-109
23	Thursday, January 21, 2010	Mozzarella cheese	79.26	$ 12.18	$ 9.56	AC44	EX-104
24	Saturday, January 23, 2010	Black olives	46.52	$ 15.24	$ 11.54	AC32	EX-104
25	Sunday, January 24, 2010	Mozzarella cheese	52.5	$ 15.26	$ 11.12	AC84	EX-109
26	Tuesday, January 26, 2010	Romaine lettuce	39.5	$ 12.55	$ 9.54	AC103	EX-104
27	Wednesday, January 27, 2010	Parmesan cheese	66.5	$ 15.98	$ 9.56	AC4	EX-104
28	Thursday, January 28, 2010	Peppers	58.26	$ 15.87	$ 9.50	AC174	EX-104
29	Thursday, January 28, 2010	Mozzarella cheese	40.15	$ 33.54	$ 22.12	AC45	EX-104
30	Friday, January 29, 2010	Tomatoes	71.56	$ 33.56	$ 22.05	AC4	EX-104
31	Friday, January 29, 2010	Peppers	18.25	$ 15.00	$ 10.25	AC174	EX-104

FIGURE 7.7

Sales Data Sample

	A	B	C	D	E	F	G	H	I	J
1	Order Date	Product Name	Quantity	Unit Price	Total Sales	Unit Cost	Total Cost	Profit	Customer	Sales Rep
2	04-Jan-10	Mozzarella cheese	41	24	984	18	738	246	The Station	Debbie Fernandez
3	04-Jan-10	Romaine lettuce	90	15	1,350	14	1,260	90	The Station	Roberta Cross
4	05-Jan-10	Red onions	27	12	324	8	216	108	Bert's Bistro	Loraine Schultz
5	06-Jan-10	Romaine lettuce	67	15	1,005	14	938	67	Smoke House	Roberta Cross
6	07-Jan-10	Black olives	79	12	948	6	474	474	Flagstaff House	Loraine Schultz
7	07-Jan-10	Romaine lettuce	46	15	690	14	644	46	Two Bitts	Loraine Schultz
8	07-Jan-10	Romaine lettuce	52	15	780	14	728	52	Pierce Arrow	Roberta Cross
9	08-Jan-10	Red onions	39	12	468	8	312	156	Mamm'a Pasta Palace	Loraine Schultz
10	09-Jan-10	Romaine lettuce	66	15	990	14	924	66	The Dandelion	Loraine Schultz
11	10-Jan-10	Romaine lettuce	58	15	870	14	812	58	Carmens	Loraine Schultz
12	10-Jan-10	Pineapple	40	33	1,320	28	1,120	200	The Station	Loraine Schultz
13	11-Jan-10	Pineapple	71	33	2,343	28	1,988	355	The Dandelion	Loraine Schultz
14	14-Jan-10	Romaine lettuce	18	15	270	14	252	18	Carmens	Loraine Schultz
15	14-Jan-10	Romaine lettuce	28	15	420	14	392	28	Flagstaff House	Debbie Fernandez
16	15-Jan-10	Pepperoni	33	53	1,749	35	1,155	594	Smoke House	Roberta Cross
17	15-Jan-10	Parmesan cheese	14	8	112	4	56	56	Smoke House	Loraine Schultz
18	16-Jan-10	Parmesan cheese	72	8	576	4	288	288	Mamm'a Pasta Palace	Roberta Cross
19	18-Jan-10	Parmesan cheese	10	8	80	4	40	40	Mamm'a Pasta Palace	Loraine Schultz
20	18-Jan-10	Romaine lettuce	42	15	630	14	588	42	Smoke House	Roberta Cross
21	20-Jan-10	Tomatoes	48	9	432	7	336	96	Two Bitts	Loraine Schultz
22	21-Jan-10	Peppers	29	21	609	12	348	261	The Dandelion	Roberta Cross
23	21-Jan-10	Mozzarella cheese	10	24	240	18	180	60	Mamm'a Pasta Palace	Debbie Fernandez
24	23-Jan-10	Black olives	98	12	1,176	6	588	588	Two Bitts	Roberta Cross
25	24-Jan-10	Mozzarella cheese	45	24	1,080	18	810	270	Carmens	Loraine Schultz
26	26-Jan-10	Romaine lettuce	58	15	870	14	812	58	Two Bitts	Loraine Schultz
27	27-Jan-10	Parmesan cheese	66	8	528	4	264	264	Flagstaff House	Loraine Schultz
28	28-Jan-10	Peppers	85	21	1,785	12	1,020	765	Pierce Arrow	Loraine Schultz
29	28-Jan-10	Mozzarella cheese	12	24	288	18	216	72	The Dandelion	Debbie Fernandez
30	29-Jan-10	Tomatoes	40	9	360	7	280	80	Pierce Arrow	Roberta Cross

FIGURE 7.8

Accounting Data Sample

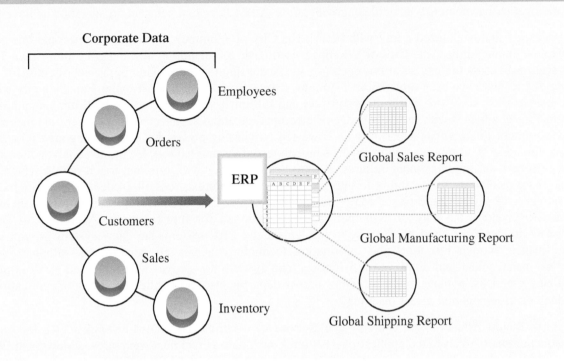

FIGURE 7.9

Enterprise Resource Planning System

Fairmont Hotels and Resorts is a world-leading company operating more than 100 hotels around the globe. Headquartered in Toronto, it boasts some of the world's great hotels, such as the Fairmont Banff Springs in Banff National Park, the Fairmont Chateau Laurier in Ottawa, and the Savoy in London. With plans to open 50 new hotels over the next five years, the Fairmont chain needed a way to help individual property owners stay on top of their businesses while still supplying the necessary data to corporate headquarters in Toronto. The solution also needed to serve as the financial data backbone to the company as a whole. The ERP solution Fairmont implemented serves its needs by allowing each of its property owners to run their hotel as a small- or medium-sized business without the need to get information from corporate headquarters, while still allowing Fairmont to operate as larger global hotel chain. The ERP system has also set up Fairmont with a good flow of data and information to obtain the business intelligence they need to make informed decisions as they expand their operations over the coming years.[30]

ERP systems provide organizations with consistency. An ERP system provides a method for the effective planning and controlling of all the resources required to take, make, ship, and account for customer orders in a manufacturing, distribution, or service organization. The key word in enterprise resource planning is *enterprise* and there are two key components to ERP:

- The heart of ERP
- The evolution of ERP

The Heart of ERP

ERP systems serve as the organization's backbone in providing fundamental decision-making support. In the past, departments made decisions independent of each other. ERP systems provide a foundation for collaboration between departments, enabling people in different business areas to communicate. ERP systems have been widely adopted in large organizations to store critical data used to make the decisions that drive performance.

To be competitive, organizations must always strive for excellence in every enterprise-wide business process, a daunting challenge if the organization has multi-site operations worldwide. To obtain operational efficiencies, lower costs, improve supplier and customer relations, and increase revenues and market share, all units of the organization must work together harmoniously toward congruent goals. An ERP system helps an organization achieve this.

One organization that has blazed a trail with ERP is the City of Winnipeg. In its quest to become one of Canada's most efficient municipalities, the City of Winnipeg used ERP to streamline and integrate more than 100 diverse systems scattered across the city's various departments. According to Rodger Guinn, project director for the City of Winnipeg, the results have been remarkable: "Winnipeg went from being the last major Canadian city without ERP to being seen as the leader with world-class software and full integration." Before the ERP implementation, the city faced numerous challenges with its hodgepodge of incompatible and disconnected applications: (1) inconsistent data and poor communication across departments; (2) wasted purchasing power due to non-integrated procurement; (3) lack of coordination of common activities such as human resources and payroll; (4) limited analytical capability; and (5) silos of functional organizational cultures and business practices with minimal touch points. The ERP system overcame these challenges by its ability to integrate the city's systems across all 14 departments, including police, transit, public works, water, and waste. Major components of the ERP system were human resources and finance. With the ERP system, the City of Winnipeg is well positioned for future growth. According to Deloitte, the professional services firm hired by the city to implement the ERP system, the "new system provides alignment between finance, human resources and information technology across all departments—along with real-time information management and employee self-service. The system also provides a stable and flexible platform for standardizing practices, policies, and procedures across departments, and for developing new applications such as competency management and career planning."[31]

In the United States, Atlanta-based United Parcel Service of America (UPS) also leveraged ERP for success. UPS developed a number of Web-based applications that track such data as recipient signatures, addresses, time in transit, and other shipping facts. These services run on an ERP foundation that UPS customers can connect to using real-time ERP data obtained from the UPS website. On a regular day, 22.4 million tracking requests pass through the company's site. This increases to 40 million during the holidays. By automating the data delivery process, UPS dramatically reduced the demand on its customer service representatives. Just as importantly, UPS improved relationships with its business partners—in effect, integrating its business with theirs—by making it easier for consumers to find delivery data without leaving the website of the merchant.

The heart of an ERP system is a central database that collects data from and feeds data into all of the ERP system's individual application components (called *modules*), supporting such diverse business functions as accounting, manufacturing, marketing, and human resources. When a user enters or updates data in one module, the data are immediately and automatically updated throughout the entire system, as illustrated in Figure 7.10.

ERP automates business processes such as order fulfillment—taking an order from a customer, shipping the purchase, and then billing for it. With an ERP system, when a customer service representative takes an order from a customer, he or she has all the data necessary to complete the order (the customer's credit rating and order history, the company's inventory levels, and the delivery schedule). Everyone else in the company sees the same data and has access to the database that holds the customer's new order. When one department finishes with the order, it is automatically routed via the ERP system to the next department. To find out where the order is at any point, a user only needs to log in to the ERP system and track down the order, as illustrated in Figure 7.11. The order process moves like a bolt of lightning through the organization, and customers get their orders faster and with fewer errors than ever before. ERP can apply that same magic to the other major business processes, such as employee benefits or financial reporting.

ERP enables employees across the organization to share data across a single, centralized database. With extended portal capabilities, an organization can also involve its suppliers and customers in the workflow process, allowing ERP to penetrate the entire value chain, and help the organization achieve greater operational efficiency (see Figures 7.12 and 7.13).

The Evolution of ERP

ERP   Originally, ERP solutions were developed to deliver automation across multiple units of an organization, to help facilitate the manufacturing process and address issues such as raw materials, inventory, order entry, and distribution. However, ERP was unable to extend to other functional areas of the company, such as sales, marketing, and shipping. It could not tie in any customer relationship management capabilities that would allow organizations to capture customer-specific data, nor did it work with websites or portals used for customer service. Call centre or quality assurance staff could not tap into the ERP solution, nor could ERP handle document management, such as cataloguing contracts and purchase orders.

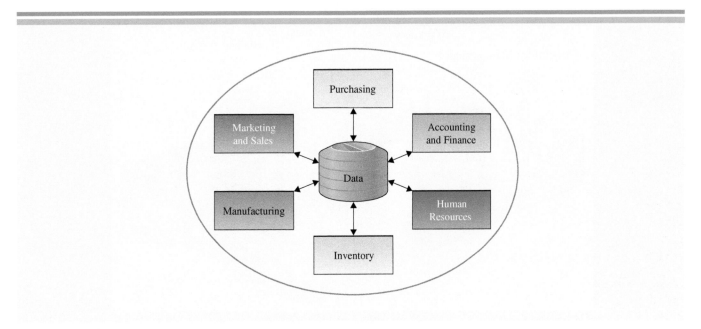

FIGURE 7.10

ERP Integrated Data Flows

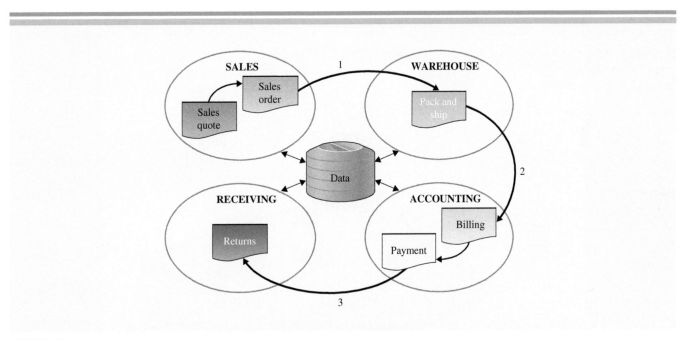

FIGURE 7.11

ERP Process Flow

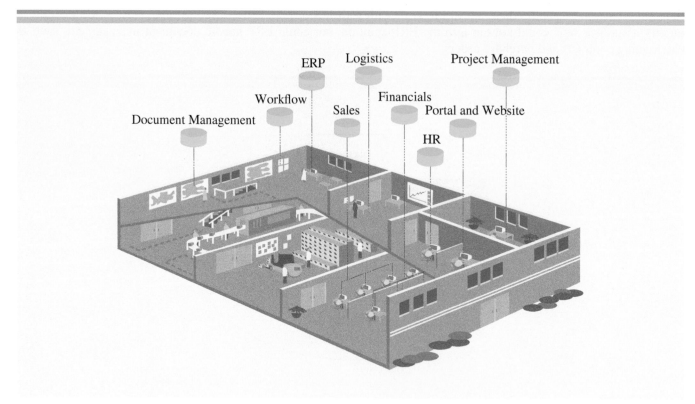

FIGURE 7.12

The Organization Before ERP with Functional "Silos"

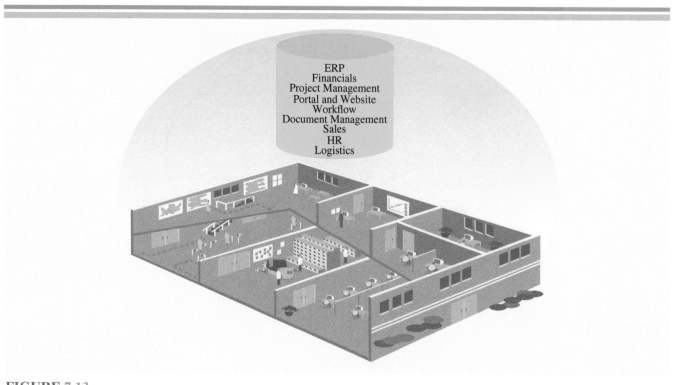

FIGURE 7.13

The Integrated Organization After ERP

Extended ERP   ERP has grown over the years to become part of the extended enterprise. From its beginning as a tool for materials planning, it has extended to warehousing, distribution, and order entry. With its next evolution, ERP expands to the front office, including customer relationship management. Now administrative, sales, marketing, and human resources staff can share a tool that is truly enterprise-wide. To compete on a functional level today, companies must adopt an enterprise-wide approach to ERP that uses the Internet and connects to every facet of the value chain. Figure 7.14 shows how ERP has grown since the 1990s to accommodate the needs of the entire organization.

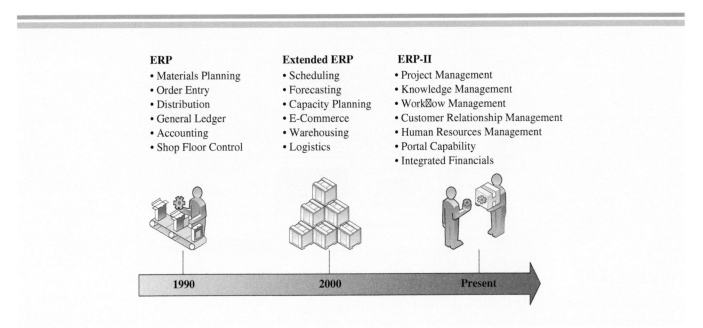

FIGURE 7.14

The Evolution of ERP

ERP II: Core and Extended   Figure 7.15 provides an example of an ERP system with its core and extended components. *Core ERP components* are the traditional components included in most ERP systems and they primarily focus on internal operations. *Extended ERP components* are the extra components that meet the organizational needs not covered by the core components and primarily focus on external operations.

LO3 | CORE ERP COMPONENTS

The three most common core ERP components focusing on internal operations are:

1. Accounting and finance

2. Production and materials management

3. Human resources

Accounting and Finance ERP Components

Headquartered in New York City, Excelsior Radio Networks is a company that syndicates music programming and morning prep services for more than 2,000 radio stations across the United States. It also provides advertising sales representation to over 40 independent radio producers. When it acquired Winstar Communications, it found it required a new ERP solution that provided robust financial reporting and accounting capabilities. It also had to combine the processes of two different organizations quickly. Furthermore, the ERP solution had to deal with a unique situation, as Winstar had declared bankruptcy just prior to the takeover. The solution is helping Excelsior make day-to-day decisions but also helping it manage its accounts.[32]

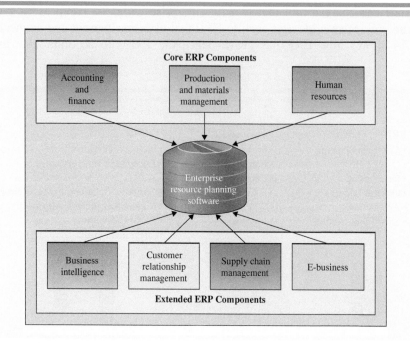

FIGURE 7.15

Core ERP Components and Extended ERP Components

Accounting and finance ERP components manage accounting data and financial processes within the enterprise with functions such as general ledger, accounts payable, accounts receivable, budgeting, and asset management. One of the most useful features included in an ERP accounting/finance component is its credit-management feature. Most organizations manage their relationships with customers by setting credit limits, or a limit on how much a customer can owe at any one time. The company then monitors the credit limit whenever the customer places a new order or sends in a payment. ERP financial systems help to correlate customer orders with customer account balances determining credit availability. Another great feature is the ability to perform product profitability analysis. ERP financial components are the backbone behind product profitability analysis and allow companies to perform all types of advanced profitability modelling techniques.

Production and Materials Management ERP Components

One of the main functions of an ERP system is streamlining the production planning process. *Production and materials management ERP components* handle the various aspects of production planning and execution such as demand forecasting, production scheduling, job cost accounting, and quality control. Companies typically produce multiple products, each of which has many different parts. Production lines, consisting of machines and employees, build the different types of products. The company must then define sales forecasting for each product to determine production schedules and materials purchasing. Figure 7.16 displays the typical ERP production planning process. The process begins with forecasting sales in order to plan operations. A detailed production schedule is developed if the product is produced, and a materials requirement plan is completed if the product is purchased.

Ponzi's Vineyards, located in Oregon, is a second-generation, family-owned vineyard that produces 15,000 cases of wine a year. Not only does Ponzi operate the vineyard but it also operates a wine bar and restaurant and a Web store, and distributes its wines across the United States. For its ERP solution it requires not only a point-of-sale system that works in both the retail and the Web environment, but also as an inventory management system for the distribution side of their business. The system also needs to deliver the sales data back to the family so they can make strategic decisions with regard to production to manage both the barrels of wine in production and the vineyard itself.[33]

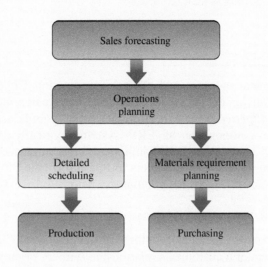

FIGURE 7.16

The Production Planning Process

Human Resources ERP Components

Human resources ERP components track employee data, including payroll, benefits, compensation, and performance assessment, and assure compliance with the legal requirements of multiple jurisdictions and tax authorities. Human resources components even offer features that allow an organization to perform detailed analyses on its employees to determine such things as identifying individuals likely to leave the company unless additional compensation or benefits are provided. These components can also identify which employees are using which resources, such as online training and long-distance telephone services, and help determine whether the most talented people are working for business units with the highest priority—or where they would have the greatest impact on profit.

YoCream International manufactures frozen yogurt mix and smoothie products for distribution across the United States. Originally a retail yogurt chain, it moved to manufacturing in 1987 and is returning to its roots. It has partnered with Dannon to sell soft-serve yogurt to food service distributors who sell to customers at convenience stores, restaurants, schools, and hospitals; Costco's food court is the most popular place for the product. With this change, YoCream needed an ERP system capable of helping its sales representatives communicate effectively with each other. Sales reps needed to track their contacts and keep their sales managers back in Portland, Oregon, informed of their activities so they could monitor overlaps and prevent the problem of multiple sales reps contacting the same customer. The ERP system helps the sales force be more productive.[34]

EXTENDED ERP COMPONENTS

Extended ERP components are the extra components that meet the organizational needs not covered by the core components and primarily focus on external operations. Many of the numerous extended ERP components are Internet-enabled and require interaction with customers, suppliers, and business partners outside the organization. The four most common extended ERP components are:

1. Business intelligence

2. Customer relationship management

3. Supply chain management

4. E-business

Business Intelligence Components

ERP systems offer powerful tools that measure and control organizational operations. Many organizations have found that these valuable tools can be enhanced to provide even greater value by adding powerful business intelligence systems. *Business intelligence* describes information that people use to support their decision-making efforts. The business intelligence components of ERP systems typically collect data used throughout the organization (including data used in many other ERP components), organize and summarize this data in a way that turns this data into information, and apply analytical tools to this information to assist managers and analysts with their decisions. Data warehouses are one of the most popular extensions to ERP systems.

Customer Relationship Management Components

ERP vendors have expanded to provide customer relationship management. *Customer relationship management (CRM)* involves managing all aspects of a customer's relationship with an organization to increase customer loyalty and retention, and profitability for the organization. CRM components provide an integrated view of customer data and interactions, allowing organizations to work more effectively with customers and be more responsive to their needs. CRM components typically include contact centres, sales force automation, and marketing functions. These improve the customer experience while identifying a company's most (and least) valuable customers to better allocate resources.

Supply Chain Management Components

ERP vendors also provide supply chain management. *Supply chain management (SCM)* involves managing data flows between and among stages in a supply chain to maximize total supply chain effectiveness and profitability. SCM components help an organization plan, schedule, control, and optimize the supply chain from its acquisition of raw materials to the receipt of finished goods by customers.

E-Business Components

The original focus of ERP systems was the internal organization. In other words, ERP systems are not fundamentally ready for the external world of e-business. The newest and most exciting extended ERP components are the e-business components.

Two of the primary features of e-business components are e-logistics and e-procurement. *E-logistics* manages the transportation and storage of goods. *E-procurement* is the business-to-business (B2B) purchase and sale of supplies and services over the Internet.

E-business and ERP complement each other by allowing companies to establish a Web presence and fulfill orders expeditiously. A common mistake made by many businesses is deploying a Web presence before the integration of back-office systems or an ERP system. For example, one large toy manufacturer announced less than a week before Christmas that it would be unable to fulfill any of its Web orders. The company had all the toys in the warehouse, but it could not organize the basic order processing function to get the toys delivered to the consumers on time.

Customers and suppliers are now demanding access to ERP data, including order status, inventory levels, and invoice reconciliation. Plus, the customers and partners want all this data in a simplified format available through a website. This is a difficult task to accomplish because most ERP systems are full of technical jargon, which is why employee training is one of the hidden costs associated with ERP implementations. Removing the jargon to accommodate untrained customers and partners is one of the more difficult tasks when Web-enabling an ERP system. To accommodate the growing needs of the e-business world, ERP vendors need to build two new channels of access into the ERP information system—one channel for customers (B2C) and one channel for businesses, suppliers, and partners (B2B).[35]

LO4 ⌉ INTEGRATING SCM, CRM, AND ERP

Applications such as SCM, CRM, and ERP are the backbone of e-business. Integrating these applications is the key to success for many companies. Integration allows the unlocking of data to make it available to any user, anywhere, anytime. There are more than 150 ERP vendors in the marketplace but the top three vendors are Oracle, SAP, and Microsoft Dynamics.

Most organizations today have no choice but to piece their applications together since no one vendor can respond to every organizational need; therefore, customers purchase applications from multiple vendors. As a result, organizations face the challenge of integrating their systems. For example, a single organization might choose its CRM components from SAP, SCM components from JDA Software, and financial and HR management components from Oracle. Figure 7.17 displays the general audience and purpose for each of these applications that have to be integrated.

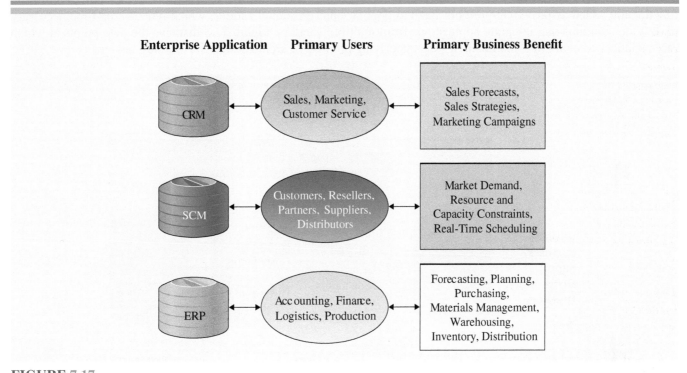

FIGURE 7.17

Primary Users and Business Benefits of Enterprise Applications

From its roots in the California gold rush era, San Francisco–based Del Monte Foods has grown to become the U.S.'s largest producer and distributor of premium quality processed fruits, vegetables, and tomato products. With annual sales of over US$3.82 billion, Del Monte is also one of that country's largest producers, distributors, and marketers of private-label food and pet products, with a powerful portfolio of brands including Del Monte, Nature's Goodness, 9Lives, and Kibbles 'n Bits.

Del Monte's acquisition of StarKist (since divested), 9Lives, and Kibbles 'n Bits from the H. J. Heinz Company required an integration between Del Monte's and Heinz's business processes. Del Monte needed to overhaul its IT infrastructure, migrating from multiple platforms, including UNIX and mainframe systems, and consolidating applications on a single system. The work required integrating business processes across manufacturing, financial, supply chain, decision support, and transactional reporting areas.

Revamping Del Monte's architecture stemmed from a strategic decision. Del Monte decided to implement an ERP system to support its entire U.S. operations, with headquarters in San Francisco, operations in Pittsburgh, and distribution centres and manufacturing facilities across the United States. The company concluded that the only way it could unite its operations and open its system to its customers, which are mainly large retailers, was by using an ERP system. Among other key factors was the need to embrace an e-business strategy. The challenge facing Del Monte was to select an ERP system to merge multiple systems quickly and cost-effectively. To achieve financial and customer service, Del Monte needed to integrate new businesses that more than doubled the size of the company. Since implementing the ERP system, customers and trading partners are now provided with a single, consistent, and integrated view of the company.[36]

Integration Tools

Effectively managing the transformation to an integrated enterprise is critical to the success of the 21st century organization. The key is the integration of the disparate IT applications. An integrated enterprise infuses support areas, such as finance and human resources, with a strong customer orientation. Integrations are achieved using *middleware*—several different types of software that sit in the middle of and provide connectivity between two or more software applications. Middleware translates data between disparate systems. *Enterprise application integration (EAI) middleware* represents a new approach to middleware by packaging together commonly used functionality, such as providing pre-built links to popular enterprise applications, which reduces the time necessary to develop solutions that integrate applications from multiple vendors. Figure 7.18 displays the data points at which these applications integrate and illustrates the underlying premise of architecture infrastructure design.

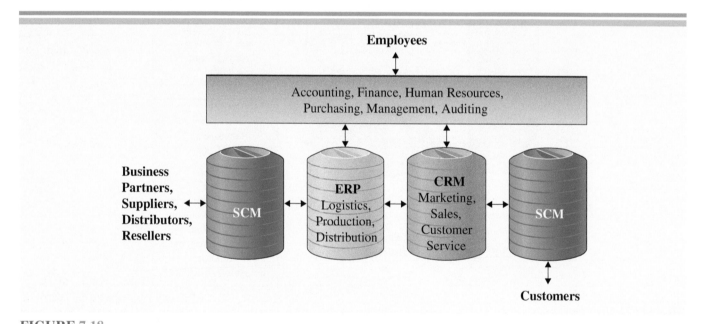

FIGURE 7.18

Integrations Between SCM, CRM, and ERP Applications

Companies run on interdependent applications, such as SCM, CRM, and ERP. If one application performs poorly, the entire customer value delivery system is affected. For example, no matter how great a company is at CRM, if its SCM system does not work and the customer never receives the finished product, the company will lose that customer. The world-class enterprises of tomorrow must be built on the foundation of world-class applications implemented today.

Coca-Cola's business model is a common one among well-known franchisers. The company gets the majority of its US$48.2 billion in annual revenue from franchise fees it earns from bottlers all over the world. Bottlers, along with the franchise, license Coca-Cola's secret recipe and many others, including recipes for Odwalla, Nestea, Minute Maid, and Sprite. Now Coca-Cola hopes that bottlers will also buy into adopting common business practices using a service-oriented architecture (SoA) ERP system.

The target platform chosen by Coca-Cola is mySAP ERP, by SAP. If it works, Coca-Cola and its bottlers stand to make and save a lot of money, and SAP will be able to position itself as one of the dominant players in SoA-enabled

ERP. Already, Coca-Cola and many of its bottlers use versions of SAP for finance, manufacturing, and a number of administrative functions, but Coca-Cola wants everyone to move to a "services" architecture environment.

Coca-Cola hopes that this standardization of its services will make its supply chain more efficient and reduce costs. In explaining why a services approach is so vitally important, Jean-Michel Ares, CIO of Coca-Cola, stated, "That will allow bottlers to converge one step at a time, one process area at a time, one module at a time, at a time that's right for the bottler. We can march across the bottling world incrementally."[37]

LO5 | MEASURING ERP SUCCESS

Measuring ERP success is extremely difficult. One of the best methods is the balanced scorecard. This approach to strategic management was developed in the early 1990s by Drs. Robert Kaplan of the Harvard Business School and David Norton of the Palladium Group. Addressing some of the weaknesses and vagueness of previous measurement techniques, the balanced scorecard approach provides a clear prescription as to what companies should measure to balance the financial perspective.[38]

The *balanced scorecard* is a management system, in addition to a measurement system, that enables organizations to clarify their vision and strategy and translate them into action. It provides feedback for both the internal business processes and external outcomes to continuously improve strategic performance and results. When fully deployed, the balanced scorecard transforms strategic planning from an academic exercise into the nerve centre of an enterprise. Kaplan and Norton describe the innovation of the balanced scorecard as follows: "The balanced scorecard retains traditional financial measures. But financial measures tell the story of past events, an adequate story for industrial age companies for which investments in long-term capabilities and customer relationships were not critical for success. These financial measures are inadequate, however, for guiding and evaluating the journey that information age companies must make to create future value through investment in customers, suppliers, employees, processes, technology, and innovation."[39]

The balanced scorecard views the organization from four perspectives, and users should develop metrics, collect data, and analyze their business relative to each of these perspectives:

- The learning and growth perspective
- The internal business process perspective
- The customer perspective
- The financial perspective (see Figure 7.19)[40]

Companies cannot manage what they cannot measure. Therefore, metrics must be developed based on the strategic plan priorities, which provides the key business drivers and criteria for metrics that managers most want to watch. Processes are then designed to collect data relevant to these metrics and reduce the data to numerical form for storage, display, and analysis. Decision makers examine the outcomes of various measured processes and strategies and track the results to guide the company and provide feedback. The value of metrics is in their ability to provide a factual basis for defining:

- Strategic feedback to show the present status of the organization from many perspectives for decision makers
- Diagnostic feedback into various processes to guide improvements on a continuous basis
- Trends in performance over time as the metrics are tracked
- Feedback around the measurement methods themselves and which metrics should be tracked
- Quantitative inputs to forecasting methods and models for decision support systems[41]

One warning about metrics—don't overdo it. The trick is to find a few important metrics that provide significant insight, and to tie them to other financial and business objectives in the firm. A good rule of thumb is to develop seven key metrics, plus or minus two.[42]

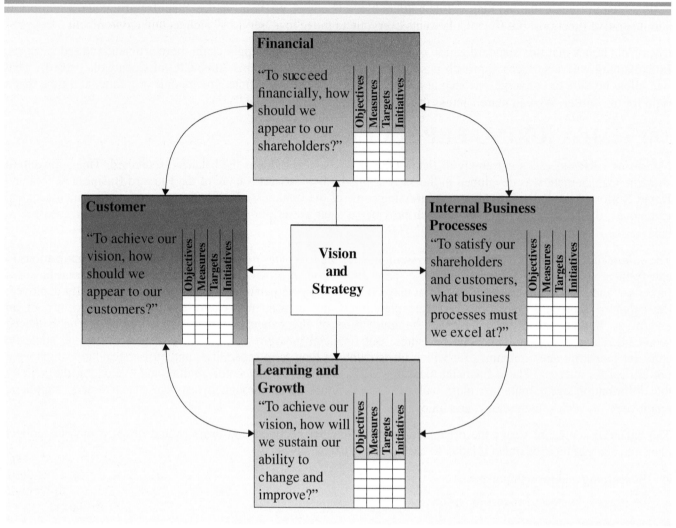

FIGURE 7.19

The Four Primary Perspectives of the Balanced Scorecard

CHOOSING ERP SOFTWARE

There are many different ERP vendors on the market today, such as SAP, Microsoft, and Oracle. Each provides different solutions but the core ERP functions for each are the same and focus on financial, accounting, sales, marketing, human resources, operations, and logistics. ERP vendors differentiate themselves by offering unique functionality such as CRM and SCM systems.

Some customers find that their chosen ERP solution does not meet their expectations. Despite many improvements in the software, the industry itself is well aware that failed ERP implementations are still far too common. According to Gartner Research, the average failure rate for an ERP project is 66 percent. No wonder some manufacturers view ERP as a necessary strategic evil. The key word here, though, is *necessary*.

ERP Failures

In the history of ERP there have always been high-profile failures, such as those at Hershey's Chocolate in 1999, Nike's in 2000, and HP in 2004, to name just a few. The U.S. Air Force, after spending US$1 billion on a seven-or eight-year project that started in 2004 and only reached about 25 percent of its original scope, wisely decided to shut down its ERP initiative. Almost every year we get articles in the press highlighting the top ERP failures of the past 12 months.

Looking back at the past few years, it is still clear that many software projects, like ERP projects, continue to fail to live up to their promises. With these failures companies lose money and productivity, and expend a lot of wasted effort. In consequence, lawsuits against software vendors and implementers are more common than ever.

Some of the high-profile ERP and software project failures in recent years include:

- The U.K. government scrapping the $18.7 billion nine-year project IT program that would enable the National Health Service to provide electronic health records.

- New York City's City Time payroll project, which saw cost overruns and a criminal kickback scheme. Costs originally pegged at $63 million have reportedly reached $760 million. Criminal proceedings have begun with some defendants making guilty pleas and paying back funds.

- Montclair State University suing Oracle over a project that was designed to replace the school's aging legacy systems. Oracle has since countersued, claiming the failure is the school's fault.

- ParknPool suing over an ERP project that turned into a "big mess." The company claims it has nothing to show for the work, which affected their business to the point where ParknPool could not even take orders.

- Marin County accusing SAP/Deloitte Consulting of bilking the county out of more than $20 million.

- Idaho State Auditors found problems with Medicad ERP software that could cost Idaho millions due to payment delays and faulty claims processing.

- Nova Scotia Victorian Order of nurses enduring at least six months of faulty paycheques with a faulty payroll system implementation.[43]

Finding the Right ERP Solution

A good ERP system is highly reflective of the business process in place at the company, and helps the company achieve industry best practices for processes. This means that the software must perform many different tasks and that makes it complex. Most companies do not carry a high degree of ERP software expertise on their staff and do not understand ERP to the degree they should. This makes it easy to choose the wrong package. The key to making an effective purchase is to have solid business processes. Successful ERP projects share three basic attributes:

1. Overall fit

2. Proper business analysis

3. Solid implementation plans[44]

Overall Fit   This refers to the measure of the gaps that exist between the system and the business process. A well-fitting ERP system has no major process gaps and very few minor ones. Think of a new ERP system as a suit. Typically, a customer buys a suit three ways:

1. Off the rack

2. Off the rack and tailored to fit

3. Custom-made

The way the solution fits the business process normally determines the client's satisfaction level. Buying ERP off the rack is equivalent to buying a canned software package. It fits some well, but some not at all. That is why a customer can tailor a suit so that it fits better. Modifications can be made to the software so that its processes line up better with the company processes. This is a good strategy, provided the chosen package supports this. The downside is that it can get very expensive. Finally, the custom system can provide a great fit, but the company must thoroughly understand what it is doing and be able to support the heavy financial burden associated with a custom build.

Proper Business Analysis   The best way to determine which fit strategy is right is to conduct a thorough business analysis. Successful companies normally spend up to 10 percent of the project budget on a business analysis. A proper analysis must result in a documented list of the business processes at work within the company. This provides a basic tool that measures vendor capability.

Solid Implementation Plans   Like the installation of any successful process or piece of machinery, a plan is needed to monitor the quality objectives and timelines. It also employs processes such as workflow analysis and job combination to harvest savings.

A thorough implementation transfers knowledge to the system users. When the project is complete the users of the new system must be able to use the tools it provides. The users must also know what to do in cases when the process fluctuates. The majority of failed systems are the result of poor-quality implementation. It is important to remember that ERP is simply a tool, and tools that people do not know how to use can be as useless as having no tools at all.

ERP AND SME MARKETS

ERP is no longer the purview of large organizations. Large-scale ERP vendors, such as SAP, Microsoft, and Oracle, are attempting to enter the small to medium enterprise (SME) market in the hopes of expanding their client base. However, despite some clever packaging and dumbing-down of the features offered, large-scale ERP vendors find it difficult to make significant headway with SMEs.

It's not that SMEs don't want ERP tools. On the contrary, ERP solutions enable SMEs to streamline operational processes and provide fully integrated financial and sales management capabilities. This is attractive to small and medium-sized business. Many SMEs still operate with manual processes where automation would be of clear benefit. However, what many ERP vendors are finding is that SMEs constitute a different marketplace than what these large-scale ERP vendors are traditionally accustomed to, for four primary reasons:

1. SMEs demand affordability and ease of use, more so than their large organizational cousins. Further, this must be achieved in an SME environment where software solutions abound, spending is frugal, IT departments are rare, and "out of the box" solutions are preferred.

2. Large-scale ERP vendors are relatively unknown to most SME organizations. These vendors must start at square one in making this market space aware of who they are and what their track records are in this domain.

3. In Canada, several large-scale ERP vendors have missed the mark when attempting to market their ERP solutions to SME companies. These vendors geared their products and prices toward an American mid-market firm rather than a Canadian mid-market one. In Canada, an SME organization compares in revenue and size with a small American company, while an American mid-sized company is comparable to some large Canadian organizations.

4. Most importantly, the SME market space demands using partners (resellers) to sell software solutions. This is new territory for large-scale ERP vendors, who have traditionally relied on using a direct sales force to market ERP solutions to companies. In this regard, large-scale ERP vendors have little, if any, experience working with channel partners.

Paul Edwards, director of Strategic Partnering and Alliances for IDC Canada, agrees. According to Edwards, "In order to get any kind of traction in the mid-market space, or gain market share, you need partners.... [The large ERP vendors are] going to have to start developing partnerships [and] SAP, as an example, doesn't have a real strong partner base."[45]

One company that seems to have made great headway in this regard is Sage Software, whose Sage ERP solution, has leveraged the success and infiltration of its accounting applications among small and medium-sized companies.[46]

Two examples of successful use of Sage ERP are Second Cup and Island Resort Group. Second Cup has grown from a kiosk in a shopping mall, selling only whole-bean coffee in 1975, to being Canada's largest franchiser of specialty coffee. With 350 cafés and 5,000 associates, Second Cup needed a powerful but easy-to-use solution to manage the business and its franchisees. Ninety-five percent of Second Cup's cafés are franchisee-owned, which means that there are still some corporate stores in its business operations, complicating its business processes even more. Its ERP system is required to manage not only royalties from franchisees but also advertising for franchisee locations, operating expenses and revenues at the corporate cafés, head-office activities, and the company's fixed assets. On top of this they are spread across Canada, so making the system Web-enabled and seamless are also key components of their successful system.[47]

Island Lake Resort operates a cat-skiing resort near Fernie, British Columbia, and a heli-skiing resort near Revelstoke, British Columbia, along with the accommodation and restaurant facilities needed to house and feed their guests. Prior to the 2010–11 winter season, it also operated a second cat-skiing operation near Fernie. As the adventure tour industry in the Canadian Rockies gets more competitive with more operators but no change in the number of skier days, Island Resort Group needed to become more efficient in its operations and improve its marketing to fill all available spaces. An important part of their ERP solution was the CRM system. With the new ERP solution, their systems now share data, so duplications have been eliminated, they can consolidate the data from all of their operations, and integrate information from their third-party point-of-sales and reservations systems into the reports they use to make better decisions. Why is the CRM system such an important business element for Island Lake Group? Well, it gives them a database of the limited pool of people interested in spending $600 to $2,000 a day to go cat skiing or heli-skiing, and therefore helps them keep their tours full. One empty seat on a helicopter is 25 percent of Island Lake Resort's revenues and all of its profits for that trip. ERP also allows them to recognize when there will be an empty seat and then they can focus their efforts on filling that seat with targeted marketing campaigns and track the results.[48]

OPENING CASE QUESTIONS

Shell Fuels Productivity with ERP

5. How did ERP help improve business operations at Shell?

6. How important was training in helping roll out the system to Shell personnel?

7. How could extended ERP components help improve business operations at Shell?

8. What advice would you give Shell if it decided to choose a different ERP software solution?

9. How can integrating SCM, CRM, and ERP help improve business operations at Shell?

SUMMARY OF KEY THEMES

The purpose of the chapter was to describe the new trends found in enterprise computing today and to explain the concept of enterprise resource planning and enterprise resource planning systems.

Enterprises need to stay abreast of new technological trends to compete successfully in today's ever-changing competitive marketplace. Companies must leverage the advantages that new technologies offer, because it is almost certain that an organization's competitors will. Enterprises must be constantly on guard for innovations in the marketplace and thinking about how these innovations can be used to improve current ways of doing things or to offer something entirely new. Recent IT trends that enterprises are paying attention to today include going green (i.e., becoming socially responsible) and leveraging social networks made affordable by recent Web 2.0 technologies. Note that new information technologies are not used simply because they are available but because they enable an organization to operate more efficiently and effectively than it otherwise could.

ERP systems help companies operate more efficiently and effectively by combining all of an organization's operational data into one central core information system. In the past, operational data were not easily shared between different departments or business units in the same organization. This resulted in silos of data across the enterprise, which often led to discrepancies and inconsistencies in the data between different departments or business units. ERP systems were the solution to this problem. ERP systems allow the integration of all a company's internal daily operational processes into a single information system or integrated set of information systems as a means of improving operational efficiencies and reducing costs. Tightly integrating operations across the enterprise through the implementation and use of ERP systems also allows for smoother work flow. An ERP system is often considered to be the core business system that drives a company's daily operations.

KEY TERMS

Accounting and finance ERP components

Balanced scorecard

Business intelligence

Core ERP components

Corporate policy

Corporate social responsibility

Customer relationship management (CRM)

E-logistics

E-procurement

E-waste

Electronic tagging

Enterprise application integration (EAI) middleware

Enterprise resource planning (ERP)

Extended ERP components

Functional systems

Human resources ERP components

Innovation

Legacy system

Middleware

Mobile commerce (m-commerce)

Production and materials management ERP components

Social responsibility

Supply chain management (SCM)

Sustainable (or "green") IT

Sustainable IT disposal

Telematics

Virtualization

CLOSING CASE ONE

ERP and Analytics Brings Germany World Cup Success

This case illustrates an innovative use of an ERP system and the big data it collects to manage the talent in an organization.

In the world of business companies often look for solutions that help them with human capital management (HCM) or talent management. Whatever you call it, there are systems that support businesses around the globe, capable of tracking and managing every aspect of a company's workforce like recruitment, training, maintaining employee data, managing payroll, employees' workflows, benefits administration, and keeping track of real-time performance. Most recently a powerful tool of HCM has appeared in the marketplace: talent/workforce analytics, which predicts how best to apply talent over time so that people's contributions to the company are maximized and the employees also get the best experience possible.

It's easy to understand the power of this kind of performance data in charting the course of employees to keep them as efficient as possible, but you might be surprised to learn how talent analytics are being used by coaches of the German Football Association (DFB).An example is given by TSG Hoffenheim, a football club in Germany's first division. The team is capturing and analyzing data in real time, including spatial analysis of player movements, to optimize training. Its players are equipped with sensors during training, and there is also a sensor in the ball. The data is then fed into SAP's HANA cloud platform for real-time analysis. The solution facilitates the analysis of training, preparation, and potentially game performance. Coaches, management, and scouts are enabled to process large amounts of data to find and assess key situations from every practice and pinpoint ways to improve player and team performance. SAP and the coaches of the German national football team have also been working together to further develop software that can enhance on-field football performance. The goal of the project between SAP and the coaches of the German national football team was to build an innovative solution that enhanced on-field performance leading up to the 2014 World Cup.

SAP Match Insights

SAP Match Insights features a simple user interface for both players and coaches that enable them to analyze individual player performance and overall game play to better shape training and improve strategic game play decisions. "Imagine this—in just 10 minutes, 10 players with three balls can produce over seven million data points. SAP HANA can process these in real time. With Match Insights, our team can analyze and act on this huge amount of data," says Oliver Bierhoff, manager of the German national team and a former player. Today each sports team is looking for innovative ways to gain a competitive edge over its rivals. "We are representing one of the most successful teams in the world. The DFB is committed to providing the German national team with the best technology to maximise their performance. SAP meets this demanding criterion."

Simon Carpenter, Chief Customer Officer at SAP Africa, said "the insights are also aimed to be beneficial for the media, enabling them to deliver a better informed commentary. Big data is an incredible resource for coaches and players to contextualise information and draw well-informed conclusions to optimise training and tactics. It is high time to make this type of information accessible to sports journalism and the fans as well."

Using Match Insights Germany managed to qualify for the 2014 FIFA World Cup Final in Brazil and surpass a 32-year-old DFB goal scoring record in the process. The German national team continued to use Match Insights for post-game analyses during the World Cup, and went on to win the championship with a 1–0 victory over Argentina in extra time.

The development of Match Insights furthers the 2013, SAP and the DFB partnership to improve the business processes of the federation which saw the successfully implemented SAP CRM and SAP Event Ticketing software. With SAP Match Insights, the partnership moves solidly into the world of software-based solutions designed to enhance on-field sports performance.

Analytics to Generate $3.7 Trillion by 2015

Based on the German national team's performance, it seems as if talent analytics has helped offer the kind of insights needed to win a World Cup. What about the business world? According to a recent report from Gartner, only 30 percent of organizations currently combine talent data with business data to measure the impact on company performance. Things are changing. Gartner expects the market for big data and analytics to reach $3.7 trillion by 2015. While most of this revenue will be from marketing and consumer business the adoption of big data analytics systems for human resources will continue to rise.

With today's big data technology, talent managers can finally analyze the huge sea of structured and unstructured data generated by their employees every day. The potential for the application of analytics in talent management is huge. With detailed data about employee performance, satisfaction, and compensation, cross-referenced with insights into current and future business needs, management can make better decisions when it comes to hiring, rewarding, and retaining the right talent.[49]

Questions

1. How can ERP software like SAP help improve business operations of the DFB and German National Team?

2. How can other football organizations like the DFB use innovation like this to fuel better performance by their athletes?

3. What lessons for dealing with the challenges of implementing an ERP information system can be passed to other football organizations adopting this technology?

CLOSING CASE TWO

Campus ERP

This case illustrates the challenges in implementing an ERP system.

When Stefanie Fillers returned to university, she needed to log in to the school's new online registration system to make certain that the courses she was taking would allow her to graduate. She also wanted to waive her participation in her school's dental insurance plan. When the system crashed the day before classes began, Fillers, a second-year undergraduate student, was annoyed. But at least she knew where her classes were—unlike most first-year students.

Schools like Stanford, the University of Massachusetts and Indiana University experienced problems with non-functioning ERP that prevented students from finding out where their classes were among other things. At the University of Massachusetts 27,000 students experienced problems registering for classes, finding classes and registering for financial aid in the fall of 2004. Said one UMass senior at the time: "The freshmen were going crazy because they didn't know where to go." After a couple of tense days and weeks, however, everyone eventually got their cheques and class schedules. At another university, financial aid was denied to 3,000 students by a buggy new ERP system, even though they had already received loan commitments. The school provided short-term loans for the cash-strapped students while the IT department and financial aid administrators scrambled to fix the complex system.

Disastrous ERP implementations have given more than a few postsecondary institutions black eyes. These recent campus meltdowns illustrate how the growing reliance on expensive ERP systems has created nightmare scenarios for some schools. In every case, the new systems were designed to centralize business processes in what has historically been a hodgepodge of discrete legacy systems. College and university administrators are drawn to ERP systems offering integrated views of finance, HR, student records, financial aid, and more.

ERP implementations are difficult, even in very top-down corporate environments. Getting them to work in academic settings, which are essentially a conglomeration of decentralized fiefdoms, has been nearly impossible. Staff members in the largely autonomous departments do not like the one-size-fits-all strategy of an ERP implementation. Plus, these non-profit organizations generally lack the talent and financial resources to create and manage a robust enterprise system. Representatives from Oracle, which dominates the higher education market for ERP, say that much of the problem results from the inexperience of college and university IT departments and their tendency to rush implementations and inadequately test the new systems.

Standardizing at Stanford

Starting in 2001, Stanford implemented student administration systems, PeopleSoft HR, OracleFinancials, and several other ancillary applications. "In hindsight, we tried to do too much in too little time," said Randy Livingston, Stanford's vice-president of business affairs and CFO.

Years later, users still complain that they have lower productivity with the new systems than with the previous ones, which were supported by a highly customized mainframe. Users have also had difficulty accessing critical information on a timely basis. Livingston said many transactions, such as initiating a purchase requisition or requesting a reimbursement, now take longer for users than with the previous legacy system.

Stanford has also not realized any of the projected savings the vendors promised. "We are finding that the new ERP applications cost considerably more to support than our legacy applications," Livingston said. He does not know how much it will cost to get the enterprise systems working at acceptable user levels.

Stanford's IT department is still trying to get campus-wide buy-in for the enterprise applications, which have necessitated new ways of doing business, leading to the new systems not being used and costly customizations to keep all users satisfied. For example, Stanford's law school operates on a semester schedule, while the other six schools operate on a trimester schedule. "This means that every aspect of the student administration system needs to be configured differently for the law school," Livingston said. Within the schools, some faculty members are paid a 12-month salary; other schools pay by 9, 10, or 11 months. "The standard HR payroll system is not designed to handle all these unusual pay schedules," Livingston said.

To resolve the issues, Livingston reorganized the IT department, which he hopes will be better able to manage the enterprise projects going forward. He also created a separate administrative systems group that reports directly to him, with responsibility for development, integration, and support of the major ERP systems.

Stanford's IT was still struggling with integrating the enterprise systems when the newly launched PeopleSoft portal crashed in 2004. The portal could not handle the load of all the returning students trying to log in to the untested Web-based system at the same time, Livingston said. Stanford was able to fix those problems relatively quickly, but Livingston and his staff continue to struggle with the enterprise projects. The university's departments remain "highly suspicious and resistant" to his efforts to standardize and centralize business processes, Livingston said.

Montclair State Sues

In 2008 Montclair State University wanted to replace its legacy systems with a new system. MSU requirements were for a system that required minimal customization. The school spent a year developing its requirements which ended up with some 3,200 items on it. The requirements were given to vendors, including Oracle, who was awarded the contract.

Montclair State sued Oracle in 2011 over the ERP implementation. MSU's suit stated that Oracle made "intentionally false statements regarding the functionality of its base ERP system, the amount of customization that would be required, and the amount of time, resources, and personnel that the University would have to devote to the project. Ultimately [the suit states], after missing a critical go-live deadline for the University's finance system, Oracle sought to extort millions of dollars from the University by advising the University that it would not complete the implementation of the … project unless the University agreed to pay millions of dollars more than the fixed fee the University and Oracle had previously agreed to." The case was settled out of court in March 2013 with no details of the settlement being released.

Cultural Hurdles

The hurdles that Stanford and other colleges and universities face with ERP systems are largely cultural ones. For instance, lean staffs and tight budgets at most campuses usually lead to a lack of proper training and systems testing. At Stanford, plenty of training was offered, but many users did not take it, Livingston said. He set up new training programs, including a group of trainers who sit with users to help them learn how to do complex tasks, periodic user group meetings, website and email lists that offer more help, and expert users embedded in the various departments who aid their colleagues.[50]

Questions

1. How could core ERP components help improve business operations at your school?

2. How could extended ERP components help improve business operations at your school?

3. How can integrating SCM, CRM, and ERP help improve business operations at your school?

4. What lessons for dealing with the challenges of implementing an ERP information system at your school can be learned from this case?

CLOSING CASE THREE

Intuitive ERP

This case highlights one specific ERP solution and its use by two separate Canadian manufacturers.

Aptean offers an ERP software application called Intuitive ERP for mid-sized manufacturers, especially those in regulated industries. It helps mid-sized manufacturing companies achieve higher operational efficiency and profitability via seamless integration of business processes on an enterprise-wide level in a user-friendly manner. The software is also designed to offer customer driven ERP solutions.

Since 1994, Intuitive ERP has been providing manufacturers with solutions that truly add value to their business. The Intuitive ERP enterprise system, built with Microsoft's .NET technology, has been designed with the future in mind. Intuitive ERP has a pure .NET-managed code framework; and over 80 percent of the standard product features have been rewritten in pure .NET.

Intuitive ERP consists of both core and extended ERP components. These include:

■ *Enterprise Resource Planning (ERP).* Handles all the front and back-office operations required by a discrete manufacturing company including planning, materials management and procurement, and financial business processes.

■ *Customer Relationship Management (CRM).* Manages contact and account information for prospects, customers, vendors, and other business partners. Handles the complete sales cycle from prospect to customer. Creates and deploys targeted marketing campaigns to potential and current customers. Automates customer support with complete incident management.

■ *Business Intelligence.* Tracks and analyzes over 50 key performance indicators (KPIs), including inventory turns, average days to pay, etc. Analyzes and reports on transactional data using advanced On Line Analytical Processing (OLAP) and data warehousing technology. Monitors a company's financial status.

■ *E-Commerce.* Allows customers to view product catalogue information, and to place and track orders, all securely over the Internet.

Companies from around the world have taken advantage of Intuitive ERP to improve their organization's daily operations, including Fibre Connections and Westwinn Group Enterprises.

1. Fibre Connections

This global company—headquartered in Schomberg, Ontario, near Toronto, with another key Canadian location in Summerside, Prince Edward Island—manufactures and markets a wide variety of fibre-optic cable assemblies, components, enclosures, and cabling connections. The company also develops polishing procedures for numerous fibre-optic connectors and components.

With Intuitive ERP, the company reaped improved efficiencies in several areas, including:

1. A reduction in administration staff from five to two people while increasing production levels

2. A 50 percent increase in their ability to generate quotes for custom products

3. An improvement in on-time deliveries from 85 to 97 percent

4. An increase in customer satisfaction, since customers now have the ability to track shipment orders in real time themselves over the Web

5. An improvement in being able to purchase components needed for custom products at the right time and in the right quantities

2. Westwinn Group Enterprises

This manufacturing company got its start making car-top boats for Sears Canada in the 1950s. Today, the company supplies premium aluminum boats across the globe. Westwinn Group employs 90 people in its manufacturing plants in Vernon, British Columbia, and Sylvan Lake, Alberta. Customers can select a variety of options and layouts for their boats, and the boats are configured and manufactured to order at these plants.

Before implementing Intuitive ERP, the company faced several challenges with the DOS-based system they used to support production and administration. For example, the DOS-based system was difficult to use and it did not have perpetual inventory tracking, MRP, or integrated accounting functionality. In fact, each sales invoice generated from this DOS-based system had to be manually re-entered into the accounting package.

With the implementation of Intuitive ERP, these problems went away. Within the first six months of using this new system, the company started seeing significant improvements to their bottom line in having a single, fully integrated system:

1. Saved over 250 hours per month of employee time by eliminating duplicate data entry.

2. Saw an instant increase in order and inventory accuracy; managed to reduce inventory stockouts to almost zero.

3. Knew exactly what to purchase and when.

4. Saw improved accuracy in their bills of materials and shop picklists.

5. Able to cross-train staff more easily since everyone used the same system.

6. Doubled production without adding more administrative staff to handle the volume.

According to Brad Armstrong, vice-president of finance, one of the most important benefits of Intuitive ERP is the ability to have instant access to information—something that was only a pipedream before the implementation of this system.[51]

Questions

1. How well do the components of the Intuitive ERP software product align with the ERP components described in this chapter?

2. What advantages did Fibre Connections and Westwinn Group Corp. realize with the introduction of Intuitive ERP? How well do these advantages resonate with the benefits of ERP described in this chapter?

3. The successful implementation of Intuitive ERP described above does not speak of any negative outcomes or drawbacks of introducing a new enterprise-wide information system in an organization. What challenges do you envision would occur in a company that decides to introduce such large-scale change? What drawbacks, if any, are there in adopting a software solution from a single vendor that serves such a critical and important role in an organization? How might one mitigate or lessen these drawbacks?

MAKING BUSINESS DECISIONS

1. Buying Green

You have recently been hired by Exclusive Recycling, an IT recycling company. The company is paid to pick up organizational IT equipment and safely dispose of the waste. After working for the company for a few weeks, you realize that the company does not dispose of the majority of the equipment. Instead, it fixes or upgrades the equipment and then sells it on eBay. The firms paying to have their IT equipment recycled are not aware of this practice. Do you believe Exclusive Recycling is acting ethically? Why or why not?

2. Building Alternatives

IBM plans to invest $1 billion a year in products and services that will help reduce IT power consumption in data centres. By using new techniques, within the next three years IBM plans to double the computing capacity of its data centres—more than 700,000 square metres worldwide—without increasing power consumption. Explain why all organizations should be interested in similar plans.

3. Implementing an ERP System

Blue Dog Inc. is a leading manufacturer in the high-end sunglasses industry, reaching record revenue levels of over $250 million last year. Blue Dog is currently deciding on the possibility of implementing an ERP system to help decrease production costs and increase inventory control. Many of the executives are nervous about making such a large investment in an ERP system due to its low success rates. As a senior manager at Blue Dog Inc., you have been asked to compile a list of the potential benefits and risks associated with implementing an ERP system, along with your recommendations for the steps the company can take to ensure a successful implementation.

4. Most Popular ERP Component

Mackenzie Coombe is currently thinking about implementing an ERP solution in her online music company, The Burford Beat. The company is generating over $12 million in revenues and is growing by 150 percent a year. Create a one-page document explaining the advantages and disadvantages of ERP systems, why ERP systems include CRM and SCM components, and why the most popular ERP component in today's marketplace is the accounting and finance core component.

5. Value-Added ERP

Pirate's Pizza is a large pizza chain that operates 700 franchises in five provinces. The company is currently contemplating implementing a new ERP system, which is expected to cost $7 million and take 18 months to implement. Once the system is completed, it is expected to generate $12 million a year as a result of decreased costs and increased revenues. You are working in the finance department for the company and your boss has asked you to compile a report detailing the different financial metrics you can use to assess the business value of the new ERP system. Once your report is completed, the company will make a decision about purchasing the ERP system.

6. Increasing Revenues with ERP

Cold Cream is one of the premier beauty supply stores in the metro Toronto area. People come from all over to sample the store's unique creams, lotions, makeup, and perfumes. The company receives its products from manufacturers around the globe. The company would like to implement an ERP system to help it better understand its customers and their purchasing habits. Create a report summarizing ERP systems and explain how an ERP system can directly influence Cold Cream's revenues.

connect   LEARNSMART

For more information on the resources available from McGraw-Hill Ryerson, go to www.mheducation.ca/he/solutions.

ENDNOTES

1. "IBM Helps Shell Canada Fuel New Productivity with PeopleSoft EnterpriseOne," case study, August 8, 2005, validated February 5, 2007, http://jobfunctions.bnet.com/ abstract.aspx?docid=256244, accessed July 9, 2010; "Shell Canada: Using IBM System i and Oracle JD Edwards EnterpriseOne for Mission-Critical Business

Applications," http://public.dhe.ibm.com/ common/ssi/ecm/en/chc00373usen/CHC00373USEN.PDF, accessed July 7, 2014.

2. *BusinessWeek: Innovation*, www.businessweek.com/innovate, accessed February 15, 2008; Matt Burns, "The World's First Carbon Fiber 3D Printer Is Now Available to Order," February 18, 2014, http://techcrunch.com/2014/02/18/the-worlds-first-carbon-fiber-3d-printer-is-now-available-to-order, accessed March 23, 2014.

3. *BusinessWeek: Innovation*, www.businessweek.com/innovate, accessed February 15, 2008.

4. http://tsologic.com, accessed March 23, 2014.

5. "Eco-Innovation: Saving Energy with HP," 2007; Patrick Thibodeau, "Inside HP's Prefab Data Center: The New Way of Building Data Centers in Containers," www.computerworld.com/s/article/9217538/Inside_HP_s_prefab_data_center, June 13, 2011, accessed July 26, 2011.

6. *BusinessWeek: Innovation*, www.businessweek.com/innovate, accessed February 15, 2008.

7. Ibid.

8. Roger Allan, "The Greening of Server Farms," September 1, 2009, http://powerelectronics.com/markets/greening-server-farms, accessed March 23, 2014.

9. *BusinessWeek: Innovation*, www.businessweek.com/innovate, accessed February 15, 2008.

10. "How VMware Virtualization Right-Sizes IT Infrastructure to Reduce Power Consumption," 2008, www.vmware.com/solutions/green-it, accessed July 26, 2011.

11. https://saveonenergy.ca/Business/Program-Overviews.aspx, accessed March 23, 2014.

12. "Eco-Innovation: Saving Energy with HP," 2007.

13. *BusinessWeek: Innovation*, www.businessweek.com/innovate, accessed July 9, 2010.

14. Ibid.

15. Ibid.

16. www.hp.com/canada/corporate/recycle/provincial.html, accessed July 26, 2011.

17. *BusinessWeek: Innovation*, www.businessweek.com/innovate, accessed July 9, 2010.

18. "Global e-Waste Crisis Is Worsening but the Tide Will Turn in 2015," www.pikeresearch.com/newsroom/global-e-waste-crisis-is-worsening-but-the-tide-will-turn-in-2015, May 6, 2009, accessed July 26, 2011; "Fact and Figure on E-Waste and Recycling," www.electronicstakeback.com/wp-content/uploads/Facts_and_Figures, June 4, 2010, accessed July 26, 2011; http://epa.gov/epawaste/conserve/materials/ecycling/manage.htm, accessed July 26, 2011; U.S. Environmental Protection Agency Office of Conservation and Recovery,"Electronic Waste Management in the United States Through 2009," EPA 550-R-11-002, May 2011; "Sun Microsystems Open Work Energy Measurement Project," February 2009.

19. *BusinessWeek: Innovation*, www.businessweek.com/innovate, accessed July 9, 2010.

20. Robert D. Hof, "Betting on the Real-Time Web: No One Knows How Twitter and Similar Social Sites Will Make Money, but Investors See a New Web Revolution," *BusinessWeek*, August 17, 2009, p. 46; www.StockTwits.com, accessed July 26, 2011.

21. "The Boomerang Effect: Rehire but Do It Right," February 18, 2014, www.hcamag.com/hr-news/the-boomerang-effect-rehire-but-do-it-right-123108.aspx, accessed February 21, 2014.

22. *BusinessWeek: Innovation*, www.businessweek.com/innovate, accessed February 15, 2008.

23. Kenneth Rapoza, "One in Five Americans Work from Home: Numbers Seen Rising over 60%," February 18, 2013, www.forbes.com/sites/kenrapoza/2013/02/18/one-in-five-americans-work-from-home-numbers-seen-rising-over-60, accessed March 6, 2014.

24. Maria Korolov, "At the Second Life Tipping Point," www.hypergridbusiness.com/2011/04/at-the-second-life-tipping-point, April 24, 2011, accessed July 26, 2011.

25. *BusinessWeek: Innovation*, www.businessweek.com/innovate, accessed February 15, 2008.

26. Ibid.

27. Ibid.

28. Margaret Wente, "For God's sake, Get a Second Life (or Not): If You're Feeling a Little Obsolete, It's Probably Time for an Avatar," *The Globe and Mail*, August 15, 2009, p. A19.

29. "Definition of a Legacy System," www.ehow.com/about_5175378_definition-legacy-system.html, accessed August 7, 2011.

30. "Sage ERP Accpac Enjoys Long-Term Stay Around the Globe at Fairmount Raffles Hotels International," www.sageaccpac.com/Resources/Success-Stories, accessed July 26, 2011.

31. "City of Winnipeg: Taking the Lead," Deloitte & Touche LLP–Canada, www.deloitte.com/dtt/case_study/0,1005,sid%253D3630%2526cid%253D80674,00.html, accessed March 28, 2007.

32. "Sage Helps Excelsior Radio Networks Boost Its Bottom Line," www.sageaccpac.com/Resources/Success-Stories, accessed July 26, 2011.

33. "Ponzi Vineyards Drives Business with Sage ERP Accpac," www.sageaccpac.com/Resources/Success-Stories, accessed July 26, 2011.

34. "Sage ERP Accpac Extend Enterprise Suite Up Smooth and Consistent Communication at YoCream," www.sageaccpac.com/Resources/Success-Stories, accessed July 26, 2011.

35. Michael Doane, "A Blueprint for ERP Implementation Readiness," www.metagroup.com, accessed October 17, 2003.

36. Megan Santosus, "In the Know," *CIO Magazine*, January 2006.

37. Ibid.

38. "The Balanced Scorecard," www.balancedscorecard.org, accessed July 27, 2011.

39. Ibid.

40. Ibid.

41. Ibid.

42. Ibid.

43. Thomas Wailgum, "10 Famous ERP Disasters, Dustups and Disappointments," CIO, March 24, 2009, www.cio.com/article/486284/10_Famous_ERP_Disasters_Dustups_and_Disappointments, accessed March 23, 2014; Robert N. Charette, "U.S. Air Force Blows $1 Billion on Failed ERP Project," *IEEE Spectrum*, November 15, 2012, http://spectrum.ieee.org/riskfactor/aerospace/military/us-air-force-blows-1-billion-on-failed-erp-project, accessed March 23, 2014; Chris Kanaracus, "10 Biggest ERP Software Failures of 2011," 2011, www.pcworld.com/businesscenter/article/246647/10_biggest_erp_software_failures_of_2011.html, accessed March 23, 2014; Nicholle Buckley and Greg B. Smith, "Three Defendants in CityTime Scandal to Repay $31 Million to City," *New York Daily News*, June 19, 2013, at www.nydailynews.com/new-york/defendants-repay-31-million-citytime-scandal-article-1.1377372, accessed March 23, 2014.

44. Michael Doane, "A Blueprint for ERP Implementation Readiness," www.metagroup.com, accessed October 17, 2003. (*Note:* The Meta Group was purchased by Gartner in April 2005.)

45. Sandra Bolan, "Keeping Everyone in the Loop: ERP Systems for the Lucrative SMB Market Has Been Nothing but Lip Service Until Now," *Computer Dealer News*, Volume 19, Issue 7, May 2, 2003, p. 16(2).

46. Alexandra DeFelice, "Sage Accpac: On the Grow," *Accounting Technology*, Volume 22, Issue 10, November 2006, p. 50.

47. "Sage ERP Accpac—A First Class Solution for The Second Cup Ltd.," www.sageaccpac.com/Resources/Success-Stories, accessed July 26, 2011.

48. "Sage ERP Accpac and Sage CRM Enable Island Lake Resort to Grow Despite Stiff Competition," www.sageaccpac.com/Resources/Success-Stories, accessed July 26, 2011.

49. "HCM Goes to the World Cup," http://it.toolbox.com/blogs/inside-erp/hcm-goes-to-the-world-cup-61791, accessed July 9, 2014; "German Football Association Focused World Cup Success with SAP," June 13, 2014, www.erpnews.net/526/german-football-association-focused-world-cup-success-sap, accessed July 9, 2014; "SAP Hopes to Help Germany Win World Cup with HANA," www.aerpi.edu.au/news/sap-hopes-to-help-germany-win-world-cup-with-hana, accessed July 9, 2014.

50. Thomas Wailgum, "Big Mess on Campus," *CIO Magazine*, May 1, 2005; Thomas Wailgum, "10 Famous ERP Disasters, Dustups and Disappointments," March 24, 2009, www.cio.com/article/2429865/enterprise-resource-planning/10-famous-erp-disasters--dustups-and-disappointments.html, July 8, 2014; Chris Kanaracus, "University Accuses Oracle of Extortion, Lies, 'Rigged' Demo in Lawsuit," December 14, 2011, www.pcworld.com/article/246238/university_accuses_oracle_of_extortion_lies_rigged_demo_in_lawsuit.html, accessed July 8, 2014; Doug Henschen, "Oracle, Montclair State University Settle Bitter Contract Dispute," March 11, 2013, www.informationweek.com/applications/oracle-montclair-state-university-settle-bitter-contract-dispute/d/d-id/1109019, accessed July 8, 2014.

51. www.automated-design.ca/erp, accessed March 29, 2007; "Intuitive ERP," www.aptean.com/products/intuitive-erp, accessed July 8, 2014; "Intuitive: End-to-End Easy," http://intuitive.consona.com/erp-system/ease-of-use.aspx, accessed July 8, 2014.

8
CHAPTER

Operations Management and Supply Chain Management

LEARNING OUTCOMES

LO 8.1 | Explain the fundamentals of operations management and its role in business.

LO 8.2 | Describe how information systems can support the operations management function.

LO 8.3 | Explain supply chain management and its role in business.

LO 8.4 | Describe the relationship between information systems and the supply chain.

LO 8.5 | Summarize the best practices for implementing a successful supply chain management system.

WHY DO I NEED TO KNOW THIS

Information systems can be used to revolutionize and transform operations and supply chain management processes. Information systems enable companies to better manage the flow of information, materials, and financial payments that occurs between and among stages in a supply chain to maximize total supply chain effectiveness and profitability.

As a business student, you need to know why a supply chain is significant to organizational success and the critical role information systems play in ensuring smooth operation of a supply chain. A supply chain consists of all direct and indirect parties involved in the procurement of a product or raw material. These parties can be internal groups or departments within an organization or external partner companies and end-customers.

This chapter emphasizes the important role information systems play in providing an underlying infrastructure and the coordination mechanisms needed for operations management and supply chains to function effectively and efficiently as possible. Knowing this, you will appreciate and understand the capabilities and limitations of operations management, the benefits and challenges of supply chain management, as well as future trends where information systems will play a critical part.

Supply Chain Management Inc. Helping Canadians Shop

Supply Chain Management

As one of Canada's largest retail logistics service companies, Supply Chain Management Inc. (SCM Inc.) operates several large, state-of-the-art distribution centres for Walmart Canada. SCM Inc.'s relationship with Walmart Canada began when Walmart entered Canada in 1994 with 122 stores, and as of 2014 they supply Walmart's 142 conventional stores and 247 Supercentres. SCM Inc. is there to support Walmart Canada's operations and commitment to its customers. "Walmart Canada's commitment to customers is to provide unbeatable prices, one-stop shopping and friendly service, and our team operates the company's ambient logistics network with this in mind," says Dan Gabbard, president of SCM Inc. "We strive to identify efficiencies that contribute to Walmart's bottom line, so it can continue to serve millions of Canadians and grow its business."

SCM Inc.'s business is logistics—the process of planning, implementing, and controlling the flow and storage of goods and materials from the point of origin to the point of consumption. In other words, SCM Inc.'s job is to get the right products to the right place in the right quantity at the right time to satisfy customer demand.

SCM Inc. was founded in 1994 by the Tibbett & Britten Group. In July 2004, SCM Inc. joined the Exel Group. Then, in December 2005, Exel was acquired by Deutsche Poste World Net, a leading integrated logistics group focused on the management and transportation of goods, information, and payments through a global network of companies.

SCM and Logistics at SCM Inc.

SCM Inc. operations include distribution centres in Cornwall, Ontario; Calgary, Alberta; and Mississauga, Ontario. When you tour one of their three large distribution centres, you will see kilometres of conveyor belts and sophisticated technology. The conveyors and the technology work together with merchandise flow planning, and highly trained and engaged employees, to provide a "gold standard" service level in logistics and supply chain management for their customers. SCM Inc. works closely with Walmart's buying and replenishment teams to ensure stock arrives in the stores and that Walmart has best-in-class quality and supply chain cost levels for general merchandise and groceries, which includes both non-perishable and perishable goods.

How It Works

The statistics of the distribution centre in Calgary show that:

- The warehouse is 1.2 million square feet.
- There are 122 shipping lanes and 91 receiving doors.
- There is enough parking for 2,500 trailers.
- The distribution centre in Calgary is responsible for supplying each of Walmart Canada's stores in western Canada.

But how does SCM Inc. supply logistics to its customer? In other words, how does SCM Inc. manage the supply chain so that the right product arrives in the right store at the right time for the retail customer to buy? This is accomplished with a combination of technology and processes. Let's look at how stock is handled at the Calgary distribution centre. The easiest way to appreciate how they do this is to look at the various areas within the distribution centre.

Staple Stock Receiving

Staple stock items are carried for stores throughout the year. Data on each store's sales made before 6 p.m. every day are collected and transmitted to Walmart's information processing centre in Bentonville, Arkansas. The information for each of the stores supplied by the Calgary distribution centre is sent back to the distribution centre that same evening. The data is used to generate labels for the product picks the next morning; the labels are then picked and placed on the conveyor, and sent to the appropriate shipping lanes.

Distribution Assembly Receiving Dock

The distribution assembly dock has 43 docks for receiving truck shipments. As the trailers are unloaded, with the aid of the Receiving Dock System (RDS), team members scan the bar codes on the vendor cases and enter the quantity for each item in the system; RDS then prints the required number of labels. The team member labels the freight and places it on the conveyor, which moves the freight to the shipping area after about a 12-minute ride on a conveyor.

Casepack Modules

At each of the seven casepack modules, freight is picked from the slots, labelled, and placed on the conveyor to travel to the shipping lanes. The modules work with all of the full-case freight created from the previous night's production (label) run with freight that has been ordered in full-case quantities.

Put to Light Department

The Put to Light department handles freight that is less than full-case quantities and that has predetermined distribution to the stores. The department has three modules, and each module is set up in sections. When the operator scans the label bar code created by the receiving department, which is on the outside of the carton, a light flashes, indicating what quantities to "put" into the container designated for a store. In this department the team member moves the stock to a stationary box.

Pick to Light Department

The Pick to Light department also handles freight that is less than full-case quantities. However, it deals with staple stock items already in the building, based on the previous day sales of the stores that are not in full-case quantities. It uses the same technology as the Put to Light department in the order filling process, but in this department the store box moves to the stationary vendor freight.

Voice

Voice is a process created by Walmart that enables the distribution of non-conveyable stock. Product is picked directly from the vendor pallet and distribution is given through voice commands to the pickers. The system tells each operator where and how many cases to put to each pallet. Each pallet represents a store.

Merge

This is the area at the top of the conveyor system where all the cases from all input lines come together. The cartons pass through two scanners. The first scanner reads the label and sorts the box to either the north or south side of the shipping building depending on its final destination. The second scanner scans the bar code for billing information and then places the freight into the proper window to be diverted into its respective shipping lane.

Shipping Lanes

Shipping is the largest department in the distribution centre and the final destination in the building for the cartons before they are moved into the trailers for shipping. This department is set up so that each door represents one store in western Canada. In this area, team members cover multiple lanes, using an overhead lighting system to determine lane priority.

Trailer Loading

Freight arrives at the shipping lanes from many input lines, in no particular order. This puts pressure on the team members that are loading the trailers as they build secure loads. Team members must build secure walls of freight in the trailers to ensure safe offloading and minimal in-transit damage to the stock when it arrives at store level. Loading safe trailers and filling them to capacity is a key initiative for SCM Inc. and Walmart alike.

The Billing Department

Even though the freight has made it to the trailer, the processing is not finished. The Billing department takes over and creates the shipping packets from the paperwork that comes to them from the Data Processing department. Once the shipping packets are created, the Billing department also prepares the bills of lading so that the carriers can deliver the freight. In addition, the Billing department processes claims, credits, additional billing, and reprinting of invoices.

The Dispatch Department

Once the dispatch team receives the shipping packets from the Billing department, they schedule the trailers using the dispatch program. When the trailers are scheduled, the dispatchers forward the information to the carriers to confirm delivery. Dispatch also emails the delivery information to the stores and processes all paperwork prior to each trailer leaving. Drivers pick up paperwork at the dispatch window prior to hooking up to their trailers.[1]

INTRODUCTION

Production is the creation of goods and services using the factors of production: land, labour, capital, entrepreneurship, and knowledge. Production has historically been associated with manufacturing, but the nature of business has changed significantly in the last 20 years. The service sector, especially Internet services, has grown dramatically. Canada now has what is called a service economy—that is, one dominated by the service sector.

Organizations that excel in operations management, specifically supply chain management, perform better in almost every financial measure of success, according to a report from AMR Research Inc. When supply chain excellence improves operations, companies experience a higher profit margin, less inventory, stronger "perfect order" ratings, and significantly shorter cycle times than their competitors. "The basis of competition for winning companies in today's economy is supply chain superiority," said Kevin O'Marah, vice-president of research at AMR Research. "These companies understand that value chain performance translates to productivity and market-share leadership. They also understand that supply chain leadership means more than just low costs and efficiency: It requires a superior ability to shape and respond to shifts in demand with innovative products and services."[2]

Collecting, analyzing, and distributing transactional information to all relevant parties, supply chain management (SCM) systems help the different entities in the supply chain work together more effectively. SCM systems provide dynamic holistic views of organizations. Users can "drill down" into detailed analyses of supply chain activities to find valuable information on organizational operations. This chapter explores the details of operations management and supply chain management.

8.1 OPERATIONS MANAGEMENT

LO1 OPERATIONS MANAGEMENT FUNDAMENTALS

Books, Blu-ray discs, downloaded music files, and dental and medical procedures are all examples of goods and services. *Production management* describes all the activities managers perform to help companies create goods. To reflect the change in importance from manufacturing to services, the term "production" is often replaced by "operations" to reflect the manufacturing of both goods and services. *Operations management (OM)* is the management of systems or processes that convert or transform resources (including human resources) into goods and services. Operations management is responsible for managing the core processes used to manufacture goods and produce services.

Essentially, creating goods or services involves transforming or converting inputs into outputs. Various inputs such as capital, labour, and information are used to create goods or services using one or more transformation processes (e.g., storing, transporting, and cutting). A *transformation process* is often referred to as the technical core, especially in manufacturing organizations, and is the actual conversion of inputs to outputs. To ensure that the desired outputs are obtained, an organization takes measurements at various points in the transformation process (feedback) and then compares them with previously established standards to determine whether corrective action is needed (control). Figure 8.1 depicts the conversion system.[3]

Figure 8.2 displays examples of inputs, transformation processes, and outputs. Although goods and services are listed separately in Figure 8.1, it is important to note that goods and services often occur jointly. For example, having the oil changed in a car is a service, but the oil that is changed is a good. Similarly, house painting is a service, but the paint is a good. The goods–service combination is a continuum. It ranges from primarily goods with little service to primarily service with few goods (see Figure 8.3). There are relatively few pure goods or pure services; therefore, organizations typically sell product packages, which are a combination of goods and services. This makes managing operations more interesting, and also more challenging.[4]

Value-added is the term used to describe the difference between the cost of inputs and the price value of outputs. OM is critical to an organization because of its ability to increase value-added during the transformation process. In non-profit and many government organizations, the value of outputs (highway construction, police, and fire protection) is their value to society; the greater the value-added, the greater the effectiveness of the operations. In for-profit organizations, the value of outputs is measured by the prices that customers are willing to pay for those goods or services. Firms use the money generated by value-added for research and development, investment in new facilities and equipment, worker salaries, and profits. Consequently, the greater the value-added, the greater the amount of funds available for these important activities.

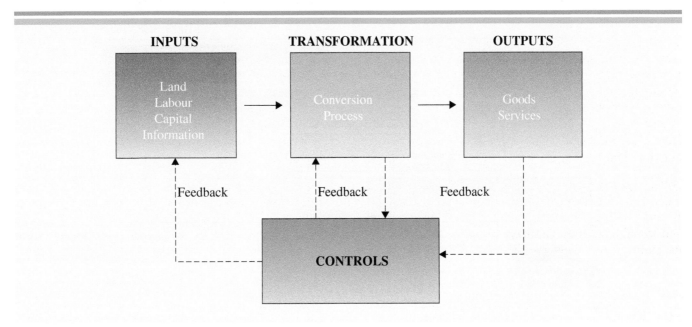

FIGURE 8.1

The Process of Converting Inputs into Outputs

Input	Transformation Process	Output
Restaurant inputs include hungry customers, food, wait staff	Well-prepared food, served well; agreeable environment	Satisfied customers
Hospital inputs include patients, medical supplies, doctors, nurses	Health care	Healthy individuals
Automobile inputs include sheet steel, engine parts, tires	Fabrication and assembly of cars	High-quality cars
College inputs include high school graduates, books, professors, classrooms	Imparting knowledge and skills	Educated individuals
Distribution centre inputs include stock keeping units, storage bins, workers	Storage and redistribution	Fast delivery of available products

FIGURE 8.2

Examples of Inputs, Transformation Processes, and Outputs

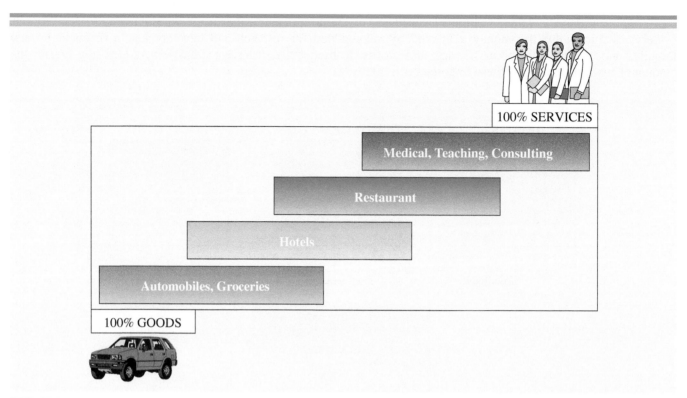

FIGURE 8.3

The Goods–Service Continuum: Most Products Are a Bundle of Goods and Services

OPERATIONS MANAGEMENT IN BUSINESS

The scope of OM ranges across the organization and includes many interrelated activities, such as forecasting, capacity planning, scheduling, managing inventories, assuring quality, motivating employees, deciding where to locate facilities, and more.

Reviewing the activities performed in an airline company makes it easy to understand how a service organization's OM team adds value. The company consists of the airplanes, airport facilities, and maintenance facilities, and typical OM activities include:

- *Forecasting.* Estimating seat demand for flights, weather and landing conditions, and estimates for growth or reduction in air travel are all included in forecasting.

- *Capacity planning.* This is the key essential metric for the airline to maintain cash flow and increase revenues. Underestimating or overestimating flights will hurt profits.

- *Scheduling.* The airline operates on tight schedules that must be maintained including flights, pilots, flight attendants, ground crews, baggage handlers, and routine maintenance.

- *Managing inventory.* Inventory of such items as food, beverages, first-aid equipment, in-flight magazines, pillows, blankets, and life jackets is essential for the airline.

- *Assuring quality.* Quality is indispensable in an airline where safety is the highest priority. Today's travellers expect high-quality customer service during ticketing, check-in, curb service, and unexpected issues where the emphasis is on efficiency and courtesy.

- *Motivating and training employees.* Airline employees must be highly trained and continually motivated, especially when dealing with frustrated airline travellers.

- *Locating facilities.* Key questions facing airlines include: in which cities to offer services, where to host maintenance facilities, and where to locate major and minor hubs.[5]

In contrast to an airline, a bike factory is typically an assembly operation: buying components such as frame tubing, tires, wheels, gears, and other items from suppliers, and then assembling bicycles. Some of the fabrication work is done in a bike factory, such as welding the frames and forks. Obviously, an airline company and a bike factory are completely different types of operations. One is primarily a service operation, the other a producer of goods. Nonetheless, these two operations have much in common. Like the airline, the bike factory must schedule production, deal with components, order parts and materials, schedule and train employees, ensure quality standards are met, and above all satisfy customers. In both organizations, the success of the business depends on short- and long-term planning and the ability of its executives and managers to make informed decisions.[6]

LO2 | INFORMATION SYSTEMS' ROLE IN OPERATIONS MANAGEMENT

Managers can use information systems (IS) to heavily influence OM decisions including productivity, costs, flexibility, quality, and customer satisfaction. One of the greatest benefits of IS on OM is in making operational decisions, because operations management exerts considerable influence over the degree to which the goals and objectives of the organization are realized. Most OM decisions involve many possible alternatives that can have varying impacts on revenues and expenses. OM information systems are critical for managers to be able to make well-informed decisions.

For example, *decision support systems* and *executive information systems* can help an organization perform what-if analysis, sensitivity analysis, drill-down, and consolidation. Numerous managerial and strategic key decisions are based on OM information systems that affect the entire organization, including:

- *What.* What resources will be needed, and in what amounts?

- *When.* When will each resource be needed? When should the work be scheduled? When should materials and other supplies be ordered? When is corrective action needed?

- *Where.* Where will the work be performed?

- *How.* How will the product or service be designed? How will the work be done (organization, methods, equipment)? How will resources be allocated?

- *Who:* Who will perform the work?

Strategic Business Systems

UPS uses package flow information systems at each of its locations. The custom-built systems combine operations strategy and mapping technology to create smart labels for packages that include not only the customer's tracking number but also the dispatch plan for the driver to "ensure that drivers are not over-dispatched and that last-minute load changes to a driver's package car are minimized." About 95 percent of packages travelling through the UPS network are smart.[7]

Operations strategy is concerned with developing a long-term plan for determining how to best use the firm's major resources so that there is a high degree of compatibility between these resources and the firm's long-term corporate strategy. Operations strategy addresses broad questions about how these major resources should be configured to achieve the desired corporate objectives. Some of the major long-term issues addressed in operations strategy include:

- How big should we make the facilities?

- Where should we locate the facilities?

- When should we build additional facilities?

- What type of process(es) should we install to make the products?

Each of these issues can be addressed by OM decision support systems. In developing an operations strategy, management needs to consider many factors. These include: (1) the level of technology that is or will be available; (2) the required skill levels of the workers; and (3) the degree of vertical integration, in terms of the extent to which outside suppliers are used.

Today, many organizations, especially larger conglomerates, operate in terms of *strategic business units (SBUs)*, which consist of several stand-alone businesses. When companies become really big, they are best thought of as being composed of a number of businesses (or SBUs). As displayed in Figure 8.4, operations strategy supports the long-range strategy developed at the SBU level.[8]

Type of Planning	Time Frame	Issues	Decisions	Systems
Strategic planning	Long range	Plant size, location, type of processes	How will we make the products? Where do we locate the facility or facilities? How much capacity do we require? When should we increase capacity?	Materials requirement planning (MRP) systems
Tactical planning	Intermediate range	Workforce size, material requirements	How many workers do we need? When do we need them? Should we work overtime or put on a second shift? When should we have material delivered? Should we have a finished goods inventory?	Global inventory management systems
Operational planning and control (OP&C)	Short range	Daily scheduling of employees, jobs, and equipment, process management, inventory management	What jobs do we work on today or this week? To whom do we assign what tasks? What jobs have priority?	Inventory management and control systems, transportation planning systems, distribution management systems

FIGURE 8.4

Hierarchy of Operational Planning

Decisions at the SBU level focus on being effective—that is, on "doing the right things." These decisions are sometimes referred to as *strategic planning*, which focuses on long-range planning such as plant size, location, and type of process to be used. One of the primary systems used for strategic planning is a material requirements planning system. *Material requirements planning (MRP) systems* use sales forecasts to make sure that needed parts and materials are available at the right time and place in a specific company. The latest versions of MRP are components of enterprise resource planning, which was discussed in Chapter 7.[9]

Strategic decisions affect intermediate-range decisions, often referred to as tactical planning, which focuses on being efficient—that is, "doing things right." *Tactical planning* focuses on producing goods and services as efficiently as possible within the strategic plan. Here the emphasis is on producing quality products, including when material should be delivered, when products should be made to best meet demand, and what size the workforce should be. One of the primary systems used in tactical planning includes global inventory management. *Global inventory management systems (GIMS)* provide the ability to locate, track, and predict the movement of every component or material anywhere upstream or downstream in the business process. Tesco in the United Kingdom has added delivery information to their GIMS by installing GPS systems in delivery vans to report back "on the location of each van, as well as providing vehicle status, driver status, and performance information." The system will also text customers shortly before their deliveries arrive.[10] These systems allow an organization to locate and analyze its inventory anywhere in its processes. At Volvo, GIMS allow the company to manage its aftermarket parts at dealers worldwide, where worldwide dealer service levels exceed 95 percent.[11]

Finally, *operational planning and control (OP&C)* deals with the day-to-day procedures for performing work, including scheduling, inventory, and process management. *Inventory management and control systems* provide control and visibility to the status of individual items maintained in inventory. The software maintains inventory record accuracy, generates material requirements for all purchased items, and analyzes inventory performance. Inventory management and control software provides organizations with the information from a variety of sources including:

- Current inventory and order status
- Cost accounting
- Sales forecasts and customer orders
- Manufacturing capacity
- New-product introductions[12]

OP&C systems comprise a number of systems, including transportation planning and distribution management. *Transportation planning systems* track and analyze the movement of materials and products to ensure the delivery of materials and finished goods at the right time, to the right place, and at the lowest cost. *Distribution management systems* coordinate the process of transporting materials from a manufacturer to distribution centres to the final customers. Transportation routes directly affect the speed and cost of delivery. An organization will use these systems to help it decide if it wants to use an effectiveness route and ship its products directly to its customers, or use an efficiency route and ship its products to a distributor that ships the products to customers.

Competitive OM Strategy

The key to developing a competitive OM strategy is understanding how to create value-added goods and services for customers. Specifically, value is added through the competitive priority or priorities that are selected to support a given strategy. Five key competitive priorities translate directly into characteristics that are used to describe various processes by which a company can add value to its OM decisions, including:

1. Cost
2. Quality
3. Delivery
4. Flexibility
5. Service

Cost Every industry has low-cost providers. However, being the low-cost producer does not always guarantee profitability and success. Products sold strictly based on cost are typically commodity-like products, including such goods as flour, petroleum, and sugar. In other words, customers cannot distinguish the products made by one firm from those of another. As a result, customers use cost as the primary determinant in making a purchasing decision.

Low-cost market segments are frequently very big, and many companies are lured by the potential for significant profits, which are associated with large unit volumes of product. As a consequence, the competition in this segment is exceedingly fierce—and so is the failure rate. After all, there can be only one lowest-cost producer, and that firm usually establishes the selling price in the market.

Quality Quality can be divided into two categories—product quality and process quality. Product quality levels vary as to the particular market that it aims to serve. For example, a generic bike is of significantly different quality than the bike of a world-class cyclist. Higher-quality products command higher prices in the marketplace. Organizations must establish the "proper level" of product quality by focusing on the exact requirements of their customers. Over-designed products with too much quality will be viewed as being prohibitively expensive. Under-designed products, on the other hand, will lose customers to products that cost a little more but are perceived by the customers as offering greater value.

Process quality is critical in every market segment. Regardless of whether the product is a generic bike or a bike for a professional cyclist, customers want products without defects. Thus, the primary goal of process quality is to produce error-free products. The investment in improving quality pays off in stronger customer relationships and higher revenues. Many organizations use modern quality control standards, including:

- *Six Sigma quality.* The goal is to detect potential problems to prevent their occurrence and achieve no more than 3.4 defects per million opportunities.

- *ISO 9000.* The common name given to quality management and assurance standards. It comes from the **International Organization for Standardization (ISO)**, a non-governmental organization established in 1947 to promote developing world standards to facilitate the international exchange of goods and services. ISO is a worldwide federation of national standards bodies from more than 140 countries. ISO 9000 standards require a company to determine customer needs, including regulatory and legal requirements. The company must also make communication arrangements to handle issues such as complaints. Other standards involve process control, product testing, storage, and delivery.[13]

- *ISO 14000.* This collection of the best practices for managing an organization's impact on the environment does not prescribe specific performance levels, but establishes environmental management systems. The requirements for certification include having an environmental policy, setting specific improvement targets, conducting audits of environmental programs, and maintaining top management review of processes. Certification in ISO 14000 displays that a firm has a world-class management system in both quality and environmental standards.[14]

- *CMMI.* Capability Maturity Model Integration is a framework of best practices. The current version, CMMI-DEV, describes best practices in managing, measuring, and monitoring software development processes. CMMI does not describe the processes themselves; it describes the characteristics of good processes, thus providing guidelines for companies developing or honing their own sets of processes.[15]

Delivery   Another key factor in purchasing decisions is delivery speed. The ability of a firm to provide consistent and fast delivery allows it to charge a premium price for its products. George Stalk, Jr., of the Boston Consulting Group, has demonstrated that both profits and market share are directly linked to the speed with which a company can deliver its products relative to its competition. In addition to fast delivery, the reliability of the delivery is also important. In other words, products should be delivered to customers with minimum variance in delivery times.[16]

Flexibility   Flexibility, from a strategic perspective, refers to the ability of a company to offer a wide variety of products to its customers. Flexibility is also a measure of how fast a company can convert its process(es) from making an old line of products to making a new product line. Product variety is often perceived by the customers to be a dimension of quality.

The flexibility of the manufacturing process at John Deere's Harvester Works allows the firm to respond to the unpredictability of the agricultural industry's equipment needs. By manufacturing such small-volume products as seed planters in "modules," or factories within a factory, John Deere can offer farmers a choice of 84 different planter models with such a wide variety of options that farmers can have planters virtually customized to meet their individual needs. Its manufacturing process allows John Deere to compete on both speed and flexibility.[17]

Currently, there appears to be a trend toward offering environmentally friendly products that are made through environmentally friendly processes. As consumers become more aware of the fragility of the environment, they are increasingly turning toward products that are safe for the environment. Several flexible manufacturers now advertise environmentally friendly products, energy-efficient products, and recycled products. Some companies have taken this further and are getting their products certified as environmentally responsible, such as with wood and paper products having Forest Stewardship Council (FSC) certification.

Service   With shortened product life cycles, products tend to migrate toward one common standard. As a consequence, these products are often viewed as commodities in which price is the primary differentiator. For example, the differences in laptops offered among PC manufactures are relatively insignificant so price is the prime selection criterion. For this reason, many companies attempt to place an emphasis on high-quality customer service as a primary differentiator. Customer service can add tremendous value to an ordinary product.

Businesses are always looking toward the future to find the next competitive advantage that will distinguish their products in the marketplace. To obtain an advantage in such a competitive environment, firms must provide "value-added" goods and services, and the primary area where they can capitalize on all five competitive priorities is in the supply chain.

OM and the Supply Chain

To understand a supply chain, consider a customer purchasing a Cervélo bike from a dealer. The supply chain begins when a customer places an order for a Cervélo bike with the dealer. The dealer purchases the bike from the manufacturer, Cervélo. Cervélo purchases the raw materials required to make the bike, such as carbon fibre, packaging, and components from different suppliers. The supply chain for Cervélo encompasses every activity and party involved in the process of fulfilling the order from the customer for the new bike.

A *supply chain* consists of all parties involved, directly or indirectly, in procuring a product or raw material. *Supply chain management (SCM)* involves managing information flows between and among stages in a supply chain to maximize total supply chain effectiveness and profitability. The four basic components of supply chain management are:

1. *Supply chain strategy.* The strategy for managing all the resources required to meet customer demand for all products and services.

2. *Supply chain partners.* The partners chosen to deliver finished products, raw materials, and services, including pricing, delivery, and payment processes along with partner relationship monitoring metrics.

3. *Supply chain operation.* The schedule for production activities, including testing, packaging, and preparation for delivery. Measurements for this component include productivity and quality.

4. *Supply chain logistics.* The product delivery processes and elements, including orders, warehouses, carriers, defective product returns, and invoicing.[18]

Dozens of steps are required to achieve and carry out each of the above components. SCM software can enable an organization to generate efficiencies within these steps by automating and improving the information flows throughout and among the different supply chain components. Figures 8.5 and 8.6 display the typical supply chains for goods and services.

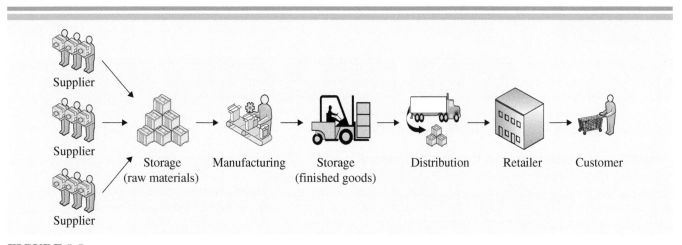

FIGURE 8.5

A Typical Goods Supply Chain

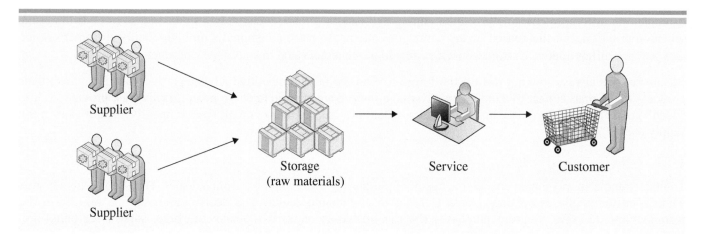

FIGURE 8.6

A Typical Service Supply Chain

Walmart and Procter & Gamble (P&G) implemented a successful SCM system that linked Walmart's distribution centres directly to P&G's manufacturing centers. Every time a Walmart customer purchases a P&G product, the system sends a message directly to the factory alerting P&G to restock the product. The system also sends an automatic alert to P&G whenever a product is running low at one of Walmart's distribution centres. This real-time information allows P&G to produce and deliver products to Walmart without having to maintain large inventories in its warehouses. The SCM system saves time, reduces inventory, and decreases order-processing costs for P&G, which P&G passes on to Walmart in the form of discounted prices.[19]

Figure 8.7 diagrams the stages of the SCM system for a customer purchasing a product from Walmart. The diagram demonstrates how the supply chain is dynamic and involves the constant flow of information between the different parties. For example, a customer purchases a product from Walmart and generates order information. Walmart supplies the order information to its warehouse or distributor. The warehouse or distributor transfers the order information to the manufacturer, who provides pricing and availability information to the store and replenishes the product. Partners transfer all payments electronically. Effective and efficient supply chain management systems can enable an organization to:

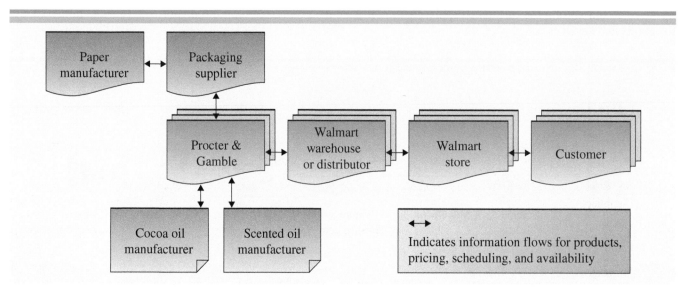

FIGURE 8.7

Supply Chain for a P&G Product Purchased from Walmart

- Decrease the power of its buyers
- Increase its own supplier power
- Increase switching costs to reduce the threat of substitute products or services
- Create entry barriers, thereby reducing the threat of new entrants
- Increase efficiencies while seeking a competitive advantage through cost leadership (see Figure 8.8)[20]

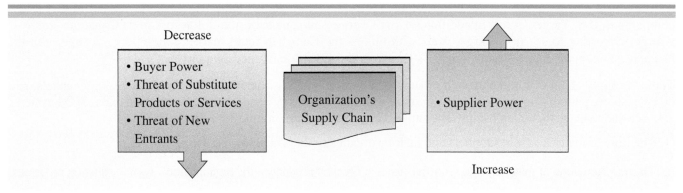

FIGURE 8.8

Effective and Efficient Supply Chain Management's Effect on Porter's Five Forces

---

OPENING CASE QUESTIONS

Supply Chain Management Inc. Helping Canadians Shop

1. How is operations management critical to SCM Inc. and its customer, Walmart Canada?

2. Given that SCM Inc. is a third-party logistics provider, contracted by Walmart Canada to provide logistics and supply chain management to all Walmart Canada locations, how does SCM Inc. use each of the three OM planning strategies to improve its operations?

3. How does SCM Inc. use the five competitive priorities to help increase the value of both its goods and services and those of Walmart Canada?

8.2 THE SUPPLY CHAIN

LO3 SUPPLY CHAIN FUNDAMENTALS

While consumers have crowded the aisles at the new Target locations in Canada, the vendors at its loading docks are causing Target to experience growing pains. Early in the move to Canada, Target realized that its supply chain management would be an important contributor to its success in Canada. It appears that Target failed to understand that supply chain management is about more than just its SCM systems; it's also about relationships with vendors. Target may have also underestimated just how competitive the Canadian retail marketplace is on the upstream supply chain side. Canada's large retailers made good use of the two years they had to prepare for the entrance of Target into the Canadian market. Not only did they make improvements for consumers with renovations, improved signage and overall friendlier stores, they also used their clout with vendors to dissuade them from selling to Target in Canada's more complicated vendor structure. Target does, however, benefit from their existing U.S. relationships with large vendors like Procter & Gamble or Unilever.

What about all of the smaller vendors in Canada that Target doesn't have this relationship with? Target's buying organization started off by damaging a non-existent relationship through bad supplier relationship processes in the start. Other questions also exist as to whether smaller vendors will be interested in supplying Target, especially if they already have most of their products going elsewhere like Hudson's Bay or Walmart. It does create a good position for the smaller vendors, as they may have the largest retailers in the country jockeying for their business.

As of August 2013, Target's stores in Canada were underperforming in customer satisfaction against the other major retailers. In a recent customer satisfaction survey, customers complained about stock shortages and higher prices compared to U.S. Target stores. In addition, in 2013 Target saw a near-billion-dollar loss in its Canadian stores. It will be interesting to see how Target deals with this as the Canadian retail market continues to change with the recent acquisitions of Safeway and Shopper's Drug market and still more new entrants.[21]

Today's supply chain is a complex web of suppliers, assemblers, logistic firms, sales and marketing channels, and other business partners linked primarily through information networks and contractual relationships. SCM systems enhance and manage the relationships. The supply chain has three main links (see Figure 8.9):

1. The flow of materials from suppliers and their upstream suppliers at all levels

2. The transformation of materials into semi-finished and finished products—the organization's own production processes

3. The distribution of products to customers and their downstream customers at all levels

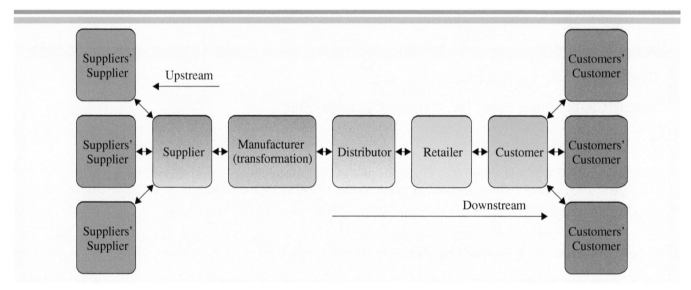

FIGURE 8.9

A Typical Supply Chain for a Manufacturer

Organizations must embrace technologies that can effectively manage and oversee their supply chains. SCM is increasingly important in creating organizational efficiencies and competitive advantages. Best Buy checks inventory levels at 1,600-plus stores and mobile stores in North America as often as every half-hour with its SCM system, taking much of the guesswork out of inventory replenishment. SCM improves ways for companies to find the raw components they need to make a product or service, manufacture that product or service, and deliver it to customers. Figure 8.10 highlights the five basic components of supply chain management.[22]

Technology advances in the five SCM components have significantly improved companies' forecasting and business operations. Businesses today have access to modelling and simulation tools, algorithms, and applications that can combine information from multiple sources to build forecasts for days, weeks, and months in advance. Better forecasts for tomorrow result in better preparedness today.

Mattel Inc. experienced a number of recalls for safety reasons since 2007, which made it re-examine its processes at all of its factories. Part of this process was adding more controls into the SCM system that tested the safety of the raw materials they were using to manufacture toys. This was in addition to the SCM strategies they had used before to cut the time it takes to design, produce, and ship everything from Hot Wheels to Barbies. Mattel also uses SCM to forecast demand so that it no longer produces more inventory than stores require and delivers inventory on request.[23]

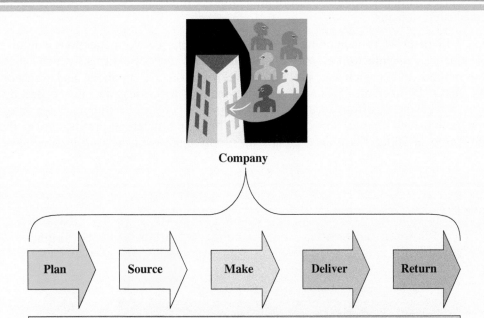

Company

| Plan | Source | Make | Deliver | Return |

THE FIVE BASIC SUPPLY CHAIN MANAGEMENT COMPONENTS
1. **Plan**—This is the strategic portion of supply chain management. A company must have a plan for managing all the resources that go toward meeting customer demand for products or services. A big piece of planning is developing a set of metrics to monitor the supply chain so that it is efficient, costs less, and delivers high quality and value to customers.
2. **Source**—Companies must carefully choose reliable suppliers that will deliver goods and services required for making products. Companies must also develop a set of pricing, delivery, and payment processes with suppliers and create metrics for monitoring and improving the relationships.
3. **Make**—This is the step where companies manufacture their products or services. This includes scheduling the activities necessary for production, testing, packaging, and preparing for delivery. This is by far the most metric-intensive portion of the supply chain, measuring quality levels, production output, and worker productivity.
4. **Deliver**—During this step, companies receive orders from customers, fulfill the orders to deliver the products, and invoice their customers.
5. **Return**—This is typically the most problematic step in the supply chain. Companies must create a network for receiving defective and excess products and support customers who have problems with delivered products.

FIGURE 8.10

Basic Supply Chain Management Components

LO4) INFORMATION SYSTEMS' ROLE IN THE SUPPLY CHAIN

As companies evolve into extended organizations, the roles of supply chain participants are changing. It is now common for suppliers to be involved in product development and for distributors to act as consultants in brand marketing. The notion of virtually seamless information links within and between organizations is an essential element of integrated supply chains.

The primary role of IS in SCM is integrating the information links between functions within a firm—such as marketing, sales, finance, manufacturing, and distribution—and between firms, which allows the smooth, synchronized flow of both information and product between customers, suppliers, and transportation providers across the supply chain. IS integrates planning, decision-making processes, business operating processes, and information sharing for business performance management (see Figure 8.11). Supply chain integration has been credited with giving companies superior supply chain capabilities and increased profits, as was the case with both General Mills and Tesco in 2009. Tesco even credits its supply chain with helping it to achieve a small carbon footprint.[24]

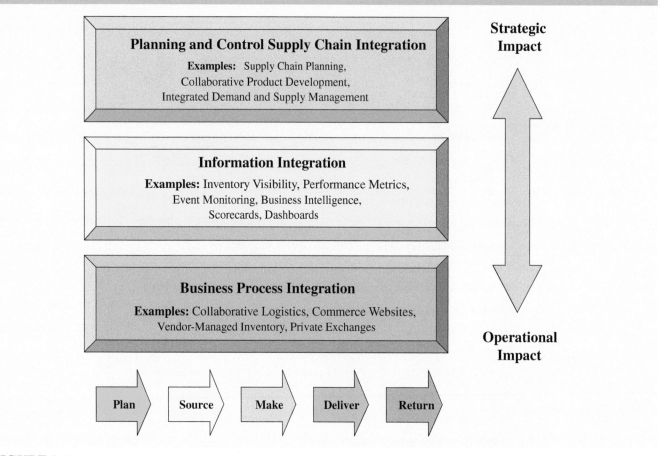

FIGURE 8.11

An Integrated Supply Chain

For example, Canadian Tire, one of Canada's leading hard goods retailers, has successfully used information systems to support its Collaborative Planning, Forecasting, and Replenishment (CPFR) strategy, which calls for increased and proactive collaboration with suppliers to improve forecast accuracy. The goal of this strategy is to enhance customer service, reduce inventory costs, and lower suppliers' costs; this is accomplished through heavy investments in IS. The first step in delivering an IS solution was implementing a demand and fulfillment management system. This system allowed Canadian Tire to move from a reactive, purchase-order-driven replenishment environment to a proactive, time-phased forecasting process in which the company was able to consider consumer demand and generate a time-phased store demand forecast. Building on the success of this system, the company has since created a Web-based environment that allows Canadian Tire to post and share information with its suppliers. As a means of engaging suppliers and building supplier commitment to use this information system, suppliers must agree to a written "collaboration contract" prior to gaining access to the system. In return, Canadian Tire shares and discusses planning, forecasting, and replenishment information with these suppliers. For instance, Canadian Tire shares its aggregate demand forecast representing the demand for 490 stores for a 39-week time horizon, information on purchase orders outstanding, planned orders, and current and projected inventory levels at its distribution centres. Through this Web-based environment, suppliers enter their own item forecast information. When items in the forecast comparison between Canadian Tire's projections and those of its suppliers fall outside acceptable tolerance ranges, the system automatically triggers an email notification so that appropriate action can be taken to prevent or mitigate future disruptions in the delivery and shipment of goods.[25]

Although people have been talking about the integrated supply chain for a long time, it has only been recently that advances in IS have made it possible to bring the idea to life and truly integrate the supply chain. Visibility, consumer behaviour, competition, and speed are a few of the changes resulting from advances in information technology that are driving supply chains (see Figure 8.12).

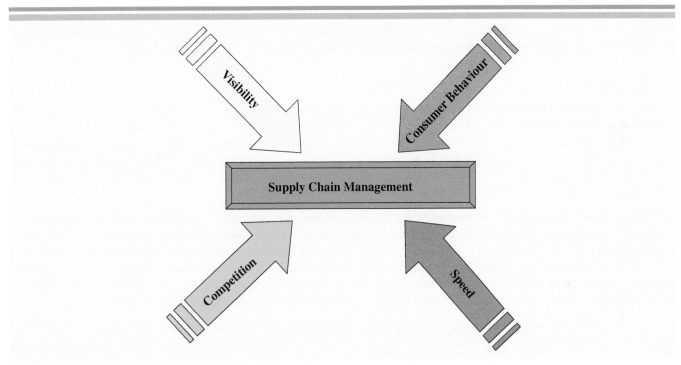

FIGURE 8.12

Factors Driving Supply Chain Management

Visibility

Supply chain visibility is the ability to view all areas up and down the supply chain. Making the change to supply chains requires a comprehensive strategy buoyed by information technology. Organizations can use technology tools that help them integrate upstream and downstream, with both customers and suppliers.

To make a supply chain work most effectively, organizations must create visibility in real time. Organizations must know about customer events triggered downstream, but so must their suppliers and their suppliers' suppliers. Without this information, partners throughout the supply chain can experience a bullwhip effect, in which disruptions intensify throughout the chain. The *bullwhip effect* occurs when distorted product demand information passes from one entity to the next throughout the supply chain. The misinformation regarding a slight rise in demand for a product could cause different members in the supply chain to stockpile inventory. These changes ripple throughout the supply chain, magnifying the issue and creating excess inventory and costs.

Today, IS allows additional visibility in the supply chain. Electronic information flows allow managers to view their suppliers' and customers' supply chains. Some organizations have completely changed the dynamics of their industries because of the competitive advantage gained from high visibility in the supply chain. Dell is the obvious example. The company's ability to get product to the customer and the impact of the economics have clearly changed the nature of competition and caused others to emulate this model.

Consumer Behaviour

The behaviour of customers has changed the way businesses compete. Customers will leave if a company does not continually meet their expectations. They are more demanding because they have information readily available, they know exactly what they want, and they know when and how they want it.

Demand planning systems generate demand forecasts using statistical tools and forecasting techniques. Companies can respond faster and more effectively to consumer demands through supply chain enhancements such as demand planning software. Once an organization understands customer demand and its effect on the supply chain it can begin to estimate the impact that its supply chain will have on its customers and ultimately the organization's performance. The payoff for a successful demand planning strategy can be tremendous. One study found that companies have achieved impressive bottom-line results from managing demand in their supply chains, averaging a 50 percent reduction in inventory and a 40 percent increase in timely deliveries, and companies such as WAM Supply Chain talk about managing demand as being fundamental to managing the supply chain.[26]

Competition

Supply chain management software can be broken down into (1) supply chain planning systems and (2) supply chain execution systems. Both increase a company's ability to compete. *Supply chain planning (SCP) systems* use advanced mathematical algorithms to improve the flow and efficiency of the supply chain while reducing inventory. SCP depends entirely on information for its accuracy. An organization cannot expect the SCP output to be accurate unless correct and up-to-date information regarding customer orders, sales information, manufacturing capacity, and delivery capability is entered into the system.

An organization's supply chain encompasses the facilities where raw materials, intermediate products, and finished goods are acquired, transformed, stored, and sold. These facilities are connected by transportation links, where materials and products flow. Ideally, the supply chain consists of multiple organizations that function as efficiently and effectively as a single organization, with full information visibility. *Supply chain execution (SCE) systems* automate the different steps and stages of the supply chain. This could be as simple as electronically routing orders from a manufacturer to a supplier. Figure 8.13 details how SCP and SCE software relate to the supply chain.

In 2013, the Toyota Camry was second in the list of the American-Made Index from **Cars.com**, where vehicles need to have 75 percent North American content to be eligible. The Camry was deemed almost as American as the Ford F-150. The link between the North American car industry and Japan for parts is huge today due to supply chain management. In 2009, the United States imported more than US$13.8 billion in parts from Japan and Japan imported US$38.3 billion from American companies. In March 2011, when a devastating tsunami and earthquake hit Japan, Toyota in the U.S. operated at 30 percent capacity for weeks, and American manufacturers such as GM and Ford temporarily closed parts plants due to the lack of demand for parts from manufacturers in Japan as it recovered from the disaster.[27]

Speed

During the past decade or more, competition has focused on speed. New forms of servers, telecommunications, wireless applications, and software are enabling companies to perform activities that were once never thought possible. These systems increase the accuracy, frequency, and speed of communication between suppliers and customers, as well as between internal users. Another aspect of speed is a company's ability to satisfy continually changing customer requirements efficiently, accurately, and quickly. Timely and accurate information is more critical to businesses than ever before. Figure 8.14 displays the three factors fostering this change.

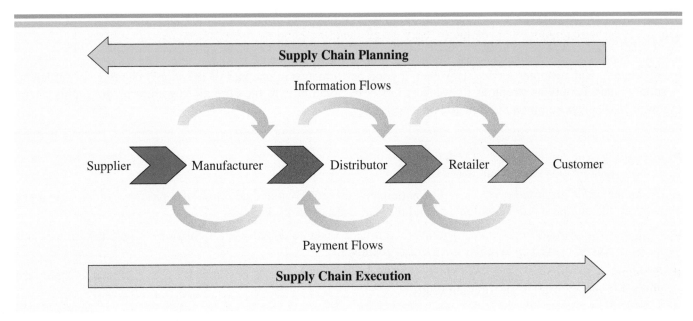

FIGURE 8.13

Supply Chain Planning and Supply Chain Execution Software's Relationship to the Supply Chain

1. Pleasing customers has become something of a corporate obsession. Serving the customer in the best, most efficient, and most effective manner has become critical, and information about issues such as order status, product availability, delivery schedules, and invoices has become a necessary part of the total customer service experience.

2. Information is crucial to managers' abilities to reduce inventory and human resources requirements to a competitive level.

3. Information flows are essential to strategic planning for and deploying resources.

FIGURE 8.14

Three Factors Fostering Speed

LO5 | SUPPLY CHAIN MANAGEMENT SUCCESS FACTORS

To succeed in today's competitive markets, companies must align their supply chains with the demands of the markets they serve. Supply chain performance is now a distinct competitive advantage for companies proficient in the SCM area. GS1 Canada is well aware of this competitive advantage. GS1 Canada is a member organization of Global Standards One (GS1)—a global organization of over 100 members charged with developing standards and solutions to improve supply chain management. GS1 Canada developed the E-Commerce Community Network (ECCnet) Registry, Canada's online, standardized product registry for synchronized data exchange. With this registry, there is now a single point of access in Canada between suppliers and retailers, streamlining and supporting the day-to-day e-commerce requirements of the supply chain. Suppliers input information for each product just one time and the registry facilitates distribution to many customers. Additions and updates are always aligned. Such data synchronization ensures that the right amount of goods is available at the right place and at the right time. To date, more than 20,000 companies—representing billions of dollars of transactions in 22 sectors—have signed on as users of ECCnet Registry.[28]

SCM Success Metrics

SCM metrics can help an organization understand how it's operating over a given time period. Supply chain measurements can cover many areas, including procurement, production, distribution, warehousing, inventory, transportation, and customer service. However, a good performance in one part of the supply chain is not sufficient. A supply chain is only as strong as its weakest link. The solution is to measure all key areas of the supply chain. Figure 8.15 displays common SCM metrics.[29]

- *Back order.* An unfilled customer order. A back order is demand (immediate or past due) against an item whose current stock level is insufficient to satisfy demand.

- *Customer order promised cycle time.* The anticipated or agreed-upon cycle time of a purchase order. It is a gap between the purchase order creation date and the requested delivery date.

- *Customer order actual cycle time.* The average time it takes to actually fill a customer's purchase order. This measure can be viewed on an order or an order-line level.

- *Inventory replenishment cycle time.* Measure of the manufacturing cycle time plus the time included to deploy the product to the appropriate distribution centre.

- *Inventory turns (inventory turnover).* The number of times that a company's inventory cycles or turns over per year. It is one of the most commonly used supply chain metrics.

FIGURE 8.15

Supply Chain Management Metrics

To achieve success such as reducing operating costs, improving asset productivity, and compressing order cycle time, an organization should follow the seven principles of SCM outlined in Figure 8.16.

1. Segment customers by service needs, regardless of industry, and then tailor services to those particular segments.

2. Customize the logistics network and focus intensively on the service requirements and on the profitability of the pre-identified customer segments.

3. Listen to signals of market demand and plan accordingly. Planning must span the entire chain to detect signals of changing demand.

4. Differentiate products closer to the customer, since companies can no longer afford to hold inventory to compensate for poor demand forecasting.

5. Strategically manage sources of supply, by working with key suppliers to reduce overall costs of owning materials and services.

6. Develop a supply chain information technology strategy that supports different levels of decision making and provides a clear view (visibility) of the flow of products, services, and information.

7. Adopt performance evaluation measures that apply to every link in the supply chain and measure true profitability at every stage.

FIGURE 8.16

Seven Principles of Supply Chain Management

Companies using these principles benefit by knowing immediately what is being transacted at the customer end of the supply chain (the end-customer's activities are visible to them). Instead of waiting days or weeks (or months) for the information to flow upstream through the supply chain, with all the pitfalls of erroneous or missing information, suppliers can react in near-real-time to fluctuations in end-customer demand.

Dell Inc. offers one of the best examples of an extremely successful SCM system. Dell's highly efficient build-to-order business model enables it to deliver customized computer systems quickly. As part of the company's continual effort to improve its supply chain processes, Dell deploys supply chain tools to provide global views of forecasted product demand and material requirements, as well as improved factory scheduling and inventory management.

Organizations should study industry best practices and follow organizational change management best practices to improve their chances of successfully implementing SCM systems. The following are keys to SCM success.

Make the Sale to Suppliers   The hardest part of any SCM system is its complexity, because a large part of the system extends beyond the company's walls. Not only will the people in the organization need to change the way they work, the people working for each supplier added to the network must also change. Be sure suppliers are on board with the benefits that the SCM system will provide.

Wean Employees off Traditional Business Practices   Operations people typically deal with phone calls, faxes, and orders scrawled on paper and will most likely want to keep it that way. Unfortunately, an organization cannot disconnect the telephones and fax machines just because it is implementing an SCM system. If the organization cannot convince people that using the software will be worth their time, they will easily find ways to work around it, which will quickly decrease the chances of success for the SCM system.

Ensure the SCM System Supports the Organizational Goals   It is important to select SCM software that gives organizations an advantage in the areas most crucial to their business success. If the organizational goals support highly efficient strategies, be sure the supply chain design has the same goals.

Deploy in Incremental Phases and Measure and Communicate Success   Design the deployment of the SCM system in incremental phases. For instance, instead of installing a complete SCM system across the company and all suppliers at once, start by getting it working with a few key suppliers, and then move on to the other suppliers. Along the way, make sure each step is adding value through improvements in the supply chain's performance. While a big-picture perspective is vital to SCM success, the incremental approach means the SCM system should be implemented in digestible bites, and also measured for success one step at a time.

Be Future-Oriented   The supply chain design must anticipate the future state of the business. Because the SCM system likely will last for many more years than originally planned, managers need to explore how flexible the systems will be when (not if) changes are required in the future. The key is to be certain that the software will meet future needs, not only current needs.[30]

SCM Success Stories

Apple initially distributed its business operations over 16 legacy applications. It quickly realized that it needed a new business model centred on an integrated supply chain to drive performance efficiencies. So it devised an implementation strategy that focused on specific SCM functions—finance, sales, distribution, and manufacturing—that would most significantly help its business. The company decided to deploy leading-edge functionality with a new business model that provided:

- Build-to-order and configure-to-order manufacturing capabilities
- Web-enabled configure-to-order order entry and order status for customers buying directly from Apple at **store.apple.com**
- Real-time credit card authorization
- Available-to-promise and rules-based allocations
- Integration to advanced planning systems

Since its SCM system went live, Apple has experienced substantial benefits in many areas, including measurable improvements in its manufacturing processes, a decrease by 60 percent in its build-to-order and configure-to-order cycle times, and the ability to process thousands of orders daily.[31]

Key supply chain practices that make Apple a top-performing company are linking the supply chain to corporate strategy and creating a lean, end-to-end value chain. It is important that when companies consider these key practices, they also consider them within the performance areas of service, cost, and inventory. Figure 8.17 lists several companies that have considered key SCM practices to drive performance in their operations.

AB World Foods	Improved forecast accuracy.
Avon	Eliminated manual production planning.
Black & Decker	Eliminated manufacturing overtime, expedited shipments, and excess inventory.
Dr Pepper Snapple Group	Mass-produced store-specific plans quickly for its retail customers.
Hallmark Cards	Reduced working stock levels significantly while increasing product availability by 2 percent.
HP	Identified environmental non-conformance with key suppliers.
Knauf Drywall	Increased stock fulfillment rate from 94.6 to 99.2 percent and eliminated out-of-stock situations.
Rite Aid	Balanced their goals of maximizing sales and maintaining supply chain costs.

FIGURE 8.17

Companies Using Supply Chain Management Practices to Drive Operations

Sources: Infor Enterprise Software Solutions, www.infor.com; JDA Software Group, Inc., www.jda.com; Hewlett-Packard Company, www.hp.com.

SUPPLY CHAIN TRENDS

In IBM's study of the future of supply chains, they found a number of key areas that chief supply chain officers will need to deal with in the future and three key areas of supply chain development. SCM is going to struggle with cost containment due to the rapid changes that will continue to happen more quickly than executives can adapt to. SCM executives will also have issues with visibility, where they will see more information than ever before but struggle to find the "right" information. They will continue to need to deal with risk management and the ongoing impacts of globalization. Lastly, SCM systems have created great connectedness between companies and their suppliers, but the connection to their customers is not as good, despite demand-driven mantras. Companies will struggle with customer intimacy (we'll look closer at this in the next chapter).

As far as SCM systems are concerned, they will see development in three key areas: instrumentation, interconnectedness, and intelligence.

Instrumentation

According to the study, the data contained within SCM systems will increasingly be machine-generated by means of RFID-enabled devices and GIS-enabled devices, meters, and actuators. Cargo containers will report contents and pallets will report location (or if they end up in the wrong place).

Interconnectedness

The entire supply chain will be interconnected. Not just the customer, suppliers, and IT systems in general but all the parts, including transportation vehicles, shipping containers, pallets, and even individual products. The system will have pinpoint accuracy in tracking where every individual product in the supply chain is at any moment on a worldwide basis.

Intelligence

Beyond the smart objects in the supply chain that can report where they are at any moment, supply chain software is becoming smarter with more advanced analytics, allowing executives to create better models and make decisions in a more complex world. These systems will be able to help decision makers evaluate alternatives with more complex and dynamic sets of risks and constraints and, in some instances, will make decisions automatically.

Airbus, the world's largest commercial aircraft manufacturer, found it increasingly difficult to track parts as they move from suppliers' warehouses to the company's 18 manufacturing sites. To increase the visibility of the parts in the supply chain, Airbus created a smart sensing system that detects when parts deviate from the intended path. Containers are fitted with RFID tags that contain important information. As parts move from the supplier to Airbus, RFID readers read the tags at important junctures and, if the shipment is in the wrong place or does not contain the right parts, an employee is immediately notified to correct the problem so that there is no impact on manufacturing. This can lead to benefits that include a reduction of human intervention (or required labour) and holding fewer inventories, which nets a reduction in operating costs.

The Army and Air Force Exchange Service (AAFES) sells merchandise and services to those on active duty, national guard and reserve members, retirees, and their families at competitive prices. It also invests two-thirds of its earnings to support morale, welfare, and recreation programs for American military personnel. While looking at ways to reduce expenses, AAFES realized that it served the same market as another peer organization: the Family, Morale and Recreation Command. The two organizations formed a joint team that identified partnering opportunities across procurement, distribution, and transportation. They found success by identifying a number of synergies, eliminating some warehousing facilities and the need to carry US $2.3 million inventory, and reducing labour expenses by US$800,000.[32]

Firms are spending to improve business processes that monitor, manage, and optimize their extended supply chains. Figure 8.18 displays the fastest-growing SCM components that can have the greatest potential impact on an organization's bottom line.[33]

Supply chain event management (SCEM)	Enables an organization to react more quickly to resolve supply chain issues. SCEM software increases real-time information sharing among supply chain partners and decreases their response time to unplanned events. SCEM demand will skyrocket as more and more organizations begin to discover the benefits of real-time supply chain monitoring.
Selling chain management	Applies technology to the activities in the order life cycle from inquiry to sale.
Collaborative engineering	Allows an organization to reduce the cost and time required during the design process of a product.
Collaborative demand planning	Helps organizations reduce their investment in inventory, while improving customer satisfaction through product availability.

FIGURE 8.18

Fast-Growing SCM Components

Another interesting project that involves using new technology for container tracking is the Canada–U.S. Cargo Security Project. This international/regional initiative has the support of Transport Canada and the ports of Halifax and Montreal, as well as American federal and state agencies. The purpose of the project is to provide a rapidly assembled prototype test-bed for elements of cargo container supply chain security. The goal is to develop technology for international container shipping that maintains open borders and facilitates commerce, while improving security practices.[34]

Above all, the system validates and tracks the movement of containerized cargo by using technology to report a container's status and post it to a website in real time where it can be analyzed by authorized agencies. The technology involves using a matchbook-sized "micro-impulse radar detector" that is so sensitive it can sense if a person is moving in a container or if an intruder has cut a hole in the side. A prototype has been developed and there are hopes to improve the system to create a small, lightweight integrated package that could be adopted by the container shipping industry en masse.[35]

OPENING CASE QUESTIONS

Supply Chain Management Inc. Helping Canadians Shop

4. How might SCM Inc. use each of the five basic SCM components?

5. How has SCM Inc. influenced visibility, consumer behaviour, competition, and speed in Walmart Canada's supply chain through the use of information systems and processes?

6. Explain the seven principles of SCM in reference to SCM Inc.'s business model.

7. As Walmart Canada introduces more Supercentres, with both perishable and non-perishable groceries, what changes may need to be made to the SCM processes prior to the introduction of groceries?

SUMMARY OF KEY THEMES

This chapter introduced the concepts of operations management and supply chain management, showcasing how information systems can be used to improve supply chain processes. As the chapter has illustrated, supply chains exist across a variety of sectors and industries. Various examples were given showcasing information systems' ability to help organizations improve their interactions with suppliers, manufacturers, distributors, warehouses, and customers.

As a business student, you should understand the pivotal role that information systems play in facilitating operations management and supply chain processes, and in supporting the basic infrastructure and coordination needed for core business operations to function.

KEY TERMS

Bullwhip effect

Collaborative demand planning

Collaborative engineering

Demand planning systems

Distribution management systems

Global inventory management systems (GIMS)

International Organization for Standardization (ISO)

Inventory management and control systems

Material requirements planning (MRP) systems

Operational planning and control (OP&C)

Operations management (OM)

Production

Production management

Selling chain management

Strategic business units (SBUs)

Strategic planning

Supply chain

Supply chain event management (SCEM)

Supply chain execution (SCE) systems

Supply chain management (SCM)

Supply chain planning (SCP) systems

Supply chain visibility

Tactical planning

Transformation process

Transportation planning systems

Value-added

CLOSING CASE ONE

Rescuing Canada's Health Care Supply Chain

This case illustrates the use of information systems in the health care sector to improve supply chain performance.

When compared with other organizations that rely on and order significant volumes of supplies and materials to run their businesses, hospitals are laggards in the deployment of information systems. Hospitals need a variety of materials, surgical instruments, and medical supplies on a daily basis. According to David Yundt, president and Chief Operation Officer at Hospital Logistics Inc., a for-profit hospital supply and logistics company launched by the University Health Network in Toronto, hospitals have historically focused their energy and capital on direct patient care as opposed to improving the supply chain. This problem is compounded when one considers the tight financial budgets that constrain hospital operations and the general inertia that exists in today's hospitals from moving away from labour-intensive, manual materials management processes. With a highly fragmented hospital industry, there is no developed standard for naming, describing, ordering, and paying for the tens of thousands of products that hospitals use. Further, most hospitals lack integrated computer systems that handle ordering, tracking, and paying for supplies. This leads to poor buying habits by hospitals, because supplies are purchased individually by physicians and clinicians rather than in volume at a greatly reduced contracted price.[36] The advent of RFID has allowed everything from shipping companies to hospitals to reduce costs and overhead by making inefficient business processes obvious. Aberdeen's research shows that 38 percent of enterprises using RFID are doing so to improve the cost, safety, and reliability of managing business processes. Organizations are leveraging RFID to improve the productivity of their workforce, all while simplifying the implementation and ongoing management costs of their networks.[37]

When Walmart announced its RFID strategy in 2003, it was just one of many retailers that had become enamoured of the technology. By placing RFID tags on cases and pallets, companies could keep close tabs on their shipments. In turn, that allowed Walmart and its suppliers to streamline their supply chains and ultimately ensure shelves were always fully stocked.

To the rescue comes CareNET Services Inc., an association of Canadian health care providers and suppliers established in 1990 that promotes, educates, facilitates, and supports using electronic commerce. CareNET's goal is to improve business processes and reduce costs throughout the health care supply chain. In 2014, CareNET membership consisted of over 625 hospitals and long-term-care facilities and 250 suppliers.

CareNET and GS1 Canada formed a strategic alliance partnership to enhance patient safety and increase the adoption of standardized supply chain and e-commerce practices within the Canadian health care sector. Through this partnership, CareNET is on board with GS1 Canada's Supply Chain Standards Project to harmonize hospital supply chains by implementing global standards. The benefits of the project have included not only the modernization of the health care supply chain, but also significant cost savings and patient safety gains. These included reducing supply chain and medication errors, deterring counterfeiting, enabling efficient and effective traceability, maximizing the intellectual capital of Canada's health care professionals, and decreasing production and supply chain costs that allow the redirection of resources toward more patient care. Key public partners of the Supply Chain Standards Project are the governments of Ontario, British Columbia, New Brunswick, Nova Scotia, and Alberta. Deliverables include purchase order and invoice electronic data interchange standards and medical/surgical product bar code standards.[38]

The benefit of standardizing the use of bar codes in hospitals and their positive impact on patient safety gained worldwide exposure during a February 2009 episode of *The Oprah Winfrey Show*,[39] which featured the story of actor Dennis Quaid's infant twins who almost died in 2007 because of an incorrect medication dosage in hospital. On the show, Quaid told Oprah that he thought the media attention garnered by this almost-tragic event helped raise public awareness of the desirability of computerized record keeping and bar coding in hospitals. Dr. Mehmet Oz agreed, and explained how bar coding systems and computerized order entry have dramatically improved how medical practice is conducted in hospitals, eliminating dosage errors. "We're not talking about a little jump here," Oz said. "We're talking about a dramatic shift."

CareNET intends to assist Canada in this dramatic shift by heading off such potentially fatal errors as what happened to Quaid. This is good news for the Canadian health care sector.[40]

Questions

1. What problems plague the delivery of efficient supply chains in the Canadian health care sector?

2. How does CareNET help mitigate these problems?

3. What aspects of the Supply Chain Standards Project help make the health care supply chain more effective and efficient?

4. SCM is experiencing explosive growth. Explain why this statement is true using the above case as an example.

5. Evaluate CareNET's effect on each of the factors that are driving SCM success.

Listerine's Journey

This case shows how information systems can enhance supply chain performance on a global scale.

When you use Listerine antiseptic mouthwash, you are experiencing the last step in a complex supply chain spanning several continents and requiring months of coordination by countless businesses and individuals. You might be astonished to know the amount of resources involved in getting a single bottle of Listerine to a consumer. As raw material transforms into finished product, what will become Listerine travels around the globe and through multiple supply chains and information systems.

The Journey Begins

A farmer in Australia is harvesting a crop of eucalyptus for eucalyptol, the oil found in its leathery leaves. The farmer sells the crop to an Australian processing company, which spends about four weeks extracting the eucalyptol from the eucalyptus.

Meanwhile, in New Jersey, Warner-Lambert (WL) partners with a distributor to buy the oil from the Australian company and transport it to WL's Listerine manufacturing and distribution facility in Lititz, Pennsylvania. The load will arrive at Lititz about three months after the harvest.

At the same time, in Saudi Arabia, a government-owned operation is drilling deep under the desert for the natural gas that will yield the synthetic alcohol that gives Listerine its 43-proof punch. Union Carbide Corp. ships the gas via tanker to a refinery in Texas, which purifies it and converts it into ethanol. The ethanol is loaded onto another tanker, and then transported from Texas through the Gulf of Mexico to New Jersey, where it is transferred to storage tanks and transported via truck or rail to WL's plant. A single shipment of ethanol takes about six to eight weeks to get from Saudi Arabia to Lititz.

SPI Polyols Inc., a manufacturer of ingredients for the confectionery, pharmaceutical, and oral care industries, buys corn syrup from farmers in the Midwest. SPI converts the corn syrup into sorbitol solution, which sweetens and adds bulk to the Cool Mint Listerine. The syrup is shipped to SPI's New Castle, Delaware, facility for processing and then delivered on a tank wagon to Lititz. The whole process, from the time the corn is harvested to when it is converted into sorbitol, takes about a month.

By now the ethanol, eucalyptol, and sorbitol have all arrived at WL's plant in Lititz, where employees test them, along with the menthol, citric acid, and other ingredients that make up Listerine, for quality assurance before authorizing storage in tanks. To mix the ingredients, flow meters turn on valves at each tank and measure out the right proportions, according to the Cool Mint formula developed by WL R&D in 1990. (The original amber mouthwash was developed in 1879.)

Next, the Listerine flows through a pipe to fillers along the packaging line. The fillers dispense the product into bottles delivered continuously from a nearby plastics company for just-in-time manufacturing. The bottles are capped, labelled, and fitted with tamper-resistant safety bands, then placed in shipping boxes that each hold one dozen 500-millilitre bottles. During this process, machines automatically check for skewed labels, missing safety bands, and other problems. The entire production cycle, from the delivery via pipe of the Listerine liquid to the point where bottles are boxed and ready to go, takes a matter of minutes. The line can produce about 300 bottles per minute—a far cry from the 80 to 100 bottles that the line produced per minute before 1994.

Each box travels on a conveyor belt to the palletizer, which organizes and shrink-wraps the boxes into 100-case pallets. Stickers with identifying bar codes are affixed to the pallets. Drivers forklift the pallets to the distribution centre, located in the same Lititz facility, from which the boxes are shipped around the world.

Finally, the journey is completed when a customer purchases a bottle of Listerine at a local drugstore or grocery store. In a few days, the store will place an order for a replacement bottle of Listerine. And so begins the cycle again.[41]

Questions

1. Explain the role of operations management for Warner-Lambert.

2. Summarize SCM and describe Warner-Lambert's supply chain strategy. Diagram the SCM components.

3. Detail Warner-Lambert's three operations management strategies and identify systems it could use to help make strategic decisions.

4. What would happen to Warner-Lambert's business if a natural disaster in Saudi Arabia depletes its natural gas resources?

5. Assess the impact to Warner-Lambert's business if the majority of the eucalyptus crop was destroyed in a natural disaster.

CLOSING CASE THREE

How Levi's Got Its Jeans into Walmart

The case illustrates how information systems can improve supply chain performance between two companies.

People around the world recognize Levi's jeans as an American icon, worn by such movie stars James Dean and Marilyn Monroe. For one reason or another, however, Levi Strauss & Co. failed to keep up with the fast-changing tastes of American teenagers. In particular, it missed the trend to baggy jeans that took hold in the mid-1990s. Levi's sales plummeted from US$7.1 billion in 1996 to US$4.1 billion in 2003, and the company's U.S. market share dropped from 18.7 percent in 1997 to 12 percent in 2003, a huge decline of almost one-third in both dollars and market share. Since that time, things have levelled off; the company reported fiscal 2008 net revenues of US$4.4 billion.[42]

Analyzing and Responding to What Happened

Competition hit Levi Strauss on both the high and low ends. Fashion-conscious buyers were drawn to such high-priced brands as Blue Cult, Juicy, and Seven, which had more fashion cachet than Levi's. On the low end, parents were buying Wrangler and Lee jeans for their kids because on average they cost about $12 less than Levi's Red Tab brand. Wrangler and Lee were also the brands they found at discount retailers such as Walmart, Target, and T. J. Maxx. David Bergen, Levi's chief information officer (CIO), described the company as "getting squeezed," and "caught in the jaws of death."

Levi Strauss's new CEO, Philip A. Marineau, came to the company from PepsiCo in 1999, a year after he had helped PepsiCo surpass Coca-Cola in sales for the first time. Marineau recruited Bergen in 2000 from **Carstation.com**. Marineau quickly realized that turning Levi Strauss around would entail manufacturing, marketing, and distributing jeans that customers demanded, particularly customers at the low end, where the mass market was located.

Bergen was eager to join Marineau's team because of his background in clothing, retailing, and manufacturing with such companies as The Gap and Esprit de Corps in the 1980s. He knew that Marineau's plan to anticipate customer wants would require such up-to-date IT applications as data warehousing, data mining, and CRM systems. He also knew that selling to mass-market retailers would require upgrades to the SCM systems, and he understood that globalization would necessitate standardized ERP systems. It was a challenge any ambitious CIO would covet: designing and installing IT systems that drive and achieve key business initiatives.

Joining Walmart

Walmart was a pioneer in SCM systems, having learned early on that driving costs out of the supply chain would let it offer products to customers at the lowest possible prices, while at the same time ensuring that products the customers demanded were always on the stores' shelves. Becoming one of Walmart's 30,000 suppliers is not easy. Walmart insists that its suppliers do business using up-to-date IT systems to manage the supply chain—not just the supply chain between Walmart and its suppliers, but the supply chains between the suppliers and their suppliers as well. Walmart has strict SCM system requirements that its business partners must meet.

Walmart's requirements presented Levi Strauss with a serious hurdle to overcome because its SCM systems were in bad shape. Executives did not even have access to key information required to track where products were moving in the supply chain. For example, they did not know how many pairs of jeans were in the factory awaiting shipment, how many were somewhere en route, or how many had just been unloaded at a customer's warehouse. According to Greg Hammann, Levi's U.S. chief customer officer, "Our supply chain could not deliver the services Walmart expected."

Bergen created a cross-functional team of key managers from IT, finance, and sales to transform Levi Strauss's systems to meet Walmart's requirements. Their recommendations included network upgrades, modifications to ordering and logistics applications, and data warehouse improvements, among others. Although Bergen realized that about half the changes required to current IT systems to accommodate the state-of-the-art demands of Walmart would be a waste of resources since these systems were being replaced by a new SAP enterprise software system over the next five years, Levi Strauss could not wait for the SAP installation if it wanted Walmart's business now, so it decided to move forward with the changes to the current systems.

The successful transformation of its SCM system allowed the company to collaborate with Walmart. The company introduced its new signature line at Walmart, which sold for around $27 and had fewer details in the finish than Levi's other lines—for example, no trademark pocket stitching or red tab. Walmart wants big-name brands to lure more affluent customers into its stores, while still maintaining the low price points customers have come to expect. Walmart senior vice-president Lois Mikita noted that Walmart "continues to tailor its selection to meet the needs of customers from a cross section of income levels and lifestyles." She also stated that she was impressed with the level of detail Levi Strauss put into its systems transformation efforts to "make the execution of this new launch 100 percent."

Achieving Business Success Through Information Systems

Bergen's changes were a success, and the percentage of products delivered on time quickly rose from 65 to 95 percent primarily because of the updated SCM system. Levi's total sales were also up in the third and fourth quarters of 2003, for the first time since 1996.

In 2003, Levi's appeared on NPD Fashionworld's top 10 list of brands preferred by young women, ending an absence of several years. NPD Group is a research group that tracks apparel and footwear market trends. Marshall Cohen, a senior industry analyst at NPD Fashionworld, noted that Levi's "hadn't been close to that for a while. Teens hadn't gravitated toward Levi's in years. That was incredible. A lot of that has to do with having the right style in the right place at the right time." The improved systems, Cohen noted, also helped the company get the right sizes to the right stores.

Another highly successful information system implemented by Levi Strauss was a digital dashboard whereby executives could display on their PC screens the status of a product as it moved from the factory floor to distribution centres to retail stores. For example, the dashboard could display how Levi's 501 jeans were selling at an individual Kohl's store compared to forecasted sales. "When I first got here I didn't see anything," Hammann said. "Now I can drill down to the product level."

The digital dashboard alerts executives to trends that under the previous systems would have taken weeks to detect. For example, in 2003 Levi Strauss started to ship Dockers Stain Defender pants. Expected sales for the pants were around 2 million pairs. The digital dashboard quickly notified key executives that the trousers were selling around 2.5 million pairs. This information enabled them to adjust production upward in time to ship more pants, meet the increased demand, and avoid lost sales. Levi Strauss also uses the systems to control supply during key seasonal sales periods such as back-to-school and Christmas.

"If I look overconfident, I'm not," Bergen said. "I'm very nervous about this change. When we trip, we have to stand up real quick and get back on the horse, as they say." As if to reinforce Bergen's point, Gib Carey, a supply chain analyst at Bain, noted, "The place where companies do fail is when they aren't bringing anything new to Walmart. Walmart is constantly looking at 'How can I get the same product I am selling today at a lower price somewhere else?'"[43]

Questions

1. How did Levi Strauss achieve business success through the use of SCM?

2. What might have happened to Levi's if its top executives had not supported investments in SCM?

3. David Bergen, Levi's CIO, put together a cross-functional team of key managers from MIS, finance, and sales to transform Levi's systems to meet Walmart's requirements. Analyze the relationships between these three business areas and SCM systems. How can an SCM system help support these three critical business areas?

4. Describe the basic SCM components in reference to Walmart's business model.

5. Explain the future trends of SCM and provide an example of how Levi Strauss could use leading-edge information systems and technologies to increase its business operations.

6. Identify any security and ethical issues that might occur for a company doing business with Walmart.

MAKING BUSINESS DECISIONS

1. Analyzing Dell's Supply Chain Management System

Dell's supply chain strategy is legendary. If you want to build a successful SCM system, your best bet is to model your SCM system after Dell's. In a team, research Dell's SCM strategy on the Web, and create a report discussing any new SCM updates and strategies the company is currently using that were not discussed in this text. Be sure to include a graphical presentation of Dell's current supply chain model.

2. Increasing Information

Galina's is a high-end auction house located in Vancouver. Galina's specializes in selling jewellery, art, and antique furniture primarily from estate sales. The owner, Galina Bucrya, would like to begin offering certain items for auction over the Internet. Galina is unfamiliar with the Internet and not quite sure how to pursue her new business strategy. You are working for Information Inc., a small business consulting company that specializes in e-business strategies. Galina has hired you to help her create her supply chain e-business strategy. Compile a report describing SCM, the potential benefits her company can receive from an SCM strategy, your recommendation for an efficient or effective SCM strategy, and your views on the future of SCM.

3. Increasing Revenues with SCM

Cold Cream is one of the premier beauty supply stores in the Metro Toronto area. People come from all over to sample the store's unique creams, lotions, makeup, and perfumes. The company receives its products from manufacturers around the globe. The company would like to implement an SCM system to help it better understand its customers and their purchasing habits. Create a report summarizing SCM systems and explain how an SCM system can directly influence Cold Cream's revenues.

connect **LEARNSMART** **SMARTBOOK**™

For more information on the resources available from McGraw-Hill Ryerson, go to www.mheducation.ca/he/solutions.

ENDNOTES

1. Supply Chain Management Inc., www.scm3pl.com, accessed August 12, 2011; Jamie Baker, General Manager, SCM Calgary, personal communication, August, 2011; "Walmart Canada Extends Contract with SCM Until 2013," May 1, 2009, www.supplychainnetwork.com/walmart-canada-extends-contract-with-scm-until-2013, accessed August 14, 2011.

2. John Hagerty, "How Best to Measure Our Supply Chain," October 21, 2005, www.oracle.com/newsletters/updates/2005-10-21/supply-chain-management/amr-measure-scm.pdf, accessed July 14, 2010.

3. Norman E. Bowie, ed., *The Blackwell Guide to Business Ethics* (Malden, MA: Blackwell, 2002).

4. Ibid.

5. Geoffrey Colvin, "Managing in the Info Era," *Fortune*, March 6, 2007, pp. F6–F9.

6. Christopher A. Bartlett and Sumantra Ghoshal, "Going Global: Lessons from Late Movers," *Harvard Business Review*, March–April 2000, pp. 132–134.

7. "Package Flow Technologies: Innovation at Work," www.pressroom.ups.com/Fact+Sheets/Package+Flow+Technologies:+Innovation+at+Work, accessed August 6, 2011.

8. James Fitzsimmons and Mona Fitzsimmons, *Service Management: Operations, Strategy, Information Technology*, 7th ed. (New York: McGraw-Hill Irwin, 2011).

9. Ibid.

10. Leo King, "Supermarket to Reduce Fuel Consumption with Driving Analytics," July 30, 2008, www.itworldcanada.com/news/supermarket-to-reduce-fuel-consumption-with-driving-analytics/03528, accessed August 6, 2008.

11. "Volvo CE Raises Customer Service with Optimized Dealer Inventory Management," www.syncron.com/en/Solutions/global-inventory-management, accessed August 8, 2011.

12. "Supply Chain Inventory Management," www.syncron.com/en/Solutions/global-inventory-management, accessed August 8, 2011.

13. "ISO 9000—Quality Management," www.iso.org/iso/iso_catalogue/management_and_leadership_standards/quality_management.htm, accessed August 6, 2011.

14. "ISO 14000—Environmental Management," www.iso.org/iso/iso_catalogue/management_and_leadership_standards/environmental_management.htm, accessed August 6, 2011.

15. www.sei.cmu.edu/cmmi, accessed August 6, 2011.

16. Christopher A. Bartlett and Sumantra Ghoshal, "Going Global: Lessons from Late Movers," *Harvard Business Review*, March/April 2000, pp. 132–134.

17. Sharon Shinn, "What About the Widgets?" *BizEd*, November/December 2004, pp. 30–35.

18. Ibid.

19. James P. Womack, Daniel Jones, and Daniel Roos, *The Machine That Changed the World* (New York: Harper Perennial, 1991).

20. Ibid.

21. Mark Brown, "Target Becomes the Targeted: Walmart and HBC Lock In Vendors, Leaving Target Shelves Bare," *Canadian Business*, April 18, 2013, www.canadianbusiness.com/companies-and-industries/target-becomes-the-targeted, accessed March 23, 2014; Hollie Shaw, *Financial Post*, November 5, 2011, http://business.financialpost.com/2011/05/26/what-we-can-expect-tony-fisher-talks-about-target-canada, accessed March 23, 2014; Marina Strauss, "Target's Canadian Effort Receives a Poor Grade from Shoppers," *Globe and Mail*, August 19, 2013, www.theglobeandmail.com/report-on-business/targets-canadian-effort-receives-a-poor-grade-from-shoppers/article13832051, accessed March 23, 2014; "Sobeys to Supply Target Stores in Canada," *Financial Post*, http://business.financialpost.com/2011/09/23/sobeys-to-supply-target-stores-in-canada, accessed March 23, 2014.

22. Andrew Binstock, "Virtual Enterprise Comes of Age," *InformationWeek*, November 6, 2004.

23. David Barboza and Louise Story, "Toymaking in China—The Mattel Way," July 26, 2007, www.nytimes.com/2007/07/26/business/26toy.html?_r=1&oref=slogin, accessed August 8, 2011; Mitch Betts, "Kinks in the Chain," *Computerworld*, December 17, 2005.

24. Steve Banker, "General Mills and Tesco: How Supply Chain Boosts Profits," February 3, 2010, http://logisticsviewpoints.com/2010/02/03/general-mills-and-tesco-how-supply-chain-boosts-profits, accessed August 8, 2011.

25. G. S. Frodsham, N. J. Miller, and L. A. Mooney, "CPFR Implementation at Canadian Tire and GlobalNetXchange (GNX)," in D. Seifert (ed.), *Collaborative Planning, Forecasting, and Replenishment* (New York: American Management Association [AMACOM], 2003), pp. 140–161.

26. Fred Hapgood, "Smart Decisions," *CIO Magazine*, www.cio.com, accessed August 15, 2001; "Managing Demand," www.wamsystems.com/library/WA%20Systems%20Datasheet%20-%20Managing%20Demand.pdf, accessed August 6, 2011.

27. Grace Ruch, "One Car Two Drivers? Part 3: Auto Parts—The Supply Chain Becomes a Web," July 13, 2011, www.japanmattersforamerica.org/2011/07/us-japan-auto-industry-part-3, accessed August 6, 2011; Kelsey Mayes, "The 2013 American-Made Index," www.cars.com/go/advice/Story.jsp?section=top&subject=ami, accessed March 24, 2014.

28. "About GS1 Canada," www.gs1ca.org/page.asp?LSM=0&intNodeID=1&in.tPageID=380, accessed March 23, 2014; "Who We Represent," www.gs1ca.org/page.asp?LSM=0&intNodeID0=8&intNodeID1=213&int NodeID2=385&intPageID=477, accessed March 23, 2014.

29. "Creating a Value Network," *Wired*, September 2003, p. S13.

30. Ibid.

31. "The e-Biz Surprise," *BusinessWeek*, May 12, 2003, pp. 60–65.

32. "The Smarter Supply Chain of the Future: Insights from the Global Chief Supply Officer Study" (Somers, NY: IBM, 2010), http://www-935.ibm.com/services/us/gbs/bus/html/gbs-csco-study.html, accessed August 25, 2014.

33. Frank Quinn, "The Payoff Potential," and William Copacino, "How to Become a Supply Chain Master," *Supply Chain Management Review*, September 1, 2001; Frank Quinn, "The Payoff Potential in Supply Chain Management," www.ascet.com/documents.asp?grID=197&d_ID=233, accessed July 9, 2010; William Copacino, "How to Become a Supply Chain Master," http://kino.iteso.mx/~genaro/howtobecomeasupplychain-master.doc.

34. "About Canada–United States Cargo Security Project," www.ni2cie.org/cuscsp/about.asp, accessed August 8, 2011.

35. R. G. Edmonson, "The U.S.–Canadian Connection," *The Journal of Commerce*, Volume 7, Issue 9, February 27, 2006, pp. 26–28.

36. J. King, "Health Care's Major Illness," *Computerworld*, May 10, 2004.

37. Mohsen Attaran, "RFID: An Enabler of Supply Chain Operations," *Supply Chain Management: An International Journal*, Volume 12, 2007, pp. 249–257.

38. www.carenet.ca, accessed August 8, 2011.

39. www.oprah.com/slideshow/oprahshow/20090219-tows-dennis-quaid/1, accessed August 8, 2011.

40. CareNet News, May 14, 2009, "Oprah Showcases Bar Coding in Healthcare," www.carenet.ca/news.php?newsitem=9#article9, accessed August 8, 2011.

41. Jennifer Bresnahan, "The Incredible Journey," *CIO Enterprise Magazine*, August 15, 1998, www.cio.com, accessed March 12, 2004; Dave Lowry, "Listerine's Supply Chain," July 3, 2006, http://lowrys-place.blogspot.ca/2006/07/listerine-supply-chain.html, accessed July 7, 2014; "An Introduction to E-Commerce and Distributed Applications," http://labspace.open.ac.uk/mod/resource/view.php?id=370328, accessed July 7, 2014; P. P. Sengupta, "Supply Chain Management: Trends in Logistics and Transportation," December 2009, www.sari-energy.org/PageFiles/What_We_Do/activities/advanced_coal_managment_dec-2009/Presentations/Day2/SupplyChainManagement-PPSengupta.pdf, accessed July 7, 2014.

42. Levi Strauss and Co. annual reports, http://levistrauss.com/investors/annual-report, accessed July 27, 2009; "Levi Strauss & Co. and Mayor Newsom Announce Company's Decision to Remain at Battery St. Headquarters in San Francisco," July 15, 2009, www.oewd.org/Levi_Strauss_and_Co_To_Remain_in_San_Francisco.aspx, accessed August 8, 2011.

43. Kim Girard, "How Levi's Got Its Jeans into Wal-Mart," *CIO Magazine*, July 15, 2003.

9
CHAPTER

Customer Relationship Management

LO 9.1 Explain the difference between customer relationship management and customer relationship management systems.

LO 9.2 Describe the business benefits of customer relationship management and how customer relationship management systems can help achieve those benefits.

LO 9.3 Explain the differences between: operational and analytical customer relationship management; the operational customer relationship management systems used by marketing departments, sales departments, and customer service departments; and the various analytical customer relationship management systems used by organizations.

LO 9.4 Identify and explain best practices in implementing CRM in organizations, including the tracking of common customer relationship management metrics by organizations.

LO 9.5 Describe the benefits of expanding customer relationship management to include suppliers, partners, and employees, as well as other future trends in CRM.

This chapter elaborates upon the concept of *customer relationship management (CRM)* and discusses how information systems can be used to support firms in their interactions with customers. At the simplest level, organizations implement CRM to gain a better understanding of customer needs and behaviours, and information systems provide companies with a new channel to communicate with customers beyond those traditionally used by organizations, such as face-to-face or paper-based methods.

CRM systems are exciting in that they can automate and personalize a company's interactions with customers at significantly reduced costs, and at times most convenient to customers. Further, CRM systems can be used to gather and assimilate data about customers regardless of the method of contact a customer chooses to interact with a company. Assimilating customer data obtained through various channels can help organizations know and better understand their customers and help improve customer relations.

Organizations recognize the importance of maintaining and fostering healthy relationships with customers. Doing so has a direct and positive effect on customer loyalty and retention. This greatly adds to a company's profitability and provides an edge over competitors who fail to foster customer relationships. This is why customer relationship management is important and why you, the business student, need to know this.

As a business student, you must understand the critical relationship your organization will have with its customers. You should also be aware of and recognize the potential value of information systems in facilitating and improving customer relationships. Information systems are at the heart of most CRM strategies used by organizations today. You need to be knowledgeable about the benefits and the various ways CRM systems can be leveraged for organizational success.

Twitter: A Social CRM tool

Social CRM is the use of social media techniques and technologies that enable organizations to engage with their customers. Today we see Social CRM in a number of formats, from sites that use social media identities to allow customers to log into their sites, to allowing customers to easily share information on sites or companies to develop strong analytics about their customers based on their social media interactions. In some instances the use of Social CRM goes beyond the customer and allows organizations to reach out to others, like fans. Social CRM is being implemented by many companies and these companies are using a number of social media platforms including Facebook, Twitter, and Google+ to name a few. Let's examine a few uses of Social CRM by examining how some companies are using Twitter as a Social CRM tool.

Using Twitter to Inform Customers

At a basic level companies like WestJet use Twitter as an opt-in customer email list, but in this case customers opt in by becoming followers. Used effectively, Twitter can boost email marketing performance by turning what was an email list into a viral marketing tool. For example, when WestJet has something to inform customers about, such as the phone scam of March 2014, or offers of deals on flights, followers can retweet this information. Given a critical mass of followers, the news can be widely spread by this means. Used in this way Twitter creates a new marketing channel for reaching, educating, and informing WestJet customers. Using Twitter allows companies like WestJet to inform their customers in an effective and efficient manner.

Using Twitter to Listen to and Engage Customers

Media giant Comcast uses Twitter to begin conversations with influencers. It also uses Twitter to listen, so that it can spot and engage detractors. While some issues can be resolved in 140 characters, others can be directed to other resources like website content or to recruiting customers to participate into interactive channels, such as chat sessions or online communities. Comcast is using Twitter to begin discussions with their customers and then direct the discussion to tools that can finish the discussion when Twitter can't.

Using Twitter to Link and Upsell Customers

A third use of Twitter adds one or more of the following: specialization, active multi-channel integration, and a goal of deeper engagement on other social channels. The idea is to take Twitter beyond a role of a two-way broadcast medium with minimal targeted customer engagement or viral marketing focus. Instead the idea is to use Twitter as a channel that links customers and companies so that more specialized audiences can be reached and followers can be drawn into the communities that are relevant to them. This means communities where the followers can view rich content targeted to them, interact with experts, or even play the role of super-user themselves. Companies may also discover active selling opportunities when they get more targeted and use Twitter as the beginning of an extended, multi-channel discussion of why followers might want to try out a premium service or the latest product offerings. Actuate Corporation accomplishes this with its @BirtyGuy Twitter account that promotes demos, workshops, and happenings on the company's BIRT Exchange, along with news on open source business intelligence.

Another example of this type of Twitter use comes from the world of professional bicycle racing: BMC Racing (@BMCProTeam) uses its Twitter account to allow followers not only to get race results for the BMC Team but also to link to live articles, unique pictures, and live video of races in progress. BMC also promotes its merchandise tent to those followers on the race site and post-race interaction with the members of the team to followers around the world. The use of Twitter to link and upsell is very noticeable when you compare BMC's Twitter use to that of a team like Garmin-Sharp (@Ride_Argyle) which usually only supplies race results and some unique pictures from the race on its account. It is interesting that Garmin-Sharp has a second Twitter account (@Shop_Argyle) to promote its merchandise but its 6,438 followers pale in comparison to the 90,100 followers of the @Ride_Argyle account.

Other Social CRM Uses for Twitter

There are many other ways of leveraging the potential of Twitter as a Social CRM tool. The three cases above let companies see what works for their customers, listen for feedback, create and distribute new offers, and let customers discover valuable links. Twitter permits companies to turn customers into followers and potentially their best promoters.[1]

9.1 CRM FUNDAMENTALS

LO1 INTRODUCTION

Customer relationship management (CRM) involves managing all aspects of a customer's relationship with an organization to increase customer loyalty and retention, and an organization's profitability. As organizations begin to migrate from the traditional product-focused organization toward customer-driven organization, they are recognizing their customers as experts, not just revenue generators. They are quickly realizing that without customers they simply would not exist, so it is critical to ensure customers' satisfaction. In an age when product differentiation is difficult, CRM is one of the most valuable assets a company can acquire. The sooner a company embraces CRM, the better off it will be, and the harder it will be for competitors to steal customers.

When dealing with sick customers, flexibility is key. That is why Walgreens in the United States has made healthy investments in customer service over the past 30 years, originating the drive-through pharmacy and pioneering a network for refilling prescriptions at any location. It should come as no surprise that Walgreens has credited much of its growth to an increased investment in customer service. The company developed new software that can print prescription labels in 14 languages and large-type labels for older patrons. Besides investing in customer-friendly technology, the chain, founded in 1901, is not forgetting the human touch. Walgreens spends more on payroll in stores where performance is below average, increasing the clerk-to-customer ratio, and it runs an online training program for all employees. In view of its recent five-plus years of earnings growth, the prescription appears to be working.

Today, most competitors are simply a mouse click away. The intense competition in today's marketplace forces organizations to switch from sales-focused to customer-focused strategies. Charles Schwab recouped the cost of a multimillion-dollar CRM system in less than two years. The system, developed by Oracle, allows the brokerage firm to trace each interaction with a customer or prospective customer and then provide services (e.g., retirement planning) to each customer's needs and interests. The system provides Schwab with a complete view of its customers, which it uses to differentiate serious investors from non-serious investors. For example, automated deposits from paycheques are a sign of a serious investor, while stagnant balances signal a non-serious investor. Once Schwab is able to make this determination, the firm allocates its resources accordingly, saving money by not investing time or resources in subsidizing non-serious investors.[2]

CRM allows an organization to gain insights into customers' shopping and buying behaviours. Kaiser Permanente, the largest nonprofit integrated health care plan and medical provider in the United States, undertook a CRM strategy to improve and prolong the lives of diabetics. After compiling CRM information on 84,000 diabetic patients, Kaiser found that only 20 percent were getting their eyes checked routinely (diabetes is the leading cause of blindness). As a result, Kaiser enforces rigorous eye-screening programs for diabetics, along with creating support groups for obesity and stress (two more factors that make diabetes even worse). This CRM-based "preventive medicine" approach saves Kaiser money and, more importantly, improves the health of diabetic patients.[3]

Figure 9.1 provides an overview of a typical CRM system for how data flows between customers and the organization itself. Customers contact an organization through various means, including call centres, Web access, email, faxes, and direct sales. A single customer may access an organization multiple times through many different channels. The CRM system tracks every communication between the customer and the organization and provides access to CRM data across different systems, from accounting to order fulfillment. Understanding all customer communications allows the organization to communicate effectively with each customer. It gives the organization a detailed understanding of each customer's products and services regardless of the customer's preferred communication channel. A customer service representative can easily view detailed account data and history through a CRM system when providing information to a customer, such as expected delivery dates, complementary product information, and customer payment and billing information. Understanding the fundamentals of CRM includes the following:

- CRM as a business strategy
- Business benefits of CRM
- The evolution of CRM
- Operational and analytical CRM

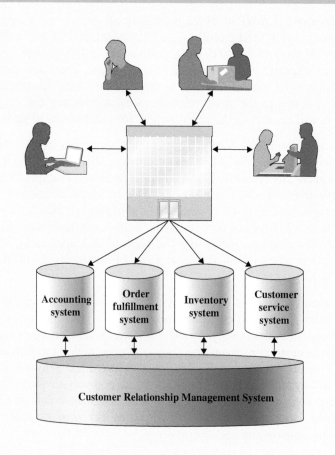

FIGURE 9.1

Customer Relationship Management Overview

CRM as a Business Strategy

ATB Financial is the largest Alberta-based financial institution, with more than 662,000 customers and $33.7 billion in assets. "ATB's challenges in recent years for its marketing organization have been to increase revenue generated by existing customers at any point in the customer cycle; to lengthen median customer tenure with ATB and reduce churn; and to reactivate customers who have already defected," says Bill Laycock, ATB Financial's Director of Marketing Information Services. Laycock's predecessor realized that ATB did not have the type of data required to do the analysis for their marketing campaigns and that they required new systems to move forward with the marketing analysis. Using the data generated by their systems in their SAP environment, ATB is able to target their campaigns so the right customer is introduced to the right product. ATB has this ability because they not only have a complete view of their customers, but also have models of their key products. With each campaign they spend their marketing budget more effectively, gain new customer insights, and do not contact the same customer repeatedly.[4]

It is important to realize that CRM is not just a type of information system, but also a strategy that an organization must embrace on an enterprise level. Although there are many technical and information systems components of CRM, it is actually a process and business goal enhanced by using information technologies. Implementing a CRM system helps an organization identify customers and design specific marketing campaigns tailored to each customer, thereby increasing customer spending. A CRM system also allows an organization to treat customers as individuals, gaining important insights into their buying preferences and behaviours, leading to increased sales, greater profitability, and higher rates of customer loyalty.

Consider Caesars Entertainment—a private gaming corporation that owns and operates casinos, hotels, and multiple golf courses, under a number of brands but primarily Caesars, Horseshoe, and Harrah's. When a "lucky ambassador" greets a Caesars guest at a video-poker machine by name, conveys a happy birthday message, and offers free tickets to a show, luck has nothing to do with it. The moment customers insert their Total Rewards loyalty card into a slot machine, the casino giant's $30-million-plus CRM system reveals every move they have ever made at any of its casino properties. "If you start to have a really unfortunate visit, you start to think, 'Man, that place is really just bad luck,'" said Gary Loveman, Caesars's chairperson and president. "If we see that coming, we can intervene" with perks to soothe the pain of gambling losses. While many companies struggle to employ CRM successfully, gathering massive amounts of data without using it to benefit customers, Caesars builds on its mastery. In the future, its slot machines will spout real-time monetary credits and dinner coupons using new customer-recognition software and hardware, leaving even its losing customers feeling a little luckier.[5]

LO2 | Business Benefits of CRM

Even small business can receive the benefits of CRM with products such as TELUS's Managed CRM. According to Kaiser Mulla-Feroze, Director of Product Marketing at **Salesforce.com**, a hosted and managed solution has a total cost of ownership one-seventh that of an in-house solution. The cost advantage happens because there is no capital outlay required for a hosted CRM solution and payment comes from operational budgets. Typically a return on investment (ROI) is seen within six months.

With Managed CRM the TELUS technical team uploads any of the client's legacy data into the application, although the client will need to "scrub" for stale data. TELUS trains the client prior to the application going live. Also included is a feature that enables clients to synchronize their contact, calendar, and task list information with Microsoft Outlook. The solution will update information automatically so clients can always access their data, even without an Internet connection.[6]

CRM is a business philosophy based on the premise that organizations that understand the needs of individual customers are best positioned to achieve sustainable competitive advantage in the future. Many aspects of CRM are not new to organizations; CRM is simply performing current business better. Placing customers at the forefront of all thinking and decision making requires significant operational and technology changes.

A customer strategy starts with understanding who the company's customers are and how the company can meet strategic goals. Alterna Savings, a Canadian credit union with branches in Ottawa, Toronto, Kingston, Pembroke, and North Bay, understands this and, in response, has rolled out a Web-based system called iSpectrum, developed by Summit Information Systems for the Canadian financial services industry. iSpectrum allows the pulling of client data into one central repository so that Alterna can deliver much faster customer service and improve the customer experience. As opposed to traditional mainframe systems that forced customer service representatives to use several different applications, each with their own password and screen, the iSpectrum empowers front-line staff with easy and quick access to all front-line staff data they need about a customer to help him or her better.[7]

As the business world increasingly shifts from product focus to customer focus, most organizations recognize that treating existing customers well is the best source of profitable and sustainable revenue growth. In this age of e-business, however, an organization is challenged more than ever to satisfy its customers. Figure 9.2 displays the benefits derived by an organization from a CRM strategy beyond increasing customer revenues.

Better customer service	Ability of sales staff to close deals faster
Improved call centre efficiency	Simplification of marketing and sales processes
Ability to cross-sell products more effectively	Ability to discover new customers

FIGURE 9.2

Benefits of a Customer Relationship Management System

CCL Industries, a world leader in the development of specialty packaging and labelling solutions for the consumer products and health care industries, recognizes the importance of adopting a CRM strategy. CCL Industries was founded in Toronto in 1951, initially under the name of Connecticut Chemicals Limited, with a single production line and three people packaging aerosol products, which were at that time new products. Since then, the company has grown substantially. Its major customers include such companies as Clorox, Dow, Gillette, Nabisco, Pfizer, Procter & Gamble, and Unilever. Part of CCL's success is its adoption of a long-term view toward building customer relationships and managing them fairly and effectively. Relationships are seen as a vital corporate asset. As part of its CRM strategy, the company created an e-commerce portal to increase its ability to interact with customers more effectively, and also to differentiate CCL from its competitors. However, CCL does not view a CRM system as a substitute for its ability to bond with customers. Rather, the company views CRM systems as something that can add value and should be used to complement and strengthen more traditional forms of CRM—not replace them.[8]

An organization can find its most valuable customers by using a formula that industry insiders call RFM for *recency*, *frequency*, and *monetary value*. In other words, an organization must ask and track the answers to the following questions:

■ How recently has a customer purchased items? (Recency)

■ How frequently does a customer purchase items? (Frequency)

■ How much does a customer spend on each purchase? (Monetary value)

Once a company has gathered this initial CRM data, it can compile the data to identify patterns and create marketing campaigns, sales promotions, and services to increase business. For example, if Ms. Smith buys only at the height of the season, then the company should send her a special offer during the off-season. If Mr. Jones always buys software but never computers, the company should offer him free software with the purchase of a new computer.

The CRM technologies discussed in this chapter can help organizations find answers to RFM and other tough questions, such as who their best customers are and which of their products are the most profitable.

LO3 | The Evolution of CRM

Knowing the customer, especially knowing the profitability of individual customers, is highly lucrative in the financial services industry. Its high transactional nature has always afforded the financial services industry more access to customer data than other industries have, but it has embraced CRM technologies only recently.

Barclays Bank, a leading financial services company operating worldwide, with about 48 million customers in 50 countries and 2013 revenues of £28.1 billion, invested in CRM systems to help it gain valuable insights into its business and customers.

With the new CRM system, Barclays managers are better able to predict the financial behaviour of individual customers and assess whether a customer is likely to pay back a loan in full and within the agreed-upon period. This helps Barclays manage its profitability with greater precision because it can charge its customers a more appropriate rate of interest based on the results of the customer's risk assessment. The company uses a sophisticated customer segmentation system to identify groups of profitable customers, both on a corporate and on a personal level, which it can then target for new financial products. Barclays also reduced the time to process applications by 15 to 30 minutes, and increased their conversion rate from 40 percent to 45 percent.[9]

There are three phases in the evolution of CRM: (1) reporting, (2) analyzing, and (3) predicting. **CRM reporting systems** help organizations identify their customers across other applications. **CRM analysis systems** help organizations segment their customers into categories such as best and worst customers. **CRM predicting systems** help organizations make predictions regarding customer behaviour, such as which customers are at risk of leaving (see Figure 9.3).

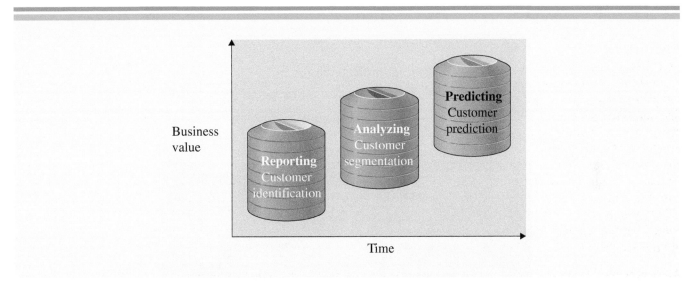

FIGURE 9.3

The Evolution of CRM Abilities

Both operational and analytical CRM systems can assist in customer reporting (identification), customer analysis (segmentation), and customer prediction. Figure 9.4 highlights a few of the important questions an organization can answer using CRM systems.

Operational and Analytical CRM

CRM is being used by banks to treat their customers better. Sun National Bank used Microsoft Dynamics CRM to increase cross-selling rates by 20 percent, reduce time to approve loans by 80 percent, and reduce the time to market for new products by 67 percent. MKB Bank also used Microsoft Dynamics CRM to reduce service times by 25 percent, decease customer churn by 5 percent, and increase the profit of the most valuable customers by 20 percent.[10]

The two primary components of a CRM strategy are operational CRM and analytical CRM. **Operational CRM** supports traditional transactional processing for day-to-day front-office operations or systems that deal directly with customers. **Analytical CRM** supports back-office operations and strategic analysis, and includes all systems that do not deal directly with the customers. The primary difference between operational CRM and analytical CRM is the direct interaction between the organization and its customers. Figure 9.5 provides an overview of operational CRM and analytical CRM.

Reporting: What Happened?	Analyzing: Why Did It Happen?	Predicting: What Will Happen?
What is the total revenue by customer?	Why did sales not meet forecasts?	What customers are at risk of leaving?
How many units did we manufacture?	Why was production so low?	What products will the customer buy?
Where did we sell the most products?	Why did we not sell as many units as last year?	Who are the best candidates for a mailing?
What were total sales by product?	Who are our customers?	What is the best way to reach the customer?
How many customers did we serve?	Why was customer revenue so high?	What is the lifetime profitability of a customer?
What are our inventory levels?	Why are inventory levels so low?	What transactions might be fraudulent?

FIGURE 9.4

Examples of Reporting, Analyzing, and Predicting Behaviours

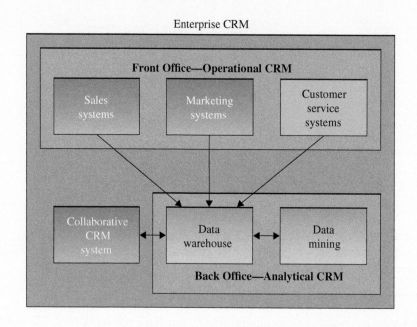

FIGURE 9.5

Components of an Enterprise CRM

USING INFORMATION TO DRIVE OPERATIONAL CRM

Figure 9.6 displays the different information systems that marketing, sales, and customer service departments can use to perform operational CRM.

Marketing CRM

Companies are no longer trying to sell one product to as many customers as possible; instead, they are trying to sell one customer as many products as possible. Marketing departments are able to adapt to this new way of doing business by using CRM systems that allow them to gather and analyze customer data to deploy successful marketing campaigns. In fact, a marketing campaign's success is directly proportional to the organization's ability to gather and analyze the right data. The three primary operational CRM systems a marketing department can implement to increase customer satisfaction are:

1. List generators

2. Campaign management systems

3. Cross-selling and upselling strategies

Marketing	Sales	Customer Service
1. List generator	1. Sales management	1. Contact centre
2. Campaign management	2. Contact management	2. Web-based self-service
3. Cross-selling and upselling	3. Opportunity management	3. Call scripting

FIGURE 9.6

Components of an Operational CRM

List Generators *List generators* compile customer data from a variety of sources and segment the data for different marketing campaigns. Data sources include website visits, website questionnaires, online and offline surveys, flyers, toll-free numbers, current customer lists, and so on. After compiling the customer list, an organization can use criteria to filter and sort the list for potential customers. Filter and sort criteria can include such things as household income, education level, and age. List generators provide the marketing department with a solid understanding of the type of customer it needs to target for marketing campaigns.

Campaign Management Systems *Campaign management systems* guide users through marketing campaigns performing such tasks as campaign definition, planning, scheduling, segmentation, and success analysis. These advanced systems can even calculate quantifiable ROI results for each campaign, and track the results to analyze and understand how the company can fine-tune future campaigns.

Cross-Selling and Upselling Strategies Two key sales strategies a marketing campaign can deploy are cross-selling and upselling. *Cross-selling* is selling additional products or services to a customer. *Upselling* is increasing the value of the sale. For example, McDonald's performs cross-selling by asking customers if they would like an apple pie with their meal. It performs upselling by asking customers if they would like large drink instead of a medium drink with their meals. CRM systems offer marketing departments all kinds of data about their customers and their products, which can help those departments identify cross-selling and upselling marketing campaigns.

Sol Melia is the largest Spanish hotel company with hotels in Europe, Latin America, and the Caribbean. It takes advantage of its CRM not only to enable it to contact its customers more often with more products, but also to increase its customer loyalty rates in the process. Sol Melia uses its CRM to cross-sell and upsell its products in the form of longer stays, more stays, and higher revenue stays by guests. This is accomplished because the CRM allows Sol Melia to contact its customers more often and in more personalized ways.[11]

Sales CRM

Sales departments were the first to begin developing CRM systems. Sales departments had two primary reasons to track customer sales data electronically. First, sales representatives were struggling with the overwhelming amount of customer account data they were required to maintain and track. Second, companies were struggling with the issue that much of their vital customer and sales data remained in the heads of their sales representatives. One of the first CRM components built to help address these issues was the sales force automation component. ***Sales force automation (SFA)*** is a system that automatically tracks all of the steps in the sales process. SFA products focus on increasing customer satisfaction, building customer relationships, and improving product sales by tracking all sales data.

Playground, an Intrawest company headquartered in Vancouver, manages the sales and marketing campaigns for luxury ownership opportunities in major resorts worldwide, including Whistler Blackcomb and Mont Tremblant. Playground took advantage of a CRM solution developed by Maximizer Software to support Playground's sales activities. Playground uses Maximizer's CRM technology to monitor the results of marketing plans, track prospects, build relationships, manage customers, complete sales, and gauge the accuracy and activity of the sales pipeline. The tool is used to control logistics of Playground's sales and marketing offices that are set up at each resort site. Playground employees like the CRM system since it is easy to learn and easy to tailor to the way Playground does its business. This frees Playground employees from having to fiddle with and manipulate the CRM system, and allows them to concentrate on the business of selling.[12]

The three primary operational CRM technologies a sales department can implement to increase customer satisfaction are:

1. Sales management CRM systems

2. Contact management CRM systems

3. Opportunity management CRM systems

Sales Management CRM Systems Figure 9.7 depicts the typical sales process, which begins with an opportunity and ends with billing the customer for the sale. Leads and potential customers are the lifeblood of all sales organizations, whether the products they are peddling are computers, clothing, or cars. How the leads are handled can make the difference between revenue growth or decline. ***Sales management CRM systems*** automate each phase of the sales process, helping individual sales representatives coordinate and organize all of their accounts. Features include calendars to help plan customer meetings, alarm reminders signalling important tasks, customizable multimedia presentations, and document generation. These systems even have the ability to provide an analysis of the sales cycle and calculate how each individual sales representative is performing during the sales process.

Contact Management CRM Systems A ***contact management CRM system*** maintains customer contact information and identifies prospective customers for future sales. Contact management systems include such features as maintaining organizational charts, detailed customer notes, and supplemental sales information. For example, a contact management system can take an incoming telephone number and display the caller's name along with notes detailing previous conversations. This allows the sales representative to answer the telephone and say, "Hi Sue, how is your new laptop working? How was your vacation to the Yukon?" without receiving any reminders of such details first from the customer. The customer feels valued since the sales associate knows her name and even remembers details of their last conversation!

With US$31 billion in sales, 3M is a leader in health care, safety, electronics, telecommunications, office, and consumer markets. The company began to focus on streamlining and unifying its sales processes with the primary goals of better customer segmentation and more reliable lead generation and qualification. To achieve these goals, the company implemented a CRM system and soon found itself receiving the following benefits:

- Cutting the time it takes to familiarize sales professionals with new territories by 33 percent
- Increasing management's visibility of the sales process
- Decreasing the time it takes to qualify leads and assign sales opportunities by 40 percent

Opportunity Management CRM Systems ***Opportunity management CRM systems*** target sales opportunities by finding new customers or companies for future sales. Opportunity management systems determine potential customers and competitors and define selling efforts, including budgets and schedules. Advanced opportunity management systems can even calculate the probability of a sale, which can save sales representatives significant time and money when attempting to find new customers. The primary difference between contact management and opportunity management is that contact management deals with existing customers and opportunity management deals with new customers. Figure 9.8 displays six pointers that a sales representative can use to increase prospective customers and that should be incorporated into a CRM.

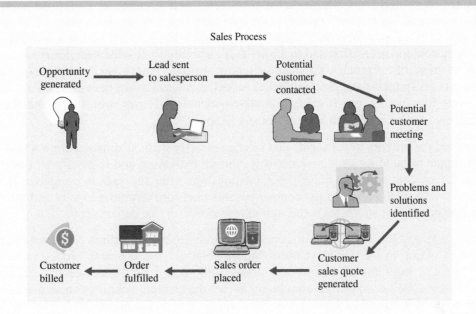

FIGURE 9.7

Overview of the Sales Process

1. Get their attention	If you have a good prospect, chances are that he or she receives dozens of offers from similar companies. Be sure your first contact is professional and gets your customer's attention.
2. Value their time	When you ask for a meeting, you are asking for the most valuable thing a busy person has—time. In exchange for your customer's time you need to provide something of value to the customer.
3. Over-deliver	If you offer a free DVD in exchange for a meeting, bring a box of microwave popcorn along with the movie. Little gestures like these tell customers that you not only keep your word, but also can be counted on to over-deliver.
4. Contact frequently	Find new and creative ways to contact your prospective customers frequently. Starting a newsletter and sending out a series of industry updates are excellent ways to keep in contact and provide value.
5. Generate a trustworthy mailing list	If you are buying a mailing list from a third party, be sure that the contacts are genuine prospects, especially if you are offering an expensive gift. Be sure that the people you are meeting have the power to authorize a sale.
6. Follow up	One of the most powerful prospecting tools is a simple thank-you note. Letting people know that their time was appreciated might even lead to additional referrals.

FIGURE 9.8

Pointers for Gaining Prospective Customers

Customer Service CRM

Andy Taylor became president of Enterprise, his father's US$76 million rental-car company, in 1980. Today, it is the largest in North America, with US$15.4 billion in revenue. How has he kept customer service a priority? By quantifying it. Every month, Enterprise measures customer satisfaction by conducting telephone surveys with hundreds of thousands of its customers. These survey results are used to create an Enterprise Service Quality index (ESQi) for each local branch. That is, each branch earns a ranking based on the percentage of its customers who say they were completely satisfied with their last Enterprise experience. ESQi is one of many ways in which Enterprise reminds itself to put customers' needs first and to ensure that its ability to provide superior customer service is never compromised. For example, if a branch's satisfaction scores are low, employees, even vice-presidents, cannot be promoted. The result is self-propagating. Seeking better scores, managers make better hires. And because Enterprise promotes almost solely from within, nearly every executive—including Taylor, who started out washing cars—has a front-line understanding of what it takes to keep customers happy.[13]

Sales and marketing are the primary departments that interact directly with customers before a sale. Most companies recognize the importance of building strong relationships during marketing and sales efforts; however, many fail to realize the importance of continuing to build these relationships after the sale is complete. It is actually more important to build post-sale relationships if the company wants to ensure customer loyalty and satisfaction. The best way to implement post-sale CRM strategies is through the customer service department.

Bell Canada, Canada's largest telecommunications company with almost 28 million customer connections, also has a CRM success story. Prior to the CRM solution implementation, the business processes and methods being employed did not fulfill or meet any of the business needs. Bell needed a customer-centric strategy that supported the company requirements. Bell encountered a problem, in that the existing solutions created a lot of extra work for employees, which resulted in decreased employee satisfaction and posed numerous problems. In addition, Bell required the front- and back-end operations of its shared services centre to be integrated. The solution was a customer service CRM and support initiatives. What did Bell ultimately witness? The result was increased and better customer service from employees along with internal efficiencies. The CRM enabled a reduction in the total case volume.[14]

One of the primary reasons a company loses customers is bad customer service experiences. Providing outstanding customer service is a difficult task, and many CRM systems are available to assist organizations with this important activity.

The three primary operational CRM systems a customer service department can implement to increase customer satisfaction are:

1. Contact centres

2. Web-based self-service systems

3. Call scripting systems

Contact Centres   Knowledge-management software, which helps call centres put consistent answers at customer service representatives' fingertips, is often long on promise and short on delivery. The problem? Representatives have to take time out from answering calls to input things they have learned—putting the "knowledge" in knowledge management.

Brad Cleveland, who heads the Incoming Calls Management Institute, said, "Software is just a tool. It doesn't do any good unless people across the organization are using it to its potential." To encourage customer service representatives to use such systems in ways they were supposed to be used, companies need to create incentives. Take, for example, Sharp Electronics. When it was building its own call management system, to encourage use of the final system, the company ensured Sharp's front-line representatives helped build the system from scratch. Further, the company tied representatives' compensation and promotions to the system's use. As a result, the customer call experience at Sharp has improved dramatically.[15]

A *contact centre (call centre)* is where customer service representatives (CSRs) answer customer inquiries and respond to problems through a number of different customer touch points. A contact centre is one of the best assets a customer-driven organization can have because maintaining a high level of customer support is critical to obtaining and retaining customers. Numerous systems are available to help an organization automate its contact centres. Figure 9.9 highlights a few of the features available in contact centre systems.

Automatic call distribution	A phone switch routes inbound calls to available agents.
Interactive voice response (IVR)	Directs customers to use touch-tone phones or keywords to navigate or provide information.
Predictive dialling	Automatically dials outbound calls, and when someone answers the call is forwarded to an available agent.

FIGURE 9.9

Common Features Included in Contact Centres

Contact centres also track customer call history along with problem resolutions—this history is critical for providing a comprehensive customer view to the CSR. CSRs who can quickly understand all of a customer's products and issues provide tremendous value to the customer and the organization. Nothing makes frustrated customers happier than not having to explain their problems to yet another CSR.

Computershare is a world leader in transfer agency and share registration, employee equity plans, proxy solicitation, and stakeholder communications. To perform these tasks better, Computershare wanted to improve customer satisfaction and agent empowerment by increasing evaluator and agent confidence in an overall quality program at their contact centres. To do this they required two things: a clearer and more holistic skill evaluation for accurately gauging improvements, and the establishment of a "coach and mentor" system. Using call recordings at their contact centres along with a quality management program, Computershare was better able to communicate with it agents about their individual performance and coach them to better performance. This has resulted in customer satisfaction rates of 90+ percent on a month-to-month basis, which is 3 to 7 percent better than the industry average and well above the rates prior to the implementation.[16]

Web-Based Self-Service Systems *Web-based self-service systems* allow customers to use the Web to find answers to their questions or solutions to their problems. FedEx and UPS both use Web-based self-service systems to allow customers to track their own packages without having to talk to a CSR. Their customers can simply log on to their websites and enter their tracking number. The site quickly displays the exact location of the package and the estimated delivery time.

Another great feature of Web-based self-service is chat buttons, which allow customers to simply click on a link and chat with a CSR via the Internet. Powerful customer-driven features like these add tremendous value to any organization by providing customers with real-time information.

Call Scripting Systems *Call-scripting systems* access organizational databases that track similar issues or questions and automatically generate the details for the CSR, who can then relay them to the customer. The system can even provide a list of questions that the CSR can ask the customer to determine the potential problem and resolution. This feature helps CSRs answer difficult questions quickly while also presenting a uniform image so that two different customers do not receive two different answers.

U.S. Bioservices provides reimbursement information about pharmaceutical products to patients and health care professionals. The company supports inquiries for pharmaceutical companies and receives over 30,000 customer calls per month. Originally, the company had a data file for each patient and for each pharmaceutical company. This inefficient process resulted in a single patient potentially having a different data file for each pharmaceutical company of which she or he was a client. To answer customer questions, a CSR had to download each customer file, causing tremendous inefficiencies and confusion. The company implemented a CRM system with a call scripting feature to alleviate the problem and provide its CSRs with a comprehensive view of every customer, regardless of the pharmaceutical company.[17]

USING INFORMATION TO DRIVE ANALYTICAL CRM

Maturing analytical CRM and behavioural modelling systems help numerous organizations move beyond legacy benefits, such as enhanced customer service and retention, to systems that can truly improve business profitability. Unlike operational CRM, which automates call centres and sales forces with the aim of enhancing customer transactions, analytical CRM solutions are designed to dig deep into a company's historical customer data and expose patterns of behaviour on which a company can capitalize. Analytical CRM is primarily used to enhance and support decision making, and works by identifying patterns in customer data collected from the various operational CRM systems.

For many organizations, the power of analytical CRM solutions provides tremendous managerial opportunities. Depending on the specific solution, analytical CRM tools can slice and dice customer data to create made-to-order views of customer value, spending, product affinities, percentile profiles, and segmentations. Modelling tools can identify opportunities for cross-selling, upselling, and expanding customer relationships.

Personalization occurs when a website knows enough about a person's likes and dislikes that it can fashion offers more likely to appeal to that person. Many organizations are now using CRM to create rules and templates that marketers can use to personalize customer messages.

The information produced by analytical CRM solutions helps companies make decisions about how to handle customers based on the value of each and every one. Analytical CRM can reveal information about which customers are worth investing in, which should be serviced at an average level, and which should not be invested in at all. For example, at the Bank of Montreal (BMO), a customer knowledge database was used by a statistical modelling group to calculate monthly customer economic profit. When the group ran their analysis to determine the relationship between "customer loyalty" and "customer spending potential" to identify potential new customers, BMO discovered that there were strategic benefits in growing existing customer relationships for new business rather than trying to find brand-new customers. David Moxley, the vice-president overseeing BMO's customer knowledge management operation, commented, "We were pleased at how many additional wallet opportunities existed within our customer lists. In most cases, we found that we needed to acquire our own customers."[18]

Data gained from customers can also reveal information about employees. Wachovia Bank (now part of Wells Fargo & Company) in the United States surveyed customers for feedback on their service experience. It asked about individual employees and used those answers in one-on-one staff coaching. A 20-minute coaching session at one branch made clear how this feedback—each customer surveyed rated 33 employee behaviours—can improve service. The branch manager urged an employee to focus on sincerity rather than on mere friendliness, to "sharpen her antenna" so she would listen to customers more intuitively, and to slow down rather than hurry up. That focus on careful, sincere, intuitive service paid off. Wachovia held the top score among banks in the American Customer Satisfaction Index since 2001 and continues high ratings as part of Wells Fargo & Company.[19]

Analytical CRM relies heavily on data warehousing systems and business intelligence to glean insights into customer behaviour. (*Note:* Data warehousing and business intelligence are more fully described in Chapter 4.) These systems quickly aggregate, analyze, and disseminate customer information throughout an organization. Figure 9.10 displays a few examples of the kind of information insights analytical CRM can help an organization gain.

UPS's data-intensive environment is supported by a database, consisting of hundreds of terabytes of data related to its analytical CRM tool. The shipping company's goal is to create one-to-one customer relationships, and it uses tools that allow it let customers tailor views of such things as shipment history, and receive notices when a package arrives or is delayed.[20]

Data warehouses provide businesses with information about their customers and products that was previously impossible to locate, and the resulting payback can be tremendous. Organizations rely on business intelligence to provide them with hard facts that can determine everything from which type of marketing and sales campaign to launch, to which customers to target, at what time. Using CRM along with business intelligence allows organizations to make better, more informed decisions and to reap amazing unforeseen rewards.

Give customers more of what they want	Analytical CRM can help an organization go beyond the typical "Dear Mr. Smith" salutation. An organization can use its analytical CRM information to make its communications more personable. For example, if staff knows a customer's shoe size and preferred brand they can notify the customer that there is a pair of size 12 shoes set aside to try on the next time the customer visits the store.
Find new customers similar to your best customers	Analytical CRM might determine that an organization does business with women 35 to 45 years old who drive SUVs and live within 50 kilometres of a certain location. The company can then find a mailing list that highlights this type of customer for potential new sales.
Find out what the organization does best	Analytical CRM can determine what an organization does better than its competitors. For example, if a restaurant caters more breakfasts to mid-sized companies than its competition does, it can purchase a specialized mailing list of mid-sized companies in the area and send them a mailing that features the breakfast catering specials.
Beat competitors to the punch	Analytical CRM can determine sales trends allowing an organization to offer the best customers deals before the competition has a chance to. For example, a clothing store might determine its best customers for outdoor apparel and send them an offer to attend a private sale right before the competition runs its outdoor apparel sale.
Reactivate inactive customers	Analytical CRM can highlight customers who have not done any business with the organization in a while. The organization can then send them a personalized letter along with a discount coupon. It will remind them of the company and may help spark a renewed relationship.
Let customers know they matter	Analytical CRM can determine what customers want and need, so an organization can contact them with this information. Anything from a private sale to a reminder that the car is due for a tuneup is excellent customer service.

FIGURE 9.10

Analytical CRM Information Examples

Loyalty Management Group Canada, a Toronto-based company, runs the Air Miles rewards program used by over half of Canadian households. With their plastic Air Miles cards in hand, consumers can get their cards scanned at cash registers of participating retailers to gain reward points that later can be redeemed for "free" travel and other reward offerings. The key to the rewards program is using analytical CRM to research how Air Miles cards are used for consumer preferences and spending habits. One key source of data is the initial signup form where members quite freely identify their private data, including age, address, family size, and total household income. These data are a treasure trove for such Air Miles corporate sponsors as Shell, Holt Renfrew, Safeway, Rona, Bank of Montreal, and the Liquor Control Board of Ontario, most of whom had never had access to such personal data. Another key source of data occurs every time a customer makes a purchase. Merging these two sources of customer data can help corporate sponsors make business decisions, such as deciding where to locate new stores and how to maximize sales to each customer. It also provides a means for sponsors to peek at one another's data and to share customer insights. Loyalty Management is, in essence, in the customer data mining business. The company operates on the principle that the more you know about a customer, the better you can service that customer.[21]

In a search for brand authenticity and using CRM to alter customer purchasing behaviour, the Air Miles program's social change division introduced a new program in 2102 that teams Air Miles up with public companies to encourage a sustained shift toward more eco-friendly consumer behaviour. Examples are:

■ In St. John's, Newfoundland, the transit authority will give its customers Air Miles every time they ride the Metrobus, using smart card technology.

■ In British Columbia, FortisBC, the province's major natural gas utility, will offer residential customers Air Miles for signing up for renewable gas, a costlier but more environmentally sustainable alternative.

The social responsibility agenda is not new for Air Miles, as it has been partnering across Canada to promote everything from the use of public transit to energy efficiency. The new program is already proving it works and is looking to change behaviours in some cases.

- At the Toronto Transit Commission a program that rewarded riders with Air Miles for purchasing annual passes rather than monthly passes lifted annual pass sales by 57 percent.

- At Sobey's an energy efficiency program that used Air Miles to increase sales of compact fluorescent light (CFL) bulbs resulted in a year-over-year increase in CFL sales of 200 percent.[22]

OPENING CASE QUESTIONS

Twitter: A Social CRM Tool

1. Summarize the evolution of CRM and provide an example of a reporting, analyzing, and predicting questions that a company using a Social CRM tool might ask its customers or followers.

2. How has BMC Racing effectively used Social CRM systems to improve its operations? What other CRM systems could a company like WestJet employ to improve its operations?

3. Define analytical CRM. How could a company effectively use analytical CRM in the context of using Social CRM? How important is analytical CRM to companies using Social CRM?

4. What is the difference between customer data, customer information, and business intelligence?

9.2   CRM BEST PRACTICES AND TRENDS

LO4) IMPLEMENTING CRM

Brother International Corporation experienced skyrocketing growth in its sales of multifunction centres, fax machines, printers, and labelling systems in the late 1990s. Along with that came a tremendous increase in customer service calls. When Brother failed to answer the phone fast enough, product returns started to increase. The company responded by increasing call centre capacity, and the rate of returns began to drop. However, Dennis Upton, CIO of Brother International, observed that all the company was doing was answering the phone. He quickly realized that the company was losing a world of valuable market intelligence about existing customers from all those telephone calls. The company decided to deploy SAP's CRM solution. The 1.8 million calls Brother handled dropped to 1.57 million, which reduced call centre staff from 180 agents to 160 agents. Since customer demographic data are now stored and displayed on the agent's screen based on the incoming telephone number, the company has reduced call duration by an average of one minute, saving $600,000 per year.[23]

To achieve such success in implementing CRM, organizations should follow best practices (see Figure 9.11). These include clearly communicating the CRM strategy, defining data needs and flows, building an integrated view of the customer, implementing in iterations, and achieving scalability for organizational growth.

The five best practices illustrated in Figure 9.11 align with Gartner Inc.'s eight building blocks of CRM. Gartner Inc. created this CRM framework, or map, after analyzing several hundred organizations over the years. The building blocks are meant to help organizations see the big picture of CRM, identify their business cases, and plan out successful implementations. The building blocks are summarized as follows:

1. *Creating a CRM vision that provides a "big picture" of what the customer-centric organization should look like.* The vision outlines the organization's value proposition in implementing CRM, clearly identifies the customers with whom the organization wants a relationship, the importance and benefits of CRM to the company's overall business strategy, and the nature of the customer experience that is desired.

2. *Defining and weaving a CRM strategy that aligns with broader marketing and sales strategies, and informs operational and production strategies.* The company's overall business strategy should drive and coordinate the interactions between all these strategies.

3. *Understanding and engaging the customer.* This means knowing who your customers are and involving them in the design and implementation of the company's CRM strategy. This can be accomplished by getting constant feedback from customers, and using that feedback to improve and fine-tune the CRM strategy and how it is operationalized.

4. *Ensuring organizational collaboration between internal groups and external business partners.* Often this involves changing processes, structures, incentives, skills, and behaviours so that the CRM strategy can be realized and implemented successfully.

5. *Focusing on improving customer processes.* Rather than creating fragmented customer processes that yield less than ideal customer experiences, organizations need to re-engineer their processes so that they are customer-centric and deliver great customer value.

6. *Achieving data integrity across the enterprise.* Since the careful and precise sharing of data between different business units and system applications is imperative for CRM to succeed, it is important that organizations are serious in their efforts to maintain high-quality data and to readily share this data across business units and between partners.

7. *Leveraging information systems to implement CRM.* Organizations should take steps to build enterprise computing architectures that facilitate using and tightly integrating information systems. Integration is key to CRM applications.

8. *Defining, collecting, and analyzing CRM metrics.* By continually measuring indicators of the customer experience, and understanding what those measures are saying, organizations can respond to those metrics by taking steps to improve the customer experience and ensure that the CRM strategy is realized.[24]

1. *Clearly communicate the CRM strategy.*   Boise Office Solutions spent $29 million implementing a successful CRM system. One of the primary reasons for the system's success was that Boise started with a clear business objective for the system: provide customers with greater economic value. Only after establishing the business objective did Boise Office Solutions invest in CRM technology to help meet the goal. Ensuring that all departments and employees understood exactly what CRM meant and how it adds value to the organization was critical. Research by Gartner Dataquest indicates that enterprises that attain success with CRM have interested and committed senior executives who set goals for what CRM should achieve, match CRM strategies with corporate objectives, and tie the measurement process to both goals and strategies.

2. *Define data needs and flows.*   People who perform successful CRM implementations have a clear understanding of how data flow in and out of their organizations. Chances are that data come into an organization in many different forms over many different touch points.

3. *Build an integrated view of the customer.*   Essential to a CRM strategy is choosing the correct CRM system that can support organizational requirements. The system must have the corresponding functional breadth and depth to support strategic goals. Do not forget to take into account the system's infrastructure, including ease of integration to current systems, discussed in greater detail later in this section.

4. *Implement in increments.*   Implement the CRM system in manageable pieces; in other words, avoid the "big bang" implementation approach. This makes it easier to manage, measure, and track the design, building, and deployment of the system. Most importantly, this allows the organization to find out early if the implementation is headed for failure, and thus gives it a chance to either kill the project or change direction.

5. *Scalability for organizational growth.*   Make certain that the CRM system meets the organization's future needs as well as its current needs. Estimating future needs is by far one of the hardest parts of any project. Understanding how the organization is going to grow, predicting how technology is going to change, and anticipating how customers are going to evolve are very difficult. Taking the time to answer tough questions up front will ensure the organization grows into, instead of out of, its CRM system.

FIGURE 9.11

Industry Best Practices for CRM Implementation

Once a CRM strategy is implemented, it still needs full-time dedication and staff. Some organizations create a specific organizational role, such as a ***CRM manager***, to ensure that somebody in the company is held accountable and is responsible for the continued successful rollout of CRM. The CRM manager's full-time responsibilities include functional management of the existing CRM solution, operational management, change management, and strategic partnership with key CRM stakeholders. Functional management involves the CRM manager acting as the single point of reference, and documenting and understanding how CRM business processes and systems work and integrate with one another. Operational management concerns the CRM manager who ensures that service-level agreements (SLAs) are met, technical support is provided, and CRM metrics are collected and analyzed. Change management involves the CRM manager in fielding and prioritizing CRM systems change requests. Strategic management requires the CRM manager to work with key CRM stakeholders to ensure that the value and benefits of the delivered CRM systems meet stakeholder expectations and requirements, as well as fulfill the CRM strategy and vision. An important aspect of strategic management is assessing emerging trends and reviewing best practices in the field to ensure that the company's CRM solutions and strategy remain relevant and agile.[25]

CRM METRICS

As mentioned above, a company must continually monitor its CRM efforts to ensure success. Without understanding CRM's impact, a business will not be able to understand whether its CRM practices are adding to its success. Using CRM metrics to track and monitor performance is a best practice for many companies.

Some companies track too many metrics and suffer from "metrics overload." To deal with this, many organizations have a framework for deciding which metrics to monitor and for figuring out how such metrics will be used to gauge CRM performance. Figure 9.12 displays a few common CRM metrics tracked by organizations.

Sales Metrics	Service Metrics	Marketing Metrics
Number of prospective customers	Cases closed the same day	Number of marketing campaigns
Number of new customers	Number of cases handled by an agent	New customer retention rates
Number of retained customers	Number of service calls	Number of responses by marketing campaign
Number of open leads	Average number of service requests by type	Number of purchases by marketing campaign
Number of sales calls	Average time to resolution	Revenue generated by marketing campaign
Number of sales calls per lead	Average number of service calls per day	Cost per interaction by marketing campaign
Amount of new revenue	Percentage compliance with service-level agreement	Number of new customers acquired by marketing campaign
Amount of recurring revenue	Percentage of service renewals	Customer retention rate
Number of proposals given	Customer satisfaction level	Number of new leads by product

FIGURE 9.12

CRM Metrics

These common metrics are relatively straightforward to collect and analyze. Several key best practices when dealing with these common metrics are: to continually collect and analyze them to identify trends and patterns; to use those metrics to assess the overall health of the CRM strategy and vision, not just the health and well-being of tactical CRM operations; and to conduct a regular review of the CRM metrics that are collected and analyzed. Are these metrics still useful (i.e., are they used as decision-making inputs)? Are they measuring what they should be measuring? Are better or new metrics available?

Some companies, as part of their best practices, include the measurement of CSR satisfaction in the metrics they monitor. This metric is important to track. If CSRs are not satisfied in their roles this often translates into poorer customer service. For example, if customers perceive the CSR they interact with to be unmotivated, rushed, poorly trained, or slow in responding, then that will result in customer dissatisfaction, and in the long run can ultimately lead to a decline in customer loyalty and retention.

Another best practice is to collect and analyze CRM metrics on customer experiences that span multiple customer interactions over different communication channels. Often such metrics are complex and difficult to measure. For instance, if a customer contacts a company to sort out a problem, first by telephone, and then later by engaging in a Web-based chat session with a CSR, it is difficult to measure the entire customer experience in dealing with that problem because it spanned two separate sessions and interactions with the company. However, companies that can link and assess independent interactions when dealing with a single customer problem or complaint as a whole often have a better understanding of what the true customer experience is and a more accurate account of the time and effort expended in dealing with a single customer issue.[26]

An important trend in measuring customer satisfaction and uptake with a product or service is to monitor external communities. For example, Google, consumer blogs, Facebook, and Twitter are some of the more popular public tools and platforms where a company can find comments about its products and services, both good and bad. Using such qualitative feedback as part of your company's repertoire of metrics can provide great insight, more so than using quantitative techniques alone. Figure 9.13 shows an example of a real-life instance of customers making poor customer experiences and poor company practices very public. Companies are well advised to regularly monitor such postings on external community websites and to incorporate such feedback into their CRM metrics analysis.

FIGURE 9.13

Customer Power

Source: "Current List of Consumer Boycotts," Ethical Consumer site, www.ethicalconsumer.org/boycotts/boycotts list.aspx, accessed August 29, 2014.

CRM APPLICATIONS AND VENDORS

Gartner predicted that the worldwide CRM market would be around US$36.5 billion by 2017 and lead all enterprise software growth through 2017.[27] This growth will be driven by organizations that decided a CRM strategy was an important pursuit to follow. Many of these organizations realized the importance of customer retention to their bottom lines, and the goal of achieving high levels of customer satisfaction at the lowest possible costs. Investments in CRM systems were seen as the most viable way of achieving these desired outcomes. In early 2014, the top three providers of CRM service providers were Salesforce.com, Oracle Sales Cloud, and Microsoft Dynamics CRM.[28]

Consolidation of the CRM application vendor market is expected to continue, as well as a focus on delivering CRM applications to small and medium-sized businesses. Growth of Software as a Service (SaaS) to deliver CRM applications continues to be a major trend, as will the use of analytical tools and the available of mobile CRM application offerings.[29]

LO5 ⌉ MANAGING OTHER RELATIONSHIPS

Organizations are discovering a wave of other key business areas where it is beneficial to take advantage of building strong relationships. These emerging areas include supplier relationship management, partner relationship management, and employee relationship management.

Building healthy relationships with key stakeholders is healthy and profitable for companies. Relationships between two parties are said to exist when the two parties interact well, have a rapport with one another, feel sympathetic toward each other, and are responsive to each other's needs. A good relationship exists when there is a reciprocal exchange of value between the two parties (i.e., they both appreciate one another), and when both parties want to be part of that relationship and avidly work at keeping the relationship strong.

Information systems can play a significant role in fostering good relationships. They are not a critical component and good relationships can certainly exist without the help or use of information systems, but information systems can be quite useful in improving relationships, especially in business. For example, information systems can provide more efficient and effective communication between stakeholders and be beneficial in monitoring stakeholder activities and measuring stakeholder performance.

Supplier Relationship Management

Supplier relationship management (SRM) focuses on keeping suppliers satisfied by evaluating and categorizing suppliers for different projects, which optimizes supplier selection. There are a couple of key reasons why an organization would want to foster its relationships with suppliers. First, by knowing suppliers well, in terms of both their good and their bad points, an organization can determine the best supplier to collaborate with at anytime. Second, by building good relationships with suppliers, an organization can work better with its suppliers to streamline processes and deliver higher-quality products and parts than it could if such relationships did not exist.

Supplier relationship management is not the same thing as an SRM system. SRM is a management activity, whereas an SRM system is an application that supports SRM. SRM applications help companies analyze vendors based on a number of key variables, including strategy, business goals, prices, and markets. The company can then determine the best supplier to collaborate with and can work on developing strong relationships with that supplier. The partners can then work together to streamline processes, outsource services, and provide products that they could not provide individually.

To do this, SRM systems need to monitor the performance of the suppliers a company works with. Do they meet deadlines? Do they under-quote on estimates? Do they deliver high-quality parts? The answers to these performance-type questions can be collected and analyzed with SRM systems to assess and rate each individual supplier. These ratings can be used by an organization when choosing potential suppliers to work with in the future. SRM systems can also collect information on new or potential suppliers, and serve as a repository or data bank of both new and existing suppliers.

SRM systems also help an organization communicate with its suppliers by providing a seamless communication channel where data can be shared and accessed by both parties. This helps facilitates supply chain management activities. For example, with the merger of the Bank of Halifax and Bank of Scotland, the new company, HBOS, implemented an SRM system to provide consistent information to its suppliers. The system integrated procurement information from the separate bank operational systems, generating a single repository of management information for consistent reporting and analysis. Other benefits HBOS derived from the SRM solution included:

- A single consolidated view of all suppliers
- Consistent, detailed management information allowing multiple views for every executive
- Elimination of duplicate suppliers[30]

Good supplier relationships ultimately translate into better supply chain efficiency and effectiveness. Good supplier relationships indirectly benefit an organization's customer satisfaction with the products delivered (e.g., they are of good quality, always in stock, delivered on time, etc.). This is good news for organizations, as happier customers mean better business and increased profits. For this reason, many organizations today are avidly fostering better relationships with suppliers and are using SRM systems to help achieve this goal.

Partner Relationship Management

Organizations have begun to realize the importance of building relationships with partners. These include alliance partner organizations, dealers, retailers, and resellers.

Alliance partners are competitor organizations who cooperate with one another because doing so allows them to compete more successfully. A global example is Star Alliance, which was founded in 1997 by five airlines: Air Canada, Lufthansa, Scandinavian Airlines System, Thai Airways International, and United Airlines. Since then, Star Alliance has grown considerably and has 28 full members.[31]

Dealers are agents who sell products or services on behalf of a company or organization, particularly in the automobile industry. A prominent example of dealers operating in Canada is Canadian Tire retail stores. There are 490 Canadian Tire retail stores in operation coast-to-coast across the country. Each store operates independently as an associate dealer. Canadian Tire owns the building and land for each of its retail stores; associate dealers own everything inside the building, from fixtures to merchandise. Canadian Tire charges rent as a percentage of sales to each associate dealer, shares the gross margin at each store with the dealers on a fixed basis, and offers extensive training, including e-learning, to associate dealers.[32]

Retailers are stores or shops operating at the end of the supply chain that acquire goods or products from manufacturers or importers, and then sell smaller quantities of these goods or products to consumers at higher prices to cover expenses and make a profit.

Resellers are companies or individuals who purchase goods and products in bulk with the intention of reselling them at a profit. Resellers are prevalent in the telecommunications industry, where companies buy excess amount of transmission capacity or call time from other carriers and resell them to smaller carriers or individual consumers.

Partner relationship management (PRM) focuses on keeping vendors satisfied by managing alliance partner, dealer, retailer, and reseller relationships that provide customers with an optimal sales channel. As with SRM, PRM is a management activity. PRM's business strategy is to select and manage partners to optimize their long-term value to an organization. In effect, it means picking the right partners, working with them to help them be successful in dealing with mutual customers, and ensuring that partners and the ultimate end customers are satisfied and successful. This makes great business sense for organizations, since partners interact with an organization's customers and provide those customers a sales channel to an organization's products.

Analogously to the relationship between SRM and SRM systems, PRM systems are information systems applications that support the management activity of PRM. Information systems can help foster good partner relationships by facilitating better communication with partners, exchanging transactional data more efficiently and effectively, and monitoring partners to see how they are performing. It is common for organizations to use PRM systems to decide which partners to keep, which to eliminate, and which to recruit. Many of the features of a PRM application include the management of real-time product data on availability, marketing materials, contracts, order details, and pricing, inventory, and shipping information.

Employee Relationship Management

Employee relationship management (ERM) is a management activity that focuses on managing an organization's relationships with its employees. As with SRM and PRM, ERM is a good business strategy, especially when it concerns managing relationships with employees who have direct customer contact. An employee who is not happy with his or her employer can easily upset or anger customers, who in turn may take their business elsewhere. Further, employees who feel good about the company they work for will actually work harder, put in longer hours, be more productive, and be more likely to engage with and contribute ideas to the company. ERM can increase employee productivity in many ways by improving employees' morale, loyalty, turnaround, communication, and change readiness.

ERM is a management activity and ERM systems are information systems applications that support ERM practice. Often, ERM systems provide employees with a subset of CRM applications available through a Web browser. Many of the ERM applications assist the employee in dealing with customers by providing detailed information on company products, services, and customer orders. There is a positive impact of implementing ERM systems on a company's bottom line. ERM systems improve employee relationships, which in turn yields happier and more knowledgeable employees who offer better service to customers and produce better quality goods and services,

At Rackspace, a Web and cloud hosting company, customer focus borders on the obsessive. Joey Parsons, 24, won the Straightjacket Award, the most coveted employee distinction at Rackspace. The award recognizes the employee who best lives up to the Rackspace motto of delivering "fanatical support," a dedication to customers that is so intense it borders on the loony. Rackspace motivates its staff by treating each team as a separate business, which is responsible for its own profits and losses and has its own ERM website. Every month, employees can earn bonuses of up to 20 percent of their monthly base salaries depending on the performance of their units, not only by financial measurements but also by customer-centric ones such as customer turnover, customer expansion, and customer referrals. Daily reports are available through the team's ERM website. It appears that such efforts are worthwhile, as customer testimonials indicate "fanatical support" works the way it's meant to—meeting and exceeding every customer's needs and expectations.[33]

FUTURE CRM TRENDS

In the future, CRM applications will continue to evolve and be used with a wide variety of partners. However, the primary purpose and goal of CRM initiatives will be to provide a consistent view of customers across the enterprise and to deliver timely and accurate customer data to all departments across an organization.

As technology advances (e.g., wireless, RFID, SaaS), CRM will remain a major strategic focus for companies, particularly in industries whose product is difficult to differentiate. Some companies approach this problem by moving to a low-cost producer strategy. CRM is an alternative way to pursue a differentiation strategy with a non-differentiable product.

CRM applications will continue to adapt wireless capabilities supporting mobile sales and mobile customers, and cloud computing will become increasingly popular. Sales professionals will be able to access email, order details, corporate information, inventory status, and opportunity information, all from a smartphone or other mobile device in their car or on a plane. Real-time interaction with human CSRs over the Internet will continue to increase.

CRM suites will also incorporate SRM, PRM, and ERM modules as enterprises seek to take advantage of these initiatives. Automating interactions with all types of partners will enhance the corporation's ability to deliver a quality experience to its customers.

One interesting area of CRM may be in the use of RFID that has allowed everything from shipping companies to hospitals to reduce costs and overhead by making inefficient business processes obvious. Aberdeen's research shows that 38 percent of enterprises using RFID are doing so to improve the cost, safety, and reliability of managing business processes. Organizations are leveraging RFID to improve the productivity of their workforce, all while simplifying the implementation and ongoing management costs of their networks.[34]

When Walmart announced its RFID strategy in 2003, it was just one of many retailers that had become enamoured of the technology. By putting RFID tags on cases and pallets shipped from manufacturers to Walmart distribution centres, companies could keep close tabs on their shipments. In turn, that allowed Walmart and its suppliers to streamline their supply chains and ultimately ensure shelves were always fully stocked.

OPENING CASE QUESTIONS

Twitter: A Social CRM Tool

5. Describe some best practices evident in the CRM industry. Discuss to what extent a company using Social CRM can following these best practices.

6. Describe the trends found in the CRM industry. Discuss to what extent a company using Social CRM can following these trends.

7. Explain SRM. Do you see a potential for Social SRM, and if so how could it be used to improve its business?

8. Explain PRM. Do you see a potential for Social PRM, and if so how could it be used to improve its business?

9. Explain ERM. Do you see a potential for Social ERM, and if so how could it be used to improve its business?

SUMMARY OF KEY THEMES

This chapter focused on customer relationship management, and the strategic importance of CRM was discussed. Two broad types of CRM applications were described: operational and analytical. Best practices and trends in CRM were also explained. CRM was shown to be a management activity where information systems play a major role. Information systems were presented as a key enabler of CRM, and as tools through which organizations can launch and run successful CRM programs.

As a business student, you should understand the instrumental role that information systems play in facilitating customer relationship management. It is important to keep in mind that CRM is first and foremost a business phenomenon, and not a technological one. Information systems—though useful, and some would say even necessary—only support CRM; they are not CRM themselves.

This is an important distinction. For example, all the benefits CRM systems offer an organization can be easily undone by a thoughtless employee, partner, or supplier, who may, by some action or word, demonstrate that the organization does not care about or understand its customers. Information systems can help organizations implement better and effective CRM, but at the end of the day, how a company's employees, partners, and suppliers interact with a customer, either directly or indirectly, is the real test of a company's ability to foster healthy customer relations.

KEY TERMS

Alliance partners

Analytical CRM

Automatic call distribution

Call-scripting systems

Campaign management systems

Contact centre (call centre)

Contact management CRM system

CRM analysis systems

CRM manager	Partner relationship management (PRM)
CRM predicting systems	Personalization
CRM reporting systems	Predictive dialling
Cross-selling	Resellers
Customer relationship management (CRM)	Retailers
Dealers	Sales force automation (SFA)
Employee relationship management (ERM)	Sales management CRM systems
Interactive voice response (IVR)	Social CRM
List generators	Supplier relationship management (SRM)
Operational CRM	Upselling
Opportunity management CRM systems	Web-based self-service systems

CLOSING CASE ONE

Harnessing Customer Relationships at Fairmont Hotels & Resorts

This case shows how one organization used a CRM solution to solve information issues.

Richard's Story

Richard Wilson was impressed during his stay at Fairmont Vancouver Airport. He had just signed up for the hospitality chain's guest recognition program, "President's Club," and couldn't remember his loyalty program number when he checked in. He ended up not needing to know. The hotel employee simply asked Richard to supply his last name and the name of the company he worked for in order to pull up his file from the hotel's computer records. With his file displayed, the hotel employee quickly noticed that Richard's company formation was out of date and that his credit card was going to expire within 30 days. So the employee asked Richard to leave his new business card at the desk so that his personal information could be updated in his records after he was checked in. Richard was thrilled with this personal care and attention, wishing other businesses could offer such a good level of service.[35]

Guest Recognition Program

Fairmont would be pleased with this story. It embarked on its guest recognition program as a means of offering special benefits and privileges to customers, as well as to reflect individual travel preferences and provide an enhanced level of service. The difficulty in doing this well, however, is a direct result of Fairmont's size and expanse. Fairmont Hotels & Resorts is a leading owner/operator of luxury hotels and resorts around the world. Through its various holdings, Fairmont is North America's largest luxury hotel management company, with several distinctive city centre and resort hotels in Canada, including the Fairmont Banff Springs in Alberta, Fairmont Le Château Frontenac in Quebec, and Fairmont Algonquin in New Brunswick.

With such a large and expansive network of hotels and resorts, Fairmont realizes that information systems are critical to the success of a customer loyalty program like President's Club or their Fairmont Gold customer relationship initiative.

Consolidating Guest Information

A case in point is how the company consolidated guest information gathered across its hotel and resort locations. When Canadian Pacific spun off Fairmont into its own independent company, Fairmont built a central repository of information about what its customers wanted. This included things like preferences for bed size, room proximity to elevators, local or national newspapers, and activities patrons might be interested in. The problem was that, at that time, each hotel maintained its own separate guest database and had no incentive or urgency to share this information with others. In response, Fairmont built one centralized database that gathered information from all its various property management systems. The result was the ability to have a single centralized, consistent view of each guest, regardless of which hotel he or she stayed in. According to Sean Taggart, Fairmont's Executive Director of Marketing Services, the project was all about capturing information about Fairmont's guests as a means of servicing them better and to deliver customized, personalized experiences for each guest at any Fairmont hotel. Moreover, according to Taggart, the guest database provided hotels with the ability to know and talk with guests, to service them on the basis of their preferences and interests, regardless of whether they were high-repeat customers or were checking into a hotel they may never have been to before.[36]

Enhancing Guest Experiences

Fairmont is committed to providing its guests with leading information systems solutions in its hotels to enhance the guest experience and foster customer relations. For example, the hotel conglomerate chose Superclick to provide dedicated 24/7 customer support to its guests using state-of-the-art high-speed Internet services at Fairmont hotel and resort locations worldwide. Fairmont's relationship with Superclick allows guests staying at to get the same online experience with their laptops they would get at home or the office.[37]

Another example of Fairmont's use of information systems to improve guest relations and the customer experience is its consideration of self-service check-in kiosks. For instance, in its Toronto hotel location, Fairmont pioneered the idea of people using a kiosk to check in, pick up hotel keys, and even choose a room. Once guests swipe their credit card at the kiosk, no extra personal details need to be entered. On leaving, guests can settle their accounts at the kiosk, drop off keys, and even obtain a boarding pass for any Air Canada flight before heading to the airport. Fairmont has expanded their guests' ability to interact with them through the Fairmont Hotels and Resorts App for iOS. The app not only allows guests to investigate Fairmont's offers but also to choose hotels, make reservations, and take advantage of special offers.[38]

By knowing its customers well, Fairmont is able to use that information to predict future demand for its rooms by categories of customers. Forecasts can be produced so that individual Fairmont hotels can easily obtain a complete view of the expected room demand by market segment and generate realistic target rates to charge its customers.[39]

Lessons for Others

So what can be taken from this? The need to harness customer intelligence. To do this, organizations must understand that customer information must be analyzed and interpreted to gain insight on customer needs, expectations, interests, and motivations. These insights can be gained from four customer data sources: (1) those that are stated ("what customers tell you"); (2) those that are observed ("how customers behave"); (3) those that are transacted ("what customers buy and how"); and (4) those that are inferred ("what customers are likely to do").

As is shown above, Fairmont Hotels & Resorts seems to be taking these lessons to heart. Through its strategic uses of information systems, such as its centralized guest repository, the company has demonstrated how information systems can be effectively employed to capture customer information and how this information can later be used to improve customer relationships and experiences. This has turned into real profits for the company. For example, Fairmont uses its customer intelligence database to predict when it needs to set up promotions. It used the database one winter to advertise a third-night-free promotion communicated through direct mail and email to selected guests who had stayed with the hotel chain before; this action generated about 20,000 room nights during a traditionally slow period.[40]

Questions

1. How can Fairmont's marketing department use operational CRM to strengthen its relationships with its customers?

2. How can Fairmont's customer service department use operational CRM to strengthen its relationships with its customers?

3. Review all of the operational CRM technologies and determine which one would add the greatest value to Fairmont's business.

4. What benefits does Fairmont gains from using analytical CRM?

5. How does Fairmont use CRM to increase efficiency in its business?

CLOSING CASE TWO

Target: CRM and Big Data

This case shows how Target uses CRM to attract consumers and engage them to become long-term customers.

Shoppers don't buy everything they need at one store. Instead, they buy toys at the toy store, and groceries at the grocery store. Consumers only visit Target when they need the items they associate with Target. This happens even though Target sells everything from milk to clothing to lawn furniture to electronics. Target's goal is to convince consumers that Target is the only store they really need, but this is a tough message to get across because consumers' shopping habits are so ingrained.

Realizing that new parents are the retailer's holy grail, Target is identifying consumers who are in this period of their life, when their routines typically fall apart and opportunities arise to change their buying habits. This happens right around the birth of a child, because parents are exhausted and overwhelmed. In this state of mind their shopping patterns and brand loyalties come up for grabs. With birth records usually being public, the moment a couple has a baby they are quickly barraged with offers and advertisements from all sorts of companies. This means that, to be successful, Target needs to reach them before any other retailers know a baby is on the way. With specially designed ads, Target wants to reach women in their second trimester, when most expectant mothers begin buying things like prenatal vitamins and maternity clothing.

According to Target's Andrew Pole, "we knew that if we can identify them in their second trimester, there's a good chance we could capture them for years. As soon as we get them buying diapers from us, they're going to start buying everything else too. If you're rushing through the store, looking for bottles, and you pass orange juice, you'll grab a carton. Oh, and there's that new DVD I want. Soon, you'll be buying cereal and paper towels from us, and keep coming back."

Many see this approach as "creepy," so Target has started to change its reach-out strategy. Target now mixes in coupons for things like wine and lawnmowers with those for pacifiers and baby wipes. With this strategy pregnant women use the coupons without realizing that Target knows they are pregnant. As Pole told *The New York Times Magazine*, "Even if you're following the law, you can do things where people get queasy."

Target collects vast amounts of data on every person who regularly walks into its stores for decades. When possible, Target assigns each shopper a unique code (Guest ID) that tracks everything they buy. "If you use a credit card or a coupon, or fill out a survey, or mail in a refund, or call the customer help line, or open an e-mail we've sent you or visit our Web site, we'll record it and link it to your Guest ID," Pole said. "We want to know everything we can." Target is then able to link demographic information (age, marital status, location of your house, etc.) to you through your Guest ID. In addition, Target can also buy data. This data can include things like:

■ Ethnicity

■ College attendance

■ Job history

■ Year of house purchase

■ Bankruptcy declaration

■ Marital status

■ Preferred brands

■ Charitable contributions

- Preferred magazines
- Political beliefs

All this information is meaningless, until someone analyzes it and makes sense of it. That is where the members of Target's Guest Marketing Analytics department come in, using "predictive analytics," which allow Target to understand not just consumers' shopping habits but also their personal habits. This understanding allows Target to market more efficiently to them. According Eric Siegel, a consultant and the chairman of a conference called Predictive Analytics World, "Target has always been one of the smartest at this and it is amazing how much they can figure out about how people think now."[41]

Questions

1. How is Target using CRM to drive consumers to its stores?

2. How would you classify what Target is doing in terms of the types of CRM systems?

3. In your opinion what types of best practices need to be adopted when companies like Target start using predictive analytics in the CRM system?

4. Read Kashmir Hill's February 16, 2012, article "How Target Figured Out a Teen Girl Was Pregnant Before Her Father Did" (www.forbes.com/sites/kashmirhill/2012/02/16/how-target-figured-out-a-teen-girl-was-pregnant-before-her-father-did). What would your reaction to this situation be?

CLOSING CASE THREE

Revving Up Customer Relationships at Harley-Davidson

This case showcases how information technology can be used to improve customer relations.

There is a mystique around a Harley-Davidson; no other motorcycle in the world has the look, feel, and sound. Demand for Harley-Davidson motorcycles outweighs supply even though the company produces 300,000 cycles per year, which generates over US$4.6 billion in revenues. Some models have a two-year waiting list.

The company has won a number of awards:

- Second in *Computerworld*'s Top 100 Best Places to Work in IT
- Fifty-first in *Fortune*'s 100 Best Companies to Work For
- First in *Fortune*'s 5 Most Admired Companies in the motor vehicles industry
- First in the Top 10 Sincerest Corporations by the *Harris Interactive Report*
- Second in the Top 10 Overall Corporations by the *Harris Interactive Report*

This success is based, in part, on Harley-Davidson's strategic concern over the maintenance and growth of its customer relationships. The company realizes that each time a customer reaches out to them, they have an opportunity to build a trusting relationship with that particular customer. They know it takes more than just building and selling motorcycles to fulfill the dreams of customers. For this reason, the company strives to deliver unforgettable experiences along with high-quality products.

One strategy to do this has been the development of a customer-centric online store, **www.Harley-Davidson.com** Bear in mind the enormity of such a task. Harley-Davidson sells more than US$580 million worth of parts and accessories to its loyal followers. Ken Ostermann, the company's manager of electronic commerce and communications, recognized that the company could increase parts and accessories sales if it could offer the products online.

However, the dilemma facing Ostermann's online strategy was that selling jackets, saddlebags, and T-shirts directly to consumers over the Web would bypass Harley-Davidson's 650 dealers, who depend on selling these high-margin accessories to fuel profits. His solution was to build an online store that prompted customers to select a participating Harley-Davidson dealership before placing any online orders; that dealership is then responsible for fulfilling them. This strategy has ensured that dealers remain the focal point of customers' buying experiences.

To date, the company gets over a million visitors a month to its online store. To guarantee that every customer has a highly satisfying buying experience, Harley-Davidson asks the dealers to agree to a number of standards, including:

- Checking online orders twice daily
- Shipping online orders within 24 hours
- Responding to customer inquiries within 24 hours

Another of Harley-Davidson's customer-centric strategies is its Harley's Owners Group (HOG), which offers an array of events, rides, and benefits to its members. With more than 600,000 members, HOG is the largest factory-sponsored motorcycle club in the world and is one of the key drivers in building a strong sense of community among Harley-Davidson owners. Harley-Davidson has built a customer following that is extremely loyal—a difficult task in any industry.[42]

Questions

1. What are the two different types of CRM, and how has Harley-Davidson used them to become a customer-centric business?

2. Which of Harley-Davidson's customer-centric strategies is most important for its business? Why?

3. Evaluate the HOG's CRM strategy, and recommend an additional benefit Harley-Davidson could provide to its HOG members to increase customer satisfaction.

4. Describe three ways Harley-Davidson can extend its customer reach even further by performing CRM functions over the Internet.

5. What benefits might Harley-Davidson gain from using analytical CRM?

6. Explain ERM, and describe how Harley-Davidson might use it to increase efficiency in its business.

MAKING BUSINESS DECISIONS

1. Customer Relationship Management Strategies

On average, it costs an organization six times more to sell to a new customer than to sell to an existing customer. As the co-owner of a medium-sized luggage distributor, you have recently been notified that sales for the past three months have decreased by an average of 17 percent. The reasons for the decline in sales are numerous, including a poor economy, people's aversion to travel because of the threat of terrorist attacks, and some negative publicity your company received regarding a defective product line. In a group, explain how implementing a CRM system can help you understand and combat the decline in sales. Be sure to justify why a CRM system is important to your business and its future growth.

2. Comparing CRM Vendors

As a team, search the Internet for at least one recent and authoritative article that compares or ranks CRM systems. Select two packages from the list and compare their functions and features as described in the article(s) you found as well as on each company's website. Find references in the literature for companies that are using each package and have reported their experiences, both good and bad. Draw on any other comparisons you can find. Prepare a presentation for delivery in class on the strengths and weaknesses of each package, which one you favour, and why.

3. Searching for Employee Loyalty

You are the CEO of Razz, a startup Web-based search company planning to compete directly with Google. The company had an exceptional first year and is currently getting over 500,000 hits a day from customers all over the world. You have hired 250 people in the past four months, doubling the size of your organization. With so many new employees starting so quickly, you are concerned about how your company's culture will evolve and whether your employees are receiving enough attention. You are already familiar with CRM and how the systems can help an organization create strong customer relationships. However, you are unfamiliar with employee relationship management and wondering what ERM systems can offer your employees and company. Research on Web, create a report detailing features and functions of ERM systems, and determine what value will be added to your organization if you decide to implement an ERM solution.

4. Employee Relationship Management

All new employees at the Shinaberry Inn & Spa wear bathing suits during orientation to experience the spa's exfoliating showers and hot mineral baths. At the Shinaberry Saskatoon, new employees get the same penthouse champagne toast the hotel uses to woo meeting planners. And at many properties, employees arriving for their first day have their cars parked by the valet or get vouchers for a free night's stay. This innovative orientation program, which lets employees experience what guests experience began two years ago after focus groups pointed to empathy as a service differentiator. As a result, the company added empathy to the attributes for which it screens and a training program that involves listening to recorded guest phone calls. Even its discounted employee travel program gives employees yet another way to understand the guest experience. Design an ERM system that would help Shinaberry further its employee-centred culture. The system must consider all employee needs.

5. Increasing Revenues with CRM

Cold Cream is one of the premier beauty supply stores in the metro Toronto area. People come from all over to sample the store's unique creams, lotions, makeup, and perfumes. The store is four storeys high with each department located on a separate floor. The company would like to implement a CRM system to help it better understand its customers and their purchasing habits. Create a report summarizing CRM systems and detail how such a system can directly influence Cold Cream's revenues.

6. Driving Up (or Driving Down?) Profits with Successful Campaigns

The Butterfly Café is a local hotspot located in downtown Calgary that offers specialty coffee, teas, and organic fruits and vegetables. It holds a number of events to attract customers: live music, poetry readings, book clubs, charity events, a local artists' night, etc. A list of all participants attending each event is tracked in a database, which the café uses for marketing campaigns and additional discount offers for customers who attend multiple events. A marketing database company, **TheKnow.ca**, has offered to pay the Butterfly Café a substantial amount of money for access to its customer database, which it will then sell to other local businesses. The owner of the Butterfly Café, Mary Conzachi, has come to you for advice. She is not sure her customers would appreciate her selling their personal information and wonders how it might affect her business. However, the amount of money The Know is offering is enough to finance her much-needed new patio for the back of the café. The Know has promised Mary that the sale will be completely confidential. What should Mary do?

7. Supporting Customers

CreativeThought.ca is an e-business that sells craft materials and supplies over the Internet. You have just started as the vice-president of customer service, and you have a team of 45 customer service representatives.

Currently, the only form of customer service is the 1-800 number and the company is receiving a tremendous number of calls regarding products, orders, and shipping information. The average wait time for a customer to speak to a customer service representative is 35 minutes. Orders are being cancelled and Creative Thought is losing business due to its lack of customer service. Create a strategy to revamp the customer service centre at Creative Thought and get the company back on track.

connect   **LEARNSMART**   **SMARTBOOK**

For more information on the resources available from McGraw-Hill Ryerson, go to www.mheducation.ca/he/solutions.

ENDNOTES

1. Allan Bonde, "Twitter Customer Service: Three Use Cases for More Social CRM," April 29, 2010, http://searchcrm.techtarget.com/news/2240018228/Twitter-Customer-Service-Three-Use-Cases-for-More-Social-CRM, accessed March 26, 2014; https://twitter.com/comcast, accessed March 26, 2014; https://twitter.com/WestJet, accessed March 26, 2014; https://twitter.com/BirtyGuy, accessed March 26, 2014; Brian Solis, "The Twitter Paradox," June 10, 2011, www.briansolis.com/2011/06/the-twitter-paradox, accessed March 26, 2014; https://twitter.com/BMCProTeam, accessed March 30, 2014. https://twitter.com/Ride_Argy, accessed March 30, 2 014. https://twitter.com/Shop_Argyle, accessed March 30, 2014.

2. "Customer Success," www.siebel.com, accessed May 5, 2003.

3. "Kaiser's Diabetic Initiative," www.businessweek.com, accessed Nov 15, 2003.

4. Bill Laycock, Director of Marketing Information Services, ATB Financial, personal communication, March 2013; "ATB Financial Uses Unica to Bring Powerful Consistency and Value to Marketing," 2009, www.unica.com/documents/us/Unica_CaseStudy_ATB_100109.pdf, accessed August 7, 2011; "Our Business," March 2014, www.atb.com/about/Pages/our-business.aspx, accessed March 9, 2014.

5. Gary Loveman, "Diamonds in the Data Mine," *Harvard Business Review*, May 2003; "About Us," www.caesars.com/corporate/about-us.html, accessed August 8, 2011.

6. "Managed CRM," www.teluscentral.com/application_ services/managed_crm_faq.html, accessed August 7, 2011.

7. Alex Anderson, "Credit Union Hopes Web Services Will Improve Customer Experience," *Computing Canada*, Volume 31, Issue 12, September 9, 2005, p. 13.

8. Ian Gordon and Connie Wente, "Customer Relationship Management at CCL," *Ivey Business Journal, Best Practice*, November/December 2001, pp. 23–25.

9. "Giving Voice to Customer-Centricity Reaps Big ROI for Barclays," www.databasesystemscorp.com/tech-telemarketing_mortgage_52.htm, accessed August 8, 2011.

10. "When Banks Use CRM Technology, Customer Service Improves," February 28, 2013, www.forbes.com/sites/microsoftdynamics/2013/02/28/banking-driving-more-profitable-customer-relationships-by-using-crm, accessed March 9, 2014.

11. "Sol Melia," www.infor.com/company/customers/inforcrm, 2010, accessed August 8, 2011.

12. "Playground Real Estate Realizes Significant Returns from Successful CRM Strategy Using Maximizer," *Electronic News Publishing*, February 13, 2007.

13. "Enterprise Holdings Fact Sheet December 2010," www.enterpriseholdings.com/siteAssets/Enterprise_Holdings_fact_sheets_DEC_2010.pdf, 2010, accessed August 8, 2011; "Culture of Customer Service," http://aboutus.enterprise.com/customer_service.html, accessed August 8, 2011.

14. "Bell Canada's Phenomenal Success with CRM," www.crminfoline.com/crm-articles/crm-bell-canada.htm, accessed August 7, 2011.

15. "Avnet Brings IM to Corporate America with Lotus Instant Messaging," http://my.advisor.com/doc/12196, accessed June 14, 2010.

16. "Computershare," www.nice.com/content/video/computershare, 2009, accessed August 7, 2011.

17. "Documedics," www.siebel.com, accessed July 10, 2003.

18. Bob Angel, "Relationship Results," *CA Magazine*, January/February 2002, www.camagazine.com/index.cfm?ci_id=6764&la_id=1, accessed March 23, 2007.

19. Bob Evans, "Business Technology: Sweet Home," *InformationWeek*, February 7, 2005; "Scores by Industry: Banks," www.theacsi.org/index.php?option=com_content&view=article&id=147&catid=&Itemid=212&i=Banks, accessed August 8, 2011.

20. "Customer Success: UPS," www.sap.com, accessed April 5, 2003.

21. Kimberly Noble, Ross Laver, Michael MacLean, and John Schofield, "The Data Game," *Maclean's*, Volume 111, Issue 33, August 17, 1998, pp. 14–19; www.airmiles.ca/arrow/SponsorDirectory?filter=1100001%3AFeatured+Sponsors__Commanditaires+en+vedette#featuredTop, accessed August 8, 2011.

22. Rachel Mendleson, "Air Miles Aims to Reward Eco-Friendly Choices with 'Change Canada' Campaign," April 24, 2012, www.huffingtonpost.ca/2012/04/24/air-miles-for-social-change_n_1447717.html, accessed March 23, 2014; Air Miles—My Planet, www.airmiles.ca/arrow/MyPlanet?splashId=6800056&changeLocale=en_CA, accessed March 23, 2014; Air Miles Aims to Reward Eco-Friendly Choices with Change Canada Campaign, http://neia.org/air-miles-aims-to-reward-eco-friendly-choices-with-change-canada-campaign, accessed March 23, 2014; "Sobeys Lights the Way on Creating a More Energy Efficient Nova Scotia, September 19, 2011, www.newswire.ca/en/story/842997/sobeys-lights-the-way-on-creating-a-more-energy-efficient-nova-scotia, accessed March 23, 2014.

23. "Customer Success: Brother," www.sap.com, accessed January 12, 2004.

24. Ed Thompson, "Applying Gartner's Eight Building Blocks of CRM," *Gartner Research*, July 23, 2009, ID Number G00169547.

25. Isher Kaila, "The Role of a CRM Manager After an Implementation," *Gartner Research*, October 2, 2006, ID Number G00142254.

26. Michael Maoz, "CRM Performance Metrics That Matter Most in the Contact Center," *Gartner Research*, July 7, 2009, ID Number G00168499.

27. Louis Columbus, "Gartner Predicts CRM Will Be a $36B Market by 2017," June 18, 2013, www.forbes.com/sites/louiscolumbus/2013/06/18/gartner-predicts-crm-will-be-a-36b-market-by-2017, accessed February 22, 2014.

28. Eric Blattburg, "The Top 10 Customer Relationship Management Services," February 11, 2014, http://venturebeat.com/2014/02/11/top-10-crm-services, accessed February 22, 2014.

29. Barney Beal, "Top 15 CRM Vendors, Emerging Trends Revealed," http://SearchCRM.com, accessed March 28, 2007.

30. "HBOS Gains a Clear View of Procurement After Merger," www.kalido.com/Collateral/Documents/English-US/CS-HBOS plc.pdf, accessed August 8, 2011.

31. www.staralliance.com/en/travellers/index.html, accessed September 9, 2009; www.staralliance.com/en/about/airlines, accessed August 8, 2011.

32. http://corp.canadiantire.ca/EN/Pages/default.aspx, accessed August 8, 2011.

33. "Customer Success," www.rackspace.com, accessed June 2005.

34. Mohsen Attaran, "RFID: An Enabler of Supply Chain Operations," *Supply Chain Management: An International Journal*, 2007, Volume 12, pp. 249–257.

35. Andy Holloway, "The Customer Is King," *Canadian Business*, Volume 78, Issue 14/15, July 18, 2005, pp. 62–65.

36. Ibid.

37. "Fairmont Hotels & Resorts Selects Superclick to Further Enhance," *Market News Publishing*, February 2, 2006.

38. Jane Knight, "How to Avoid the Angry Man with the Big Bill Bar: A Modern Mystery Solved," Travel 2 section, *The Times*, August 13, 2005; https://itunes.apple.com/ca/app/fairmont-hotels-resorts/id386982247?mt=8, accessed March 30, 2014.

39. Adam Kirby, "Getting the Missing Business," *Hotels*, February 2008, pp. 55–56.

40. Andy Holloway, "The Customer Is King," *Canadian Business*, Volume 78, Issue 14/15, July 18, 2005, pp. 62–65.

41. Charles Duhigg, "How Companies Learn Your Secrets," February 16, 2012, www.nytimes.com/2012/02/19/magazine/shopping-habits.html?pagewanted=all, accessed March 24, 2014; Kashmir Hill, "How Target Figured Out a Teen Girl Was Pregnant Before Her Father Did," February 16, 2012, www.forbes.com/sites/kashmirhill/2012/02/16/how-target-figured-out-a-teen-girl-was-pregnant-before-her-father-did, accessed March 30, 2014; Alice E. Marwick, "How Your Data Are Being Deeply Mined," January 9, 2014, www.nybooks.com/articles/archives/2014/jan/09/how-your-data-are-being-deeply-mined, accessed March 30, 2014.

42. www.investor.harley-davidson.com, accessed October 10, 2003; Bruce Caldwell, "Harley-Davidson Revs Up IT Horsepower," *Internetweek.com*, accessed December 7, 2000; "Computerworld 100 Best Places to Work in IT 2003," *Computerworld*, June 9, 2003, pp. 36–48; Leroy Zimdars, "Supply Chain Innovation at Harley-Davidson: An Interview with Leroy Zimdars," *Ascet*, Volume 2, April 15, 2000; "Customer Trust: Reviving Loyalty in a Challenging Economy," Pivotal webcast, September 19, 2002; "Harley-Davidson Announces Go-Live: Continues to Expand Use of Manugistics Supplier Relationship Management Solutions," www.manugistics.com, accessed May 7, 2002; Roger Villareal, "Docent Enterprise Increases Technician and Dealer Knowledge and Skills to Maximize Sales Results and Customer Service," www.docent.com, August 13, 2002.

MIS Business Concerns and Information Systems Development

Module 5 first explains some of the concerns that come with information systems such as privacy and security concerns, and goes on to explain how organizations go about building and developing information systems while keeping the concerns in mind. It's a complex task requiring an in-depth understanding of user needs and enterprise computing infrastructures, and the ability to translate user requirements into a technical design that works for people. It also requires extensive planning and people skills to make it all happen. Easier said than done. Too often, information systems development projects are criticized for going over budget, being delayed, or lacking in desired functionality.

The purpose of this module is to describe the various ways information systems can be developed in organizations, the challenges that come along with the process, and the beauty of how well things turn out if systems are built according to good design principles and sound management practices while protecting the information they contain.

This module begins by highlighting the treatment of information. As a key organizational resource, information must be protected from misuse and harm. This involves addressing ethical concerns about the collection, storage, and use of information, protecting information privacy, and ensuring that information is secure against unauthorized access and attack.

Next, an overview of how enterprise applications are developed in companies and the traditional systems development life cycle that is used to build information systems is presented. This part of the module also discusses information systems development from a project management perspective.

Lastly, how enterprise architectures, in all their variety, support information systems' functionality and success is examined. The module then goes on to describe the architecture trends that are revolutionizing the way organizations deploy information systems across today's enterprises.

Information Ethics, Privacy, and Security

LEARNING OUTCOMES

LO 10.1 Explain what information ethics is and its importance in the workplace.

LO 10.2 Describe what information privacy is and the differences in privacy legislation around the world.

LO 10.3 Identify the differences between various information ethics and privacy policies in the workplace.

LO 10.4 Describe information security, and explain why people are the first line of defence for protecting information.

LO 10.5 Describe how information technologies can be used to enhance information security.

WHY DO I NEED TO KNOW THIS ?

This chapter discusses protecting information from potential misuse. Organizations must ensure they collect, capture, store, and use information in an ethical manner. This can be any sort of information they collect and use, including information about customers, partners, and employees. Companies must ensure that personal information collected about someone remains private. This is not just a nice thing to do—Canadian law requires it. And perhaps most importantly, information must be kept physically secure to prevent access and possible dissemination and use by unauthorized sources.

As a business student, you must understand information ethics, privacy, and security issues because they are the top concerns voiced by customers today. These concerns directly influence a customer's likelihood of embracing electronic technologies and conducting business over the Web. In that sense, these concerns affect a company's bottom line. You can find evidence in recent news reports about how the stock price of organizations dramatically falls when information privacy and security breaches are made known. Organizations also face potential litigation if they fail to meet their ethical, privacy, and security obligations concerning the handling of information in their companies.

opening case study

The Privacy Commissioner of Canada's Work

PIPEDA is Canada's *Personal Information Protection and Electronic Documents Act*, which is enforced by Canada's privacy commissioner. Canadians can make formal complaints to the commissioner when they feel a company has violated sections of the act.

The Complaint

An individual requested that he be removed from an online dating service's mailing list and have his personal information deleted after he had cancelled his membership. After making his request he continued to receive marketing emails. Under the provisions of PIPEDA he also requested access to his personal information held by the online dating service. The response to this request was that his information was the property of the service, and that they could not find his personal profile information in any database.

The Investigation

When the privacy commissioner became involved in the investigation, the owner of the dating service claimed that all of the complainant's personal information had been removed from their computer systems and information that was on paper had been shredded, and they had supplied the complainant with his online profile. During the investigation the dating service was sold and the new owner inherited all the client profiles and contacts.

When the office followed up with the new owner, it was revealed that the complainant's information had been transferred to the new owner, including his profile and email address. The new owner then provided the complainant with access to a portion of his personal information. Not included in this information were the photographs, which the new owner had deleted from the system, and shortly afterwards all the complainant's personal information was removed from the system. Once the complainant received confirmation that the information was destroyed, he contacted the commissioner to determine whether the dating service had failed to retain the information for as long as necessary to allow him to exhaust any recourse under the *Act*.

What the Privacy Commissioner Found

The complainant alleged that he had not been provided with access to all his personal information by the dating service. He also received marketing emails that he alleged showed the dating service had not respected his request to stop the collection, use, and disclosure of his personal information after he cancelled his contract.

The investigation found that the dating service had:

- Denied the complainant access to his personal information

- Failed to respect the 30-day time limit set out under subsection

- Limited the complainant's ability for recourse by destroying the photographs

- Retained the complainant's information after it was no longer required to deliver dating services

- Continued to use the complainant's personal information, specifically his email address, to send marketing emails, after he had clearly withdrawn his consent for any such purposes

Also, the dating service had had no privacy policy in place at the time of the complainant's initial dealings. It was also found that the dating service had failed to safeguard the complainant's personal information.

Lessons Learned

The lessons learned in this complaint include:

- Organizations must let individuals know of the existence, use, and disclosure of their personal information. Individuals also need to be given access to that information, unless there is a valid exception in PIPEDA.

- The consent principle allows individuals to withdraw their consent at any time. This is subject to legal and contractual restrictions and reasonable notice.

- A person's information can be retained only as long as necessary for the purpose identified by the organization. After that time, the information needs to be destroyed, erased, or made anonymous. An exception is that when an organization has personal information that is the subject of an access request made to the privacy commissioner, it must kept for as long as is necessary to allow the individual to exhaust any recourse related to the request.

- Security safeguards must protect personal information against loss, theft, unauthorized access, disclosure, copying, use, or modification. Polices in relation to security safeguards must be publicly available and people must be able to acquire information about an organization's policies and practices without unreasonable effort.[1]

10.1 INFORMATION ETHICS AND PRIVACY

INTRODUCTION

The ethical issues surrounding copyright infringement and intellectual property rights are consuming the business world. Advances in technology make it easier for people to copy everything from music to pictures. Technology continually poses new challenges for our *ethics*—the principles and standards that guide our behaviour toward other people. Figure 10.1 lists a few of the concepts and ethical issues stemming from advances in technology.

Intellectual property	Intangible creative work that is embodied in physical form.
Copyright	The legal protection afforded an expression of an idea, such as a song, video game, and some types of proprietary documents.
Fair dealing	The principle by which, in certain situations, it is legal to use copyrighted material.
Pirated software	Copyrighted software that is used, duplicated, distributed, or sold without authorization by the copyright holder.
Counterfeit software	Software that is manufactured to look like the real thing and sold as such.

FIGURE 10.1

Technology-Related Ethical Issues and Concepts

One of the biggest issues today is ***privacy***—the right to be left alone when you want to be, to have control over your own personal possessions, and not to be observed without your consent. Privacy is related to ***confidentiality***, which is the assurance that messages and information are available only to those who are authorized to view them. Some of the most problematic decisions facing organizations today lie in the murky and turbulent waters of privacy. The burden comes from the knowledge that whenever employees make a decision regarding issues of privacy, the outcome might possibly sink the company.

Trust between companies, customers, partners, and suppliers is the support structure of business and in particular e-business, and one of the main ingredients in trust is privacy. Privacy continues to be one of the primary barriers to the growth of e-business. People are concerned that their privacy will be violated because of interactions on the Web. Unless an organization can effectively address this issue, its customers, partners, and suppliers might lose trust in the organization, which would hurt its business. Figure 10.2 displays the results from a survey of CIOs regarding how privacy issues reduce trust for e-businesses.

1. There is loss of personal privacy.

2. Internet users are a lot more inclined to purchase a product on a website that has a privacy policy.

3. Effective privacy would convert more Internet users to Internet buyers.

FIGURE 10.2

Primary Reasons Privacy Issues Reduce Trust for E-Business

LO1) INFORMATION ETHICS

Information ethics concerns the ethical and moral issues arising from the development and use of information technologies and systems, as well as the creation, collection, duplication, distribution, and processing of information itself (with or without the aid of computer technologies and information systems).

Individuals determine how to use information and how information affects them. How individuals behave toward each other, how they handle information, computer technologies, and information systems, is largely influenced by their ethics. Ethical dilemmas do not usually arise in simple, clear-cut situations but out of a clash between competing goals, responsibilities, and loyalties. Inevitably, the decision process has more than one socially acceptable "correct" decision. Figure 10.3 contains examples of ethically questionable or unacceptable uses of information systems.

Individuals copy, use, and distribute software.

Employees search organizational databases for sensitive corporate and personal information.

Organizations collect, buy, and use information without checking the validity or accuracy of the information.

Individuals create and spread viruses that cause trouble for those using and maintaining information systems.

Individuals hack into computer systems to steal proprietary information.

Employees destroy or steal proprietary organization information such as schematics, sketches, customer lists, and reports.

FIGURE 10.3

Examples of Ethically Questionable or Unacceptable Use of Information Systems

Even though people make arguments for or against—justify or condemn—the behaviours in Figure 10.3, there are few hard-and-fast rules for determining what is and is not ethical. Knowing the law will not always help, because what is legal might not always be ethical, and what is ethical is not always legal (see Figure 10.4). Because technology and information systems are so new and pervasive in unexpected ways, the ethics surrounding information is still being defined. The ideal goal for organizations is to make decisions that are both legal and ethical (i.e., within quadrant I in the figure).

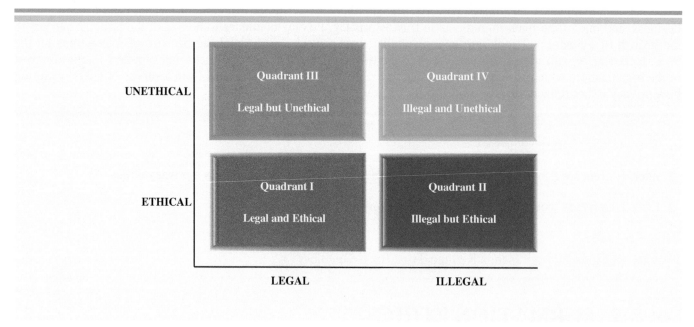

FIGURE 10.4

Acting Ethically and Legally Are Not Always the Same

Information Has No Ethics

Jerry Rode, CIO of Saab Cars USA, realized he had a public relations fiasco on his hands when he received an email from an irate customer. Saab had hired four Internet marketing companies to distribute electronic information about Saab's new models to its customers. Saab specified that the marketing campaign be opt-in, that is, it would contact only people who had agreed to receive promotions and marketing material via email. Unfortunately, one of the marketing companies had a different definition of "opt-in," and was emailing all customers regardless of their opt-in decision.

Rode fired the errant marketing company and immediately developed a formal policy for using customer information. "The customer doesn't see ad agencies and contracted marketing firms. They see Saab USA spamming them," Rode said. "Finger-pointing after the fact won't make your customers feel better."[2]

Information has no ethics. Information does not care how it is used. It will not stop itself from spamming customers, sharing itself if it is sensitive or personal, or revealing details to third parties. Information cannot delete or preserve itself. Therefore, it falls on the shoulders of those who own the information to develop ethical guidelines on how to manage the information.

Information Ethics in the Workplace

The rampant introduction and use of information systems in the workplace have led to many ethical concerns for employers. For instance, information systems have reduced or eliminated some types of jobs; not everyone gets retrained when an information system changes job roles. Though information systems have eliminated numerous monotonous tasks and jobs in organizations, they have also introduced brand-new monotonous tasks. You have only to visit any large organization's accounts receivable and payable departments to see row on row of employees in cubicles doing manual data entry day in, day out. Not fun.

Systems and Respect of Human Dignity

Another ethical issue concerns the dehumanization of workers through the introduction of new information systems. Sometimes, in the "wisdom" of information systems designers to build systems that maximize profit and reduce costs, new systems that are introduced into organizations make tasks too easy. Users are not challenged, or they are forced not to think, causing them to feel dehumanized. For example, "pickers" at a Canadian Tire Distribution Centre in Brampton, Ontario, were given handheld devices that instructed them to pick up certain items in a certain order and to place those items into totes for loading onto trucks. The handheld technology was so specific it even told workers when to "turn right" or "turn left" in order to make optimal use of their time. Workers were annoyed and rejected the new technology, because they found it depersonalizing, taking away the elements of the job that made it interesting.

Sometimes, information systems deployed in organizations are overly regimented and inflexible, causing employees to endure painful screen navigations or wait for long times between transactions. Building information systems with poor interfaces creates an ethical issue for employers if they allow and condone such development on a regular basis.

Several things can be done to circumvent or mitigate these information technology–related ethical concerns. For example, systems designers can build information systems that respect worker intelligence and dignity. The systems design process can also get end-users directly involved in the design of these systems to ensure that human–computer interfaces are amenable to the people who will eventually use these systems.

Tracking People's Activities

Even though there are many types of technology available to track a person's computer-based activities online, there are also other ways of tracking activities. In the workplace these can effect an employee in different ways (see Figure 10.5). Consider status updates on Facebook—letting everyone know that you will be away in Las Vegas next week, or about sensitive family circumstances, such as a death. This information might be of interest to the criminal elements. An extreme example was the experience of Ghyslain Raza from Quebec. Ghyslain was 14 years old when he innocently swung a golf-ball retriever around in a quiet corner of his high school, pretending he was the Phantom Menace's Darth Maul. He videotaped it and left the tape at school, where it was found several months later. Not long after that, Raza became an Internet sensation, known today as the "Star Wars kid," with fans adding light-sabre effects and music, and creating video revisions that number over a hundred. The embarrassing footage has since become one of the Internet's most popular, having been spoofed on TV shows ranging from *American Dad* to *The Colbert Report* to *Arrested Development*. Raza sued the individuals who posted the video online, and the case was eventually settled.

Protecting Digital Content

Canada's *Copyright Modernization Act* was passed and received royal assent on June 29, 2012. General details on Canada's update to copyright legislation can be found on the Government of Canada's publications site at **http://laws-lois.justice.gc.ca/eng/AnnualStatutes/2012_20/FullText.html.** The key changes were as follows:

- Legalizing format shifting (copying of content from one device to another, such as a CD to an iPod).
- Legalizing time shifting, or recording television programs for viewing at later time but not for the building up of a library.
- Allowing for making a backup copy of content to protect against loss or damage.
- Allowing for people to "mash up" (create a blend of different) media under certain circumstances, as long as it's not for commercial gain.
- Enacting a system in which copyright holders can inform Internet service providers (ISPs) of possible piracy by their customers. The ISP would then be required to notify the customer that he or she is violating copyright law and the violator's personal information could then be released to the copyright holder with a court order.
- Protecting search engines and ISPs from the copyright violations of their users.
- Differentiating commercial and individual copyright violation with respect to penalties involved. Individuals would see penalties ranging from $100 to $5,000 instead of the current $20,000 maximum penalty.

- Expanding the meaning of "fair dealing" to include the purposes of parody, satire, and education.

- Criminalizing cracking a digital lock placed on a device, disc, or file. For example, a television broadcaster could air a program with a digital lock that prevents it from being recorded, or deletes it from a PVR after a certain amount of time; it would be illegal for consumers to attempt to circumvent those codes.

---

1. Employee absenteeism reached its highest point in several years in 2009. The lesson here might be that more employees are missing work to take care of personal business. Perhaps losing a few minutes here or there—or even a couple of hours—is cheaper than losing entire days.

2. Studies indicate that electronic monitoring results in lower job satisfaction, in part because people begin to believe the quantity of their work is more important than the quality.

3. Electronic monitoring also induces what psychologists call "psychological reactance": the tendency to rebel against constraints. If you tell your employees they cannot shop, use corporate networks for personal business, or make personal phone calls, then their desire to do all these things will likely increase.

FIGURE 10.5

Effects of Employee Monitoring

This bill included a number of measures that allow educators and students to take advantage of digital technologies by expanding access to copyrighted materials. This enriched the educational experience for Canadian students and allowed teachers to be more creative in their lesson planning. At the same time it introduced safeguards to protect the interests of copyright owners. A few of the measures for education include:

- Expanding the definition of "fair dealing" to recognize education in a structured context as a legitimate purpose.

- Permitting educators to use publicly available material from the Internet, via a special exemption.

- Enabling teachers to connect with students in remote communities across the country through technology-enhanced learning, and allowing schools to offer the same educational opportunities to a student in the remote northern Yukon as to a student in Calgary.

- Allowing libraries to deliver interlibrary loan material in paper and other forms.

Fair dealing is a long-standing feature of Canadian copyright law that permits certain uses of copyrighted material in ways that do not threaten the interests of copyright owners, but which could have significant social benefits. Currently, fair dealing in Canada is limited to five purposes: research, private study, news reporting, criticism, and review, and the new law recognizes the important societal benefits of education, parody, and satire.

In December 2010, Access Copyright, a body that manages copyright permissions in Canada, made a ruling that significantly increases the tariff on gaining copyright permissions for things like articles or cases for use in the classroom. Many Canadian universities opted out of the tariff program, which led to many rules regarding what can and cannot be used in research, used in print and electronic form in the classroom, and delivered to the student through classroom management systems. Many of the universities that opted out of the new agreement have implemented their own systems to ensure copyright compliance and in some instances these systems have been integrated with the classroom management systems.

LO2 | INFORMATION PRIVACY

The protection of personal information has become a real concern for everyday Canadians. In April 2014 the Canadian government introduced new legislation to help protect Canadian's online data. For the most part the legislation is aimed at reporting data breaches, regulating how businesses share personal data, and having better explanations of how personal data will be used.[3]

Information privacy concerns the legal right or general expectation of individuals, groups, or institutions to determine for themselves when, and to what extent, information about them is communicated to others. In essence, information privacy is about how personal information is collected and shared.

Issues or concerns about collecting and sharing personal information occur in companies whenever uniquely identifiable data or information relating to a person is collected and stored. These concerns exist regardless of the format in which personal information is stored. That is, information privacy breaches pertain to personal data and information stored electronically or otherwise.

Breaches in information privacy occur when improper disclosure of personal information is made. This often stems from a lack of proper controls in organizations that protect how personal information is collected, stored, accessed, and distributed. Most often, information privacy pertains to personally sensitive information about individuals, such as health information, police records, financial information (income, purchases, spending habits), genetic information, and demographic information (e.g., name, age, weight, height, religion, ethnic origin, place of birth, number of dependants).

Information privacy is not about preventing the collection and sharing of personal information; often, personal information has to be collected to complete a business transaction. For example, if a customer orders a product off the Web, a company needs to collect and share personal information, such as an address and credit card number, internally or with business partners, to facilitate delivery of the ordered product. Rather, information privacy is about recognizing the sensitivity of personal information and protecting that information from inappropriate disclosure or unauthorized access.

Protecting Your Personal Data

Have you thought about what happens when those risqué photos you are sending to your current significant other make it to the Web on a social media site like Tumblr, Instagram, or Facebook? Advances in facial recognition technology mean that you could be identified years later when you are in a position of power. Or have you thought about why technology-savvy individuals don't post pictures of their kids online? Many digital photographs contain embedded information about when and where the picture was taken. This data can be extracted, telling a stalker what park your child plays at, the route she takes home from school, and even what school she attends.

There are a number of simple things you can do while on the Internet to protect your personal brand. Know the Net, a U.K. organization that promotes "Manners on the Net," has developed an infographic that keeps it pretty simple: **www.knowthenet.org.uk/infographic/be-careful-trolling-can-happen-anyone**. Know the Net has also produced a number of online tests, one of which is the Threat Test, designed to help people learn how to spot online scams. See **http://threattest.knowthenet.org.uk**.

The Canadian Bankers Association has put together an extensive and regularly updated section on its website discussing all the threats to your money and personal data: **www.cba.ca/en/component/content/category/42-safeguarding-your-money**.

It is also good, as you surf the Web, to keep in the back of your mind that tech companies and others have a vested interest in getting as much data about you as possible, because the more data they have, the better they understand you and better they can target you with advertising.[4] To facilitate information privacy, many countries have established legislation to protect the collection and sharing of personal information. However, this legislation varies greatly around the world.

Europe

At one end of the spectrum lie European nations with their strong information privacy laws. Most notably, all member countries of the European Union adhere to a *directive* on the protection of personal data—a legislative act of that requires member states to achieve a particular result without dictating the means.

The directive on the protection of personal data grants the citizens of European Union members the following rights:

- The right to know the source of personal data processing and the purposes of such processing
- The right to access and/or rectify inaccuracies in one's personal data

■ The right to disallow the use of personal data

These rights are based on eight key principles concerning the collection or storage of personal data. The directive defines personal data as covering both facts and opinions about an individual. Any organization processing the personal data of a person living in the European Union must comply with these eight key principles as outlined in the directive. These state that the data must be:

■ Fairly and lawfully processed

■ Processed for limited purposes

■ Adequate, relevant, and not excessive

■ Accurate

■ Not kept longer than necessary

■ Processed in accordance with the data subject's rights

■ Secure

■ Not transferred to countries without adequate protection

This last right restricts the flow of personal information outside the European Union by permitting its transfer only to countries that provide an "adequate" level of privacy protection—adequate in the sense that these other countries have to offer a level of privacy protection equivalent to that of the European Union. When first implemented, this part of the directive caused some concerns since other countries outside the European Union had much weaker privacy protection laws. Organizations in the United States were greatly concerned. Such organizations were at a legal risk if the personal data of European citizens were transferred to computer servers in the U.S.—a likely scenario in today's global world of electronic business. This led to extensive negotiations. The result was the establishment of a "safe harbour" program in the United States that provides a framework for organizations in the U.S. to show evidence of compliance with the directive. In this way, American companies can self-declare compliance with the key principles and do business with European Union nations without worrying about European citizens suing them.

All European member states have adopted legislation pursuant to the directive or adapted their existing laws to comply with the directive. Each country also has its own supervisory authority to monitor the levels of protection afforded by the legislation.

The United States

At the other end of the spectrum lies the United States, where information privacy is not highly legislated or regulated. There is no all-encompassing law that regulates the use of personal data or information. In many cases, access to public information is considered culturally acceptable, such as obtaining credit reports for employment or housing purposes. The reason for this may be historical. In the U.S., the first amendment protects free speech and in many instances the protection of privacy conflicts with this amendment.

There are some exceptions. Though very few states recognize an individual's right to privacy, California's legislature has enshrined an inalienable right to privacy in its constitution, enacting several pieces of legislation aimed at protecting citizen information privacy. For example, California's *Online Privacy Protection Act*, established in 2003, requires commercial websites or online services that collect personal information of California residents to clearly post a privacy policy on the site or online service and to comply with this policy. Other exceptions are the *Children's Online Privacy Protection Act* (COPPA) and the *Health Insurance Portability and Accountability Act* (HIPAA).

COPPA is a U.S. federal law established in 1998 that applies to collecting personal information from American children who are under 13. The *Act* outlines what a website should include in its privacy policy, how to go about seeking consent from a parent or guardian, and the responsibilities of an operator of a site to protect children's online safety and privacy. This law applies to any site perceived to be targeting American children. So, if a toy company established in Canada wants to sells its toys in the United States, that company's website has to comply with the collection and use of information as outlined in COPPA. To show compliance requires a substantial amount of paperwork. As a result, many sites completely disallow underage users from joining online communities and sites. One of COPPA's largest impacts has been the complete shutdown of websites that cater to children and a large number of general-audience sites deciding not to offer services to children at all. Not complying with COPPA can be costly. For example, in September 2006, the site **Xanga.com** was fined US$1 million for violating COPPA legislation.

HIPAA was enacted by the U.S. Congress in 1996. There are provisions in HIPPA that establish national standards for the electronic data interchange of health care–related transactions between health care providers, insurance plans, and employers. Embedded in these standards are rules for the handling and protection of personal health care information.[5]

Canada

Canada is also concerned about protecting the personal information of its citizens and its privacy laws follow the European model very closely. Canada's primary privacy law is the *Personal Information Protection and Electronic Documents Act* (PIPEDA).

Its precursor was the *Privacy Act*, established in 1983, which imposed restrictions on the handling of personal information within federal government departments and agencies only. This information concerned such things as:

- Pension and employment insurance files
- Medical records
- Tax records
- Security clearances
- Student loan applications
- Military records

PIPEDA came into effect in January 2001 and, like the *Privacy Act*, applied only to federally regulated organizations. By January 2004, PIPEDA's reach extended beyond government environments and applied to all other types of organizations, including commercial businesses. By doing so, Canada's PIPEDA law brought Canada into compliance with the European Union's Directive on the protection of personal data. As of January 2004, Canada no longer needed to implement safe harbour provisions, like those found in the United States, for organizations wishing to collect and store personal information on citizens of the European Union. In April 2014, the government introduced the *Digital Privacy Act*, which will give the Privacy Commissioner improved and more flexible powers.[6]

The purpose of PIPEDA is to provide Canadians with a right of privacy for how their personal information is collected, used, or disclosed by an organization. This is most important today, especially in the private sector, when information technology increasingly facilitates the collection and free flow of information.

The privacy provisions encapsulated within PIPEDA are based on the Canadian Standards Association's Model Code for the Protection of Personal Information, recognized as a national standard in 1996. The Code addresses ways organizations can collect, use, and disclose personal information. It also addresses the rights of individuals to have access to their personal information and to have it corrected if necessary.

Figure 10.6 outlines the 10 guiding principles of PIPEDA as they apply to organizations. The gist of these can be easily remembered as the "3Cs": the notion of informed *consent*; the notion of *choice*; and the notion of *control*.

Sometimes, information privacy concerns are overruled. For example, law enforcement agencies and journalists need to collect, use, and disclose personal information without obtaining the consent of the individuals in question. PIPEDA allows such exceptions, which include:

- Personal information collected, used, or disclosed solely for journalistic, artistic, or literary purposes
- If the action clearly benefits the individual or if obtaining permission could infringe on the information's accuracy
- Where such data can contribute to a legal investigation or aid in an emergency where people's lives and safety could be at stake

■ If, in times of emergency, disclosure aids matters of legal investigation, or facilitates the conservation of historically important records[7]

Guiding Principle	Description	
1.	Accountability	An organization is responsible for personal information under its control and shall designate an individual or individuals who are accountable for the organization's compliance with the following principles.
2.	Identifying purposes	The purposes for which personal information is collected shall be identified by the organization at or before the time the information is collected.
3.	Consent	The knowledge and consent of the individual are required for the collection, use, or disclosure of personal information, except when inappropriate.
4.	Limiting collection	The collection of personal information shall be limited to that which is necessary for the purposes identified by the organization. Information shall be collected by fair and lawful means.
5.	Limiting use, disclosure, and retention	Personal information shall not be used or disclosed for purposes other than those for which it was collected, except with the consent of the individual or as required by the law. Personal information shall be retained only as long as necessary for fulfillment of those purposes.
6.	Accuracy	Personal information shall be as accurate, complete, and up to date as is necessary for the purposes for which it is to be used.
7.	Safeguards	Personal information shall be protected by security safeguards appropriate to the sensitivity of the information.
8.	Openness	An organization shall make readily available to individuals specific information about its policies and practices relating to the management of personal information.
9.	Individual access	Upon request, an individual shall be informed of the existence, use, and disclosure of his or her personal information and shall be given access to that information. An individual shall be able to challenge the accuracy and completeness of the information and have it amended as appropriate.
10.	Challenging compliance	An individual shall be able to address a challenge concerning compliance with the above principles to the designated individual or individuals for the organization's compliance.

FIGURE 10.6

Ten Guiding Principles of PIPEDA for Organizations

Source: Office of the Privacy Commissioner of Canada.

As a citizen of Canada, what does PIPEDA mean for you? Several things. First, it *requires* organizations to:

- Obtain consent when they collect, use, or disclose your personal information
- Supply you with a product or service even if you refuse consent for the collection, use, or disclosure of your personal information unless the information is essential to the transaction
- Collect information by fair and lawful means
- Provide personal information policies that are clear, understandable, and readily available

Second, it *encourages* organizations to:

- Destroy personal information that is no longer needed for the purposes for which it was collected

Third, it *gives* you (the citizen) the right to:

- Know why an organization collects, uses, or discloses your personal information
- Expect an organization to collect, use, or disclose your personal information reasonably and appropriately and not to use the information for any purposes other than that to which you have consented
- Know who in the organization is responsible for protecting your personal information
- Expect an organization to protect your personal information by taking appropriate security measures
- Expect the personal information about you to be accurate, complete, and up to date
- Obtain access to your personal information and ask for corrections
- Complain about how an organization handles your personal information by first going to the privacy officer within the organization and, if not satisfied, to then seek intervention first from the Provincial Privacy Commissioner, and if not satisfied then the Privacy Commissioner of Canada

Each province has enacted privacy legislation based on the guiding principles of PIPEDA.

LO3 | DEVELOPING INFORMATION MANAGEMENT POLICIES

Treating sensitive corporate information as a valuable resource is good management. Building a corporate culture based on ethical principles that employees can understand and implement is responsible management. Organizations should develop written policies establishing employee guidelines, employee procedures, and organizational rules for information. These policies set employee expectations about the organization's practices and standards and protect the organization from misuse of computer systems and IT resources. If an organization's employees use computers at work, the organization should, at a minimum, implement e-policies. *E-policies* are policies and procedures that address information management along with the ethical use of computers and the Internet in the business environment. Figure 10.7 displays the e-policies a firm should implement to set employee expectations.

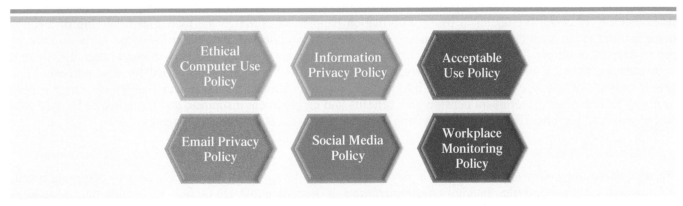

FIGURE 10.7

Overview of E-Policies

Ethical Computer Use Policy

In a case that illustrates the perils of online betting, a leading Internet poker site reported that a hacker had exploited a security flaw to gain an insurmountable edge in high-stakes, no-limit Texas Hold-'em tournaments—the ability to see his opponents' hole cards. The cheater, whose illegitimate winnings were estimated at between $400,000 and $700,000 by one victim, was an employee of **AbsolutePoker.com** who had hacked the system to show it could be done. Regardless of what business a company operates—even one that many view as unethical—the company must protect itself from unethical employee behaviour.[8]

Cyberbullying includes threats, negative remarks, or defamatory comments transmitted via the Internet or posted on the website. *Click-fraud* is the abuse of pay-per-click, pay-per-call, and pay-per-conversion revenue models by repeatedly clicking on a link to increase charges or costs for the advertiser. *Competitive click-fraud* is a computer crime in which a competitor or disgruntled employee increases a company's search advertising costs by repeatedly clicking on the advertiser's link. Cyberbullying and click-fraud are just a few examples of the many types of unethical computer use found today.

One essential step in creating an ethical corporate culture is establishing an *ethical computer use policy*—principles to guide computer user behaviour. Such a policy ensures that users know how to behave at work and that the organization has a published standard to deal with infractions. It might, for example, explicitly state that users should refrain from playing computer games during working hours, and that after appropriate warnings the company will terminate an employee who continues to do so.

Organizations can legitimately vary in how they expect employees to use computers, but in any approach to controlling such use, the overriding principle should be informed consent. The users should be *informed* of the rules and, by agreeing to use the system on that basis, *consent* to abide by them.

Managers should make a conscientious effort to ensure all users are aware of the policy through formal training and other means. If an organization were to have only one e-policy, it should be an ethical computer use policy, because that is the starting point and the umbrella for any other policies the organization might establish.

Information Privacy Policy

An organization that wants to protect its information should develop an *information privacy policy*, which contains general principles regarding information privacy. Visa created Inovant to handle all its information systems including its coveted customer information, which details how people are spending their money, in which stores, on which days, and even at what time of day. Just imagine what a sales and marketing department could do if it gained access to this information. For this reason, Inovant bans the use of Visa's customer information for anything outside its intended purpose—billing. Inovant's privacy specialists developed a strict credit card information privacy policy, which it follows.

Now Inovant is being asked if it can guarantee that unethical use of credit card information will never occur. In a large majority of cases, the unethical use of information happens not through the malicious scheming of a rogue marketer, but rather unintentionally. For instance, information is collected and stored for some purpose, such as record keeping or billing. Then, a sales or marketing professional figures out another way to use it internally, share it with partners, or sell it to a trusted third party. The information is "unintentionally" used for new purposes. The classic example of this type of unintentional information reuse is the Social Insurance Number, which started simply as a way to administer government pension plan benefits and employment insurance, and has come to be used as a sort of universal personal ID, found on everything from drivers' licences to savings accounts.

Acceptable Use Policy

An *acceptable use policy (AUP)* requires a user to agree to follow it to be provided access to corporate email, information systems, and the Internet. *Nonrepudiation* is a contractual stipulation to ensure that e-business participants do not deny (repudiate) their online actions. A nonrepudiation clause is typically contained in an acceptable use policy. Many businesses and educational facilities require employees or students to sign an acceptable use policy before gaining network access. When signing up with an email provider, each customer is typically presented with an AUP, which states the user agrees to adhere to certain stipulations:

- Not to use the service as part of violating any law
- Not to attempt to break the security of any computer network or user
- Not to post commercial messages to groups without prior permission
- Not to repudiate any of their online actions

Some organizations go so far as to create a unique information management policy focusing solely on Internet use. An ***Internet use policy*** contains general principles to guide the proper use of the Internet. Because of the large amounts of computing resources that Internet users can expend, it is essential that such use be legitimate. In addition, the Internet contains numerous materials that some believe are offensive, making regulation in the workplace a requirement. ***Cybervandalism*** is the electronic defacing of an existing website. ***Typosquatting*** is a problem that occurs when someone registers purposely misspelled variations of well-known domain names. These variants sometimes lure consumers who make typographical errors when entering a URL. ***Website name stealing*** is the theft of a website's name that occurs when someone, posing as a site's administrator, changes the ownership of the domain name assigned to the website to another website owner. These are all examples of unacceptable Internet use. ***Internet censorship*** is government attempts to control Internet traffic, thus preventing some material from being viewed by a country's citizens. Generally, an Internet use policy:

- Describes the Internet services available to users
- Defines the organization's position on the purpose of Internet access and what restrictions, if any, are put on that access
- Describes user responsibility for citing sources, properly handling offensive material, and protecting the organization's good name
- States the ramifications if the policy is violated

Email Privacy Policy

An ***email privacy policy*** details the extent to which email messages may be read by others. Email is so pervasive in organizations that it requires its own specific policy. Most working professionals use email as their preferred means of corporate communications. While email and instant messaging are common business communication tools, there are risks associated with using them. For instance, a sent email is stored on at least three or four computers (see Figure 10.8). Simply deleting an email from one computer does not delete it from the others. Companies can mitigate many of the risks of using electronic messaging systems by implementing and adhering to an email privacy policy.

One major problem with email is the user's expectations of privacy. To a large extent, this expectation is based on the false assumption that email privacy protection exists somehow analogously to that of U.S. first-class mail. Generally, the organization that owns the email system can operate the system as openly or as privately as it wishes. Surveys indicate that the majority of large firms regularly read and analyze employees' email looking for confidential data leaks such as unannounced financial results or the sharing of trade secrets that result in the violation of an email privacy policy and eventual termination of the employee. That means that if the organization wants to read everyone's email, it can do so. Basically, using work email for anything other than work is not a good idea. A typical email privacy policy:

- Defines legitimate email users and explains what happens to accounts after a person leaves the organization
- Explains backup procedure so users will know that at some point, even if a message is deleted from their computer, it is still stored by the company
- Describes the legitimate grounds for reading email and the process required before such action is performed
- Discourages sending junk email or spam to anyone who does not want to receive it
- Prohibits attempting to mail-bomb a site—that is, send a massive amount of email to a specific person or system that can cause that user's server to stop functioning
- Informs users that the organization has no control over email once it has been transmitted outside the organization

Spam is unsolicited email. It plagues employees at all levels within an organization, from receptionist to CEO, and clogs email systems and siphons MIS resources away from legitimate business projects. An ***anti-spam policy*** simply states that email users will not send unsolicited emails (or spam). It is difficult to write anti-spam policies, laws, or software, because there is no such thing as a universal litmus test for spam. One person's spam is another person's newsletter. End-users have to decide what spam is, because it can vary widely, not just from one company to the next but also from one person to the next. A user can *opt out* of receiving emails by choosing to deny permission to incoming emails. ***Teergrubing*** is an anti-spamming approach where the receiving computer launches a return attack against the spammer, sending email messages back to the computer that originated the suspected spam.

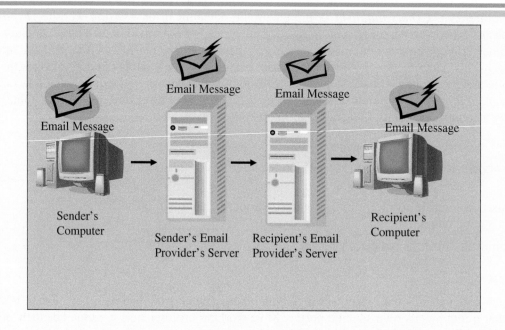

FIGURE 10.8

Email Is Stored on Multiple Computers

Social Media Policy

Have you seen the YouTube video showing two Domino's Pizza employees violating health codes while preparing food by passing gas on sandwiches? Millions of people did and the company took notice when disgusted customers began posting negative comments all over Twitter. Not having a Twitter account, corporate executives at Domino's did not know about the damaging tweets until it was too late. The use of social media can contribute many benefits to an organization, and implemented correctly it can become a huge opportunity for employees to build brands. But there are also tremendous risks, as a few employees can cause tremendous brand damage. Companies can protect themselves by implementing a ***social media policy*** outlining guidelines or principles that should govern employee online communications.

A single social media policy might not be enough to ensure the company's online reputation is protected. Additional, more specific social media policies a company might choose to implement include:[9]

- Employee online communication policy detailing brand communication
- Employee blog and personal blog policies
- Employee social network and personal social network policies
- Employee, corporate, and personal Twitter policies
- Employee LinkedIn policy

- Employee Facebook usage and brand usage policy
- Corporate YouTube policy

The Canadian Broadcasting Company (CBC) has issued a social networking policy directing journalists to avoid adding sources or contacts as friends on social networking sites such as Facebook or LinkedIn. Basic rules state that reporters never allow one source to view what another source says and reporters want to ensure private conversations with sources remain private. Adding sources as "friends" can compromise a journalist's work by allowing friends to view other friends in the network. It may also not be in a journalist's best interest to become a "friend" in a source's network. The CBC also discourages posting any political preferences in personal profiles, commenting on bulletin boards or people's "Facebook wall."[10]

Organizations must protect their online reputations and continuously monitor blogs, message boards, social networking sites, and media sharing sites. However, monitoring the hundreds of different social media sites can quickly become overwhelming. To combat these issues, a number of companies specialize in online social media monitoring; for example, **Trackur.com** creates digital dashboards allowing executives to view at a glance the date published, source, title, and summary of every item tracked. The dashboard not only highlights what's being said, but also the influence of the particular person, blog, or social media site.

Workplace Monitoring Policy

Increasingly, employee monitoring is not a choice; it is a risk management obligation. Michael Soden, CEO of the Bank of Ireland, issued a mandate stating that company employees could not surf illicit websites with company equipment. Next, he hired Hewlett-Packard to run the MIS department and illicit websites were discovered on Soden's own computer, forcing Soden to resign. Monitoring employees is one of the biggest challenges CIOs face when developing information management policies. Soden recovered from this indiscretion by being appointed to the Irish Central Bank Commission in 2010.[11]

Physical security is tangible protection such as alarms, guards, fireproof doors, fences, and vaults. New technologies make it possible for employers to monitor many aspects of their employees' jobs, especially on telephones, computer terminals, through electronic and voice mail, and when employees are using the Internet. Such monitoring is virtually unregulated. Therefore, unless company policy specifically states otherwise, your employer may listen, watch, and read most of your workplace communications. *Workplace MIS monitoring* tracks people's activities by such measures as number of keystrokes, error rate, and number of transactions processed (see Figure 10.9 for an overview). The best path for an organization planning to engage in employee monitoring is open communication including an *employee monitoring policy* stating explicitly how, when, and where the company monitors its employees. Several common stipulations an organization can follow when creating an employee monitoring policy are:

- Be as specific as possible stating when and what (email, IM, Internet, network activity, etc.) will be monitored.
- Expressly communicate that the company reserves the right to monitor all employees.
- State the consequences of violating the policy.
- Always enforce the policy in the same way for everyone.

Many employees use their company's high-speed Internet access to shop, browse, and surf the Web. Most managers do not want their employees conducting personal business during working hours, and they implement a Big Brother approach to employee monitoring. Many management gurus advocate that organizations whose corporate cultures are based on trust are more successful than those whose corporate cultures are based on mistrust. Before an organization implements monitoring technology, it should ask itself, "What does this say about how we feel about our employees?" If the organization really does not trust its employees, then perhaps it should find new ones. If an organization does trust its employees, then it might want to treat them accordingly. An organization that follows its employees' every keystroke might be unwittingly undermining the relationships with its employees, and it might find the effects of employee monitoring are often worse than lost productivity from employee surfing.

Common Internet Monitoring Technologies	
Key logger, or key trapper, software	A program that records every keystroke and mouse click.
Hardware key logger	A hardware device that captures keystrokes on their journey from the keyboard to the motherboard.
Cookie	A small file deposited on a hard drive by a website containing information about customers and their Web activities. Cookies allow websites to record the comings and goings of customers, usually without their knowledge or consent.
Adware	Software that generates ads that install themselves on a computer when a person downloads some other program from the Internet.
Spyware (sneakware or stealthware)	Software that comes hidden in free downloadable software and tracks online movements, mines the information stored on a computer, or uses a computer's CPU and storage for some task the user knows nothing about.
Web log	Consists of one line of information for every visitor to a website and is usually stored on a Web server.
Clickstream	Records information about a customer during a Web surfing session such as what websites were visited, how long the visit was, what ads were viewed, and what was purchased.

FIGURE 10.9

Internet Monitoring Technologies

OPENING CASE QUESTIONS

The Privacy Commissioner of Canada's Work

1. Why is protecting personal information in the best interest of both Canadians and the Government of Canada?

2. What policies has the Government of Canada implemented to protect citizen information privacy?

3. What lessons can be learned from the opening case study that will help other organizations better protect the personal information they collect?

4. How does the recent trend of government allowing public access to data raise awareness of the need for governments to embrace privacy planning as a part of normal, everyday business practice?

10.2 INFORMATION SECURITY

LO4 INTRODUCTION

Data security breaches and privacy issues are in our newsfeeds on a pretty regular basis these days. These continue to take different forms, but in many cases we have seen security breaches by password theft. For instance, six million LinkedIn passwords showed up on underground sites that are frequented by hackers. The company, according to many experts, was slow to respond and appears to not be as sophisticated in its data security practices and recovery plan as one would expect from a large corporation. On the privacy side we have seen the practice of employers and academic institutions asking potential employees and student athletes for their Facebook usernames and passwords, then using the information they find on these accounts in their decision-making processes concerning hiring and offering tryouts. Since July 2012, many U.S. states have made this practice illegal; some of the first movers were California, Illinois, Maryland, Michigan, New Jersey, and Delaware. In Canada, it is the opinion of lawyers that due to strong labour laws, privacy practices, and legislation, Canadians are protected from this practice even though Canada has no specific laws that address the situation. U.S. job hunters should be aware that some companies use third-party apps for people to apply through and generally these are accessed with a social media account. These apps can give the potential employers access to the content posted on your social media account. In Canada, third-party apps are not commonly used for job applications.[12]

How Much Will Downtime Cost Your Business?

The old business maxim "Time is money" needs to be updated to more accurately reflect the crucial interdependence between information systems and business processes. To reflect the times, it should be "Uptime is money." The leading cause of downtime is software failure, followed by human error, according to Infonetics Research. Unplanned downtime can strike at any time from any number of causes, ranging from tornadoes to sink overflows to network failures to power outages. Although natural disasters might appear to be the most devastating causes of information systems outages, they are hardly the most frequent or the biggest threats to uptime. Figure 10.10 highlights some possible sources of unplanned downtime.

Bomb threat	Fraud	Shredded data
Burst pipe	Frozen pipe	Snowstorm
Chemical spill	Hacker	Sprinkler malfunction
Construction	Hail	Static electricity
Corrupted data	Hurricane	Strike
Earthquake	Ice storm	Theft
Electrical short	Insects	Tornado
Epidemic	Lightning	Train derailment
Equipment failure	Network failure	Smoke damage
Evacuation	Plane crash	Vandalism
Explosion	Power outage	Vehicle crash
Fire	Power surge	Virus
Flood	Rodents	Water damage (various)
Flu season	Sabotage	Wind

FIGURE 10.10

Sources of Unplanned Downtime

According to CA Technologies, IT downtime costs tens of billions in lost revenue across North America and Europe.[13] Figure 10.11 displays the four categories associated with downtime, according to Gartner. A few questions companies should ask when determining the cost of downtime are:

- How many transactions can the company afford to lose without significantly affecting business?

- Does the company depend upon one or more mission-critical application(s) to conduct business?

- How much revenue will the company lose for every hour a critical application is unavailable?

- What is the productivity cost associated with each hour of downtime?

- How will collaborative business processes with partners, suppliers, and customers be affected by an unexpected information systems outage?

- What is the total cost of lost productivity and lost revenue during unplanned downtime?

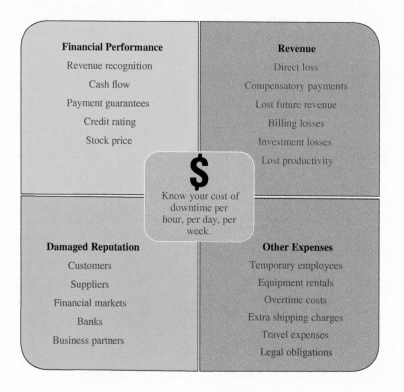

FIGURE 10.11

The Cost of Downtime

The reliability and resilience of information systems have never been more essential for success as businesses cope with the forces of globalization, 24/7 operations, government and trade regulations, and overextended information systems budgets and resources. Any unexpected information systems downtime in today's business environment has the potential to cause both short- and long-term costs with far-reaching consequences. This section explains how you can use security to combat the threat of downtime. Understanding how to secure a business network is critical to keeping downtime to a minimum and uptime to a maximum.

PROTECTING INFORMATION

Smoking is not just bad for a person's health; it seems that it is also bad for company security. With companies banning smoking inside their offices, smokers are forced outside—usually to specific smoking areas in the back of the building. The doors leading out to them are a major security hole, according to a study undertaken by NTA Monitor Ltd., a U.K.-based Internet security tester. An NTA tester was able to easily get inside a corporate building through a back door that was left open so smokers could easily and quickly get out and then back in, according to the company. Once inside, the tester asked an employee to take him to a meeting room, claiming the IS department had sent him. Even without a pass, he reportedly gained access unchallenged and was then able to connect his laptop to the company's network. In Canada, 69 percent of businesses believe that have had some type of a cyberattack in the last year.[14]

Organizational information is a key resource. Just as organizations protect their assets—keeping their money in an insured bank or providing a safe working environment for employees—they must also protect their information. With security breaches on the rise and computer hackers everywhere, an organization must put in place strong information security measures to survive. In May 2104, there was a data breach at eBay with the theft of information on 100 million user accounts, and in late 2103 Target lost 40 million credit card and debit card users' data. Following are some more examples that demonstrate why such measures are important:

■ On June 1, 2011, Scotiabank reportedly lost three data CDs in its internal mail, which contained personal information such as social insurance numbers and account numbers for an undisclosed number of customers. According to the bank, "the loss is a rare incident and only a small percentage of customers are affected." The CDs were being transferred to the Canada Revenue Agency as part of the bank's reporting requirements. According to the bank, at least one customer was concerned "that someone might steal his identity and apply for fraudulent credit cards."[15]

■ The Privacy Commissioner of Canada, Jennifer Stoddart, launched an investigation into a CIBC personal information breach involving nearly half a million people. The issue was the loss of a backup computer file containing personal information on approximately 470,000 clients of a subsidiary of the bank, Talvest Mutual Funds. The missing data were in a file that disappeared "while in transit" between offices. The information may have included client names, addresses, signatures, dates of birth, bank account numbers, beneficiary information, and social insurance numbers.[16]

■ An information security breach occurred when hundreds of Rogers's cable and Internet customer orders, containing personal information such as driver's licence numbers and social insurance numbers, were found abandoned in a downtown Toronto parking lot near Ryerson University. In its defence, Rogers blamed an employee of the company it had hired to sell its cable TV and Internet services.[17]

Though these breaches made national news, what is troubling is that Canada really does not know the extent of privacy and security breaches. This is because PIPEDA legislation does not make it mandatory for organizations to notify people of data breaches involving personal information. However, Stoddart called for amendments to PIPEDA to make public notification of security breaches mandatory by companies. This suggested change would give consumers advance notice to take action (such as verifying their credit card history and possibly cancelling credit cards). The amendment would also encourage business to take privacy matters more seriously and take measures that would better protect sensitive customer information. There is some apathy among Canadian private-sector companies in complying with Canadian data and information protection laws. One study indicates that Canadian retailers generally fail to adequately understand or deal with accountability, openness, access, and consent; the capacity of retailers to safeguard personal information, or even know if a security breach has occurred, is also suspect.[18]

Interestingly, though the United States has weaker privacy legislation than Canada, more than 30 American states have already introduced mandatory notification laws. This is due in large part to a major privacy and security breach in 2005 involving a data company that inadvertently sold personal information on thousands of U.S. residents to a criminal organization.[19]

The message here is that all businesses must understand the importance of information security, whether or not it is enforceable by law. ***Information security*** is a broad term that encompasses the protection of information from accidental or intentional misuse by persons inside or outside an organization. The typical size of an organization's information security budget relative to the organization's overall IT budget ranges but in most cases the trend has been that CIO are gaining more control over IT security spending.[20]

Security is perhaps the most fundamental and critical of all the technologies/disciplines an organization must have squarely in place to execute its business strategy. Without solid security processes and procedures, none of the other technologies can develop business advantages.

PROTECTING DATA

Backup and Recovery

Every year, businesses lose time and money because of system crashes and failures. One way to minimize the damage of a crash is to have a backup, recovery, and business continuity strategy in place (see Figure 10.12). A ***backup*** is an exact copy of a system's data. ***Recovery*** is the ability to get a system up and running again in the event of a crash or failure and includes restoring the backup. Many different types of backup and recovery media are available, including redundant storage servers, tapes, disks, and even CDs and DVDs. All the different types of backup and recovery media are reliable; their primary differences are the speed and associated costs.

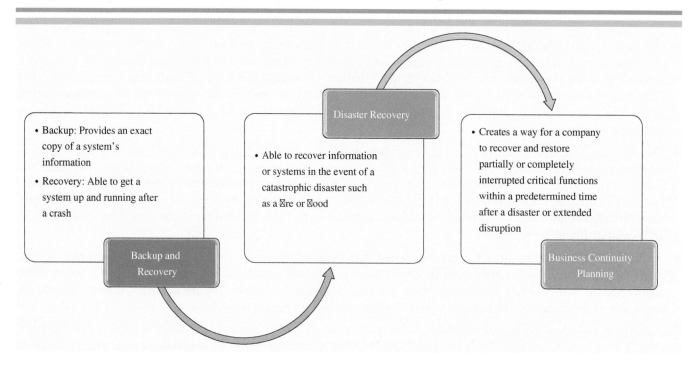

FIGURE 10.12

Data Backup and Recovery, Disaster Recovery, and Business Continuity Planning

7-Eleven Taiwan, a chain of more than 4,000 franchise locations, uploads backup and recovery data from its central location to all its locations daily. The company implemented a new technology solution that can quickly and reliably download and upload backup and recovery data to all its stores. In addition, when a connection fails during the download or upload, the technology automatically resumes the download without having to start over, saving valuable time.[21]

Organizations should choose a backup and recovery strategy that is in line with its business goals. If the organization deals with large volumes of critical data, it will require daily, perhaps even hourly, backups to storage servers. If the organization deals with small amounts of non-critical data, then it might require only weekly backups to tapes, CDs, or DVDs. Deciding how often to back up data and what media to use is a critical business decision. If an organization decides to back up only weekly, it is taking the risk that, if a total crash occurs, it might lose a week's worth of work. If this risk is acceptable, a weekly backup strategy will work. If this risk is unacceptable, the organization needs to move to daily backup. Some organizations find the risk of losing a day's worth of work too high and move to an hourly backup strategy.

Two techniques used to help in case of system failure are fault tolerance and failover. *Fault tolerance* is a computer system designed so that in the event a component fails, a backup component or procedure can immediately take its place with no loss of service. Fault tolerance can be provided with software or embedded in hardware, or provided by some combination. *Failover* is a backup operational mode in which the functions of a computer component (such as a processor, server, network, or database) are assumed by secondary system components when the primary component becomes unavailable through either failure or scheduled downtime. A failover procedure involves automatically offloading tasks to a standby system component so that the procedure is as seamless as possible to the end-user. Failover makes systems more fault-tolerant, and is typically an integral part of mission-critical systems that must be constantly available, such as systems used in the financial industry.[22]

Disaster Recovery

A northern Ohio power company, FirstEnergy, missed signs that there were potential problems in its portion of North America's electrical grid. The events that followed left an estimated 50 million people in the United States and Canada in the dark. The failings are laid out in the widely reported findings of a joint U.S./Canada task force that investigated the causes of the blackout and recommended what to do to avoid future large-scale outages. The report detailed many procedures or best practices, including:

■ Mind the enterprise architectures

■ Monitor the quality of computer networks that provide data on power suppliers and demand

■ Make sure the networks can be restored quickly in the case of downtime

■ Set up disaster recovery plans

■ Provide adequate staff training, including verbal communication protocols so that operators are aware of any IT-related problems that may be affecting their situational awareness of the power grid

Disasters such as power outages, floods, fires, and even harmful hacking strike businesses every day. To prepare for such occurrences, organizations must develop a *disaster recovery plan*, a detailed process for recovering data or an IT system in the event of a catastrophic event such as a fire or flood. Spending on disaster recovery is rising worldwide among financial institutions.

Such a plan takes into consideration the location of the backup data. Many organizations store it at an off-site facility. There are vendors that specialize in off-site data storage and disaster recovery solutions. A comprehensive plan also foresees the possibility that not only the computer equipment but also the building where employees work might be destroyed. Organizations might establish either a *hot site*, a separate and fully equipped facility where the company can move immediately after a disaster and resume business, or a *cold site*, a separate facility that does not have any computer equipment, but to which employees can move after a disaster.

A *disaster recovery cost curve* charts (1) the cost to the organization of the unavailability of data and technology and (2) the cost to the organization of recovering from a disaster over time. Figure 10.13 displays a disaster recovery cost curve and shows that where the two lines intersect is the best recovery plan in terms of cost and time. Creating an organization's disaster recovery cost curve is no small task. It must consider the cost of losing data and technology within each department or functional area, and the cost of losing data and technology across the whole enterprise. During the first few hours of a disaster, those costs will be low, but they become increasingly higher over time. With those costs in mind, an organization must then determine the costs of recovery. Cost of recovery during the first few hours of a disaster is exceedingly high and diminishes over time.

On April 18, 1906, San Francisco was rocked by an earthquake that destroyed large swaths of the city and claimed the lives of more than 3,000 inhabitants of the San Francisco Bay area. More than a century later, a bigger, bolder, rebuilt, and more resilient San Francisco is more important than ever. Now it serves as the heart of the global IT industry and is a major world financial centre. However, San Francisco remains well aware of the terrible potential that exists along the San Andreas Fault.

The vast skyscrapers downtown may now be built to withstand huge pressures, but what about the infrastructure and the systems that keep modern business ticking—and the people who must be able to access them? A **business continuity plan (BCP)** is a plan for recovery and restoration of partly or completely interrupted critical functions within a predetermined time after a disaster or extended disruption. A BCP typically includes five key pieces:

1. Business continuity plan governance that establishes a governance structure in the form of committees that make sure control is established during a disaster

2. Business impact analysis that identifies an organization's goals and critical services or products; ranks the order of priority of services or products for continuous delivery or rapid recovery; and identifies internal and external impacts of disruptions

3. The plans, measures, and arrangements required for business continuity

4. Readiness procedures that allow for the training of staff about the BCP and also outline the exercises staff undertake during training

5. Quality assurance techniques that assess the plan's accuracy, relevance, and effectiveness and uncover which parts of the plan need improvement

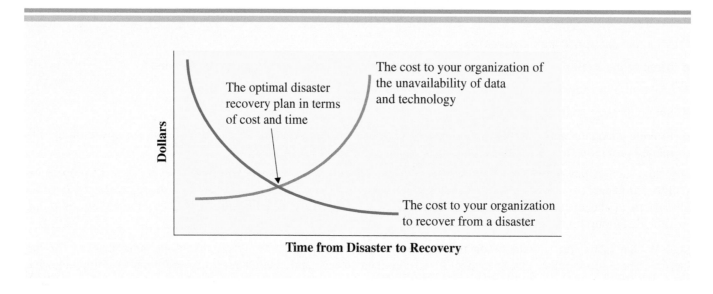

FIGURE 10.13

The Disaster Recovery Cost Curve

When an organization experiences a disruption, the key elements that need to be undertaken in the incident response are the response (which includes incident management), communications management, and operations management. These are followed by continuing the critical services as identified by the BCP, and then restoration and recovery of normal business operations.[23]

Business continuity and disaster recovery are serious issues for all organizations in the San Francisco Bay area, including the Union Bank of California, which is based in the heart of downtown San Francisco.[24] Barry Cardoza, head of business continuity planning and disaster recovery at Union Bank of California, said, "You have disasters that you can see coming and you've got disasters that you can't see coming and an earthquake is an example of [the latter]. And you don't know how bad it's going to be until it hits."[25]

Businesses must have processes in place ahead of such an event to mitigate the threat. Simply reacting is not a strategy. The continuity department must also understand every aspect of the business and weigh downtime for each in terms of financial and reputational damage. Union Bank of California created a disaster recovery plan that includes multiple data centres in diverse locations, mirrored sites that can take over at the flick of a switch, hot sites where staff can walk in and start working exactly as they would if they were in their normal location, and a vast amount of redundancy. In addition, the bank created real-time mirroring between data centres. It is now a matter of minutes, not hours, for Union Bank of California to be up and running in the event of a disaster.

Securing Data

Security professionals are under increasing pressure to do the job right and cost-effectively as networks extend beyond organizations to remote users, partners, and customers, and to smartphones, tablets, and other mobile devices. Regulatory requirements to safeguard data have increased. Concerns about identity theft are at an all-time high. Hacking and other unauthorized access contribute to the approximately 10 million instances of identity theft each year, according to the U.S. Federal Trade Commission. A good data architecture includes a strong data security plan, along with managing user access and up-to-date antivirus software and patches.[26]

Managing user access to data is a critical piece of the data architecture, and passwords may still be the weakest link in the security chain. At VITAS Innovative Hospice Care, with a workforce of 11,000 and operations in the U.S. across 17 states, authorized employees enter as many as a half-dozen passwords a day to access multiple systems. While it is important to maintain password discipline to secure customers' data, maintaining and managing the situation is a drag on the IT department. "Our help desk spends 30 percent of their time on password management and provisioning," said John Sandbrook, senior IT director. The company began using an identity management suite to manage passwords and comply with data access regulations. The ID management product includes automated audit, reporting, and compliance capabilities and a common platform for password management, provisioning, and self-service. With the software, VITAS can enforce stronger passwords with seven, eight, or nine characters, numbers, and capital letters that frequently change. The company anticipates curbing help desk password time by 50 percent.[27]

Security is a top priority for business managers, regardless of the size of their company. Among Fortune 500 companies, more than 80 percent of those surveyed described updating security procedures, tools, and services as a key business priority. That desire holds true for small, mid-size, or large companies and for IT managers and corporate managers.

The main focus for most managers is preventing hackers, spammers, and other mischief-makers from entering their networks, and nearly two-thirds are looking to enhance their network security management, intrusion detection, content-filtering, and anti-spam software. More than half also plan to upgrade their encryption software.[28]

Microsoft issues patches for its software on the second Tuesday of every month. If a company wants to keep its systems protected, these must be downloaded and installed on all systems across the enterprise. At OMD, a media buying and planning subsidiary of Omnicom Group Inc., the network administrator had to manually install critical patches on all 100 servers, taking more than a week to deploy the patch. Now, OMD uses automated installation software for patches and upgrades. The company purchased software that let it move ahead with applying patches without taking down entire systems and balancing patch-deployment timing among servers so that all departments were not down at once during a patch install. Given everything else that security professionals need to think about, automated installation software is a welcome relief.[29]

PEOPLE: THE FIRST LINE OF DEFENCE

With current advances in information systems and business strategies such as CRM, organizations are able to determine valuable information, such as who are the top 20 percent of the customers that produce 80 percent of all revenues. Most organizations view this type of information as critical, and are implementing security measures to prevent the information from walking out the door or falling into the wrong hands. Enterprises can implement information security lines of defence through people first and through technology second.

Adding to the complexity of information security is the fact that organizations must enable employees, customers, and partners to access information electronically to be successful in this electronic world. Doing business electronically automatically creates tremendous information security risks for organizations. Surprisingly, the biggest issue surrounding information security is not a technical issue, but a people issue.

The last Computer Security Institute survey reported that 41.1 percent of respondents had experienced a security incident and 43.2 percent had reported that at least some of their losses could be attributed to insider attacks. *Insiders* are legitimate users who purposely or accidentally misuse their access to the environment and cause some kind of business-affecting incident. Most information security breaches result from people misusing an organization's information either intentionally or inadvertently. For example, many individuals freely give out their passwords or write them on sticky notes next to their computers, leaving the door wide open to intruders.[30]

In the past there have been a number of incidents of patients dying when they received overdoses of radiation treatment while being treated for cancer. The more famous of these incidents were the Therac-25 accidents in the late 1980s, where an investigation found that part of the cause of the accidents were related to software problems. These types of findings raise a new set of questions around liability and who is responsible. For example, is the software designer responsible or is the radiotherapist responsible, and what about the responsibilities of the hospital manager or the hospital itself?[31]

The director of information security at a large health care company discovered how easy it was to create an information security breach when she hired outside auditors to test her company's security awareness. In one instance, auditors found that staff members testing a new system had accidentally exposed the network to outside hackers. In another, auditors were able to obtain the passwords of 16 employees when the auditors posed as support staff using a technique called *social engineering*, which means using one's social skills to trick people into revealing access credentials or other information valuable to the attacker. Dumpster diving, or looking through people's trash, is another way social engineers obtain information.[32]

Information security policies identify the rules required to maintain information security. An *information security plan* details how an organization will implement the information security policies. Figure 10.14 displays some common considerations for an information security plan.

Things an information security plan should do:

- Identify and assess risks to customer information
- Identify security plan roles and assign responsibilities
- Provide ways to identify and assess risk
- Develop written policies and procedures to manage and control identified risks
- Identify mechanisms to implement and assess the plan

Areas that should be addressed by an information security plan:

- Employee management and training
- Physical security of the data and information
- Safeguards
- Service providers

FIGURE 10.14

Information Security Plan Considerations

The first line of defence an organization should follow is to create an information security plan detailing the various information security policies. Such a plan can alleviate people-based information security issues. Five steps for creating an information security plan are displayed in Figure 10.15.

1.	**Develop the information security policies**	Identify who is responsible and accountable for designing and implementing the organization's information security policies. Simple, yet highly effective types of information security policies include requiring users to log off of their systems before leaving for lunches or meetings, never sharing passwords with anyone, and changing personal passwords every 60 days. The chief security officer (CSO) is typically responsible for designing these information security policies.
2.	**Communicate the information security policies**	Train all employees on the policies and establish clear expectations for following the policies. For example, let all employees know that they will receive a formal reprimand for leaving a computer unsecured.
3.	**Identify critical information assets and risks**	Require the use of user IDs, passwords, and antivirus software on all systems. Ensure any systems that contain links to external networks have the appropriate technical protections such as firewalls or intrusion detection software. A firewall is hardware and/or software that guards a private network by analyzing the information leaving and entering the network. Intrusion detection software (IDS) searches out patterns in information and network traffic to indicate attacks and quickly responds to prevent any harm.
4.	**Test and reevaluate risks**	Continually perform security reviews, audits, background checks, and security assessments.
5.	**Obtain stakeholder support**	Gain the approval and support of the information security polices from the board of directors and all stakeholders.

FIGURE 10.15

Five Steps for Creating an Information Security Plan

Figure 10.16 provides the top 10 questions that managers should ask to ensure their information is secure.

LO5 | THE SECOND LINE OF DEFENCE: TECHNOLOGY

The Arkansas State University (ASU) network upgrade brought gigabit-speed network capacity to every dorm room and office on its campus. The university was concerned that the new network would be a tempting playground for hackers. To reduce its fear, the university installed intrusion detection software (IDS) to stay on top of security and potential network abuses. Whenever the IDS spots a potential security threat, such as a virus or a hacker, it alerts the central management system. The system automatically pages the IT staff, who deal with the attack by shutting off access to the system, identifying the hacker's location, and calling campus security.[33]

Once an organization has protected its intellectual capital by arming its people with a detailed information security plan, it can begin to focus its efforts on deploying the right types of information security technologies such as the IDS installed at ASU.

It is estimated that worldwide spending on IT security software, hardware, and services will top US$86 billion by the end of 2016.[34] Organizations can deploy numerous technologies to prevent information security breaches. When determining which types of technologies to invest in, it helps to understand the three primary information security areas:

1. Authentication and authorization

2. Prevention and resistance

3. Detection and response[35]

1. Does our board of directors recognize that information security is a board-level issue that cannot be left to the IT department alone?

2. Is there clear accountability for information security in our organization?

3. Do our board members articulate an agreed-upon set of threats and critical assets? How often do we review and update these?

4. How much is spent on information security and what is it being spent on?

5. What is the impact on the organization of a serious security incident?

6. Does our organization view information security as an enabler? (For example, by implementing effective security, could we enable our organization to increase business over the Internet?)

7. What is the risk to our business of getting a reputation for low information security?

8. What steps have we taken to ensure that third parties will not compromise the security of our organization?

9. How do we obtain independent assurance that information security is managed effectively in our organization?

10. How do we measure the effectiveness of our information security activities?

FIGURE 10.16

Top 10 Questions Managers Should Ask Regarding Information Security

Authentication and Authorization

Authentication is a method for confirming users' identities. Once a system has determined the authentication of a user, it can then determine the access privileges (or authorization) for that user. *Authorization* is the process of giving someone permission to do or have something. In multiple-user computer systems, user access or authorization determines such things as file access, hours of access, and amount of allocated storage space. Authentication and authorization techniques are broken down into three categories, and the most secure type involves a combination of all three:

1. Something the user knows, such as a user ID and password

2. Something the user has, such as a smart card or token

3. Something that is part of the user, such as a fingerprint or voice signature

Something the User Knows, Such as a User ID and Password The first type of authentication, using something the user knows, is the most common way to identify individual users and typically consists of a unique user ID and password. However, this is actually one of the most *ineffective* ways for determining authentication, because passwords are not secure. All it typically takes to crack a password is enough time. More than 50 percent of help-desk calls are password-related, which can cost an organization significant money, and passwords are vulnerable to being coaxed out of somebody by a "social engineer with goals of accomplishing things like identity theft.

Identity theft is the forging of someone's identity for the purpose of fraud. The fraud is often financial fraud, such as applying for and using credit cards in the victim's name or applying for a loan. Figure 10.17 displays several examples.

A man and a woman were arrested for redirecting people's mail using a change of address form from Canada Post. Redirecting mail provides thieves with an abundant source of personal information about people and gives thieves more time to engage in fraudulent activity before victims are even suspicious. To entice people to provide enough personal information so that a change of address form could be filled out, the man and woman posted a fake online job offer and just waited for people to send them their personal information.[36]

The security of information is often only as good as the integrity of employees working in organizations who have access to personal information of customers and fellow employees. An instance of such insider theft occurred at the Bank of Canada where two people employed by EDS Canada—a third-party systems outsourcer that provided back-office administration and support for the Bank of Canada's Canada Savings Bond (CSB) program—were arrested. These two individuals victimized eight account holders of the CSB Payroll Savings Program for a total of about $100,000.[37]

An 82-year-old woman in Fort Worth, Texas, discovered that her identity had been stolen when the woman using her name was involved in a four-car collision. For 18 months, she kept getting notices of lawsuits and overdue medical bills that were really meant for someone else. It took seven years for her to get her financial good name restored after the identity thief charged over $100,000 on the 12 fraudulently acquired credit cards.

A 42-year-old retired army captain in Rocky Hill, Connecticut, found that an identity thief had spent $260,000 buying goods and services that included two trucks, a Harley-Davidson motorcycle, and a timeshare vacation home in South Carolina. He discovered the problem only when his retirement income was garnisheed to pay the outstanding bills.

FIGURE 10.17

Examples of Identity Theft

Phishing is a common technique to gain personal or corporate information for the purpose of identity theft, usually by means of fraudulent email. Perpetrators might send out email messages that look as though they come from legitimate businesses such as the Royal Bank of Canada or Desjardins Financial Security. The messages seem genuine, with official-looking formats and logos. They typically ask for verification of important information like passwords and account numbers. Recently, Chinese military officials have been accused of using phishing to gain backdoor access to corporate information.[38] Since the emails look authentic, up to one in five recipients responds with the information, and subsequently becomes a victim of identity theft and other fraud.

Something the User Has, Such as a Smart Card or Token   The second type of authentication, using something that the user has, offers a much more effective way to identify individuals than a user ID and password. Tokens and smart cards are two of the primary forms of this type of authentication. *Tokens* are small electronic devices that change user passwords automatically. The user enters his or her user ID and token-displayed password to gain access to the network. A *smart card*, about the size of a credit card, contains embedded technologies that store information and small amounts of software to perform some limited processing. Smart cards act as identification instruments, a form of digital cash, or a data storage device with the ability to store an entire medical record.

Something That Is Part of the User, Such As a Fingerprint or Voice Signature   The third kind of authentication, using something that is part of the user, is by far the best and most effective way to manage authentication. *Biometrics* is the identification of a user based on a physical characteristic, such as a fingerprint, iris, face, voice, or handwriting. Unfortunately, biometric authentication can be costly and intrusive. For example, iris scans are expensive and considered intrusive by most people. Fingerprint authentication is less intrusive and inexpensive but is also not 100 percent accurate. Biometrics are used with the NEXUS card to help frequent travellers cross the Canada/U.S. border more quickly. In Canada it also enables cardholders to clear airport security faster by using the Trusted Traveller CATSA Security Lane. The NEXUS card stores biometrics of the person's irises and fingerprints, and includes an RFID chip. At specifically equipped border crossings and airports, cardholders use the card in a special kiosk that reads their biometrics. Cardholders can use the Trusted Traveller security line at eight major Canadian airports and 24 land ports of entry. The card is available to qualified Canadians through Canada Border Services Agency.[39]

Prevention and Resistance

Prevention and resistance technologies stop intruders from accessing intellectual capital. A division of Sony Inc., Sony Pictures Entertainment (SPE), defends itself from attacks by using an intrusion detection system to detect new attacks as they occur. SPE develops and distributes a wide variety of products including movies, television, videos, and DVDs. A compromise to SPE security could result in costing the company valuable intellectual capital as well as millions of dollars and months of time. The company needed an advanced threat management solution that would take fewer resources to maintain and require limited resources to track and respond to suspicious network activity. The company installed an advanced intrusion detection system allowing it to monitor all of its network activity, including any potential security breaches.[40]

Content Filtering

Content filtering occurs when organizations use software that filters content to prevent the transmission of unauthorized information. Organizations can use content filtering technologies to filter email and prevent emails containing sensitive information from transmitting, whether the transmission was malicious or accidental. It can also filter emails and prevent any suspicious files from transmitting such as potential virus-infected files. Email content filtering can also filter for spam.

"Sean Lane Bought 14k White Gold 1/5 ct Diamond Eternity Flower Ring from **Overstock.com**" was the Facebook status shown to Sean Lane's network of friends including his wife. So much for the surprise of his wife's Christmas gift. This was all thanks to Beacon, a feature that shared members' online purchases with their friends. Beacon's goal was to turn Facebook users into effective word-of-mouth promoters of the products they were buying online, but it was sharing this information without users' consent. The outcomes included a 50,000-user-signed petition calling on Facebook to discontinue the use of Beacon and a class-action lawsuit. Beacon was shut down in September 2009 and a US$9.5 million fund was set up to pay for online privacy initiatives as a result of the lawsuit settlement.[41]

Encryption

Encryption scrambles information into an alternative form that one requires a key or password to decrypt. Even if the information is stolen, it will be unreadable. Encryption can switch the order of characters, replace characters with other characters, insert or remove characters, or use a mathematical formula to convert the information into some sort of code. Companies that transmit sensitive customer information over the Internet, such as credit card numbers, frequently use encryption.

Some encryption technologies use multiple keys such as public key encryption. *Public key encryption (PKE)* is an encryption system that uses two keys: a public key that everyone can have and a private key for only the recipient (see Figure 10.18). When implementing security using multiple keys, the organization provides the public key to all of its customers (end consumers and other businesses). The customers use the public key to encrypt their information and send it on the Internet. When it arrives at its destination, the organization uses the private key to unscramble the encrypted information.

Firewalls

One of the most common defences for preventing a security breach is a *firewall*, hardware and/or software that guards a private network by analyzing the information entering and leaving it. Unless a message has the correct markings, a firewall prevents it from entering the network. Firewalls can even detect computers communicating with the Internet without approval. As Figure 10.19 illustrates, organizations typically put a firewall between a server and the Internet.

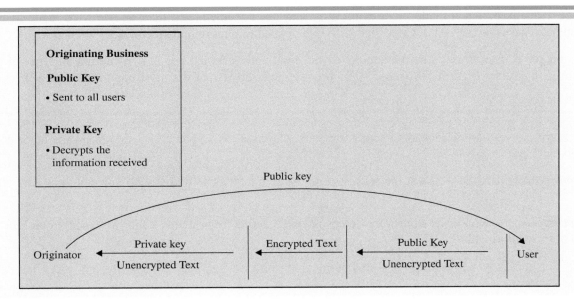

FIGURE 10.18

Public Key Encryption (PKE) System

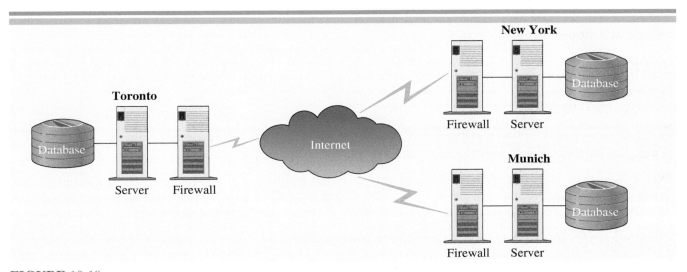

FIGURE 10.19

Sample Firewall Architecture Connecting Systems Located in Toronto, New York, and Munich

Detection and Response

The final area where organizations can allocate resources is in detection and response technologies. If prevention and resistance strategies fail and there is a security breach, an organization can use detection and response technologies to mitigate the damage. The most common type of defence within detection and response technologies is antivirus software.

The world has seen a number of widespread malware and vulnerabilities in software in the past decades. Recent instances include the Heartbleed bug and the BlackShades malware. Heartbleed is a bug within OpenSSL encryption that allows anyone on the Internet to read the memory of the vulnerable OpenSSL system, which can include usernames and passwords as well as content.[42] BlackShades is malware that can be purchased and downloaded and used to remotely control and view another person's computer. Jared Abrahams was sentenced to 18 months in jail for blackmailing Miss Teen USA Cassidy Wolf in a case of what's being called "sextortion." In this case

BlackShades was used to take nude pictures of Wolf and other women, and then threats were made to post the pictures online unless they agreed to video chat with him or send him more nude pictures.[43]

Typically, people equate viruses (the malicious software) with hackers (the people). While not all types of hackers create viruses, many do. Figures 10.20 and 10.21 provide an overview of the most common types of hackers and viruses.

Hacker. Someone very knowledgeable about computers who uses his or her knowledge to invade other people's computers.

White-hat hacker. One who works at the request of the system owners to find system vulnerabilities and plug the holes.

Black-hat hacker. Someone who breaks into other people's computer systems; might just look around, or might steal and destroy information.

Hactivist. Someone who has philosophical and political reasons for breaking into systems and will often deface a website as a protest.

Script kiddies or *script bunnies*. Someone who finds hacking code on the Internet and clicks-and-points his or her way into systems to cause damage or spread viruses.

Cracker. A hacker with criminal intent.

Cyberterrorist. Someone who seeks to cause harm to people or to destroy critical systems or information and use the Internet as a weapon of mass destruction.

FIGURE 10.20

Types of Hackers

Virus. Software written with malicious intent to cause annoyance or damage.

Worm. A type of virus that spreads itself, not only from file to file, but also from computer to computer. The primary difference between a virus and a worm is that a virus must attach to something, such as an executable file, in order to spread. Worms do not need to attach to anything to spread and can tunnel themselves into computers.

Denial-of-service attack (DoS). Floods a website with so many requests for service that it slows down or crashes the site.

Distributed denial-of-service attack (DDoS). Attacks from multiple computers that flood a website with so many requests for service that it slows down or crashes. A common type is the Ping of Death, in which thousands of computers try to access a site at the same time, overloading it and shutting it down.

Trojan-horse virus. Hides inside other software, usually as an attachment or a downloadable file.

Backdoor programs. Viruses that open a way into a network for future attacks.

Polymorphic viruses and worms. Viruses and worms that change their form as they propagate.

FIGURE 10.21

Types of Viruses

Some of the most damaging forms of security threats to e-business sites include malicious code, hoaxes, spoofing, and sniffers (see Figure 10.22).

Elevation of privilege is a process by which a user misleads a system into granting unauthorized rights, usually for the purpose of compromising or destroying the system. For example, an attacker might log onto a network by using a guest account, and then exploit a weakness in the software that lets the attacker change the guest privileges to "Administrative."

Hoaxes attack computer systems by transmitting a virus hoax, with a real virus attached. By masking the attack in a seemingly legitimate message, unsuspecting users more readily distribute the message and send the attack on to their co-workers and friends, infecting many users along the way.

Malicious code includes a variety of threats such as viruses, worms, and Trojan horses.

Spoofing is the forging of the return address on an email so that the email message appears to come from someone other than the actual sender. This is not a virus but rather a way by which virus authors conceal their identities as they send out viruses.

Spyware is software that comes hidden in free downloadable software and tracks online movements, mines the information stored on a computer, or uses a computer's CPU and storage for some task the user knows nothing about. According to the National Cyber Security Alliance, 91 percent of those in the study had spyware on their computers that could cause extremely slow performance, excessive pop-up ads, or hijacked home pages.

A *sniffer* is a program or device that can monitor data travelling over a network. Sniffers can show all the data being transmitted over a network, including passwords and sensitive information. Sniffers tend to be a favourite weapon in the hacker's arsenal.

Packet tampering consists in altering the contents of packets (blocks of data) as they travel over the Internet or altering data on computer disks after penetrating a network. For example, an attacker might put a tap on a network line to intercept packets as they leave the computer. The attacker could eavesdrop or alter the information as it leaves the network.

Phishing is a technique used to gain personal information for the purpose of identity theft, usually by means of fraudulent emails that look as though they came from legitimate businesses.

Pharming reroutes requests for legitimate websites to false ones. For example, if you were to type in your bank's URL, pharming could redirect you to a fake site that collects your information.

FIGURE 10.22

Security Threats to E-Business

Implementing information security lines of defence through people first and technology second is the best way for an organization to protect its vital information. The first line of defence is securing information by creating an information security plan detailing the various information security policies. The second line of defence is investing in technology to help secure information through authentication and authorization, prevention and resistance, and detection and response.

OPENING CASE QUESTIONS

The Privacy Commissioner of Canada's Work

5. In the example, how can the company's embrace of privacy mitigate future information security problems?

6. What is the biggest information security roadblock facing organizations attempting to achieve compliance with privacy legislation?

7. Can technology alone guarantee that information is kept secure? Why or why not?

8. Unfortunately, privacy and security breaches are a common occurrence in organizations today. What recent privacy and security breaches have been in the media lately? Do you think things will get worse before they get better? How can organizations better prepare themselves against future privacy and security breaches?

SUMMARY OF KEY THEMES

The purpose of the chapter was to highlight the need for organizations to protect information from misuse. Specifically, this chapter discussed:

- *Information ethics and its importance in the workplace.* Organizations need to be aware of the ethical and moral issues surrounding information and information systems. These issues are largely influenced by people's individual ethical beliefs—there are no hard-and-fast rules for determining what is and is not ethical. In the workplace, ethical issues include the design and deployment of information systems that do not respect human dignity, and using information technology to monitor employee performance in inappropriate ways.

- *Information privacy and the differences in privacy legislation around the world.* Information privacy concerns the protection of unauthorized access to personal information. Around the world, different privacy legislations exist. European countries tend to favour strong privacy legislation, while the United States tends to adopt a more laissez-faire attitude toward privacy legislation, often promoting self-regulation rather than hard, steadfast polices. Canada's laws closely follow the European model. PIPEDA is Canada's premier privacy legislation— it imposes strict rules on how businesses of all shapes and sizes must protect and handle personal (customer) information. The gist of PIPEDA is the notions of consent, choice, and control. The legislation gives organizations rules on how personal information is collected, shared, and stored.

- *The differences between various information ethics and privacy policies in the workplace.* A variety of policies exist in organizations to help enforce proper information ethics and information privacy behaviours. Typical policies include ethical computer use, information privacy, acceptable use privacy, email privacy, Internet use, anti-spam, and employee monitoring.

- *Information security and why people are the first line of defence in terms of protecting information.* Information security is about protecting information from harm or misuse. The biggest issue facing information security is not a technical issue, but a people one. Even the tightest technical security measures and the most severe information privacy policies can be severely compromised by just one lackadaisical or corrupt worker (an "insider") who has access to confidential or private information and is careless or malicious about how this information is used. The effectiveness of information security measures and information polices is highly dependent upon the people in the organization who enforce and enact these measures and policies.

- *How information technologies can be used to enhance information security.* A variety of information technology solutions are available to organizations to help keep information protected and secure. These include user IDs and passwords, smart cards or tokens, biometrics, intrusion detection software, encryption, and corporate firewalls.

As a business student, you must understand that information ethics, privacy, and security are of paramount importance in organizations today. This is particularly true in Canada, where PIPEDA privacy legislation puts legal pressure on companies to guarantee that the personal information they collect remains private and secure. Companies that fail to do so not only face legal repercussions, but also the wrath of consumers who have high expectations about how their personal information is handled by companies.

KEY TERMS

Acceptable use policy (AUP)

Anti-spam policy

Authentication

Authorization

Backdoor programs

Backup

Biometrics

Black-hat hacker

Business continuity plan

Click-fraud

Competitive click-fraud

Confidentiality

Content filtering

Copyright

Counterfeit software

Cracker

Cyberbullying

Cyberterrorist

Cybervandalism

Denial-of-service attack (DoS)

Disaster recovery plan

Disaster recovery cost curve

Distributed denial-of-service attack (DDoS)

Elevation of privilege

Email privacy policy

Encryption

e-Policies

Ethical computer use policy

Ethics

Failover

Fair dealing

Fault tolerance

Firewall

Hacker

Hactivist

Hoaxes

Identity theft

Information ethics

Information privacy

Information privacy policy

Information security

Information security plan

Information security policies

Insiders

Intellectual property

Internet censorship

Internet use policy

Malicious code

Nonrepudiation

Packet tampering

Pharming

Phishing

Physical security

Pirated software

Polymorphic viruses and worms

Privacy

Public key encryption (PKE)

Recovery

Script kiddies (script bunnies)

Smart card

Sniffer

Social engineering

Social media policy

Spam

Spoofing

Spyware

Teergrubing	Website name stealing
Tokens	White-hat hacker
Trojan-horse virus	Workplace MIS monitoring
Virus	Worm

CLOSING CASE ONE

WestJet Accepts Blame for Spying on Air Canada

This case illustrates the ethics and ramifications of breaching private information.

In May 2006, a resolution was reached in a corporate espionage case between WestJet and Air Canada. WestJet admitted culpability in accessing confidential information via an Air Canada website.

Accessing this information, Air Canada claimed, allowed WestJet to identify Air Canada's most profitable routes and plan their expansion accordingly. Being privy to this information, Air Canada claimed, allowed WestJet to unfairly adjust its own scheduling and pricing information and to gain a valuable springboard to start new routes and terminating others. In addition, Air Canada claimed, it allowed WestJet to identify booking trends, information tremendously valuable to any airline.

In a press release jointly issued with Air Canada, WestJet accepted "full responsibility," stating that "the conduct was both unethical and unacceptable." In the press release, WestJet admitted that certain members of its management team had "engaged in an extensive practice of covertly accessing a password-protected proprietary employee website maintained by Air Canada to download detailed and commercially sensitive information without authorization or consent from Air Canada."[44]

What was truly alarming about this incident was that this corporate spying occurred with the knowledge and direction of the highest management levels at WestJet and did not stop until the breach was discovered by Air Canada.

Here is the sequence of events, according to the *Calgary Herald*:

- In 2002, Jeffrey Lafond joined WestJet as a financial analyst. Lafond had worked at Canadian Airlines for five years; that employment ended when Canadian Airlines was bought by Air Canada.

- As part of Lafond's severance package, he could receive two free trips per year, which could be booked through an Air Canada employee website.

- Realizing the importance of Air Canada's bookings, Lafond showed the site to Scott Butler, WestJet's director of Strategic Planning. Butler told Mark Hill, a vice-president and WestJet founder.

- Hill and Butler asked for Lafond's Air Canada employee number and personal code; Lafond asked them for indemnity against potential legal liability.

- From his home computer in Victoria, B.C., Hill started using Lafond's code to access the site. Each night, he spent about 90 minutes checking Air Canada's load factors on different routes. However, this proved too time-consuming, and in response another WestJet employee created an automated "screen scraper" program to collect and parse Air Canada's information. Sometimes this program hit Air Canada's website over 1,000 times a day. Hill would scan the material, sometimes passing it on to other WestJet employees.

- In the summer of 2003, Air Canada was beginning to get suspicious of WestJet's access to Air Canada passenger load information.

- In December 2003, a whistleblower from WestJet informed Air Canada management about the situation. Air Canada corporate security began investigating.

- In early February 2004, investigators reported an unusually high number of accesses—243,630—to the system over a 10-month period via Lafond's employee number.

- On April 6, 2004, Air Canada launched a $5 million lawsuit against WestJet and its two employees, Mark Hill and Jeffrey Lafond, alleging unauthorized access to private information from its site.

- On July 14, 2004, Hill resigned from WestJet.

- On July 22, 2004, Air Canada upped the lawsuit to $220 million.

- In 2006, two years after the original lawsuit was filed, an out-of-court settlement was reached with all legal proceedings dropped. The settlement had WestJet agreeing to pay settlement costs of $15.5 million. This amount included a $10 million donation made in Air Canada's name to children's charities across the nation and payment of Air Canada's $5.5 million litigation costs.[45]

Clive Beddoe, co-founder of Calgary-based WestJet in 1996 and former president of WestJet Airlines, admits that WestJet learned painful lessons. In direct response to the fallout from Air Canada's lawsuit, WestJet quickly introduced a whistleblower policy and beefed up its "code of business conduct."[46]

Questions

1. Was WestJet's access to Air Canada's website information ethical? Legal? Explain.

2. How common in organizations is unauthorized access to private competitor information?

3. Does Air Canada have any responsibility in WestJet's ability to access Air Canada's private information? Explain.

4. What people measures could Air Canada implement to prevent future unauthorized access to private information?

5. What technology measures might Air Canada implement to prevent future unauthorized access to private information?

CLOSING CASE TWO

Information Ethics and Privacy Issues with Facebook Make Headlines

This case examines information ethics and privacy issues confronting Facebook users that made national and international headlines.

Facebook, the popular global social networking website, received much attention in the popular press for a variety of information ethics and privacy issues. Take, for instance, what happened to an employee of Nationale Suisse, a Swiss insurance company, who was fired for using Facebook on a day she called in sick. The 31-year-old woman had called her employer saying she was desperately ill with a migraine and that she needed to lie in the dark. However, that very same day, one of her work colleagues saw her signed onto Facebook and reported this activity to the woman's boss. The woman was immediately let go. In her defence, the woman said she was surfing Facebook in bed on her iPhone, not her computer, and that it was utterly ridiculous for a company to expect someone who calls in sick to be so sick that they must be totally incapacitated and not do anything at all. When the public found out about the firing, there was uproar that Nationale Suisse was playing "Big Brother" by monitoring its employees' personal activities online. This type of monitoring is not an isolated case. There have been other reports in the press of terminations and firings when people posted negative things on Facebook about their employers, such as "it is a boring place to work."

In the summer of 2009, Facebook was in hot water in Canada when Jennifer Stoddart, Canada's Privacy Commissioner, claimed that Facebook was only paying lip service to protecting its members' privacy. She claimed that it needed to do more. The Commissioner's year-long investigation into Facebook was instigated by a complaint from the Canadian Internet Policy and Public Interest Clinic. One of the issues with which Stoddart had concerns was that it was not clear how users could delete their accounts, or even if it was possible. In reality, users could only deactivate their accounts, which meant Facebook could collect and retain the personal information of Canadians indefinitely. This was a serious concern, especially given that, at the time of the investigation, approximately 12 million Canadians (about one-third of the population) had accounts. Another issue was that Facebook gave too much personal information about users to third-party developers, who installed applications. It is estimated that over one million third-party developers exist worldwide. It was this last issue that was the Privacy Commissioner's top concern. "The notion that some teenager working in a basement halfway around the globe could have access to all of this personal information was unsettling, to say the least," said Elizabeth Denham, Assistant Privacy Commissioner.

In response, confronted with the possibility of litigation, Facebook promised to make a series of changes to its operations and privacy policies. First, it promised to make clearer to users what the difference is between deleting an account and deactivating it. Second, Facebook agreed to designate a specific time period after which data from an inactive account would be permanently deleted. Third, Facebook said it would retrofit its website with new controls that limit the amount of personal information of Facebook users accessible to third-party developers. This change prevents third-party applications from accessing the information unless users had provided explicit consent. Fourth, Facebook stated it would launch a new privacy tool for its site whose purpose was to give users more control over who gets to see each item on their pages.

Stoddart stated she was "very pleased" with the way Facebook addressed her concerns. At a news conference in Ottawa she said, "We're satisfied that with these changes, Facebook is on the way to meeting the requirements of Canada's privacy laws."[47]

Questions

1. Was Nationale Suisse justified in its online monitoring of the employee who called in sick? If companies want to conduct such monitoring activities, what steps can they take to lessen negative backlash from the public and their employees? What steps can employees take?

2. Do you think the Privacy Commissioner went too far in her demands? Is this a bit of "much ado about nothing"?

3. Will the changes that Facebook implements to address the Commissioner's concerns negatively affect the site in any way? What do you think the average Facebook user thinks of the new features?

4. Do you know of any other examples in the popular press that showcase information ethics or privacy issues with the use of social networking sites like Facebook?

5. Does the above case make you wish to change how you use Facebook in any way?

CLOSING CASE THREE

Thinking Like the Enemy

This case illustrates how some organizations are preparing themselves against hacking threats.

David and Barry Kaufman, the founders of the Intense School, offer several security courses, such as the five-day "Professional Hacking Boot Camp" and "Ethical Hacking" in their school's curriculum that teach information systems security specialists how to hack into computer systems. The Intense School also offers such courses to prepare its students for certification exams. Students are flocking to these courses worldwide in hopes of achieving the EC-Council's Certified Ethical Hacker (CEH) or Certified Penetration Tester (CPT) designations. These designations are becoming increasingly important as organizations look to hire qualified security specialists to help protect their organization's information assets from harm. Many organizations are sending existing IT staff to these courses to help strengthen the organization's first line of defence—people.

The concept of sending IT professionals to a hacking school may seem counterintuitive; it is somewhat similar to sending accountants to an Embezzling 101 course. The Intense School does not strive to breed the next generation of hackers, but to teach its students how to be "ethical" hackers—to use their skills to build better locks, and to understand the minds of those who would attempt to crack them.

The main philosophy of the security courses at the Intense School is simply "Know thy enemy." In fact, one of the teachers at the Intense School is none other than Kevin Mitnick, the famous hacker imprisoned five years for hacking activities. Teaching security from the hacker's perspective, as Mitnick does, is more difficult than teaching hacking itself. A hacker just needs to know one way into a system, David Kaufman notes, but a security professional needs to know all of the system's vulnerabilities. The two courses analyze those vulnerabilities from different perspectives.

The hacking course teaches ways to protect against the mischief typically associated with hackers: worming through computer systems via vulnerabilities that are susceptible to technical, or computer-based, attacks. Mitnick's social engineering course, by contrast, teaches the more frightening art of worming through the vulnerabilities of the people using and maintaining systems—getting passwords and access through duplicity, not technology. People who take this class, or read Mitnick's book *The Art of Deception*, never think of passwords or the trash bin the same way again.

So how does the Intense School teach hacking? With sessions on dumpster diving (the unsavoury practice of looking for passwords and other bits of information on discarded papers), with field trips to case target systems, and with practice runs at the company's in-house "target range," a network of computers set up to thwart and educate students.

One feature of the Intense School that raises a few questions is that anyone paying the tuition can attend the school. Given the danger an unchecked graduate of a hacking school might represent, it is surprising that police authorities do not collect the names of graduates. But perhaps it gets them anyhow—several governmental agencies have sent students to the school.[48]

Questions

1. How could an organization benefit from attending one of the courses offered at the Intense School?

2. What are the two primary lines of security defence, and how can organizational employees use the information taught by the Intense School when drafting an information security plan?

3. If your employer sent you to take a course at the Intense School, what type of course would you interest you and why?

4. What ethical dilemmas are involved in having such a course offered by a private company?

MAKING BUSINESS DECISIONS

1. Firewall Decisions

You are the CEO of Inverness Investments, a medium-sized venture capital firm that specializes in investing in high-tech companies. The company receives over 30,000 email messages per year. On average, there are two viruses and three successful hackings against the company each year, which result in losses to the company of about $250,000 per year. Currently, the company has antivirus software installed but does not have any firewalls.

Your CIO suggests implementing 10 firewalls for a total cost of $80,000. The estimated life of each firewall is about three years. The chances of hackers breaking into the system with the firewalls installed are about 3 percent. Annual maintenance costs on the firewalls are estimated around $15,000. Build an argument for or against supporting your CIO's recommendation to purchase the firewalls. Are there any considerations in addition to finances?

2. Preventing Identity Theft

Identity theft is one of the fastest-growing crimes. If you are a victim of identity theft, your financial reputation can be ruined, making it impossible for you to cash a cheque or receive a bank loan. Learning how to avoid identity theft can be a valuable activity. Research the following websites and draft a document stating the best ways to prevent identity theft.

- **www.publicsafety.gc.ca/aid/index-eng.aspx**—The Government of Canada's site providing information and services on public safety

- **www.priv.gc.ca/fs-fi/index_e.cfm#contenttop**—The Office of the Privacy Commissioner of Canada's fact sheets on personal privacy

- **www.ic.gc.ca/eic/site/cmc-cmc.nsf/eng/fe00170.html**—Canada's Consumer Measures Committee's site about identity theft.

- **www.canadapost.ca/cpo/mc/business/help/privacy.jsf**—How Canada Post keeps its customer information private and safeguarded as a means of preventing identity theft

- **www.cippic.ca/identity-theft**—The Canadian Internet Policy and Public Interest Clinic's information about identity theft

3. Discussing the Three Areas of Information Security

Great Granola Inc. is a small business operating out of Saskatchewan. The company specializes in selling homemade granola, and its primary sales vehicle is its website. The company is growing exponentially and expects its revenues to triple this year to $15 million. The company also expects to hire 60 additional employees to support its growing number of customers. Sally Smith, the CEO, is aware that if her competitors discover the recipe for her granola, or who her primary customers are, it could easily ruin her business. Sally has hired you to draft a document discussing the different areas of information security, along with your recommendations for providing a secure e-business environment.

4. Information Privacy

A study by the Annenberg Public Policy Center at the University of Pennsylvania shows that 95 percent of people who use the Internet at home think they should have a legal right to know everything about the information that websites collect from them. Research also shows that 57 percent of home Internet users incorrectly believe that when a site has an information privacy policy, it will not share personal information with other sites or companies. In fact, the research found that after showing the users how companies track, extract, and share website information to make money, 85 percent found the methods unacceptable, even for a highly valued site. Write a short paper arguing for or against an organization's right to use and distribute personal information gathered from its website.

5. Spying on Email

Technology advances now allow individuals to monitor computers that they do not even have physical access to. New types of software can capture an individual's incoming and outgoing email and then immediately forward that email to another person. For example, if you are at work and your child is home from school and she receives an email from John at 3 p.m., at 3:01 you will receive a copy of that email sent to your email address. A few minutes later, if she replies to John's email, within seconds you will receive a copy of what she sent to John. Describe two scenarios (other than the above) for the use of this type of software: (1) where the use is ethical and (2) where the use is unethical.

6. Stealing Software

The software industry fights against pirated software on a daily basis. The major centres of software piracy are in places such as Russia and China, where salaries and disposable income are comparatively low. People in developing and economically depressed countries will fall behind the industrialized world technologically if they cannot afford access to new generations of software. Considering this, is it reasonable to blame someone for using pirated software when it could potentially cost him or her two months' salary to purchase a legal copy? Build an argument for or against the following statement: "Individuals who are economically less fortunate should be allowed access to software free of charge to ensure that they are provided with an equal technological advantage."

7. Acting Ethically

Assume you are an IS manager, and one of your projects is failing. You have been against the project from the start; however, the project had powerful sponsorship from all of the top executives. You know you are doomed and so is the project. The reasons for the failure are numerous, including the fact that the initial budget was drastically understated, the technology is evolving and not stable, the architecture was never scaled for growth, and your resources do not have the necessary development skills for the new technology. One of your team leads has come to you with a plan to sabotage the project that would put the project out of its misery without assigning any blame to the individuals on the project. Outline and describe how you would handle this situation.

connect   LEARNSMART®   SMARTBOOK™

For more information on the resources available from McGraw-Hill Ryerson, go to www.mheducation.ca/he/solutions.

ENDNOTES

1. "Online Dating Service Used Former Customer's Personal Information Without Consent and Failed to Provide Him Access to His Personal Information," December 18, 2013, www.priv.gc.ca/cf-dc/2013/2013_015_1218_e.asp, accessed May 24, 2014; www.priv.gc.ca/resource/tool-outil/security-securite/english/AssessRisks.asp?x=1, accessed May 24, 2014; www.priv.gc.ca/leg_c/legislation/02_06_07_e.asp, accessed May 24, 2014.

2. Scott Berianato, "The CIO Code of Ethical Data Management," *CIO Magazine*, July 1, 2002, www.cio.com/article/31171/The_CIO's_Code_of_Ethical_Data_Management, accessed August 31, 2011.

3. "Harper Government Introduces New Law to Protect the Personal Information of Canadians Online," http://news.gc.ca/web/article-en.do?nid=836559, accessed May 23, 2014.

4. Julia McKinnell, "Needed: An 'Eraser' Button to Right Internet Wrongs, May 30, 2012, www2.macleans.ca/2012/05/30/control-alt-erase, accessed July 15, 2013; www.knowthenet.org.uk/infographic/be-careful-trolling-can-happen-anyone, accessed August 20, 2013; http://threattest.knowthenet.org.uk, accessed August 20, 2013; Safeguarding Your Money, March 2013, www.cba.ca/en/component/content/category/42-safeguarding-your-money, accessed August 20, 2013.

5. Alice Dragoon, "Eight (Not So) Simple Steps to the HIPAA Finish Line," *CIO Magazine*, July 1, 2003, www.cio.com, accessed July 7, 2003; Susannah Patton, "Small Firms Still Having Trouble Complying with HIPAA," October 15, 2006, www.cio.com/article/25787/Small_Firms_Still_Having_Trouble_Complying_with_HIPAA, accessed August 31, 2011.

6. "Harper Government Introduces New Law to Protect the Personal Information of Canadians Online," http://news.gc.ca/web/article-en.do?nid=836559, accessed May 23, 2014.

7. "Privacy Provision Highlights," www.ic.gc.ca/eic/site/ecic.nsf/eng/gv00214.html, accessed June 22, 2010.

8. Mike Brunker, "Online Poker Cheating Blamed on Employee," MSNBC.com, October 19, 2007, www.msnbc.msn.com/id/21381022, accessed May 20, 2014.

9. Raymund Flandez, "Domino's Response Offers Lessons in Crisis Management," *The Wall Street Journal*, April 20, 2009, http://blogs.wsj.com/independentstreet/2009/04/20/dominos-response-offers-lessons-in-crisis-management, accessed May 20, 2014.

10. "CBC Tells Journalists How to Behave on Facebook," ReportR.net, August 3, 2007, www.reportr.net/2007/08/03/cbc-tells-journalists-how-to-behave-on-facebook, accessed May 20, 2014.

11. Andy McCue, "Bank Boss Quits After Porn Found on PC," www.businessweek.com, accessed June 2004; www.independent.ie/business/irish/newsletter-mike-soden-central-bank-commission-member-26685961.html, accessed May 14, 2014.

12. Jim Finkle and Jennifer Saba, "LinkedIn Breach Puts Site's Reputation on the Line," June 11, 2012, http://in.reuters.com/article/2012/06/11/us-linkedin-breach-idINBRE85A0IN20120611, accessed July 15, 2013; David Kravets, "6 States Bar Employers from Demanding Facebook Passwords," Wired.com, January 2, 2013, www.wired.com/threatlevel/2013/01/password-protected-states, accessed August 15, 2013; Knowlton Thomas, "Lawyer: It's Illegal for Employers to Ask Job Seekers for Facebook Passwords in Canada," March 27, 2012, www.techvibes.com/blog/draft-lawyer-its-illegal-for-employers-to-ask-job-seekers-for-facebook-passwords-in-canada-2012-03-27, accessed August 15, 2013; "Facebook-Snooping Employers Limited in Canada," March 26, 2012, www.cbc.ca/news/technology/story/2012/03/26/technology-facebook-job-seekers.html, accessed August 15, 2013.

13. Chandler Harris, "IT Downtime Costs $26.5 Billion in Lost Revenue," May 24, 2011, www.informationweek.com/news/storage/disaster_recovery/229625441, accessed September 6, 2011.

14. www.cybersecurityinstitute.com/index.php/weblog/C8, accessed May 23, 2014.

15. Canadian Press, "Scotiabank Loses Data CDs with SIN Numbers," June 6, 2011, www.cbc.ca/news/business/story/2011/06, accessed August 29, 2011.

16. "CIBC Loses Data on 470,000 Talvest Fund Customers," January 18, 2007, www.cbc.ca/money/story/2007/01/18/cibc.html, accessed August 29, 2011.

17. "Rogers Blames Document Dumping on Third-Party Company," April, 9, 2007, www.cbc.ca/consumer.story/2007/04/09/rogers-documents.html, accessed April 27, 2007.

18. "Compliance with Canadian Data Protection Laws: Are Retailers Measuring Up?" *The Canadian Internet Policy and Public Interest Clinic*, April 2006, www.cippic.ca/documents/bulletins/compliance_report_06-07-06_(color)_(cover-english).pdf, accessed August 31, 2011.

19. Laura Bobak, "Rogers Data Leak Shows Need for Mandatory Customer Notification Law, Expert Says," *The Canadian Press*, April 9, 2007.

20. "2014 IT Security Budget Forecast Roundup for CIOS and CISOS/CSOS," www.tripwire.com/register/it-security-budget-forecast-roundup-2014-for-csos-and-ciocisos/showMeta/2, accessed May 23, 2014.

21. "Distribution of Software Updates of Thousands of Franchise Locations Was Slow and Unpredictable," www.fountain.com, accessed October 10, 2003.

22. Christopher Koch, "A New Blueprint for the Enterprise," *CIO Magazine*, March 1, 2005.

23. "A Guide to Business Continuity Planning," November 23, 2010, www.publicsafety.gc.ca/prg/em/gds/bcp-eng.aspx, accessed September 25, 2011.

24. "New Coalitions Increasing America's Crisis Preparedness," March 2007, www.usfst.com/article/New-coalitions-increasing-Americas-crisis-preparedness, accessed September 21, 2011.

25. Ibid.

26. Kristin M. Finklea, "Identity Theft: Trends and Issues" (Washington, DC: Congressional Research Service, January 5, 2010), www.fas.org/sgp/crs/misc/R40599.pdf, accessed September 19, 2011.

27. Martin Garvey, "Health-Care Organization Manages Passwords to Protect Identities," May 20, 2005, *InformationWeek*, www.informationweek.com/news/163106055?queryText=Health-Care+Organization+Manages+Passwords+To+Protect+Identities#, accessed September 21, 2011.

28. Ibid.

29. Ibid.

30. www.gocsi.com.

31. Nancy Leveson and Clark S. Turner, "An Investigation of the Therac-25 Accidents," *IEEE Computer*, Volume 26, Number 7, July 1993, pp. 18–41.

32. www.ey.com, accessed November 25, 2003.

33. "The Security Revolution," *CIO Magazine*, www.cio.com, accessed June 6, 2003.

34. "Global Security Spending to Hit $86B in 2016," September 14 , 2012, www.infosecurity-magazine.com/view/28219/global-security-spending-to-hit-86b-in-2016, accessed May 23, 2014.

35. Alice Dragoon, "Eight (Not So) Simple Steps to the HIPAA Finish Line," *CIO Magazine*, www.cio/com/article/29781/HIPAA_Security_Rule_Compliance_Checklist, accessed June 22, 2010.

36. Gloria Galloway, "Canada Post Tip Leads to Arrests in Identity Scam," *The Globe and Mail*, March 9, 2006.

37. Mari-Len De Guzman, "Bank Fraud Trail Leads to Former Outsourcing Help," *ITWorld Canada News*, April 27, 2006, http://www.itworldcanada.com/article/bank-fraud-trail-leads-to-former-outsourcing-help/5691, accessed August 31, 2014.

38. Ellen Nakashima and William Wan, "Chinese Military Unit Charged with Cyber-Espionage Against U.S. Firms," May 19, 2014, www.washingtonpost.com/world/national-security/us-to-announce-first-criminal-charges-against-foreign-country-for-cyberspying/2014/05/19/586c9992-df45-11e3-810f-764fe508b82d_story.html, accessed May20, 2014.

39. "Nexus," www.cbsa-asfc.gc.ca/prog/nexus/menu-eng.html, accessed May 20, 2014; "Trusted Traveller CATSA Security Line," www.catsa.gc.ca/Page.aspx?ID= 91&pname=Nexus_Nexus&lang=en, accessed August 31, 2011.

40. "Losses from Identity Theft to Total $221 Billion Worldwide," www.cio.com, accessed May 23, 2003.

41. Pete Cashmore, "RIP Facebook Beacon," September 19, 2009, http://mashable.com/2009/09/19/facebook-beacon-rip, accessed August 31, 2011.

42. http://heartbleed.com, accessed May 20, 2014.

43. Andrea Janus, "Canada at 'Top of the Target List' for BlackShades," May 20, 2014, www.ctvnews.ca/sci-tech/canada-at-top-of-the-target-list-for-blackshades-1.1829756, accessed May 20, 2014.

44. Joaquim P. Menezews, "WestJet Accepts Blame, Settles with Air Canada in Espionage Case," *IT World Canada*, May 28, 2006, www.itworldcanad.com/news/westjet-accepts-blame-settles-with-air-canada-in-espionage-case/99049, accessed June 22, 2010.

45. Lisa Schmidt, "WestJet Admits Spying on Rival: How the Upstart Airline Ended Up Paying $15.5M over an Espionage Caper with Air Canada," *Calgary Herald*, May 30, 2006.

46. Brent Jagg, "WestJet Chief Talks Exit Strategy," *The Globe and Mail* (Update), June 1, 2006.

47. Tech-Ex, "Surfing Facebook While Ill Earns Employee a Pink Slip," http://technologyexpert.blogspot.com/2009/04/surfing-facebook-while-ill-earns.html, accessed June 22, 2010; Caroline McCarthy, "Canadian Official Takes Issue with Facebook Privacy," *The Social—CNET News*, July 17, 2009; CTV.ca News Staff, "Ottawa Announces Changes to Facebook Operations," www.ctvtoronto.ca, accessed Aug 27, 2009; "Facebook Privacy Ruling Could Be New Precedent," *The Canadian Press*, August 26, 2009, http://montreal.ctv.ca/servlet/an/local/CTVNews/20090826/Facebook_Privacy_090826?hub=OttawaHome, accessed June 22, 2010.

48. Berinato and Scalet, "The ABCs of Information Security," *CIO Magazine*, www.cio.com, accessed July 7, 2003; "InfoSec Institute Announces 95% Pass Rate for Certified Penetration Tester (CPT) Examination," October 15, 2008, www.infosecinstitute.com/releases/infosec-cpt-pass.html, accessed August 31, 2011; Eric Grier, "How to Become an Ethical Hacker," www.pcworld.com/article/250045/how_to_become_an_ethical_hacker.html, accessed July 8, 2014.

11 CHAPTER

Systems Development and Project Management

LO 11.1 Explain the business benefits associated with successful systems development and how the issues and challenges developing domestic information systems amplify with global systems development.

LO 11.2 Describe and understand the relationships between each of the seven phases of the systems development life cycle.

LO 11.3 Summarize and compare different systems development methodologies.

LO 11.4 Explain the importance of good project management practice.

LO 11.5 Describe the benefits and challenges of outsourcing systems development projects.

This chapter provides an overview of how organizations go about developing information systems. As a business student, you need to know this since information systems are the underlying foundation of how companies operate. Having a basic understanding of the principles of building information systems will make you a more valuable employee. You will be able to identify trouble spots early on and make suggestions during the design process that will result in a better delivered information systems project—one that satisfies both you and your organization.

Building an information system is analogous to constructing a house. You could sit back and let the developers do all the design work, construction, and testing on their own with the hope that the finished house will meet all your needs. However, participating in the house building process helps guarantee that your needs are not only being heard, but also being met. It is good business practice to have direct user input steering the development of the finished product.

The same is true for building information systems. Your knowledge of the systems development process allows you to participate and ensures you are building information systems that support not only current business needs but future ones as well.

Project Management

The Project

Marie Westley was sitting at her office one day, reviewing her company's documents for the annual general meeting. She sat back in her chair and thought to herself: "I wish more of our stakeholders understood what went into creating these documents and how time-consuming it is for the company to ensure the accuracy and readability of the information." Having taught management courses at the local university, Sunshine City College, she wondered if there was another way to teach students of all ages how to understand a company's official trade securities documents. Marie was motivated to do more than think about this subject. She investigated whether any of the publishing companies for university learning materials would be interested in funding her to develop an e-learning tool for understanding and reading these documents. After speaking with a few publishers' representatives, Marie put together a proposal and sent it to University Learning Publishers. Shortly thereafter, her proposal was approved. She received $25,000 to develop her e-learning concept. Now the real work began. How was she going to set up her project development team? She assessed her own strengths and weaknesses and understood that she knew the content of these documents very well. However, she knew very little about writing for or designing the platform for e-learning. There were so many different types of electronic platforms, she could feel her heart beat faster just thinking about how little she knew about choosing the type of platform to use for the e-learning tool. And what about creative design? She went to the Internet to review a few websites. There were so many different formats, colours, and methods for setting up tabs, menus, and navigation bars that she immediately became concerned that she had taken on more than she could handle. She didn't know where to begin. Enough of thinking about this project for now! Marie headed for the fitness centre to clear her mind.

Putting the Parts Together

Even though Marie tried to concentrate on her exercise program, thoughts of that project and how it would all come together kept popping into her mind. As she pedalled her stationary bike faster, causing her heart rate to rise, beads of sweat started to run down her face. She leaned forward on the handle bars of her bike to help her through the last few minutes of her ride ... and then as her legs were moving through those final turns on the cycle, her eyes began to move slowly from one part of her bike to another and she thought: "What an amazing piece of equipment!" Each part had a function that fulfilled an objective: the chain, the handlebars, the wheels, the pedals, and more. Even though the pressure on the pedals made the bike move and the pedals were the main driving force, the bike could not function without the other parts. All of a sudden she realized that her project was similar to the bike. She was the main driving force, but she needed other parts ... other persons ... to fulfill the other functions that she could not accomplish by herself. Now her mind was racing as fast as the pedals on her bike. She eased into her cool-down, and then hurried to the locker room where she started jotting down capabilities that she needed to complete her project: management information systems expertise; securities commission experts; knowledge about writing for e-learning; instructional designers; and educational experts. She then started jotting down names of her contacts who had the capabilities that she needed, and wrote above these categories and names in large letters: ADVISORY COMMITTEE. She could approach each of these individuals in each of the project phases as she needed advice.

Putting Advisors in Place

Marie had much work to do. She needed to form her Advisory Committee, determine her target audience, get quotes for various phases of development of the e-learning tool (and identify those phases), hire someone who could manage the project while she wrote the content, determine the timeline for software development and implementation, and decide how to assess the quality of the software throughout the development and implementation phases. Perhaps she needed a Testing Committee (consisting of a combination of different audiences that could benefit from the e-learning tool) to provide feedback when the product was completed, but before it was released to the public. Marie proceeded to discuss the project with a couple of design companies and asked them for price quotations. However, their quotes were far above Marie's budget and lacked detail. None drew up prototypes of what the final product would look like even though Marie provided a draft of the content for the first module. From the quotes, it was impossible for her to determine what the final product would look like or what characteristics it would have. As well, the companies wanted to complete a Discovery Phase for $5,000, consisting of determining what the end-users would like in the product. While Marie agreed that a Discovery Phase was necessary, through her own experience and discussions with various stakeholders in the business community, she did not want to pay for a Discovery Phase that would include information she already had. The design companies wanted to take an all-or-nothing approach and were not interested in doing just a piece of the product. Marie then searched for companies interested in completing those parts of the project that she wanted to outsource. Finally, she found one, Star Communications, that was willing to accommodate her budget. However, it was difficult to judge the quality of Star's work and the capabilities of the designers, as Star provided no work samples to help determine what the possibilities were for the final product.

Adding Project Management

After much consideration of the risks associated with partial outsourcing versus full service, Marie decided to let Star create the first module. She and her Advisory Committee would then review it and provide feedback at an early stage before proceeding to develop the other three modules in the e-learning product.

It took four weeks before the first module was ready to view. During this time, Marie had many meetings with the designers to try to convey her ideas as to how the final product should look. Unfortunately, Marie thought the designers would be forthcoming with suggestions on how to format various information items to ensure user engagement, but she was not receiving many ideas from the designers, except that the sentences should not be long, the wording should be interesting, and there should be examples. She was already behind in the timeline for completion, but she felt it was important to ensure the first module was of high quality and reviewed by the potential users before proceeding to the next stage.

Disappointment

When Marie clicked on the link to view the first module of her e-learning product, she was quite disappointed. She had hoped the designers would take her words and use Internet and e-learning characteristics to make them come alive and engage the readers. She did not know how to tell the designers that it was not the quality she expected. Maybe she was a poor judge. She decided to go to her Advisory Committee and ask their suggestions. They gave her good, detailed feedback about how the module could be improved, noting especially that she needed a better overall template that the designers could follow.

Already over her budget and way behind on her timeline, Marie agreed with the advice but did not know exactly how to "start over" at this point. To proceed to meet budget and her timeline was useless if the final product was of low quality.[1]

11.1   SYSTEMS DEVELOPMENT

INTRODUCTION

Every type of organization in business today, from farming to pharmaceuticals to franchising, is affected by information systems and, in particular, the software developed to operate, improve, or innovate these systems. Companies are affected by IS solutions that enable them to improve their cost structure, manage people better, and develop and deliver new products to market. These organizational improvements help companies sustain their competitive advantage and position in the marketplace. They can solve complex problems, dislodge competitors, or create exciting opportunities to pursue. Organizations must learn and mature in their ability to identify, build, and implement information systems to remain competitive.

Information systems built correctly can support nimble organizations and can transform as the organization and its business transform. Systems that effectively meet employee needs will help an organization become more productive and enhance decision making. Systems that do not meet employee needs may have a damaging effect on productivity and can even cause a business to fail. Employee involvement, along with using the right implementation methodology when developing systems, is critical to the success of an organization.

LO1 ⟩ DEVELOPING INFORMATION SYSTEMS

Nike's SCM system failure, which spun out of control to the tune of $400 million, is legendary. Nike blamed it on its SCM vendor, i2 Technologies, saying its demand and supply planning module created serious inventory problems. The i2 deployment, part of a multimillion-dollar e-business upgrade, caused Nike CEO Philip Knight to famously say, "This is what we get for our $400 million?" The SCM vendor saw its stock plummet with the Nike disaster, along with its reputation. Katrina Roche, i2's chief marketing officer, asserted that Nike failed to use the vendor's implementation methodology and templates, which contributed to the problem.[2]

If information systems do not work, then the organization will not work. Traditional business risk models typically ignored systems development, largely because most organizations considered the impact from systems development on the business to be minor. In the digital age, however, system success, or failure, can lead directly to business success or failure. Almost every large organization in the world relies on information systems, either to drive its business operations or to make its products work. As organizations' reliance on systems grows, so do the business-related consequences of system successes and failures, as displayed in Figure 11.1.

Increase or decrease revenues. Organizations have the ability to directly increase profits by implementing successful IT systems. Organizations can also lose millions when software fails or key information is stolen or compromised.

Repair or damage to brand reputation. Technologies such as CRM can directly enhance a company's brand reputation. Software can also severely damage a company's reputation if it fails to work as advertised or has security vulnerabilities that affect its customers' trust.

Prevent or incur liabilities. Technology such as CAT scans, MRIs, and mammograms can save lives. Faulty technology used in airplanes, automobiles, pacemakers, or nuclear reactors can cause massive damage, injury, or death.

Increase or decrease productivity. CRM and SCM software can directly increase a company's productivity. Large losses in productivity can also occur when software malfunctions or crashes.

FIGURE 11.1

Consequences of System Success and Failure

Source: Gary McGraw, "Making Essential Software Work: Why Software Quality Management Makes Good Business Sense," *Cigital* (Dulles, VA: 2003), www.cigital.com/whitepapers/dl/Making_Essential_Software_Work.pdf, accessed September 12, 2011.

The lucrative advantages of successful information systems implementations provide significant incentives to manage systems development risks. It is estimated that nearly have the systems development projects done take longer than planned or are over budget, and over half of the completed projects contained fewer features and functions than originally specified. Therefore, understanding the basics of systems development methodologies will help organizations avoid potential systems development pitfalls, and ensure that systems development efforts are successful.[3]

Global Information Systems Development

It is difficult to develop a domestic information system, but the added complexity of developing a global information system quadruples the effort. Global information systems must support a diverse base of customers, users, products, languages, currencies, laws, and so on. Developing efficient, effective, and responsive information systems for multiple countries, differing cultures, and global e-businesses is an enormous challenge for any organization. Managers should expect conflicts over local versus global system requirements and difficulties agreeing on common system features. For the project to succeed, the development environment should promote involvement and ownership by all local system users.

One of the most important global IS development issues is the global standardization of data definitions. Common data definitions are necessary for sharing data among the parts of an international business. Differences in language, culture, and technology platforms can make global data standardization quite difficult. For example, what Canadians call a "sale" may be called "an order booked" in the U.K., an "order scheduled" in Germany, and an "order produced" in France. These all refer to the exact same business event, but could cause problems if global employees have different versions of the data definition. This is even more important as businesses incorporate more and more XML in their reporting with the adoption of standards like International Financial Reporting Standards (IFRS) and Global Reporting Initiatives (GRI). Businesses are being required to standardize data definitions and business processes, and many organizations are implementing corporate wikis where all global employees can post and maintain common business definitions.

Organizations can use several strategies to solve some of the problems that arise in global IS development:

1. Transform and customize an information system used by the home office into a global application. This ensures that the system uses the established business processes and supports the primary needs of the end-users.

2. Set up a multinational development team with key people from several subsidiaries to ensure that the system design meets the needs of all local sites as well as corporate headquarters.

3. Use centres of excellence where an entire system might be assigned for development to a particular subsidiary based on its expertise in the business or technical dimensions needed for successful development.

4. Outsource the development work to global or offshore development countries that have the required skills and experience to build global information systems.

All of these approaches still require development team collaboration and managerial oversight to meet the global needs of the business.[4]

LO2 THE SYSTEMS DEVELOPMENT LIFE CYCLE (SDLC)

The *systems development life cycle (SDLC)* is the overall process for developing information systems from planning and analysis through implementation and maintenance. SDLC is the foundation for all systems development methodologies, and literally hundreds of different activities associated with each phase in the SDLC. Typical activities include determining budgets, gathering systems requirements, and writing detailed user documentation. The activities performed during each systems development project vary.

The SDLC begins with a business need, followed by an assessment of the functions a system must have to satisfy the need, and ends when the benefits of the system no longer outweigh its maintenance costs. This is why it is referred to as a life cycle. The SDLC comprises seven distinct phases: *planning*, *analysis*, *design*, *development*, *testing*, *implementation*, and *maintenance* (see Figure 11.2).

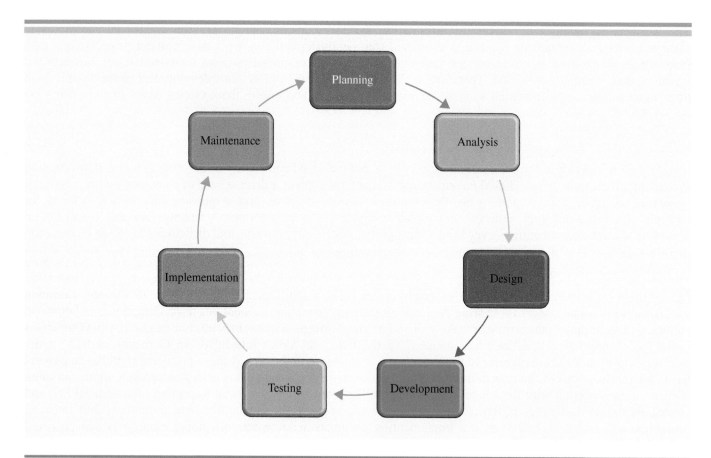

Phase	Associated Activity
Planning	■ Brainstorm issues and identify opportunities for the organization ■ Prioritize and choose projects for development ■ Set the project scope ■ Develop the project plan
Analysis	■ Gather the business requirements for the system ■ Define any constraints associated with the system
Design	■ Design the technical architecture required to support the system ■ Design the system models
Development	■ Build the technical architecture ■ Build the database ■ Build the applications
Testing	■ Write the test conditions ■ Perform system testing
Implementation	■ Write detailed user documentation ■ Provide training for the system users
Maintenance	■ Build a help desk to support the system users ■ Provide an environment to support system changes

FIGURE 11.2

The Systems Development Life Cycle and Its Associated Activities

LO3) SYSTEMS DEVELOPMENT METHODOLOGIES

Today, systems are so large and complex that teams of architects, analysts, developers, testers, and users must work together to create the millions of lines of custom-written code that drive enterprises. For this reason, developers have created a number of different SDLC methodologies. A ***methodology*** is a set of policies, procedures, standards, processes, practices, tools, techniques, and tasks that people apply to technical and management challenges. It is used to manage the deployment of information systems with work plans, requirements documents, and test plans. It is also used to deploy information systems. A formal methodology can include coding standards, code libraries, development practices, and much more.

Waterfall Methodology

The oldest of these, and the best known, is the waterfall methodology: a sequence of phases in which the output of each phase becomes the input for the next (see Figure 11.3). The traditional ***waterfall methodology*** is a sequential, activity-based process in which each phase in the SDLC is performed sequentially from planning through implementation and maintenance. The traditional method no longer serves most of today's development efforts; the success rate for software development projects that follow this approach is about 1 in 10. Paul Magin, a senior executive with Epicor Software, a leading provider of ERP and POS software, states, "Waterfall is a punishing technology. It forces people to be accurate when they simply cannot. It is dangerous and least desirable in today's development environment. It does not accommodate mid-course changes; it requires that you know exactly what you want to do on the project and a steady-state until the work is done; it requires guarantees that requirements will not change. We all know that it is nearly impossible to have all requirements up front. When you use a cascading method, you end up with cascading problems that are disastrous if not identified and corrected early in the process."5

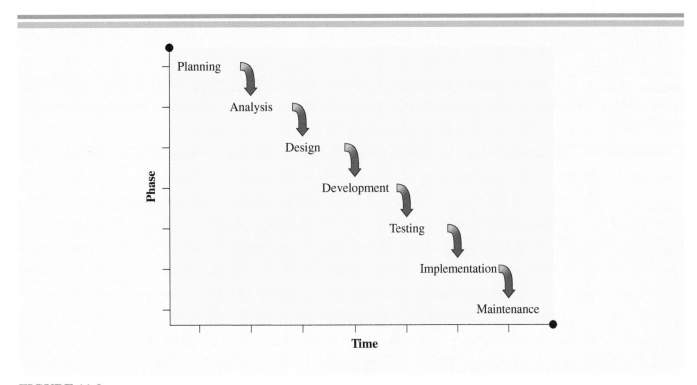

FIGURE 11.3

The Traditional Waterfall Methodology

The waterfall methodology is inflexible and expensive, and requires rigid adherence to the sequentially based steps in the process. Figure 11.4 explains some issues related to the waterfall methodology.

The business problem	Any flaws in accurately defining and articulating the business problem in terms of what the business users actually require flow onward to the next phase.
The plan	Managing costs, resources, and time constraints is difficult in the waterfall sequence. What happens to the schedule if a programmer quits? How will a schedule delay in a specific phase impact the total cost of the project? Unexpected contingencies may sabotage the plan.
The solution	The waterfall methodology is problematic in that it assumes users can specify all business requirements in advance. Defining the appropriate IT infrastructure that is flexible, scalable, and reliable is a challenge. The final IT infrastructure solution must meet not only current but also future needs in terms of time, cost, feasibility, and flexibility. Vision is inevitably limited at the head of the waterfall.

FIGURE 11.4

Issues Related to the Waterfall Methodology

Today's business environment is fierce. The desire and need to outsmart and outplay competitors remains intense. Given this drive for success, leaders push internal development teams and external vendors to deliver agreed-upon systems faster and cheaper so they can realize benefits as early as possible. Even so, systems remain large and complex. The traditional waterfall methodology no longer serves as an adequate systems development methodology in most cases. Because this development environment is the norm and not the exception anymore, development teams use a new breed of alternative development methods to achieve their business objectives.

Agile Software Development Methodologies

Standish Group's CHAOS research clearly shows that the smaller the project, the greater the success rate. The iterative development style is the ultimate in small projects. *Iterative development* consists of a series of tiny projects and has become the foundation of multiple agile types of methodologies. Figure 11.5 displays an iterative approach.[6]

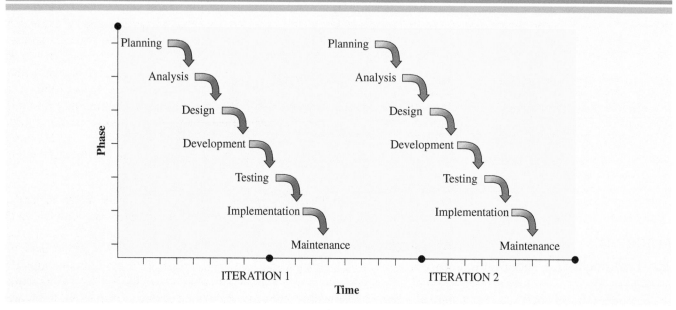

FIGURE 11.5

The Iterative Approach

An *agile methodology* aims for customer satisfaction through early and continuous delivery of useful software components developed by an iterative process with a design point that uses the bare minimum requirements. Agile is what it sounds like: fast and efficient, small and nimble, lower cost, fewer features, shorter projects. Using agile methods helps refine feasibility and supports the process for getting rapid feedback as functionality is introduced. Developers can adjust as they move along and better clarify unclear requirements. Gartner Research estimates that 65 percent of agile projects are successful. This success rate is extraordinary compared with the 10 percent success rate of waterfall projects.

The key to delivering a successful product or system is to deliver value to users as soon as possible—give them something they want and like early to create buy-in, generate enthusiasm, and, ultimately, reduce scope. Using agile methodologies helps maintain accountability and helps to establish a barometer for the satisfaction of end-users. It does no good to accomplish something on time and on budget if it does not satisfy the end user. The primary forms of agile methodologies include:

- Rapid prototyping or rapid application development methodology

- Extreme programming methodology

- Rational unified process (RUP) methodology

- Scrum methodology[7]

It is important not to get hung up on the names of the methodologies—some are proprietary brand names, others are generally accepted names. It is more important to know how these alternative methodologies are used in today's business environment and the benefits they can deliver.

Rapid Application Development Methodology (RAD)   In response to the faster pace of business, rapid application development has become a popular route for accelerating systems development. *Rapid application development (RAD)* (also called *rapid prototyping*) *methodology* emphasizes extensive user involvement in the rapid and evolutionary construction of working prototypes of a system to accelerate the systems development process. Figure 11.6 displays the RAD approach.

A *prototype* is a smaller-scale representation or working model of the users' requirements, or a proposed design for an information system. The prototype is an essential part of the analysis phase when using the RAD methodology.

SwimAmerica runs swimming lessons for more than 3,000 students on an annual basis. When program director Robert Polley was given a three-ring binder to run the program, he began to look for a solution that would eliminate the paper, the back-and-forth snail mail, and all the inefficiencies of the paper-based system. Polley created a customized database system that works on both a desktop and the Web, and manages all of SwimAmerica's data. The system includes an email registration system that manages the thousands of student records. Data entry that took hours now takes minutes. Children can be registered in classes and have their T-shirt size selected in just a few mouse clicks. The three-ring binders, the paper, and the filing cabinets have been eliminated. In addition, lost records have been eliminated thanks to online registration, and children can be signed up for classes right up until the day before lessons begin. The information is easily searchable and Polley is able to maximize the program's profitability because the information allows him to fill existing classes before creating new classes. He has also expanded his use of the databases by building in automated payroll and automatically generated email reminders of swim lessons for parents.[8]

Extreme Programming Methodology   *Extreme programming (XP) methodology*, like other agile methods, breaks a project into tiny phases, and developers cannot continue on to the next phase until the first phase is complete. XP emphasizes the fact that the faster the communication or feedback the better the results. There are four parts: planning, designing, coding, and testing. Unlike other methodologies, these are not phases; they work in tandem with each other. Planning includes user stories, stand-up meetings, and small releases. The design segment stresses not adding functionally until it is needed. During coding, the user is always available for feedback, developers work in pairs, and the code is written to an agreed standard. For testing, the tests are written before the code. XP users are embedded into the development process. This technique is powerful because of the narrow communication gap between developers and users—it is a direct link. This saves valuable time and, again, continues to clarify needed (and unneeded) requirements.

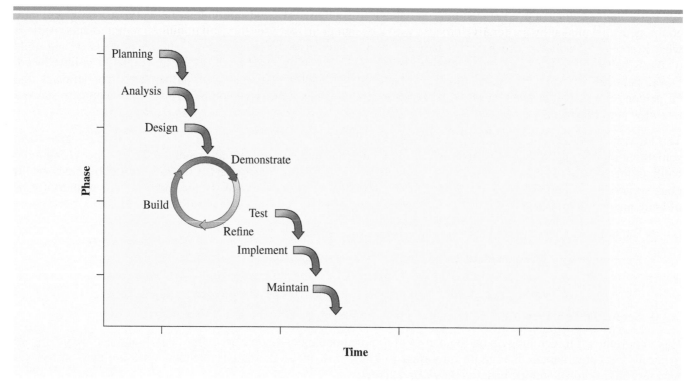

FIGURE 11.6

The RAD Approach

One reason for XP's success is its stress on customer satisfaction. XP empowers developers to respond to changing customer and business requirements, even late in the SDLC, and XP emphasizes teamwork. Managers, customers, and developers are all part of a team dedicated to delivering quality software. XP implements a simple yet effective way to enable groupware-style development. Kent Beck, the father of XP, proposes conversation as the paradigm and suggests using index cards as a means of creating dialogue between business and technology. XP is a lot like a jigsaw puzzle: there are many small pieces. Individually the pieces make no sense, but when they are combined (again and again), they become effective mechanisms by which to build a new system that meets changing customer and business requirements.[9]

Rational Unified Process (RUP) Methodology The *rational unified process (RUP) methodology*, owned by IBM, provides a framework for breaking down the development of software into four gates. Each gate consists of executable iterations of the software in development. A project stays in a gate until the stakeholders are satisfied, and then it either moves to the next gate or is cancelled. The gates include:

- *Gate One: Inception.* This phase includes inception of the business case; it ensures that all stakeholders have a shared understanding of the system.

- *Gate Two: Elaboration.* This phase provides a rough order of magnitude. Primary questions answered in this phase deal with agreed-upon details of the system, including the ability to provide an architecture to support and build the system.

- *Gate Three: Construction.* This phase includes building and developing the product.

- *Gate Four: Transition.* Primary questions answered in this phase address ownership of the system and training of key personnel.[10]

Because RUP is an iterative methodology, the user can reject the product and force the developers to go back to

Gate One. Approximately 500,000 developers have used RUP in software projects of varying sizes in the 20 years it has been available, according to IBM. RUP helps developers avoid reinventing the wheel and focuses on rapidly adding or removing reusable chunks of processes addressing common problems.

Scrum Methodology   Another agile methodology, *scrum methodology*, uses small teams to produce small pieces of deliverable software using sprints, or 30-day intervals, to achieve an appointed goal. In rugby, a scrum is a team pack and everyone in the pack works together to move the ball down the field. Under this methodology, each day ends or begins with a stand-up meeting to monitor and control the development effort.

Primavera Systems, Inc., a software solutions company, was finding it increasingly difficult to use the traditional waterfall methodology for development, so it moved to an agile methodology. Scrum's insistence on delivering complete increments of business value in 30-day learning cycles helped the teams learn rapidly. It forced teams to test and integrate experiments and encouraged them to release them into production. Primavera's shift resulted in highly satisfied customers and a highly motivated, energetic development environment. Dick Faris, CTO of Primavera, said, "Agile programming is very different and new. It is a different feel to the way programming happens. Instead of mindlessly cranking out code, the process is one of team dialogue, negotiation around priorities and time and talents. The entire company commits to a 30-day sprint and delivery of finished, tested software. Maybe it is just one specific piece of functionality but it's the real thing, including delivery and client review against needs and requirements. Those needs and requirements, by the way, change. That is the strength we saw in the Scrum process."[11]

Implementing Agile Methodologies   Amos Auringer, an executive advisor for prestigious Gartner Inc., said, "Concepts such as agile, RAD, and XP are all various approaches to the same model—idea, production, delivery. These models represent consolidated steps, skipped steps for project size, and compressed steps to achieve the same result—a delivered product. Emerging process engineering models tend to focus on eliminating or reducing steps. The SDLC phases do not change—we just learn how to do our jobs better and more efficiently."[12]

If organizations choose to adopt agile methodologies, it is important to educate those involved. For an agile process to work, it must be simple and quick. The Agile Alliance is a group of software developers whose mission is to improve software development processes; elements from the group's manifesto are displayed in Figure 11.7. Decisions must be made quickly without analysis paralysis. The best way to do this is to involve stakeholders, develop excellent communication processes, and implement strong project management skills. Understanding that communication is the most crucial aspect of a project is the core of collaborative development. Standish Group reports that projects in which users or user groups have a good understanding of their true needs have a better rate of return and lower risk. Strong project management is key to building a successful enterprise.

THE AGILE ALLIANCE MANIFESTO

We are uncovering better ways of developing software by doing it and helping others do it. Through this work we have come to value:

Individuals and interactions over processes and tools

Working software over comprehensive documentation

Customer collaboration over contract negotiation

Responding to change over following a plan

That is, while there is value in the items on the right, we value the items on the left more.

FIGURE 11.7

The Agile Alliance Manifesto

Source: "The Agile Manifesto," Agile Alliance site, www.agilealliance.org/the-alliance/the-agile-manifesto, accessed January 10, 2012.

Participatory Design Methodology

The *participatory design (PD) methodology* is different from the waterfall and agile methodologies, not in terms of the type of work that is done, but rather who is in control and does most of the design work. PD promotes the active involvement of users in the IS development process. It is an approach toward systems design that originated in Scandinavia, where there is a history of direct and effective participation of workers in design activities and decision making. With PD, "the people destined to *use* the system play a critical role in *designing* it."[13]

Here, the traditional designer/user relationship is reversed: users are viewed as the experts—the ones with the most knowledge about what they do and what they need—and the designers are viewed as technical consultants or coaches.

Two oft-cited benefits of PD are the development of systems that better match user needs, and heightened user trust and acceptance of the system.

The PD approach is based on several tenets:

■ The design process makes a difference for participants.

■ Implementing the results from the design process is likely.

■ It is fun to participate.[14]

The first two points refer to the political side of having users participate in design. The project must make a difference for participants. If they perceive the system as having little benefit or relevance to their daily lives, the likelihood of engaging users actively in the project is remote at best. And if participants perceive their inclusion in the process as only a gesture of goodwill or a half-hearted attempt at understanding user needs, participants will not "buy in." Participants need to feel their contributions are meaningful and will be put into action, not just recorded and put aside.

The last point concentrates on the design process itself; it must be fun for users to participate. To secure the active engagement of users in design, steps must be taken to overcome obstacles of hard work and boredom that are inherently part of any systems project.

To encourage healthy cooperation between user and designer, PD advocates suggest:

1. Creating opportunities for mutual learning between users and traditional systems designers (e.g., each has knowledge from which the other can benefit)

2. Using design tools that are familiar to users (e.g., using pens, paper, and flip charts instead of entity-relationship or data flow diagrams)

3. Employing language that end-users know (no technobabble allowed!)

4. Starting the design process with the current practice of users; that is, understanding how users currently conduct activities that the future system will help users perform, and using that knowledge as a springboard for determining ways to make improvements.

5. Facilitating other design activities in a way that encourages users to envision future situations of working with the final system, which will allow users to experience and contemplate how the emerging design may affect their lives in practice[15]

Self-Sourcing

In addition to the methods discussed, *self-sourcing*—or end-user development—also happens in many organizations today. In this method the systems are developed by the people who use the systems. Self-sourcing and end-user development are processes where the end user builds and maintains the information system themselves without much support from IT specialists. The complexity of these techniques range greatly. In some instances a knowledge worker may write a macro for an Excel spreadsheet to automate a work process. In other cases, a group of end-users follow a more formal SDLC approach that includes prototyping. There are a number of advantages to this technique that include improved requirements determination, increased sense of system ownership, and faster development. There are also some disadvantages. These include lack of development expertise, lack of organizational focus, lack of alternative analysis, and lack of documentation.

DEVELOPING SUCCESSFUL SYSTEMS

Regardless of the type of systems development methodology chosen, there are some key primary principles an organization should follow for successful systems development, as follows.[16]

Slash the Budget

Small budgets force developers and users to focus on the essentials. Small budgets also make it easier to kill a failing project. For example, imagine that a project that has already cost $20 million is going down the tubes. With that much invested, it is tempting to invest another $5 million to rescue it rather than take a huge loss. All too often, the system fails and the company ends up with an even bigger loss.

If It Doesn't Work, Kill It   Bring all key stakeholders together at the beginning of a project and as it progresses bring them together again to evaluate the software. Is it doing what the business wants and, more importantly, requires? Eliminate any software that is not meeting business expectations. This is called triage, and it's "the perfect place to kill a software project," said Pat Morgan, senior program manager at Compaq's Enterprise Storage Group (now owned by Hewlett-Packard). He held monthly triage sessions and said they can be brutal. "At one [meeting], engineering talked about a cool process they were working on to transfer information between GUIs. No one in the room needed it. We killed it right there. In the Compaq environment, you could burn a couple of million dollars in a month only to realize what you're doing isn't useful."[17]

Keep Requirements to a Minimum   Start each project with what the software absolutely must do. Do not start with a list of everything the software should do. Every software project traditionally starts with a requirements document that often has hundreds or thousands of business requirements. The Standish Group estimates that only 7 percent of the business requirements are needed for any given application. Keeping requirements to a minimum also means that scope creep and feature creep must be closely monitored. *Scope creep* occurs when the scope of the project increases. *Feature creep* occurs when developers add extra features that were not part of the initial requirements.

Test and Deliver Frequently   As often as once a week, and not less than once a month, complete a part of the project or a piece of software. The part must be working and it must be bug-free. Then have the customers test and approve it. This is the agile methodology's most radical departure from traditional development. In some traditional software projects, the customers did not see any working parts or pieces for years.

Assign Non-IT Executives to Software Projects   Non-IT executives should coordinate with the technical project manager, test iterations to make sure they are meeting user needs, and act as liaisons between executives and IT. Having the business side involved full-time brings project ownership and a desire to succeed to all parties involved.

OPENING CASE QUESTIONS

Project Management

1. Did this project use any development methodologies?

2. What development methodology would you have recommended for the project development and why?

3. What are some of the key elements of the information requirements for this project?

4. What was done to ensure that a wide and representative set of end-users were involved in the design process?

11.2 PROJECT MANAGEMENT AND GOVERNANCE

INTRODUCTION

According to the Project Management Institute, there continues to be uncertainty in the economics of project management, but there are signs of potential improvement. The number of delayed projects and employment for project managers continues to fluctuate, but the number of reinstated projects is increasing.[18]

In the weeks leading up to the devastating floods in Calgary and other southern Alberta communities in June 2013, a hint of the impending disaster was apparent in data from observations by the Gravity Recovery and Climate Experiment (GRACE). The data was showing groundwater at progressively higher levels than average, which left the land with little extra capacity to take up any additional water that might come from rainfall or snow melt. The resulting disaster suggests that groundwater monitoring should be a higher priority so that officials can include it in their planning. The question then becomes: How can a system be developed that would allow officials to plan better? This question is particularly important given that even though GRACE collects data for and produces generalized maps a worldwide basis while highly detailed data maps are only being produced for the United States. What this means for Canada is that Canada is well behind the United States in mapping out its primary aquifers.[19] It can be suggested that project management which offers a strategic framework for coordinating the activities associated with organizational projects could help Canada develop its own maps. Today, business leaders face a rapidly moving and unforgiving global marketplace that will force them to use every possible tool to sustain competitiveness—project management is one of those tools.

LO4 MANAGING SOFTWARE DEVELOPMENT PROJECTS

Analysts estimate that tens of billions of dollars are lost annually in development costs and this does not include lost revenues. This is due to failed system development projects. According to McKinsey & Company, a global management consulting firm, "17 percent of large IT projects go so badly that they can threaten the very existence of the company" and "On average, large IT projects run 45 percent over budget and 7 percent over time, while delivering 56 percent less value than predicted." This is the grim reality of business face with many of their projects today.[20] Companies from Nestlé to Nike have experienced additional consequences of failed projects—a damaged brand, lost goodwill, the dissolution of partnerships, lost investment opportunities, and the effects of low morale.[21]

With so many skilled and knowledgeable IS professionals at the helm of IS projects, how can this happen? Every day, organizations adopt projects that do not align with mission-critical initiatives; they overcommit financial and human capital; they sign off on low-value projects that consume valuable and scarce resources; and they agree to support projects that are poorly defined from requirements to planning.

IS projects typically fail because, in most instances, they are complex, made even more so by poor planning and unrealistic expectations; they are rushed, due to increasingly demanding market pressure; and their scope becomes too unmanageable. Because this is today's reality, it is important to apply solid project management techniques and tools to increase the success rate of IS projects.

The Triple Constraint

A project's vision needs to be clear, concise, and comprehensible, but it also has to be the same for all stakeholders. It is imperative that everyone be on the same page. From a business perspective, everyone has to be aligned with the direction of the overall business and the project's overall objectives. It is key for members of an organization who want to make meaningful contributions to understand the company's investment and selection strategy for projects, and how it determines and prioritizes the project pipeline. Projects consume vast amounts of resources. It is imperative to understand how the organization allocates its scarce and valuable resources to get the big picture.

Figure 11.8 displays the relationships between the three primary variables in any project—time, cost, and scope. These three variables are interdependent; all projects are limited in some way by these three constraints. The Project Management Institute calls the framework for evaluating these competing demands the triple constraint.

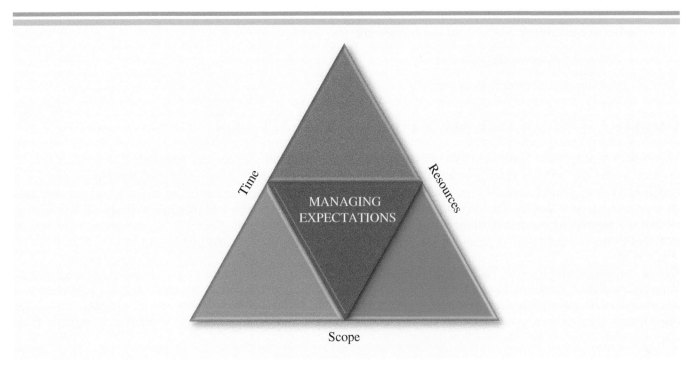

FIGURE 11.8

Project Management's Triple Constraints

If any one of the three factors changes, at least one other factor is likely to be affected. For example, moving up a project's finish date could result in either increasing costs to hire more staff or decreasing the scope to eliminate features or functions. Increasing a project's scope to include additional customer requests could result in extending the project's time to completion or increasing the project's cost—or both—to accommodate the scope changes. Project quality is affected by the project manager's ability to balance these competing demands. High-quality projects deliver the agreed-upon product or service on time and on budget.

Project management is the science of making intelligent trade-offs between time, cost, and scope. All three of the factors combined determine a project's quality. Benjamin Franklin's timeless advice—by failing to prepare, you prepare to fail—applies to many of today's software development projects. The failure rate of IS projects is much higher in organizations that do not exercise disciplined project management. A successful project is on time, within budget, meets the business's requirements, and fulfills the customer's needs. The Hackett Group, an Atlanta-based consultancy in the United States, analyzed its client database, which includes 2,000 companies, including 81 Fortune 100 companies, and discovered:

- Three in 10 major IS projects fail.

- Twenty-one percent of the companies state that they cannot adjust rapidly to market changes.

- Only one in four companies validates a business case for IT projects after completion.[22]

About 54 percent of project failures result from project management challenges and only 3 percent are the result of technical challenges. In the area of project management challenges the top seven challenges that appear in failed projects are:

- Poor project planning and direction

- Insufficient communication

- Ineffective management

- Failure to align with project constituents and stakeholders

- Ineffective involvement of executive management

- Lack of soft skills or ability to adapt

- Poor or missing methodology or tools[23]

PROJECT MANAGEMENT FUNDAMENTALS

The Project Management Institute (PMI) defines a ***project*** as a temporary endeavour undertaken to create a unique product or service. ***Project management*** is the application of knowledge, skills, tools, and techniques to project activities to meet project requirements. Projects are short-term efforts such as removing old servers, developing a custom e-commerce site, or merging databases. The PMI offers the Project Management Body of Knowledge (PMBOK), which sets the standards for project management on a global basis. Figure 11.9 provides an overview of PMI and its fundamental project management terms all managers should know and understand.[24]

Before its merger with Hewlett-Packard, Compaq decided to analyze and prioritize its system development projects. Knowing that the CIO wanted to be able to view every project, project management leaders quickly identified and removed non-strategic projects. At the end of the review process, the company cancelled 39 projects, saving the organization $15 million. Most Fortune 100 companies receive bottom-line benefits similar to Compaq's from implementing a project management solution.[25]

The ***Project Management Institute (PMI)*** develops procedures and concepts necessary to support the profession of project management (**www.pmi.org**). It has three areas of focus:

1. The distinguishing characteristics of a practising professional (ethics)

2. The content and structure of the profession's body of knowledge (standards)

3. Recognition of professional attainment (accreditation)

Project deliverables are any measurable, tangible, verifiable outcome, result, or item that is produced to complete a project or part of a project. Examples of project deliverables include design documents, testing scripts, and requirements documents.

Project milestones represent key dates when a certain group of activities must be performed. For example, completing the planning phase might be a project milestone. If a project milestone is missed, then chances are the project is experiencing problems.

Project manager is an individual who is an expert in project planning and management, defines and develops the project plan, and tracks the plan to ensure the project is completed on time and on budget. The project manager is the person responsible for executing the entire project plan.

Project management office (PMO) is an internal department that oversees all organizational projects. This group must formalize and professionalize project management expertise and leadership. One of the primary initiatives of the PMO is to educate the organization on techniques and procedures necessary to run successful projects.

FIGURE 11.9

Project Management Terms

Most business managers are not project managers; however, it is inevitable that all managers will be part of a project team. Therefore, it is important to understand how a business manages its project and how the culture supports the effort. The art and science practised by a project manager involves coordinating numerous things, as displayed in Figure 11.10. The remainder of this section focuses on four of these primary activities:

1. Choosing strategic projects

2. Understanding project planning

3. Managing projects

4. Outsourcing projects

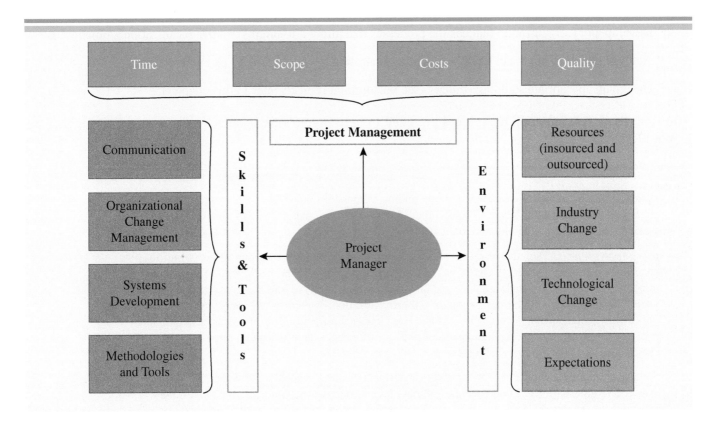

FIGURE 11.10

The Art and Science of a Project Manager Role

CHOOSING STRATEGIC PROJECTS AND IT GOVERNANCE

One of the most difficult decisions organizations make is determining the projects in which to invest time, energy, and resources. An organization must identify what it wants to do and how it is going to do it. The "what" part of this question focuses on issues such as justification for the project, the project definition, and expected results of the project. The "how" part of the question deals with such issues as project approach, project schedule, and analysis of project risks. Determining which projects to focus corporate efforts on is as necessary to projects as each project is to an organization.

In addition to project management there is a need to use *IT governance* to help create value from projects. In the governance process responsibilities and authority is clearly assigned and defined. IT governance is a set of processes that ensure the effective and efficient use of IT in enabling an organization to achieve its goals. IT governance helps

IT project teams create projects that align IT and business strategies and support the objectives of the business. IT governance helps mitigate project risk by placing IT leaders at the executive table when it comes to decisions about projects, and strengthens overall corporate governance practices which leads to enhanced regulatory compliance. Ideally to be effective governance needs to help IT leaders work more creatively, proactively, strategically and innovatively rather than just working to protect the IT assets of the organization. In this way IT can assume greater responsibility for enhancing competitiveness. According to Deloitte companies need to embrace the following steps to move toward developing stronger IT governance, which in turn can assist companies in choosing more strategic and successful IT projects.

- Determine the governance processes, structures and mechanisms needed to increase business-IT alignment.

- Examine the current IT governance processes, structures, and mechanisms to find opportunities for improvements.

- Develop an IT organization that has the processes that allow it to align IT to the organization's objectives.

- Analyze which IT costs can be reduced without harming the quality of the IT environment.

- Design an appropriate sourcing strategy (see outsourcing projects later in this chapter).[26]

Additionally, a few common techniques are used to help organizations select more strategic projects (see Figure 11.11).[27]

1. *Focus on organizational goals.* Managers are finding tremendous value in choosing projects that align with the organization's goals. Projects that address organizational goals tend to have a higher success rate since they are important to the entire organization.

2. *Categorize projects.* There are various categories that an organization can group projects into to determine a project's priority. One type of categorization includes problem, opportunity, and directives. Problems are undesirable situations that prevent an organization from achieving its goals. Opportunities are chances to improve the organization. Directives are new requirements imposed by management, government, or some other external influence. It is often easier to obtain approval for projects that address problems or directives, because the organization must respond to these categories to avoid financial losses.

3. *Perform a financial analysis.* A number of different financial analysis techniques can be performed to help determine a project's priority. A few of these include net present value, return on investment, and payback analysis. These financial analysis techniques help determine the organization's financial expectations for the project.

FIGURE 11.11

Techniques for Choosing Strategic Projects

Project Stakeholders

Project stakeholders are individuals and organizations actively involved in the project or whose interests might be affected as a result of project execution or project completion. Stakeholders are not necessarily involved in the completion of project deliverables. For example, a chief financial officer (CFO) will probably not help test a new billing system, but she will expect the successful completion of the project and exert influence over the project's objectives and outcomes. It is important for all stakeholders to understand the business objective of the project—once again, it is about getting the big picture. Stakeholders measure projects based on such factors as customer satisfaction, increased revenue, or decreased cost.

The project management team must identify stakeholders, determine their requirements and expectations, and, to the extent possible, manage their influence in relationship to the requirements to ensure a successful project. While all stakeholders are important, one stands out as having the most impact on the success or failure of a project: the executive sponsor. PMI defines the ***executive sponsor*** as the person or group that provides the financial resources for the project. Research has shown that the leadership strength of the executive sponsor has more to do with the success or failure of a project than any other critical success factor. In fact, the executive sponsor should be accountable to the project team for much more than the financial backing. The executive sponsor communicates up the chain on behalf of the project; he or she supports the project manager by championing the project to others who share the vision and benefit of the successfully completed project; and the executive sponsor also demonstrates the commitment and accountability necessary to survive a project! If a team has a hands-off sponsor who merely reviews invoices and inquires as to the status of a project, then that project is surely in trouble from the start.[28]

Another part of the equation is influence. If the executive sponsor has influence, he or she can use that influence to gain and direct essential resources needed to accomplish the project. A highly connected executive sponsor could mean the difference between success and failure. The executive sponsor should be committed to use this influence to ensure the health of the project. Executive management support influences the process and progress of a project. No matter what the case, the lack of executive support and input can place a project at a severe disadvantage.

UNDERSTANDING PROJECT PLANNING

Once an organization has selected strategic projects and identified its project manager, it is time to build the critical component—the project plan. Building a project plan involves two key components:

- Project charter

- Project plan

Project Charter

Many project professionals believe that a solid project is initiated with documentation that includes a project charter, a scope statement, and the project management plan. A ***project charter*** is a document issued by the project initiator or sponsor that formally authorizes the existence of a project and provides the project manager with the authority to apply organizational resources to project activities. In short, this means someone has stepped up to pay for and support the project. A project charter typically includes several elements.

- ***Project scope*** defines the work that must be completed to deliver a product with the specified features and functions. A project scope statement describes the business need, justification, requirements, and current boundaries for the project. The business need can be characterized by the problem that will be satisfied by the results of the project. This is important in linking the project with the organization's overall business goals. The project scope statement includes constraints, assumptions, and requirements—all components necessary for developing accurate cost estimates.

- ***Project objectives*** are quantifiable criteria that must be met for the project to be considered a success.

- ***Project constraints*** are specific factors that can limit options. They include budget, delivery dates, available skilled resources, and organizational policies.

- ***Project assumptions*** are factors that are considered to be true, real, or certain without proof or demonstration. Examples include hours in a work week or time of year the work will be performed.

The project objectives are one of the most important areas to define, because they are essentially the major elements of the project. When an organization achieves the project objectives, it has accomplished the major goals of the project and the project scope is satisfied. Project objectives must include metrics so that the project's success can be measured. The metrics can include cost, schedule, and quality metrics, along with a number of other metrics. Figure 11.12 displays the SMART criteria—useful reminders on how to ensure that the project has created understandable and measurable objectives.

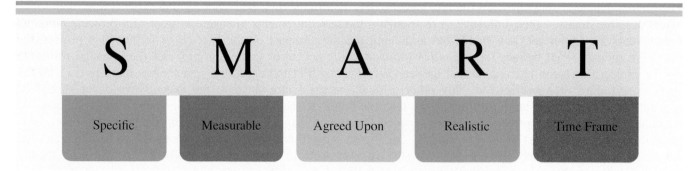

FIGURE 11.12

SMART Criteria for Successful Objective Creation

Project Plan

The *project plan* is a formal, approved document that manages and controls project execution. Figure 11.13 displays the characteristics of a well-defined project plan. The project plan should include a description of the project scope, a list of activities, a schedule, time estimates, cost estimates, risk factors, resources, assignments, and responsibilities. In addition to these basic components, most project professionals also include contingency plans, review and communications strategies, and a *kill switch*—a trigger that enables a project manager to close the project prior to completion.

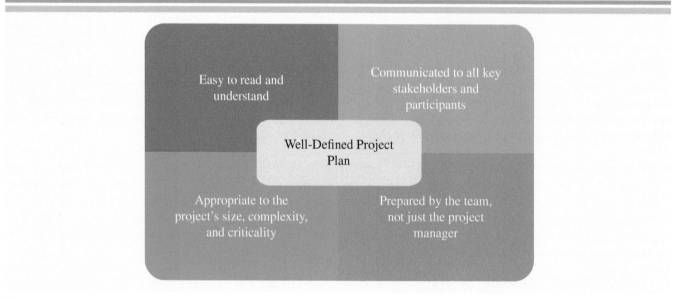

FIGURE 11.13

Well-Defined Project Plan Characteristics

A good project plan should include estimates for revenue and strategic necessities. It should also include measurement and reporting methods and details as to how top leadership will engage in the project. A good plan informs stakeholders of the benefits of the project and justifies the investment, commitment, and risk of the project in relation to the overall mission of the organization.[29]

An organization must build in continuous self-assessment, which allows earlier termination decisions on failing projects, with the associated cost savings. This frees capital and personnel for dedication to projects that are worth pursuing. Eliminating a project should be viewed as successful resource management, not as an admission of failure.

The most important part of the plan is communication. The project manager must communicate the plan to every member of the project team and to any key stakeholders and executives. The project plan must also include any project assumptions and be detailed enough to guide the execution of the project. A key to achieving project success is earning consensus and buy-in from all key stakeholders. By including key stakeholders in project plan development, the project manager allows them to have ownership of the plan. This often translates to greater commitment, which in turn results in enhanced motivation and productivity. The two primary diagrams most frequently used in project planning are PERT and Gantt charts.

PERT Chart   A *PERT (Program Evaluation and Review Technique) chart* is a graphical network model that depicts a project's tasks and the relationships between those tasks. In a PERT chart, a *dependency* is a logical relationship that exists between the project tasks, or between a project task and a milestone. PERT charts define dependency between project tasks before those tasks are scheduled (see Figure 11.14). The boxes in Figure 11.14 represent project tasks, and the project manager can adjust the contents of the boxes to display various project attributes, such as schedule and actual start and finish times. The arrows indicate that one task is dependent on the start or completion of another task. Today, PERT is often referred to as PERT/CPM, where CPM stands for critical path method. The *critical path* is a path from the start to the finish that passes through all the tasks that are critical to completing the project in the shortest amount of time. PERT/CPM charts frequently display a project's critical path.

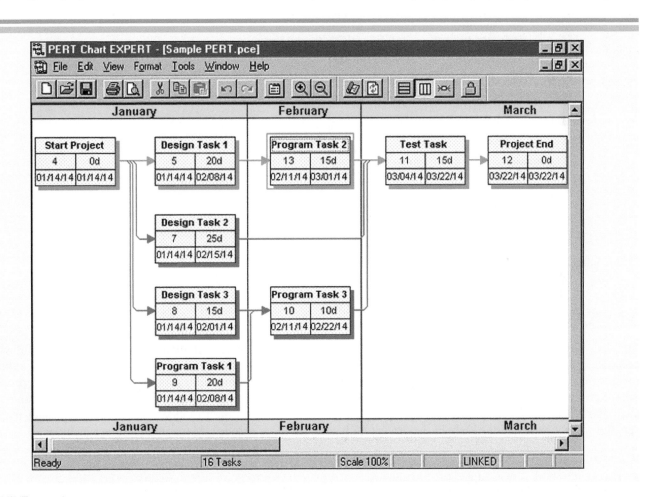

FIGURE 11.14
PERT/CPM Chart Example

Gantt Chart   A *Gantt chart* is a simple bar chart that depicts project tasks against a calendar. In a Gantt chart, tasks are listed vertically and the project's time frame is listed horizontally. A Gantt chart works well for representing the project schedule. It also shows actual progress of tasks against the planned duration. Figure 11.15 displays a software development project using a Gantt chart.

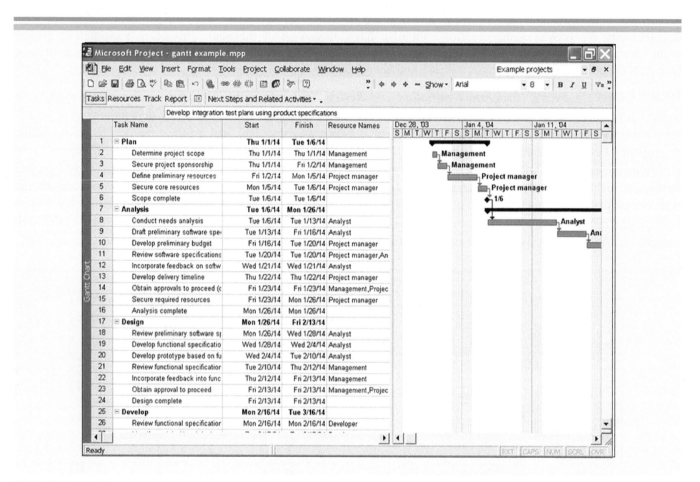

FIGURE 11.15

Gantt Chart Example

MANAGING PROJECTS

Standish Group research clearly shows that projects are likely to be less challenged and more successful with a competent and skilled project manager on board. Again, a project manager is an individual who is an expert in project planning and management, defines and develops the project plan, and tracks the plan to ensure the project is completed on time and on budget. A project manager can, of course, bring enormous benefits to an organization, such as reduced project expense, high company morale, and quicker time to market. A competent project manager sets the correct expectations early in the project with achievable milestones. Managing a project includes:

■ Identifying requirements

■ Establishing clear and achievable objectives

■ Balancing the competing demands of quality, scope, time, and cost

■ Adapting the specifications, plans, and approach to the different concerns and expectations of the various stakeholders[30]

In addition to managing these objectives, a successful project manager possesses a variety of hard and soft skills. Standish Group research also shows that successful project managers have basic business operational knowledge and good business skills. When a project manager has a good grasp of the business operations, he or she can improve critical communication among the designers, developers, user community, and top leadership. An experienced project manager should be able to minimize scope and create a better estimate. He or she knows how to say no without creating controversy. And a good project manager should have learned that a happy stakeholder is one who is under-promised and over-delivered! A project manager must focus on managing three primary areas to ensure success:

1. People

2. Communications

3. Change

Managing People

Managing people is one of the hardest and most critical efforts a project manager undertakes. Resolving conflicts within the team and balancing the needs of the project with the personal and professional needs of the team are two of the challenges facing project managers. More and more project managers are the main (and sometimes sole) interface with a client during the project. This being so, communication, negotiation, marketing, and salesmanship are just as important to the project manager as financial and analytical acumen. Often, the people management side of project management makes the difference in pulling off a successful project.

Managing Communications

While many companies develop unique project management frameworks based on familiar project management standards, all of them agree that communication is the key to excellent project management. This is easy to state, but not easy to accomplish! It is extremely helpful if a project manager plans what and how he or she will communicate as a formal part of the project management plan. This plan, most often a document, is referred to as a *communications plan*. A project manager distributes timely, accurate, and meaningful information regarding project objectives that involve time, cost, scope, and quality, and the status of each. The project manager also shares small wins as the project progresses, informs others of needed corrections, makes requests known for additional resources, and keeps all stakeholders informed of the project schedule.

Another important aspect of a project management communications plan is to provide a method for continually obtaining and monitoring feedback from and for all stakeholders. This is not to say that a project manager needs to spend countless hours answering every email and responding to every question posed. Rather, managers should develop a method for asking for specific feedback as part of the plan and responding to it in a timely, organized manner. Team members remain close to the project and should be encouraged to share open and honest feedback. It is the project manager's role and responsibility to foster an environment of trust so that members feel safe to contribute their knowledge and ideas—even if it means relaying bad news or offering an opposing viewpoint.

Managing Change

Change, whether it comes in the form of a crisis, a market shift, or a technological development, is challenging for all organizations. Successful organizations and successful people learn to anticipate and react appropriately to change. For example, Snap-on, a maker of tools and equipment for specialists such as car mechanics, is successful at managing change. In the past, the company increased profits by 12 percent while sales were down 6.7 percent. Dennis Leitner, vice-president of IT, runs the IT group on a day-to-day basis and leads the implementation of all major software development initiatives. Each software development initiative is managed by both the business and IT. In fact, business resources are on the IT group's payroll, and they spend as much as 80 percent of their time learning what a business unit is doing and how IT can help make it happen. Leitner's role focuses primarily on strategic planning, change management, and setting up metrics to track performance.[31]

Dynamic organizational change is inevitable, and an organization must effectively manage change as it evolves. With the numerous challenges and complexities that organizations face in today's rapidly changing environment, effective change management thus becomes a critical core competency. ***Change management***, or ***organizational change management*** as it is commonly called, is a set of techniques that aid in evolution, composition, and policy management of the design and implementation of a system. Figure 11.16 displays a few of the more common reasons change occurs.[32]

1. An omission in defining initial scope

2. A misunderstanding of the initial scope

3. An external event, such as government regulations that create new requirements

4. Organizational changes, such as mergers, acquisitions, or partnerships, that create new business problems and opportunities

5. Availability of better technology

6. Shifts in planned technology that force unexpected and significant changes to the business organization, culture, and/or processes

7. The users or management simply wanting the system to do more than they originally requested or agreed to

8. Management reducing the funding for the project or imposing an earlier deadline

FIGURE 11.16

Common Reasons for Change

Before organizations implement change management systems, they need to consider the steps required to make change happen. Since the late 1990s, organizations that specialize in organizational change management have looked at processes for leading change like those in ProSci's 3 Steps for Change Management or the seven-step program introduced by John Kotter. In the case of ProSci, they have developed the ADKAR® model, which focuses on empowering the individual person within the organization by equipping them to adapt to change successfully.[33] With John Kotter's model, the change management steps are still people-focused, but they also involve the broader organization in most of the steps to manage change. Once organizations understand how change works, they can proceed to developing their procedures for creating change and developing change management systems.[34]

A *change management system* includes a collection of procedures to document a change request, and define the steps necessary to consider the change based on the expected impact of the change. Most change management systems require that a change request form be initiated by one or more project stakeholders (systems owners, users, customers, analysts, developers). Ideally, these change requests are considered by a *change control board (CCB)* that is responsible for approving or rejecting all change requests. The CCB's composition typically includes a representative from each business area that has a stake in the project. The CCB's decision to accept or reject each change is based on an impact analysis of the change. For example, if one department wants to implement a change to the software that will increase both deployment time and cost, then the other business owners need to agree that the change is valid and that it warrants the extended time frame and increased budget.

Change is an opportunity, not a threat. Realizing that change is the norm rather than the exception will help an organization stay ahead. Becoming a change leader and accepting the inevitability of change can help ensure that an organization can survive and even thrive in times of change. Figure 11.17 displays the three important guidelines change leaders can follow to make change effective both inside and outside their organizations.[35]

MEASURING PROJECT VALUE

IS has become an important part of an organization's strategy, competitive advantage, and profitability. There is management pressure to build information systems faster, better, and at minimum cost. The return on investment that an organization can achieve from the money it spends on IS has come under increased scrutiny from senior business executives and directors. Consequently, IS now has to operate like other parts of the organization, being aware of its performance and its contribution to the organization's success and opportunities for improvement. So what is it that managers need to know about measuring the success of information systems?

1. *Institute change management policies.* Create clearly defined policies and procedures that must be followed each time a request for change is received.

2. *Anticipate change.* View change as an opportunity and embrace it both individually and as an organization.

3. *Seek change.* Every 6 to 12 months look for changes that may be windows of opportunity. Review successes and failures to determine if there are any opportunities for innovation.

FIGURE 11.17

Three Important Guidelines for Effective Change Management

The first thing managers need to understand about project success is that it is incredibly difficult to measure. Determining the return on investment (ROI) of a project like a new software application is difficult. For example, what is the ROI of a fire extinguisher? If the fire extinguisher is never used, the return on the investment is low. If the extinguisher puts out a fire that could destroy the entire building, then its ROI is high. This is similar to information systems. If a company implements a $5,000 firewall to prevent virus attacks on the organization's computers and it never stops a virus, the company has lost $5,000. However, if the firewall stops viruses that could have cost the organization millions of dollars, then the ROI of that firewall is significantly greater than $5,000. Other questions executives can ask regarding their information systems' project success include:

- Are IS operations performing satisfactorily?

- How is my IS outsource provider performing?

- What are the risk factors to consider in an IS project?

- What questions should be asked to ensure an IS project proposal is realistic?

- What are the characteristics of a healthy IS project?

- Which factors are most critical to monitor to ensure an IS project remains on track?

To offer detailed information to all layers of management, General Electric Co. (GE) invested $1.5 billion in employee time, hardware, software, and other technologies to implement a real-time operations monitoring information system. GE executives use the new system to monitor sales, inventory, and savings across the company's 13 global business operations every 15 minutes. This allows GE to respond to changes, reduce cycle times, and improve risk management on an hourly basis instead of waiting for monthly or quarterly reports. GE estimates that the $1.5 billion investment will provide a 33 percent return over five years.[36]

IS professionals know how to install and maintain information systems. Business professionals know how to run a successful business. But how does a company decide if an information system helps make a business successful? Peter Drucker, a famous management guru, once stated that if you cannot measure it, you cannot manage it. Managers need to ask themselves how they are going to manage IS projects when it is so incredibly difficult to measure IS projects.[37]

The answer lies in the metrics as discussed in Chapter 2. Designing metrics requires an expertise that neither IS nor business professionals usually possess. Metrics ask questions such as: How do you define success? How do you apply quantifiable measures to business processes, especially qualitative ones such as customer service? What kind of information best reflects progress, or the lack of it?

LO5) OUTSOURCING PROJECTS

In the high-speed global business environment, an organization needs to maximize its profits, enlarge its market share, and restrain its ever-increasing costs. Businesses need to make every effort to rethink and adopt new processes, especially the prospective resources regarding insourcing and outsourcing. Two basic options are available to organizations wishing to develop and maintain their information systems—insourcing and outsourcing.

Insourcing (in-house development) is a common approach using the professional expertise within an organization to develop and maintain the organization's IT systems. Insourcing has been instrumental in creating a viable supply of IT professionals, and in creating a better quality workforce combining both technical and business skills.

Outsourcing is an arrangement by which one organization provides a service or services for another organization that chooses not to perform them in-house. In some cases, the entire IS department is outsourced, including planning and business analysis as well as the installation, management, and servicing of the network and workstations. Outsourcing can range from a large contract under which an organization such as IBM manages IS services for a company such as Xerox, to the practice of hiring contractors and temporary office workers on an individual basis. Figure 11.18 shows functions companies typically outsource, while Figure 11.19 displays the primary reasons companies outsource. The IT outsourcing market hit a value of about $288 billion in 2013, a 2.8 percent increase over 2012, and Gartner is predicting continued growth through 2017.[38]

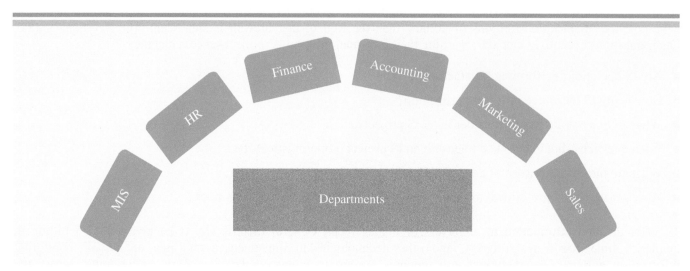

FIGURE 11.18

Departments Commonly Outsourced by Organizations

IS outsourcing enables organizations to keep up with market and technology advances—with less strain on human and financial resources and more assurance that the IS infrastructure will keep pace with evolving business priorities (see Figure 11.20). Planning, deploying, and managing IS environments is both a tactical and a strategic challenge that must take into account a company's organizational, industrial, and technological concerns. The three different forms of outsourcing options are *onshore*, *nearshore*, and *offshore*:

1. *Onshore outsourcing* is the process of engaging another company within the same country for services.

2. *Nearshore outsourcing* refers to contracting an outsourcing arrangement with a company in a nearby country. Often this country will share a border with the native country.

3. *Offshore outsourcing* is using organizations from developing countries to write code and develop systems. In offshore outsourcing the country is geographically far away.

Tap outside sources of expertise	70%
Concentrate resources on core business	66%
Reduce head count and related expenses	53%
Eliminate the need to reinvest in technology	48%
Reduce costs	39%
Better manage the costs of internal processes	32%
Other	3%

FIGURE 11.19

Primary Reasons Companies Outsource

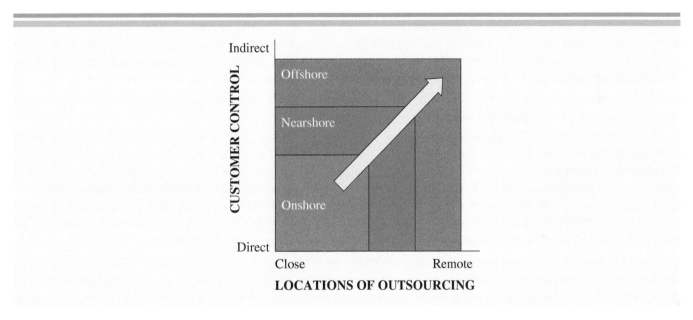

LOCATIONS OF OUTSOURCING

FIGURE 11.20

Outsourcing Models and Cost Savings

Major Canadian companies send significant portions of their software development work offshore—primarily to vendors in India, but also to vendors in China, Eastern Europe (including Russia), Ireland, Israel, and the Philippines. The big selling point for offshore outsourcing is inexpensive good work. Companies can easily realize cost savings through offshore outsourcing and still get the same, if not better, quality of service.

Developed and developing countries throughout Europe and Asia offer some IS outsourcing services, but most are hampered to some degree by language, telecommunications infrastructure, or regulatory barriers. The first and largest offshore marketplace is India, whose English-speaking and technologically advanced population has built its IS services into a business that continues to grow at 25 to 30 percent annually.[39]

Ever since Eastman Kodak announced in 1988 that it was outsourcing its IS function to IBM, DEC, and Businessland, large organizations have found it acceptable to transfer their IT assets, leases, and staff to outsourcers. In view of the changes in sourcing, the key question now is not "Should we outsource IS?" but rather "Where and how can we take advantage of the rapidly developing market of IS service providers?" Some of the influential drivers affecting the growth of the outsourcing market include:

- *Core competencies.* Many companies have recently begun to consider outsourcing as a means to fuel revenue growth rather than just a cost-cutting measure. Outsourcing enables an organization to maintain an up-to-date technology infrastructure while freeing it to focus on revenue growth goals by reinvesting cash and human capital in areas offering the greatest return on investment.

- *Financial savings.* It is typically cheaper to hire workers in China and India than similar workers in Canada. Technology is advancing at such an accelerated rate that companies often lack the resources, workforce, or expertise to keep up. It is close to impossible for an IS department to maintain a "best-of-breed" status, especially for small- and medium-sized enterprises where cost is a critical factor.

- *Rapid growth.* A company's sustainability depends on both speed to market and ability to react quickly to changes in market conditions. By taking advantage of outsourcing, an organization is able to acquire best practices process expertise. This facilitates the design, building, training, and deployment of business processes or functions.

- *Industry changes.* High levels of reorganization across industries have increased demand for outsourcing to better focus on core competencies. The significant increase in merger and acquisition activity created a sudden need to integrate multiple core and non-core business functions into one business, while the deregulation of the utilities and telecom industries created a need to ensure compliance with government rules and regulations. Companies in either situation turned to outsourcing so they could better focus on industry changes at hand.

- *The Internet.* The pervasive nature of the Internet as an effective sales channel has allowed clients to become more comfortable with outsourcing. Barriers to entry, such as lack of capital, are dramatically reduced in the world of e-business due to the Internet. New competitors enter the market daily.

- *Globalization.* As markets open worldwide, competition heats up. Companies may engage outsourcing service providers to deliver international services.

Best Buy Co. Inc. is a leading specialty retailer for consumer electronics, personal computers, entertainment software, and appliances. Best Buy needed to find a strategic IS partner that could help the company leverage its IS functions to meet its business objectives. The company also wanted to integrate its disparate enterprise systems and minimize its operating expenses. It outsourced these functions to Accenture, a global management consulting, technology services, and outsourcing company. The comprehensive outsourcing relationship that drove Best Buy's transformation produced spectacular results that were measurable in every key area of its business, such as a 20 percent increase in key category revenue that translated into a $25 million profit improvement.[40]

According to PricewaterhouseCoopers's survey of CEOs from 452 of the fastest-growing American companies, "Businesses that outsource are growing faster, larger, and more profitably than those that do not. In addition, most of those involved in outsourcing say they are saving money and are highly satisfied with their outsourcing service providers." Figure 11.21 lists common areas for outsourcing opportunities across industries.[41]

Outsourcing Benefits

The many benefits associated with outsourcing include:

- Increased quality and efficiency of a process, service, or function
- Reduced operating expenses
- Focusing resources on core profit-generating competencies
- Reduced exposure to risks involved with large capital investments
- Access to outsourcing service provider's economies of scale
- Access to outsourcing service provider's expertise and best-in-class practices
- Access to advanced technologies
- Increased flexibility with the ability to respond quickly to changing market demands
- Avoiding costly outlay of capital funds

- Reduced head count and associated overhead expense
- Reduced frustration and expense related to hiring and retaining employees in an exceptionally tight job market
- Reduced time to market for products or services[42]

Industry	Outsourcing Opportunities
Banking and finance	Cheque and electronic payment processing, credit report issuance, delinquency management, securities, trades processing
Insurance	Claims reporting and investigation, policy administration, cheque processing, risk assessment
Telecommunications	Invoice and bill production, transaction processing
Health care	Electronic data interchange, database management, accounting
Transportation	Ticket and order processing
Government	Loan processing, fine payment processing
Retail	Electronic payment processing

FIGURE 11.21
Outsourcing Opportunities

The Challenges of Outsourcing

Outsourcing comes with several challenges. These arguments are valid and should be considered when a company is thinking about outsourcing. Many challenges can be avoided with proper research on the outsourcing service provider. The challenges include:

- *Contract length.* Most of the outsourced IS contracts are for a relatively long period (several years). This is because of the high cost of transferring assets and employees as well as maintaining technological investment. The long contract causes three particular issues:

   1. Difficulties in getting out of a contract if the outsourcing service provider turns out to be unsuitable

   2. Problems in foreseeing what the business will need over the next five or ten years (typical contract lengths), creating difficulties in establishing an appropriate contract

   3. Problems in reforming an internal IS department after the contract period is finished

- *Competitive edge.* Effective and innovative use of information systems can give an organization a competitive edge over its rivals. A competitive business advantage provided by an internal IS department that understands the organization and is committed to its goals can be lost in an outsourced arrangement. In an outsourced arrangement, IS staff are striving to achieve the goals and objectives of the outsourcing service provider, which may conflict with those of the organization.

- *Confidentiality.* In some organizations, the information stored in the computer systems is central to the enterprise's success or survival, such as information about pricing policies, product mixing formulas, or sales analysis. Some companies decide against outsourcing for fear of placing confidential information in the hands of the provider, particularly if the outsourcing service provider offers services to companies competing in the same marketplace. Although the organization usually dismisses this threat, claiming it is covered by confidentiality clauses in a contract, the organization must assess the potential risk and costs of a confidentiality breach in determining the net benefits of an outsourcing agreement.

■ *Scope definition.* Most IS projects suffer from problems associated with defining the scope of the system. The same problem afflicts outsourcing arrangements. Many difficulties result from contractual misunderstandings between the organization and the outsourcing service provider. In such circumstances, the organization believes that the service required is within the contract scope whereas the service provider is sure it is outside the scope, so is subject to extra fees.[43]

OPENING CASE QUESTIONS

Project Management

5. Did this project benefit from project management principles and techniques?

6. What project management principles and techniques could have been followed to improve the project?

7. How could the concept of governance be applied to the management of this project?

8. What are the opportunities for outsourcing in this project both in the development and maintenance stages of the project?

SUMMARY OF KEY THEMES

The purpose of this chapter was to provide you, the business student, with a detailed overview of the various ways in which organizations go about developing information systems. Specifically, this chapter described:

■ *The business benefits associated with successful systems development, and how the issues and challenges developing domestic information systems amplify with global systems development.* Successful systems development leads to information systems that meet business and user requirements, and thus contribute directly to an organization's strategic and operational success. Systems development projects that occur in global environments have specific political, cultural, and geographical challenges that can add to the difficulty in yielding the development and rollout of successful information systems.

■ *The seven phases of the systems development life cycle and the relationships between each of these phases to one another.* The seven phases of the SDLC are planning, analysis, design, development, testing, implementation, and maintenance.

■ *Different systems development methodologies.* The traditional systems development approach is the waterfall methodology. Due to criticisms of inflexibility and the time intensiveness of the waterfall method, other methodologies have been proposed that are more agile (i.e., more flexible, less time-intensive). These include rapid prototyping, extreme programming, RUP, and Scrum. Participatory design (PD) is a completely different systems development methodology approach from the waterfall and agile methods. With PD, users lead design and systems developers serve as coaches or facilitators.

■ *The importance of good project management practice.* Project management is the application of knowledge, skills, tools, and techniques to project activities to meet project requirements. Organizations today recognize the art and science of project management and the need to manage and coordinate projects across organizations in ways that maximize limited organizational resources (e.g., staff, dollars, equipment) and support organizational goals and business needs. This requires implementing and supporting good project management practices in the organization, such as implementing a centralized project management office, and hiring project managers who not only are able to create sound project plans and feasible technical schedules, but also can lead and motivate project staff.

■ *The benefits and challenges of outsourcing systems development projects.* Outsourcing is an arrangement where an outside organization is hired to provide a service or services to a company. Benefits include gaining outside expertise that the company may lack, reduced operating expenses, and the ability to get services done more quickly. Challenges include negotiating contracts, ensuring confidentiality of information, and the loss of competitive edge companies may have if they developed and supported the outsourced service or services themselves.

You should now have sufficient knowledge of the systems development process that you can participate and contribute toward the successful design and implementation of information systems. You should also be familiar with project management basics—these will help you successfully steer the completion of any project.

KEY TERMS

Agile methodology

Analysis

Change control board (CCB)

Change management

Change management system

Critical path

Dependency

Design

Development

Executive sponsor

Extreme programming (XP) methodology

Feature creep

Gantt chart

Implementation

Insourcing (in-house development)

IT governance

Iterative development

Kill switch

Maintenance

Methodology

Nearshore outsourcing

Offshore outsourcing

Onshore outsourcing

Organizational change management

Outsourcing

Participatory design (PD) methodology

PERT (Program Evaluation and Review Technique) chart

Planning

Project

Project assumptions

Project charter

Project constraints

Project deliverables

Project management

Project Management Body of Knowledge (PMBOK)

Project Management Institute (PMI)

Project management office (PMO)

Project manager

Project milestones

Project objectives

Project plan

Project scope

Project stakeholders

Prototype

Rapid application development (RAD) (rapid prototyping)

Rational unified process (RUP) methodology

Scope creep

Scrum methodology

Self-sourcing

Systems development life cycle (SDLC)

Testing

Waterfall methodology

CLOSING CASE ONE

HP's Software Problems

This case showcases how easy it is for a systems development project to go awry and cause major problems for an organization.

With IS projects, pessimism—otherwise known as contingency planning—is the only way to keep small information systems problems from becoming full-blown business disasters. Christina Hanger had little reason to be pessimistic in May 2004, when she was moving one of Hewlett-Packard's (HP) biggest North American divisions onto a centralized ERP system from SAP. As the leader of an IS consolidation project rooted in HP's acquisition of Compaq two years earlier, Hanger, HP senior vice-president of Americas operations and IT, had an unbroken record of success migrating five product groups within the two former companies onto one of two SAP systems.

Hanger had every reason to believe that the sixth would go well too. Even so, she knew to be prepared for problems. At approximately $7.5 billion in annual revenue, Industry Standard Servers (ISS), the division involved with this latest project, was much larger than any of the others that Hanger had migrated to SAP to that point. Hanger took the contingency plan that her team had developed for the other five migrations and adjusted it to accommodate the ISS division's larger sales volume. She planned for three weeks of IS snafus, mostly focused on what might happen as a result of tweaking a legacy order-entry system to work with the new SAP system. The contingency plan addressed business impacts too. HP banked three weeks' worth of extra servers and took over an empty portion of an HP factory in Omaha to stand by for any overflow of orders that needed special configurations (e.g., an unusual component or software combination) and could not be stockpiled ahead of time.

"We had a series of small problems, none of which individually would have been too much to handle. But together they created the perfect storm," stated Gilles Bouchard, CIO and executive vice-president of global operations. Starting when the system went live at the beginning of June and continuing throughout the rest of the month, as many as 20 percent of customer orders for servers stopped dead in their tracks between the legacy order-entry system and the SAP system. As IS problems go, this was not too big. Some data modelling issues between the legacy system and the SAP system prevented the SAP system from processing some orders for customized products; these programming errors were fixed within four or five weeks. However, Hanger and her business colleagues from the ISS division who were on the project steering committee never envisioned the degree to which these programming glitches would affect the business.

Orders began to backlog quickly, and HP did not have enough manual workarounds to keep servers flowing fast enough to meet customer demand. Angry customers picked up the phone and called HP—or worse, competitors Dell and IBM. In a commodity market such as servers, customer loyalty is built upon a company's ability to configure products to order and get them delivered on time. HP could do neither for much of the summer. In a third-quarter conference call on August 12, HP chair and CEO Carly Fiorina pegged the financial impact at $160 million: a $120 million order backlog that resulted in $40 million in lost revenue. That was more than the cost of the project itself, which AMR Research estimated to be $30 million. The headlines all claimed an IS disaster, but in fact HP's disaster resulted from a few relatively small problems in IS that snowballed into a much bigger problem for the business: the inability to cope with the order backlog. This was a disaster that could have been prevented—not by trying to eliminate every possibility for error in a major information systems migration, which is virtually impossible, but by taking a much broader view of the impact that these projects can have on a company's supply chain.[44]

Questions

1. Which of the seven phases of the systems development life cycle is least important to HP? The most important? Why?

2. Which of the different software development methodologies should HP use to implement successful systems? Why?

3. Identify the primary reasons for systems project failure and explain which ones HP experienced on its ERP build.

4. Review the buy-versus-build decision and explain why HP chose to buy its ERP system.

5. Review the project charter and explain how HP could benefit by using one.

6. Review the three outsourcing options and identify the pros and cons HP should consider if it chooses to outsource its systems development effort.

CLOSING CASE TWO

Disaster at Denver International Airport

This case showcases how looking at past problems can help an organization develop a new solution.

One good way to learn how to develop successful systems is to review past failures. One of the most infamous system failures is Denver International Airport's (DIA) baggage system. When the automated baggage system design for DIA was introduced, it was hailed as the saviour of modern airport design. The design relied on a network of 300 computers to route bags and 4,000 cars to carry luggage across 34 kilometres of track. Laser scanners were to read bar-coded luggage tags, while advanced scanners tracked the movement of toboggan-like baggage carts.

When DIA finally opened its doors for reporters to witness its revolutionary baggage handling system, the scene was rather unpleasant. Bags were chewed up, lost, and misrouted in what has since become a legendary systems nightmare. One of the biggest mistakes made in the fiasco was that not enough time was allowed to properly develop the system. In the beginning of the project, DIA assumed it was the responsibility of individual airlines to find their own way of moving the baggage from the plane to the baggage claim area. The automated system was not involved in the initial planning of the DIA project. By the time the DIA developers decided to create an integrated system, the time frame for designing and implementing such a complex and huge system was not achievable.

Another common mistake that occurred during the project was that the airlines kept changing their business requirements. This caused numerous issues, including the implementation of power supplies that were not properly updated for the revised system design, which caused overloaded motors and mechanical failures. Besides the power supply design problem, the optical sensors did not read the bar codes correctly, causing issues with baggage routing.

Finally, BAE, the company that designed and implemented the automated baggage system for DIA, had never created a baggage system of this size before. BAE had created a similar system in an airport in Munich, Germany, where the scope was much smaller. Essentially, the baggage system had an inadequate IT infrastructure because it was designed for a much smaller system.

DIA simply could not open without a functional baggage system, so the city had no choice but to delay the opening date for more than 16 months, costing taxpayers roughly $1 million per day, which totalled around $500 million.[45]

Questions

1. One problem with DIA's baggage system was inadequate testing. Why is testing important to a project's success? Why do so many projects decide to skip testing?

2. Evaluate the different systems development methodologies. Which one would have most significantly increased the chances of the project's success?

3. How could more time spent in the analysis and design phase have saved Colorado taxpayers hundreds of millions of dollars?

4. Why could BAE not take an existing IT infrastructure and simply increase its scale and expect it to work?

CLOSING CASE THREE

Staying on Track: Toronto Transit

This case illustrates the benefits of using project management software for project success.

Schedules are at the heart of the Toronto Transit Commission's (TTC) celebrated transit system, which services over a million customers daily. More than 50 large engineering and construction projects were completed to expand, upgrade, and maintain Toronto's transit systems and structures. One such project was the Sheppard project, which consisted of constructing a new 6 kilometre line north of the city. The Sheppard took more than five years to complete at a total cost of $970 million.

The TTC's challenge was to keep its 50 individual projects, most of which fell within the $2 million to $110 million price range and spanned an average of five years, on schedule and under budget. Staying on top of so many multi-faceted, multi-year, and often interdependent projects added complexity for the company. In response, the TTC used Primavera Project Planner (P3) to create a single master schedule for all of its engineering and construction projects.

The TTC's 50 individual projects averaged 100 to 150 activities each, with some projects encompassing as many as 500 to 600 activities. According to Vince Carroll, head scheduler for the Engineering and Construction branch, "Seeing the big picture was important, not only for the 300 people who worked in the Engineering and Construction branch of the TTC, but for the entire 9,000-person organization. Engineering managers needed to see how other projects may have impacted their own. Materials and procurement managers needed to track project progress. Senior managers needed to be able to communicate with city government to secure funding. Marketing and public relations people needed the latest information to set public expectations. And most important of all," Carroll said, "the operations group needed to stay informed of what was happening so that they could adjust the schedules that ran the trains."

Carroll and his team of 25 people created, updated, and published a master schedule that summarized the individual status of each project, showing the logical links between projects, and providing an integrated overview of all projects. The master schedule helped the team effectively and regularly communicate the status of all projects throughout the Toronto Transit system.

The master schedule organized projects according to their location in the capital budget. For example, projects could be organized according to those that had been allotted funding for expansion, state of good repair, legislative reasons, or environmental reasons. Each project was organized by its logical flow—from planning, analysis, and design, through the maintenance phase. The final report showed positive and negative balances for each project and a single overview of the status of all the engineering and construction projects. Carroll and his team used PERT charts to create time-scaled logic diagrams and then converted this information to bar charts for presentation purposes in the master schedule. The TTC also linked its master schedule directly to its payroll system, enabling it to track the number of hours actually worked versus hours planned.

Today customers can easily access these schedules and more information about moving around the greater Toronto area at **GOTransit.com**. The system also takes advantage of Google Transit Trip Planner.[46]

Questions

1. How was project management software used by the TTC for better project management?

2. Describe Gantt charts and explain how the TTC could have used one to communicate project status.

3. Describe PERT charts and explain how the TTC could have used one to communicate project status.

4. Using this case study of the TTC as a guide, under what circumstances should organizations use project management software to help manage projects?

MAKING BUSINESS DECISIONS

1. Selecting a Systems Development Methodology

Exus Incorporated is an international billing outsourcing company. Exus currently has revenues of $5 billion, over 3,500 employees, and operations on every continent. You have recently been hired as the CIO. Your first task is to increase the software development project success rate, which is currently at 20 percent. To ensure that future software development projects are successful, you want to standardize the systems development methodology across the entire enterprise. Currently, each project determines which methodology it uses to develop software.

Create a report detailing three additional system development methodologies that were not covered in this text. Compare each of these methodologies to the traditional waterfall approach. Finally, recommend which methodology you want to implement as your organizational standard. Be sure to highlight any potential roadblocks you might encounter when implementing the new standard methodology.

2. Understanding Project Failure

You are the director of project management for Stello, a global manufacturer of high-end writing instruments. The company sells to primarily high-end customers, and the average price for one of its fine writing instruments is about $350. You are currently implementing a new customer relationship management system and you want to do everything you can to ensure a successful systems development effort. Create a document summarizing the five primary reasons why this project could fail, along with your strategy for eliminating the possibility of system development failure on your project.

3. Missing Phases in the Systems Development Life Cycle

Hello Inc. is a large concierge service for executives operating in Vancouver, Montreal, and Toronto. The company performs all kinds of services, from dog walking to airport transportation. Your manager, Dan Martello, wants to skip the testing phase during the company's financial ERP implementation. Dan feels that since the system came from a vendor it should work correctly. To meet the project's looming deadline he wants to skip the testing phase. Draft a memo explaining to Dan the importance of following the SDLC and the ramifications to the business if the financial system is not tested.

4. Refusing to Sign Off

You are the primary client on a large extranet development project. After carefully reviewing the requirements definition document, you are positive that there are missing, ambiguous, inaccurate, and unclear requirements. The project manager is pressuring you for your sign-off since he has already received sign-off from five of your co-workers. If you fail to sign off on the requirements, you are going to put the entire project at risk since the time frame is non-negotiable. What would you do? Why?

5. Saving Failing Systems

Crik Candle Company manufactures low-end candles for restaurants. The company generates over $40 million in annual revenues and has more than 300 employees. You are in the middle of a large multimillion-dollar supply chain management implementation. Your project manager has just come to you with the information that the project might fail for the following reasons:

- Several business requirements were incorrect and the scope has to be doubled.

- Three developers recently quit.

- The deadline has been moved up a month.

Develop a list of options that your company can follow to ensure the project remains on schedule and within budget.

6. Explaining Project Management

Prime Time Inc. is a large consulting company that specializes in outsourcing people with project management capabilities and skills. You are in the middle of an interview for a job with Prime Time. The manager performing the interview asks you to explain why managing a project plan is critical to a project's success. The manager also wants you to explain scope creep and feature creep, and your tactics for managing them on a project. Finally, the manager wants you to elaborate on your strategies for delivering successful projects and reducing risks.

7. Applying Project Management Techniques

You have been hired by a medium-sized airline company, Sun Best. Sun Best currently flies over 30 routes in the Maritime provinces. The company is experiencing tremendous issues coordinating its 100 pilots, 200 flight attendants, and 65 daily flights. Determine how Sun Best could use a Gantt chart to help it coordinate pilots, flight attendants, and daily flights. Using Excel, create a sample Gantt chart highlighting the different types of activities and resources Sun Best could track with the tool.

8. GUS Software Offshores

Founded in 2007, GUS Software provides innovative search software, website demographics, and testing software. All serve as part of its desktop and enterprise resource planning solutions for government, corporate, educational, and consumer markets. Website publishers, digital media publishers, content managers, document managers, business users, consumers, software companies, and consulting services companies use GUS solutions. The company is currently thinking about offshore-outsourcing its call centre functions, e-business strategies, and application development. Describe how GUS could use outsourcing along with the potential advantages it might receive.

connect   **LEARNSMART**   **SMARTBOOK**

For more information on the resources available from McGraw-Hill Ryerson, go to www.mheducation.ca/he/solutions.

ENDNOTES

1. Irene Herremans, professor, University of Calgary, personal communication, September 23–29, 2011.

2. Tim Wilson, "Nike: i2 Software Just Didn't Do It," *Internet Week*, January 1, 2003, http://corvelle.com/library/ebuscouse/caseStudies/Nike_i2.doc, accessed September 12, 2011.

3. Mark McDonald, "McKinsey Report Highlights Failure of Large Projects: Why It Is Better to Be Small, Particularly in IT," October 29, 2012, http://blogs.gartner.com/mark_mcdonald/2012/10/29/mckinsey-report-highlights-failure-of-large-projects-why-it-is-better-to-be-small-particularly-in-it, accessed May 29, 2014.

4. "Python Project Failure," www.systemsdev.com, accessed November 14, 2003; Mathias Kirchmer, "How to Create Successful IT Projects with Value-Driven BPM," February 27, 2013, www.cio.com/article/729518/How_to_Create_Successful_IT_Projects_With_Value_Driven_BPM, accessed May 29, 2014.

5. Jim Johnson, *My Life Is Failure: 100 Things You Should Know to Be a Successful Project Leader* (Boston: MA: Standish Group International, 2006), p. 46.

6. www.standishgroup.com, accessed December 12, 2003.

7. Gary McGraw, "Making Essential Software Work: Why Software Quality Management Makes Good Business Sense," *Cigital* (Dulles: VA), 2003, www.cigital.com/whitepapers/dl/Making_Essential_Software_Work.pdf, accessed September 12, 2011.

8. "SwimAmerica Has Smooth Sailing with Alpha Five," www.alphasoftware.com/alphafive/casestudies, accessed September 12, 2011.

9. Meredith Levinson, "When Failure Is Not an Option," *CIO Magazine*, June 1, 2006; "The Project Manager in the IT Industry," www.si2.com, accessed December 15, 2003; www.standishgroup.com; Jim Johnson, *My Life Is Failure: 100 Things You Should Know to Be a Successful Project Leader* (Boston: MA: Standish Group International, 2006); Gary McGraw, "Making Essential Software Work: Why Software Quality Management Makes Good Business Sense," *Cigital* (Dulles: VA), 2003, www.cigital.com/whitepapers/dl/Making_Essential_Software_Work.pdf, accessed September 12, 2011.

10. Ibid.

11. Ibid.

12. Ibid.

13. D. Schuler and A. Namioka (eds.), *Participatory Design: Principles and Practices* (Hillsdale, NJ: Lawrence Erlbaum Associates, 1993).

14. P. Ehn and D. Sjogren, "From System Descriptions to Scripts for Action," in J. Greenbaum and M. Kyng (eds.), *Design at Work: Cooperative Design of Computer Systems* (Hillsdale, NJ: Lawrence Erlbaum Associates, 1991), pp. 241–268.

15. J. Greenbaum and M. Kyng (eds.), *Design at Work: Cooperative Design of Computer Systems* (Hillsdale, NJ: Lawrence Erlbaum Associates, 1991).

16. "Building Events," www.microsoft.com, accessed November 15, 2003.

17. "Building Software That Works," www.compaq.com, accessed November 14, 2003.

18. "PMI Economic Snapshot," www.pmi.org/Knowledge-Center/Surveys-PMI-Pulse-Surveys.aspx, accessed August 14, 2013.

19. *ESSA Weekly Newsletter*, June 28, 2013, www.esaa.org/files/EWN062813.pdf, accessed August 12, 2013; "Groundwater and Soil Moisture Conditions from GRACE Data Assimilation," http://drought.unl.edu/MonitoringTools/NASAGRACEDataAssimilation.aspx, accessed August 29, 2013; GRACE, http://science1.nasa.gov/missions/grace, accessed August 29, 2013.

20. Why Projects Fail: Facts and Figures," http://calleam.com/WTPF/?page_id=1445, accessed May 27, 2014.

21. Gary McGraw, "Making Essential Software Work: Why Software Quality Management Makes Good Business Sense," *Cigital* (Dulles: VA), 2003, www.cigital.com/whitepapers/dl/Making_Essential_Software_Work.pdf, accessed September 12, 2011; Meredith Levinson, "When Failure Is Not an Option," *CIO Magazine*, June 1, 2006; "Software Project Failure Costs Billions. Better Estimation and Planning Can Help," June 7, 2008, www.galorath.com/wp/software-project-failure-costs-billions-better-estimation-planning-can-help.php, accessed September 12, 2011.

22. www.standishgroup.com; Jim Johnson, *My Life Is Failure: 100 Things You Should Know to Be a Successful Project Leader* (Boston: MA: Standish Group International, 2006); "Making Essential Software Work: Why Software Quality Management Makes Good Business Sense," *Cigital* (Dulles: VA), 2003, www.cigital.com/whitepapers/dl/Making_Essential_Software_Work.pdf, accessed September 12, 2011.

23. Joseph Gulla, "Seven Reasons IT Projects Fail," February 2012, www.ibmsystemsmag.com/power/Systems-Management/Workload-Management/project_pitfalls/?page=3, accessed September 1, 2014.

24. *A Guide to the Project Management Book of Knowledge*, 4th ed. (Atlanta, GA: Project Management Institute, 2008).

25. Gary McGraw, "Making Essential Software Work: Why Software Quality Management Makes Good Business Sense," *Cigital* (Dulles: VA), 2003, www.cigital.com/whitepapers/dl/Making_Essential_Software_Work.pdf, accessed September 12, 2011.

26. "IT Governance Risk," www.deloitte.com/view/en_ca/ca/services/enterprise-risk/technology-risk-governance/it-governance-risk/index.htm, accessed May 29, 2014.

27. www.standishgroup.com; Jim Johnson, *My Life Is Failure: 100 Things You Should Know to Be a Successful Project Leader* (Boston: MA: Standish Group International, 2006); Gary McGraw, "Making Essential Software Work: Why Software Quality Management Makes Good Business Sense," *Cigital* (Dulles: VA), 2003, www.cigital.com/whitepapers/dl/Making_Essential_Software_Work.pdf, accessed September 12, 2011.

28. *A Guide to the Project Management Book of Knowledge*, 4th ed. (Atlanta, GA: Project Management Institute, 2008); "The Project Manager in the IT Industry," www.standishgroup.com; Jim Johnson, *My Life Is Failure: 100 Things You Should Know to Be a Successful Project Leader* (Boston: MA: Standish Group International, 2006); Gary McGraw, "Making Essential Software Work: Why Software Quality Management Makes Good Business Sense," *Cigital* (Dulles: VA), 2003, www.cigital.com/whitepapers/dl/Making_Essential_Software_Work.pdf, accessed September 12, 2011.

29. K. C. Jones, "Poor Communications, Unrealistic Scheduling Lead to IT Project Failure," *InformationWeek*, March 12, 2007, www.informationweek.com/news/198000251, accessed September 12, 2011; Frank Winters, "The Top Ten Reasons Projects Fail (Part 7)," August 11, 2003, www.gantthead.com/article/cfm?ID=187449, accessed September 12, 2011; www.calpine.com, accessed December 14, 2003; "The Project Manager in the IT Industry," www.si2.com, accessed December 15, 2003; www.standishgroup.com, accessed December 12, 2003; www.snapon.com, accessed December 13, 2003.

30. Ibid.

31. Ibid.

32. Ibid.

33. www.prosci.com/adkar-model/overview-3, accessed July 26, 2014.

34. "The 8-Step Process for Leading Change," http://kotterinternational.com/kotterprinciples/changesteps, accessed September 19, 2011; John Kotter, *Leading Change* (Boston, MA: Harvard Business Press, 1996).

35. K. C. Jones, "Poor Communications, Unrealistic Scheduling Lead to IT Project Failure," March 12, 2007, *InformationWeek*, www.informationweek.com/news/198000251, accessed September 12, 2011; Frank Winters, "The Top Ten Reasons Projects Fail (Part 7)," August 11, 2003, www.gantthead.com/article/cfm?ID=187449, accessed September 12, 2011; www.calpine.com, accessed December 14, 2003; "The Project Manager in the IT Industry," www.si2.com, accessed December 15, 2003; www.standishgroup.com, accessed December 12, 2003; www.snapon.com, accessed December 13, 2003.

36. Dave Lindorff, "General Electric and Real Time," November 11, 2002, www.cioinsight.com/article2/o,3959,686147,00.asp, accessed September 19, 2011.

37. Peter Drucker, *The Essential Drucker: The Best of Sixty Years of Peter Drucker's Essential Writings on Management* (New York: Harper Business, 2003).

38. "Gartner Says Worldwide IT Outsourcing Market to Reach $288 Billion in 2013," July 17, 2013, www.gartner.com/newsroom/id/2550615, accessed May 27, 2014

39. www.outsource2india.com/why_india/why_india.asp, accessed May 28, 2014.

40. "REI Pegs Growth on Effective Multi-Channel Strategy," February, 17, 2005, *Internet Retailer*, www.internetretailer.com/2005/02/17/rei-pegs-growth-on-effective-multi-channel-strategy-executive-s, accessed June 24, 2010; Alison Overholt, "Smart Strategies: Putting Ideas to Work," *Fast Company*, April 2004, p. 63, www.fastcompany.com/magazine/81/smartstrategies.html.

41. *CIO Magazine*, June 1, 2006; "The Project Manager in the IT Industry," www.si2.com, accessed December 15, 2003; www.standishgroup.com, accessed December 12, 2003; Jim Johnson, *My Life Is Failure: 100 Things You Should Know to Be a Successful Project Leader* (Boston: MA: Standish Group International, 2006); Gary McGraw, "Making Essential Software Work: Why Software Quality Management Makes Good Business Sense," *Cigital* (Dulles: VA), 2003, www.cigital.com/whitepapers/dl/Making_Essential_Software_Work.pdf, accessed September 12, 2011.

42. Ibid.

43. Ibid.

44. "Overcoming Software Development Problems," www.samspublishing.com, accessed October 2005; Thomas Wailgum, "10 Famous ERP Disasters, Dustups and Disappointments," March 24, 2009, www.cio.com/article/486284/10_Famous_ERP_Disasters_Dustups_and_Disappointments, accessed May 12, 2014; Christopher Koch, "When Bad Things Happen to Good Projects," December 2004, http://web.eng.fiu.edu/ronald/EIN6117/ContingencyPlanningAtHP.pdf, accessed May 12, 2014.

45. "Case Study. Denver International Airport Baggage Handling System: An Illustration of Ineffectual Decision Making," 2008, http://calleam.com/WTPF/wp-content/uploads/articles/DIABaggage.pdf, accessed May 27, 2014; Kirk Johnson, "Denver Airport Saw the Future. It Didn't Work," August 27, 2005, www.nytimes.com/2005/08/27/national/27denver.html?pagewanted=all&_r=0, accessed May 27, 2014; Kirk Johnson, "Denver Airport to Mangle Last Bag," August 27, 2005, www.nytimes.com/2005/08/26/world/americas/26iht-denver.html, accessed May 27, 2014.

46. "Staying on Track at the Toronto Transit Commission," www.primavera.com, accessed June 20, 2010; www.gotransit.com/publicroot/en/default.aspx, accessed May 27, 2014; www.ttc.ca/Service_Advisories/index.jsp, accessed May 27, 2014.

Infrastructure

LEARNING OUTCOMES

LO 12.1 Explain enterprise architecture and how global concerns can magnify the challenges associated with enterprise architecture management.

LO 12.2 Describe agile MIS architecture.

LO 12.3 Describe the business value in deploying a service-oriented architecture and Web services.

LO 12.4 Describe a virtualized environment and its business benefits.

LO 12.5 Explain the business benefits of grid computing and cloud computing.

As a business student, why do you need to understand the underlying technology of any business? Isn't this technical stuff something that businesses hire nerds and geeks for? The fact is, every manager in the 21st century must have a base-level appreciation of what technology can and cannot do for the business. The information presented in this chapter attempts to create a more level playing field between managers and information systems staff, who are already ingrained in technology terms and acronyms.

If you understand the concepts of planning and developing information systems, you can think about how information technology can be used to support business decisions. This is a critical skill for any businesspersons, whether they are just starting out or are a seasoned Fortune 500 employee. Learning about enterprise architectures gives you a competitive advantage because understanding how information systems work can provide you with feedback on overall business performance.

After reading this chapter, you should have many of the skills needed to become directly involved in analyzing current business systems, in recommending needed changes in business processes, in evaluating alternative hardware and software options, and in judging the technical feasibility of an information systems project.

Cloud Computing in Canada

Cloud computing is on the rise, with companies such as SAP taking business analytics into the cloud with applications like HANA Enterprise Cloud, the Canadian government implementing plans to consolidate more than 100 different email systems used by more than 300,000 employees into a single, outsourced email system, and a 2014 TELUS-IDC report finding that 73 percent of cloud-reliant businesses are reporting improved ability in their IT strategy as a direct result of cloud computing. However, this same report indicates that managers of nearly two-thirds (63 percent) of non-public cloud users simply don't know enough about the cloud, indicating a general lack of knowledge around the nebulous terminology involved. At the same time 71 percent of IT managers dismissed alternative choices to cloud computing.

Cloud computing allows for the storage, access, and sharing of data by outsourcing the information to a remote server. Software as a Service, in which vendors grant access to already-built programs like Google Docs, accounts for most of the cloud adoptions among Canadian businesses. Cloud computing uses a computing infrastructure that relies on computer server farms and high-speed network connections that allow users to access their content from any device connected to the Internet. Cloud services offer convenience and cost savings. However, the drawbacks include reduced control over your own content, reliance on third-party providers, and privacy risks. Additionally, there is a risk of the data being disclosed to law enforcement agencies without appropriate notice or oversight.

Concerns over Data Transfers

In 2011, the Canadian government was clearly concerned by dangers associated with storing potentially sensitive emails outside the country on a cloud-based email service. As a result, the government used a national security exception and made one of its requirements for the proposed single email system that it be hosted in Canada. The concerns of the Canadian officials were over privacy issues around the *Patriot Act* in the United States.

These privacy concerns raise questions for millions of Canadians that use U.S. cloud services, as well as organizations such as Canadian universities that are contemplating switching their email or document management services to U.S.-based providers. If U.S. cloud services are not good enough for the Canadian government, why should they be good enough for Canadian organizations or individual Canadians? With the Edward Snowden revelations of widespread surveillance by the National Security Agency in the United States, many Internet users feel increasingly uncomfortable with the loss of control over their data. These types of events have led several countries to explore mandating local cloud providers to ensure that domestic data stays within their country. In Canada, the majority of websites are hosted outside Canada and data often travels through the U.S. networks.

Canadian Businesses and the Cloud

In Canada, it is estimated that cloud adoption rates trail the United States by about 10 percent. There are numerous theories on why this situation exits. TELUS-IDC report author Mark Schrutt says, "users have come back [to IDC] to say between 40 to 45% of the time, they believe there are regulations that inhibit their ability to use the cloud. They have concerns that are unfounded, or not based on fact."

IDC estimates that the entire IT services market in Canada will grow to $22.5 billion in 2014. With cloud services expected to generate $1 billion in 2014, this puts the size of the cloud services market into sharp perspective. Cloud technology does not even account for 5 percent of IT spending in Canada. In Canada, small and medium-sized businesses adopt cloud at higher rates than larger enterprises, particularly than those in the financial services, government, and health care sectors. These organizations have concerns about data governance, security and privacy, and negligence on the part of cloud providers that lessens their adoption rates, whereas, according to Schrutt, "SMBs don't have too many choices. They don't have large enough IT staff. They may not be embedded in older technology so they can make the switch easier."

David Brassor, cloud lead for Deloitte Consulting in Canada, suggests that instead of focusing on cost savings, companies need to focus on the productivity improvement and business agility that cloud computing can deliver. "It could take eight to 12 weeks to get a server installed and configured. With some of the cloud solutions, it could take you eight to 12 minutes," said Mr. Brassor.

Chris Weitz, a cloud computing technology expert at Deloitte, believes Canada's lagging adoption rate compared to that of the United States comes down to supply and demand, and cloud providers are investing in the world's largest market first. "The coverage [in the U.S.] is better compared to other markets, with more competition among providers, more aggressive pricing, and a more fluid market; therefore, the choices are broader for customers," said Mr. Weitz. "Enterprises particularly are faced with a lot of good market options, so the prices are going to be more competitive with more attractive offers in the U.S. simply based on the market maturity and the size of the market."

"Concerns surrounding Canadian businesses reliant on U.S.-based cloud computing providers being vulnerable to American spying under the provisions of the *Patriot Act* are overemphasized," according to Mr. Brassor. "The issues around the *Patriot Act* are overblown," he says. Mr. Weitz agrees. "Most global companies are sophisticated enough to segregate their data. If you are designing a system for cross-border use, you're going to typically factor that into the design of your system. You'll just have to design around anything that could be subject to different regulatory or jurisdictional regimes."[1]

12.1   MANAGING INFRASTRUCTURE

INTRODUCTION

Enterprise architecture lies at the heart of most companies' operating capabilities. Changes in IT, therefore, lead to fundamental changes in how businesses operate. Since many companies depend on these technologies, no longer is IT simply nice to have; no longer is IT just value-adding. It has become vital.

Recent advances have led to major changes in how IT services are delivered. Low-cost computing power has driven a shift toward more distributed processing. Internet working technologies, which provide a low-cost way to connect virtually everyone on the same network, present new possibilities for addressing business computing needs. The operational mechanisms at the heart of many businesses continue to evolve; new technologies add to, improve, and interconnect older systems to yield architectures with complex operational characteristics.

More importantly, new approaches to system design and development now enable large, complex applications to be built from reusable modules linked through shared services and common interfaces. This approach dramatically increases the ability to reuse data, information, and applications and to share a common infrastructure, which further increases the flexibility and speed with which new value-creating IT-enabled business initiatives can be launched and globally deployed.

While enterprise architecture alone cannot convey a sustainable proprietary advantage, businesses that remain chained to a legacy of incompatible and inflexible proprietary architectures find themselves at a significant strategic disadvantage as they attempt to keep pace with increasingly shorter cycles of innovation, productivity, and return on investment.

This chapter covers the basics of enterprise architecture, including terminology, characteristics, and associated managerial responsibilities for building a solid enterprise architecture.

LO1 | ENTERPRISE ARCHITECTURE

In the United States, a 66-hour failure of an FBI database that performed background checks on gun buyers was long enough to allow criminals to buy guns. The database failed at 1 p.m. on a Thursday and was not restored until 7:30 a.m. Sunday. The FBI must complete a gun check within three days; if it fails to do so, a merchant is free to make the sale. During this outage, any gun checks that were in progress were not finished, allowing merchants to complete those gun sales at their own discretion.[2]

To support the volume and complexity of today's user and application requirements, information technology needs to take a fresh approach to enterprise architecture by constructing smarter, more flexible environments that protect from system failures and crashes. *Enterprise architecture (EA)* includes the plans for how an organization builds, deploys, uses, and shares its data, processes, and IT assets. A unified EA will standardize enterprise-wide hardware and software systems, with tighter links to the business strategy. A solid enterprise architecture can decrease costs, increase standardization, promote reuse of IT assets, and speed development of new systems, the end result being that the right enterprise architecture can make IT cheaper, strategic, and more responsive. The primary business goals of enterprise architecture are displayed in Figure 12.1.

Enterprise architectures are never static; they continually change. Organizations use enterprise architects to help manage change. An *enterprise architect* is a person grounded in technology, fluent in business, and a patient diplomat, and he or she provides the important bridge between IT and the business. T-Mobile International's enterprise architects review projects to ensure they are soundly designed, meet the business objectives, and fit in with the overall enterprise architecture. One T-Mobile project was to create software that would let subscribers customize the ring tones on their cellphones. The project group assumed it would have to create most of the software from scratch. However, T-Mobile's EAs found software already written elsewhere at T-Mobile that could be reused to create the new application. The reuse reduced the development cycle time by eight months, and the new application was available in less than six weeks.[3]

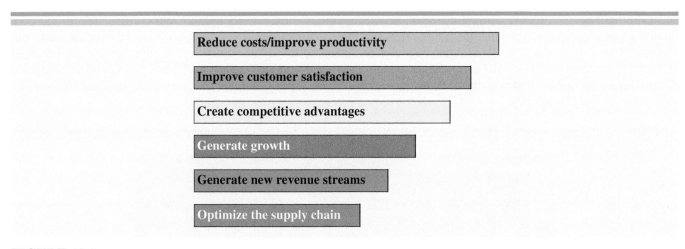

FIGURE 12.1

Primary Business Goals of Enterprise Architecture

Global Enterprise Architectures

As companies expand their boundaries and conduct business around the world, organizations must be mindful of managing their global EA to support their global business operations. Managing a global EA is not only technically complex, but also has major political and cultural implications. For example, hardware choices are difficult in some countries because of high prices, high tariffs, import restrictions, long lead times for government approvals, lack of local service or replacement parts, and lack of documentation tailored to local conditions. Software choices also present issues. For example, European data standards differ from North American or Asian standards, even when purchased from the same vendor. Some software vendors also refuse to offer service and support in countries that disregard software licensing and copyright agreements.

The Internet and the World Wide Web are critical to international business. This interconnected matrix of computers, data, and networks that reaches tens of millions of user in hundreds of countries is a business environment free of traditional boundaries and limits. Linking to online global businesses offers companies unprecedented potential for expanding markets, reducing costs, and improving profit margins at a price that is typically a small percentage of the corporate communications budget. The Internet provides an interactive channel for direct communication and data exchange with customers, suppliers, distributors, manufacturers, product developers, financial backers, information providers—in fact, with all parties involved in an international organization.[4]

Threats The Paris-based organization Reporters Without Borders restrict their citizens' access to the Internet. "At its most fundamental, the struggle between Internet censorship and openness at the national level revolves around three main means: controlling the conduits, filtering the flows, and punishing the purveyors. In countries such as Burma, Libya, North Korea, Syria, and the countries of Central Asia and the Caucasus, Internet access is either banned or subject to tight limitations through government-controlled ISPs. These countries face a lose-lose struggle against the information age. By denying or limiting Internet access, they stymie a major engine of economic growth. But by easing access, they expose their citizenry to ideas potentially destabilizing to the status quo. Either way, many people will get access to the electronic information they want. In Syria, for example, people go to Lebanon for the weekend to retrieve their email," said Virginie Locussol, Reporters Without Borders desk officer for the Middle East and North Africa.[5]

Figure 12.2 displays the top international telecommunication issues as reported by the IT executives at 300 Fortune 500 multinational companies. Political issues dominate the listing over technology issues, clearly emphasizing their importance in the management of global enterprise architectures.[6]

Estimating the operational expenses associated with international IT operations is another global challenge. Companies with global business operations usually establish or contract with systems integrators for additional IT facilities for their subsidiaries in other countries. These IT facilities must meet local and regional computing needs, and even help balance global computing workloads through communications satellite links. However, offshore IT facilities can pose major problems in headquarters' support, hardware and software acquisition, maintenance, and security. This is why many global companies prefer to outsource these facilities to application service providers or systems integrators such as IBM or Accenture to manage overseas operations. Managing global enterprise architectures, including Internet, intranet, extranet, and other telecommunication networks, is a key global IT challenge for the 21st century.

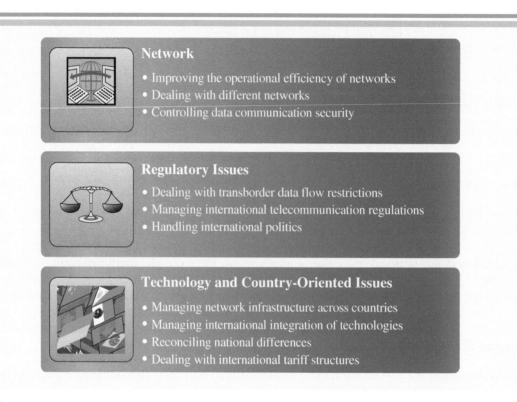

FIGURE 12.2

Top International Telecommunication Issues

Companies that have created solid enterprise architectures, such as T-Mobile, are reaping huge rewards in savings, flexibility, and business alignment.

LO2) AGILE MIS INFRASTRUCTURE

Agile MIS infrastructure includes the hardware, software, and telecommunications equipment that, when combined, provides the underlying foundation to support the organization's goals. If a company grows by 50 percent in a single year, its infrastructure and systems must be able to handle a 50 percent growth rate. If they cannot, they can severely hinder the company's ability not only to grow but also to function.

The future of a company depends on its ability to meet its partners, suppliers, and customers any time of the day in any geographic location. Imagine owning an e-business and everyone on the Internet is tweeting and collaborating about how great your business idea is and how successful your company is going to be. Suddenly, you have 5 million global customers interested in your website. Unfortunately, you did not anticipate this many customers so quickly, and the system crashes. Users typing in your URL find a blank message stating the website is unavailable and to try back soon. Or even worse, they can get to your website but it takes three minutes to reload each time they click on a button. The buzz soon dies about your business idea as some innovative Web-savvy fast follower quickly copies your idea and creates a website that can handle the massive number of customers. The characteristics of agile MIS infrastructures can help ensure your systems can meet and perform under any unexpected or unplanned changes. Figure 12.3 lists the seven abilities of an agile infrastructure.

Accessibility	• Varying levels allow system users to access, view, or perform operational functions.
Availability	• The system is operational during different time frames.
Maintainability	• The system quickly transforms to support environmental changes.
Portability	• The system is available to operate on different devices or software platforms.
Reliability	• The system functions correctly and provides accurate information.
Scalability	• The system can "scale up" or adapt to the increased demands of growth.
Usability	• The system is easy to learn and efficient and satisfying to use.

FIGURE 12.3

Agile MIS Infrastructure Characteristics

Accessibility

Accessibility refers to the varying levels that define what a user can access, view, or perform when operating a system. Imagine the people at your college accessing the main student information system. Each person that accesses the system will have different needs and requirements; for example, a payroll employee will need to access vacation information and salary information, or a student will need to access course information and billing information. Each system user is provided with an access level that details which parts of the system the user can and cannot access and what the user can do when in the system. For example, you would not want your students to be able to view payroll information or professor's personal information; also, some users can only view information and are not allowed to create or delete information. Top-level MIS employees require *administrator access*, or unrestricted access to the entire system. Administrator access can perform functions such as resetting passwords, deleting accounts, and shutting down entire systems.

Tim Berners-Lee, W3C director and inventor of the World Wide Web, has stated, "the power of the Web is in its universality. Access by everyone regardless of disability is an essential aspect." *Web accessibility* means that people with disabilities, including visual, auditory, physical, speech, cognitive, and neurological disabilities, can use the Web. The *web accessibility initiative (WAI)* brings together people from industry, disability organizations, government, and research labs from around the world to develop guidelines and resources to help create Web accessibility. For example, Apple includes screen magnification and VoiceOver on its iPhone, iPad, and iPod, which allows the blind and visually impaired to use the devices.

Availability

In a 24/7/365 e-business environment, business professionals need to use their systems whenever they want from wherever they want. *Availability* refers to the time frames when the system is operational. A system is called *unavailable* when it is not operating and cannot be used. *High availability* occurs when a system is continuously operational at all times. Availability is typically measured relative to "100 percent operational" or "never failing." A widely held but difficult-to-achieve standard of availability for a system is known as "five 9s" (99.999 percent) availability. Some companies have systems available around the clock to support e-business operations, global customers, and online suppliers.

Sometimes systems must be taken down for maintenance, upgrades, and fixes, which are completed during downtime. One challenge with availability is determining when to schedule system downtime if the system is expected to operate continuously. Performing maintenance during the evening might seem like a great idea, but evening in one city is morning somewhere else in the world, and business professionals scattered around the globe may not be able to perform specific job functions if the systems they need are unavailable. This is where companies deploy *failover* systems (see Chapter 10) so they can take the primary system down for maintenance and activate the secondary system to ensure continuous operations.

Maintainability

Companies must watch today's needs, as well as tomorrow's, when designing and building systems that support agile infrastructures. Systems must be flexible enough to meet all types of company changes, environmental changes, and business changes. *Maintainability* (or *flexibility*) refers to how quickly a system can transform to support environmental changes. Maintainability helps to measure how quickly and effectively a system can be changed or repaired after a failure. For example, when starting a small business you might not consider that you will have global customers, a common mistake. When building your systems, you might not design them to handle multiple currencies and different languages, which might make sense if the company is not currently performing international business. Unfortunately, when the first international order arrives, which happens easily with e-business, the system will be unable to handle the request because it does not have the flexibility to be easily reconfigured for a new language or currency. When the company does start growing and operating overseas, the system will need to be redeveloped, which is not an easy or cheap task, to handle multiple currencies and different languages.

Building and deploying flexible systems allow easy updates, changes, and reconfigurations for unexpected business or environmental changes. Just think what might have happened if Facebook had had to overhaul its entire system to handle multiple languages. Another social networking business could easily have stepped in and become the provider of choice. That certainly would not be efficient or effective for business operations.

Portability

Portability refers to the ability of an application to operate on different devices or software platforms, such as different operating systems. Apple's iTunes is readily available to users of Mac computers and also users of PC computers, smartphones, iPods, iPhones, iPads, and so on. It is also a portable application. Because Apple insists on compatibility across its products, both software and hardware, Apple can easily add to its product, device, and service offerings without sacrificing portability. Many software developers are creating programs that are portable to all three devices—the iPhone, iPod, and iPad—which increases their target market and, they hope, revenue.

Reliability

Reliability (or *accuracy*) ensures a system is functioning correctly and providing accurate information. Inaccuracy can occur for many reasons, from the incorrect entry of information to the corruption of information during transmissions. Many argue that the information contained in Wikipedia is unreliable. Because the Wikipedia entries can be edited by any user, there are examples of rogue users inaccurately updating information. Many users skip over Google search findings that correlate to Wikipedia for this reason. Housing unreliable information on a website can put a company at risk of losing customers, placing inaccurate supplier orders, or even making unreliable business decisions. A *vulnerability* is a system weakness, such as a password that is never changed or a system left on while an employee goes to lunch, that can be exploited by a threat. Reliable systems ensure that vulnerabilities are kept at a minimum to reduce risk.

Scalability

Estimating company growth is a challenging task, in part because growth can occur in a number of different forms—the firm can acquire new customers, new product lines, or new markets. *Scalability* describes how well a system can scale up, or adapt to the increased demands of growth. If a company grows faster than anticipated, it might experience a variety of problems, from running out of storage space to taking more time to complete transactions. Anticipating expected, and unexpected, growth is key to building scalable systems that can support that development.

Performance measures how quickly a system performs a process or transaction. Performance is a key component of scalability as systems that can't scale suffer from performance issues. Just imagine your college's content management system suddenly taking five minutes to return a page after a button is pushed. Now imagine if this occurs during your midterm exam and you miss the two-hour deadline because the system is so slow. Performance issues experienced by firms can have disastrous business impacts causing loss of customers, loss of suppliers, and even loss of help desk employees. Most users will wait only a few seconds for a website to return a request before getting frustrated and either calling the support desk or giving up and moving on to another website.

Capacity represents the maximum throughput a system can deliver; for example, the capacity of a hard drive represents its size or volume. *Capacity planning* determines future environmental infrastructure requirements to ensure high-quality system performance. If a company purchases connectivity software that is outdated or too slow to meet demand, its employees will waste a great deal of time waiting for systems to respond to user requests. It is cheaper for a company to design and implement agile infrastructure that envisions growth requirements than to update all the equipment after the system is already operational. If a company with 100 workers merges with another company and suddenly there are 400 people using the system, performance time could suffer. Planning for increases in capacity can ensure systems perform as expected. Waiting for a system to respond to requests is not productive. Web 2.0 is a big driver for capacity planning to ensure agile infrastructures can meet the business's operational needs. Delivering videos over the Internet requires enough bandwidth to satisfy millions of users during peak periods such as Friday and Saturday evenings. Video transmissions over the Internet cannot tolerate packet loss (blocks of data loss), and allowing one additional user to access the system could degrade the video quality for every user.

Usability

Usability is the degree to which a system is easy to learn and efficient and satisfying to use. Providing hints, tips, shortcuts, and instructions for any system, regardless of its ease of use, is recommended. Apple understood the importance of usability when it designed the first iPod. One of the iPod's initial attractions was the usability of the click wheel. One simple and efficient button operates the iPod, making it usable for all ages. And to ensure ease of use, Apple also made the corresponding iTunes software intuitive and easy to use. *Serviceability* is how quickly a third party can change a system to ensure it meets user needs and the terms of any contracts, including agreed levels of reliability, maintainability, or availability. When using a system from a third party, it is important to ensure the right level of serviceability for all users, including remote employees.

OPEN SYSTEMS

Open system is a broad, general term that describes non-proprietary IT hardware and software made available by the standards and procedures by which their products work, making it easier to integrate them. In general, *open source* refers to any program whose source code is made available for use or modification as users or other developers see fit. Historically, the makers of proprietary software have generally not made source code available. Open source software is usually developed as a public collaboration and made freely available. **Amazon.com** embraced open source technology, converting from Sun's proprietary operating system to Linux. The switch to an open source operating system, such as Linux, is simplifying the process by which Amazon.com associates can build links to Amazon.com applications into their websites.[7]

The design of open systems allows for data sharing. In the past, different systems were independent of each other and operated as individual islands of control. Sharing data was accomplished through software drivers and devices that routed data, allowing data to be translated and shared between systems. Although this method is still widely used, its limited capability and added cost are not an effective solution for most organizations. Another drawback to the stand-alone system is it can communicate only with components developed by a single manufacturer. The proprietary nature of these systems usually results in costly repair, maintenance, and expansion because of a lack of competitive forces. On the other hand, open system integration is designed to:

- *Allow systems to seamlessly share data.* Sharing data reduces the total number of devices, resulting in an overall decrease in cost.

- *Capitalize on enterprise architectures.* This avoids installing several independent systems, which creates duplication of devices.

- *Eliminate proprietary systems and promote competitive pricing.* Often a sole-source vendor can demand its price and may even provide the customer with less than satisfactory service. Using open systems allows users to purchase systems competitively.[8]

OPENING CASE QUESTIONS

Cloud Computing in Canada

1. How can an organization use cloud as its enterprise architecture to protect its IT investment?

2. How can an organization protect the security of its data in the cloud?

3. What are the benefits for Canadian companies of developing a cloud computing strategy?

4. How can Canadian companies use cloud computing to deliver on the seven aspects of agile MIS infrastructure?

12.2 INFRASTRUCTURE TRENDS

INFRASTRUCTURE TRENDS

Keeping business systems up and running 24/7/365 while continuing to be flexible, scalable, reliable, and available is no easy task. In this era of BYOD (bring your own device), maintaining a functioning architecture is even more challenging. Organizations today must continually watch new architecture trends to ensure they can keep up with new and disruptive technologies. This section discusses four architecture trends that are quickly becoming requirements for all businesses:

- Service-oriented architecture
- Virtualization
- Grid computing
- Cloud computing

Companies are paying attention to trends in computing. Take, for example, Ford Motor Company. Since 2007, it has had a BYOD program in place that now is available to more than 70,000 salaried employees in 20 countries. According to Randy Nunez, a senior engineer at Ford, the BYOD program was put in place due to trends in computing. "It was really caused by what's happening in the corporate environment, especially around the concept of the consumerization of IT. Instead of technology being brought in from a corporate standpoint and people using it, people are starting to be able to bring these types of technologies in from their personal lives. They have direct access to technology, and it's affordable. They're able to use it and assimilate it much faster than the corporate environment can."[9]

LO3) SERVICE-ORIENTED ARCHITECTURE

Service-oriented architecture (SOA) is a business-driven IT architectural approach that supports integrating a business as linked, repeatable tasks or services. SOA helps today's businesses innovate by ensuring that IT systems can adapt quickly, easily, and economically to support rapidly changing business needs. It helps businesses increase the flexibility of their processes, strengthen their underlying IT architecture, and reuse their existing IT investments by creating connections among disparate applications and information sources.

SOA is not a concrete architecture—it is something that leads to a concrete architecture (as illustrated in Figure 12.4). SOA is not a concrete tool or framework to be purchased. It is an approach, a way of thinking, a value system that leads to certain concrete decisions when designing a concrete architecture.

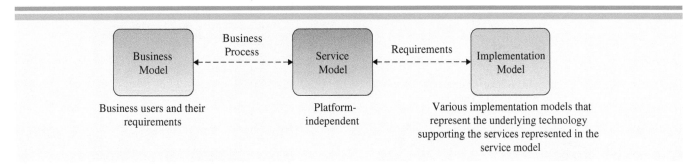

FIGURE 12.4

The Service-Oriented Architecture

The Canadian Institute for Scientific and Technical Information (CISTI) implemented an SOA to revitalize itself to meet the needs of the digital world. The Institute wanted to move away from supplying paper-based document delivery services to libraries, and toward an electronic infrastructure that supported end-users with "on the fly" digital document search and retrieval functionality. CISTI also wanted to do this right, and plan and implement a sound enterprise architecture. In the past, technology projects were reactionary, spawned from one-off client requests or done haphazardly from perceived information requirements. A key part of the solution was the decision to create an SOA. This put the focus on services that could be used simultaneously in more than one application at a time. Thus, most applications became a collection of services operating together, rather than a large monolithic black box application that was difficult to integrate or impossible to communicate with. These services could now also be used with patrons' applications, intranets, and desktops, not just CISTI's applications or its website. If enough libraries (including CISTI) adopted an SOA, users at their local libraries could then use the library's site to access the appropriate services from these remote library sites, as the local library felt was appropriate for their patrons.[10]

SOA Business Benefits

The reality is that architectures vary across operating systems, applications, system software, and application infrastructure. Some existing applications are used to run current business processes, so starting from scratch to build a new architecture is not an option. Enterprises should quickly respond to business changes with agility, leverage existing investments in applications and application infrastructure to address newer business requirements, and support new channels of interactions with customers, partners, and suppliers. SOA, with its loosely coupled nature, allows enterprises to plug in new services or upgrade existing services in a granular fashion. This enables businesses to address the new business requirements, provides the option to make the services consumable across different channels, and exposes the existing enterprise and legacy applications as services, thereby safeguarding existing IT infrastructure investments (see Figure 12.5). The key technical concepts of SOA are:

- ■ *Services*. A business task
- ■ *Interoperability*. The capability of two or more computer systems to share data and resources, even though they are made by different manufacturers

■ *Loose coupling*. The capability of services to be joined together on demand to create composite services, or disassembled just as easily into their functional components[11]

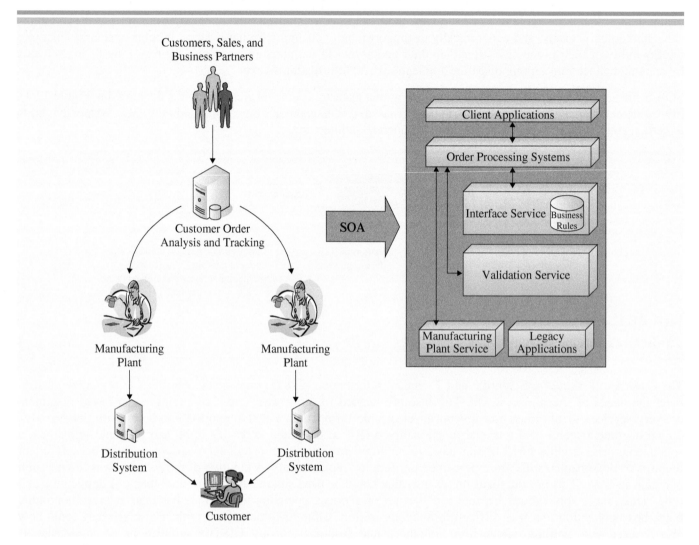

FIGURE 12.5
SOA Integration

Services   SOA begins with a service—an *SOA service* being simply a business task, such as checking a potential customer's credit rating when opening a new account. It is important to stress that this is part of a business process. As mentioned in the previous section, services are "like" software products; however, when describing SOA, do not think about software or IT. Think about what a company does on a day-to-day basis, and break up those business processes into repeatable business tasks or components.

SOA provides the technology underpinnings for working with services that are not just software or hardware, but rather business tasks. It is a pattern for developing a more flexible kind of software application that can promote loose coupling among software components while reusing existing investments in technology in new, more valuable ways across the organization. SOA is based on standards that enable interoperability, business agility, and innovation to generate more business value for those who use these principles.

SOA helps companies become more agile by aligning business needs and the IT capabilities that support these needs. Business drives requirements for IT; SOA enables the IT environment to effectively and efficiently respond to these requirements. SOA is about helping companies apply reusability and flexibility that can lower cost (of development, integration, maintenance), increase revenue, and obtain sustainable competitive advantage through technology.

It is important to note that SOA is an evolution. Although its results are revolutionary, it builds on many technologies used in the marketplace, such as Web services, transactional technologies, data-driven principles, loose coupling, components, and object-oriented design. The beauty of SOA is that these technologies exist together in SOA through standards, well-defined interfaces, and organizational commitments to reuse key services instead of reinventing the wheel. SOA is not just about technology, but about how technology and business link themselves for a common goal of business flexibility.

Businesses have become increasingly complex over the past couple of decades. Factors such as mergers, regulations, global competition, outsourcing, and partnering have resulted in a massive increase in the number of applications any given company might use. These applications were implemented with little knowledge of the other applications with which they would be required to share data in the future. As a result, many companies are trying to maintain information systems that coexist but are not integrated.

SOA can help provide solutions to companies that face a variety of business issues; Figure 12.6 lists some of them.[12]

Business Issues	SOA Solutions
■ Employees unable to see customer data remotely ■ Calls/faxes used to get data from other divisions ■ Customer data stored on paper ■ Complex access to design drawings	Integrate data to make it more accessible to employees
■ High cost of handling customer calls ■ Reconciliation of invoice deductions and rebates ■ Hours on hold to determine customer eligibility for a program or service ■ High turnover leading to excessive hiring and training costs	Understand how business processes interact to better manage administrative costs
■ Decreasing customer loyalty due to incorrect invoices ■ Customers placed on hold to check order status ■ Inability to quickly update customer data ■ Poor service levels	Improve customer retention and deliver new products and services through reuse of current investments
■ Time wasted reconciling separate databases ■ Manual processes ■ Inability to detect quality flaws early in cycle ■ High percentage of scrap and rework	Improve people productivity with better business integration and connectivity

FIGURE 12.6

Business Issues and Associated SOA Solutions

Interoperability As previously defined, interoperability is the capability of two or more computer systems to share data and resources, even though they are made by different manufacturers. Businesses today use a variety of systems that have resulted in a heterogeneous environment. This heterogeneity has inundated businesses with the lack of interoperability. However, since SOA is based on open standards, businesses can create solutions that draw upon functionality from these existing, previously isolated systems that are portable and/or interoperable, regardless of the environment in which they exist.

Loose Coupling   Part of the value of SOA is that it is built on the premise of loose coupling of services. Loose coupling is the capability of services to be joined on demand to create composite services or disassembled just as easily into their functional components.

Loose coupling is a way of ensuring that the technical details such as language, platform, and so on are decoupled from the service. For example, look at currency conversion. Today, all banks have multiple currency converters, all with different rate refreshes at different times. By creating a common service "conversion of currency" that is loosely coupled to all banking functions that require conversion, the rates, times, and samplings can be averaged to ensure floating the treasury in the most effective manner possible. Another example is common customer identification. Most businesses lack a common customer ID and, therefore, have no way to determine who the customers are and what they buy for what reason. Creating a common customer ID that is independent of applications and databases allows loosely coupling the service "Customer ID" to data and applications, without the application or database ever knowing who it is or where it is.

The difference between traditional, tightly bound interactions and loosely coupled services is that, before the transaction occurs, the functional pieces (services) operating within the SOA are dormant and disconnected. When the business process initiates, these services momentarily interact with each other. They do so for just long enough to execute their piece of the overall process, and then they go back to their dormant state, with no long-standing connection to the other services with which they just interacted. The next time the same service is called, it could be as part of a different business process with different calling and destination services.

A great way to understand this is through the analogy of the telephone system. At the dawn of widespread phone usage, operators had to physically plug in a wire to create a semi-permanent connection between two parties. Callers were "tightly bound" to each other. Today you pick up your cellphone and put it to your ear, and there's no dial tone—it's disconnected. You enter a number, push "Talk," and only then does the process initiate, establishing a loosely coupled connection just long enough for your conversation. Then, when the conversation is over, your cellphone goes back to dormant mode until a new connection is made with another party. As a result, supporting a million cellphone subscribers does not require that the cellphone service provider support a million live connections; it requires supporting only the number of simultaneous conversations at any given time. It allows for a much more flexible and dynamic exchange.[13]

Web Services

Gartner Inc. research indicates that application problems are the single largest source of downtime, causing 40 percent of annual downtime hours and 32 percent of average downtime costs. Application architecture determines how applications integrate and relate to each other. Advances in integration technology—primarily Web services and open systems—are providing new ways to design more agile, more responsive application architectures that provide the kind of value businesses need. With these new architectures, IS departments can build new business capabilities faster, cheaper, and in a vocabulary the business can understand.[14]

Web services promise to be the next major frontier in computing. *Web services* contain a repertoire of Web-based data and procedural resources that use shared protocols and standards permitting different applications to share data and services. The major application of Web services is the integration among different applications (see Figure 12.7). Before Web services, organizations had trouble with interoperability. If a manufacturing system can talk to (share data with) a shipping system, interoperability exists between the two systems. The traditional way that organizations achieved interoperability was to build integrations. Now, an organization can use Web services to perform the same task.

In the United States, Verizon's massive enterprise architecture includes three different companies, GTE, Bell Atlantic, and Nynex, each with its own complex systems. To find a customer record in any of the three companies' systems, Verizon turns to its search engine, called Spider. Spider is Verizon's version of Google, and it's helping Verizon's business to thrive.

Spider contains a vital customer data Web service that encapsulates Verizon's business rules, which help it to access the correct data repository when looking for customer data. Whenever a new system is built that needs to link to customer data, all the developer has to do is reuse the Web service that links to the customer records. Because

Verizon has the Web service in place as part of its enterprise architecture, development teams can build new applications within a month, as opposed to six months.[15]

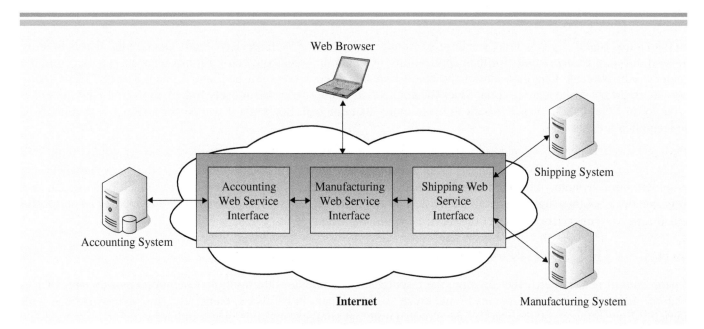

FIGURE 12.7

Web Services

Web services encompass all the technologies that are used to transmit and process data on and across a network, most specifically the Internet. It is easiest to think of an individual Web service as software that performs a specific task, with that task being made available to any user who needs its service. For example, a "deposit" Web service for a banking system might allow customers to perform the task of depositing money to their accounts. The Web service could be used by a bank teller, by the customer at an ATM, and/or by the customer performing an online transaction through a Web browser.

The deposit Web service demonstrates one of the great advantages of using the Web service model to develop applications. Developers do not have to reinvent the wheel every time they need to incorporate new functionality. A Web service is really a piece of reusable software code. A software developer can quickly build a new application by using many of these pieces of reusable code. The two primary parts of Web services are *events* and *services*.

Events Events are the eyes and ears of the business expressed in technology—they detect threats and opportunities and alert those who can act on the information. Pioneered by telecommunication and financial services companies, this involves using information systems to monitor a business process for events that matter—a stockout in the warehouse or an especially large charge on a consumer's credit card—and automatically alert the people best equipped to handle the issue. For example, a credit monitoring system automatically alerts a credit supervisor and shuts down an account when the system processes a $7,000 charge on a credit card with a $6,000 limit.

Services Services are more like software products than they are coding projects. They must appeal to a broad audience, and they need to be reusable if they are going to have an impact on productivity. Early forms of services were defined at too low a level in the architecture to interest the business, such as simple "Print" and "Save" services. The new services are being defined at a higher level; they describe such things as "Credit Check," "Customer Information," and "Process Payment." These services describe a valuable business process. For example, "Credit Check" has value not just for programmers who want to use that code in another application, but also for businesspeople who want to use it across multiple products—say auto loans and mortgages—or across multiple business.

The trick to building services is finding the right level of granularity. T-Mobile builds services starting at the highest level and then works its way down to lower levels, helping to ensure it does not build services that no one uses. The company first built a "Send Message" service and then built a "Send SMS Message" service that sends messages in special formats to different devices such as cellphones and pagers.

In the United States, Lydian Trust's enterprise architects designed a Web service called "Get Credit" that is used by several different business units for loan applications. "Get Credit" seeks out credit ratings over the Internet from the major credit bureaus. One day, one of the credit bureaus' Web servers crashed, and Lydian Trust's "Get Credit" service could not make a connection. Since the connection to the server was loosely linked, the system did not know what to do. "Get Credit" was not built to make more than one call. So, while it waited for a response, hundreds of loan applications sat idle.

Lydian Trust's loan officers had to work overnight to ensure that all of the applications were completed within 24 hours as promised by the company. Fortunately, Lydian Trust's customers never felt the pain; however, its employees did. Systems must be designed to deal with the existence of certain events, or the lack of an event, in a way that does not interrupt the overall business. The "Get Credit" service has been modified to include an automatic email alert to a supervisor whenever the service encounters a delay.[16]

LO4) VIRTUALIZATION

Virtualization is a framework of dividing the resources of a computer into multiple execution environments. It is a way of increasing physical resources to maximize the investment in hardware. Generally, this process is done with virtualization software, running on the one physical unit that emulates multiple pieces of hardware.

In a virtualized environment, the logical functions of computing, storage, and network elements are separated from their physical functions. Functions from these resources can then be manually or automatically allocated to meet the changing needs and priorities of a business. These concepts can be applied broadly across the enterprise, from data-centre resources to PCs and printers.

Through virtualization, people, processes, and technology work together more efficiently to meet increased service levels. Since capacity can be allocated dynamically, chronic over-provisioning is eliminated and an entire IT architecture is simplified (see Figure 12.8).

Even something as simple as partitioning a hard drive is considered virtualization, because you take one drive and partition it to create two separate hard drives. Another example is a virtual machine with a different operating system, like running Windows on a Mac. Devices, applications, and users are able to interact with the virtual machines as if it were a real single logical resource.

What Are Virtual Machines?

System virtualization (often referred to as "server virtualization" or "desktop virtualization," depending on the role of the virtualized system) is the ability to present the resources of a single computer as if it is a collection of separate computers ("virtual machines"), each with its own virtual CPUs, network interfaces, storage, and operating system.

Virtual machine technology was first implemented on mainframes in the 1960s to allow the expensive systems to be partitioned into separate domains and used more efficiently by more users and applications. As standard PC servers became more powerful in the past decade, virtualization has been brought to the desktop and notebook processors to provide the same benefits.[17]

Virtual machines appear both to the user within the system and the world outside as separate computers, each with its own network identity, user authorization and authentication capabilities, operating system version and configuration, applications, and data. The hardware is consistent across all virtual machines: while the size or number of them may differ, devices are used that allow virtual machines to be portable, independently of the actual hardware type on the underlying systems.

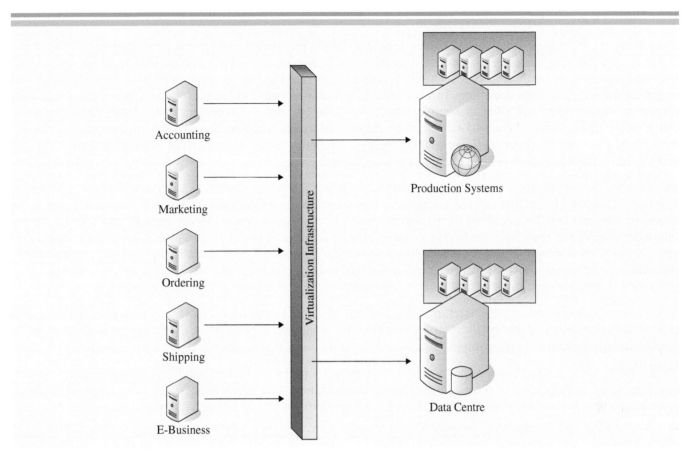

FIGURE 12.8
Virtualization Architecture

Figure 12.9 shows an overview of what a system virtualization looks like on a Mac computer.

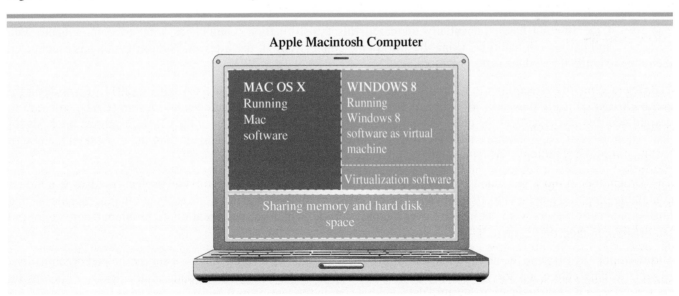

FIGURE 12.9
Virtualization Allows an Apple Macintosh Computer to Run Mac OS X and Windows 8

Virtualization Business Benefits

Virtualization is by no means a new technology. As previously mentioned, mainframe computers have offered the ability to host multiple operating systems for over 30 years. However, several trends have moved virtualization into the spotlight, such as hardware being underused, data centres running out of space, energy costs increasing, and system administration costs mounting. In 2008, the U.S. Environmental Protection Agency proclaimed that data centres consumed 61 billion kilowatt-hours of electricity. That is roughly 1.6 percent of total American electricity consumption and is worth about $4.5 billion. With the current trends continue, the national energy consumption by data centres is continuing to increase, making energy efficiency a top priority.[18] In September 2011, Google announced it continually uses enough energy to power 200,000 homes.

The first major virtualization trend highlights hardware being underused. In the April 1965 issue of *Electronics* magazine, Gordon Moore first offered his observation about processor computing power, which has come to be known as Moore's law. In describing the increasing power of computing power, Moore stated: "The complexity for minimum component costs has increased at a rate of roughly a factor of two per year." What he means is that every year (actually, most people estimate the time frame at around 18 months), for a given size processor, twice as many individual components can be squeezed onto a similarly sized piece of silicon. Put another way, every new generation of chip delivers twice as much processing power as the previous generation—at the same price.

Moore's law demonstrates increasing returns—the amount of improvement itself grows over time because there's an exponential increase in capacity for every generation of processor improvement. That exponential increase is responsible for the mind-boggling improvements in computing—and the increasing need for virtualization.[19]

Today, many data centres have machines running at only 10 to 15 percent of total processing capacity, which translates to 85 to 90 percent of the machine's power being unused. In a way, Moore's law is no longer relevant to most companies, because they are not able to take advantage of the increased power available to them.

Moore's law not only enables virtualization, but also effectively makes it mandatory. Otherwise, increasing amounts of computing power will go to waste every year.

A second virtualization trend concentrates on data centres running out of space. The business world has undergone an enormous transformation over the past 25 years. In the late 1980s, the vast majority of business processes were paper-based. Computerized systems were confined to so-called backroom automation: payroll, accounting, and the like. That has all changed, thanks to the steady march of Moore's law. Business process after business process has been captured in software and automated, moving from paper to computers.[20]

The rise of the Internet has exponentially increased this transformation. Companies want to communicate with customers and partners in real time, using the worldwide connectivity of the Internet. Naturally, this has accelerated the move to computerized business processes.

The first Boeing 787 Dreamliner to go into service rolled out of the paint hangar on August 6, 2011. It was designed and built in a radically new way. Boeing and each of its suppliers used computer-aided design (CAD) software to design their respective parts of the plane. All communication about the project used the CAD designs as the basis for discussion. Using CAD software enabled testing to be done in computer models rather than the traditional method of building physical prototypes, speeding completion of the plane by a year or more.[21]

The Dreamliner project generated enormous amounts of data. Just one piece of the project—a data warehouse containing project plans—ran to 19 terabytes. The net effect of all this and similar projects at other companies is that huge numbers of servers were put into use over the past decade, which caused a real estate problem—companies ran out of space in their data centres.[22]

Virtualization, by offering the ability to host multiple guest systems on a single physical server, helped organizations to reclaim data centre territory, thereby avoiding the expense of building more data centre space. This was an enormous benefit of virtualization, because data centres cost in the tens of millions of dollars to construct.

Rapidly escalating energy costs are also furthering the trend toward virtualization. The cost of running computers, coupled with the fact that many of the machines filling up data centres are running at low usage rates, means that virtualization's ability to reduce the total number of physical servers can significantly reduce the overall cost of energy for companies. Data centre power is such an issue that energy companies are putting virtualization programs into place to address it.

These trends reveal why virtualization is a technology whose time has come. The exponential power growth of computers, the substitution of automated processes for manual work, the increasing cost to power the multitude of computers, and the high personnel cost to manage that multitude all cry out for a less expensive way to run data centres. In fact, a newer, more efficient method of running data centres is critical because, given the trends mentioned above, the traditional methods of delivering computing are becoming cost-prohibitive.

Virtualization enables data centre managers to make far better use of computer resources than in non-virtualized environments, and also enables an enterprise to maximize its investment in hardware. Underused hardware platforms and server sprawl—today's norm—can become things of the past. By virtualizing a large deployment of older systems on a few highly scalable, highly reliable, enterprise-class servers, businesses can substantially reduce costs related to hardware purchases, provisioning, and maintenance.

Additional Virtualization Benefits

Virtualization offers more than server consolidation benefits as described in the previous section. Rapid application deployment, dynamic load balancing, and streamlined disaster recovery top the list of additional benefits. Virtualization technologies can reduce application test and deployment time from days or weeks to a matter of hours by enabling users to test and qualify software in isolation but also in the same environment as the production workload.

Virtualization, in all its forms, is a highly disruptive yet clearly beneficial technology. Enterprises are deploying virtualization for a number of real and significant benefits. The strongest driver—business continuity—is surprising, but many of the other drivers, such as flexibility and agility, server consolidation, and reduced administration costs, are fully expected.

Other advantages of virtualization include a variety of security benefits (stemming from centralized computing environments); improved service-level management (i.e., the ability to manage resource allocation against service levels for specific applications and business users); the ability to more easily run legacy systems; greater flexibility in locating staff; and reduced hardware and software costs.

Bell Canada uses virtual servers to lower costs. A virtual server uses the hardware of one physical computer to provide the appearance, services, and capabilities of multiple servers. Before adopting this technology, Bell Canada found it difficult to manage different geographically distributed servers centrally. These distributed servers were also all being underused. Virtual servers offered a solution, since they allow multiple distributed servers running under capacity to run on one central physical computer at a much higher capacity. Having one physical server instead of many reduced costs since only one server needed to be maintained, updated, and secured, and fewer servers were required to handle and process the same workload.[23]

LO5 | GRID COMPUTING

When you turn on the light, the power grid delivers exactly what you need, instantly. Computers and networks can now work that way using grid computing. *Grid computing* is an aggregation of geographically dispersed computing, storage, and network resources, coordinated to deliver improved performance, higher quality of service, better usage, and easier access to data.

Grid computing enables the virtualization of distributed computing and data resources such as processing, network bandwidth, and storage capacity to create a single system image, granting users and applications seamless access to vast IT capabilities. Virtualizing these resources yields a scalable, flexible pool of processing and data storage that the enterprise can use to improve efficiency. Moreover, it will help create a sustainable competitive advantage by streamlining product development and allowing focus to be placed on the core business. Over time, grid environments enable the creation of virtual organizations and advanced Web services, as partnerships and collaborations become more critical in strengthening each link in the value chain.

The uses of grid computing are numerous, including the creative environment of animated movies. DreamWorks Animation used grid computing to complete many of its hit films, including *Antz, Shrek, Madagascar,* and *How to*

Train Your Dragon. The third *Shrek* film required more than 20 million computer hours to make (compared to 5 million for the first *Shrek* and 10 million for the second). At peak production times, DreamWorks dedicated more than 4,000 computers to its *Shrek* grid, allowing it to complete scenes in days and hours instead of months. With the increased grid computing power, the DreamWorks's animators were able to add more realistic movement to water, fire, and magic scenes (see Figure 12.10). With grid computing a company can work faster or more efficiently, providing a potential competitive advantage and additional cost savings.[24]

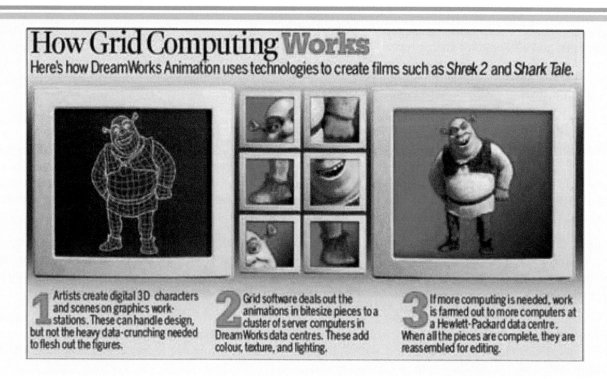

FIGURE 12.10

Using Grid Computing to Create *Shrek*

Grid Computing Business Benefits

At its core, grid computing is based on an open set of standards and protocols (e.g., Open Grid Services Architecture) that enable communication across heterogeneous, geographically dispersed environments, as shown in Figure 12.11. With grid computing, organizations can optimize computing and data resources, pool them for large-capacity workloads, share them across networks, and enable collaboration.

Google, the secretive, extraordinarily successful $55.5 billion global search engine company, is one of the most recognized brands in the world. Yet it selectively discusses its innovative information management architecture—which is based on one of the largest grid computing systems in the world. Google runs on hundreds of thousands of servers—by one estimate, more than 900,000—racked up in thousands of clusters in dozens of data centres around the world. It has data centres in Ireland, Virginia, and California. It recently opened a new centre in Atlanta and built two football-field-sized centres in The Dalles, Oregon. By having its servers and data centres widely distributed, Google delivers faster performance to its worldwide audience.[25]

Grid computing goes far beyond sheer computing power. Today's operating environments must be resilient, flexible, and integrated as never before. Organizations around the world are experiencing substantial benefits by implementing grids in critical business processes to achieve both business and technology benefits. These business benefits include:

- Improving productivity and collaboration of virtual organizations and respective computing and data resources

- Allowing widely dispersed departments and businesses to create virtual organizations to share data and resources

FIGURE 12.11
Virtualization of Grid Computing

- Building robust and infinitely flexible and resilient operational architectures
- Providing instantaneous access to massive computing and data resources
- Leveraging existing capital investments, which in turn help to ensure optimal usage and costs of computing capabilities[26]

Many organizations have started identifying the major business areas for grid computing business applications. Some examples of major business areas include:

- Financial services, for running long, complex financial models and arriving at more accurate decisions
- Higher education, for enabling advanced, data- and computation-intensive research
- Engineering services, including automotive and aerospace, for collaborative design and data-intensive testing
- Government, for enabling seamless collaboration and agility in both civil and military departments and other agencies
- Collaborative games, for replacing the existing single-server online games with more highly parallel, massively multi-player online games

In this pervasive need for information anytime and anywhere, the explosive grid computing environments have now proven to be so significant that they are often referred to as being the world's single most powerful computer solutions.

CLOUD COMPUTING

The Expansion of Cloud Computing

Forty-nine percent of executive-level managers see cloud computing as transformational to their business strategies, according to IDG Enterprise and its *Cloud Computing Trends and Future Effects Report* released in late June 2013. Although cloud spending is increasing, the survey found that though CFOs still need to be convinced that cloud spending is money well spent, companies are seeing some benefits. Some of the other key takeaways from the survey include the following:

1. Of the other 51 percent of executive-level managers:

    a) 40 percent currently have their IT staff investigating the potential contribution of cloud computing to their businesses

    b) 5 percent don't see cloud as an option

    c) 6 percent aren't sure

2. The top four drivers of cloud computing investments are:

    a) Enabling business continuity (43 percent)

    b) Greater flexibility to react to changing market conditions (40 percent)

    c) Speed of deployment (39 percent)

    d) Improving customer support or services (38 percent)

3. The top four benefits for cloud-based applications are:

    a) Accelerating business value through the access to critical data and applications (56 percent)

    b) Serving as a source of IT innovation (56 percent)

    c) Enabling better employee collaboration (54 percent)

    d) Enabling higher levels of IT agility (54 percent)

4. A lower total cost of ownership is one of the top selling points for cloud computing.[27]

Now imagine a cyclical business that specializes in Halloween decorations and how its sales trends and orders vary depending on the time of year. The majority of sales occur in September and October, and the remaining 10 months have relatively small sales and small system usage. The company does not want to invest in massive expensive servers that sit idle 10 months of the year just to meet its capacity spikes in September and October. The perfect solution for this company is cloud computing, which makes it easier to gain access to the computing power that was once reserved for large corporations. Small to medium-size companies no longer have to make big capital investments to access the same powerful systems that large companies run.

You have probably already used cloud computing. Free email services such as **Live.com** and Gmail are all examples of cloud computing applications where you use an Internet browser on any client machine to manage your email. The email application is installed and run "on the cloud"—that is, on a server machine on the Net managed by a third-party organization like Google or Microsoft. The data the application uses (your email messages) are also stored on the server machine. You have access to all your email messages from any client (e.g., your laptop, your parents' PC, a computer in an Internet café), since the email program and data (your email messages) are stored on a server on the cloud. Newer cloud applications include data storage and synchronization services like those offered with Microsoft's OneDrive, or online office applications like Google Docs or Microsoft's Office 365.

According to the national institute of standards and technology (NIST), cloud computing is a model for enabling ubiquitous, convenient, on-demand network access to a shared pool of configurable computing resources (e.g., networks, servers, storage, applications, and services) that can be rapidly provisioned and released with minimal management effort or service provider interaction. It offers new ways to store, access, process, and analyze information, and connect people and resources from any location in the world where an Internet connection is available.

As shown in Figure 12.12, users connect to the cloud from their personal computers or portable devices using a client, such as a Web browser. To these individual users, the cloud appears as their personal application, device, or document. All you need is a device to access the cloud; no more hard drives, software, or processing power. Users are not physically bound to a single computer or network; they can access their programs and documents from wherever they are, whenever they need to. The best part is that even if your machine crashes, or is lost or stolen, the information hosted in the cloud is safe and always available.

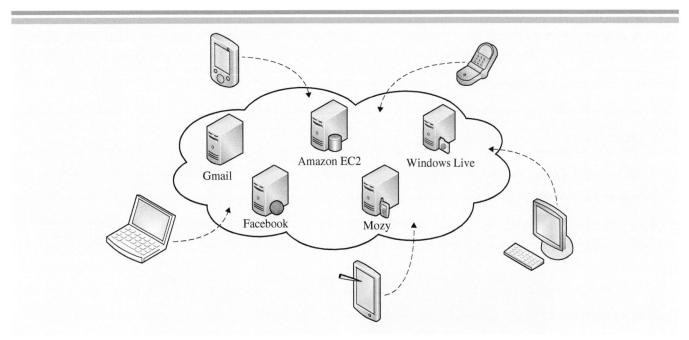

FIGURE 12.12
Cloud Computing Example

Multi-tenancy in the cloud means that a single instance of a system serves multiple customers. In the cloud, each customer is called a *tenant* and multiple tenants can access the same system. Multi-tenancy helps to reduce operational costs associated with implementing large systems, as the costs are dispersed across many tenants, in contrast to single-tenancy, in which each customer or tenant has to purchase and maintain an individual system. In the multi-tenancy approach, the service provider has only one place to update its system. In the single-tenancy approach, the service provider would have to update its system in every company where the software was running.

The *cloud fabric* is the software that makes all these benefits possible. A *cloud fabric controller* is an individual who monitors and provisions cloud resources, similarly to a server administrator at an individual company. Cloud fabric controllers provision resources, balance loads, manage servers, update systems, and ensure all environments are available and operating correctly. Cloud fabric is the primary reason cloud computing promotes all of the seven abilities of an agile infrastructure, allowing a business to make its data and applications accessible, available, maintainable, portable, reliable, scalable, and usable. Figure 12.13 displays the benefits of cloud computing.

The cloud offers a company higher availability, greater reliability, and improved accessibility—all with affordable high-speed access. For flexibility, scalability, and cost-efficiency, cloud computing is quickly becoming a viable option for companies of all sizes. With the cloud, you could simply purchase a single licence for software such as Microsoft Office or Outlook at a discounted rate without the hassle of installing and upgrading on your computer. No more worries that you don't have enough memory to run a new program, because the hardware is provided in the cloud along with the software. You simply pay for access. Think of this the same way you do your telephone service. You simply pay to access a vendor's service, and you do not have to pay for the equipment required to carry the call around the globe. You also don't have to worry about scalability, because the system automatically handles peak loads, which can be spread out among the systems in the cloud. Because additional cloud resources are always available, companies no longer have to purchase systems for infrequent computing tasks that need intense processing power, such as preparing tax returns during tax season or increased sales transactions during certain holiday seasons. If a company needs more processing power, it is always there in the cloud—and available on a cost-efficient basis. With cloud computing, individuals or businesses pay only for the services they need, when they need them, and where, much as we use and pay for electricity. In the past, a company would have to pay millions of dollars for the hardware, software, and networking equipment required to implement a large system such as payroll or sales management. A cloud computing user can simply access the cloud and request a single licence to a payroll application. The user does not have to incur any hardware, software, or networking expenses. As the business grows and the user requires more employees to have access to the system, the business simply purchases additional licences. Rather than running software on a local computer or server, companies can now reach to the cloud to combine software applications, data storage, and considerable computing power. Utility computing offers a pay-per-use revenue model similar to a metered service such as gas or electricity. Many cloud computing service providers use utility computing cloud infrastructures, which are detailed in Figure 12.14.

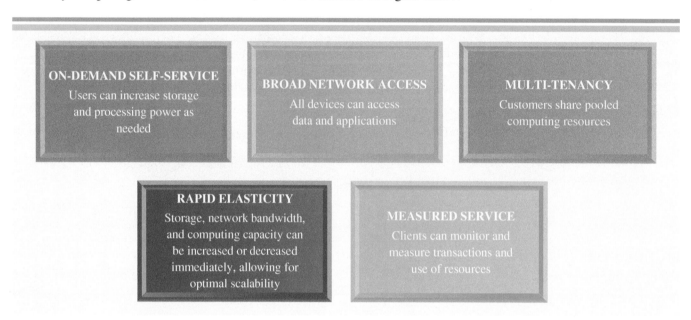

FIGURE 12.13

Benefits of Cloud Computing

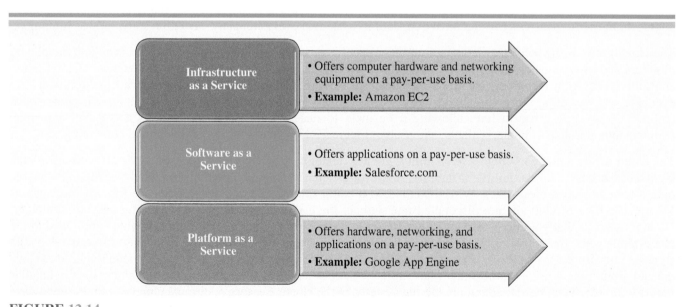

FIGURE 12.14

Cloud Service Delivery Models

Infrastructure as a Service (IaaS) delivers hardware networking capabilities, including the use of servers, networking, and storage, over the cloud using a pay-per-use revenue model. With IaaS the customer rents the hardware and provides its own custom applications or programs. IaaS customers save money by not having to spend a large amount of capital purchasing expensive servers, which is a great business advantage considering some servers cost more than $100,000. The service is typically paid for on a usage basis, much like a basic utility service such as electricity or gas. IaaS offers a cost-effective solution for companies that need their computing resources to grow and shrink as business demand changes. This is known as *dynamic scaling*, which means the MIS infrastructure can be automatically scaled up or down based on needed requirements.

Currently the most popular IaaS operation is Amazon's Elastic Compute Cloud, generally known as Amazon EC2, or simply EC2. EC2 provides a Web interface through which customers can load and run their own applications on Amazon's computers. Customers control their own operating environment, so they can create, run, and stop services as needed, which is why Amazon describes EC2 as elastic. IaaS is a perfect fit for companies with research-intensive projects that need to process large amounts of information at irregular intervals, such as those in the scientific or medical fields. Cloud computing services offer these companies considerable cost savings; they can perform testing and analysis at levels not possible without access to additional and very costly computing infrastructure.

Software as a Service (SaaS) delivers applications over the cloud using a pay-per-use revenue model. Before its introduction, companies often spent huge amounts of money implementing and customizing specialized applications to satisfy their business requirements. Many of these applications were difficult to implement, expensive to maintain, and challenging to use. Usability was one of the biggest drivers for creating interest in and success for cloud computing service providers.

SaaS offers a number of advantages; the most obvious is tremendous cost savings. The software is priced on a per-use basis with no upfront costs, so companies get the immediate benefit of reducing capital expenditures. They also get the added benefits of scalability and flexibility to test new software on a rental basis. **Salesforce.com** is one of the most popular SaaS providers. Salesforce built and delivered a sales automation application, suitable for the typical salesperson, that automates functions such as tracking sales leads and prospects and forecasting. Tapping the power of SaaS can provide access to a large-scale, secure infrastructure, along with any needed support, which is especially valuable for a startup or small company with few financial resources.

Platform as a Service (PaaS) supports the deployment of entire systems including hardware, networking, and applications using a pay-per-use revenue model. PaaS is a perfect solution for a business, as it passes on to the service provider the headache and challenges of buying, managing, and maintaining Web development software. With PaaS the development, deployment, management, and maintenance is based entirely in the cloud and performed by the PaaS provider, allowing the company to focus resources on its core initiatives. Every aspect of development, including the software needed to create it and the hardware to run it, lives in the cloud. PaaS helps companies minimize operational costs and increase productivity by providing all the following without upfront investment:

- Increased security
- Access to information anywhere and anytime
- Centralized information management
- Easy collaboration with partners, suppliers, and customers
- Increased speed to market with significantly less cost

One of the most popular PaaS services is Google's App Engine, which builds and deploys Web applications for a company. The App Engine is easy to build, easy to maintain, and easy to scale as a company's Web-based application needs grow. It is free and offers a standard storage limit and enough processing power and network usage to support a Web application serving about 5 million page views a month. When a customer scales beyond these initial limits, it can pay a fee to increase capacity and performance. This can turn into some huge costs savings for a small business that does not have enough initial capital to buy expensive hardware and software for its Web applications. Just think: a two-person company can access the same computing resources as Google. That makes good business sense. Regardless of which cloud model a business chooses, it can select from four different cloud computing environments—public, private, community, and hybrid (see Figure 12.15).

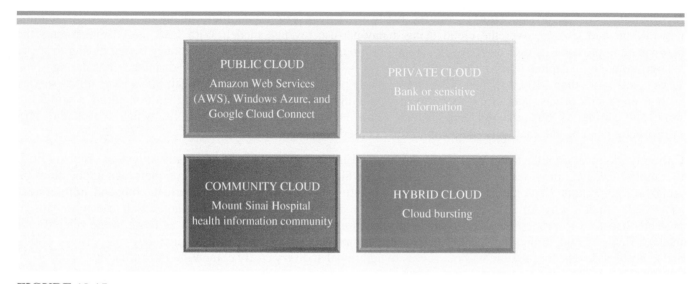

FIGURE 12.15

Cloud Computing Environments

The *public cloud* environment promotes massive, global, and industry-wide applications offered to the general public. In a public cloud, customers are never required to provision, manage, upgrade, or replace hardware or software. Pricing is utility-style and customers pay only for the resources they use. A few great examples of public cloud computing include Amazon Web Services (AWS), Windows Azure, and Google Cloud Connect.

The *private cloud* environment serves only one customer or organization, and can be located either on the customer's premises or off. A private cloud is the optimal solution for an organization such as the government that has high data security concerns and values information privacy. Private clouds are far more expensive than public ones, because costs are not shared across multiple customers.

The *community cloud* environment serves a specific community with common business models, security requirements, and compliance considerations. Community clouds are emerging in highly regulated industries such as financial services and pharmaceutical companies.

The *hybrid cloud* environment includes two or more private, public, or community clouds, but each cloud remains separate and is only linked by technology that enables data and application portability. For example, a company might use a private cloud for critical applications that maintain sensitive data and a public cloud for non-sensitive data. A company is engaged in *cloud bursting* when it uses its own computing infrastructure for normal usage and accesses the cloud only when it needs to scale for peak load requirements, ensuring that a sudden spike in usage does not result in poor performance or system crashes.

The trend to MIS infrastructure in the cloud forever changes the way an organization's MIS systems are developed, deployed, maintained, and managed. It is a fundamental shift from an MIS infrastructure a physical to a logical world, making irrelevant the notion of which individual server applications or data reside on. As a result, organizations and MIS departments need to change the way they view systems and the new opportunities to find competitive advantages.

There are many advantages for organizations in adopting a cloud computing approach. First, employees have convenient access to applications and data from any client machine or device that has an Internet connection. Second, there are significant cost savings. Cloud computing offsets the need for organizations to purchase software and software licences for applications, and mitigates the need for IT personnel to install this software on individual employees' PCs or laptops. It also lessens the need for organizations to purchase expensive, robust client machines, since most of the processing power needed resides on the server side of things, not the client, and reduces the need for organizations to invest in digital storage devices and servers to store application data and run applications, since these exist on the cloud. In short, organizations adopting a cloud computing approach avoid many capital expenditures, because they basically rent application use and data storage from a third-party provider. They consume resources as a service and pay only for resources that they use.

Cloud computing is not without disadvantages. One is the loss of control over the applications. Organizations are at the mercy of the third-party providers with regard to any changes in the software and the software's availability. Another disadvantage is that data are physically housed on the third-party providers' servers, not on a server controlled by the organization. Organizations have to trust the providers to arrange for adequate privacy and security protection of data. Because of this, many corporate executives hesitate to take advantage of cloud computing. Others question who actually owns the data that resides on computing cloud servers—the organization or the third-party provider? Theoretically, a cloud computing provider could deny an organization access to its own data.

Despite these disadvantages, Gartner Inc. forecasts cloud computing to be the fastest-growing form of computing, with a projected market size of $195 billion in 2012. Such popular software companies as Salesforce.com, Microsoft, and Google all offer software applications over a cloud computing infrastructure. One of the most well-known is Google Docs, mentioned above—a suite of standard office productivity applications including spreadsheets, calendars, and word processing applications.

Note that cloud computing is closely related to grid computing. In grid computing, networked computers access and use the resources of every other computer on the network (grid). With cloud computing, this access and use is restricted to computers on the cloud (not client computers that access the cloud).[28]

OPENING CASE QUESTIONS
Cloud Computing in Canada

5. Explain advantages in using a cloud computing architecture.

6. Explain the business drivers for using cloud computing.

7. What business benefits might Canadian businesses experience deploying grid computing?

8. What business benefits might Canadian businesses experience deploying virtualization?

SUMMARY OF KEY THEMES

The purpose of this chapter was to provide you, the business student, with a detailed overview of enterprise architectures and an understanding of the various activities that surround the regular maintenance and upkeep of enterprise architectures in organizations. Note that many organizations today pay special attention to their enterprise architectures, since these architectures form the underlying foundation that support a firms information systems, and serve as integral components of an organizations overall business strategy and competitive advantage. Specifically, this chapter described:

- *Enterprise architecture and how global concerns can magnify the challenges associated with enterprise architecture management. Enterprise architecture includes the plans for how an organization will build, deploy,* use, and share its data, processes, and IT assets. A unified enterprise architecture reaps business benefits through standardization of hardware and software across the company, decreased costs, the reuse of IT resources, and increased speed in the development and rollout of new systems. Political and cultural factors increase the difficulty of successfully implementing technically complex enterprise architectures in international organizations.

- *The characteristics of agile MIS infrastructure. Infrastructure identifies the hardware, systems software, and* telecommunications equipment that together provide the underlying foundation of the computing environment for the organization. This infrastructure must be accessible, available, maintainable, scalable, reliable, portable, and usable and offer good computing performance.

- *The business value in deploying a service-oriented architecture. A service-oriented architecture is an* architectural approach that supports the use of linaked, repeatable tasks or services. These services communicate with each other to create a working software application. The benefit of such an architecture is that it allows companies to plug in new services or upgrade existing ones in a granular fashion, and overcome hardware or software incompatibility issues.

- *Virtualized environments and their business benefits. Virtualized system environments are ones where the* logical functions of a computing system are separated from the physical ones. These environments allow for much better computer resource use, and maximize a companys investment in its IT hardware.

- *The business benefits of grid computing and cloud computing. Grid computing is the aggregation of* geographically dispersed computing resources coordinated in a way to offer improved performance and higher quality of service. Grid computing allows organizations to optimize computing by distributing workloads across geographically dispersed resources. Cloud computing is a form of client/server computing in which applications and data reside on servers on the Net and thin clients use minimal software, such as a Web browser, to access the applications and data they need. This architecture offers cheap and convenient access to applications and data on any Internet-enabled computer or device.

KEY TERMS

Accessibility	Enterprise architecture (EA)
Agile MIS infrastructure	Grid computing
Availability	High availability
Capacity	Hybrid cloud
Capacity planning	Infrastructure as a service (IaaS)
Cloud computing	Interoperability
Community cloud	Loose coupling
Enterprise architect	Maintainability

Multi-tenancy	Service-oriented architecture (SOA)
Open source	Serviceability
Open system	Services
Performance	Software as a service (SaaS)
Platform as a service (PaaS)	SOA service
Portability	System virtualization
Private cloud	Virtualization
Public cloud	Web accessibility
Reliability	Web services
Scalability	

CLOSING CASE ONE

Virtualization at Ontario's Workplace Safety and Insurance Board

This case illustrates how virtual infrastructure can benefit the organization's operations.

The role of Ontario's Workplace Safety and Insurance Board (WSIB), headquartered in Toronto, is to promote workplace health and safety. It also provides Ontario workers and employers with a workers' compensation system. In 2009, the WSIB developed a mission called the Road to Zero ("the elimination of all workplace fatalities, injuries and illnesses"). To support this mission the WSIB provided disability benefits, assisted with return to work, and developed education programs to help companies improve their work safety practices.

The WSIB develops, creates, and maintains software that more than 4,300 employees depend upon to process some 340,000 claims a year. Another 200 staff rely on the software to deliver workplace safety programs.

At one time, the data centre housed approximately 200 servers with an approximate 12 percent usage rate. With the data centre nearing capacity and a need to reduce costs in order to redirect funds into the injury prevention program, something needed to be done.

Starting in 2007, the WSIB began looking at virtualization as a solution, and to help them prepare for their 2009 mission change. The goal was to virtualize 35 percent of their data centre and 50 percent in 2008 by implementing a Microsoft virtualized environment. According to the WSIB, the immediate impact would be a $300,000 savings in licensing costs and better results.

According to the WSIB officials, the better results would stem from other benefits of virtualization. These benefits included the quick provisioning of both testing and development environments, the freeing of space in the data centre, and improved data centre efficiency with usage increasing from 12 to 70 percent. There were also immediate plans to reduce the number of physical servers by 25–35 percent.

The WSIB firmly believed that the greater efficiency of the data centre, reduced number of servers, and improved consistency in user interfaces would lead to reduced data centre costs. The interface consistency would result in lower training costs and savings through the leveraging of a full life cycle management approach, which would result in rapid patching and more efficient monitoring. In addition, the WSIB claimed that developers could quickly update software, which would result in improved claims services and worker safety programs. WSIB followed this up in 2013 by virtualizing their storage with a homogenous central storage solution.[29]

Questions

1. Review the five characteristics of infrastructure architecture and rank them in order of their potential impact on the WSIB's business.

2. What precautions did the WSIB need to take to ensure 100 percent security?

3. If the WSIB decided to go to 100 percent virtualization in their data centre, what concerns beyond security would they need to address?

4. Explain how the data centre enabled the WSIB's new business mission.

5. How might the WSIB be able to take advantage of cloud computing and/or grid computing to further its business strategy?

CLOSING CASE TWO

Pandora's Music Box

This case shows how a proper computing infrastructure can benefit the organization.

Napster was one of the first service providers for sharing online music. Many other companies have attempted to jump legally into the online music business, and most found little success. However, Pandora, the Internet radio site, is becoming the exception. Pandora provides users with the ability to choose specific artists or categories of music and then creates individualized playlists. Based on user feedback to Pandora's suggestions of similar tracks, the site "learns" what selections each listener prefers for his or her playlist and uses that information to generate a unique customized listening experience for each. In addition, Pandora is driving its listeners to custom content provided by its advertisers through it Promoted Stations program.

At the heart of Pandora's business is the Music Genome Project (MGP), a computerized jukebox of more than 700,000 works by 80,000 artists, with new ones added every day. Each selection within the MGP is categorized by hundreds of characteristics, including artist and genre and covering the qualities of melody, harmony, rhythm, form, composition, and lyrics. For example, if someone is looking for a song with a certain tempo or wants to know what the lyrics are about, Pandora can supply that information. The company has 50 employees whose sole job is to listen to and analyze music along with assigning more than 400 characteristics to each track.

Computing Merges with Connectivity

Pandora is a perfect example of cloud computing as a result of three major trends:

1. The marriage of computing and connectivity can now occur without having to be tethered to a single location. It's among the biggest disruptive forces of modern times; one that will redefine business models for decades to come.

2. The mobile Internet is now pervasive.

3. There is now the availability of low-cost, always-on computers—smartphones—that allow sophisticated software to conduct complex tasks on the go.

Pandora is strategically planning to reach a broad, global market by embedding itself in all sorts of Internet-enabled electronic devices that can access its services directly through the cloud. Its music offerings are now being made available in everything from thin LED televisions to Blu-ray players to digital frames. Customers are listening to Pandora through their Blu-ray players, iPods, iPhones, and BlackBerrys, and soon cars will come with Pandora preinstalled.

The Pandora team envisions Pandora playing everywhere, enabling users to create as many as 100 stations, allowing for a nearly infinite list of musical opportunities. Since its founding in 2000, Pandora has registered more than 50 million listeners and adds thousands more every day. A basic membership, which includes an occasional advertisement or two, is free. Members are allowed 40 hours a month to listen to their personal stations. If users want more than 40 hours, they can purchase unlimited playing time for 99 cents per month. Users can upgrade even further to a Pandora One account for $36 a year that includes unlimited playing time, no advertisements, and higher-quality sound. What drives Pandora's business? Other than its valued customer base, it is the company's solid MIS infrastructure that supports its growth, operations, and profits. So far, Pandora's investment in MIS infrastructure has delivered wonderful results as well as future opportunities. The company can now develop new applications that support its core functions more rapidly than ever. And since Pandora is located in the cloud, the company has created an MIS infrastructure that is accessible, available, flexible, scalable, reliable, and usable and that performs to meet the needs of its growing customer community.[30]

Questions

1. List the ways that an agile MIS infrastructure supports Pandora's business.

2. Describe the reasons Pandora would create a disaster recovery plan and a business continuity plan.

3. Apply the concepts of cloud computing to Pandora's business model.

4. Develop a way that Pandora could benefit from grid computing.

5. Assess the use of virtualization to support Pandora's business growth while helping the environment.

CLOSING CASE THREE

The U.S. Open Supports SOA

This case illustrates how an organization can leverage service-oriented architecture for business benefits.

The U.S. Open is a tennis event sponsored by the United States Tennis Association (USTA), a not-for-profit organization with more than 665,000 members. It devotes 100 percent of its proceeds to the advancement of tennis. At last count, more than five million viewers checked out the U.S. Open online.

The USTA created an integrated scoring system for the U.S. Open that helps collect data from all tennis courts, and then stores and distributes the data to **USOpen.org**, the official site of the U.S. Open. The ability to immediately and simultaneously distribute scoring data, supporting more than 156 million scoring updates, illustrates how the USTA leverages SOA to support its business goals. SOA helped the USTA use its existing computing systems to become more responsive and more closely aligned with the needs of its customers and partners.

For example, umpires officiating at each of the U.S. Open matches hold a device they use to keep score. These devices feed into a database that holds the collective tournament scores. From there, the constantly changing scoring data is fed to numerous servers that can be accessed through the U.S. Open site. When visitors go to USOpen.org and click the "Live Scores" link, they see the scoreboards for all 18 courts, which are updated before their eyes. This is then used to present them with instantly updated scoring data presented on the site's On Demand Scoreboards and the "matches in progress" pages.

Scores and statistics can also be instantly viewed on the website and compared with past U.S. Open events and similar competitions. Additionally, SOA is helping support the integration of data and statistics related to the tournament, such as individual scores and how they compare with current and past performances of the competitors.

Linking all of the tournament's data and delivering scores in real time requires a sophisticated information technology infrastructure that can be easily accessed and understood by USTA subscribers, many of whom are not IT professionals. The USTA is at the beginning stages of an SOA, and the USOpen.org site will be able to accommodate a growing audience of tennis fans worldwide.

The U.S. Open is the world's largest annually attended sporting event, and USOpen.org is among the top five most-trafficked sports event websites. The site has seen a 62 percent year-over-year traffic increase, with 5 million unique users, 27 million visits, and 79,000 concurrent real-time scoreboards. Since SOAs are scalable and flexible, they can easily meet the demands of the constantly changing site and the anticipated heavy traffic produced by 27 million visits—with each visitor spending nearly an hour and a half per visit.[31]

Questions

1. Review the five characteristics of infrastructure architecture and rank them in order of their potential impact on USOpen.org.

2. What are the USTA security concerns regarding interoperability between the tournament database and its website?

3. How could the USTA benefit from virtualization?

4. Identify the value of integrating the tournament data with the USTA site, USOpen.org.

5. Why would a sudden surge in server usage during the middle of the U.S. Open spell disaster for the USTA?

6. Why is loose coupling a critical business component to the USTA architecture?

MAKING BUSINESS DECISIONS

1. Purchasing a Computer

Dell is considered the fastest company on earth and specializes in computer customization. Connect to Dell's website at **www.dell.ca**. Go to the portion of Dell's site that allows you to customize either a laptop or a desktop computer. First, choose an already prepared system and note its price and capability in CPU speed, RAM size, monitor quality, and storage capacity. Now, customize that system to increase CPU speed, add RAM, increase monitor size and quality, and add storage capacity. What is the difference in price between the two? Which system is more in your price range? Which system has the speed and capacity you need?

2. Web-Enabled Cellphones

When categorizing computers by size for personal needs, we focused on tablets, laptops, and desktop computers. Other variations include smartphones and netbooks. For this project, you will need a group of four people, which you will then split into two groups of two. Have the first group research smartphones, their capabilities and costs. Have that group make a purchase recommendation based on price and capability. Have the second group do the same for tablets. What is your vision of the future? Will we ever get rid of clunky laptops and desktops in favour of more portable and cheaper devices such as smartphones and tablets? Why or why not?

3. Small Business Computers

Many different types of computers are available for small businesses. Use the Internet to find three different vendors of laptops or notebooks that are good for small businesses. Find the most expensive and the least expensive that the vendor offers and create a table comparing the different computers based on the following:

- CPU
- Memory
- Hard drive
- Optical drive
- Operating system
- Utility software
- Application software
- Support plan

Determine which computer you would recommend for a small business looking for (a) an inexpensive laptop and (b) an expensive laptop.

4. Planning for Infrastructure

You are the new senior analyst in the IT department at Beltz, a large snack food manufacturing company. The company is located on the beautiful south shoreline in Halifax. The company's location is one of its best and also worst features. The weather and surroundings are beautiful, but the threat of severe storms is high. Compile an infrastructure plan that minimizes any data loss risks involved with a natural disaster.

5. Comparing Cloud Computing Providers

Use the Internet to find three different vendors of cloud computing systems. Compare and contrast the systems, and determine which one you would recommend if you were installing a cloud computing provider for a medium-sized business with 3,500 employees that maintains information on the stock market. Compile your findings in a presentation to your class that details the three systems strengths and weaknesses, along with your recommendation.

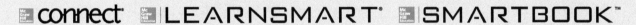

For more information on the resources available from McGraw-Hill Ryerson, go to www.mheducation.ca/he/solutions.

ENDNOTES

1. Michael Giest, "Time for Consumers to Think Local for Cloud Computing: Geist," March 7, 2014, www.thestar.com/business/2014/03/07/time_for_consumers_to_think_local_for_cloud_computing_geist.html, accessed May 18, 2014; Mashoka Maimona, "Canadian Businesses Still Searching for Silver Lining in Cloud: IDC-TELUS Report," June 11, 2013, http://business.financialpost.com/2013/06/11/canadian-businesses-still-searching-for-silver-lining-in-cloud-idc-telus-report/?__lsa=e724-1981, accessed May 18, 2014; Andre Brooks, "SAP Takes Business Analytics to the Cloud," May 15, 2014, www.itworldcanada.com/article/sap-takes-business-analytics-to-the-cloud/93354, accessed May 18, 2014.

2. Christine McGeever, "FBI Database Problem Halts Gun Checks," May 22, 2000, www.computerworld.com/s/article/45101/FBI_Database_Problem_Halts_Gun_Checks, accessed September 15, 2011.

3. www.cio.com, accessed November 2005.

4. "BusinessWeek: Innovation," www.businessweek.com/innovate, accessed February 15, 2008.

5. "The New Media: Between Revolution and Repression—Net Solidarity Takes On Censorship," March 10, 2011, http://en.rsf.org/the-new-media-between-revolution-11-03-2011,39764.html, accessed September 19, 2011; "Internet Enemies" (Paris, France: Reporters without Borders, March 2011); "BusinessWeek: Innovation," www.businessweek.com/innovate, accessed February 15, 2008.

6. BusinessWeek: Innovation, www.businessweek.com/innovate, accessed February 15, 2008.

7. Ibid.

8. Tim O'Reilly, "Open Source Paradigm Shift," http://tim.oreilly.com/articles/paradigmshift_0504.html, accessed January 11, 2008.

9. Christina Torode, "A Manufacturing-Floor Look at Ford's Bring-Your-Own-Device Program," August 31, 2011, http://searchcio.techtarget.com/news/2240074296/A-manufacturing-floor-look-at-Fords-bring-your-own-device-program, accessed September 21, 2011; Christina Torode, "Securing and Supporting a Bring-Your-Own-Device Program at Ford," September 1, 2011, http://searchcio.techtarget.com/news/2240074385/Securing-and-supporting-a-bring-your-own-device-program-at-Ford, accessed September 19, 2011.

10. Stephen Kevin Anthony, "Implementing Service Oriented Architecture at the Canada Institute for Scientific and Technical Information," *The Serials Librarian*, Volume 55, Issue 1/2 (2008), pp. 235–253.

11. Dirk Slama and Robert Paluch, "Key Concepts of Service-Oriented Architecture," www.csc.com/cscworld/012006/web/web002.html, accessed January 4, 2008.

12. Ibid.

13. "Achieving a Single Customer View," www.sun.com, accessed January 12, 2008.

14. Erick Schonfeld, "Linux Takes Flight," *Business 2.0*, January 2003, pp. 103–105.

15. "Looking at the New," *Information Week*, May 2005.

16. John Fontana, "Lydian Revs Up with Web Services," *Network World*, March 10, 2004.

17. "VMware—History of Virtualization," www.virtualizationworks.com/Virtualization-History.asp, accessed January 23, 2008.

18. James Glanz, "Google Details, and Defends, Its Use of Electricity," September 8, 2011, www.nytimes.com/2011/09/09/technology/google-details-electricity-output-of-its-data-centers.html, accessed September 19, 2011; "EPA Report to Congress on Server and Data Center Energy Efficiency," www.energystar.gov/ia/partners/prod_development/downloads/EPA_Report_Exec_Summary_Final.pdf, accessed January 23, 2008.

19. Paul Krill, "Impending Death of Moore's Law Calls for Software Development Changes," *InfoWorld*, May 24, 2005.

20. Ibid.

21. "Boeing, ANA Roll Out the First 787 Dreamliner That Will Enter into Service," August 6, 2011, http://boeing.mediaroom.com/index.php?s=13&item=1633, accessed August 31, 2011.

22. Geoffrey Thomas, "Seeing Is Believing," *Air Transport World*, June 2007, p. 54.

23. www.vmware.com/files/pdf/customers/06Q3_cs_vmw_Bell_Canada_English.pdf, accessed April 13, 2010.

24. "Switch on the Benefits of Grid Computing," h20338.www2.hp.com/enterprise/downloads/7_Benefits%20of%20grid%20computing.pdf, accessed April 2, 2010; "Talking to the Grid," www.technologyreview.com/energy/23706, accessed April 3, 2010; "Tech Update: What's All the Smart Grid Buzz About?," www.fieldtechnologiesonline.com/download.mvc/Whats-All-The-Smart-Grid-Buzz-About-0001, accessed April 3, 2010.

25. "Google Announces Fourth Quarter and Fiscal Year 2010 Results and Management Changes," January 20, 2011, http://investor.google.com/earnings/2010/Q4_google_earnings.html, accessed September 19, 2011; Rich Miller, "Who Has the Most Web Servers?," May 14, 2009 with August 2011 update, www.datacenterknowledge.com/archives/2009/05/14/whos-got-the-most-web-servers, accessed September 19, 2011; "Google Groans Under Data Strain," www.byteandswitch.com/document.asp?doc_id585804, accessed January 30, 2008.

26. Alan Joch, "Grid Gets Down to Business," *Network World*, December 27, 2004.

27. www.forbes.com/sites/louiscolumbus/2013/08/13/idg-cloud-computing-survey-security-integration-challenge-growth, accessed August 14, 2013; www.idgenterprise.com/report/cloud-research-2013, accessed August 14, 2013; www.computerworld.com/pdfs/editorial/2013IDGEnterpriseCloud.pdf, accessed August 19, 2013.

28. Merrill Lynch, "The Cloud Wars: $100+ Billion at Stake," *Merrill Lynch Report*, August 5, 2008; "Predicts 2009: Cloud Computing Beckons," *Gartner Research Report*, December 2008; Jonathon Strickland, "How Cloud Computing Works," http://communication.howstuffworks.com/cloud-computing.htm, accessed September 25, 2011.

29. "Workplace Safety and Insurance Board," October 9, 2008, www.microsoft.com/casestudies/Case_Study_Detail.aspx?CaseStudyID=4000002824, accessed September 25, 2011; "Storage Strategy Helps Organization Manage Data Growth," 2013, www.flexity.ca/wp-content/uploads/CaseStudies/flexity_WSIB_CaseStudy%20final.pdf, accessed May 24, 2014; "Safety Board Uses Virtualization to Stop Server Sprawl, Support Test Environment," www.techrepublic.com/resource-library/casestudies/safety-board-uses-virtualization-to-stop-server-sprawl-support-test-environment, accessed May 24, 2014.

30. Om Malik, "Pandora: Streaming Everywhere on Everything," *Bloomberg BusinessWeek*, January 12, 2010, www.businessweek.com/technology/content/jan2010/tc20100112_584610.htm, accessed May 24, 2014; www.pandora.com/about, accessed May 24, 2104; "Pandora Introduces Promoted Stations," May 10, 2014, http://press.pandora.com/phoenix.zhtml?c=251764&p=irol-newsArticle&ID=1928168&highlight=, accessed May 24, 2014.

31. www.usopen.org, accessed January 28, 2008; "US Open and SOA," September 6, 2006, www.ibm.com/developerworks/community/blogs/SOA_Off_the_Record/entry/us_open_and_soa2?lang=en, accessed May 24, 2014; "Benefit the U.S. Open SOA Technology," May 19, 2012, www.databaseskill.com/3159836, accessed May 24, 2014.

A

Acceptable use policy (AUP)   A policy that a user must agree to follow to be provided access to a network or to the Internet.

Accessibility   The varying levels that define what a user can access, view, or perform when operating a system.

Accounting and finance ERP components   Manage accounting data and financial processes within the enterprise with functions such as general ledger, accounts payable, accounts receivable, budgeting, and asset management.

Affinity grouping   Determination of which things go together.

Agile methodology   A type of software development methodology that aims for customer satisfaction through early and continuous delivery of useful software components, developed by an iterative process with a design point that uses the bare minimum requirements.

Agile MIS infrastructure   The hardware, software, and telecommunications equipment that, when combined, provides the underlying foundation to support the organization's goals.

Alliance partners   Competitor organizations that cooperate with one another, allowing them to compete more successfully with other competitors.

Analysis   A phase of the systems development life cycle (SDLC), consisting in analyzing end-user business requirements and refining project goals into defined functions and operations of the intended system.

Analysis latency   The time from when data are made available to when analysis is complete.

Analytical CRM   Supports back-office operations and strategic analysis and includes all systems that do not deal directly with the customers.

Analytical information   Encompasses all summarized or aggregated transactional data; its primary purpose is to support the performing of higher-level analysis tasks.

Anti-spam policy   States that email users will not send unsolicited emails (or spam).

Application programming interface (API)   A set of routines, protocols, and tools for building software applications.

Application service provider (ASP)   A company that offers an organization access over the Internet to systems and related services that would otherwise have to be located in personal or organizational computers.

Artificial intelligence (AI)   A simulation of human thinking and behaviour, such as the ability to reason and learn with the ultimate goal of building a system that can mimic human intelligence.

As-Is process models   Represent the current state of the operation that has been mapped, without any specific improvements or changes to existing processes.

Associate (affiliate) program   A type of marketing initiative that allows a business to generate commissions or referral fees when a customer visiting its website clicks on a link to another merchant's site.

Association detection   Reveals the degree to which variables are related and the nature and frequency of these relationships in the information.

Asynchronous communications   Communications that occur at different times, such as email.

Attributes   Characteristics or properties of an entity class.

Augmented reality   Viewing of the physical world with computer-generated layers of information added to it.

Authentication   A method for confirming users' identities.

Authorization   The process of giving someone permission to do or have something.

Automatic call distribution   A common feature in contact centres in which a phone switch routes inbound calls to available agents.

Availability   The time frames when an information system is operational and can be accessed by users.

B

Backdoor programs   Viruses that open a way into the network for future attacks.

Backup   An exact copy of a system's data.

Backward integration   Takes information entered into a given system and sends it automatically to all upstream systems and processes.

Balanced scorecard   A management system (not only a measurement system) that enables organizations to clarify their vision and strategy and translate them into action.

Bandwidth   The difference between the highest and the lowest frequencies that can be transmitted on a single communication medium; a measure of a communication medium's capacity.

Banner ad   A small ad on a website that advertises the products and services of another business, usually another e-business.

Benchmarking   The process of continuously measuring system results, comparing those results to optimal system performance (benchmark values), and identifying steps and procedures to improve system performance.

Benchmarks   Baseline values the system seeks to attain.

Best practices   The most successful solutions or problem-solving methods developed by a specific organization or industry.

Biometrics   The identification of a user based on a physical characteristic, such as a fingerprint, iris, face, voice, or handwriting.

Bits per second (bps)   A measure of upload or download speed measured in the number of signals (bits) sent per second.

Black-hat hacker   One who breaks into other people's computer systems and may just look around or steal and destroy information.

Bluetooth   A telecommunications industry specification that describes how mobile phones, computers, tablets, etc. can be easily interconnected using a short-range wireless connection.

Broadband   Describing high-speed Internet connections that transmit data at speeds greater than 200 kilobytes per second (Kbps), as against the 56 Kbps maximum speed offered by traditional dial-up connections.

Bullwhip effect   Occurs when distorted product demand information passes from one entity to the next throughout the supply chain.

Business analytics (BA)   The practice of using iterative, methodical techniques to explore an organization's data with emphasis on predictive, applied, and statistical analysis.

Business continuity plan   A plan for how an organization will recover and restore partially or completely interrupted critical function(s) within a predetermined time after a disaster or extended disruption.

Business-critical integrity constraints   Enforce business rules vital to an organization's success and often require more insight and knowledge than relational integrity constraints.

Business-driven information systems   Systems implemented to support a company's competitive business strategy.

Business-facing processes   Activities invisible to the external customer but essential to the effective management of the business; include goal setting, day-to-day planning, performance feedback, rewards, and resource allocation.

Business intelligence (BI)   A broad term denoting information that people use to support their analytical and strategic decision-making efforts.

Business process   A standardized set of activities that accomplishes a specific task, such as processing a customer's order.

Business process improvement   Attempts to understand and measure a business process and make performance improvements on that process accordingly.

Business process management (BPM)   Integrates all of an organization's business processes to make individual processes more efficient.

Business process model   A graphic description of a process showing the sequence of process tasks, which is developed for a specific purpose and from a selected viewpoint.

Business process modelling (mapping)   The activity of creating a detailed flowchart, workflow diagram, use case diagram, or process map of a work process showing its inputs, tasks, and activities, in a structured sequence.

Business process patent   A patent that protects a specific set of procedures for conducting a particular business activity.

Business process re-engineering (BPR)   The analysis and redesign of workflow within and between enterprises.

Business-to-business (B2B)   Applies to businesses buying from and selling to each other over the Internet.

Business-to-business (B2B) marketplace   An Internet-based service that brings together many buyers and sellers.

Business-to-consumer (B2C)   Applies to any business that sells its products or services to consumers over the Internet.

Buyer power   High when buyers have many choices of whom to buy from and low when their choices are few.

C

Call-scripting systems   Access organizational databases that track similar issues or questions and automatically generate the details for the customer service representative (CSR) who can then relay them to the customer.

Campaign management systems   One of the three primary operational CRM systems a marketing department can implement to increase customer satisfaction; guide users through marketing campaigns, performing such tasks as campaign definition, planning, scheduling, segmentation, and success analysis.

Capacity   The maximum throughput a system can deliver. For example, the capacity of a hard drive represents its size or volume.

Capacity planning   Determines the future IT infrastructure requirements for new equipment and additional network capacity.

Change control board (CCB)   Responsible for approving or rejecting all change requests.

Change management   A set of techniques that aid in evolution, composition, and policy management of the design and implementation of a system.

Change management system   Includes a collection of procedures to document a change request and define the steps necessary to consider the change based on the expected impact of the change.

Chief information officer (CIO)   Responsible for (1) overseeing all uses of information systems and (2) ensuring the strategic alignment of IT with business goals and objectives.

Chief knowledge officer (CKO)   Responsible for collecting, maintaining, and distributing the organization's knowledge.

Chief privacy officer (CPO)   Responsible for ensuring the ethical and legal use of information within an organization.

Chief security officer (CSO)   Responsible for ensuring the security of IT systems and developing strategies and IT safeguards against attacks from hackers and viruses.

Chief technology officer (CTO)   Responsible for ensuring the throughput, speed, accuracy, availability, and reliability of an organization's information technology.

Click-fraud   The abuse of pay-per-click, pay-per-call, and pay-per-conversion revenue models by repeatedly clicking on a link to increase charges or costs for the advertiser.

Classification   The assignment of records to one of a predefined set of classes.

Clickstream data   Exact pattern of a consumer's navigation through a site.

Click-through   A count of the number of people who visit one site and click on an advertisement that takes them to the site of the advertiser.

Cloud computing   A form of client/server computing operating over the Internet; "cloud" is used as a metaphor for the Internet.

Cluster analysis   A technique used to divide an information set into mutually exclusive groups such that the members of each group are as close together as possible to one another and the different groups are as far apart as possible.

Clustering Segmentation of a heterogeneous population of records into a number of more homogeneous subgroups.

Collaboration system An IT-based set of tools that supports the work of teams by facilitating the sharing and flow of information.

Collaborative demand planning Helps organizations reduce their investment in inventory, while improving customer satisfaction through product availability.

Collaborative engineering Allows an organization to reduce the cost and time required during the design process of a product.

Community cloud A cloud environment that serves a specific community with common business models, security requirements, and compliance considerations.

Competitive advantage A product or service that an organization's customers place a greater value on than similar offerings from a competitor.

Competitive click-fraud A computer crime in which a competitor or disgruntled employee increases a company's search advertising costs by repeatedly clicking on the advertiser's link.

Confidentiality The assurance that messages and information are available only to those who are authorized to view them.

Consolidation Involves the aggregation of information and features simple rollups to complex groupings of interrelated information.

Consumer-to-business (C2B) Applies to any consumer that sells a product or service to a business over the Internet.

Consumer-to-consumer (C2C) Applies to sites primarily offering goods and services to assist consumers interacting with each other over the Internet.

Contact centre (call centre) Customer service representatives (CSRs) answer customer inquiries and respond to problems through a number of different customer touch points.

Contact management CRM system Maintains customer contact information and identifies prospective customers for future sales.

Content filtering Occurs when organizations use software that filters content to prevent the transmission of unauthorized information.

Content management system Provides tools to manage the creation, storage, editing, and publication of information in a collaborative environment.

Cookie A small file deposited on a hard drive by a website containing information about customers and their Web activities.

Copyright The legal protection afforded an expression of an idea, such as a song, video game, and some types of proprietary documents.

Core competency An organization's key strength or business function that it does better than any of its competitors.

Core competency strategy Followed when an organization chooses to focus specifically on what it does best (its core competency) and forms partnerships and alliances with other specialist organizations to handle non-strategic business processes.

Core ERP components Traditional components included in most ERP systems that primarily focus on internal operations.

Core processes Business processes, such as manufacturing goods, selling products, and providing services, that make up the primary activities in a value chain.

Corporate policy A dimension of social responsibility that refers to the position a firm takes on social and political issues.

Corporate social responsibility A dimension of social responsibility that includes everything from hiring minority workers to making safe products.

Counterfeit software Software manufactured to look like other software and sold as such.

Cracker A hacker with criminal intent.

Critical path A path from the start to the finish that passes through all the tasks that are critical to completing the project in the shortest amount of time.

Critical success factors (CSF) The crucial steps companies perform to achieve their goals and objectives and implement their strategies.

CRM Customer relationship management.

CRM analysis systems Help organizations segment their customers into categories such as best and worst customers.

CRM manager A person in an organization who is held accountable and is responsible for the continued successful rollout of CRM in that organization.

CRM predicting systems Help organizations make predictions regarding customer behaviour, such as which customers are at risk of leaving.

CRM reporting systems Help organizations identify their customers across other applications.

Cross-selling Selling additional products or services to a customer. One of the three primary operational CRM systems a marketing department can implement to increase customer satisfaction.

Crowdsourcing Getting needed services, ideas, or content by asking for input from a large group of people. The most common form of collective intelligence found outside the organization.

Cube The common term for the representation of multidimensional information.

Customer-facing processes The result in a product or service that is received by an organization's external customer.

Customer relationship management (CRM) Involves managing all aspects of a customer's relationship with an organization to increase customer loyalty and retention, and an organization's profitability.

Cyberbullying Threats, negative remarks, or defamatory comments transmitted via the Internet or posted on a website.

Cybermediation The creation of new kinds of intermediaries that simply could not have existed before the advent of e-business, including comparison-shopping sites such as Kelkoo and bank account aggregation services such as Citibank.

Cyberterrorist One who seeks to cause harm to people or to destroy critical systems or information; uses the Internet for destructive purposes.

Cybervandalism The electronic defacing of an existing website.

D

Data   Raw facts that describe the characteristics of an event.

Database   Maintains information about various types of objects (inventory), events (transactions), people (employees), and places (warehouses).

Database-based workflow systems   Store documents in a central location and automatically ask the team members to access the document when it is their turn to edit the document.

Database management system (DBMS)   Software through which users and application programs interact with a database.

Data-driven website   An interactive website kept constantly updated and relevant to the needs of its customers through the use of a database.

Data governance   The way an organization manages the availability, usability, integrity, and security of its data.

Data integrity   A measure of the quality of data.

Data latency   The time duration to make data ready for analysis (i.e., the time for extracting, transforming, cleansing, and loading the data into a database).

Data mart   Contains a subset of data warehouse information.

Data mining   The process of analyzing data to extract information not offered by the raw data alone.

Data mining tools   The techniques used to find patterns and relationships in large volumes of information and infer rules from them that predict future behaviour and guide decision making.

Data redundancy   The duplication of data, or storing the same data in multiple places.

Data warehouse   A logical collection of information—gathered from many different operational databases—that supports business analysis activities and decision-making tasks.

Dealers   Agents who sell products or services on behalf of a company or organization, particularly in the automobile industry.

Decision latency   The time it takes a human to comprehend the analytic result and determine an appropriate action.

Decision support system (DSS)   Models data and information to support managers, analysts, and other business professionals during the decision-making process for more analytical purposes.

Demand planning systems   Generates demand forecasts using statistical tools and forecasting techniques.

Denial-of-service attack (DoS)   Floods a website with so many requests for service that it slows down or crashes the site.

Dependency   A logical relationship that exists between the project tasks, or between a project task and a milestone.

Design   A phase of the systems development life cycle (SDLC) that involves describing the desired features and operations of the system including screen layouts, business rules, process diagrams, and other documentation.

Development   A phase of the systems development life cycle (SDLC) that involves taking all of the detailed design documents from the design phase and transforming them into the actual system.

Digital asset management system (DAM)   Similar to a document management system (DMS), but generally works with binary rather than text files, such as multimedia file types.

Digital Darwinism   The principle that organizations unable to adapt to the new demands made on them for surviving in the information age are doomed to extinction.

Digital dashboard   Integrates information from multiple components and tailors the information to individual preferences.

Digital divide   The situation of those with access to technology having great advantages over those without such access.

Digital wallet   Both software and information—the software provides security for a transaction and the information includes payment and delivery information (e.g., the credit card number and expiration date).

Dimension   A particular attribute of some information.

Disaster recovery cost curve   Charts (1) the cost to the organization of the unavailability of information and technology and (2) the cost to the organization of recovering from a disaster over time.

Disaster recovery plan   A detailed process for recovering information or an IT system in the event of a catastrophic disaster such as a fire or flood.

Disintermediation   Occurs when a business sells directly to the customer online and cuts out the intermediary.

Disruptive technology   A new way of doing things that initially does not meet the needs of existing customers.

Distributed denial-of-service attack (DDoS)   Attacks from multiple computers that flood a website with so many requests for service that it slows down or crashes.

Distribution management systems   Coordinate the process of transporting materials from a manufacturer to distribution centres to the final customer.

Document management system (DMS)   Supports the electronic capturing, storage, distribution, archival, and accessing of documents.

Drill-down   Enables users to view details, and details of details, of information.

E

E-business   The conducting of business on the Internet, not only buying and selling, but also serving customers and collaborating with business partners.

E-business model   An approach to conducting electronic business on the Internet.

E-commerce   The buying and selling of goods and services over the Internet.

Effectiveness IS metrics   Measures the impact IS has on business processes and activities including customer satisfaction, conversion rates, and sell-through increases.

Efficiency IS metrics   Measures the performance of the IS itself such as throughput, speed, and availability.

E-government   Involves the use of strategies and technologies to transform government(s) by improving the delivery of services and enhancing the quality of interaction between the citizen-consumer within all branches of government.

Electronic bill presentment and payment (EBPP)   System that sends bills over the Internet and provides an easy-to-use mechanism (such as clicking on a button) to pay the bill.

Electronic catalogue   Presents customers with information about goods and services offered for sale, bid, or auction on the Internet.

Electronic data interchange (EDI)   A standard format for exchanging business data.

Electronic marketplaces (e-marketplaces)   Interactive business communities providing a central marketspace where multiple buyers and suppliers can engage in e-business.

Electronic tagging   A technique for identifying and tracking assets and individuals via technologies, such as radio frequency identification and smart cards.

Elevation of privilege   Process by which a user misleads a system into granting unauthorized rights, usually for the purpose of compromising or destroying the system.

E-logistics   Manages the transportation and storage of goods.

Email privacy policy   Details the extent to which email messages may be read by others.

Employee relationship management (ERM)   A management activity that focuses on managing an organization's relationships with its employees.

Encryption   The scrambling of information into an alternative form that requires a key or password to read.

Enterprise application integration (EAI) middleware Represents a new approach to middleware by packaging together commonly used functionality, such as providing pre-built links to popular enterprise applications, which reduces the time necessary to develop solutions that integrate applications from multiple vendors.

Enterprise architect   Person who is grounded in technology, fluent in business, and a patient diplomat, and who provides the important bridge between IT and the business.

Enterprise architecture (EA)   Plans for how an organization will build, deploy, use, and share its data, processes, and IT assets.

Enterprise portals   Single-point Web browser interfaces used within an organization to promote the gathering, sharing, and dissemination of information throughout an enterprise.

Enterprise resource planning (ERP)   Integrates all departments and functions throughout an organization into a single information system (or integrated set of information systems) so that employees can make decisions by viewing enterprise-wide data on all business operations.

Entity   A person, place, thing, transaction, or event about which information is stored.

Entity class   A collection of similar entities.

Environmental scanning   The acquisition and analysis of events and trends in the environment external to an organization.

E-policies   Policies and procedures that address the ethical use of computers and Internet usage in the business environment.

E-procurement   The B2B purchase and sale of supplies and services over the Internet.

ERP   Enterprise resource planning.

Estimation   Determines values for an unknown continuous variable behaviour or estimated future value.

Ethical computer use policy   Contains general principles to guide computer user behaviour.

Ethics   Principles and standards that guide our behaviour toward other people.

E-waste   Old electronics and computer equipment.

Executive information system (EIS)   A specialized DSS that supports senior level executives within the organization.

Executive sponsor   The person or group who provides the financial resources for the project.

Expert systems   Computerized advisory programs that imitate the reasoning processes of experts in solving difficult problems.

Explicit knowledge   Knowledge that can be documented, archived, and codified, often with the help of information systems.

Extended ERP components   The extra components that meet the organizational needs not covered by the core components and that primarily focus on external operations.

Extraction, transformation, and loading (ETL)   A process that extracts information from internal and external databases, transforms the information using a common set of enterprise definitions, and loads the information into a data warehouse.

Extranet   An intranet that is available to strategic allies (such as customers, suppliers, and partners).

Extreme programming (XP) methodology   An agile software development methodology breaks a project up into tiny phases, and prevents developers from moving on to the next phase until the previous one has been completed.

F

Fact   The confirmation or validation of an event or object.

Failover   Backup operational mode in which the functions of a computer component (such as a processor, server, network, or database) are assumed by secondary system components when the primary component becomes unavailable through either failure or scheduled downtime.

Fair dealing   The principle that, in certain situations, it is legal to use copyrighted material.

Fault tolerance   A computer system designed so that, in the event a component fails, a backup component or procedure can immediately take its place with no loss of service.

Feature creep   Occurs when developers add extra features that were not part of the initial requirements.

Field   Characteristics or properties of a table. Also referred to as attributes or columns.

Financial cybermediary   Internet-based company that facilitates payments over the Internet.

Financial EDI (financial electronic data interchange)   Standard electronic process for business-to-business market purchase payments.

Firewall   Hardware and/or software that guards a private network by analyzing the information leaving and entering the network.

First-mover advantage   An organization can significantly impact its market share by being first to market with a competitive advantage.

Five Forces Model   Tool to aid organizations facing the decision of entering a new industry or industry segment; helps determine the relative competitive attractiveness of an industry.

Forecasts Predictions made on the basis of time series information.

Foreign key A primary key of one table that appears as an attribute in another table and provides a logical relationship between the two tables.

Forward integration Takes information entered into a given system and sends it automatically to all downstream systems and processes.

Functional systems Information systems that serve a single business unit, such as accounting.

Fuzzy logic A mathematical method of handling imprecise or subjective information.

G

Gantt chart A simple bar chart that depicts project tasks against a calendar.

Genetic algorithm An artificial intelligence system that mimics the evolutionary, survival-of-the-fittest process to generate increasingly better solutions to a problem.

Geographic information system (GIS) An information system designed to work with information that can be shown on a geographic map.

Global inventory management systems (GIMS) Provide the ability to locate, track, and predict the movement of every component or material anywhere upstream or downstream in the supply chain.

Global positioning system (GPS) A constellation of 24 well-spaced satellites that orbit Earth and make it possible for people with ground receivers to pinpoint their geographic location.

Goal-seeking analysis Finds the inputs necessary to achieve a goal such as a desired level of output.

Granularity The extent of detail within data and information (e.g., it can be fine and detailed or coarse and abstract)

Grid computing An aggregation of geographically dispersed computing, storage, and network resources, coordinated to deliver improved performance, higher quality of service, better utilization, and easier access to data.

Groupware Software that supports team interaction and dynamics, including calendaring, scheduling, and videoconferencing.

H

Hacker Someone very knowledgeable about computers, who uses his or her knowledge to invade other people's computers.

Hactivist Someone with philosophical and political reasons for breaking into systems and who often defaces a website as a protest.

Hertz A measure of processor speed in cycles per second.

Hierarchical database model Information is organized into a treelike structure that allows repeating information using parent-child relationships, in such a way that it cannot have too many relationships.

High availability Refers to a system or component that is continuously operational for a desirably long length of time.

Hoaxes Attack computer systems by transmitting a virus hoax, with a real virus attached.

Human resources ERP components Track employee data including payroll, benefits, compensation, and performance assessment, and assure compliance with the legal requirements of multiple jurisdictions and tax authorities.

Hybrid cloud Combination of two or more private, public, or community clouds, in which each cloud remains separate and is only linked by technology that enables data and application portability.

Hypertext transfer protocol (HTTP) The Internet standard that supports the exchange of information on the World Wide Web.

I

Identity theft The forging of someone's identity for the purpose of fraud.

Implementation A phase of the systems development life cycle (SDLC) that involves placing the system into production so users can begin to perform actual business operations with the system.

Information Data converted into a meaningful and useful context.

Information age Time when infinite quantities of facts are widely available to anyone who can use a computer.

Information cleansing (scrubbing) A process that weeds out and fixes or discards inconsistent, incorrect, or incomplete information.

Information ethics The moral principles concerning the creation, collection, duplication, distribution, and processing of information, as well as the development and use of information technologies.

Information partnership Occurs when two or more organizations cooperate by integrating their information systems, thereby providing customers with the best of what each can offer.

Information privacy policy Contains general principles regarding information privacy.

Information reach Refers to the number of people a business can communicate with, on a global basis.

Information richness Refers to the depth and breadth of information transferred between customers and businesses.

Information security The protection of information from accidental or intentional misuse by persons inside or outside an organization.

Information security plan Details how an organization will implement the information security policies.

Information security policies The rules required to maintain information security.

Information systems (IS) Computer-based tools that people use to work with information and that support the information and information processing needs of an organization.

Information technology (IT) The acquisition, processing, storage, and dissemination of vocal, pictorial, textual, and numerical information by a microelectronics-based combination of computing and telecommunications.

Infrastructure as a service (IaaS) Delivers hardware networking capabilities, including the use of servers, networking, and storage, over the cloud using a pay-per-use revenue model.

Innovation The introduction of new equipment or methods.

Insiders Legitimate users who purposely or accidentally misuse their access to the environment and cause some kind of business-affecting incident.

Insourcing (in-house development) A common approach using the professional expertise within an organization to develop and maintain the organization's information technology systems.

Instances (records) The data about each entity in a table.

Instant messaging (IM, IMing) A type of communications service that enables someone to create a kind of private chat room with another individual in order to communicate in real time over the Internet.

Integration Allows separate systems to communicate directly with each other.

Integrity constraints The rules that help ensure the quality of information.

Intellectual property Intangible creative work that is embodied in physical form.

Intelligent agent A special-purpose knowledge-based information system that accomplishes specific tasks on behalf of its users.

Intelligent systems Various commercial applications of artificial intelligence.

Interactive voice response (IVR) A common feature in contact centres that directs customers to use touch-tone phones or keywords to navigate or provide information.

Interactivity Measures the visitor interactions with the target ad.

Intermediaries Agents, software, or businesses that provide a trading infrastructure to bring buyers and sellers together. Examples are distributors or wholesalers.

International Organization for Standardization (ISO) A non-governmental organization established in 1947 to promote the development of world standards to facilitate the international exchange of goods and services.

Internet A global public network of computer networks that pass information from one to another using common computer protocols.

Internet censorship A government attempt to control Internet traffic, preventing some material from being viewed by a country's citizens.

Internet service provider (ISP) A company that provides individuals and other companies access to the Internet along with additional related services, such as website-building.

Internet use policy Contains general principles to guide the proper use of the Internet.

Interoperability Capability of two or more computer systems to share data and resources, even though they are made by different manufacturers.

Intranet An internalized portion of the Internet, protected from outside access, that allows an organization to provide access to information and application software to only its employees.

Inventory management and control systems Provide control and visibility to the status of individual items maintained in inventory.

Iterative development A series of tiny projects, which has become the foundation of multiple agile types of methodologies.

IT governance Defines and assigns responsibilities and authority so that project value can be created; a set of processes that ensure the effective and efficient use of IT in enabling an organization to achieve its goals.

J

Joint problem solving A process of knowledge transfer in which an expert and a novice work actively together on a task or problem as a way of disseminating the expert's knowledge to the novice.

K

Key performance indicators (KPIs) Measures that are tied to business drivers.

Kill switch A trigger that enables a project manager to close the project prior to completion.

Kiosk Publicly accessible computer system that has been set up to allow interactive information browsing.

Knowledge Actionable information.

Knowledge management (KM) Involves capturing, classifying, evaluating, retrieving, and sharing information assets in a way that provides context for effective decisions and actions.

Knowledge management system (KMS) Supports the capturing, organization, and dissemination of knowledge (i.e., know-how) throughout an organization.

L

Legacy system Older computer technology that remains in use even though there are newer systems available.

List generators One of the three primary types of operational CRM systems a marketing department can implement to increase customer satisfaction; compile customer information from a variety of sources and segment the information for different marketing campaigns.

Local area network (LAN) A network designed to connect a group of computers in close proximity to each other such as in an office building, a school, or a home.

Location-based services (LBS) Wireless mobile content services that provide location-specific data to mobile users moving from location to location.

Logical view A way database users can view data that focuses on how users logically access information to meet their particular business needs.

Long tail The tail of a typical sales curve.

Loose coupling The capability of services to be joined together on demand to create composite services or disassembled just as easily into their functional components.

Loyalty programs Programs that reward customers on the basis of the amount of business they do with a particular organization.

M

Maintainability How quickly a system can transform to support environmental changes. Helps to measure how quickly and effectively a system can be changed or repaired after a failure.

Maintenance   A phase of the systems development life cycle (SDLC) that involves performing changes, corrections, additions, and upgrades to ensure the system continues to meet the business goals.

Maintenance, repair, and operations (MRO) materials (indirect materials)   Materials that are necessary for running an organization but that do not relate to the company's primary business activities.

Malicious code   Any of a variety of threats such as viruses, worms, and Trojan horses.

Management information systems (MIS)   The function that plans for, develops, implements, and maintains IT hardware, software, and applications that people use to support the goals of an organization.

Market basket analysis   Analyzes such items as websites and checkout scanner information to detect customers' buying behaviour and predict future behaviour by identifying affinities among customers' choices of products and services.

Market share   A common external key performance indicator (KPI) that indicates the proportion of the market a firm captures. Calculated by dividing a firm's sales by the total market sales for the entire industry.

Mashup editors   Software editing tool for mashups.

Mass customization   Ability of an organization to give its customers the opportunity to tailor its products or services to the customers' specifications.

Material requirements planning (MRP) systems   Uses sales forecasts to make sure that needed parts and materials are available at the right time and place in a specific company.

Messaging-based workflow systems   Systems that send work assignments by email.

Methodology   A set of policies, procedures, standards, processes, practices, tools, techniques, and tasks that people apply to technical and management challenges.

Metropolitan area network (MAN)   A large computer network usually spanning a city.

Microwave transmitter   A transmitter that uses the atmosphere (or outer space) as the transmission medium to send the signal to a microwave receiver.

Middleware   Different types of software that sit in the middle of and provide connectivity between two or more software applications.

M-learning   The use of portable computing devices with wireless capability to enable mobile learning.

Mobile commerce (m-commerce)   The ability to purchase goods and services through a wireless Internet-enabled device.

Multi-dimensional databases   In data warehouses and data marts, information that contains layers of columns and rows.

Multi-tenancy   In the cloud environment, the existence of a single instance of a system that serves multiple customers.

N

Nearshore outsourcing   Contracting an outsourcing agreement with a company in a nearby country.

Network   A communications, data exchange, and resource-sharing system created by linking two or more computers and establishing standards, or protocols, so that they can work together.

Network database model   A flexible way of representing objects and their relationships.

Neural network (artificial neural network)   A category of artificial intelligence that attempts to emulate the way the human brain works.

Nonrepudiation   A contractual stipulation to ensure that e-business participants do not deny (repudiate) their online actions.

O

Offshore outsourcing   Using organizations from developing countries to write code and develop systems.

Online analytical processing (OLAP)   The analysis of summarized or aggregated information sourced from transaction processing systems data, and sometimes external information from outside industry sources, to create business intelligence in support of strategic decision making.

Online service provider (OSP)   A firm that offers an extensive array of unique services, such as its own version of a Web browser.

Online transaction processing (OLTP)   The capturing of transaction and event data using information systems to (1) process the data according to defined business rules, (2) store the data, and (3) update existing data to reflect the new information.

Onshore outsourcing   The process of engaging another company within the same country for services.

Open source   Describes any program whose source code is made available for use or modification as users or other developers see fit.

Open system   A broad, general term that describes non-proprietary IT hardware and software made available by the standards and procedures by which their products work, making it easier to integrate them.

Operational CRM   Supports traditional transactional processing for day-to-day front-office operations or systems that deal directly with the customers.

Operational planning and control (OP&C)   Deals with the day-to-day procedures for performing work, including scheduling, inventory, and process management.

Operations management (OM)   The management of systems or processes that convert or transform resources (including human resources) into goods and services.

Opportunity management CRM systems   Target sales opportunities by finding new customers or companies for future sales.

Organizational change management   A set of techniques that aid in evolution, composition, and policy management of the design and implementation of a system.

Outsourcing   An arrangement by which one organization provides a service or services for another organization that chooses not to perform them in-house.

P

Packet tampering Altering the contents of packets as they travel over the Internet or altering data on computer disks after penetrating a network.

Participatory design (PD) methodology A systems design approach originating in Scandinavia that calls for the active involvement of users in design, in which users are the experts and systems development staff are coaches or facilitators.

Partner relationship management (PRM) Focuses on keeping vendors satisfied by managing alliance partner and reseller relationships that provide customers with the optimal sales channel.

Performance Measures how quickly a system performs a certain process or transaction (in terms of efficiency IT metrics of both speed and throughput).

Personalization Occurs when a website can know enough about a person's likes and dislikes that it can fashion offers that are more likely to appeal to that person.

PERT (Program Evaluation and Review Technique) chart A graphical network model that depicts a project's tasks and the relationships between those tasks.

Pharming Reroutes requests for legitimate websites to false websites.

Phishing Technique to gain personal information for the purpose of identity theft, usually by means of fraudulent email.

Physical security Tangible protection such as alarms, guards, fireproof doors, fences, and vaults.

Physical view A way database users can view data that looks at the physical storage of information on a storage device such as a hard disk.

Pirated software The unauthorized use, duplication, distribution, or sale of copyrighted software.

Planning A phase of the systems development life cycle (SDLC) that involves establishing a high-level plan of the intended project and determining project goals.

Platform as a service (PaaS) A cloud-based service in which the entire system, including hardware, networking, and applications, is deployed using a pay-per-use revenue model.

Polymorphic viruses and worms Viruses and worms that change their form as they propagate.

Pop-under ad A form of pop-up ad that users do not see until they close the current Web browser screen.

Pop-up ad A small Web page containing an advertisement that appears on the page outside of the current website loaded in the browser.

Portability The ability of an application to operate on different devices or software platforms, such as different operating systems.

Portal A website that offers a broad array of resources and services, such as email, online discussion groups, search engines, and online shopping malls.

Predictive dialling A common feature in contact centres that automatically dials telephone calls and, when someone answers, forwards the call to an available agent.

Primary key A field (or group of fields) that uniquely identifies a given entity in a table.

Privacy The right to be left alone when you want to be, to have control over your own personal possessions, and not to be observed without your consent.

Private cloud A cloud environment that serves only one customer or organization, and can be located either on the customer's premises or off.

Private exchange A business-to-business marketplace in which a single buyer posts its need and then opens the bidding to any supplier who would care to bid.

Process collaboration A type of collaboration in which participants share in the business processes where knowledge is hard-coded as rules, improving automation and the routing of information.

Production The creation of goods and services using the factors of production: land, labour, capital, entrepreneurship, and knowledge.

Production and materials management ERP components ERP components that handle the various aspects of production planning and execution, such as demand forecasting, production scheduling, job cost accounting, and quality control.

Production management Describes all the activities managers perform to help companies create goods.

Project A temporary endeavour undertaken to create a unique product or service.

Project assumptions Factors that are considered to be true, real, or certain without proof or demonstration.

Project charter A document issued by the project initiator or sponsor that formally authorizes the existence of a project and provides the project manager with the authority to apply organizational resources to project activities.

Project constraints Specific factors that can limit options for a project.

Project deliverables Any measurable, tangible, verifiable outcome, result, or item that is produced to complete a project or part of a project.

Project management The application of knowledge, skills, tools, and techniques to project activities in order to meet project requirements.

Project Management Body of Knowledge (PMBOK) Sets the standards for project management on a global basis.

Project Management Institute (PMI) Develops procedures and concepts necessary to support the profession of project management.

Project management office (PMO) An internal department that oversees all organizational projects.

Project manager An individual who is an expert in project planning and management, defines and develops the project plan, and tracks the plan to ensure all key project milestones are completed on time.

Project milestones Key dates in the progress of a project when a certain group of activities must have been performed.

Project objectives Quantifiable criteria that must be met for the project to be considered a success.

Project plan   A formal, approved document that manages and controls project execution.

Project scope   A definition of the work that must be completed to deliver a product with the specified features and functions.

Project stakeholders   Individuals and organizations actively involved in the project or whose interests might be affected as a result of project execution or project completion.

Protocols   Standards that specify the format of data as well as the rules to be followed during transmission.

Prototype   A smaller-scale representation or working model of the user's requirements, or a proposed design for an information system.

Public cloud   A cloud environment that promotes massive, global, and industry-wide applications offered to the general public.

Public key encryption (PKE)   Encryption system that uses two keys: a public key that everyone can have and a private key for the recipient only.

R

Radio frequency identification (RFID)   Technologies using active or passive tags in the form of chips or smart labels that can store unique identifiers and relay this information to electronic readers.

Rapid application development (RAD) (rapid prototyping)   An agile software development methodology that emphasizes extensive user involvement in the rapid and evolutionary construction of working prototypes of a system to accelerate the systems development process.

Rational unified process (RUP) methodology   An agile software development methodology that provides a framework for breaking down the development of software into four gates—inception, elaboration, construction, and transition— each of which consists of executable iterations of the software in development. A project stays in a gate until the stakeholders are satisfied, and then it either moves to the next gate or is cancelled.

Real-time data   Immediate, up-to-date data.

Real-time information   Immediate, up-to-date information.

Real-time system   Provides real-time information in response to query requests.

Records (instances)   The data about each entity in a table.

Recovery   The ability to get a system up and running in the event of a system crash or failure and includes restoring the data backup.

Reintermediation   Steps added to the value chain as new players find ways to add value to the business process.

Relational database model   A type of database that stores information in the form of logically related two-dimensional tables.

Relational integrity constraints   The rules that enforce basic and fundamental data constraints.

Reliability   Ensures all systems are functioning correctly and providing accurate information.

Resellers   Companies or individuals who purchase goods and products in bulk with the intention of reselling them at a profit.

Retailers   Stores or shops operating at the end of the supply chain that acquire goods or products from manufacturers or importers, and then sell smaller quantities of these goods or products to consumers at higher prices to cover expenses and make a profit.

Return on investment (ROI)   A common internal KPI that indicates the earning power of a project. Measured by dividing the profitability of a project by its costs.

Reverse auction   An auction format in which increasingly lower bids are solicited from organizations willing to supply the desired product or service at an increasingly lower price.

RFID tags   Contain a microchip and an antenna.

Rivalry among existing competitors   High when competition is fierce in a market and low when competition is more complacent.

S

Sales force automation (SFA)   A system that automatically tracks all of the steps in the sales process.

Sales management CRM systems   Automate each phase of the sales process, helping individual sales representatives coordinate and organize all of their accounts.

Satellite   A large microwave device located high in the sky that contains one or more transponders that listen to a particular portion of the electromagnetic spectrum, amplifying incoming signals and retransmitting them back to Earth.

Scalability   Refers to how well a system can adapt to increased demands.

Scope creep   Gradual increase in the scope of a project.

Script kiddies (script bunnies)   Persons who find hacking code on the Internet and click-and-point their way into systems to cause damage or spread viruses.

Scrum methodology   An agile software development methodology that uses small teams to produce bits of deliverable software at 30-day intervals to achieve an appointed goal.

Secure electronic transaction (SET)   A communications protocol standard that ensures transactions are secure and legitimate.

Secure socket layer (SSL)   A protocol for encrypting information over the Internet that (1) creates a secure and private connection between a client and server computer, (2) encrypts the information, and (3) sends the information over the Internet.

Self-sourcing   Development of systems by the people who use them (the end-users).

Selling chain management   Applies technology to the activities in the order life cycle from inquiry to sale.

Semantic Web   An evolving extension of the World Wide Web in which content can be expressed not only in natural language, but also in a format that can be read and used by software agents, thus permitting them to find, share, and integrate information more easily.

Semi-structured decisions   Managerial decisions that occur in situations in which a few established processes help to evaluate potential solutions, but not enough to lead to a definite recommendation.

Sensitivity analysis The study of the impact that changes in one (or more) parts of the model have on other parts of the model.

Serviceability A measure of how quickly a third party can change a system to ensure it meets user needs and the terms of any contracts, including agreed levels of reliability, maintainability, or availability.

Service level agreements (SLAs) Define the specific responsibilities of the service provider and set the customer expectations.

Service-oriented architecture (SOA) A business-driven IT architectural approach that supports integrating business as linked, repeatable tasks or services.

Services Business tasks.

Shadowing A process of knowledge transfer in which less experienced staff observe more experienced workers as a means of teaching the less experienced staff how more experienced counterparts approach their work.

Shopping bot Software that will search several retailer websites and provide a comparison of each retailer's offerings including price and availability.

Slice-and-dice The ability to look at information from different perspectives.

Smart card A device, about the same size as a credit card, containing embedded technologies that can store information and small amounts of software to perform limited processing.

Sniffer A program or device that can monitor data travelling over a network.

SOA service A business task, such as checking a potential customer's credit rating when opening a new account.

Social CRM The use of social media techniques and technologies that enable organizations to engage with their customers.

Social engineering Using one's social skills to trick people into revealing access credentials or other information valuable to the attacker.

Social media policy Guidelines or principles that outline or govern employee online communications.

Social networking analysis (SNA) A process of mapping a group's contacts (whether personal or professional) to identify who knows whom and who works with whom.

Social responsibility Implies that an entity, whether it is a government, corporation, organization, or individual, has a responsibility to society.

Software as a service (SaaS) Delivers applications over the cloud using a pay-per-use revenue model.

Spam Unsolicited email.

Spoofing Forging the return address on an email so that the email message appears to come from someone other than the actual sender.

Spyware Software that comes hidden in free downloadable software and tracks online movements, mines the information stored on a computer, or uses a computer's CPU and storage for some task the user knows nothing about.

Statistical analysis Performs such functions as information correlations, distributions, calculations, and variance analysis.

Strategic business units (SBUs) Businesses that consist of several stand-alone businesses. SBUs are typically found in large conglomerates.

Strategic planning Focuses on long-range planning such as plant size, location, and types of processes to be used.

Structured collaboration (process collaboration) Involves shared participation in business processes, such as workflow, in which knowledge is hard-coded as rules.

Structured decisions Operational decisions that arise in situations in which established processes offer potential solutions.

Supplier power High when buyers have few choices of whom to buy from and low when their choices are many.

Supplier relationship management (SRM) Focuses on keeping suppliers satisfied by evaluating and categorizing suppliers for different projects, which optimizes supplier selection.

Supply chain The progression of all parties involved, directly or indirectly, in the procurement of a product or raw material.

Supply chain event management (SCEM) Enables an organization to react more quickly to resolve supply chain issues.

Supply chain execution (SCE) systems Systems that automate the different steps and stages of the supply chain.

Supply chain management (SCM) Involves the management of information flows between and among stages in a supply chain to maximize total supply chain effectiveness and profitability.

Supply chain planning (SCP) systems Use advanced mathematical algorithms to improve the flow and efficiency of the supply chain while reducing inventory.

Supply chain visibility The ability to view all areas up and down the supply chain.

Sustainable ("green") IT The manufacture, management, use, and disposal of information technology in a way that minimizes damage to the environment, which is a critical part of a corporation's responsibility.

Sustainable IT disposal The safe disposal of IT assets at the end of their life cycle.

Sustaining technology Produces an improved product customers are eager to buy, such as a faster car or larger hard drive.

Switching costs The costs that can make customers reluctant to switch to another product or service.

System virtualization The ability to present the resources of a single computer as if it is a collection of separate computers ("virtual machines"), each with its own virtual CPUs, network interfaces, storage, and operating system.

Systems development life cycle (SDLC) The overall process for developing information systems from planning and analysis through implementation and maintenance.

T

Table A collection of similar entities.

Tablet A mobile computer, larger than a mobile phone, that is primarily operated by tapping and/or stroking the screen.

Tacit knowledge The knowledge that resides in people's minds.

Tactical planning   Focuses on producing goods and services as efficiently as possible within the strategic plan.

Teergrubing   An anti-spamming approach in which the receiving computer launches a return attack against the spammer, sending email messages back to the computer that originated the suspected spam.

Telecommunication systems   Enable the transmission of data over public or private networks.

Telematics   The blending of computers and wireless telecommunications technologies with the goal of efficiently conveying information over vast networks to improve business operations.

Testing   A phase of the systems development life cycle (SDLC) that involves bringing all the project pieces together into a special testing environment to test for errors, bugs, and interoperability and verify that the system meets all of the business requirements defined in the analysis phase.

Threat of new entrants   High when it is easy for new competitors to enter a market and low when there are significant entry barriers to entering a market.

Threat of substitute products or services   High when there are many alternatives to a product or service and low when there are few alternatives from which to choose.

Time series information   Time-stamped information collected at a particular frequency.

To-Be process models   Shows the results of applying change improvement opportunities to the current (As-Is) process model.

Tokens   Small electronic devices that change user passwords automatically.

Transaction processing system (TPS)   The basic business system that serves the operational level (clerks and analysts) in an organization.

Transactional data   Encompasses all of the information contained within a single business process or unit of work, and its primary purpose is to support the performing of daily operational tasks.

Transformation process   The actual conversion of inputs to outputs; often referred to as the *technical core*, especially in manufacturing organizations.

Transportation planning systems   Track and analyze the movement of materials and products to ensure the delivery of materials and finished goods at the right time, the right place, and the lowest cost.

Trojan-horse virus   A virus that hides inside other software, usually as an attachment or a downloadable file.

Typosquatting   Registering purposely misspelled variations of well-known domain names.

U

Unstructured collaboration (information collaboration)   Includes document exchange, shared whiteboards, discussion forums, and email.

Unstructured decisions   Strategic decisions that occur in situations in which no procedures or rules exist to guide decision makers to the correct choice.

Upselling   Increasing the value of a sale. One of the three primary operational CRM systems a marketing department can implement to increase customer satisfaction.

V

Value-added   The difference between the cost of inputs and the price value of outputs.

Value-added network (VAN)   A private network, provided by a third party, for exchanging information through a high-capacity connection.

Value chain   Views an organization as a series of processes, each of which adds value to the product or service for each customer.

Videoconferencing   The use of telecommunications to virtually bring people at different sites together for a meeting. It uses a set of interactive telecommunication technologies that allow persons at two or more locations to interact via two-way video and audio transmissions simultaneously.

Viral marketing   Technique that induces websites or users to pass on a marketing message to other websites or users, creating exponential growth in the message's visibility and effect.

Virtual private network (VPN)   A way to use a public telecommunication infrastructure (such as the Internet) to provide secure access to an organization's network.

Virtual reality   A computer-generated environment that can be a simulated version of either the real or an imaginary world.

Virtualization   A framework of dividing the resources of a computer into multiple execution environments.

Virtual workforce   A workforce not located in one physical space that uses networked technology to produce work products without regard for geographical location or time.

Virus   A type of software written with malicious intent to cause annoyance or damage.

Visualization   Graphical displays of patterns and complex relationships in large amounts of data.

Voice over Internet Protocol (VoIP)   Uses TCP/IP technology to transmit voice calls over long-distance telephone lines.

W

Waterfall methodology   A sequential, activity-based process in which each phase in the systems development life cycle is performed sequentially from planning through implementation and maintenance.

Web 2.0   A set of economic, social, and technology trends that collectively form the basis for the next generation of the Internet—a more mature, distinctive medium characterized by user participation, openness, and network effects.

Web 3.0   Describes the evolution of Web usage and interaction among several separate paths. These include transforming the Web into a database, a move toward making content accessible by multiple non-browser applications, the leveraging of artificial intelligence technologies, and the semantic Web.

Web accessibility   A feature that enables people with visual, auditory, physical, speech, cognitive, or neurological disabilities to use the Web.

Web-based self-service systems   Systems that allow customers to use the Web to find answers to their questions or solutions to their problems.

Web conferencing   Blends audio, video, and document-sharing technologies to create virtual meeting rooms.

Web content management system (WCM)   Adds a layer to document and digital asset management that enables publishing content both to intranets and to public websites.

Web mashup   A website or Web application that uses content from more than one source to create a completely new service.

Web services   Contain a repertoire of Web-based data and procedural resources that use shared protocols and standards permitting different applications to share data and services.

Website name stealing   Theft that occurs when someone, posing as a site's administrator, changes the ownership of the domain name assigned to the website to another website owner.

What-if analysis   Checks the impact of a change in an assumption on the proposed solution.

White-hat hacker   A hacker who works at the request of the system owners to find system vulnerabilities and plug the holes.

Wide area network (WAN)   A network that spans a large geographic area, such as a state, province, or country.

Wikis   Web-based tools that make it easy for users to add, remove, and change online content.

WiMAX   The Worldwide Interoperability for Microwave Access is a telecommunications technology aimed at providing wireless data over long distances in a variety of ways, from point-to-point links to full mobile cellular type access.

Wireless fidelity (Wi-Fi)   A means of linking computers using infrared or radio signals.

Wireless Internet service provider (WISP)   An ISP that allows subscribers to connect to a server at designated hotspots or access points using a wireless connection.

Workflow   All the steps or business rules, from beginning to end, required for a business process.

Workflow management systems   Facilitate the automation and management of business processes and control the movement of work through the business process.

Workplace MIS monitoring   Tracks people's activities using measures such as number of keystrokes, error rate, and number of transactions processed.

World Wide Web (WWW)   A global hypertext system that uses the Internet as its transport mechanism.

Worm   A type of virus that spreads itself, not only from file to file, but also from computer to computer.

PHOTO CREDITS